Artificial Higher Order Neural Networks for Economics and Business

Ming Zhang
Christopher Newport University, USA

INFORMATION SCIENCE REFERENCE

Hershey · New York

Director of Editorial Content: Kristin Klinger
Senior Managing Editor: Jennifer Neidig
Managing Editor: Jamie Snavely
Assistant Managing Editor: Carole Coulson
Typesetter: Sean Woznicki
Cover Design: Lisa Tosheff
Printed at: Yurchak Printing Inc.

Published in the United States of America by
        Information Science Reference (an imprint of IGI Global)
        701 E. Chocolate Avenue, Suite 200
        Hershey PA 17033
        Tel: 717-533-8845
        Fax: 717-533-8661
        E-mail: cust@igi-global.com
        Web site: http://www.igi-global.com

and in the United Kingdom by
        Information Science Reference (an imprint of IGI Global)
        3 Henrietta Street
        Covent Garden
        London WC2E 8LU
        Tel: 44 20 7240 0856
        Fax: 44 20 7379 0609
        Web site: http://www.eurospanbookstore.com

Library of Congress Cataloging-in-Publication Data

Artificial higher order neural networks for economics and business / Ming Zhang, editor.

    p. cm.

  Summary: "This book is the first book to provide opportunities for millions working in economics, accounting, finance and other business areas education on HONNs, the ease of their usage, and directions on how to obtain more accurate application results. It provides significant, informative advancements in the subject and introduces the HONN group models and adaptive HONNs"--Provided by publisher.

  ISBN-13: 978-1-59904-897-0 (hbk.)
  ISBN-13: 978-1-59904-898-7 (e-book)
  1. Finance--Computer simulation. 2. Finance--Mathematical models. 3. Finance--Computer programs. 4. Neural networks (Computer science) I. Zhang, Ming, 1949 July 29-
  HG106.A78 2008
  332.0285'632--dc22

                          2007043953

British Cataloguing in Publication Data
A Cataloguing in Publication record for this book is available from the British Library.

All work contributed to this book set is original material. The views expressed in this book are those of the authors, but not necessarily of the publisher.

To My Wife,

Zhao Qing Zhang

Table of Contents

Section I
Artificial Higher Order Neural Networks for Economics

Chapter I
Ming Zhang, Christopher Newport University, USA

Chapter II
Adam Knowles, Liverpool John Moores University, UK
Abir Hussain, Liverpool John Moores University, UK
Wael El Deredy, Liverpool John Moores University, UK
Paulo G. J. Lisboa, Liverpool John Moores University, UK
Christian L. Dunis, Liverpool John Moores University, UK

Chapter III
Da Shi, Peking University, China
Shaohua Tan, Peking University, China
Shuzhi Sam Ge, National University of Singapore, Singapore

Chapter IV
John Seiffertt, Missouri University of Science and Technology, USA
Donald C. Wunsch II, Missouri University of Science and Technology, USA

Section II
Artificial Higher Order Neural Networks for Time Series Data

Detailed Table of Contents

Section I
Artificial Higher Order Neural Networks for Economics

Chapter I

  Ming Zhang, Christopher Newport University, USA

This chapter delivers general format of Higher Order Neural Networks (HONNs) for nonlinear data analysis and six different HONN models. This chapter mathematically proves that HONN models could converge and have mean squared errors close to zero. This chapter illustrates the learning algorithm with update formulas. HONN models are compared with SAS Nonlinear (NLIN) models and results show that HONN models are 3 to 12% better than SAS Nonlinear models. Moreover, this chapter shows how to use HONN models to find the best model, order and coefficients, without writing the regression expression, declaring parameter names, and supplying initial parameter values.

Chapter II

  Adam Knowles, Liverpool John Moores University, UK
  Abir Hussain, Liverpool John Moores University, UK
  Wael El Deredy, Liverpool John Moores University, UK
  Paulo G. J. Lisboa, Liverpool John Moores University, UK
  Christian L. Dunis, Liverpool John Moores University, UK

Multi-Layer Perceptrons (MLP) are the most common type of neural network in use, and their ability to perform complex nonlinear mappings and tolerance to noise in data is well documented. However, MLPs also suffer long training times and often reach only local optima. Another type of network is Higher Order Neural Networks (HONN). These can be considered a 'stripped-down' version of MLPs, where joint activation terms are used, relieving the network of the task of learning the relationships between the inputs. The predictive performance of the network is tested with the EUR/USD exchange rate and evaluated using standard financial criteria including the annualized return on investment, showing a 8% increase in the return compared with the MLP. The output of the networks that give the highest annualized return in each category was subjected to a Bayesian based confidence measure.

Chapter III

Real-world financial systems are often nonlinear, do not follow any regular probability distribution, and comprise a large amount of financial variables. Not surprisingly, it is hard to know which variables are relevant to the prediction of the stock return based on data collected from such a system. In this chapter, we address this problem by developing a technique consisting of a top-down part using an artificial Higher Order Neural Network (HONN) model and a bottom-up part based on a Bayesian Network (BN) model to automatically identify predictor variables for the stock return prediction from a large financial variable set. Our study provides an operational guidance for using HONN and BN in selecting predictor variables from a large amount of financial variables to support the prediction of the stock return, including the prediction of future stock return value and future stock return movement trends.

Chapter IV

As the study of agent-based computational economics and finance grows, so does the need for appropriate techniques for the modeling of complex dynamic systems and the intelligence of the constructive agent. These methods are important where the classic equilibrium analytics fail to provide sufficiently satisfactory understanding. In particular, one area of computational intelligence, Approximate Dynamic Programming, holds much promise for applications in this field and demonstrate the capacity for artificial Higher Order Neural Networks to add value in the social sciences and business. This chapter provides an overview of this area, introduces the relevant agent-based computational modeling systems, and suggests practical methods for their incorporation into the current research. A novel application of HONN to ADP specifically for the purpose of studying agent-based financial systems is presented.

Chapter V

Forecasting exchange rates is an important financial problem that is receiving increasing attention especially because of its difficulty and practical applications. In this chapter, we apply Higher Order Flexible Neural Trees (HOFNTs), which are capable of designing flexible Artificial Neural Network (ANN) architectures automatically, to forecast the foreign exchange rates. To demonstrate the efficiency of HOFNTs, we consider three different datasets in our forecast performance analysis. The data sets used are daily foreign exchange rates obtained from the Pacific Exchange Rate Service. The data comprises of the US dollar exchange rate against Euro, Great Britain Pound (GBP) and Japanese Yen (JPY). Under the HOFNT framework, we consider the Gene Expression Programming (GEP) approach and the Grammar Guided Genetic Programming (GGGP) approach to evolve the structure of HOFNT. The particle swarm optimization algorithm is employed to optimize the free parameters of the two different HOFNT models. This chapter briefly explains how the two different learning paradigms could be formulated using various methods and then investigates whether they can provide a reliable forecast model for foreign exchange rates. Simulation results shown the effectiveness of the proposed methods.

Chapter VI

Yuehui Chen, University of Jinan, China
Peng Wu, University of Jinan, China
Qiang Wu, University of Jinan, China

Artificial Neural Networks (ANNs) have become very important in making stock market predictions. Much research on the applications of ANNs has proven their advantages over statistical and other methods. In order to identify the main benefits and limitations of previous methods in ANNs applications, a comparative analysis of selected applications is conducted. It can be concluded from analysis that ANNs and HONNs are most implemented in forecasting stock prices and stock modeling. The aim of this chapter is to study higher order artificial neural networks for stock index modeling problems. New network architectures and their corresponding training algorithms are discussed. These structures demonstrate their processing capabilities over traditional ANNs architectures with a reduction in the number of processing elements. In this chapter, the performance of classical neural networks and higher order neural networks for stock index forecasting is evaluated. We will highlight a novel slide-window method for data forecasting. With each slide of the observed data, the model can adjusts the variable dynamically. Simulation results show the feasibility and effectiveness of the proposed methods.

Section II
Artificial Higher Order Neural Networks for Time Series Data

Chapter VII

Ming Zhang, Christopher Newport University, USA

This chapter develops a new nonlinear model, Ultra high frequency Trigonometric Higher Order Neural Networks (UTHONN), for time series data analysis. Results show that UTHONN models are 3 to 12%

better than Equilibrium Real Exchange Rates (ERER) model, and 4 – 9% better than other Polynomial Higher Order Neural Network (PHONN) and Trigonometric Higher Order Neural Network (THONN) models. This study also uses UTHONN models to simulate foreign exchange rates and consumer price index with error approaching 0.0000%.

The research described in this chapter is concerned with the development of a novel artificial higher order neural networks architecture called the second-order pipeline recurrent neural network. The proposed artificial neural network consists of a linear and a nonlinear section, extracting relevant features from the input signal. The structuring unit of the proposed neural network is the second-order recurrent neural network. The architecture consists of a series of second-order recurrent neural networks, which are concatenated with each other. Simulation results in one-step ahead predictions of the foreign currency exchange rates demonstrate the superior performance of the proposed pipeline architecture as compared to other feedforward and recurrent structures.

Chapter IX

The research described in this chapter is concerned with the development of a novel artificial higher-order neural networks architecture called the recurrent Pi-sigma neural network. The proposed artificial neural network combines the advantages of both higher-order architectures in terms of the multi-linear interactions between inputs, as well as the temporal dynamics of recurrent neural networks, and produces highly accurate one-step ahead predictions of the foreign currency exchange rates, as compared to other feedforward and recurrent structures.

Generalized correlation higher order neural network designs are developed. Their performance is compared with that of first order networks, conventional higher order neural network designs, and higher order linear regression networks for financial time series prediction. The correlation higher order neural network design is shown to give the highest accuracy for prediction of stock market share prices and share indices. The simulations compare the performance for three different training algorithms, stationary versus non-stationary input data, different numbers of neurons in the hidden layer and several generalized correlation higher order neural network designs. Generalized correlation higher order linear regression networks are also introduced and two designs are shown by simulation to give good correct direction prediction and higher prediction accuracies, particularly for long-term predictions, than other linear regression networks for the prediction of inter-bank lending risk Libor and Swap interest rate yield curves. The simulations compare the performance for different input data sample lag lengths.

Chapter XI

Real world problems are described by nonlinear and chaotic processes, which makes them hard to model and predict. This chapter first compares the neural network (NN) and the artificial higher order neural network (HONN) and then presents commonly known neural network architectures and a number of HONN architectures. The time series prediction problem is formulated as a system identification problem, where the input to the system is the past values of a time series, and its desired output is the future values of a time series. The polynomial neural network (PNN) is then chosen as the HONN for application to the time series prediction problem. This chapter presents the application of HONN model to the nonlinear time series prediction problems of three major international currency exchange rates, as well as two key U.S. interest rates—the Federal funds rate and the yield on the 5-year U.S. Treasury note. Empirical results indicate that the proposed method is competitive with other approaches for the exchange rate problem, and can be used as a feasible solution for interest rate forecasting problem. This implies that the HONN model can be used as a feasible solution for exchange rate forecasting as well as for interest rate forecasting.

Chapter XII

This chapter discusses the use of two artificial Higher Order Neural Networks (HONNs) models; the Pi-Sigma Neural Networks and the Ridge Polynomial Neural Networks, in financial time series forecasting. The networks were used to forecast the upcoming trends of three noisy financial signals; the exchange rate between the US Dollar and the Euro, the exchange rate between the Japanese Yen and the Euro, and the United States 10-year government bond. In particular, we systematically investigate a method of pre-processing the signals in order to reduce the trends in them. The performance of the networks is benchmarked against the performance of Multilayer Perceptrons. From the simulation results, the predictions clearly demonstrated that HONNs models, particularly Ridge Polynomial Neural Networks generate higher profit returns with fast convergence, therefore show considerable promise as a decision making tool. It is hoped that individual investor could benefit from the use of this forecasting tool.

Section III
Artificial Higher Order Neural Networks for Business

Chapter XIII

Edgar N. Sanchez, CINVESTAV, Unidad Guadalajara, Mexico
Alma Y. Alanis, CINVESTAV, Unidad Guadalajara, Mexico
Jesús Rico, Universidad Michoacana de San Nicolas de Hidalgo, Mexico

In this chapter, we propose the use of Higher Order Neural Networks (HONNs) trained with an extended Kalman filter based algorithm to predict the electric load demand as well as the electricity prices, with beyond a horizon of 24 hours. Due to the chaotic behavior of the electrical markets, it is not advisable to apply the traditional forecasting techniques used for time series; the results presented here confirm that HONNs can very well capture the complexity underlying electric load demand and electricity prices. The proposed neural network model produces very accurate next day predictions and also, prognosticates with very good accuracy, a week-ahead demand and price forecasts.

Chapter XIV

Shuxiang Xu, University of Tasmania, Australia

Business is a diversified field with general areas of specialisation such as accounting, taxation, stock market, and other financial analysis. Artificial Neural Networks (ANN) have been widely used in applications such as bankruptcy prediction, predicting costs, forecasting revenue, forecasting share prices and exchange rates, processing documents and many more. This chapter introduces an Adaptive Higher Order Neural Network (HONN) model and applies the adaptive model in business applications such as simulating and forecasting share prices. This adaptive HONN model offers significant advantages over traditional Standard ANN models such as much reduced network size, faster training, as well as much improved simulation and forecasting errors, due to their ability to better approximate complex, non-smooth, often discontinuous training data sets. The generalisation ability of this HONN model is explored and discussed.

Chapter XV

Jean X. Zhang, George Washington University, USA

This chapter proposes nonlinear models using artificial neural network models to study the relationship between chief elected official (CEO) tenure and debt. Using Higher Order Neural Network (HONN) simulator, this study analyzes debt of the municipalities as a function of population and CEO tenure, and compares the results with that from SAS. The linear models show that CEO tenure and the amount of debt vary inversely. Specifically, a longer length of CEO tenure leads to a decrease in debt, while a shorter tenure leads to an increase in debt. This chapter shows nonlinear model generated from HONN out performs linear models by 1%. The results from both models reveal that CEO tenure is negatively associated with the level of debt in local governments.

This chapter investigates the soybean-oil "crush" spread, that is the profit margin gained by processing soybeans into soyoil. Soybeans form a large proportion (over 1/5th) of the agricultural output of US farmers and the profit margins gained will therefore have a wide impact on the US economy in general. The chapter uses a number of techniques to forecast and trade the soybean crush spread. A traditional regression analysis is used as a benchmark against more sophisticated models such as a Multilayer Perceptron (MLP), Recurrent Neural Networks and Higher Order Neural Networks. These are then used to trade the spread, the implementation of a number of filtering techniques as used in the literature are utilised to further refine the trading statistics of the models. The results show that the best model before transactions costs both in- and out-of-sample is the Recurrent Network generating a superior risk adjusted return to all other models investigated. However in the case of most of the models investigated the cost of trading the spread all but eliminates any profit potential.

Section IV
Artificial Higher Order Neural Networks Fundamentals

In this chapter, we aim to describe fundamental principles of artificial higher order neural units (AHONUs) and networks (AHONNs). An essential core of AHONNs can be found in higher order weighted combinations or correlations between the input variables. By using some typical examples, this chapter describes how and why higher order combinations or correlations can be effective.

This chapter concentrates on studying the dynamics of artificial higher order neural networks (HONNs) with delays. Both stability analysis and periodic oscillation are discussed here for a class of delayed

HONNs with (or without) impulses. Most of the sufficient conditions obtained in this chapter are presented in linear matrix inequalities (LMIs), and so can be easily computed and checked in practice using the Matlab LMI Toolbox. In reality, stability is a necessary feature when applying artificial neural networks. Also periodic solution plays an important role in the dynamical behavior of all solutions though other dynamics such as bifurcation and chaos do coexist. So here we mainly focus on questions of the stability and periodic solutions of artificial HONNs with (or without) impulses. Firstly, stability analysis and periodic oscillation are analyzed for higher order bidirectional associative memory (BAM) neural networks without impulses. Secondly, global exponential stability and exponential convergence are studied for a class of impulsive higher order bidirectional associative memory neural networks with time-varying delays. The main methods and tools used in this chapter are linear matrix inequalities (LMIs), Lyapunov stability theory and coincidence degree theory.

Chapter XIX

Aiming to develop a systematic approach for optimizing the structure of artificial higher order neural networks (HONN) for system modeling and function approximation, a new HONN topology, namely polynomial kernel networks, is proposed in this chapter. Structurally, the polynomial kernel network can be viewed as a three-layer feedforward neural network with a special polynomial activation function for the nodes in the hidden layer. The new network is equivalent to a HONN; however, due to the underlying connections with polynomial kernel support vector machines, the weights and the structure of the network can be determined simultaneously using structural risk minimization. The advantage of the topology of the polynomial kernel network and the use of a support vector kernel expansion paves the way to represent nonlinear functions or systems, and underpins some advanced analysis of the network performance. In this chapter, from the perspective of network complexity, both quadratic programming and linear programming based training of the polynomial kernel network are investigated.

Chapter XX

This chapter describes the progress in using optical technology to construct high-speed artificial higher order neural network systems. The chapter reviews how optical technology can speed up searches within large databases in order to identify relationships and dependencies between individual data records, such as financial or business time-series, as well as trends and relationships within them. Two distinct approaches in which optics may be used are reviewed. In the first approach, the chapter reviews current research replacing copper connections in a conventional data storage system, such as a several terabyte RAID array of magnetic hard discs, by optical waveguides to achieve very high data rates with low crosstalk interference. In the second approach, the chapter reviews how high speed optical correlators with feedback can be used to realize artificial higher order neural networks using Fourier Transform free space optics and holographic database storage.

This chapter deals with the analysis problem of the global exponential stability for a general class of stochastic artificial higher order neural networks with multiple mixed time delays and Markovian jumping parameters. The mixed time delays under consideration comprise both the discrete time-varying delays and the distributed time-delays. The main purpose of this chapter is to establish easily verifiable conditions under which the delayed high-order stochastic jumping neural network is exponentially stable in the mean square in the presence of both the mixed time delays and Markovian switching. By employing a new Lyapunov-Krasovskii functional and conducting stochastic analysis, a linear matrix nequality (LMI) approach is developed to derive the criteria ensuring the exponential stability. Furthermore, the criteria are dependent on both the discrete time-delay and distributed time-delay, hence less conservative. The proposed criteria can be readily checked by using some standard numerical packages such as the Matlab LMI Toolbox. A simple example is provided to demonstrate the effectiveness and applicability of the proposed testing criteria.

This chapter introduces trigonometric polynomial higher order neural network models. In the area of financial data simulation and prediction, there is no single neural network model that could handle the wide variety of data and perform well in the real world. A way of solving this difficulty is to develop a number of new models, with different algorithms. A wider variety of models would give financial operators more chances to find a suitable model when they process their data. That was the major motivation for this chapter. The theoretical principles of these improved models are presented and demonstrated and experiments are conducted by using real-life financial data.

Preface

Artificial Neural Networks (ANNs) are known to excellence in pattern recognition, pattern matching and mathematical function approximation. However, they suffer from several limitations. ANNs are often stuck in local, rather than global minima, as well as taking unacceptable long times to converge in the real word data. Especially from the perspective of economics and financial time series predictions, ANNs are unable to handle non-smooth, discontinuous training data, and complex mappings. Another limitation of ANN is a 'black box' nature. It means that explanations for their decisions are not hard to use expressions to describe. This then is the first motivation for developing Higher Order Neural Networks (HONNs), since HONNs are 'open-box' models and each neuron and weight are mapped to function variable and coefficient.

SAS Nonlinear (NLIN) procedure produces least squares or weighted least squares estimates of the parameters of a nonlinear model. SAS Nonlinear models are more difficult to specify and estimate than linear models. Instead of simply generating the parameter estimates, users must write the regression expression, declare parameter names, and supply initial parameter values. Some models are difficult to fit, and there is no guarantee that the procedure can fit the model successfully. For each nonlinear model to be analyzed, users must specify the model (using a single dependent variable) and the names and starting values of the parameters to be estimated. However, the objective of the users is to find the model and its coefficients. This is the second motivation for using HONNs in economics and business, since HONNs can automatically select the initial coefficients for nonlinear data analysis.

Let millions of people working in economics and business areas know that HONNs are much easier to use and can have better simulation results than SAS NLIN, and understand how to successfully use HONNs software packages for nonlinear data simulation and prediction. HONNs will challenge SAS NLIN procedures and change the research methodology that people are currently using in economics and business areas for the nonlinear date simulation and prediction.

Millions of people who are using SAS and who are doing nonlinear model research, in particular, professors, graduate students, and senior undergraduate students in economics, accounting, finance and other business departments, as well as the professionals and researchers in these areas.

The book is organized into four sections and a total of twenty two chapters. Section 1, Artificial Higher Order Neural Networks for Economics, includes chapter I to chapter VI. Section 2, Artificial Higher Order Neural Networks for Time Series Data, is from chapter VII to chapter XII. Section 3, Artificial Higher Order Neural Networks for Business, contains chapter XIII to chapter XVI. Section 4, Artificial Higher Order Neural Networks Fundamentals, consists of chapter XVII to chapter XXII. A brief description of each of the chapters are as follows.

Chapter I, "Artificial Higher Order Neural Network Nonlinear Model - SAS NLIN or HONNs", delivers general format of Higher Order Neural Networks (HONNs) for nonlinear data analysis and six different HONN models. This chapter mathematically proves that HONN models could converge and have mean squared errors close to zero. This chapter illustrates the learning algorithm with update formulas. HONN models are compared with SAS Nonlinear (NLIN) models and results show that HONN models are 3 to 12% better than SAS Nonlinear models. Moreover, this chapter shows how to use HONN models to find the best model, order and coefficients, without writing the regression expression, declaring parameter names, and supplying initial parameter values.

Chapter II, "Higher Order Neural Networks with Bayesian Confidence Measure for the Prediction of the EUR/USD Exchange Rate", presents another type of network which is Higher Order Neural Networks (HONN). These can be considered a 'stripped-down' version of MLPs, where joint activation terms are used, relieving the network of the task of learning the relationships between the inputs. The predictive performance of the network is tested with the EUR/USD exchange rate and evaluated using standard financial criteria including the annualized return on investment, showing a 8% increase in the return compared with the MLP. The output of the networks that give the highest annualized return in each category was subjected to a Bayesian based confidence measure.

Chapter III, "Automatically Identifying Predictor Variables for Stock Return Prediction", addresses nonlinear problem by developing a technique consisting of a top-down part using an artificial Higher Order Neural Network (HONN) model and a bottom-up part based on a Bayesian Network (BN) model to automatically identify predictor variables for the stock return prediction from a large financial variable set. Our study provides an operational guidance for using HONN and BN in selecting predictor variables from a large amount of financial variables to support the prediction of the stock return, including the prediction of future stock return value and future stock return movement trends.

Chapter IV, "Higher Order Neural Network Architectures for Agent-Based Computational Economics and Finance", studies the agent-based computational economics and finance grows, so does the need for appropriate techniques for the modeling of complex dynamic systems and the intelligence of the constructive agent. These methods are important where the classic equilibrium analytics fail to provide sufficiently satisfactory understanding. In particular, one area of computational intelligence, Approximate Dynamic Programming, holds much promise for applications in this field and demonstrates the capacity for artificial Higher Order Neural Networks to add value in the social sciences and business. This chapter provides an overview of this area, introduces the relevant agent-based computational modeling systems, and suggests practical methods for their incorporation into the current research. A novel application of HONN to ADP specifically for the purpose of studying agent-based financial systems is presented.

Chapter V, "Foreign Exchange Rate Forecasting using Higher Order Flexible Neural Tree", establishes that Forecasting exchange rates is an important financial problem that is receiving increasing attention especially because of its difficulty and practical applications. In this chapter, we apply Higher Order Flexible Neural Trees (HOFNTs), which are capable of designing flexible Artificial Neural Network (ANN) architectures automatically, to forecast the foreign exchange rates. To demonstrate the efficiency of HOFNTs, we consider three different datasets in our forecast performance analysis. The data sets used are daily foreign exchange rates obtained from the Pacific Exchange Rate Service. The data comprises of the US dollar exchange rate against Euro, Great Britain Pound (GBP) and Japanese Yen (JPY). Under the HOFNT framework, we consider the Gene Expression Programming (GEP) approach and the Grammar Guided Genetic Programming (GGGP) approach to evolve the structure of HOFNT. The particle swarm optimization algorithm is employed to optimize the free parameters of the two different HOFNT models. This chapter briefly explains how the two different learning paradigms could be formulated using various methods and then investigates whether they can provide a reliable forecast model for foreign exchange rates. Simulation results shown the effectiveness of the proposed methods.

Chapter VI, "Higher Order Neural Networks for Stock Index Modeling", has the aim which is to study higher order artificial neural networks for stock index modeling problems. New network architectures and their corresponding training algorithms are discussed. These structures demonstrate their processing capabilities over traditional ANNs architectures with a reduction in the number of processing elements. In this chapter, the performance of classical neural networks and higher order neural networks for stock index forecasting is evaluated. We will highlight a novel slide-window method for data forecasting. With each slide of the observed data, the model can adjusts the variable dynamically. Simulation results show the feasibility and effectiveness of the proposed methods.

Chapter VII, "Ultra High Frequency Trigonometric Higher Order Neural Networks for Time Series Data Analysis", develops a new nonlinear model, Ultra high frequency Trigonometric Higher Order Neural Networks (UTHONN), for time series data analysis. Results show that UTHONN models are 3 to 12% better than Equilibrium Real Exchange Rates (ERER) model, and 4 – 9% better than other Polynomial Higher Order Neural Network (PHONN) and Trigonometric Higher Order Neural Network (THONN) models. This study also uses UTHONN models to simulate foreign exchange rates and consumer price index with error approaching 0.0000%.

Chapter VIII, "Artificial higher order pipeline recurrent neural networks for financial time series prediction", is concerned with the development of a novel artificial higher order neural networks architecture called the second-order pipeline recurrent neural network. The proposed artificial neural network consists of a linear and a nonlinear section, extracting relevant features from the input signal. The structuring unit of the proposed neural network is the second-order recurrent neural network. The architecture consists of a series of second-order recurrent neural networks, which are concatenated with each other. Simulation results in one-step ahead predictions of the foreign currency exchange rates demonstrate the superior performance of the proposed pipeline architecture as compared to other feedforward and recurrent structures.

Chapter IX, "A novel recurrent polynomial neural network for financial time series prediction", is concerned with the development of a novel artificial higher-order neural networks architecture called the recurrent Pi-sigma neural network. The proposed artificial neural network combines the advantages of both higher-order architectures in terms of the multi-linear interactions between inputs, as well as the temporal dynamics of recurrent neural networks, and produces highly accurate one-step ahead predictions of the foreign currency exchange rates, as compared to other feedforward and recurrent structures.

Chapter X, "Generalized correlation higher order neural networks for financial time series prediction", develops a generalized correlation higher order neural network designs. Their performance is compared with that of first order networks, conventional higher order neural network designs, and higher order linear regression networks for financial time series prediction. The correlation higher order neural network design is shown to give the highest accuracy for prediction of stock market share prices and share indices. The simulations compare the performance for three different training algorithms, stationary versus non-stationary input data, different numbers of neurons in the hidden layer and several generalized correlation higher order neural network designs. Generalized correlation higher order linear regression networks are also introduced and two designs are shown by simulation to give good correct direction prediction and higher prediction accuracies, particularly for long-term predictions, than other linear regression networks for the prediction of inter-bank lending risk Libor and Swap interest rate yield curves. The simulations compare the performance for different input data sample lag lengths.

Chapter XI, "Artificial Higher Order Neural Networks in Time Series Prediction", describes real world problems of nonlinear and chaotic processes, which make them hard to model and predict. This chapter first compares the neural network (NN) and the artificial higher order neural network (HONN) and then presents commonly known neural network architectures and a number of HONN architectures. The time series prediction problem is formulated as a system identification problem, where the input to the system is the past values of a time series, and its desired output is the future values of a time series.

The polynomial neural network (PNN) is then chosen as the HONN for application to the time series prediction problem. This chapter presents the application of HONN model to the nonlinear time series prediction problems of three major international currency exchange rates, as well as two key U.S. interest rates—the Federal funds rate and the yield on the 5-year U.S. Treasury note. Empirical results indicate that the proposed method is competitive with other approaches for the exchange rate problem, and can be used as a feasible solution for interest rate forecasting problem. This implies that the HONN model can be used as a feasible solution for exchange rate forecasting as well as for interest rate forecasting.

Chapter XII, " Application of Pi-Sigma Neural Networks and Ridge Polynomial Neural Networks to Financial Time Series Prediction", discusses the use of two artificial Higher Order Neural Networks (HONNs) models; the Pi-Sigma Neural Networks and the Ridge Polynomial Neural Networks, in financial time series forecasting. The networks were used to forecast the upcoming trends of three noisy financial signals; the exchange rate between the US Dollar and the Euro, the exchange rate between the Japanese Yen and the Euro, and the United States 10-year government bond. In particular, we systematically investigate a method of pre-processing the signals in order to reduce the trends in them. The performance of the networks is benchmarked against the performance of Multilayer Perceptrons. From the simulation results, the predictions clearly demonstrated that HONNs models, particularly Ridge Polynomial Neural Networks generate higher profit returns with fast convergence, therefore show considerable promise as a decision making tool. It is hoped that individual investor could benefit from the use of this forecasting tool.

Chapter XIII, "Electric Load Demand and Electricity Prices Forecasting using Higher Order Neural Networks Trained by Kalman Filtering", proposes the use of *Higher Order Neural Networks* (HONNs) trained with an *extended Kalman filter* based algorithm to predict the electric load demand as well as the electricity prices, with beyond a horizon of 24 hours. Due to the *chaotic behavior* of the electrical markets, it is not advisable to apply the traditional forecasting techniques used for time series; the results presented here confirm that HONNs can very well capture the complexity underlying electric load demand and electricity prices. The proposed neural network model produces very accurate next day predictions and also, prognosticates with very good accuracy, a week-ahead demand and price forecasts.

Chapter XIV, "Adaptive Higher Order Neural Network Models and Their Applications in Business", introduces an Adaptive Higher Order Neural Network (HONN) model and applies the adaptive model in business applications such as simulating and forecasting share prices. This adaptive HONN model offers significant advantages over traditional Standard ANN models such as much reduced network size, faster training, as well as much improved simulation and forecasting errors, due to their ability to better approximate complex, non-smooth, often discontinuous training data sets. The generalization ability of this HONN model is explored and discussed.

Chapter XV, "CEO Tenure and Debt: An Artificial Higher Order Neural Network Approach", proposes nonlinear models using artificial neural network models to study the relationship between chief elected official (CEO) tenure and debt. Using Higher Order Neural Network (HONN) simulator, this study analyzes debt of the municipalities as a function of population and CEO tenure, and compares the results with that from SAS. The linear models show that CEO tenure and the amount of debt vary inversely. Specifically, a longer length of CEO tenure leads to a decrease in debt, while a shorter tenure leads to an increase in debt. This chapter shows nonlinear model generated from HONN out performs linear models by 1%. The results from both models reveal that CEO tenure is negatively associated with the level of debt in local governments.

Chapter XVI, "Modeling and Trading the Soybean-Oil Crush Spread with Recurrent and Higher Order Networks: A Comparative Analysis", investigates the soybean-oil "crush" spread, that is the profit margin gained by processing soybeans into soy oil. Soybeans form a large proportion (over 1/5th) of the agricultural output of US farmers and the profit margins gained will therefore have a wide impact on the US economy in general. The chapter uses a number of techniques to forecast and trade the soybean crush spread. A traditional regression analysis is used as a benchmark against more sophisticated models such as a Multi-Layer Perceptron (MLP), Recurrent Neural Networks and Higher Order Neural Networks. These are then used to trade the spread, the implementation of a number of filtering techniques as used in the literature are utilized to further refine the trading statistics of the models. The results show that the best model before transactions costs both in- and out-of-sample is the Recurrent Network generating a superior risk adjusted return to all other models investigated. However in the case of most of the models investigated the cost of trading the spread all but eliminates any profit potential.

Chapter XVII, "Fundamental Theory of Artificial Higher Order Neural Networks", aims to describe fundamental principles of artificial higher order neural units (AHONUs) and networks (AHONNs). An essential core of AHONNs can be found in higher order weighted combinations or correlations between the input variables. By using some typical examples, this chapter describes how and why higher order combinations or correlations can be effective.

Chapter XVIII, "Dynamics in Artificial Higher Order Neural Networks with Delays", concentrates on studying the dynamics of artificial higher order neural networks (HONNs) with delays. Both stability analysis and periodic oscillation are discussed here for a class of delayed HONNs with (or without) impulses. Most of the sufficient conditions obtained in this chapter are presented in linear matrix inequalities (LMIs), and so can be easily computed and checked in practice using the Matlab LMI Toolbox. In reality, stability is a necessary feature when applying artificial neural networks. Also periodic solution plays an important role in the dynamical behavior of all solutions though other dynamics such as bifurcation and chaos do coexist. So here we mainly focus on questions of the stability and periodic solutions of artificial HONNs with (or without) impulses. Firstly, stability analysis and periodic oscillation are analyzed for higher order bidirectional associative memory (BAM) neural networks without impulses. Secondly, global exponential stability and exponential convergence are studied for a class of impulsive higher order bidirectional associative memory neural networks with time-varying delays. The main methods and tools used in this chapter are linear matrix inequalities (LMIs), Lyapunov stability theory and coincidence degree theory.

Chapter XIX, "A New Topology for Artificial Higher Order Neural Networks — Polynomial Kernel Networks", is aiming to develop a systematic approach for optimizing the structure of artificial higher order neural networks (HONN) for system modeling and function approximation, a new HONN topology, namely polynomial kernel networks, is proposed in this chapter. Structurally, the polynomial kernel network can be viewed as a three-layer feed-forward neural network with a special polynomial activation function for the nodes in the hidden layer. The new network is equivalent to a HONN; however, due to the underlying connections with polynomial kernel support vector machines, the weights and the structure of the network can be determined simultaneously using structural risk minimization. The advantage of the topology of the polynomial kernel network and the use of a support vector kernel expansion paves the way to represent nonlinear functions or systems, and underpins some advanced analysis of the network performance. In this chapter, from the perspective of network complexity, both quadratic programming and linear programming based training of the polynomial kernel network are investigated.

Chapter XX, "High Speed Optical Higher Order Neural Networks for Discovering Data Trends and Patterns in Very Large Database", describes the progress in using optical technology to construct high-speed artificial higher order neural network systems. The chapter reviews how optical technology can speed up searches within large databases in order to identify relationships and dependencies between individual data records, such as financial or business time-series, as well as trends and relationships within them. Two distinct approaches in which optics may be used are reviewed. In the first approach, the chapter reviews current research replacing copper connections in a conventional data storage system, such as a several terabyte RAID array of magnetic hard discs, by optical waveguides to achieve very high data rates with low crosstalk interference. In the second approach, the chapter reviews how high speed optical correlators with feedback can be used to realize artificial higher order neural networks using Fourier Transform free space optics and holographic database storage.

Chapter XXI, "On Complex Artificial Higher Order Neural Networks: Dealing with Stochasticity, Jumps and Delays", deals with the analysis problem of the global exponential stability for a general class of stochastic artificial higher order neural networks with multiple mixed time delays and Markovian jumping parameters. The mixed time delays under consideration comprise both the discrete time-varying delays and the distributed time-delays. The main purpose of this chapter is to establish easily verifiable conditions under which the delayed high-order stochastic jumping neural network is exponentially stable in the mean square in the presence of both the mixed time delays and Markovian switching. By employing a new Lyapunov-Krasovskii functional and conducting stochastic analysis, a linear matrix inequality (LMI) approach is developed to derive the criteria ensuring the exponential stability. Furthermore, the criteria are dependent on both the discrete time-delay and distributed time-delay, hence less conservative. The proposed criteria can be readily checked by using some standard numerical packages such as the Matlab LMI Toolbox. A simple example is provided to demonstrate the effectiveness and applicability of the proposed testing criteria.

Chapter XXII, "Trigonometric Polynomial Higher Order Neural Network Group Models and Weighted Kernel Models for Financial Data Simulation and Prediction", introduces trigonometric polynomial higher order neural network models. In the area of financial data simulation and prediction, there is no single neural network model that could handle the wide variety of data and perform well in the real world. A way of solving this difficulty is to develop a number of new models, with different algorithms. A wider variety of models would give financial operators more chances to find a suitable model when they process their data. That was the major motivation for this chapter. The theoretical principles of these improved models are presented and demonstrated and experiments are conducted by using real-life financial data.

Acknowledgment

The editor would like to acknowledge the help of all involved in the collation and the review process of the book, without whose support the project could not have been satisfactorily completed. Deep appreciation and gratitude are due to Prof. Douglas Gordon, Dean of College of Liberal Arts and Science, Christopher Newport University, for giving me three Dean's Office Grants to support my research and the editing this book. Deep appreciation and gratitude are also due to Prof. David Doughty, Chair of Department of Physics, Computer Science and Engineering, Christopher Newport University, for signing my book contract with the publisher and my copyright agreement forms to support my research and the editing this book. My appreciations are also due to Dr. A. Martin Buoncristiani, Dr. Randall Caton, Dr. David Hibler, and Dr. George Webb, Professors of Department of Physics, Computer Science and Engineering, Christopher Newport University, for always strongly supporting my research. I would like thank my distinction supervisor, Dr. Rod Scofield, Senior Scientist of National Oceanic and Atmospheric Administration (NOAA), Washington DC, USA for supporting my artificial neural network research and awarding me as an USA National Research Council Postdoctoral Fellow (1991-1992) and a Senior USA National Research Council Research Associate (1999-2000). I would like to thank Dr. John Fulcher, Professor of University of Wollongong Australia, for a long time of research cooperation in the artificial neural network area since 1992.

I wish to thank all of the authors for their insights and excellent contributions to this book. Most of the authors of chapters included in this book also served as referees for chapters written by other authors. Thanks go to all the reviewers who provided constructive and comprehensive reviews and suggestions

Special thanks also go to the publishing team at IGI Global, whose contributions throughout the whole process from inception of the initial idea to final publication have been invaluable. In particular to Jessica Thompson, Kristin Roth, and Meg Stocking, who continuously prodded via e-mail for keeping the project on schedule and to Mehdi Khosrow-Pour and Jan Travers whose enthusiasm motivated me to initially accept his invitation for taking on this project.

Special thanks go to my family for their continuous support and encouragement, in particular, to my wife, Zhao Qing Zhang, for her unfailing support and encouragement during the years it took to give birth to this book.

Ming Zhang, Editor, PhD
Christopher Newport University, Newport News, VA, USA
October 2007

Section I
Artificial Higher Order Neural Networks for Economics

Chapter I
Artificial Higher Order Neural Network Nonlinear Models:
SAS NLIN or HONNs?

Ming Zhang
Christopher Newport University, USA

ABSTRACT

This chapter delivers general format of Higher Order Neural Networks (HONNs) for nonlinear data analysis and six different HONN models. This chapter mathematically proves that HONN models could converge and have mean squared errors close to zero. This chapter illustrates the learning algorithm with update formulas. HONN models are compared with SAS Nonlinear (NLIN) models and results show that HONN models are 3 to 12% better than SAS Nonlinear models. Moreover, this chapter shows how to use HONN models to find the best model, order and coefficients, without writing the regression expression, declaring parameter names, and supplying initial parameter values.

INTRODUCTION

Background of Higher-Order Neural Networks (HONNs)

Although traditional Artificial Neural Network (ANN) models are recognized for their great performance in pattern matching, pattern recognition, and mathematical function approximation, they are often stuck in local, rather than global minima. In addition, ANNs take unacceptably long time to converge in practice (Fulcher, Zhang, and Xu 2006). Moreover, ANNs are unable to manage non-smooth, discontinuous training data, and complex mappings in financial time series simulation and prediction. ANNs are 'black box' in nature, which means the explanations for their output are not obvious. This leads to the motivation for studies on Higher Order Neural Networks (HONNs).

HONN includes the neuron activation functions, preprocessing of the neuron inputs, and connections to more than one layer (Bengtsson, 1990). In this chapter, HONN refers to the neuron type, which can be linear, power, multiplicative, sigmoid, logarithmic, etc. The first-order neural networks can be formulated by using linear neurons that are only capable of capturing first-order correlations in the training data (Giles & Maxwell, 1987). The second order or above HONNs involve higher-order correlations in the training data that require more complex neuron activation functions (Barron, Gilstrap & Shrier, 1987; Giles & Maxwell, 1987; Psaltis, Park & Hong, 1988). Neurons which include terms up to and including degree-k are referred to as k*th*-order neurons (Lisboa and Perantonis, 1991).

Rumelhart, Hinton, and McClelland (1986) develop 'sigma-pi' neurons where they show that the generalized standard BackPropagation algorithm can be applied to simple additive neurons. Both Hebbian and Perceptron learning rules can be employed when no hidden layers are involved (Shin 1991). The performance of first-order ANNs can be improved by utilizing sophisticated learning algorithms (Karayiannis and Venetsanopoulos, 1993). Redding, Kowalczy and Downs (1993) develop a constructive HONN algorithm. Zhang and Fulcher (2004) develop Polynomial, Trigonometric and other HONN models. Giles, Griffin and Maxwell (1988) and Lisboa and Pentonis (1991) show that the multiplicative interconnections within ANNs have been used in many applications, including invariant pattern recognition.

Others suggest groups of individual neurons (Willcox, 1991; Hu and Pan, 1992). ANNs can simulate any nonlinear functions to any degree of accuracy (Hornik, 1991; and Leshno, 1993).

Zhang, Fulcher, and Scofield (1997) show that ANN groups offer superior performance compared with ANNs when dealing with discontinuous and non-smooth piecewise nonlinear functions. Compared with Polynomial Higher Order Neural Network (PHONN) and Trigonometric Higher Order Neural Network (THONN), Neural Adaptive Higher Order Neural Network (NAHONN) offers more flexibility and more accurate approximation capability. Since using NAHONN the hidden layer variables are adjustable (Zhang, Xu, and Fulcher, 2002). In addition, Zhang, Xu, and Fulcher (2002) proves that NAHONN groups are capable of approximating any kinds of piecewise continuous function, to any degree of accuracy. In addition, these models are capable of automatically selecting both the optimum model for a particular time series and the appropriate model order.

Applications of HONNs in Computer Areas

Jeffries (1989) presents a specific HONN design which can store any of the binomial n-strings for error-correcting decoding of any binary string code. Tai and Jong (1990) show why the probability of the states of neurons being active and passive can always be chosen equally. Manykin and Belov (1991) propose an optical scheme of the second order HONN, and show the importance of an additional time coordinate inherent in the photo-echo effect.

Venkatesh and Baldi (1991) study the estimation of the maximum number of states that can be stable in higher order extensions of the HONN models. Estevez and Okabe (1991) provide a piecewise linear HONN with the structure consisting of two layers of modifiable weights. HONN is seven times faster than that of standard feedforward neural networks when simulating the XOR/parity problem.

Spirkovska and Reid (1992) find that HONNs can reduce the training time significantly, since distortion invariance can be built into the architecture of the HONNs. Kanaoka, Chellappa, Yoshitaka, and Tomita (1992) show that a single layer of HONN is effective for scale, rotation, and shift invariance recognition. Chang, Lin, and Cheung (1993) generalize back propagation algorithm for multi-layer HONNs, and discuss the two basic structures, the standard form and the polynomial form. Based on their simulation results, both standard and polynomial HONNs can recognize noisy data under rotation up to 70% and noisy irrational data up to 94%. Spirkovska and Reid (1994) point out that invariances can be built directly into the architecture of a HONN. Thus, for 2D object recognition, the HONN needs to be trained on just one view of each object class and HONNs have distinct advantages for position, scale, and rotation-invariant object recognition. By modifying the constraints imposed on the weights in HONNs (He and Siyal, 1999) the performance of a HONN with respect to distortion can be improved. Park, Smith, and Mersereau (2000) combine maximally decimated directional filter banks with HONNs. The new approach is effective in enhancing the discrimination power of the HONN inputs. Chen, Jiang, and Xu (2003) deduce a higher order projection learning mechanism. Numerical simulations to clarify the merits of the HONN associative memory and the potential applications of the new learning rule are presented.

Applications of HONNs in Economics, Finance, and Accounting

Many researchers in the economics, finance, and accounting areas use artificial neural networks in their studies, however, only a few studies use HONN. Lee, Lee, and Park (1992) use HONNs to identify and control the nonlinear dynamic systems. The computer simulation results reveal that HONN models are more effective in controlling nonlinear dynamic systems. Karayiannis and Venetsanopoulos (1995) study the architecture, training, and properties of neural networks of order higher than one. They also study the formulation of the training of HONNs as a nonlinear associative recall problem that provides the basis for their optimal least squares training. Bouzerdoum (1999) presents a class of HONNs, shunting inhibitory artificial neural networks (SIANNs). These HONNs are capable of producing classifiers with complex nonlinear decision

boundaries, ranging from simple hyperplanes to very complex nonlinear surfaces. The author also provides a training method for SIANNs. Li, Hirasawa, and Hu (2003) present a constructive method for HONNs with multiplication units. The proposed method provides a flexible mechanism for incremental network growth.

Zhang, Zhang, and Fulcher (1997) develop trigonometric polynomial higher order neural network (THONN) group models for financial data prediction. Results show that THONN group models can handle nonlinear data that has discontinuous points. Xu and Zhang (1999) develop adaptive HONNs with adaptive neuron functions to approximate continuous data. Lu, Zhang, and Scofield (2000) generate Polynomial and Trigonometric Higher Order Neural Network (PTHONN) models for multi-polynomial function simulation. Crane and Zhang (2005) provide a SINC Higher Order Neural Network (SINCHONN) models, which use SINC function as active neurons. These models successfully simulate currency exchange rates.

Ghazali (2005) use HONN for financial time series prediction and find HONN out performs traditional multilayer neural network models. Knowles, Hussain, Deredy, Lisboa, and Dunis (2005) use HONNs with Bayesian confidence measure for prediction of EUR/USD exchange rates. They show that the simulation results for HONNs are 8% better than multilayer neural network. In the accounting area, Zhang (2005) uses HONN to estimate misclassification cost for different financial distress prediction models. Moreover, HONN has been used to generate nonlinear models for the power of chief elected officials and debt (Zhang, 2006). Dunis, Laws, and Evans (2006) use HONN to build a nonlinear model for modeling and trading the gasoline crack spread. The results show that the spread does indeed exhibit asymmetric adjustment, with movements away from fair value being nearly three times larger on the downside than on the upside.

Zhang, Murugesan and Sadeghi (1995), and Zhang, Zhang and Keen (1999) use both Polynomial and Trigonometric HONNs to simulate and predict financial time series data from the Reserve Bank of Australia Bulletin www.abs.gov.au/ausstats/abs@.nsf/w2.3 to around 90% accuracy. Zhang and Lu (2001) develop the Polynomial and Trigonometric HONN (PTHONN) and Multiple Polynomial functions HONN (MPHONN) models for improved performance. In financial time series prediction, PHONN groups produce around 1.2% error for simulation compared with 11% for HONNs (Zhang, Zhang, and Fulcher, 2000). Improvements in performance are also observed with THONN groups (Zhang, Zhang, and Fulcher, 2000). Currently, multi-PHONN (Zhang 2001, 2002, 2005, and 2006) is capable of simulating not only polynomial and/or trigonometric functions, but also a combinations of these and sigmoid and/or logarithmic functions. As a result, they are able to better approximate real world economic time series data.

SAS

The overview (http://support.sas.com/documentation/onlinedoc/index.html) of SAS Nonlinear (NLIN) procedure is as follows:

The NLIN procedure produces least squares or weighted least squares estimates of the parameters of a nonlinear model. Nonlinear models are more difficult to specify and estimates than linear models. Instead of simply listing regression variables, you must write the regression expression, declare parameter names, and supply initial parameter values. Some models are difficult to fit, and there is no guarantee that the procedure can fit the model successfully. For each nonlinear model to be analyzed, you must specify the model (using a single dependent variable) and the names and starting values of the parameters to be estimated.

The first difficulty in using SAS NLIN is that users have to provide the correct regression expression. However, this step is troublesome since there are different possible models (polynomial, trigonometric polynomial, etc.) and order that the users can select.

The second difficulty to use SAS NLIN is that you have to provide the starting values of the parameters to be estimated. If you give the wrong starting values, SAS NLIN procedure may not converge and users may waste time in guessing the initial values. The key point is SAS NLIN can not guarantee that the procedure will fit the model successfully. In most cases, the starting values of the parameters that users provide must be very close to the actual parameters, otherwise SAS NLIN will not converge.

Motivations, Contributions, and Outline of this Chapter

The purpose of this chapter is to develop easy to use and always convergent technique in building nonlinear models. Since HONNs are open-box models and the traditional neural networks are black-box models, people working in economics and business areas may feel more comfortable working with HONN. So the first motivation is to introduce open-box HONN models to people working in economics and business areas. The goal of using SAS NLIN procedure is to find the nonlinear models and the coefficients. However, this goal is difficult to achieve since most of the SAS users cannot provide the expression or the initial values for the coefficients. The second motivation is to develop new nonlinear models, which are easy to use and always convergent, for time series data analysis.

The contributions of this chapter will be:

- Introduce the background of HONNs with the applications of HONNs
- Introduce 6 different types of HONN models

- Provide the HONN learning algorithm and weight update formulae
- Compare HONNs with SAS NLIN and show that HONNs can produce more accurate simulation results than SAS NLIN models
- Show detailed steps in how to use HONNs to find the best model, order, and coefficients

Section 1 introduces the background and applications of HONNs and SAS. Section 2 provides the structure of HONN and different types of nonlinear models of HONN. The third section will introduce the convergence theories of HONN and explain why HONNs can out perform SAS NLIN procedure. Section 4 provides the learning formulae for training HONN and the detailed learning algorithm of HONN models and weights update formulae. Section 5 studies six different HONN Nonlinear Models: PHONN (Polynomial Higher Order Neural Network), THONN (Trigonometric Higher Order Neural Network), UCSHONN (Ultra High Frequency Cosine and Sine Trigonometric Higher Order Neural Network), SXSHONN (SINC and Trigonometric Higher Order Neural Network), and SPHONN (Sigmoid Polynomial Higher Order Neural Network). Section 6 shows the HONN simulation system. Section 7 compares SAS nonlinear models with HONN nonlinear models. Section 8 introduces how to find model, order, and coefficients by HONN nonlinear models. Section 9 concludes this chapter. Appendix A, B, and C give the detail proof for HONN learning weight update.

HONN STRUCTURE AND NONLINEAR MODLES

Formula (1), (2) and (3) are the HONN models 1b, 1 and 0 respectively. Model 1b has three layers of changeable weights, Model 1 has two layers of changeable weights, and model 0 has one layer of changeable weights. For models 1b, 1 and 0, Z is the output while x and y are the inputs of

HONN. $a_{kj}{}^{o}$ is the weight for the output layer, $a_{kj}{}^{hx}$ and $a_{kj}{}^{hy}$ are the weights for the second hidden layer, and $a_{k}{}^{x}$ and $a_{j}{}^{y}$ are the weights for the first hidden layer. The output layer node of HONN is a linear function of $f^{o}(net^{o}) = net^{o}$, where net^{o} equals the input of output layer node. The second hidden layer node of HONN is a multiple neuron. It means that the neuron activity function is a linear function of $f^{h}(net_{kj}{}^{o}) = net_{kj}{}^{o}$, where $net_{kj}{}^{o}$ equals the multiplication of two inputs from the first hidden layer. The first hidden layer neuron function could be any nonlinear function. HONN is an open neural network model, each weight of HONN has its corresponding coefficient in the model formula, similarly, each node of HONN has its corresponding function in the model formula. The structure of HONN is built by a nonlinear formula. It means, after training, there is rationale for each component of HONN in the nonlinear formula.

HONN   Model   1b :

$$Z = \sum_{k,j=0}^{n} a_{kj}{}^{o} \{a_{kj}{}^{hx} f_{k}{}^{x}(a_{k}{}^{x}x)\} \{a_{kj}{}^{hy} f_{j}{}^{y}(a_{j}{}^{y}y)\} \quad (1)$$

HONN   Model   1 :

$$Z = \sum_{k,j=0}^{n} a_{kj}{}^{o} \{f_{k}{}^{x}(a_{k}{}^{x}x)\} \{f_{j}{}^{y}(a_{j}{}^{y}y)\}$$

where :

$$a_{kj}{}^{hx} = a_{kj}{}^{hy} = 1 \quad (2)$$

HONN   Model   0 :

$$z = \sum_{k,j=0}^{n} a_{kj}{}^{o} \{f_{k}{}^{x}(x)\} \{f_{j}{}^{y}(y)\}$$

where : $(a_{kj}{}^{hx}) = (a_{kj}{}^{hy}) = 1$

and $a_{k}{}^{x} = a_{j}{}^{y} = 1 \quad (3)$

For equations 1, 2, and 3, values of k and j ranges from 0 to n, where n is an integer. The HONN model can simulate any nonlinear function. This property of the model allows it to easily simulate and predicate any nonlinear functions and ultra high frequency time series data, since both k and j increase when there is an increase in n. The following (see Equation (4)) is an expansion of model HONN with order two.

Figure 1 A and B show the "HONN Architecture". This model structure is used to develop the model learning algorithm, which ensures the convergence of learning.

CONVERGENCE THEORIES OF HONN

How can HONNs out perform SAS NLIN? This chapter proves mathematically that HONNs can always converge and have better accuracy than SAS NLIN. Fortunately, there are a few very good convergence theories proved mathematically in the artificial neural network modeling area.

Hornik (1991) proves the following general result:

Equation (4).

$$
\begin{aligned}
z = {}&a_{00}{}^{o}\, a_{00}{}^{hx}\, a_{00}{}^{hy} + a_{01}{}^{o}\, a_{01}{}^{hx}\, a_{01}{}^{hy}\, f_1{}^{y}(a_1{}^{y}\, y) + a_{02}{}^{o}\, a_{02}{}^{hx}\, a_{02}{}^{hy}\, f_2{}^{y}(a_2{}^{y}\, y) \\
&+ a_{10}{}^{o}\, a_{10}{}^{hx}\, a_{10}{}^{hy}\, f_1{}^{x}(a_1{}^{x}\, x) + a_{11}{}^{o}\, a_{11}{}^{hx}\, a_{11}{}^{hy}\, f_1{}^{x}(a_1{}^{x}\, x)\, f_1{}^{y}(a_1{}^{y}\, y) \\
&+ a_{12}{}^{o}\, a_{12}{}^{hx}\, a_{12}{}^{hy}\, f_1{}^{x}(a_1{}^{x}\, x)\, f_2{}^{y}(a_2{}^{y}\, y) + a_{20}{}^{o}\, a_{20}{}^{hx}\, a_{20}{}^{hy}\, f_2{}^{x}(a_2{}^{x}\, x) \\
&+ a_{21}{}^{o}\, a_{21}{}^{hx}\, a_{21}{}^{hy}\, f_2{}^{x}(a_2{}^{x}\, x)\, f_1{}^{y}(a_1{}^{y}\, y) + a_{22}{}^{o}\, a_{22}{}^{hx}\, a_{22}{}^{hy}\, f_2{}^{x}(a_2{}^{x}\, x)\, f_2{}^{y}(a_2{}^{y}\, y)
\end{aligned} \tag{4}
$$

Figure 1a. HONN Architecture Model 1b (two inputs and one output)

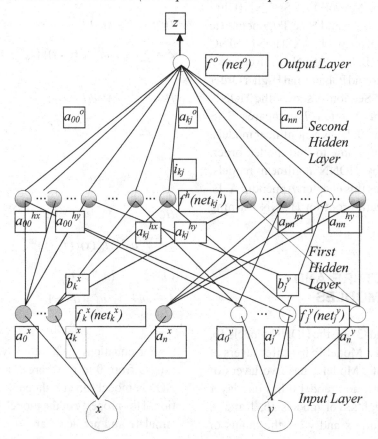

Figure 1b. HONN Architecture Model 1b (two inputs and one output)

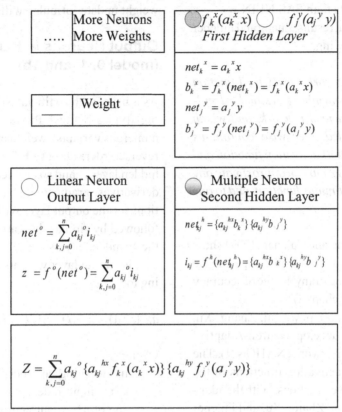

Whenever the activation function is continuous, bounded and nonconstant, then for an arbitrary compact subset $X \subseteq R^n$, standard multilayer feedforward networks can approximate any continuous function on X arbitrarily well with respect to uniform distance, provided that sufficiently many hidden units are available.

Since HONNs are a subset of artificial neural networks, and HONNs are multilayer feedforward networks and the activation functions are continuous, bounded and nonconstant. Therefore, HONNs meet all the requirements of the above result.

Leshno (1993) shows a more general result:

A standard multilayer feedforward network with a locally bounded piecewise continuous activation function can approximate any continuous function to any degree of accuracy if and only if the network's activation function is not a polynomial.

Since HONNs are standard multiplayer feedforward networks with locally bounded piecewise continuous functions, HONNs can approximate any continuous function to any degree of accuracy. Polynomial Higher Order Network uses polynomial function as network's activation function on the first hidden layer, but use other functions on the second layer and the output layer, so PHONNs still meet the conditions of the above result. Thus, PHONNs can approximate any continue function to any degree of accuracy.

Inferring from Hornik (1991) and Leshno (1993), HONNs can simulate any continuous function to any degree of accuracy, since HONNs are a subset of ANN. This is the reason why HONNs can have better results than SAS NLIN.

Given these general results, Zhang and Fulcher (1997) infer the following:

Consider a neural network Piecewise Function Group, in which each member is a standard multilayer feedforward neural network, and which has a locally bounded, piecewise continuous (rather than polynomial) activation function and threshold. Each such group can approximate any kind of piecewise continuous function, and to any degree of accuracy.

Results from Zhang and Fulcher (1997) show HONN group can simulate any kind of piecewise continuous function and to any degree of accuracy (not discussed in this chapter).

To make HONN more powerful, Zhang, Xu, and Fulcher (2002) develop Neuron-Adaptive Higher Order Neural Network (NAHONN). The key point is that the activation functions in the NAHONN are adaptive functions. With the adaptive function as neuron, Zhang, Xu, and Fulcher (2002) generate the following theorem:

A NAHONN (Neuron-Adaptive Higher Order Neural Network) with a neuron-adaptive activation function can approximate any piecewise continuous function with infinite (countable) discontinuous points to any degree of accuracy.

This theorem shows that one NAHONN can approximate any piecewise continuous function with infinite (countable) discontinuous points to any degree of accuracy. This result is stronger than the results from Hornik (1991), Leshno (1993), and Zhang and Fulcher (1997).

LEARNING ALGORITHM OF HONN MODEL

This section will mathematically provide weight update formulae for each weight in different layers.

Then the HONN learning algorithm based on the weight update formulae will be provided.

Output Neurons in HONN Model (model 0, 1, and 1b)

As is usual with Artificial Neural Network training (typically Back-Propagation or one of its numerous variants), weight adjustment occurs in reverse order: output ➜ 2nd hidden layer ➜ 1st hidden layer …and so on. Accordingly, the error, derivatives, gradients and weight update equations for the output layer will be derived. This is followed by similar derivations for the 2nd, then the 1st hidden layers.

The output layer weights are updated according to:

$$a_{kj}{}^{o}(t+1) = a_{kj}{}^{o}(t) - \eta(\partial E \ / \ \partial a_{kj}{}^{o}) \qquad (5)$$

where:

η = learning rate (positive and usually < 1)
k, j = input index (k, j=0, 1, 2,…,n means one of n*n input neurons from the second hidden layer)
E = error
t = training time
o = output layer
a = weight

In formula (5), the updated weights will be smaller than the original value, if the value of gradient is positive. The updated weights will become greater than the original value, if the value of gradient is negative. So based on formula (5), after many updates of the weights, HONN could go to minimum compare to the desired output and actual output. The learning algorithm of the output layer weights is in the following formula. Appendix A provides the detailed derivation.

$$a_{kj}^{\;o}(t+1) = a_{kj}^{\;o}(t) - \eta(\partial E / \partial a_{kj}^{\;o})$$
$$= a_{kj}^{\;o}(t) + \eta(d - z)f^{o\,'}(net^o)i_{kj}$$
$$= a_{kj}^{\;o}(t) + \eta\delta^{\,ol}i_{kj}$$

where:

$$\delta^{\,ol} = (d-z)$$
$$f^{o\,'}(net^o) = 1 \qquad (linear \qquad neuron) \qquad (6)$$

where:

d: desired output

z: actual output from output neuron

I_{kj}: input to the output neuron (output from 2nd hidden layer)

Second-Hidden Layer Neurons in HONN Model (Model 1b)

The second hidden layer weights are updated according to:

$$a_{kj}^{\;hx}(t+1) = a_{kj}^{\;hx}(t) - \eta(\partial E / \partial a_{kj}^{\;hx}) \qquad (7)$$

where:

η = learning rate (positive and usually < 1)

k, j = input index (k, j=0, 1, …,n means one of 2*n*n input combinations from 1st hidden layer)

E = error

t = training time

hx = hidden layer, related to x input

$a_{kj}^{\;hx}$ = hidden layer weight

In formula (7), the updated weight will be smaller than the original value, if the value of gradient is positive. The updated weight will become greater than the original value, if the value of gradient is negative. So based on the formula (7), after repeating this procedure for many times, HONN could go to minimum compare the desired output and actual output. The learning algorithm of the second hidden layer weights will be based on the following formula. Appendix B provides more detailed derivation.

$$a_{kj}^{\;hx}(t+1) = a_{kj}^{\;hx}(t) - \eta(\partial E / \partial a_{kj}^{\;hx})$$
$$= a_{kj}^{\;hx}(t) + \eta((d-z)f^{o\,'}(net^{\,o})a_{kj}^{\;o}f^{h\,'}(net_{kj}^{\;hx})a_{kj}^{\;hy}b_j^{\;y}b_k^{\;x})$$
$$= a_{kj}^{\;hx}(t) + \eta(\delta^{\,ol}a_{kj}^{\;o}\delta_{kj}^{\;hx}b_k^{\;x})$$

where: $\qquad \delta^{\,ol} = (d-z)$
$$\delta_{kj}^{\;hx} = a_{kj}^{\;hy}b_j^{\;y}$$
$$f^{o\,'}(net^o) = 1 \qquad (linear \qquad neuron)$$
$$f^{h\,'}(net_{kj}^{\;hx}) = 1 \qquad (linear \qquad neuron)$$
$$\qquad (8)$$

Using the same rules, weight update equations for y input neurons are:

$$a_{kj}^{\;hy}(t+1) = a_{kj}^{\;hy}(t) - \eta(\partial E / \partial a_{kj}^{\;hy})$$
$$= a_{kj}^{\;hy}(t) + \eta((d-z)f^{o\,'}(net^{\,o})a_{kj}^{\;o}f^{h\,'}(net_{kj}^{\;hy})a_{kj}^{\;hx}b_k^{\;x}b_j^{\;y})$$
$$= a_{kj}^{\;hy}(t) + \eta(\delta^{\,ol}a_{kj}^{\;o}\delta_{kj}^{\;hy}b_j^{\;y})$$

where: $\qquad \delta^{\,ol} = (d-z)$
$$\delta_{kj}^{\;hy} = a_{kj}^{\;hx}b_k^{\;x}$$
$$f^{o\,'}(net^o) = 1 \qquad (linear \qquad neuron)$$
$$f^{h\,'}(net_{kj}^{\;hy}) = 1 \qquad (linear \qquad neuron)$$
$$\qquad (9)$$

First Hidden Layer Neurons in HONN Models (Model 1 and Model 1b)

The 1st hidden layer weights are updated according to:

$$a_k^{\;x}(t+1) = a_k^{\;x}(t) - \eta(\partial E_p / \partial a_k^{\;x}) \qquad (10)$$

where:

η = learning rate (positive & usually < 1)

k = kth neuron of first hidden layer

E = error

t = training time

$a_k^{\;x}$ = 1st hidden layer weight for input x

Similarly, in formula (10), the updated weights will be smaller than the original value, if the value of gradient is positive. The updated weight will become greater than the original value, if the value of gradient is negative. So based on the formula

(10), after updating the weights for many times, HONN could go to minimum compare the desired output and actual output. The learning algorithm of the first hidden layer weights will be based on the following formula. Appendix C presents more detailed derivation.

Using the procedure displayed in Equation (11), we get Equation (12).

HONN Learning Algorithm

We summarize the procedure for performing the learning algorithm:

Step 1: Initialize all weights (coefficients) of the neurons (activation functions).
Step 2: Input a sample from the data pool.
Step 3: Calculate the actual outputs of all neurons using present values of weights (coefficients), according to equations (1), (2), and (3).
Step 4: Compare the desired output and actual output. If mean squared error reaches to the desired number, stop. Otherwise go to Step 5.

Equation (11).

$$a_k^x(t+1) = a_k^x(t) - \eta(\partial E_p / \partial a_k^x)$$
$$= a_x^x(t) + \eta(d-z)f^o{}'(net^o)a_{kj}^o * f^h{}'(net_{kj}^h)a_{kj}^{hy}b_j^y a_{kj}^{hx}f_k^x{}'(net_k^x)x$$
$$= a_x^x(t) + \eta * \delta^{ol} * a_{kj}^o * \delta_{kj}^{hx} * a_{kj}^{hx} * f_k^x{}'(net_k^x) * x$$
$$= a_x^x(t) + \eta * \delta^{ol} * a_{kj}^o * \delta_{kj}^{hx} * a_{kj}^{hx} * \delta_k^x * x$$

where:

$$\delta^{ol} = (d-z)$$
$$f^o{}'(net^o) = 1 \quad (linear \quad neuron)$$
$$\delta_{kj}^{hx} = a_{kj}^{hy}b_j^y$$
$$f^h{}'(net_{kj}^h) = 1 \quad (linear \quad neuron)$$
$$\delta_k^x = f_k^x{}'(net_k^x)$$

Equation (12).

$$a_j^y(t+1) = a_j^y(t) - \eta(\partial E_p / \partial a_j^y)$$
$$= a_j^y(t) + \eta(d-z)f^o{}'(net^o)a_{kj}^o * f^h{}'(net_{kj}^h)a_{kj}^{hx}b_k^x a_{kj}^{hy}f_j^y{}'(net_j^y)y$$
$$= a_j^y(t) + \eta * \delta^{ol} * a_{kj}^o * \delta^{hy} * a_{kj}^{hy} * f_j^y{}'(net_j^y) * y$$
$$= a_j^y(t) + \eta * \delta^{ol} * a_{kj}^o * \delta_{kj}^{hy} * a_{kj}^{hy} * \delta_j^y * y$$

where:

$$\delta^{ol} = (d-z)$$
$$f^o{}'(net^o) = 1 \quad (linear \quad neuron)$$
$$\delta_{kj}^{hy} = a_{kj}^{hx}b_k^x$$
$$f^h{}'(net_{kj}^{hy}) = 1 \quad (linear \quad neuron)$$
$$\delta_j^y = f_j^y{}'(net_j^y)$$

Step 5: Adjust the weights (coefficients) according to the iterative formulae in (6), (8), (9), (11), and (12).

Step 6: Input another sample from the data pool, go to step 3.

The above learning algorithm is the back propagation learning algorithm, the formulae in the above steps are developed in this chapter.

HONN NONLINEAR MODELS

PHONN Model

Polynomial Higher Order Neural Networks (PHONN) are defined when neuron functions $(f_k^x$ and $f_j^y)$ select polynomial functions. PHONN models are defined as follows:

PHONN   Model   1b :

let

$$f_k^x(a_k^x x) = (a_k^x x)^k$$

$$f_j^y(a_j^y y) = (a_j^y y)^j$$

Then

$$Z = \sum_{k,j=0}^{n} (a_{kj}^o)\{a_{kj}^{hx}(a_k^x x)^k\}\{a_{kj}^{hy}(a_j^y y)^j\} \quad (13)$$

PHONN   Model   1 :

$$z = \sum_{k,j=0}^{n} a_{kj}^o \ (a_k^x x)^k (a_j^y y)^j$$

where : $(a_{kj}^{hx}) = (a_{kj}^{hy}) = 1$ \quad (14)

PHONN   Model   0 :

$$z = \sum_{k,j=0}^{n} a_{kj}^o \ (x)^k (y)^j$$

where : $(a_{kj}^{hx}) = (a_{kj}^{hy}) = 1$

   and $a_k^x = a_j^y = 1$ \quad (15)

The learning formulae of the output layer weight for PHONN and all other HONN model is the same as the learning formula (6) of the output layer weight for HONN. Similarly, the learning formulae of the second hidden layer weight for

Equation (16).

> *Since*
>
> $f_k^x = (a_k^x x)^k$ *and* $net_k^x = a_k^x x$
>
> $f_k^{x\,'}(net_k^x) = k(net_k^x)^{k-1} = k(a_k^x x)^{k-1}$
>
> *Then*
>
> $a_k^x(t+1) = a_k^x(t) - \eta(\partial E_p / \partial a_k^x)$
>
> $= a_x^x(t) + \eta(d-z)f^{o\,'}(net^o)a_{kj}^o * f^{h\,'}(net_{kj}^h)a_{kj}^{hy}b_j^y a_{kj}^{hx} f_k^{x\,'}(net_k^x)x$
>
> $= a_x^x(t) + \eta * \delta^{ol} * a_{kj}^o * \delta_{kj}^{hx} * a_{kj}^{hx} * f_k^{x\,'}(net_k^x) * x$
>
> $= a_x^x(t) + \eta * \delta^{ol} * a_{kj}^o * \delta_{kj}^{hx} * a_{kj}^{hx} * k(a_k^x x)^{k-1} * x$
>
> $= a_x^x(t) + \eta * \delta^{ol} * a_{kj}^o * \delta_{kj}^{hx} * a_{kj}^{hx} * \delta_k^{x} * x$
>
> *where* :
>
> $\delta^{ol} = (d-z)$ *and* $f^{o\,'}(net^o) = 1$ (linear   neuron)
>
> $\delta_{kj}^{hx} = a_{kj}^{hy}b_j^y$ *and* $f^{h\,'}(net_{kj}^h) = 1$ (linear   neuron)
>
> $\delta_k^x = f_k^{x\,'}(net_k^x) = k(net_k^x)^{k-1} = k(a_k^x x)^{k-1}$

Equation (17).

since

$$f_j^y(a_j^y y) = (a_j^y y)^j \quad and \quad net_j^y = a_j^y y$$

$$f_j^y{}'(net_j^y) = j(net_j^y)^{j-1} = j(a_j^y y)^{j-1}$$

Then

$$a_j^y(t+1) = a_j^y(t) - \eta(\partial E_p / \partial a_j^y)$$

$$= a_j^y(t) + \eta(d-z) f^o{}'(net^o) a_{kj}^o * f^h{}'(net_{kj}^h) a_{kj}^{hx} b_k^x a_{kj}^{hy} f_j^y{}'(net_j^y) y$$

$$= a_j^y(t) + \eta * \delta^{ol} * a_{kj}^o * \delta^{hy} * a_{kj}^{hy} * f_j^y{}'(net_j^y) * y$$

$$= a_j^y(t) + \eta * \delta^{ol} * a_{kj}^o * \delta^{hy} * a_{kj}^{hy} * j(a_j^y y)^{j-1} * y$$

$$= a_j^y(t) + \eta * \delta^{ol} * a_{kj}^o * \delta_{kj}^{hy} * a_{kj}^{hy} * \delta_j^y * y$$

where :

$$\delta^{ol} = (d-z) \quad and \quad f^o{}'(net^o) = 1 \quad (linear \quad neuron)$$

$$\delta_{kj}^{hy} = a_{kj}^{hx} b_k^x \quad and \quad f^h{}'(net_{kj}^{hy}) = 1 \quad (linear \quad neuron)$$

$$\delta_j^y = f_j^y{}'(net_j^y) = j(net_j^y)^{j-1} = j(a_j^y y)^{j-1}$$

PHONN and all other HONN model are the same as learning formula (8) and (9) of the second layer weight for HONN. The first hidden layer weight learning formulae for PHONN are shown in Equations (16) and (17).

THONN Model

Trigonometric Higher Order Neural Networks (THONN) are defined when neuron functions (f_k^x and f_j^y) chose trigonometric function. THONN models are defined as follows:

THONN   Model   1b:
let

$$f_k^x = \cos^k(a_k^x x)$$

$$f_j^y = \sin^j(a_j^y y)$$

$$Z = \sum_{k,j=0}^n (a_{kj}^o)\{a_{kj}^{hx} \cos^k(a_k^x x)\}\{a_{kj}^{hy} \sin^j(a_j^y y)\}$$

$$(18)$$

THONN   Model   1:

$$z = \sum_{k,j=0}^n a_{kj}^o \ \cos^k(a_k^x x)\sin^j(a_j^y y)$$

where : $(a_{kj}^{hx}) = (a_{kj}^{hy}) = 1$

$$(19)$$

THONN   Model   0:

$$z = \sum_{k,j=0}^n a_{kj}^o \ \cos^k(x)\sin^j(y)$$

where : $(a_{kj}^{hx}) = (a_{kj}^{hy}) = 1$

and $a_k^x = a_j^y = 1$

$$(20)$$

Learning formulae of THONN nonlinear models are shown in Equations (21) and (22).

UCSHONN Model

Nyquist Rule says that a sampling rate must be at least twice as fast as the fastest frequency (Synder 2006). In simulating and predicating nonstationary time series data, the new nonlinear models of UCSHONN should have frequency twice as high

Equation (21).

Since

$$f_k{}^x = \cos^k(a_k{}^x x) \quad and \quad net_k{}^x = a_k{}^x x$$

$$f_k{}^x{}'(net_k{}^x) = -k\cos^{k-1}(a_k{}^x x)\sin(a_k{}^x x)$$

Then

$$a_k{}^x(t+1) = a_k{}^x(t) - \eta(\partial E_p / \partial a_k{}^x)$$

$$= a_x{}^x(t) + \eta(d-z)f^o{}'(net^o)a_{kj}{}^o * f^h{}'(net_{kj}{}^h)a_{kj}{}^{hy}b_j{}^y a_{kj}{}^{hx}f_k{}^x{}'(net_k{}^x)x$$

$$= a_x{}^x(t) + \eta * \delta^{ol} * a_{kj}{}^o * \delta_{kj}{}^{hx} * a_{kj}{}^{hx} * f_k{}^x{}'(net_k{}^x) * x$$

$$= a_x{}^x(t) + \eta * \delta^{ol} * a_{kj}{}^o * \delta_{kj}{}^{hx} * a_{kj}{}^{hx} * [-k\cos^{k-1}(a_k{}^k x)\sin(a_k{}^x x)] * x$$

$$= a_x{}^x(t) + \eta * \delta^{ol} * a_{kj}{}^o * \delta_{kj}{}^{hx} * a_{kj}{}^{hx} * \delta_k{}^x * x$$

$where:$

$$\delta^{ol} = (d-z) \quad and \quad f^o{}'(net^o) = 1 \quad (linear \quad neuron)$$

$$\delta_{kj}{}^{hx} = a_{kj}{}^{hy}b_j{}^y \quad and \quad f^h{}'(net_{kj}{}^h) = 1 \quad (linear \quad neuron)$$

$$\delta_k{}^x = f_k{}^x{}'(net_k{}^x) = -k\cos^{k-1}(a_k{}^x x)\sin(a_k{}^x x)$$

Equation (22).

since

$$f_j{}^y(a_j{}^y y) = \sin^j(a_j{}^y y) \quad and \quad net_j{}^y = a_j{}^y y$$

$$f_j{}^y{}'(net_j{}^y) = j\sin^{j-1}(a_j{}^y y)\cos(a_j{}^y y)$$

Then

$$a_j{}^y(t+1) = a_j{}^y(t) - \eta(\partial E_p / \partial a_j{}^y)$$

$$= a_j{}^y(t) + \eta(d-z)f^o{}'(net^o)a_{kj}{}^o * f^h{}'(net_{kj}{}^h)a_{kj}{}^{hx}b_k{}^x a_{kj}{}^{hy}f_j{}^y{}'(net_j{}^y)y$$

$$= a_j{}^y(t) + \eta * \delta^{ol} * a_{kj}{}^o * \delta^{hy} * a_{kj}{}^{hy} * f_j{}^y{}'(net_j{}^y) * y$$

$$= a_j{}^y(t) + \eta * \delta^{ol} * a_{kj}{}^o * \delta^{hy} * a_{kj}{}^{hy} * [j\sin^{j-1}(a_j{}^y y)\cos(a_j{}^y y)] * y$$

$$= a_j{}^y(t) + \eta * \delta^{ol} * a_{kj}{}^o * \delta_{kj}{}^{hy} * a_{kj}{}^{hy} * \delta_j{}^y * y$$

$where:$

$$\delta^{ol} = (d-z) \quad and \quad f^o{}'(net^o) = 1 \quad (linear \quad neuron)$$

$$\delta_{kj}{}^{hy} = a_{kj}{}^{hx}b_k{}^x \quad and \quad f^h{}'(net_{kj}{}^{hy}) = 1 \quad (linear \quad neuron)$$

$$\delta_j{}^y = f_j{}^y{}'(net_j{}^y) = j\sin^{j-1}(a_j{}^y y)\cos(a_j{}^y y)$$

as the ultra high frequency of the time series data. To achieve this purpose, Ultra high frequency Cosine and Sine Trigonometric Higher Order Neural Network (UCSHONN) has neurons with cosine and sine functions. Ultra high frequency Cosine and Cosine Trigonometric Higher Order Neural Network (UCCHONN) has neurons with cosine functions. Ultra high frequency Sine and Sine Trigonometric Higher Order Neural Network (USSHONN) has neurons with sine functions. Except for the functions in the neuron all other parts of these three models are the same. The Ultra

High Frequency Cosine and Sine Higher Order Neural Networks (UCSHONN) are defined when neuron functions (f_k^x and f_j^y) chose trigonometric functions with k times x and j times y. The UC-SHONN models are defined as follows:

UCSHONN   Model   1b :

let

$$f_k^x = \cos^k(k * a_k^x x)$$

$$f_j^y = \sin^j(j * a_j^y y)$$

then

$$Z = \sum_{k,j=0}^{n} (a_{kj}^{o})\{a_{kj}^{hx}\cos^k(k * a_k^x x)\}\{a_{kj}^{hy}\sin^j(j * a_j^y y)\}$$

(23)

Equation (26).

Since

$$f_k^x = \cos^k(k * a_k^x x) \qquad and \qquad net_k^x = a_k^x x$$

$$f_k^x{}'(net_k^x) = -k^2 \cos^{k-1}(k * a_k^x x)\sin(k * a_k^x x)$$

Then

$$a_k^x(t+1) = a_k^x(t) - \eta(\partial E_p / \partial a_k^x)$$

$$= a_x^x(t) + \eta(d-z)f^o{}'(net^o)a_{kj}^o * f^h{}'(net_{kj}^h)a_{kj}^{hy}b_j^y a_{kj}^{hx}f_k^x{}'(net_k^x)x$$

$$= a_x^x(t) + \eta * \delta^{ol} * a_{kj}^o * \delta_{kj}^{hx} * a_{kj}^{hx} * f_k^x{}'(net_k^x) * x$$

$$= a_x^x(t) + \eta * \delta^{ol} * a_{kj}^o * \delta_{kj}^{hx} * a_{kj}^{hx} * [-k^2 \cos^{k-1}(k * a_k^x x)\sin(k * a_k^x x)] * x$$

$$= a_x^x(t) + \eta * \delta^{ol} * a_{kj}^o * \delta_{kj}^{hx} * a_{kj}^{hx} * \delta_k^x * x$$

where :

$$\delta^{ol} = (d-z) \qquad and \qquad f^o{}'(net^o) = 1 \qquad (linear \qquad neuron)$$

$$\delta_{kj}^{hx} = a_{kj}^{hy}b_j^y \qquad and \qquad f^h{}'(net_{kj}^h) = 1 \qquad (linear \qquad neuron)$$

$$\delta_k^x = f_k^x{}'(net_k^x) = -k^2 \cos^{k-1}(k * a_k^x x)\sin(k * a_k^x x)$$

Equation (27).

---

since

$$f_j^y(a_j^y y) = \sin^j(j * a_j^y y) \qquad and \qquad net_j^y = a_j^y y$$

$$f_j^y{}'(net_j^y) = j^2 \sin^{j-1}(j * a_j^y y)\cos(j * a_j^y y)$$

Then

$$a_j^y(t+1) = a_j^y(t) - \eta(\partial E_p / \partial a_j^y)$$

$$= a_j^y(t) + \eta(d-z)f^o{}'(net^o)a_{kj}^o * f^h{}'(net_{kj}^h)a_{kj}^{hx}b_k^x a_{kj}^{hy}f_j^y{}'(net_j^y)y$$

$$= a_j^y(t) + \eta * \delta^{ol} * a_{kj}^o * \delta^{hy} * a_{kj}^{hy} * f_j^y{}'(net_j^y) * y$$

$$= a_j^y(t) + \eta * \delta^{ol} * a_{kj}^o * \delta^{hy} * a_{kj}^{hy} * [j^2 \sin^{j-1}(j * a_j^y y)\cos(j * a_j^y y)] * y$$

$$= a_j^y(t) + \eta * \delta^{ol} * a_{kj}^o * \delta_{kj}^{hy} * a_{kj}^{hy} * \delta_j^y * y$$

where :

$$\delta^{ol} = (d-z) \qquad and \qquad f^o{}'(net^o) = 1 \qquad (linear \qquad neuron)$$

$$\delta_{kj}^{hy} = a_{kj}^{hx}b_k^x \qquad and \qquad f^h{}'(net_{kj}^{hy}) = 1 \qquad (linear \qquad neuron)$$

$$\delta_j^y = f_j^y{}'(net_j^y) = j^2 \sin^{j-1}(j * a_j^y y)\cos(j * a_j^y y)$$

UCSHONN   Model   1:

$$z = \sum_{k,j=0}^{n} a_{kj}{}^{o} \ \cos^{k}(k*a_{k}{}^{x}x)\sin^{j}(j*a_{j}{}^{y}y)$$

$$where: \qquad (a_{kj}{}^{hx}) = (a_{kj}{}^{hy}) = 1 \qquad (24)$$

UCSHONN   Model   0:

$$z = \sum_{k,j=0}^{n} a_{kj}{}^{o} \ \cos^{k}(k*x)\sin^{j}(j*y)$$

$$where: \qquad (a_{kj}{}^{hx}) = (a_{kj}{}^{hy}) = 1$$

$$and \qquad a_{k}{}^{x} = a_{j}{}^{y} = 1 \qquad (25)$$

Learning formulae of UCSHONN nonlinear models are shown in Equations (26) and (27).

SXSPHONN Model

Similarly, SINC and Sine Polynomial Higher Order Neural Networks (SXSPHONN) are defined when neuron functions ($f_{k}{}^{x}$ and $f_{j}{}^{y}$) chose SINC and trigonometric functions. SXSPHONN models are defined as follows:

SXSPHONN   Model   1b:

let

$$f_{k}{}^{x} = [\sin c(a_{k}{}^{x}x)]^{k} = [\sin \ (a_{k}{}^{x}x)/(a_{k}{}^{k}x)]^{k}$$

$$f_{j}{}^{y} = \sin^{j}(a_{j}{}^{y}y)$$

then

$$Z = \sum_{k,j=0}^{n} (a_{kj}{}^{o})\{a_{kj}{}^{hx}[\sin \ (a_{k}{}^{x}x)/(a_{k}{}^{k}x)]^{k}\}\{a_{kj}{}^{hy}\sin^{j}(a_{j}{}^{y}y)\}$$

$$(28)$$

SXSPHONN   Model   1:

$$z = \sum_{k,j=0}^{n} a_{kj}{}^{o} \ [\sin(a_{k}{}^{x}x)/(a_{j}{}^{k}x)]^{k}\sin^{j}(a_{j}{}^{y}y)$$

$$where: \qquad (a_{kj}{}^{hx}) = (a_{kj}{}^{hy}) = 1 \qquad (29)$$

SXSPHONN   Model   0:

$$z = \sum_{k,j=0}^{n} a_{kj}{}^{o} \ [\sin(x)/x]^{k}\sin^{j}(y)$$

$$where: \qquad (a_{kj}{}^{hx}) = (a_{kj}{}^{hy}) = 1$$

$$and \qquad a_{k}{}^{x} = a_{j}{}^{y} = 1 \qquad (30)$$

Learning formulae of SXSPHONN nonlinear model are shown in Equations (31) and (32):

Equation (31).

Since

$$f_{k}{}^{x} = [\sin \ (a_{k}{}^{x}x)/(a_{k}{}^{k}x)]^{k} \qquad and \qquad net_{k}{}^{x} = a_{k}{}^{x}x$$

$$f_{k}{}^{x}{}'(net_{k}{}^{x}) = k[\sin \ (a_{k}{}^{x}x)/(a_{k}{}^{k}x)]^{k-1} * [\cos(a_{k}{}^{x}x)/(a_{k}{}^{x}x) - \sin \ (a_{k}{}^{x}x)/(a_{k}{}^{k}x)^{2}]$$

Then

$$a_{k}{}^{x}(t+1) = a_{k}{}^{x}(t) - \eta(\partial E_{p}/\partial a_{k}{}^{x})$$

$$= a_{x}{}^{x}(t) + \eta(d-z)f^{o}{}'(net^{o})a_{kj}{}^{o} * f^{h}{}'(net_{kj}{}^{h})a_{kj}{}^{hy}b_{j}{}^{y}a_{kj}{}^{hx}f_{k}{}^{x}{}'(net_{k}{}^{x})x$$

$$= a_{x}{}^{x}(t) + \eta * \delta^{ol} * a_{kj}{}^{o} * \delta_{kj}{}^{hx} * a_{kj}{}^{hx} * f_{k}{}^{x}{}'(net_{k}{}^{x}) * x$$

$$= a_{x}{}^{x}(t) + \eta * \delta^{ol} * a_{kj}{}^{o} * \delta_{kj}{}^{hx} * a_{kj}{}^{hx}$$

$$\qquad * [k[\sin \ (a_{k}{}^{x}x)/(a_{k}{}^{k}x)]^{k-1} * [\cos(a_{k}{}^{x}x)/(a_{k}{}^{x}x) - \sin \ (a_{k}{}^{x}x)/(a_{k}{}^{k}x)^{2}]] * x$$

$$= a_{x}{}^{x}(t) + \eta * \delta^{ol} * a_{kj}{}^{o} * \delta_{kj}{}^{hx} * a_{kj}{}^{hx} * \delta_{k}{}^{x} * x$$

where:

$$\delta^{ol} = (d-z) \qquad and \qquad f^{o}{}'(net^{o}) = 1 \qquad (linear \qquad neuron)$$

$$\delta_{kj}{}^{hx} = a_{kj}{}^{hy}b_{j}{}^{y} \qquad and \qquad f^{h}{}'(net_{kj}{}^{h}) = 1 \qquad (linear \qquad neuron)$$

$$\delta_{k}{}^{x} = f_{k}{}^{x}{}'(net_{k}{}^{x}) = k[\sin \ (a_{k}{}^{x}x)/(a_{k}{}^{k}x)]^{k-1} * [\cos(a_{k}{}^{x}x)/(a_{k}{}^{x}x) - \sin \ (a_{k}{}^{x}x)/(a_{k}{}^{k}x)^{2}]$$

Equation (32).

since

$$f_j^{\ y}(a_j^{\ y}y) = \sin^j(a_j^{\ y}y) \qquad and \qquad net_j^{\ y} = a_j^{\ y}y$$

$$f_j^{\ y}{}'(net_j^{\ y}) = j\sin^{j-1}(a_j^{\ y}y)\cos(a_j^{\ y}y)$$

Then

$$a_j^{\ y}(t+1) = a_j^{\ y}(t) - \eta(\partial E_p / \partial a_j^{\ y})$$

$$= a_j^{\ y}(t) + \eta(d-z)f^{o}{}'(net^{o})a_{kj}^{\ o} * f^{h}{}'(net_{kj}^{\ h})a_{kj}^{\ hx}b_k^{\ x}a_{kj}^{\ hy}f_j^{\ y}{}'(net_j^{\ y})y$$

$$= a_j^{\ y}(t) + \eta * \delta^{ol} * a_{kj}^{\ o} * \delta^{hy} * a_{kj}^{\ hy} * f_j^{\ y}{}'(net_j^{\ y}) * y$$

$$= a_j^{\ y}(t) + \eta * \delta^{ol} * a_{kj}^{\ o} * \delta^{hy} * a_{kj}^{\ hy} * [j\sin^{j-1}(a_j^{\ y}y)\cos(a_j^{\ y}y)] * y$$

$$= a_j^{\ y}(t) + \eta * \delta^{ol} * a_{kj}^{\ o} * \delta_{kj}^{\ hy} * a_{kj}^{\ hy} * \delta_j^{\ y} * y$$

where :

$$\delta^{ol} = (d-z) \qquad and \qquad f^{o}{}'(net^{o}) = 1 \qquad (linear \qquad neuron)$$

$$\delta_{kj}^{\ hy} = a_{kj}^{\ hx}b_k^{\ x} \qquad and \qquad f^{h}{}'(net_{kj}^{\ hy}) = 1 \qquad (linear \qquad neuron)$$

$$\delta_j^{\ y} = f_j^{\ y}{}'(net_j^{\ y}) = j\sin^{j-1}(a_j^{\ y}y)\cos(a_j^{\ y}y)$$

SINCHONN

SINC Higher Order Neural Networks (SIN-CHONN) are defined when neuron functions ($f_k^{\ x}$ and $f_j^{\ y}$) all chose SINC functions. SINCHONN models are defined as follows:

SINCHONN   Model   1b :

let

$$f_k^{\ x} = [\sin c(a_k^{\ x}x)]^k = [\sin(a_k^{\ x}x) / (a_k^{\ k}x)]^k$$

$$f_j^{\ y} = [\sin c(a_j^{\ y}y)]^j = [\sin(a_j^{\ y}y) / (a_j^{\ y}y)]^j$$

then

$$Z = \sum_{k,j=0}^{n} (a_{kj}^{\ o})\{a_{kj}^{\ hx}[\sin\ (a_k^{\ x}x) / (a_k^{\ k}x)]^k\}$$

$$\{a_{kj}^{\ hy}[\sin(a_j^{\ y}y) / (a_j^{\ y}y)]^j\} \qquad (33)$$

SINCHONN   Model   1 :

$$z = \sum_{k,j=0}^{n} a_{kj}^{\ o}\ [\sin(a_k^{\ x}x) / (a_j^{\ k}x)]^k[\sin(a_j^{\ y}y) / (a_j^{\ y}y)]^j$$

where : $(a_{kj}^{\ hx}) = (a_{kj}^{\ hy}) = 1$

(34)

SINCHONN   Model   0 :

$$z = \sum_{k,j=0}^{n} a_{kj}^{\ o}\ [\sin(x) / x]^k[\sin(y) / y]^j$$

where : $(a_{kj}^{\ hx}) = (a_{kj}^{\ hy}) = 1$

and $a_k^{\ x} = a_j^{\ y} = 1$ (35)

Learning formulae of SINCHONN nonlinear model are shown in Equations (36) and (37).

SPHONN

The Sigmoid Polynomial Higher Order Neural Networks (SPHONN) are defined when neuron functions ($f_k^{\ x}$ and $f_j^{\ y}$) all chose SIGMOID functions. SPHONN models are defined as follows, starting with Equation (38):

Equation (36).

Since

$$f_k^x = [\sin\,(a_k^x x)\,/\,(a_k^k x)]^k \qquad and \qquad net_k^x = a_k^x x$$

$$f_k^x{}'(net_k^x) = k[\sin\,(a_k^x x)\,/\,(a_k^k x)]^{k-1} * [\cos(a_k^x x)\,/\,(a_k^x x) - \sin\,(a_k^x x)\,/\,(a_k^k x)^2]$$

Then

$$a_k^x(t+1) = a_k^x(t) - \eta(\partial E_p\,/\,\partial a_k^x)$$

$$= a_x^x(t) + \eta(d-z)f^o{}'(net^o)a_{kj}^o * f^h{}'(net_{kj}^h)a_{kj}^{hy}b_j^y a_{kj}^{hx} f_k^x{}'(net_k^x)x$$

$$= a_x^x(t) + \eta * \delta^{ol} * a_{kj}^o * \delta_{kj}^{hx} * a_{kj}^{hx} * f_k^x{}'(net_k^x) * x$$

$$= a_x^x(t) + \eta * \delta^{ol} * a_{kj}^o * \delta_{kj}^{hx} * a_{kj}^{hx}$$

$$* [k[\sin\,(a_k^x x)\,/\,(a_k^k x)]^{k-1} * [\cos(a_k^x x)\,/\,(a_k^x x) - \sin\,(a_k^x x)\,/\,(a_k^k x)^2]] * x$$

$$= a_x^x(t) + \eta * \delta^{ol} * a_{kj}^o * \delta_{kj}^{hx} * a_{kj}^{hx} * \delta_k^x * * x$$

where :

$$\delta^{ol} = (d-z) \qquad and \qquad f^o{}'(net^o) = 1 \qquad (linear \qquad neuron)$$

$$\delta_{kj}^{hx} = a_{kj}^{hy}b_j^y \qquad and \qquad f^h{}'(net_{kj}^h) = 1 \qquad (linear \qquad neuron)$$

$$\delta_k^x = f_k^x{}'(net_k^x) = k[\sin\,(a_k^x x)\,/\,(a_k^k x)]^{k-1} * [\cos(a_k^x x)\,/\,(a_k^x x) - \sin\,(a_k^x x)\,/\,(a_k^k x)^2]$$

Equation (37).

since

$$f_j^y(a_j^y y) = [\sin(a_j^y y)\,/\,(a_j^y y)]^j \qquad and \qquad net_j^y = a_j^y y$$

$$f_j^y{}'(net_j^y) = j[\sin(a_j^y y)\,/\,(a_j^y y)]^{j-1} * [\cos(a_j^y y)\,/\,(a_j^y y) - \sin(a_j^y y)\,/\,(a_j^y y)^2]$$

Then

$$a_j^y(t+1) = a_j^y(t) - \eta(\partial E_p\,/\,\partial a_j^y)$$

$$= a_j^y(t) + \eta(d-z)f^o{}'(net^o)a_{kj}^o * f^h{}'(net_{kj}^h)a_{kj}^{hx}b_k^x a_{kj}^{hy} f_j^y{}'(net_j^y)y$$

$$= a_j^y(t) + \eta * \delta^{ol} * a_{kj}^o * \delta^{hy} * a_{kj}^{hy} * f_j^y{}'(net_j^y) * y$$

$$= a_j^y(t) + \eta * \delta^{ol} * a_{kj}^o * \delta^{hy} * a_{kj}^{hy}$$

$$* [j[\sin(a_j^y y)\,/\,(a_j^y y)]^{j-1} * [\cos(a_j^y y)\,/\,(a_j^y y) - \sin(a_j^y y)\,/\,(a_j^y y)^2]] * y$$

$$= a_j^y(t) + \eta * \delta^{ol} * a_{kj}^o * \delta_{kj}^{hy} * a_{kj}^{hy} * \delta_j^y * y$$

where :

$$\delta^{ol} = (d-z) \qquad and \qquad f^o{}'(net^o) = 1 \qquad (linear \qquad neuron)$$

$$\delta_{kj}^{hy} = a_{kj}^{hx}b_k^x \qquad and \qquad f^h{}'(net_{kj}^{hy}) = 1 \qquad (linear \qquad neuron)$$

$$\delta_j^y = f_j^y{}'(net_j^y) = j[\sin(a_j^y y)\,/\,(a_j^y y)]^{j-1} * [\cos(a_j^y y)\,/\,(a_j^y y) - \sin(a_j^y y)\,/\,(a_j^y y)^2]$$

Equation (38).

SPHONN Model 1b :

let

$$f_k^x = [1\,/\,(1+\exp(-net_k^x))]^k = [1\,/\,(1+\exp(-a_k^x x))]^k \qquad and \qquad net_k^x = a_k^x$$

$$f_j^y = [1\,/\,(1+\exp(-net_j^y))]^j = [1\,/\,(1+\exp(-a_j^y y))]^j \qquad and \qquad net_j^y = a_j^y$$

then

$$Z = \sum_{k,j=0}^{n} (a_{kj}^o)\{a_{kj}^{hx}[1\,/\,(1+\exp(-a_k^x x))]^k\}\{a_{kj}^{hy}[1\,/\,(1+\exp(-a_j^y y))]^j\}$$

SPHONN   Model   1:

$$z = \sum_{k,j=0}^{n} a_{kj}^{\ o} \ \{[1 / (1 + \exp(-a_k^{\ x} x))]^k\} \{[1 / (1 + \exp(-a_j^{\ y} y))]^j\}$$

where: $(a_{kj}^{\ hx}) = (a_{kj}^{\ hy}) = 1$

(39)

SPHONN   Model   0:

$$z = \sum_{k,j=0}^{n} a_{kj}^{\ o} \ \{[1 / (1 + \exp(-x))]^k\} \{[1 / (1 + \exp(-y))]^j\}$$

where: $(a_{kj}^{\ hx}) = (a_{kj}^{\ hy}) = 1$

and $a_k^{\ x} = a_j^{\ y} = 1$

(40)

Learning formulae of SPHONN nonlinear model are shown in Equations (41) and (42).

COMPARISONS OF SAS NONLINEAR MODELS AND HONN NONLINEAR MODELS

This section compares SAS NLIN and HONN nonlinear models by using the data provided by the SAS NLIN manual. Two examples (45.1 and 45.2) are chosen from the SAS NLIN manual.

Comparison using Quadratic with Plateau Data (45.1)

The Quadratic with Plateau data has 16 inputs. The desired output numbers are from 0.46 to 0.80, with the last three outputs 0.80, 0.80, and 0.78. SAS uses two functions to simulate these data, Quadratic function and Plateau function. SAS provide 0.0101 as the sum of squared error and 0.000774 as the residual mean squared error (MSE). Table 1 uses HONN nonlinear models to simulate the data from SAS NLIN document, and list both HONN and SAS simulating results. Six HONN models have smaller residual mean squared error than that of SAS NLIN model. UC-SHONN model 0 Order 4 produces the smallest residual mean squared error (0.0007096). Comparing the residual mean squared error (0.000774) from SAS NLIN, HONN model is 8.32% more accurate using the following formula:

Equation (41).

Since

$$f_k^{\ x} = [1 / (1 + \exp(-net_k^{\ x}))]^k = [1 / (1 + \exp(-a_k^{\ x} x))]^k \qquad and \qquad net_k^{\ x} = a_k^{\ x}$$

$$f_k^{\ x}{}'(net_k^{\ x}) = k[1 / (1 + \exp(-a_k^{\ x} x))]^{k-1} * (1 + \exp(-a_k^{\ x} x))^{-2} * \exp(-a_k^{\ x} x)$$

Then

$$a_k^{\ x}(t+1) = a_k^{\ x}(t) - \eta (\partial E_p / \partial a_k^{\ x})$$

$$= a_x^{\ x}(t) + \eta (d-z) f^o{}'(net^o) a_{kj}^{\ o} * f^h{}'(net_{kj}^{\ h}) a_{kj}^{\ hy} b_j^{\ y} a_{kj}^{\ hx} f_k^{\ x}{}'(net_k^{\ x}) x$$

$$= a_x^{\ x}(t) + \eta * \delta^{\ ol} * a_{kj}^{\ o} * \delta_{kj}^{\ hx} * a_{kj}^{\ hx} * f_k^{\ x}{}'(net_k^{\ x}) * x$$

$$= a_x^{\ x}(t) + \eta * \delta^{\ ol} * a_{kj}^{\ o} * \delta_{kj}^{\ hx} * a_{kj}^{\ hx}$$

$$\qquad * [k[1 / (1 + \exp(-a_k^{\ x} x))]^{k-1} * (1 + \exp(-a_k^{\ x} x))^{-2} * \exp(-a_k^{\ x} x)] * x$$

$$= a_x^{\ x}(t) + \eta * \delta^{\ ol} * a_{kj}^{\ o} * \delta_{kj}^{\ hx} * a_{kj}^{\ hx} * \delta_k^{\ x} * x$$

where:

$$\delta^{\ ol} = (d-z) \qquad and \qquad f^o{}'(net^o) = 1 \qquad (linear \qquad neuron)$$

$$\delta_{kj}^{\ hx} = a_{kj}^{\ hy} b_j^{\ y} \qquad and \qquad f^h{}'(net_k^{\ h}) = 1 \qquad (linear \qquad neuron)$$

$$\delta_k^{\ x} = f_k^{\ x}{}'(net_k^{\ x}) = k[1 / (1 + \exp(-a_k^{\ x} x))]^{k-1} * (1 + \exp(-a_k^{\ x} x))^{-2} * \exp(-a_k^{\ x} x)$$

(SAS MSE - HONN MSE)/(SAS MSE) *100%

The key point is when using HONN, the initial coefficients are automatically selected by the HONN system, while SAS NLIN procedure requires the user to input the initial coefficients. Moreover, the simulations can always converge using HONN, but may not converge under SAS NLIN. The reason is that in SAS NLIN, the convergence range for the initial coefficient is small and sensitive. It is very hard for the user to guess the initial coefficients in the convergence range.

Table 2 shows the coefficient for the minimum convergence range. SAS provides the initial coefficients a, b, and c. The coefficients are increased or decreased to test whether SAS can still converge using the new coefficients. When changing these coefficients by +0.002 or -0.015, SAS NLIN still can converge. However, when changing these

coefficients to +0.003 or -0.02, SAS NLIN provides the same output values for different inputs. The residual mean squared error increases from 0.000774 to 0.0125. For the Quadratic with Plateau data, the convergence range for the coefficient is less than 0.023. There are two problems in using SAS NLIN. First, users might accept the wrong results where sum of squared error equals to 0.1869. Second, users might discontinue guessing for the correct initial coefficients after a couple trial and errors. Users have less chance to guess correct initial coefficients, since the convergence range is small.

Comparison Using US Population Growth Data

The US population growth data has a total of 21 inputs from 1790 to 1990. The desired output numbers are population amounts from 3.929 to

Equation (42).

since

$$f_j^y(a_j^y y) = f_j^y = [1/(1+\exp(-net_j^y))]^j = [1/(1+\exp(-a_j^y y))]^j \quad\quad and \quad\quad net_j^y = a_j^y$$

$$f_j^y{}'(net_j^y) = j[1/(1+\exp(-a_j^y y))]^{j-1} * (1+\exp(-a_j^y y))^{-2} * \exp(-a_j^y y)]$$

Then

$$a_j^y(t+1) = a_j^y(t) - \eta(\partial E_p / \partial a_j^y)$$

$$= a_j^y(t) + \eta(d-z)f^o{}'(net^o)a_{kj}^o * f^h{}'(net_{kj}^h)a_{kj}^{hx}b_k^x a_{kj}^{hy} f_j^y{}'(net_j^y)y$$

$$= a_j^y(t) + \eta * \delta^{ol} * a_{kj}^o * \delta^{hy} * a_{kj}^{hy} * f_j^y{}'(net_j^y) * y$$

$$= a_j^y(t) + \eta * \delta^{ol} * a_{kj}^o * \delta^{hy} * a_{kj}^{hy}$$

$$\quad * [j[1/(1+\exp(-a_j^y y))]^{j-1} * (1+\exp(-a_j^y y))^{-2} * \exp(-a_j^y y)]] * y$$

$$= a_j^y(t) + \eta * \delta^{ol} * a_{kj}^o * \delta_{kj}^{hy} * a_{kj}^{hy} * \delta_j^y * y$$

where :

$$\delta^{ol} = (d-z) \quad\quad and \quad\quad f^o{}'(net^o) = 1 \quad\quad (linear \quad neuron)$$

$$\delta_{kj}^{hy} = a_{kj}^{hx}b_k^x \quad\quad and \quad\quad f^h{}'(net_{kj}^{hy}) = 1 \quad\quad (linear \quad neuron)$$

$$\delta_j^y = f_j^y{}'(net_j^y) = j[1/(1+\exp(-a_j^y y))]^{j-1} * (1+\exp(-a_j^y y))^{-2} * \exp(-a_j^y y)]$$

Table 1 Quadratic with Plateau Data Modeling Accuracy - SAS NLIN or HONNs? Input and desired output data are chosen from SAS NLIN Document Example 45.1, page 30. 6 HONN models have better modeling accuracy than SAS NLIN modeling result. UCSHONN Model 0 Order 4 has the best accuracy which is 8.32% better than SAS NLIN model

Input*	Desired Output*	SAS NLIN Output	PHONN M0O5 Output	UCSHONN M0O3 Output	UCSHONN M0O4 Output
1	0.46	0.450207	0.447760	0.461038	0.459786
2	0.47	0.503556	0.502626	0.493809	0.494116
3	0.57	0.552161	0.552784	0.541046	0.541922
4	0.61	0.596023	0.597898	0.593829	0.593482
5	0.62	0.635143	0.637699	0.643296	0.641043
6	0.68	0.669519	0.672012	0.682927	0.680231
7	0.69	0.699152	0.700779	0.710014	0.709530
8	0.78	0.724042	0.724084	0.725899	0.729204
9	0.70	0.744189	0.742177	0.734944	0.740915
10	0.74	0.759593	0.755500	0.742575	0.747891
11	0.77	0.770254	0.764709	0.753038	0.754511
12	0.78	0.776172	0.770699	0.767594	0.764455
13	0.74	0.777497	0.774632	0.783726	0.778102
13**	0.80	0.777497	0.774632	0.783726	0.778102
15	0.80	0.777497	0.782433	0.795838	0.795214
16	0.78	0.777497	0.790162	0.777513	0.782444
Sum of Squared Error		0.0101*	0.009665	0.009416	**0.009225**
Residual Mean Squared Error		0.000774*	0.0007435	0.0007243	**0.0007096**
HONN better than SAS***			3.94%	6.42%	*8.32%*

*: These numbers are published in the SAS NLIN manual.
**: This is 13, based on SAS NLIN manual.
***: HONN better than SAS (%) = (SAS MSE - HONN MSE) /(SAS MSE)*100%

Table 2 Quadratic with Plateau Data Modeling Convergence – SAS NLIN or HONNs? Input and desired output data are chosen from SAS NLIN Document Example 45.1, page 30. SAS coefficient global minimum convergence range < |0.003-(-0.02)| = 0.023

Coefficient	SAS value *	HONN initial Coefficient value	SAS initial Coefficient value (SAS value -0.1)	SAS initial Coefficient value (SAS value **-0.02**)	SAS initial Coefficient value (SAS Value **+0.003**)	SAS initial Coefficient value (SAS value +0.1)
a	0.3029	(HONN automatically chose coefficients)	0.2029	0.2829	0.3059	0.4029
b	0.0605		-0.0395	0.0405	0.0635	0.1605
c	-0.0024		-0.10237	-0.02237	0.00063	0.09763
Input*	Desired Output*	UCSHONN M0O4 Output	SAS NLIN Output	SAS NLIN Output	SAS NLIN Output	SAS NLIN Output
1	0.46	0.459786	0.686880	0.686880	0.686880	0.686880
2	0.47	0.494116	0.686880	0.686880	0.686880	0.686880
3	0.57	0.541922	0.686880	0.686880	0.686880	0.686880
4	0.61	0.593482	0.686880	0.686880	0.686880	0.686880
5	0.62	0.641043	0.686880	0.686880	0.686880	0.686880
6	0.68	0.680231	0.686880	0.686880	0.686880	0.686880
7	0.69	0.709530	0.686880	0.686880	0.686880	0.686880
8	0.78	0.729204	0.686880	0.686880	0.686880	0.686880
9	0.70	0.740915	0.686880	0.686880	0.686880	0.686880
10	0.74	0.747891	0.686880	0.686880	0.686880	0.686880
11	0.77	0.754511	0.686880	0.686880	0.686880	0.686880
12	0.78	0.764455	0.686880	0.686880	0.686880	0.686880
13	0.74	0.778102	0.686880	0.686880	0.686880	0.686880
13**	0.80	0.778102	0.686880	0.686880	0.686880	0.686880
15	0.80	0.795214	0.686880	0.686880	0.686880	0.686880
16	0.78	0.782444	0.686880	0.686880	0.686880	0.686880
Sum of Squared Error		0.009225	0.186900	0.186900	0.186900	0.186900
Residual Mean Squared Error		0.0007096	0.0125	0.0125	0.0125	0.0125

*: These numbers are published in the SAS NLIN manual.
**: This is 13, based on SAS NLIN manual.

248.710 million. SAS NLIN uses a polynomial function with order 2 to model these data. Using the NLIN procedure, the sum of squared error is 159.9628 and the residual mean squared error equals to 8.8868. Table 3 shows the actual data and the results generated from both SAS NLIN

Table 3. US Population Growth Modeling Accuracy – SAS NLIN or HONNs? Input and desired output data are chosen from SAS NLIN Document Example 45.2, page 33. HONN models have better modeling accuracy than SAS NLIN modeling result. UCSHONN M0O5 has the best accuracy which is 45.10% better than SAS NLIN model.

input* (Year)	Desired Output * (Population Million)	SAS NLIN Output Error (pop-model. pop)*	UCS HONN M0O4 Output Error	UCS HONN M0O5 Output Error	THONN M0O2 Output Error
1790	3.929	-0.93711	0.35839	0.28030	-0.22135
1800	5.308	0.46091	0.92843	0.88043	0.59541
1810	7.239	1.11853	0.61332	0.62924	0.83865
1820	9.638	0.95176	-0.25145	-0.18753	0.41783
1830	12.866	0.32159	-0.93167	-0.85929	-0.31611
1840	17.069	-0.62597	-1.22365	-1.16794	-1.23087
1850	23.191	-0.94692	-0.52154	-0.48896	-1.39974
1860	31.443	-0.43027	0.82224	0.82224	-0.63197
1870	39.818	-1.08302	0.33476	0.28726	-0.95803
1880	50.155	-1.06615	-0.22558	-0.31661	-0.56407
1890	62.947	0.11332	0.00771	-0.08406	1.01573
1900	75.994	0.25539	-0.52975	-0.56805	1.55319
1910	91.972	2.03607	1.37711	1.40919	3.69558
1920	105.710	0.28436	0.69017	0.75608	2.24361
1930	122.775	0.56725	2.60822	2.65523	2.73656
1940	131.669	-8.61325	-5.05453	-5.04682	-6.34957
1950	151.325	-8.32415	-4.02885	-4.04303	-6.10558
1960	179.323	-0.98543	2.93528	2.92383	1.02742
1970	203.211	0.95088	3.49835	3.49562	2.58186
1980	226.542	1.03780	1.62358	1.62557	2.09787
1990	248.710	-1.33067	-2.86763	-2.85942	-1.03737
Sum of Squared Error		159.9628**	87.85605	**87.82611**	126.9089
Residual Mean Squared Error		8.8868**	4.8809	**4.8792**	7.0505
HONN better than SAS***			45.08%	**45.10%**	20.66%

: These numbers are published in the SAS NLIN manual.
**: These numbers are calculated base on the data in the SAS NLIN manual.*
***: HONN better than SAS (%) = (SAS MSE - HONN MSE) /(SAS MSE)*100%*

and HONN. This table lists 4 HONN models that have a smaller residual mean squared error than that of SAS NLIN model. The smallest residual mean squared error from UCSHONN model 0 Order 5 is 4.8792, while SAS NLIN has a residual mean squared error of 8.8868. This shows HONN is 45.10% better (SAS MSE - HONN MSE)/(SAS MSE) *100%.

Table 4 shows the convergence range for the coefficients. The coefficients for b0, b1, and b2, are modified and these new values are used as the initial coefficient in SAS NLIN. When modifying these coefficients by +0.0000051 or -0.000001, SAS can still converge. However, when changing these coefficients by +0.0000052 or -0.000002, SAS cannot converge or provides no observation. The residual mean squared error of 8.8868 is increased to 527.7947. For the US population growth data, the convergence range for the coefficients is less than 0.0000072.

Comparison Using Japanese vs. US Dollar Exchange Data

The monthly Japanese vs. US dollar exchange rate from November 1999 to December 2000 is shown in Table 5. The input R_{t-2} uses exchange rates from November 1999 to October 2000. The input R_{t-1} uses exchange rates from December 1999 to November 2000. The desired output R_t numbers are exchange rates from January 2000 to December 2000. UCSHONN simulator with Model 0 and Order 5 is used to simulate these data. The simulation results and coefficients are shown in Table 5. Sum of squared error for UCSHONN is 9.04E-08 and the mean squared error is 7.53E-09. Using the same data, SAS also converges with sum of squared error of 6.04E-05 and mean squared error of 5.05E-06. Clearly, HONN model is more accurate than SAS NLIN. The Japanese vs. US dollar exchange rate data has been tested using different order. Table 5 uses UCSHONN Model 0 Order 4 in SAS, SAS system converges with sum of squared error of 4.7E-05

and mean squared error of 3.92E-06. When using UCSHONN Model 0 Order 3 in SAS, SAS system converges with a sum of squared error of 1.25E-05 and mean squared error of 1.052E-06. This shows that HONN model is still more accurate than the SAS model. When using UCSHONN Model 0 Order 2 in SAS, SAS system converges with a sum of squared error of 8.986128 and mean squared error of 0.748844 (not shown in Table 5). This means Order 2 is definitely not suitable for simulating the year 2000 Japanese vs. US dollar exchange rate.

UCSHONN Model 0 Order 5:

$$R_t = \sum_{k=0, j=0}^{5} a_{kj}\ \cos^k(k*R_{t-2})\sin^j(j*R_{t-1})$$

UCSHONN Model 0 Order 5 Coefficient Values are shown in Box 1.

Comparison Using US Consumer Price Index 1992-2004 Data

The yearly US Consumer Price Index 1992-2004 is shown in Table 6. The input C_{t-2} uses Consumer Price Index data from November 1990 to October 2002. The input C_{t-1} uses Consumer Price Index data from 1991 to November 2003. The desired output, R_t, is the Consumer Price Index from 1992 to December 2004. UCSHONN simulator with Model 0 and Order 5 has been used for simulating these data. The simulation results and coefficients are shown in Table 6. UCSHONN has a sum of squared error of 2.1E-05 and a mean squared error of 1.61E-06. Using the same data, SAS converges with sum of squared error of 7.93-04 and mean squared error of 6.1E-05. Clearly, HONN model is still more accurate than SAS model. SAS is also tested by using different models with the same order. When using the THONN Model 0 Order 5 in SAS NLIN, the procedure converges with a sum of squared error of 2.647E-02 and mean squared error of 2.036E-03. When using PHONN

Table 4. US Population Growth Modeling Convergence- SAS NLIN or HONNs? Input and desired output data are chosen from SAS NLIN Document Example 45.2, page 33. SAS coefficient global minimum convergence range <|0.0064625-0.006458|=0.0000072

Coefficient	SAS value *	HONN initial Coefficient value	SAS initial Coefficient value (SAS Value -0.000002)	SAS initial Coefficient (SAS Value -0.000001)	SAS initial Coefficient (SAS Value +0.0000052)
b0	20828.7		20828.699998	20828.699999	20828.7000052
b1	-23.2004	HONN automatically chose coefficients	-23.200402	-23.200401	-23.2003949
b2	0.00646		**0.006458**	0.006459	**0.0064652**
Input* (Year)	Desired Output* (Population Million)	UCSHONN M0O5 Output	SAS NLIN Output	SAS NLIN Output	SAS NLIN Output
1790	3.929	3.649	-8.29042	4.866109	No Observation
1800	5.308	4.428	-8.00767	4.847093	No Observation
1810	7.239	6.610	-6.43241	6.120471	No Observation
1820	9.638	9.826	-3.56462	8.686243	
1830	12.866	13.725	0.595686	12.54441	
1840	17.069	18.237	6.04851	17.69497	
1850	23.191	23.680	12.79385	24.13792	
1860	31.443	30.621	20.83172	31.87327	
1870	39.818	39.531	30.1621	40.90101	
1880	50.155	50.472	40.785	51.22115	
1890	62.947	63.031	52.70042	62.83368	
1900	75.994	76.562	65.90836	75.73861	
1910	91.972	90.563	80.40882	89.93593	
1920	105.710	104.954	96.2018	105.4256	
1930	122.775	120.120	113.2873	122.2077	
1940	131.669	136.716	131.6653	140.2822	
1950	151.325	155.368	151.3358	159.6491	
1960	179.323	176.399	172.2989	180.3084	
1970	203.211	199.715	194.5545	202.2601	
1980	226.542	224.916	218.1026	225.5042	
1990	248.710	251.569	242.9432	250.0407	No Observation
Sum of Squared Error		87.82611	2111.17886	159.962906	
Residual Mean Squared Error		4.8792	527.7947	8.8868277	
Convergence		Yes	No	yes	No

: These numbers are published in the SAS NLIN manual.

Table 5. Japanese vs. US Dollar Exchange Rate 2000 Simulation Accuracy - SAS NLIN or HONNs?

Original Data		Input		Desired Output R_t	UCS HONN M0O5 Output	SAS NLIN UCS M0O5 Output
Date	JA/US Exchange Rate 2000	R_{t-2}	R_{t-1}			
11/99	104.65					
12/99	102.58					
01/00	105.30	104.65	102.58	105.30	105.29995	105.30189
02/00	109.39	102.58	105.30	109.39	109.38980	109.39005
03/00	106.31	105.30	109.39	106.31	106.31003	106.31270
04/00	105.63	109.39	106.31	105.63	105.62997	105.63321
05/00	108.32	106.31	105.63	108.32	108.31998	108.32189
06/00	106.13	105.63	108.32	106.13	106.13000	106.13061
07/00	108.21	108.32	106.13	108.21	108.20997	108.21188
08/00	108.08	106.13	108.21	108.08	108.07998	108.08179
09/00	106.84	108.21	108.08	106.84	106.83992	106.84377
10/00	108.44	108.08	106.84	108.44	108.43997	108.44230
11/00	109.01	106.84	108.44	109.01	109.00993	109.01237
12/00	112.21	108.44	109.01	112.21	112.20982	112.21186
Sum of Squared Error					**9.04E-08**	6.04E-05
Mean Squared Error					**7.53E-09**	5.04E-06
Convergence					Yes	Yes

Box 1.

a_{kj}	k=0	k=1	k=2	k=3	k=4	k=5
j=0	0.593760	-0.535650	-0.338650	0.654490	-0.322780	-0.219680
j=1	0.638860	1.258700	-0.423250	-0.433140	-0.572700	-0.292430
j=2	-0.681450	-0.603180	0.080626	-0.494270	0.161860	-0.376570
j=3	-0.818090	0.973730	0.447020	-0.237580	0.903690	-0.335620
j=4	-0.462390	-0.067789	0.230140	-0.182000	0.385220	0.076637
j=5	-0.495590	0.679350	-0.458800	1.935000	0.301420	-0.458880

Model 0 Order 5, SAS procedure also converges with sum of squared error of 1.41E04 and mean squared error of 1.08E-05. This table shows HONN model is more accurate than SAS NLIN.

UCSHONN Model 0 Order 5:

$$R_t = \sum_{k=0, j=0}^{5} a_{kj} \cos^k(k * C_{t-2}) \sin^j(j * C_{t-1})$$

UCSHONN Model 0 Order 5 Coefficients are shown in Box 2.

Table 6: US Consumer Price Index 1992-2004 Simulation Accuracy -SAS NLIN or HONNs?

Original Data		Input		Desired Output C_t	UCS HONN MOO5 Output	SAS NLIN UCS MOO5 Output
Year	US CPI 1992-2004	C_{t-2}	C_{t-1}			
1990	130.7					
1991	136.2					
1992	140.3	130.70	136.20	140.30	140.29781	140.29514
1993	144.5	136.20	140.30	144.50	144.49874	144.49474
1994	148.2	140.30	144.50	148.20	148.19833	148.20409
1995	152.4	144.50	148.20	152.40	152.40005	152.41332
1996	156.9	148.20	152.40	156.90	156.89931	156.90537
1997	160.5	152.40	156.90	160.50	160.50033	160.49693
1998	163.0	156.90	160.50	163.00	162.99956	163.01259
1999	166.6	160.50	163.00	166.60	166.60021	166.60187
2000	172.2	163.00	166.60	172.20	172.19995	172.19802
2001	177.1	166.60	172.20	177.10	177.10061	177.1059
2002	179.9	172.20	177.10	179.90	179.90124	179.91536
2003	184.0	177.10	179.90	184.00	184.00205	184.00772
2004	188.9	179.90	184.00	188.90	188.90221	188.89646
Sum of Squared Error					2.1E-05	7.93E-04
Mean Squared Error					1.61E-06	6.1E-05
Convergence					Yes	Yes

Box 2.

a_{kj}	k=0	k=1	k=2	k=3	k=4	k=5
j=0	0.040466	0.282650	0.332090	-1.023600	0.320600	0.047749
j=1	0.692880	-0.414550	0.352800	0.160460	-0.407040	0.469310
j=2	0.786420	-0.515200	0.654160	0.271940	-0.458820	-0.187380
j=3	0.199470	-0.786580	0.454880	0.241370	1.055600	0.161010
j=4	0.041666	-0.340980	-0.124510	0.546370	0.122520	-0.443290
j=5	-0.027490	0.216360	-0.305750	-0.714690	-0.203870	-0.809710

FINDING MODEL, ORDER, & COEFFICIENT BY HONN NONLINEAR MODELS

To find the model, order, and coefficients of HONN, the following functions and data are used:

- A linear function: $z = 0.402x + 0.598y$
- A nonlinear function with order 1: $z = 0.2815682 - 0.2815682\cos(x) + 1.0376218*\sin(y)$
- Japanese Yen vs. US Dollars (2000 and 2004)
- US Consumer Price Index (1992-2004)
- Japanese Consumer Price Index (1992-2004)

There are two reasons why these examples have been selected. First, some simple and easy to understand functions are chosen, i.e. $z = 0.402x + 0.598y$ and $z = 0.2815682 - 0.2815682\cos(x) + 1.0376218*\sin(y)$, for testing HONN nonlinear models. The second reason is that these data are used as examples for the Nobel Prize in Economics in 2003 (Vetenskapsakademien, 2003).

The test time will depend on the computer system used. The computer system for the test has the following properties:

- **Computer Model:** Personal computer, DELL OPTIPLEX GX260, made by 2003
- **Central Processing Unit:** Pentium 4 CPU, 2.66GHz
- **Random Access Memory:** 512 MB
- **Operation System:** Microsoft Window XP, Professional, Version 2002
- **VNC Viewer:** Version 3.3.3.2, for running UNIX on the PC
- **SUN Operation System:** Solaris 9
- **Common Desktop Environment:** Version 1.5.7
- **Computer Language:** c
- **Test time unit:** second.

HONN can Choose the Best Model in a Pool of HONN Nonlinear Models for Different Data

The first question a user might ask is what model is the best nonlinear model for the data. Should a polynomial model or a trigonometric polynomial model be used for simulating data? Or should a sigmoid polynomial model or a SINC (sin(x)/x) polynomial model be used?

From SAS manual:

The (SAS) NLIN procedure produces least squares or weighted least squares estimates of the parameters of a nonlinear model...For each nonlinear model to be analyzed, you must specify the model (using a single dependent variable)...

Users may feel that this is a complicated task since they do not know which model is the best model for their data. This section shows that users can select the best model in a pool of HONN nonlinear models for different data.

Table 7 shows that in 530 seconds HONN selects the best model for $z = 0.402x + 0.598y$ as PHONN order 1 model. The mean squared error for PHONN order 1 model is only 7.371E-13, while the mean squared errors for PHONN nonlinear models are more than 2.30E-6. The mean squared errors of all other models (THONN, UCSHONN, SXSPHONN, SINCHONN, and SPHONN) are more than 1.33E-6.

Table 7 also shows that in around 502 seconds, HONN can recognize the best model for $z = 0.2815682 - 0.2815682\cos(x) + 1.0376218*\sin(y)$ which is THONN or UCSHONN order 1. Since the mean squared error for THONN order 1 is only 2.965E-8 and 2.841E-8 for UCSHONN order 1. Actually, THONN order 1 and UCSHONN order 1 have the same expression. The mean squared error for THONN order 2 or more is above is more than 3.27E-6. The mean squared error of UCSHONN order 2 or more is above 2.21E-6. The mean squared error for all other models (PHONN, SXSPHONN, SINCHONN, and SPHONN) are more than 3.27E-6.

The Table 8 shows that the best model for the Yen vs. US dollar exchange rate (year 2000) is UCSHONN order 5, with the mean squared error of 8.999E-10. The mean squared error of all other models (PHONN, THONN, UCSHONN order 1 to 4, SXSPHONN, SINCHONN, and SPHONN) is more than 4.9E-5. This means HONN can recognize the year 2000 Yen vs. US dollar exchange rate in around 2241 seconds. Moreover, Table 8 also shows that the best model for the year 2004 Yen vs. US dollar exchange rate is UCSHONN order 5 with the mean squared error of 3.604E-21. The mean squared error of all other models (PHONN, THONN, UCSHONN order 1 to 4, SXSPHONN, SINCHONN, and SPHONN) is more than 5.185E-3. That means HONN can

Table 7. Linear and Nonlinear Function Simulation Analysis – 20,000 Epochs

		Z=0.402*x + 0.598*y Mean Squared Error	Running Time Seconds	Z = 0.2815682 - 0.2815682*COS(x) + 1.0376218*SIN(y) - 0.0056414*COS(x)*SIN(y) Mean Squared Error	Running Time Seconds
PHONN (Model 0)	Order 1	0.0000000000007371	7	0.00001616	6
	Order 2	0.00006853	10	0.00002722	10
	Order 3	0.00000230	16	0.00010718	14
	Order 4	0.00000320	18	0.00009285	19
	Order 5	0.00000866	27	0.00006714	28
THONN (Model 0)	Order 1	0.00001351	8	0.00000002965	7
	Order 2	0.00002849	12	0.00000983	10
	Order 3	0.00000241	17	0.00000327	14
	Order 4	0.00005881	22	0.00000437	19
	Order 5	0.00001503	28	0.00000851	25
UCSHONN (Model 0)	Order 1	0.00000309	8	0.00000002841	6
	Order 2	0.00000133	14	0.00001162	11
	Order 3	0.00004071	18	0.00012063	14
	Order 4	0.00009228	24	0.00000221	19
	Order 5	0.00004116	30	0.00001962	27
SXSPHONN (Model 0)	Order 1	0.00063820	9	0.00014997	10
	Order 2	0.00022918	12	0.00014330	12
	Order 3	0.00003515	16	0.00001520	15
	Order 4	0.00000392	22	0.00003035	22
	Order 5	0.00002715	28	0.00002728	30
SINCHONN (Model 0)	Order 1	0.00556992	8	0.00747188	7
	Order 2	0.00430713	14	0.00470922	13
	Order 3	0.00266424	17	0.00345466	17
	Order 4	0.00163071	25	0.00199684	24
	Order 5	0.00172761	32	0.00192670	34
SPHONN (M0del 0)	Order 1	0.00001199	9	0.00013751	8
	Order 2	0.00001996	12	0.000120826	12
	Order 3	0.00040773	17	0.00053905	16
	Order 4	0.00029652	21	0.000151535	23
	Order 5	0.00008046	29	0.00016194	30
Total Time			530		502

Table 8. Japanese Yen vs. US Dollar Exchange Rate Analysis – 100,000 Epochs

		Year 2000, Mean Squared Error	Running Time Seconds	Year 2004, Mean Squared Error	Running Time Seconds
PHONN (Model 0)	Order 1	0.044682	29	0.046985	28
	Order 2	0.021795	36	0.042055	34
	Order 3	0.005409	61	0.028939	54
	Order 4	0.003894	84	0.021681	79
	Order 5	0.002886	119	0.018649	116
THONN (Model 0)	Order 1	0.047336	28	0.047920	21
	Order 2	0.023417	36	0.041571	35
	Order 3	0.017139	63	0.041396	60
	Order 4	0.013265	92	0.040135	88
	Order 5	0.011807	125	0.037297	124
UCSHONN (Model 0)	Order 1	0.047322	23	0.047635	20
	Order 2	0.038550	42	0.043269	40
	Order 3	0.002560	66	0.005185	65
	Order 4	0.000049	99	0.00000025	98
	Order 5	0.0000000008999	135	3.604E-21	141
SXSPHONN (Model 0)	Order 1	0.057007	34	0.053115	32
	Order 2	0.026508	46	0.046244	43
	Order 3	0.020817	67	0.042628	66
	Order 4	0.018062	101	0.041210	99
	Order 5	0.015119	138	0.040873	136
SINCHONN (Model 0)	Order 1	0.067045	31	0.063458	27
	Order 2	0.060276	48	0.062408	45
	Order 3	0.045554	76	0.059483	72
	Order 4	0.040522	112	0.051622	108
	Order 5	0.038970	157	0.049495	152
SPHONN (Model 0)	Order 1	0.062906	33	0.053220	26
	Order 2	0.052687	45	0.051223	43
	Order 3	0.043711	70	0.048336	72
	Order 4	0.038198	100	0.046790	103
	Order 5	0.035725	145	0.046638	143
Total Time			2241		2170

recognize 2004 Yen vs. US dollar exchange rate in about 2170 seconds.

Table 9 shows that in about 2360 seconds HONN can select the best model for US Consumer Price Index (1992-2004), which is UCSHONN order 5 with the mean squared error of 4.910E-7. The mean squared errors for all other models (PHONN, THONN, UCSHONN order 1 to 4,

Table 9. Consumer Price Index Analysis (1992-2004) – 100,000 Epochs

		US, Mean Squared Error	Running time Seconds	Japan, Mean Squared Error	Running Time Seconds
PHONN (Model 0)	Order 1	0.000268	23	0.018847	18
	Order 2	0.000272	38	0.018221	33
	Order 3	0.000249	64	0.017771	56
	Order 4	0.000238	95	0.017517	87
	Order 5	0.000220	125	0.016992	122
THONN (Model 0)	Order 1	0.000293	22	0.019113	24
	Order 2	0.000277	34	0.019016	40
	Order 3	0.000283	68	0.018384	62
	Order 4	0.000271	97	0.018370	102
	Order 5	0.000250	137	0.018030	142
UCSHONN (Model 0)	Order 1	0.000295	24	0.019113	23
	Order 2	0.000271	43	0.019113	42
	Order 3	0.000080	72	0.013411	71
	Order 4	0.000009	108	0.006024	107
	Order 5	0.0000004910	148	0.00002360	149
SXSPHONN (Model 0)	Order 1	0.000295	28	0.0022522	29
	Order 2	0.000272	46	0.018958	47
	Order 3	0.000289	71	0.018711	72
	Order 4	0.000279	102	0.018793	109
	Order 5	0.000285	151	0.018868	156
SINCHONN (Model 0)	Order 1	0.004945	29	0.028309	30
	Order 2	0.002652	51	0.025280	52
	Order 3	0.001572	80	0.020918	83
	Order 4	0.001492	119	0.020263	118
	Order 5	0.001480	167	0.020081	166
SPHONN (M0del 0)	Order 1	0.000442	27	0.022215	27
	Order 2	0.000355	47	0.019550	47
	Order 3	0.000295	77	0.018764	78
	Order 4	0.000300	110	0.018735	114
	Order 5	0.000287	157	0.018643	158
Total Time			2360		2364

SXSPHONN, SINCHONN, and SPHONN) are more than 9.0E-6. Moreover, the best model for Japan Consumer Price Index (1992- 2004) is UCSHONN order 5 with the mean squared error of 2.360E-5. The mean squared errors of all other models (PHONN, THONN, UCSHONN order 1 to 4, SXSPHONN, SINCHONN, and SPHONN) are more than 6.024E-3. This means HONN can

Table 10. Finding the best order for different models (best order mean squared error numbers are align left)

		Z=0.402X+0.598 Mean Squared Error	Z=0.2815682 - 0.2815682*cos(x) + 1.0376216*sin(y) Mean Square Error	US Consumer Price Index (1992-2004) Mean Squared Error	Japan Consumer Price Index (1992-2004) Mean Squared Error
PHONN	Order 1	7.371E-13	0.00001616	0.000268	0.018847
(Model 0)	Order 2	0.00006853	0.00002722	0.000272	0.018221
	Order 3	0.00000230	0.00010718	0.000249	0.017771
	Order 4	0.00000320	0.00009285	0.000238	0.017517
	Order 5	0.00000866	0.00006714	0.000220	0.016992
THONN	Order 1	0.00001351	2.965E-08	0.000293	0.019113
(Model 0)	Order 2	0.00002849	0.00000983	0.000277	0.019016
	Order 3	0.00000241	0.00000327	0.000283	0.018384
	Order 4	0.00005881	0.00000437	0.000271	0.018370
	Order 5	0.00001503	0.00000851	0.000250	0.018030
UCSHONN	Order 1	0.00000309	2.841E-08	0.000295	0.019113
(Model 0)	Order 2	0.00000133	0.00001162	0.000271	0.019113
	Order 3	0.00004071	0.00012063	0.000080	0.013411
	Order 4	0.00009228	0.00000221	0.000009	0.006024
	Order 5	0.00004116	0.00001962	0.000000491	0.000024
SXSPHONN	Order 1	0.00063820	0.00014997	0.000295	0.002252
(Model 0)	Order 2	0.00022918	0.00014330	0.000272	0.018958
	Order 3	0.00003515	0.00001520	0.000289	0.018711
	Order 4	0.00000392	0.00003035	0.000279	0.018793
	Order 5	0.00002715	0.00002728	0.000285	0.018868
SINCHONN	Order 1	0.00556992	0.00747188	0.004945	0.028309
(Model 0)	Order 2	0.00430713	0.00470922	0.002652	0.025280
	Order 3	0.00266424	0.00345466	0.001572	0.020918
	Order 4	0.00163071	0.00199684	0.001492	0.020263
	Order 5	0.00172761	0.00192670	0.001480	0.020081
SPHONN	Order 1	0.00001199	0.00013751	0.000442	0.022215
(Model 0)	Order 2	0.00001996	0.00012083	0.000355	0.019550
	Order 3	0.00040773	0.00053905	0.000295	0.018764
	Order 4	0.00029652	0.00015154	0.000300	0.018735
	Order 5	0.00008046	0.00016194	0.000287	0.018643

recognize Japan Consumer Price Index (1992-2004) in around 2364 seconds.

The above tests show that the average time to select the best model for linear or simple nonlinear data is about 516 seconds (8.6 minutes). The above tests also show that the average time to decide on the best model for nonlinear data is about 2284 seconds (38 minutes) under the computer environment given above. The computer speed could be 10 times quicker than the computer used today within several years. If the computer speed increases 10 times, only 0.86 minutes are needed to find the best model for linear or simple nonlinear data, and 3.8 minutes for more complicated data, which will make HONN more acceptable for nonlinear data modeling.

HONN Can Select the Best Order for the Data Simulation

Knowing which model is the best for the data, the second question should be asked is what order is the best order for these specific data? In some cases, the higher order model might give you better simulation result, but it does not mean the higher the better. For different data, to find the best order is one of the important steps to build a good model. Since SAS can never guarantee to converge in finding the order, user cannot be sure if the order selected yields the optimal solution. The following results show that HONN can easily find the best order in a pool of potential orders for different data.

Table 10 shows HONN can find the best order for different data. When simulating data, it does not always mean that higher order yield better results. To simulate linear data, Z = 0.402x+0.598y, the best orders are order 1, 3, 2, 4, and 2 for models PHONN, THONN, UCSHONN, SXSPHONN, and SPHONN, respectively. To simulate simple nonlinear data, Z = 0.2815682-0.2815682*cos(x) +1.0376216sin(y), the best orders are order 1, 1, 3, and 2 for models THONN, UCSHONN, SXS-PHONN, and SPHONN, respectively. To simulate US consumer price index (1992-2004), the best orders are order 5 for model UCSHONN, and order 2 for SXSPHONN model. To simulate data for Japanese consumer price index (1992-2004), the best orders are order 5 for model UCSHONN and order 1 for SXSPHONN model. Table 10 clearly shows that HONN can find the best order.

Table 11 shows the average convergence time for each model and order. Based on the average convergence time, Table 11 calculates the average time for finding the order that produces the best results. If you know the model for the data, time to find order are 325, 350, 379, 393, 431, and 406 seconds for model PHONN, THON, UCSHONN, SXSPHON, SINCHONN, and SPHONN respectively. As a result, in only 5 to 7 minutes, users can find the order that produce the best result for different data. Another key point is that users do not need to guess what coefficients they should provide. HONN will select the coefficients to make the simulation converge.

HONN Can Find the Coefficients for Data Simulation

After finding the best model and the order for the data, the third question is how to find the coefficients for the data? SAS requires the users to supply the initial parameter values. The problem is that the users cannot guess the correct initial parameter values, given that these values are what the users are trying to obtain. In most cases, SAS NLIN does not converge when the initial parameter values are not in the convergence range. In this section, this chapter demonstrates that HONN can easily find the coefficients for different models and orders, and converge all the time.

Table 11 illustrates the average time to find the coefficients, after providing the model and order. Average time for finding the coefficients are 27, 42, 69, 101, and 142 seconds for orders 1, 2, 3, 4, and 5 of HONN model 0. HONN can automatically choose the initial coefficients for simulation and can always converge.

FUTHER RESEARCH DIRECTIONS

As the next step of HONN model research, more HONN models for different data simulations will be built to increase the pool of HONN models. Theoretically, the adaptive HONN models can be

Table 11. Average Convergence Time.* (100,000 Epochs, Nonstationary Data, Model 0, Time Unit: second)

	P HONN	T HONN	UCS HONN	SXSP HONN	SINC HONN	SP HONN	Average Time for Finding Coefficients (seconds)
Order 1	25	24	23	31	29	28	27
Order 2	35	36	42	46	49	46	42
Order 3	59	63	69	69	78	74	69
Order 4	86	95	103	103	114	107	101
Order 5	121	132	143	145	161	151	142
Average Convergence Time	325	350	379	393	431	406	

* Under the computer environment as follows:

Computer Model: Personal computer, DELL OPTIPLEX GX260, made by 2003

Central Process Unit: Pentium 4CPU, 2.66GHz

Random Access Memory: 512 MB

Operation System: Microsoft Window XP, Professional, Version 2002

VNC Viewer: Version 3.3.3.2, for running UNIX on the PC

SUN Operation System: Solaris 9

Common Desktop Environment: Version 1.5.7

Computer Language: c

built and allow the computer automatically choose the best model, order, and coefficients. Making the adaptive HONN models easier to use is one of the future research topics.

SAS Nonlinear (NLIN) procedure produces least squares or weighted least squares estimates of the parameters of a nonlinear model. SAS Nonlinear models are more difficult to specify and estimate than linear models. Instead of simply generating the parameter estimates, users must write the regression expression, declare parameter names, and supply initial parameter values. Some models are difficult to fit, and there is no guarantee that the procedure can fit the model successfully. For each nonlinear model to be analyzed, users

must specify the model (using a single dependent variable) and the names and starting values of the parameters to be estimated. Therefore, SAS NLIN method is not user-friendly in finding nonlinear models using economics and business data.

HONNs can automatically select the initial coefficients for nonlinear data analysis.

The next step of this study is to allow people working in economics and business areas to understand that HONNs are much easier to use and can have better simulation results than SAS NLIN. Moreover, further research will develop HONNs software packages for people working in nonlinear data simulation and prediction area. HONNs will challenge SAS NLIN procedures and change the research methodology that people are currently using in economics and business areas for the nonlinear data simulation and prediction. Some detail steps are to:

- Introduce HONNs to people working in the fields of economics and business.
- Tell all SAS users that HONNs are much better tools than SAS NLIN models.
- Develop HONN software packages, and let more people use HONNs software packages.
- Write a good HONNs user manual, which provides the detailed information for people working in the economics and business areas to successfully use these HONNs software packages.
- Explain why HONNs can approximate any nonlinear data to any degree of accuracy, and make sure people working in economics and

business areas can understand why HONNs are much easier to use, and HONNs can have better nonlinear data simulation accuracy than SAS nonlinear (NLIN) procedures.
- Introduce the HONN group models and adaptive HONNs, and make sure people working in economics and business areas can understand HONN group models and adaptive HONN models, which can simulate not only nonlinear data, but also discontinuous and unsmooth nonlinear data.

CONCLUSION

The chapter presents HONN models (PHONN, THONN, UCSHONN, SINCHONN, SXS-PHONN, and SHONN). This chapter mathematically proves that HONN models can have mean squared error close to zero, and provide the

Box 3.

	SAS NLIN	HONN Models
Easy to use	No	Yes
	Users should provide the model, order, and initial coefficients.	Users select a model and order. The system will automatically choose initial coefficients.
Finding the best model	Users find the best model by trial and error.	Users run existing models and select the best model.
Finding the best order	Users find the best order by trial and error.	Users run existing orders and decide on the best order.
Providing the initial coefficients	Users find the initial coefficients by trial and error.	The HONN system, rather than the users, chooses the initial coefficients.
Convergence	SAS cannot guarantee convergence. If the user give the wrong model, wrong order, or/ and wrong initial coefficient, SAS NLIN will not converge.	Always converge.
Accuracy	If converges, SAS NLIN may use the average value for the outputs and the mean squared error could be very big.	Theoretically, mean squared error is close to zero.
Market	SAS NLIN not free.	As of May 2006, the authors cannot find HONN commercial software in the market.

learning algorithm with update formulas. HONN models are compared with SAS NLIN procedures. How to use HONN models to find the best model, order and coefficients are shown. The findings of this chapter are summarized in Box 3.

As the next step of HONN model research, more HONN models for different data simulations will be built for increasing the pool of HONN models. Theoretically, the adaptive HONN models can be built and allow the computer automatically choose the best model, order, and coefficients. Making the adaptive HONN models easier to use can be one of the research topics.

ACKNOWLEDGMENT

I would like to acknowledge the financial assistance of the following organizations in the development of Higher-Order Neural Networks: Fujitsu Research Laboratories, Japan (1995-1996), Australian Research Council (1997-1998), the US National Research Council (1999-2000), and the Applied Research Center grants and Dean's Office Grants of Christopher Newport University (2001-2007).

REFERENCES

Barron, R., Gilstrap, L., & Shrier, S. (1987). Polynomial and Neural Networks: Analogies and Engineering Applications. *Proceedings of the International Conference on Neural Networks,* (Vol. II, pp. 431-439). New York, NY.

Bengtsson, M. (1990). *Higher Order Artificial Neural Networks,* Diano Pub Co.

Bouzerdoum, A. (1999). A new class of high-order neural networks with nonlinear decision boundaries. *Proceedings of ICONIP'99 6th International Conference on Neural Information Processing* (Vol. 3, pp.1004-1009). 16-20 November 1999, Perth, WA, Australia.

Chang, C. H, Lin, J. L., & Cheung. J. Y. (1993). Polynomial and Standard higher order neural network, *Proceedings of IEEE International Conference on Neural Networks* (Vol.2, pp.989–994). 28 March – 1 April, 1993, San Francisco, CA.

Chen, Y., Jiang, Y. & Xu, J. (2003). Dynamic properties and a new learning mechanism in higher order neural networks, *Neurocomputing, 50*(Jan 03), 17-30.

Crane, J., & Zhang, M. (2005).Data simulation using SINCHONN model, *Proceedings of IASTED International Conference on Computational Intelligence* (pp. 50-55). Calgary, Canada.

Dunis, C. L., Laws, J., & Evans, B. (2006). *Modeling and trading the gasoline crack spread: A Non-linear story.* Working paper retrieved from http://www.ljmu.ac.uk/AFE/CIBEF/67756.htm, and paper accepted by Journal of Derivatives Use, Trading and Regulation, Forthcoming.

Estevez, P. A., & Okabe, Y. (1991). Training the piecewise linear-high order neural network through error back propagation (Vol. 1, pp.711-716). *Proceedings of IEEE International Joint Conference on Neural Networks,* 18-21 November, 1991.

Fulcher, J., Zhang, M. & Xu, S. (2006). The Application of Higher-Order Neural Networks to Financial Time Series, In J. Kamruzzaman (Ed.), *Artificial Neural Networks in Finance, Health and Manufacturing: Potential and Challenges* (pp. 80-108). Hershey, PA: IGI.

Ghazali, R. (2005). Higher order neural network for financial time series prediction, *Annual Postgraduate Research Conference,* March 16-17, 2005, School of Computing and Mathematical Sciences, Liverpool John Moores University, UK. Retrieved from http://www.cms.livjm.ac.uk/research/doc/ConfReport2005.doc

Giles, L., & Maxwell, T. (1987). Learning, invariance and generalization in high-order neural networks. *Applied Optics, 26*(23), 4972-4978.

Giles, L., Griffin, R., & Maxwell, T. (1988). Encoding geometric invariances in high-order neural networks. *Proceedings Neural Information Processing Systems*, 301-309.

He, Z., & and Siyal, M. Y. (1999). Improvement on higher-order neural networks for invariant object recognition. *Neural Processing Letters, 10*(1), 49-55.

Hornik, K. (1991). Approximation capabilities of multilayer feedforward networks. *Neural Networks, 4*, 251-257.

Hu, S., & Yan, P. (1992). Level-by-level learning for artificial neural groups. *Electronica Sinica, 20*(10), 39-43.

Jeffries, C. (1989). High order neural networks. *Proceedings of IJCNN International Joint Conference on Neural Networks* (Vol.2. pp.59). 18-22 June, 1989, Washington DC, USA.

Kanaoka, T., Chellappa, R., Yoshitaka M., & Tomita, S. (1992). A higher-order neural network for distortion unvariant pattern recognition, *Pattern Recognition Letters, 13*(12), 837-841.

Karayiannis, N. B., & Venetsanopoulos, A. N. (1995). On the training and performance of High-order neural networks, *Mathematical Biosciences, 129*(2), 143-168.

Karayiannis, N., & Venetsanopoulos, A. (1993). *Artificial neural networks: Learning algorithms, performance evaluation and applications.* Boston, MA: Kluwer.

Knowles, A., Hussain, A., Deredy, W. E., Lisboa, P. G. J., & Dunis, C. (2005). higher-order neural network with Bayesian confidence measure for prediction of EUR/USD exchange rate. *Forecasting Financial Markets Conference*, 1-3 June, 2005, Marseilles, France.

Lee, M., Lee, S. Y., & Park, C. H. (1992). Neural controller of nonlinear dynamic systems using higher order neural networks. *Electronics Letters, 28*(3), 276-277.

Leshno, M., Lin, V., Pinkus, A., & Schoken, S. (1993). Multi-layer feedforward networks with a non-polynomial activation can approximate any function. *Neural Networks, 6*, 861-867.

Li, D., Hirasawa K., & Hu, J. (2003). A new strategy for constructing higher order neural networks with multiplication units (Vol. 3, pp.2342-2347). *SICS 2003 Annual Conference.*

Lisboa, P., & Perantonis, S. (1991). Invariant pattern recognition using third-order networks and zernlike moments. *Proceedings of the IEEE International Joint Conference on Neural Networks* (Vol. II, pp. 1421-1425). Singapore.

Lu, B., Qi, H., Zhang, M., Scofield, R. A. (2000). Using PT-HONN models for multi-polynomial function simulation, Proceedings of *IASTED International Conference on Neural Networks* (pp.1-5). Pittsburg, USA,

Manykin, E. A., & Belov, M. N. (1991). Higher-order neural networks and photo-echo effect, *Neural networks, 4*(3), 417-420.

Park, S., Smith, M. J. T., & Mersereau, R. M. (2000). Target recognition based on directional filter banks and higher-order neural network. *Digital Signal Processing, 10*(4), 297-308.

Psaltis, D., Park, C., & Hong, J. (1988). Higher order associative memories and their optical implementations. *Neural Networks, 1*, 149-163.

Redding, N., Kowalczyk, A., & Downs, T. (1993). Constructive higher-order network algorithm that is polynomial time. *Neural Networks, 6*, 997-1010.

Rumelhart, D., Hinton, G., & McClelland, J. (1986). Learning internal representations by error propagation. In Rumelhart, D., & McClelland, J.

(Eds.) *Parallel distributed processing: explorations in the microstructure of cognition, Volume 1: Foundations.* Cambridge, MA: MIT Press.

Shin, Y. (1991). The Pi-Sigma network: An efficient higher-order neural network for pattern classification and function approximation. *Proceedings of the International Joint Conference on Neural Networks* (Vol. I, pp.13-18). Seattle, WA.

Spirkovska L., & Reid, M. B. (1994). Higher-order neural networks applied to 2D and 3D object recognition. *Machine Learning, 15*(2), 169-199.

Spirkovska, L., & Reid, M. B. (1992). Robust position, scale, and rotation invariant object recognition using higher-order neural networks. *Pattern Recognition, 25*(9), 975-985.

Synder, L. (2006). *Fluency with information technology.* Boston, MA: Addison Wesley.

Tai, H., & Jong, T. (1990). Information storage in high-order neural networks with unequal neural activity. *Journal of the Franklin Institute, 327*(1), 129-141.

Venkatesh, S. S., & Baldi, P. (1991). Programmed interactions in higher-order neural networks: Maximal capacity. *Journal of Complexity, 7*(3), 316-337.

Wilcox, C. (1991). Understanding hierarchical neural network behavior: A renormalization group approach. *Journal of Physics A, 24*, 2644-2655.

Xu, S., & Zhang, M. (1999). Approximation to continuous functions and operators using adaptive higher order neural networks, *Proceedings of International Joint Conference on Neural Networks '99*, Washington, DC, USA.

Zhang, J. (2005). Polynomial full naïve estimated misclassification cost models for financial distress prediction using higher order neural network. *14th Annual Research Work Shop on Artificial Intelligence and Emerging Technologies in Accounting, Auditing, and Ta.* San Francisco, California, USA.

Zhang, J. (2006), Linear and nonlinear models for the power of chief elected officials and debt. *Mid-Atlantic Region American Accounting Association.* Pittsburgh, PA, USA.

Zhang, J. C., Zhang, M., & Fulcher, J. (1997). Financial prediction using higher order trigonometric polynomial neural network group models. *Proceedings of ICNN/IEEE International Conference on Neural Networks* (pp. 2231-2234). Houston, Texas, USA.

Zhang, M., Murugesan, S., & Sadeghi, M. (1995). Polynomial higher order neural network for economic data simulation. *Proceedings of International Conference On Neural Information Processing* (pp. 493-496). Beijing, China.

Zhang, M., Fulcher, J., & Scofield, R. (1997). Rainfalll estimation using artificial neural network group. *International Journal of Neurlcomputing, 16*(2), 97-115.

Zhang, M., Zhang, J. C., & Keen, S. (1999). Using THONN system for higher frequency non-linear data simulation & prediction. *Proceedings of IASTED International Conference on Artificial Intelligence and Soft Computing* (pp.320-323). Honolulu, Hawaii, USA.

Zhang, M., Zhang, J. C., & Fulcher, J. (2000). Higher order neural network group models for financial simulation. *International Journal of Neural Systems, 10*(2), 123-142.

Zhang, M. (2001). Financial data simulation using A-PHONN model. *International Joint Conference on Neural Networks '01* (pp.1823 – 1827). Washington DC, USA.

Zhang, M. (2002) Financial data simulation using PL-HONN model. *Proceeding of IASTED International Conference on Modeling and Simulation (NS2002).* Marina del Rey, CA, USA.

Zhang, M., & Lu, B. (2001). Financial data simulation using M-PHONN model. *International Joint Conference on Neural Networks' 2001* (pp. 1828 – 1832). Washington DC, USA.

Zhang, M., Xu, S., & Fulcher, J. (2002). Neuron-adaptive higher order neural network models for automated financial data modeling, *IEEE transactions on Neural Networks, 13*(1), 188-204.

Zhang, M., & Fulcher, J. (2004). Higher order neural networks for satellite weather prediction, In J. Fulcher and L. C. Jain (Eds.), *Applied Intelligent Systems* (pp. 17-57). Springer-Verlag Publisher.

Zhang, M. (2005). A data simulation system using sinx/x and sinx polynomial higher order neural networks. *Proceedings of IASTED International Conference on Computational Intelligence* (pp. 56 – 61). Calgary, Canada.

Zhang, M. (2006). A data simulation system using CSINC polynomial higher order neural networks. *Proceedings of The 2006 International Conference on Artificial Intelligenc (Vol. I, pp. 91-97).* Las Vegas, USA.

ADDITIONAL READING

Azoff, E. (1994). *Neural network time series forecasting of financial markets.* New York: Wiley.

Balke, N. S., & Fomby, T. B. (1997). Threshold cointegration. *International Economic Review, 38,* 627-645.

Bierens, H. J., & Ploberger, W. (1997). Asymptotic theory of integrated conditional moment tests. *Econometrica. 65*(5), 1129-1151.

Blum, E., & Li, K. (1991). Approximation theory and feed-forward networks, *Neural Networks, 4,* 511-515.

Box, G. E. P. & Jenkins, G. M. (1976). *Time series analysis: Forecasting and control.* San Fransisco: Holden-Day.

Chakraborty, K., Mehrotra ,K., Mohan, C., & Ranka, S. (1992). Forecasting the behavior of multivariate time series using neural networks. *Neural Networks, 5,* 961-970.

Chang, Y., & Park, J. Y. (2003). Index models with integrated time series. *Journal of Econometrics, 114,* 1, 73-106.

Chen, C. T., & Chang, W. D. (1996) A feed-forward neural network with function shape autotuning. *Neural Networks, 9*(4), 627-641.

Chen, T., & Chen, H. (1993). Approximations of continuous functional by neural networks with application to dynamic systems. *IEEE Trans on Neural Networks, 4*(6), 910-918.

Chen, T., & Chen, H. (1995). Approximation capability to functions of several variables, nonlinear functionals, and operators by radial basis function neural networks. *IEEE Trans on Neural Networks, 6*(4), 904-910.

Chen, X., & Shen, X. (1998). Sieve extremum estimates for weakly dependent data. *Econometrica, 66*(2), 289-314.

Chenug, Y. W., & Chinn, M. D. (1999). *Macroeconomic implications of the Beliefs and Behavior of Foreign exchange Traders.* NBER, Working paper no. 7414.

Elbradawi, I. A. (1994). Estimating long-run equilibrium real exchange rates. In J. Williamson (Ed), *Estimating equilibrium exchange rates* (pp. 93-131). Institute for International Economics.

Fahlman, S. (1988). Faster-learning variations on back-propagation: An empirical study. *Proceedings of 1988 Connectionist Models Summer School.*

Gardeazabal, J., & Regulez, M. (1992). *The monetary model of exchange rates and cointegration.* New York:Springer-Verlag.

Gorr, W. L. (1994). Research prospective on neural network forecasting, *International Journal of Forecasting, 10*(1), 1-4.

Granger, C. W. J. & Weiss, A. A. (1983). Time series analysis of error-correction models. In S. Karlin, T. Amemiya and L. A. Goodman (Eds), *Studies in Econometrics, Time Series and Multivariate Statistics* (pp. 255-278). In Honor of T. W. Anderson. San Diego: Academic Press.

Granger, C. W. J. & Bates, J. (1969). The combination of forecasts. *Operations Research Quarterly*, 20, 451-468.

Granger, C. W. J., & Lee, T. H. (1990). Multicointegration. In G. F. Rhodes, Jr and T. B. Fomby (Eds.), *Advances in Econometrics: Cointegration, Spurious Regressions and Unit Roots* (pp.17-84). New York: JAI Press.

Granger, C. W. J. & Swanson, N. R. (1996). Further developments in study of cointegrated variables. *Oxford Bulletin of Economics and Statistics*, 58, 374-386.

Granger, C. W. J., & Newbold, P. (1974). Spurious regressions in econometrics. *Journal of Econometrics, 2*, 111-120.

Granger, C. W. J. (1995). Modeling nonlinear relationships between extended-memory variables, *Econometrica, 63*(2), 265-279.

Granger, C. W. J. (2001) Spurious regressions in econometrics. In B. H. Baltagi (Ed.), *A companion to theoretical econometrics* (pp.557-561). Blackwell: Oxford.

Granger, C. W. J. (1981). Some properties of time series data and their use in econometric model specification. *Journal of Econometrics, 16*, 121-130.

Hans, P., & Draisma, G. (1997). Recognizing changing seasonal patterns using artificial neural networks. *Journal of Econometrics, 81*(1), 273-280.

Hornik, K. (1993). Some new results on neural network approximation. *Neural Networks, 6*, 1069-1072.

Kilian, L., & Taylor, M. P. (2003). Why is it so difficult to beat the random walk forecast of exchange rate? *Journal of International Economics, 60*, 85-107.

MacDonald, R., & Marsh, I. (1999). *Exchange Rate Modeling* (pp. 145 – 171). Boston: Kluwer Academic Publishers.

Meese, R., and Rogoff, K. (1983A). Empirical exchange rate models of the seventies: Do they fit out of sample. *Journal of International Economics, 14*, 3-24.

Meese, R., and Rogoff, K. (1983B). The out-of-samples failure of empirical exchange rate models: sampling error or misspecification. In Frenkel, J. A., (Ed.), *Exchange rate and International macroeconomics*. Chicago and Boston: Chicago University Press and National Bureau of Economic Research.

Scarselli, F., & Tsoi, A. C. (1998). Universal approximation using feed-forward neural networks: a survey of some existing methods, and some new results. *Neural Networks, 11*(1),15-37.

Shintani, M., & Linton, O. (2004). Nonparametric neural network estimation of Lyapunov exponents and direct test for chaos. *Journal of Econometrics, 120*(1), 1-33.

Taylor, M. P. (1995). The economics of exchange rates. *Journal of Economic Literature, 33*, 13-47.

Taylor, M. P., & Peel, D. A. (2000). Nonlinear adjustment, long run equilibrium and exchange rate fundamentals. *Journal of International Money and Finance*, 19, 33-53.

Taylor, M. P., Peel, D. A., & Sarno, L. (2001). Nonlinear adjustments in real exchange rate: towards a solution to the purchasing power parity puzzles. *International Economic Review, 42*, 1015-1042.

Vetenskapsakademien, K. (2003). Time-series econometrics: Co-integration and Autoregressive conditional heteroskedasticity, *Advanced information on the Bank of Sweden Prize in Economic Sciences in Memory of Alfred Nobel*, 8 October, 2003.

Werbos, P. (1994). *The roots of backpropagation: From ordered derivatives to neural networks and political forecasting.* New York: Wiley.

Williamson, J. (1994). *Estimating equilibrium exchange rates.* Institute for International Economics.

Zell, A. (1995). *Stuttgart Neural Network Simulator V4.1.* University of Stuttgart, Institute for Parallel & Distributed High Performance Systems. Retrieved from ftp.informatik.uni-stuttgart.de

Zhang, M., Fulcher, J., & Scofield, R. A. (1996) Neural network group models for estimating rainfall from satellite images. *Proceedings of World Congress on Neural Networks* (pp.897-900). San Diego, CA.

APPENDICES

Appendix A: Output Neurons in HONN Model (model 0, 1, and 1b)

The output layer weights are updated according to:

$$a_{kj}^{\ o}(t+1) = a_{kj}^{\ o}(t) - \eta\,(\partial E\ /\ \partial a_{kj}^{\ o})$$
(A.1)

where:

η = learning rate (positive and usually < 1)

a_{kj} = weight; index k an j = input index (k, j=0, 1, 2,…,n means one of n*n input neurons from the second hidden layer)

E = error

t = training time

o = output layer

The output node equations are:

$$net^{\ o} = \sum_{k,j=1}^{n} a_{kj}^{\ o} i_{kj}$$

$$z = f^{\ o}(net^{\ o}) = \sum a_{kj}^{\ o} i_{kj}$$
(A.2)

where:

i_{kj} = input to the output neuron (= output from 2nd hidden layer)

z = actual output from the output neuron

$f^{\ o}$ = output neuron activity function

The error at a particular output unit (neuron) will be:

$$\delta = (d - z)$$
(A.3)

where d = desired output value.

The total error is the error of output unit, namely:

$$E = 0.5 * \delta^{\ 2} = 0.5 * (d - z)^{2}$$
(A.4)

The derivatives $f^{\ o\prime}(net^{o})$ are calculated as follows. The output neuron function is linear function $(f^{\ o}(net^{o}) = net^{o})$:

$$f^{\ o\prime}(net^{\ o}) = \partial f^{\ o}\ /\ \partial(net^{\ o}) = \partial(net^{\ o})\ /\ \partial(net^{\ o}) = 1$$
(A.5)

41

Gradients are calculated as follows:

$$\partial E \ / \ \partial a_{kj}{}^{o} = (\partial E \ / \ \partial z \ )(\partial z \ / \ \partial (net^{o}))(\partial (net^{o}) \ / \ \partial a_{kj}{}^{o}) \tag{A.6}$$

$$\partial E \ / \ \partial z = \partial (0.5 * (d \ - z \ )^{2}) \ / \ \partial z$$
$$= 0.5 * (-2(d \ - z \ )) = -(d \ - z \ ) \tag{A.7}$$

$$\partial z \ / \ \partial (net^{o}) = \partial f^{o} \ / \ \partial (net^{o}) = f^{o} \, '(net^{o}) \tag{A.8}$$

$$\partial (net^{o} \ ) \ / \ \partial a^{o}{}_{kj} = \partial (\sum_{k,j=0}^{n} a^{o}{}_{kj} i_{kj}) \ / \ \partial a^{o}{}_{kj} = i_{kj} \tag{A.9}$$

Combining Eqns. A.6 through A.9, the negative gradient is:

$$-\partial E \ / \ \partial a_{kj}{}^{o} = (d \ - z \ ) f^{o} \, '(net^{o}) i_{kj} \tag{A.10}$$

For a linear output neuron, this becomes, by combining Eqns. A.10 and A.5:

$$-\partial E \ / \ \partial a_{kj}{}^{o} = (d \ - z \ ) f^{o} \, '(net^{o}) i_{kj}$$
$$= (d \ - z \ )(1) i_{kj} = (d \ - z) i_{kj} \tag{A.11}$$

The weight update equations are formulated as follows. For linear output neurons, let:

$$\delta^{ol} = (d \ - z \ ) \tag{A.12}$$

Combining Formulae A.1, A.11, and A.12:

$$a_{kj}{}^{o} (t+1) = a_{kj}{}^{o} (t) - \eta (\partial E \ / \ \partial a_{kj}{}^{o})$$
$$= a_{kj}{}^{o} (t) + \eta (d \ - z \ ) f^{o} \, '(net^{o}) i_{kj}$$
$$= a_{kj}{}^{o} (t) + \eta \delta^{ol} i_{kj}$$
$$where:$$
$$\delta^{ol} = (d - z)$$
$$f^{o'}(net^{o}) = 1 \qquad (linear \qquad neuron) \tag{A.13}$$

Appendix B: Second-Hidden Layer Neurons in HONN Model (Model 1b)

The second hidden layer weights are updated according to:

$$a_{kj}{}^{hx} (t+1) = a_{kj}{}^{hx} (t) - \eta (\partial E \ / \ \partial a_{kj}{}^{hx}) \tag{B.1}$$

where:

η = learning rate (positive & usually < 1)

k,j = input index (k, j=0, 1, 2, …,n means one of 2*n*n input combinations from the first hidden layer)

E = error

t = training time

hx = hidden layer, related to x input

$a_{kj}^{\ hx}$ = hidden layer weight related to x input

The equations for the 2nd hidden layer node are:

$$net_{kj}^{\ h} = \{a_{kj}^{\ hx}b_k^{\ x}\}\{a_{kj}^{\ hy}b_j^{\ y}\}$$
$$i_{kj} = f^h(net_{kj}^{\ h}) \tag{B.2}$$

where:

i_{kj} = output from 2nd hidden layer (= input to the output neuron)

$b_k^{\ x}$ and $b_j^{\ y}$ = input to 2nd hidden layer neuron (= output from the 1st hidden layer neuron)

fh= hidden neuron activation function

hy = hidden layer, related to y input

$a_{kj}^{\ hy}$ = hidden layer weight related to y input

We call the neurons at the second layer are multiple neurons. Their activity function is linear and their inputs are the multiplication of two outputs of the first layer neuron output time their weights.

The error of a single output unit will be:

$$\delta = (d - z) \tag{B.3}$$

where:

d = desired output value of output layer neuron

z = actual output value of output layer neuron

The total error is the sum of the squared errors across all output units, namely:

$$E_p = 0.5*\delta^2 = 0.5*(d-z)^2$$
$$= 0.5*(d - f^o(net^o))^2$$
$$= 0.5*(d - f_k^o(\sum_j a_{kj}^{\ o}i_{kj}))^2 \tag{B.4}$$

The derivatives $f^{h\prime}(net_{pj}^h)$ are calculated as follows, for a linear function of second layer neurons:

$$i_{kj} = f^h(net_{kj}^{\ h}) = net_{kj}^{\ h}$$
$$f^{h\prime}(net_{kj}^{\ h}) = 1 \tag{B.5}$$

The gradient $(\partial E/\partial a_{kj}^{hx})$ is given by:

$$\partial E \ / \partial a_{kj}^{hx} = \partial (0.5*(d-z)^2)/\partial a_{kj}^{hx}$$
$$= (\partial(0.5*(d-z)^2)/\partial z \ )(\partial z \ / \partial(net^o))$$
$$(\partial(net^o)/\partial i_{kj})(\partial i_{kj}/\partial(net_{kj}^h))(\partial(net_{kj}^h)/\partial a_{kj}^{hx}) \tag{B.6}$$

$$\partial(0.5*(d-z)^2)/\partial z \ = -(d-z) \tag{B.7}$$

$$\partial z \ / \partial(net^o) = (\partial f^o \ / \partial(net^o) = f_k^{o}{}'(net^o) \tag{B.8}$$

$$\partial(net^o)/\partial i_{kj} = \partial(\sum_{k,j=1}^{n}(a_{kj}^o i_{kj}))/\partial i_{kj} = a_{kj}^o \tag{B.9}$$

$$\partial i_{kj}/\partial(net_{kj}^h) = \partial(f^h(net_{kj}^h))/\partial(net_{kj}^h) = f^h{}'(net_{kj}^h) \tag{B.10}$$

$$\partial(net_{kj}^h)/\partial a_{kj}^{hx} = \partial(\{a_{kj}^{hx}b_k^x\}\{a_{kj}^{hy}b_j^y\})/\partial a_{kj}^{hx}$$
$$= b_k^x a_{kj}^{hy}b_j^y = \delta_{kj}^{hx}b_k^x$$
$$where: \delta_{kj}^{hx} = a_{kj}^{hy}b_j^y \tag{B.11}$$

Combining Eqns. B.6 through B.11, the negative gradient is:

$$-\partial E \ / \partial a_{kj}^{hx} = (d-z)f^o{}'(net^o)a_{kj}^o f^h{}'(net_{pj}^h)\delta^{hx}b_k^x \tag{B.12}$$

The weight update equations are formulated as follows. Let output neuron is a linear neuron:

$$\delta^{ol} = (d-z)\ f^o_k{}'(net^o) = (d-z) \tag{B.13}$$

and also let the second layer neurons are linear neurons. Combining Formulae B.1, B.5, B.12 and B.13:

$$a_{kj}^{hx}(t+1) = a_{kj}^{hx}(t) - \eta(\partial E/\partial a_{kj}^{hx})$$
$$= a_{kj}^{hx}(t) + \eta((d-z)f^o{}'(net^o)a_{kj}^o f^h{}'(net_{kj}^{hx})a_{kj}^{hy}b_j^y b_k^x)$$
$$= a_{kj}^{hx}(t) + \eta(\delta^{ol}a_{kj}^o\delta_{kj}^{hx}b_k^x)$$
$$where: \qquad \delta^{ol} = (d-z)$$
$$\delta_{kj}^{hx} = a_{kj}^{hy}b_j^y$$
$$f^o{}'(net^o) = 1 \qquad (linear \qquad neuron)$$
$$f^h{}'(net_{kj}^{hx}) = 1 \qquad (linear \qquad neuron) \tag{B.14}$$

Use the same rules, the weight update question for y input neurons is:

$$a_{kj}^{hy}(t+1) = a_{kj}^{hy}(t) - \eta(\partial E / \partial a_{kj}^{hy})$$
$$= a_{kj}^{hy}(t) + \eta((d-z)f^{o\,\prime}(net^o)a_{kj}^o f^{h\,\prime}(net_{kj}^{hy})a_{kj}^{hx}b_k^x b_j^y)$$
$$= a_{kj}^{hy}(t) + \eta(\delta^{ol}a_{kj}^o \delta_{kj}^{hy}b_j^y)$$

$$where: \qquad \delta^{ol} = (d-z)$$
$$\delta_{kj}^{hy} = a_{kj}^{hx}b_k^x$$
$$f^{o\,\prime}(net^o) = 1 \qquad (linear \qquad neuron)$$
$$f^{h\,\prime}(net_{kj}^{hy}) = 1 \qquad (linear \qquad neuron) \tag{B.15}$$

Appendix C: First Hidden Layer Neurons in HONN (Model 1 and Model 1b)

The 1st hidden layer weights are updated according to:

$$a_k^x(t+1) = a_k^x(t) - \eta(\partial E / \partial a_k^x) \tag{C.1}$$

where:
  η = learning rate (positive & usually < 1)
  k = kth neuron of first hidden layer
  E = error
  t = training time
  a_k^x = 1st hidden layer weight for input x

The equations for the kth and jth node in the first hidden layer are:

$$net_k^x = a_k^x x$$
$$b_k^x = f_k^x(net_k^x)$$
$$or$$
$$net_j^y = a_j^y y$$
$$b_j^y = f_j^y(net_j^y) \tag{C.2}$$

where:
  i_{kj} = output from 2nd hidden layer (= input to the output neuron)
  b_k^x and b_j^y = output from the 1st hidden layer neuron (= input to 2nd hidden layer neuron)
  f_k^x and f_j^y are 1st hidden layer neuron activation functions.
  x and y = input to 1st hidden layer

The total error is the sum of the squared errors across all hidden units, namely:

$$E = 0.5 * \delta^2 = 0.5 * (d - z)^2$$
$$= 0.5 * (d - f^o(net^o))^2$$
$$= 0.5 * (d - f^o(\sum_j a_{kj}^o i_{kj}))^2 \tag{C.3}$$

The gradient $(\partial E / \partial a_k^x)$ is given by:

$$\partial E / \partial a_k^x = \partial(0.5 * (d - z)^2) / \partial a_k^x$$
$$= (\partial(0.5 * (d - z)^2) / \partial z)(\partial z / \partial(net^o))$$
$$(\partial(net^o) / \partial i_{kj})(\partial i_{kj} / \partial(net_{kj}^h))(\partial(net_{kj}^h) / \partial b_k^x)$$
$$(\partial b_k^x / \partial(net_k^x))(\partial(net_k^x) / \partial a_k^x) \tag{C.4}$$

$$\partial(0.5 * (d - z)^2 / \partial z = -(d - z) \tag{C.5}$$

$$\partial z / \partial(net^o) = \partial f^o / \partial(net^o) = f^o{}'(net^o) \tag{C.6}$$

$$\partial(net^o) / \partial i_{kj} = \partial(\sum_{k,j=1}^{L} (a_{kj}^o i_{kj}) / \partial i_{kj} = a_{kj}^o \tag{C.7}$$

$$\partial i_{kj} / \partial(net_{kj}^h) = \partial(f^h(net_{kj}^h))\partial(net_{kj}^h) = f^h{}'(net_{kj}^h) \tag{C.8}$$

$$\partial net_{kj}^h / \partial b_k^x = \partial((a_{kj}^{hx} * b_k^x) * (a_{kj}^{hy} * b_j^y)) / \partial b_k^x = a_{kj}^{hx} * a_{kj}^{hy} * b_j^y$$
$$= \delta_{kj}^{hx} a_{kj}^{hx}$$
$$where : \delta_{kj}^{hx} = a_{kj}^{hy} * b_j^y \tag{C.9}$$

$$\partial b_k^x / \partial(net_k^x) = f_k^x{}'(net_k^x) \tag{C.10}$$

$$\partial(net_k^x) / \partial a_k^x = \partial(a_k^x * x) / \partial a_k^x = x \tag{C.11}$$

Combining Formulae C.4 through C.11, the negative gradient is:

$$-\partial E_p / \partial a_k^x = (d - z)f^o{}'(net^o)a_{kj}^o * f^h{}'(net_{kj}^{hx})\delta_{kj}^{hx} a_{kj}^{hx} f_k^x{}'(net_k^x)x \tag{C.12}$$

The weight update equations are calculated as follows. For linear output neurons, this becomes:

$$\delta^{ol} = (d - z) \tag{C.13}$$

Whereas for linear neurons of second hidden layer, this becomes:

$$f^h{}'(net_{kj}^{hx}) = 1 \tag{C.14}$$

The negative gradient is:

$$-\partial E_p / \partial a_k^{\ x} = (d-z)f^{o\ '}(net^{\ o})a_{kj}^{\ \ o} * f^{h\ '}(net_{kj}^{\ \ h})\delta_{kj}^{\ \ hx}a_{kj}^{\ \ hx}f^{x}_{\ k}{}'(net_k^{\ x})x$$

$$= \delta^{\ ol} * a_{kj}^{\ \ o} * \delta_{kj}^{\ \ hx} * a_{kj}^{\ \ hx} * f^{x}_{\ k}{}'(net_k^{\ x}) * x \qquad\qquad (C.15)$$

We have, for a linear 1st hidden layer neuron:

$$a_k^{\ x}(t+1) = a_k^{\ x}(t) - \eta(\partial E_p / \partial a_k^{\ x})$$

$$= a_x^{\ x}(t) + \eta(d-z)f^{o\ '}(net^{\ o})a_{kj}^{\ \ o} * f^{h\ '}(net_{kj}^{\ \ h})a_{kj}^{\ \ hy}b_j^{\ y}a_{kj}^{\ \ hx}f_k^{\ x\ '}(net_k^{\ x})x$$

$$= a_x^{\ x}(t) + \eta * \delta^{\ ol} * a_{kj}^{\ \ o} * \delta_{kj}^{\ \ hx} * a_{kj}^{\ \ hx} * f_k^{\ x\ '}(net_k^{\ x}) * x$$

$$= a_x^{\ x}(t) + \eta * \delta^{\ ol} * a_{kj}^{\ \ o} * \delta_{kj}^{\ \ hx} * a_{kj}^{\ \ hx} * \delta_k^{\ x} * x$$

where : $\qquad\qquad\qquad\qquad\qquad\qquad\qquad\qquad\qquad\qquad$ (C.16)

$$\delta^{\ ol} = (d-z)$$

$$f^{o\ '}(net^{\ o}) = 1 \qquad (linear \qquad neuron)$$

$$\delta_{kj}^{\ \ hx} = a_{kj}^{\ \ hy}b_j^{\ y}$$

$$f^{h\ '}(net_{kj}^{\ \ h}) = 1 \qquad (linear \qquad neuron)$$

$$\delta_k^{\ x} = f_k^{\ x\ '}(net_k^{\ x})$$

Using the above procedure:

$$a_j^{\ y}(t+1) = a_j^{\ y}(t) - \eta(\partial E_p / \partial a_j^{\ y})$$

$$= a_j^{\ y}(t) + \eta(d-z)f^{o\ '}(net^{\ o})a_{kj}^{\ \ o} * f^{h\ '}(net_{kj}^{\ \ h})a_{kj}^{\ \ hx}b_k^{\ x}a_{kj}^{\ \ hy}f_j^{\ y\ '}(net_j^{\ y})y$$

$$= a_j^{\ y}(t) + \eta * \delta^{\ ol} * a_{kj}^{\ \ o} * \delta^{\ hy} * a_{kj}^{\ \ hy} * f_j^{\ y\ '}(net_j^{\ y}) * y$$

$$= a_j^{\ y}(t) + \eta * \delta^{\ ol} * a_{kj}^{\ \ o} * \delta_{kj}^{\ \ hy} * a_{kj}^{\ \ hy} * \delta_j^{\ y} * y$$

where : $\qquad\qquad\qquad\qquad\qquad\qquad\qquad\qquad\qquad\qquad$ (C.17)

$$\delta^{\ ol} = (d-z)$$

$$f^{o\ '}(net^{\ o}) = 1 \qquad (linear \qquad neuron)$$

$$\delta_{kj}^{\ \ hy} = a_{kj}^{\ \ hx}b_k^{\ x}$$

$$f^{h\ '}(net_{kj}^{\ \ hy}) = 1 \qquad (linear \qquad neuron)$$

$$\delta_j^{\ y} = f_j^{\ y\ '}(net_j^{\ y})$$

Chapter II
Higher Order Neural Networks with Bayesian Confidence Measure for the Prediction of the EUR/USD Exchange Rate

Adam Knowles
Liverpool John Moores University, UK

Paulo G. J. Lisboa
Liverpool John Moores University, UK

Abir Hussain
Liverpool John Moores University, UK

Christian L. Dunis
Liverpool John Moores University, UK

Wael El Deredy
Liverpool John Moores University, UK

ABSTRACT

Multi-Layer Perceptrons (MLP) are the most common type of neural network in use, and their ability to perform complex nonlinear mappings and tolerance to noise in data is well documented. However, MLPs also suffer long training times and often reach only local optima. Another type of network is Higher Order Neural Networks (HONN). These can be considered a 'stripped-down' version of MLPs, where joint activation terms are used, relieving the network of the task of learning the relationships between the inputs. The predictive performance of the network is tested with the EUR/USD exchange rate and evaluated using standard financial criteria including the annualized return on investment, showing a 8% increase in the return compared with the MLP. The output of the networks that give the highest annualized return in each category was subjected to a Bayesian based confidence measure. This performance improvement may be explained by the explicit and parsimonious representation of high order terms in Higher Order Neural Networks, which combines robustness against noise typical of distributed models, together with the ability to accurately model higher order interactions for long-term forecasting. The effectiveness of the confidence measure is explained by examining the distribution of each network's output. We speculate that the distribution can be taken into account during training, thus enabling us to produce neural networks with the properties to take advantage of the confidence measure.

INTRODUCTION

Most research on time series prediction has traditionally concentrated on linear methods, which are mathematically convenient and computationally inexpensive. Unfortunately, most systems that are of interest are nonlinear. An important class of nonlinear systems appear in financial forecasting, which typically include the prediction of exchange rates and share prices. These have generally received a large amount of attention, due to the financial incentive from even small accuracy improvements in predicting market changes. So with the growth of cheap computing power, there has been in recent years an increased interest in nonlinear models, and particularly neural networks as noted, amongst others, by Dunis and Williams (2002).

Multi-Layer Perceptrons (MLPs) are the most common type of network in use, and their ability to perform complex nonlinear mappings and tolerance to noise in data is well documented, eg. Haykin (1999). However, MLPs also suffer long training times and often reach only local optima. In addition, larger MLPs are prone to overfitting, where excess capacity is used to learn irrelevant details of the training data set, decreasing the network's performance upon testing and validation. Another type of networks is Higher Order Neural Networks (henceforth HONN). These can be considered a 'stripped-down' version of MLPs, where higher order terms are used, relieving the network of the task of learning the relationships between the inputs. Thus, HONNs are simpler than MLPs to train and implement, while still having access to joint activations between inputs that are learned by the hidden layer in MLPs.

The motivation for this chapter is to determine if HONNs can give a greater return on investment than MLPs, using as a basis previous research from Dunis and Williams (2002) and Lindemann *et al.* (2005) which benchmarked the financial results of MLPs and Gaussian mixture networks with traditional forecasting techniques.

The rest of this chapter is organised as follows: section 2 introduces the HONN architecture, the Bayesian confidence measure and how it interacts with the trading strategy. Section 3 discusses the simulation conditions and presents the results of the HONN models. Finally, section 4 analyses the results and discusses the implications.

METHODS AND MODELS

Higher Order Neural Network Architecture

HONNs were first introduced by Giles and Maxwell (1987) and further analyzed by Pao (1989) who referred to them as 'tensor networks' and regarded them as a special case of his functional-link models. HONNs have already enjoyed some success in the field of pattern recognition, as with Giles and Maxwell (1987) and Schmidt and Davis (1993) and associative recall as with Karayiannis (1995), but their application to financial time series prediction has just started with contributions such as Dunis *et al.* (2006-a,b,c). The typical structure of a HONN is given in Figure 1b.

HONNs use joint activations between inputs, thus removing the task of establishing relationships between them during training. For this reason, a hidden layer is commonly not used. The reduced number of free weights compared with MLPs means that the problems of overfitting and local optima can be migrated to a large degree. In addition, as noted by Pao (1989), a HONN is faster to train and execute when compared to a MLP. It is, however, necessary for practical reasons to limit both the order of the network and the number of inputs, to avoid the curse of dimensionality.

Confidence Measure and Trading Strategy

The models used in their research by Dunis and Williams (2002) were attached to a simple

Figure 1 – (a) Left, MLP with three inputs and two hidden nodes. (b) Right, Second Order HONN with three inputs

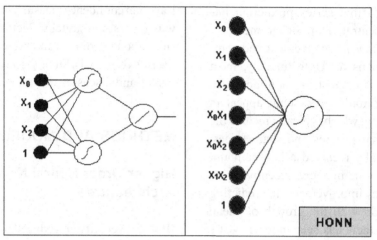

trading strategy to assess its profitability: if the return forecast is an increase, then a buy signal is produced, otherwise a signal is sent to sell. In addition to testing this strategy, we also introduce a third option called "don't know," when the model does not send either a buy or sell signal, effectively opting out of making any transaction. In order to do this, we need a confidence measure which can give us a probability of the network .

The method selected was Bayesian based on the method suggested by Masters (1993) with equation (1). With this method, the output of the network during the last epoch of training is separated into two categories; the output when the signal change is positive and the output when the signal change is negative or unchanged. These become the data for the two hypotheses (buy and sell). The distances are calculated between the current observed value and the sample data of both hypotheses. The distance is weighted by σ before being put into a Gaussian function (see equations (2) and (3)). The mean of this function is then calculated for each sample, the relative values of the means of the two hypotheses are used to give a percent probability of the signal change being positive or negative. Note that since

there are only two mutually exclusive hypotheses, H1 and H2, then Hi = 100 - Hj, where i ≠ j. If the confidence from a hypothesis is >= 60%, the respective signal is sent, otherwise no action is taken in that time period.

$$P(H_k|x) = \frac{p_k L(x|H_k)}{\sum_i (p_i L(x|H_i))} \tag{1}$$

$$g(x) = \frac{1}{n\sigma} \sum_i W(\frac{x - x_i}{\sigma}) \tag{2}$$

where x represents the observed value and x_i represents the sampled value of hypotheses i and σ is the weighting. W(.) is the window function determined according to the following equation:

$$W(d) = e^{-d^2} \tag{3}$$

This method owes more to pattern classification and game theory than traditional forecasting error techniques. However, its advantage is in its generality, as it can be used by any model where there exists prior information about the distribution of the output.

SIMULATION

The EUR/USD Exchange Rate

The target dataset that is used in the simulation is the EUR/USD exchange rate, i.e. the number of US Dollars for 1 Euro. The exchange rate time series is the daily closing prices with 1749 samples taken between 17th October 1994 to 3rd July 2001. Since the Euro was not traded until 4th January 1999, the earlier samples are a retropolated synthetic series using the USD/DEM daily exchange rate combined with the fixed EUR/DEM conversion rate agreed at the EU Summit in Brussels in May 1998 for the conversion rates to be applied between European currencies merging into the Euro and the Euro on 31st December 1998.

In Dunis and Williams (2002), the explanatory variables used were chosen by a variable selection procedure involving linear cross-correlation analysis from 27 possible exchange rates, interest rates, stock price indexes and commodity prices. The 10 variables identified as giving the best neural network performance, along with their time lagged values, are given in Table 1. In addition to using exploratory variables, we also tested the networks using only the time-lagged values of the exchange rate itself. We refer to these models as the autoregressive models.

Since the datasets were non-stationary, it was necessary to transform them into stationary series. This is because neural networks require continuous training to deal with non-stationary data. As mentioned by Haykin (1999), traditional networks with separate training and prediction algorithms cannot adapt to changes in the nature of the statistical environment. The transformation used is the following rate of return:

$$R_t = \frac{P_t}{P_{t-1}} - 1 \tag{4}$$

where R_t is the rate of return at time t and P_t is the closing price at time t. This transformation has been shown to achieve better results Dunis and Williams (2002). The one step relative change in price is very much used in financial time series prediction since R_t has a relative constant range of values even if the input data represents many years financial values, while the original data P_t can vary so much which make it very difficult to use a valid model for a long period of time, as mentioned by Hellstrom and Holmstrom (1998). Another advantage of using this transformation is that the distribution of the transformed data will become more symmetrical and will follow more closely a normal distribution as shown in Figure 2. This modification to the data distribution may

Table 1. Input variables selected for MLP by Dunis and Williams (2002), a mark indicates a variable used for HONN

	Mnemonics	Variable	Lag (days)
•	USDOLLR	US $ to UK £ exchange rate	12
•	JAPAYE$	Japanese YEN to US $ exchange rate	1
	JAPAYE$	Japanese YEN to US $ exchange rate	10
	OILBREN	Brent Crude Oil US $	1
•	GOLDBLN	Gold Bullion US $ per ounce	19
	FRBRYLD	France Benchmark Bond 10 Year	2
	ITBRYLD	Italy Benchmark Bond 10 Year	6
•	JPBRYLF	Japan Benchmark Bond 10 Year	9
	JAPDOWA	NIKKEI 225 stock average price index	1
	JAPDOWA	NIKKEI 225 stock average price index	15

Figure 2. Histograms (a) of the EUR/USD signal; (b) the relative change for the EUR/USD signal.

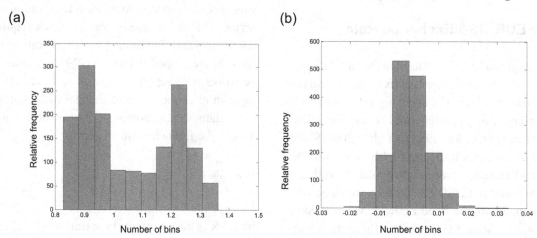

(a)

(b)

Equation 5.

$$\triangle_{ij}^{(t)} = \begin{cases} \eta^+ * \triangle_{ij}^{(t-1)} & , \quad \text{if } \frac{\partial E}{\partial w_{ij}}^{(t-1)} * \frac{\partial E}{\partial w_{ij}}^{(t)} > 0 \\ \eta^- * \triangle_{ij}^{(t-1)} & , \quad \text{if } \frac{\partial E}{\partial w_{ij}}^{(t-1)} * \frac{\partial E}{\partial w_{ij}}^{(t)} < 0 \\ \triangle_{ij}^{(t-1)} & , \quad \text{else} \end{cases}$$

improve the predictive power of the neural networks as underlined by Cao and Tay (2003).

Model Training

Two different algorithms were used to train the networks: the first was standard back-propagation and the second was resilient back-propagation.

Following Riedmiller and Braun (1993), resilient back-propagation was used due to its ability to converge towards good results in a short amount of time. As the slope of any sigmoid activation function approaches zero with inputs of a large magnitude, this can lead to smaller changes to the free weights during training, regardless of the distance from their optimum values. In resilient back-propagation, the derivative is used only to determine the direction of the weight update, the size of the weight change is controlled by other adaptive parameters. If a weight changes in the same direction for a given number of iterations,

then the size of the change is increased. If a weight starts to oscillate between different directions, then the size of the change is decreased. The formula to calculate the weight changes is given in Equation (5), where:

Δ	Individual weight update value
$\eta+, \eta-$	Step size for weight changes
w	Weight matrix
E	Error

The other training parameters include a learning rate of 0.05 and a maximum number of epochs at 5000, although this was rarely reached before a test stop. All of these networks were trained with early stopping and then evaluated on the out-of-sample validation data. This was repeated 100 times to find average and best values on networks of 2, 3 and 4 inputs with 2nd and 3rd order terms used.

Empirical Results

We judge the networks primarily on annualized return, as this is of more practical use than the network error. Risk-adjusted returns are also considered when comparing our results to previous work (see the section below).

Autoregressive Results

The results obtained using the FX time-lagged values are given in Table 2.

In the best case, the 2 inputs 2nd order networks performed poorly and both the 3 input models performed better. For the 4 input models, the 2nd order networks did worse then the 3 input networks, but the 4 inputs 3rd order networks did best, giving the highest return at 37.54%.

In the average case, the majority of the networks performed poorly, with only two models making a profit as can be seen from Figure 3. Also, the networks training with standard backpropagation (BP) give a better average result. T-testing shows that only two models are significantly different statistically. These are the 2 inputs 2nd order model (which was the best model on average) and the 4 inputs 3rd order model (which was the worst model on average) both using linear activation functions and trained with standard backpropagation.

Multi-Variable Results

These are shown in Table 3. In the best case, again the 2 inputs 2nd order models did worse. The 3 input models have three return rates above 30% and the 4 inputs models have two. The best result came from the 4 input 2nd order model, giving 37.95% return. This network was training with standard standard backpropagation and used a logsig activation function, the same as the best model for the autoregressive results.

Table 2. Annualized return given by best autoregressive models. The order is the maximum number of inputs used for each joint activation. A model of a given order also uses the joint activations of all lower orders.

	2 Inputs, Order 2	3 Inputs, Order 2	3 Inputs, Order 3	4 Inputs, Order 2	4 Inputs, Order 3
Linear, Standard BP	25.69%	31.62%	30.13%	24.43%	26.12%
Linear, Resilient BP	24.67%	31.39%	23.62%	28.55%	29.10%
Logsig, Standard BP	21.09%	29.39%	27.20%	27.14%	37.54%
Logsig, Resilient BP	18.76%	23.90%	35.90%	25.56%	25.23%

Figure 3. Mean and standard deviation of annualized return for autoregressive HONN

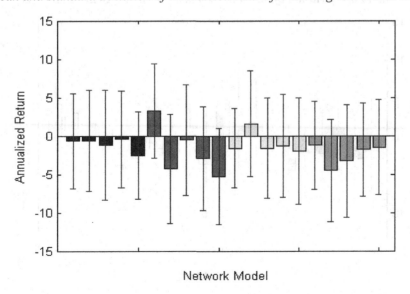

In the average case, the results were better than for the autoregressive results. As can be seen from Figure 4, many of the networks made a profit, although still not very high. The networks trained using resilient backpropagation performed better on average then the networks trained with standard backpropagation, the reverse of the autoregressive models. T-testing shows much greater differences between the models than is the case with the autoregressive networks.

Comparison with Previous Work

In Table 4, the best autoregressive and multi-variable HONNs are compared with the MLP tested in Dunis and Williams (2002) along with a naïve strategy (which predicts the rate of return for time period t is the same as the actual rate of return at time period $t-1$) and an ARMA (Auto-Regressive Moving Average) model for comparison. Both the best HONN models show a profit increase over the MLP of around 8%. Also, both models show a reduced maximum drawdown, i.e. the maximum potential loss that could be incurred during the paper trading exercise, for just over 4% less then the MLP. This is despite the HONNs all using only 2, 3 or 4 inputs compared with the MLP's 10 inputs. The only criterion on which the HONNs did less well was the annualized volatility, with a marginal 0.14-0.15% increase.

Table 3. Annualized return given by best multi-variable models. The order is the maximum number of inputs used for each joint activation. The model of a given order also uses the joint activations of all lower orders.

	2 Inputs, Order 2	3 Inputs, Order 2	3 Inputs, Order 3	4 Inputs, Order 2	4 Inputs, Order 3
Linear, Standard BP	28.81%	33.84%	37.27%	25.97%	27.39%
Linear, Resilient BP	26.69%	32.57%	31.62%	30.01%	36.36%
Logsig, Standard BP	31.07%	31.86%	29.21%	37.95%	27.13%
Logsig, Resilient BP	25.12%	27.51%	32.92%	28.47%	30.30%

Figure 4. Mean and standard deviation of annualized return for multi-variable HONNs

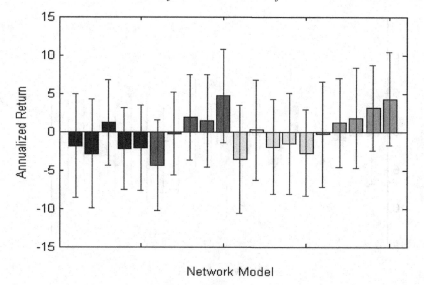

Table 4. Dunis and Williams (2002) with best autoregressive and multi-variable HONN results compared

	Naïve	ARMA	MLP	Auto HONN	Multi HONN
Annualized Return	21.34%	4.99%	29.68%	37.54%	37.95%
Annualized Volatility	11.64%	11.71%	11.56%	11.71%	11.70%
Sharpe Ratio	1.83	0.43	2.57	3.27	3.31
Maximum Drawdown	-9.06%	-10.66%	-9.12%	-5.05%	-5.02%
Correct Directional Change	55.85%	52.76%	57.24%	56.99%	58.97%

Table 5. Best HONNs according to annualized returns using confidence measure (return changes highlighted in grey). (a) top, for autoregressive HONNs; (b) bottom, for multi-variable HONNs

(a)

	2 Inputs, Order 2	3 Inputs, Order 2	3 Inputs, Order 3	4 Inputs, Order 2	4 Inputs, Order 3
Linear, Standard BP	5.73%	32.48%	22.56%	64.30%	16.29%
	-19.95%	0.86%	-7.56%	39.87%	-9.83%
Linear, Resilient BP	-2.32%	3.95%	3.24%	-1.72%	3.82%
	-26.98%	-27.44%	-20.38%	-30.27%	-25.28%
Logsig, Standard BP	53.19%	14.14%	0.00%	12.33%	48.92%
	32.10%	-15.25%	-27.20%	-14.82%	11.38%
Logsig, Resilient BP	37.72%	0.00%	8.17%	-0.10%	-1.87%
	18.96%	-23.90%	-27.73%	-25.66%	-27.10%

(b)

	2 Inputs, Order 2	3 Inputs, Order 2	3 Inputs, Order 3	4 Inputs, Order 2	4 Inputs, Order 3
Linear, Standard BP	30.15%	35.17%	38.88%	27.31%	28.73%
	1.34%	1.34%	1.61%	1.34%	1.34%
Linear, Resilient BP	28.03%	34.18%	33.24%	31.34%	36.92%
	1.34%	1.61%	1.63%	1.34%	0.56%
Logsig, Standard BP	32.41%	33.19%	30.55%	39.10%	27.98%
	1.34%	1.34%	1.34%	1.15%	0.85%
Logsig, Resilient BP	26.45%	28.84%	34.85%	29.51%	30.88%
	1.34%	1.34%	1.93%	1.04%	0.58%

Confidence Measure Results

The networks that give the highest annualized return in each category were subjected to the Bayesian confidence measure described in section Confidence Measure and Trading Strategy. The trading signal was sent only when the confidence in the prediction was above or equal to 60%. The results are presented in Table 5.

For the autogressive networks, depending on the exact model, the confidence measure either increases or decreases the annualized return by a large amount. It appears to work best on the models trained with standard backpropagation. It performs worst on linear models which use resil-

ient BP, the highest return with confidence being slightly less then the return without confidence of the same model. The largest increase was the 4 input 2nd order linear model trained with standard backpropagation, which increased by 39.87% to give an annualized return of 64.30%.

For every model of the multi-variable HONN that the confidence measure was applied to, the annualized return increased by 1-2%. This happened to all the networks in all categories without exception.

DISCUSSION

Being Right versus Making Money

As mentioned in section Confidence Measure and Trading Strategy, the trading strategy is to buy when the price is predicted to rise, and sell when the price is predicted to fall. It is then an important goal of the network to predict the correct direction of change (CDC) of the signal. Certainly, any model that could predict the CDC to 100% would be optimal from a profit point of view, regardless of what the error was.

It would appear that the number of direction changes that are correctly predicted are not as important to the annualized return as the size of the changes that are correctly predicted. If a model is accurate at predicting many smaller changes, it will lose profitability if it fails on the larger changes. Conversely, if a model is accurate at predicting the larger changes, its profitability will be eroded if it fails on many smaller changes. This trade-off is not reflected in the root mean square error, but can be largely circumvented by including transaction costs as in Dunis and Williams (2002)[1] and more sophisticated trading strategies as in Lindemann *et al.* (2005). Such refinements are nevertheless beyond the scope of this chapter.

Why Some Networks are 'More Confident' than Others

Two interesting questions that arise when examining the results for the confidence measure are:

- Why do the results for the multi-variable models always show small increases while the result for the autoregressive models show large changes, both positive and negative?
- What is the cause for the dramatic differences between those autoregressive networks where the confidence measure improves return, and where return is reduced?

To answer the first question, we can look at the distribution of the outputs of the networks. Figure 5 shows the distribution of the positive and negative sets for the out-of-sample data. The difference between the mean of the two sets was very small, in all of the multi-variable networks. It appears that the confidence measure behaves like a buffer, only using the 'hold' option on a very small set of the data (0.3 - 3%), which is borderline between indicating an increase or decrease.

In answer to the second question, the difference between the mean of the positive and negative sets was much larger. The networks which worked well with the confidence measure showed a largely normal distribution in both sets, which were also negatively skewed. Conversely, the networks which did poorly had data sets with either more uniform distributions or which were positively skewed. This is not surprising as they mimic the distribution of the targets, but it does explain why some networks work better and not others. Another interesting difference between the improved models and the poorer models was that the improved models used the 'hold' option much less (between 3 - 8% compared with 34 - 92% for the poorer models).

CONCLUSION

This research has explored the use of HONN for the prediction of financial time-series. It has been shown that HONNs can outperform MLPs on most criteria, including profitability, with out-of-sample data. This enhanced performance is due to the network's robustness caused by the reduced number of free weights compared with MLPs, while still having the higher order terms. This also makes HONNs easier to train and execute.

Further research remains to be done in the use of HONNs for time-series prediction; the use of joint activations and other functional-link terms in feed-forward networks is a promising area,

Figure 5. Histograms show the distribution of target samples and network output, red indicates negative set and blue indicates positive set. X axis shows class interval, Y axis shows frequency. (a) top left, distribution of out-of-sample targets. (b) top right, output of multi-variable network. (c) bottom left, output of autoregressive network where confidence measure performed well. (d) bottom right, output of autoregressive network where confidence measure performed poorly.

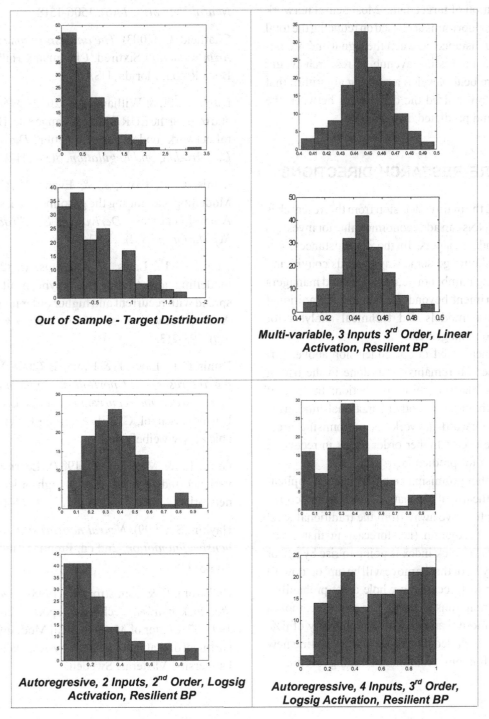

Out of Sample - Target Distribution

Multi-variable, 3 Inputs 3rd Order, Linear Activation, Resilient BP

Autoregresive, 2 Inputs, 2nd Order, Logsig Activation, Resilient BP

Autoregressive, 4 Inputs, 3rd Order, Logsig Activation, Resilient BP

as is the use of higher order terms in recurrent networks for prediction.

The Bayesian-based confidence measure has demonstrated its usefulness, however it relies on a distribution of the network output mimicking the distribution of target data. Most neural network training algorithms are based on reducing the total or mean distance between the signal and prediction. An interesting avenue of research would therefore be to develop a training algorithm that instead minimised the differences between the actual and predicted distributions.

FUTURE RESEARCH DIRECTIONS

Overall, the main conclusion from this research is that HONNs can add economic value for investors and fund managers. In the circumstances, our results should go some way towards convincing a growing number of quantitative fund managers to experiment beyond the bounds of traditional regression models and technical analysis for portfolio management.

As mentioned in our conclusion above, further research remains to be done in the use of HONNs for time-series prediction: the use of joint activations and other functional-link terms in feed-forward networks is a promising area, as is the use of higher order terms in recurrent networks for prediction.

Another promising area for financial applications is the use of alternative model architectures in order to move away from the traditional level or class prediction (i.e. forecasting that , say, tomorrow's stock index is going to rise by x% or drop by y%, or that its move will be 'up' or 'down') in order to forecast the whole asset probability distribution, thus enabling one to predict moves of, say, more than α% with a probability of β%. We have included references of this exciting new approach in our 'Additional Reading' section.

REFERENCES

Cao, L. J., & Tay, F. E. H. (2003). Support vector machine with adaptive parameters in financial time series forecasting. *IEEE Transaction on Neural Networks, 14*(6), 1506-1518.

Chatfield, C. (2003). *The analysis of time series: An Introduction,* Sixth ed., Chapman & Hall/CRC, Boca Raton, Florida, USA.

Dunis, C. L., & Williams, M. (2002). Modelling and trading the EUR/USD exchange rate: Do neural network models perform better? *Derivatives Use, Trading and Regulation, 8*(3), 211-239.

Dunis, C. L, Laws, J., & Evans, B. (2006a). Modelling and trading the gasoline crack spread: A non-linear story. *Derivatives Use, Trading & Regulation, 12*(1-2), 126-145.

Dunis, C. L., Laws, J., & Evans, B. (2006b). modelling and trading the soybean-oil crush spread with recurrent and higher order networks: A comparative analysis. *Neural Network World, 3*(6), 193-213.

Dunis, C. L., Laws, J., & Evans, B. (2006c). *Trading futures spread portfolios: Applications of higher order and recurrent networks.* Liverpool Business School, CIBEF. Working Paper, available at www.cibef.com

Giles, L., & Maxwell, T. (1987). Learning, invariance and generalization in high-order neural networks. *Applied Optics, 26*(23), 4972-4978.

Haykin, S. (1999). *Neural networks: A comprehensive foundation,* 2nd ed. Prentice-Hall, New Jersey, USA.

Hellstrom, T., & Holmstrom, K. (1998). *Predicting the stock market.* Technical report IMa-TOM-1997-07, Center of Mathematical Modeling, Department of Mathematics and Physics, Mälardalen University, Västeras, Sweden.

Karayiannis, N. B. (1995). On the training and performance of higher-order neural networks. *Mathematical Biosciences, 129*, 143-168.

Lindemann, A., Dunis, C. L., & Lisboa, P. (2005). Level estimation, classification and probability distribution architectures for trading the EUR/USD exchange rate. *Neural Computing & Applications, 14*(3), 256-271.

Masters, T. (1993). *Practical neural network recipes in C++*. San Francisco, CA: Morgan Kaufmann.

Pao, Y. (1989). *Adaptive pattern recognition and neural networks*. Boston: Addison-Wesley.

Riedmiller, M., & Braun, H. (1993). A direct adaptive method of faster back-propagation learning: The RPROP algorithm. *Proc. of the IEEE Intl. Conf. on Neural Networks*, San Francisco, CA, pp. 586 -591.

Schmidt, W. A. C., & Davis, J. P. (1993). Pattern Recognition Properties of Various Feature Spaces for Higher Order Neural Networks. *IEEE Transactions on Pattern Analysis and Machine Intelligence*, 15 (8), 795-801.

ADDITIONAL READING

Dunis, C., Laws, J., & Naim, P. (2003). *Applied quantitative methods for trading and investment*. John Wiley.

Dunis, C. L., & Chen, Y. X. (2005). Alternative volatility models for risk management and trading: An application to the EUR/USD and USD/JPY rates. *Derivatives Use, Trading & Regulation, 11*(2), 126-156.

Dunis, C. L, Laws, J., & Evans, B. (2005). Modelling with recurrent and higher order networks: A comparative analysis. *Neural Network World, 6*(5), 509-523.

Dunis, C. L, Laws, J., & Evans, B. (2006). Trading futures spreads: An application of correlation and threshold filters. *Applied Financial Economics, 16*, 1-12.

Dunis, C. L., & Nathani, A. (2007). *Quantitative trading of gold and silver using nonlinear models*. Available at www.cibef.com.

Dunis, C. L., & Morrison, V. (forthcoming). The economic value of advanced time series methods for modelling and trading 10-year government bonds. *European Journal of Finance*.

Lindemann, A., Dunis, C.L., & Lisboa, P. (2004). Probability distributions, trading strategies and leverage: An application of gaussian mixture models. *Journal of Forecasting, 23*(8), 559-585.

Lindemann, A., Dunis, C. L., & Lisboa, P. (2005). Probability distributions and leveraged trading strategies: An application of gaussian mixture models to the morgan stanley technology index tracking fund. *Quantitative Finance, 5*(5), 459-474.

Lindemann, A., Dunis, C. L., & Lisboa, P. (2005). Probability distribution architectures for trading silver. *Neural Network World, 5*(5), 437-470.

Lindemann, A., Dunis, C. L., & Lisboa, P. (2005). Level estimation, classification and probability distribution architectures for trading the EUR/USD exchange rate. *Neural Computing & Applications, 14*(3), 256-271.

ENDNOTE

[1] On the same data, Dunis and Williams (2002) estimate total transaction costs over the out-of-sample period to less than 5%.

Chapter III
Automatically Identifying Predictor Variables for Stock Return Prediction

Da Shi
Peking University, China

Shaohua Tan
Peking University, China

Shuzhi Sam Ge
National University of Singapore, Singapore

ABSTRACT

Real-world financial systems are often nonlinear, do not follow any regular probability distribution, and comprise a large amount of financial variables. Not surprisingly, it is hard to know which variables are relevant to the prediction of the stock return based on data collected from such a system. In this chapter, we address this problem by developing a technique consisting of a top-down part using an artificial Higher Order Neural Network (HONN) model and a bottom-up part based on a Bayesian Network (BN) model to automatically identify predictor variables for the stock return prediction from a large financial variable set. Our study provides an operational guidance for using HONN and BN in selecting predictor variables from a large amount of financial variables to support the prediction of the stock return, including the prediction of future stock return value and future stock return movement trends.

INTRODUCTION

The stock return prediction, including both the future stock return value prediction and the future stock return movement trends prediction, has gained unprecedented popularity in financial market forecasting research in recent years (Keim & Stambaugh, 1986; Fama & French, 1989; Basu, 1977; Banz, 1980; Jegadeesh, 1990; Fama & French, 1992; Jegadeesh &Titman, 1993; Lettau

& Ludvigson, 2001; Avramov & Chordia, 2006a; Avramov & Chordia, 2006b). Because any current stock market is not "efficient," researchers believe that appropriate techniques can be developed for the prediction of the stock return for a certain period of time to allow investors to benefit from the market inefficiency. Actually, some previous works have proved this point of view to a certain extent (Fama & French, 1989; Fama & French, 1992; Avramov & Chordia, 2006b, Ludvigson & Ng, 2007). In general, stock return prediction can be divided into two steps:

1. Identifying those predictor variables which can explain the stock return closely
2. Setting up a linear or nonlinear model which expresses qualitative or quantitative relationships between those predictor variables and the stock return. The stock return is then predicted by computing these models.

Obviously, the first step is the foundation of the prediction. However, there has not been a systematic technique developed in the past to effectively implement this step. This chapter focuses on developing an effective technique for this purpose.

There exist a large number of financial variables for a stock market (typically, over 100 variables or more), but not all of them are directly relevant to the stock return. Researchers always want to identify, among this large set of variables, those underlying predictor variables with a prominent influence on the stock return to support their further prediction. However, in the past two decades, because there have not been effective tools to fulfill this task, researchers have to select predictor variables manually according to their domain knowledge and experience or simply forced to use all the available financial variables when they want to predict the stock return (Fama & French, 1989; Fama & French, 1992; Kandel & Stambaugh, 1996; Lettau &

Ludvigson, 2001; Avramov & Chordia, 2006a; Avramov & Chordia, 2006b).

Although the domain knowledge and experience may provide some help in selecting predictor variables, relying on them alone often causes the following two problems which prevent them from obtaining quality predictive results:

1. Because different researchers may have different domain knowledge and experiences, selecting predictor variables manually may introduce researchers' subjective biases, even some wrong information into the prediction procedure.
2. Another problem of manual selection is that in many cases, the domain knowledge or experience may not at all be sufficient to determine whether some financial variables will influence the stock return or not. A trial and error approach is often resorted to in order to test out each of these variables and their combinations to ascertain the relevance, leading to too large a test problem to handle computationally.

Our main objective in this study is to develop a constructive technique that can effectively select predictor variables for stock return prediction from a large number of financial variables (typically, over 100 variables or more) automatically to overcome the above disadvantages caused by manual selection. The technique consists of a top-down part and a bottom-up part. In the top-down part, we define an information credit for each candidate financial variable based on an artificial Higher Order Neural Network (HONN) model. A heuristic selection procedure will go through all the candidate variables, compute the information credit value for each of them and select the k variables with the highest value. Simultaneously, in the bottom-up part, a Bayesian Network (BN) is used to build up all the relationships that exist among all these variables using a directed acyclic graph. Using the generated BN graph, a validation set is then formed to validate the variables selected by the top-down part to further eliminate those variables with low relevance to deliver the final result.

Our experiments show that the technique we develop can effectively and efficiently select meaningful predictor variables for the prediction of the stock return. We believe that a prediction model based on the predictor variables selected by our technique will deliver more accurate results than that of the models based on manually selected predictor variables.

The remaining part of this chapter is organized as follows: In Section 2, we focus on the background of our study and review some relevant previous work on stock return prediction. Section 3 discusses the property of the candidate financial variables we will use in our study. A detailed description about our technique, including both the top-down part and bottom-up part will be provided in Section 4. Experimental results are given in Section 5. Discussions and future work follow in Section 6 and 7.

BACKGROUND

Stock return prediction has been a key research topic for a number of years with a great deal of excellent work appearing in the past (Kandel & Stambaugh, 1996; Lettau & Ludvigson, 2001; Avramov & Chordia, 2006a; Fama & French, 1989; Fama & French, 1992; Jegadeesh & Titman, 1993). Unfortunately, most of them have concentrated on seeking a powerful prediction model, and the predictor variables were always selected manually based on experts' domain knowledge and experience.

Recently, researchers have introduced some sophisticated models, such as Support Vector Machine (SVM), and especially Neural Network models into the stock return prediction to improve the prediction accuracy (Huang, Nakamori, & Wang, 2005; Saad, Prokhorov, & Wunsch, 1998;

Saad, Prokhorov, & Wunsch, 1996; Kutsurelis, 1998; Zirilli, 1997). However, most of these models are also proposed as prediction models, and the key issue of predictor variable selection is often eluded.

The objective of our study is to explore this key issue and develop a systematic technique based on both HONN and BN to allow the selection to be done automatically. Although some researchers have applied HONN models and BN models to financial problems (Dunis, Laws, & Evans, 2006a; Dunis, Laws, & Evans, 2006b; Knowles et. al., 2005), fewer researchers have noted that these two models have powerful capability in selection of predictor variables for stock return prediction. Our technique makes use of HONN for a top-down computation and BN for a bottom-up computation to automatically reveal the relevant predictor variables from a large number of financial variables.

LEARNING ENVIRONMENT

One challenge in applying our technique to predictor variable selection is determining the candidate financial variables and gathering enough data for these variables. Theoretically, any financial variable adopted to describe the financial status of a company traded in a stock market can be used as a candidate variable. In general, these variables can be divided into two categories:

1. **Systematic Financial Variables:** A small number of commonly used variables which are treated as proxies for financial events that affect almost all stocks in stock markets, such as changes in interest rates, inflation, productivity, and so on. It is no doubt that this kind of variable will influence the prediction of the stock return.

2. **Non-Systematic Financial Variables:** Many variables that are unique to a cer-

tain company also influence stock return prediction. We call these variables non-systematic variables, most of which are firm-level variables. Examples for these variables are new product innovations, changes in management, lawsuits, labor strikes, and so on.

Some financial variables commonly used may not be "atomic," we call them "combinational" variables, in the sense that they can be derived by applying some operations to other "atomic" or even "combinational" variables, such as some technical indicators (moving average, trend line indicators, etc.) or fundamental indicators (intrinsic share value, economic environment, etc.). Combinational variables can also be used as candidate variables.

In our study, we mainly collect non-systematic variables as candidate variables, although systematic variables can also be seamlessly accommodated by our technique after applying some scaling techniques. About 100 non-systematic financial variables will be used in our study, such as sales, cost of sales, net income, short term debt, long term debt, and so on.

PREDICTOR VARIABLES SELECTION ALGORITHM

The outline of the predictor variables selection algorithm is shown in Algorithm 1 below, and the detailed descriptions about the top-down part and the bottom-up part will be detailed in the following sections.

Algorithm 1: Predictor Variables Selection Procedure Algorithm.

Input: D, the data set containing N candidate variables; k, the number of the selected predictor variables ($k < N$).

Output: The k selected predictor variables

BEGIN

1. **The Top-Down part:**
   a. Going through all the candidate variables and using the HONN model to compute each variable's information credit value.
   b. Selecting k variables with the highest information credit value, $v_1, v_2, ..., v_k$ as the possible predictor variables.

2. **The Bottom-Up part:**
   a. Building all the relationships among candidate variables using a directed acyclic graph G.
   b. Extracting the validation set V.

3. **If** $\forall v_i \in V, 1 \leq i \leq k$, outputting $v_1, v_2, ..., v_k$ as the final result. EXIT.

4. **If** $\exists v_{i_1}, v_{i_2}, ..., v_{i_d} \notin V, 1 \leq i_1, i_2, ..., i_d \leq k$, using $v_{j_1}, v_{j_2}, ..., v_{j_d} \in V, j_1, j_2, ..., j_d > k$ which have higher information credit values (defined by us in the following section) to replace $v_{i_1}, v_{i_2}, ..., v_{i_d}$, and outputting the new selected k predictor variables as the final result. EXIT.

END

The Top-Down Procedure

HONN was first introduced by Giles and Maxwell (1987) who referred to them as "Tensor networks." While it has already scored some success in the field of pattern recognition and associative recall, HONN has not been used extensively in financial applications. In this subsection, the HONN model is used to select possible predictor variables for stock return prediction as used in the above algorithm. The architecture design and training of the HONN model is discussed along with a description about the definition and computation of the information credit. The whole heuristic possible predictor variables selection procedure is also proposed in this subsection.

Design and Training of HONN

Architecture of HONN

In our study, a second order HONN model is used to select possible predictor variables for two reasons:

1. The second order items in the HONN model can be used to represent the dependencies between different candidate variables.
2. The number of inputs can be very large for architectures whose orders are higher than two. Actually, orders of 4 and over are rarely used in real applications.

The top-down part aims to select k (a preset value) possible predictor variables for stock return prediction from candidate variables. Accordingly, we select k candidate variables to train the HONN model each time in the heuristic selection procedure. Each second order item formed by two different candidate variables is kept to represent the dependency between these two variables and all the square items are ignored.

One hidden layer HONN model is adopted in our study. To determine the number of the neurons in the hidden layer, the following steps are adopted:

1. Randomly selecting k candidate variables as the inputs of the HONN model.
2. Setting the number of hidden neurons from half the number of input neurons to two times the number of input neurons. For each setting, the HONN model is trained and it is recorded if it performs better.

The above two steps are repeated 100 times and a number can be chosen which performs better in most cases.

The stock return is discretized into three categories to represent three states of the stock return movement: Rise, Fall and Unchanged, respectively. We set two output neurons in the

output layer to encode the three categories, and each output neuron only delivers 0 or 1. If the two outputs are 0 and 1, it means the current stock return belongs to the second category. Figure 1 shows the architecture of the HONN model. Detailed descriptions about HONN can be found in (Ge et al., 2001; Zhang, Ge, & Lee, 2005).

Training of HONN

As in Figure 1, the output neurons are linear and the activation function used in hidden neurons is hyperbolic tangent function:

$$S(x) = \frac{e^x - e^{-x}}{e^x + e^{-x}} \tag{1}$$

When training the HONN model, the classic Back Propagation algorithm is used (Werbos, 1994). The other training parameters include an input layer to hidden layer learning rate of 0.7, a hidden layer to output layer learning rate of 0.07, and a maximum number of epochs of 500.

Figure 1. Three-layer second order HONN with three input neurons and two output neurons

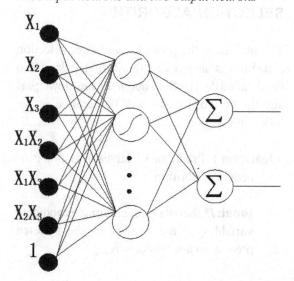

Heuristic Selection Procedure

Our study is based on the work proposed by Sindhwani et al. (2004) which treats the classic multilayer perceptron (MLP) model as a feature selector. We extend their work to the second order HONN model. Below is a brief introduction of their work, including the output information and their definition of the information credit with some extensions which will be used in our work.

Output Information

Output information is a new criterion to measure the capability of classic MLP proposed in (Sindhwani et al., 2004). In considering the HONN model as a classifier, a pattern $x = (x_1, x_2, ..., x_n)$ drawn from a dataset $X = (X_1, X_2, ..., X_n)$, is associated with a category whose label belongs to the set $v = (1, 2, ..., k)$. In our case, $X_1, X_2, ..., X_n$ represent n input variables of the HONN model, and x is a real valued instantiation of these n variables. Given a finite training data set consisting of a finite number of pairs of patterns and corresponding class labels, the HONN model aims to discover a function $f: X \rightarrow v$, which exhibits good generalization for unseen patterns. Let Y, Y_f $(=f(x), x \in X)$ be the discrete variables over v describing the unknown true label and the label predicted by the classifier, respectively.

The mutual information between Y and Y_f, $I(Y; Y_f)$, is defined as the output information by Sindhwani et al. (2004), which is the average rate of information delivered by the classifier via its outputs. In order to compute the output information, Sindhwani et al. also gave some other definitions. Let $|v| = k$ be the number of classes, let Q_f be the confusion matrix, where q_{ij} is the number of times over the labeled data set, an input pattern belonging to class i is classified by f as belonging to class j. According to these definitions, we can estimate the following probabilities:

$$\hat{P}(Y = i) = \frac{\sum_j q_{ij}}{S}$$

$$\hat{P}(Y_f = j) = \frac{\sum_i q_{ij}}{S}$$

$$\hat{P}(Y = i \mid Y_f = j) = \frac{q_{ij}}{\sum_i q_{ij}}$$

where $S = \sum_{ij} q_{ij}$, are the total number of patterns, and $\hat{P}(Y = i)$ is the empirical prior probability of class i; $\hat{P}(Y_f = j)$ is the frequency with which the classifier outputs class j, and $\hat{P}(Y = i \mid Y_f = j)$ is the empirical probability of the true label being class i when the classifier outputs class j. According to these probabilities, Sindhwani et al. deduced the relevant empirical entropies to be given by:

$$\hat{H}(Y) = \sum_i -\hat{P}(Y = i) \log(\hat{P}(Y = i))$$

$$\hat{H}(Y \mid Y_f = j) = \sum_i -\hat{P}(Y = i \mid Y_f = j) \log(\hat{P}(Y = i \mid Y_f = j))$$

$$\hat{H}(Y \mid Y_f) = \sum_j \hat{P}(Y_f = j) \hat{H}(Y \mid Y_f = j)$$

The estimated value of the mutual information between class labels and classifier outputs is given in terms of above entropies, simply by $\hat{I}(Y; Y_f) = \hat{H}(Y) - \hat{H}(Y \mid Y_f)$. Note that this mutual information computation involves only discrete variables that typically assume a small number of values (Sindhwani et al., 2004).

Information Backpropagation

Sindhwani et al. (2004) proposed an information backpropagation procedure which back-propagated the output information from the output neurons to the input neurons. They defined the information each input neuron obtained as the information credit for this input neuron. Our information backpropagation procedure is generally the same as the one proposed by Sindhwani et al. with some minor modifications:

1. Distribute the computed output information equally to the two output neurons. As each output neuron only represents a bit of the code word which represents the class label, the two outputs are equivalent in representing the class labels.

2. Consider the neuron J in the layer indexed by j and let the layer being fed by this layer indexed by k. Denoting the output of a neuron in layer k as O_k and the weight of the interconnection between neurons k and j as ω_{kj}, we define the information credit back-propagated from layer k to neuron J as:

$$I_J = \sum_k \left(I_k \frac{|c_{kJ}|}{\sum_j |c_{kj}|} \right) \qquad (2)$$

where $c_{kj} = \mathrm{Cov}(O_k, \omega_{kj} O_j)$.

Following the above two rules, the information credit can be computed for each input neuron of our HONN model.

Possible Predictor Variables Selection

The information credit provides us a new efficient way to measure the influence of a certain financial variable on the stock return prediction. However, purely relying on the definition of information credit proposed by Sindhwani et al. to select predictor variables is not enough. Some variables have high information credit not because they are more influential with respect to the stock return prediction, but because they have high relevance to other variables which have direct prominent influence on stock return prediction. One should note, however, that the variables which do not directly influence stock return prediction may still contain contributing information that is not contained in those variables that have direct influence. In this sense, the information contained for the first set of variables is not redundant (In

the work proposed by Sindhwani et al. (2004), they have proposed effective techniques to deal with redundant information).

To select possible predictor variables exactly and efficiently, we redefine the information credit for each candidate variable. Our new definition is inspired by the mRMR algorithm proposed in (Peng, Long, & Ding, 2005). Before presenting the new definition, some primary rules that the selected possible predictor variables should follow will be described:

$$\max D(S) \qquad D(S) = \frac{1}{|S|} \sum_{x_i \in S} I_{x_i} \qquad (3)$$

$$\min R(S) \qquad R(S) = \frac{1}{|S|^2} \sum_{x_i, x_j \in S} I_{x_i, x_j} \qquad (4)$$

$$\max \phi(D, R) \qquad \phi(D, R) = D - R \qquad (5)$$

where S represents a set containing selected possible predictor variables, I_{x_i} represents the information credit value of the input variable x_i following the definition proposed by Sindhwani et al., and I_{x_i, x_j} represents the information credit value of the input second order item formed by variables x_i and x_j. Equation (3) means that we should choose those variables which have a larger information credit value than other variables to maximize $D(S)$. Just as mentioned above, in selected possible predictor variables, if some predictors highly depend on other predictors, the prediction capability will not change much if they are removed. In our study, the information credit value of a certain second order input item, such as I_{x_i, x_j}, is used to represent the dependency between the two variables in forming this item. Equation (4) requires us to minimize the dependencies among these selected possible predictor variables to avoid selecting those variables highly dependent on others. Combining equation (3) and (4) is quite similar to the criterion called "minimal-redundancy-maximal-relevance" (mRMR) (Ding & Peng, 2003; Peng, Long, & Ding, 2005). We define the same operator $\phi(D,R)$ in equation (5) to combine D and R to the one in (Peng, Long, & Ding, 2005).

For each variable x_j, we redefine the information credit as follows:

$$I_{x_j} - \frac{1}{|S_{m-1}|} \sum_{x_i \in S_{m-1}} I_{x_j, x_i} \qquad (6)$$

where I_{x_j} and I_{x_j, x_i} have the same meaning as in equation (3) and (4).

With the above definition, we ascertain that variables should be selected as possible predictor variables with the highest information credit value defined by equation (6) by maximizing the equation (5).

In our selection procedure, there are altogether two cases in which we need to compute the new information credit according to equation (6):

1. *To determine the least informative predictor.* In this case, x_j is also in current selected possible predictor variable set, and S_{m-1} means the selected possible predictor variable set excluding x_j.

2. *To replace a current selected predictor variable.* In this case, the new information credit value for a non-predictor variable x_j need to be computed. Let S_{m-1} be the possible predictor variable set excluding the least informative predictor located by the above rule.

The above discussion is summarized in the following algorithm.

Algorithm 2: The selection of possible predictor variables for the stock return prediction.

Input: Training dataset D_{train}, testing data set D_{test}, the number of selected possible predictor variables k ($< N$, the number of candidate variables).
Output: Selected possible predictor variable set F, the trained HONN model using F.

BEGIN

1. Randomly selecting k variables to form an initial feature set F.
2. RESET := 0.
3. Using D_{train} to train the HONN model whose inputs are the variables in F.
4. Estimating the output information on D_{test}.
5. **If** current HONN's performance is satisfactory, EXIT.
6. Calculating the information credit for each input neuron following the definition proposed by Sindhwani et al.
7. **If** current HONN gives the best performance so far, setting $\hat{F} = F$ and RESET = 0.
8. **If** there are untested variables, replacing the least informative selected possible predictor variable (measured by equation (6), rule 1) in F by the next untested variable.
9. **If** all the candidate variables have been tried once, determining the financial variable A, the best variable not currently being used (measured by equation (6), rule 2) and the financial variable B, the worst variable currently being used (measured by equation (6), rule 1)
    1. **If** New Information Credit (A) > New Information Credit (B): replacing variable B by variable A, go to step 2.
    2. **If** New Information Credit (A) < New Information Credit (B) and $\hat{F} = F$, EXIT.
    3. **If** New Information Credit (A) < New Information Credit (B) and $\hat{F} \neq F$, setting $F = \hat{F}$ and RESET := RESET + 1.
10. **If** RESET = 2, EXIT, **else** go to step 3.
EXIT: Return current selected variable set F, and the trained HONN model.

END

The Bottom-Up Procedure

In this subsection, a Bayesian Network (BN) model is developed to build up all the relationships among the financial variables using a directed acyclic graph as the bottom-up procedure of our algorithm. First of all, the design and learning of the BN model will be introduced, and then a validation set will be deduced to validate the possible predictor variables selected by the top-down part from the generated graph.

Design and Learning of BN

A Bayesian network is a graphical model for probabilistic relationships among a set of variables (Pearl, 1988). The structure of a Bayesian network is a directed acyclic graph in which nodes represent domain variables and arcs between nodes represent probabilistic dependencies (Cooper, 1989; Horvitz, Breese, & Henrion, 1988; Lauritzen & Spiegelhalter, 1988; Neapolitan, 1990; Pearl, 1986; Pearl, 1988; Shachter, 1988). For each node x_i in a Bayesian network, there may be some other nodes with arcs pointing to it, and such nodes are the parents of x_i. We shall use π_i to denote the parent nodes of variable x_i. A node and its parents form a family with a corresponding conditional probability table containing all the conditional probabilities of this family. In our case, the nodes in the Bayesian network are used to represent the candidate financial variables and the stock return.

A large number of learning algorithms of BN have been developed in recent years. Many of them deliver excellent structures which match the given data quite well (Lauritzen & Spiegelhalter, 1988; Cooper & herskovits, 1992; Teyssier & Koller, 2005; Cheng et. al, 2002; Moore & Wong, 2003). For simplicity, a Hill-Climbing based learning algorithm is chosen with the classic *MDL* score function to build our BN structure (Neapolitan, 2004). The learning procedure is detailed in the following algorithm.

Algorithm 3: The learning algorithm of the Bayesian Network structure.

Input: D, the data set containing N candidate financial variables and the stock return.

Output: A BN, in which, nodes represent financial variables and arcs represent probabilistic dependencies among these variables.

BEGIN
1. Randomly initializing a BN B_{ini}, or using empty BN. Using classic *MDL* score function to evaluate B_{ini}, and obtaining $MDL(B_{ini})$.
2. Setting current BN $B_{current} = B_{ini}$, and $MDL(B_{current}) = MDL(B_{ini})$.
3. Operating one of the following two operations on $B_{current}$,
   a. Adding an arc between two nodes x_i and x_j, making sure not introducing cycles.
   b. Deleting an arc between two nodes x_i and x_j.
   Then we obtain a new BN $B'_{current}$.
4. **If** $MDL(B'_{current}) > MDL(B_{current})$, $B_{current} = B'_{current}$ and go to step 3.
   ELSE finding another possible operation, then go to step 3.
5. If all the possible operations have been tried once, outputting $B_{current}$. EXIT.

END

Validation Set

In this section, a validation set based on the BN model to validate the possible predictor variables selected by the top-down part is discussed. Before explaining the validation set, the definition of Markov Blanket is required for clarification (Neapolitan, 2004):

Definition 1(Markov Blanket): For a node x_i in a BN model, its Markov Blanket consists of its parent nodes, child nodes and the parent nodes of its child nodes.

According to the Bayesian Network theory, all the true predictor variables should be in the

Markov blanket of the stock return (Neapolitan, 2004). However, because of the noise in the data set and the information loss when discretizing the data, there may be some errors in the generated BN structure. Although errors exist, we believe that those true predictor variables should be in the Markov blanket of the stock return or the Markov blankets of the stock return's parent nodes. Therefore, it makes sense to extract both the nodes in the Markov blankets of the stock return and the stock return's parent nodes to form the validation set. If some possible predictor variables selected by the top-down part are not in the validation set, other variables which are in this set may replace them.

Unfortunately, the learned Bayesian network is always complex and the validation set defined above may become quite huge. In this chapter, a compact version of the validation set is used by extracting the nodes in the Markov blanket of the stock return and the parent nodes and children nodes of the stock return's parent nodes.

EXPERIMENTAL RESULTS

Data Preparation

The test data set used in our study is collected from the three US stock exchanges: American Stock Exchange, New York Stock Exchange and NASDAQ Stock Exchange from 12/1998 to 07/2004 containing 93 different variables and 13125 instances (detailed description about these variables can be found in the Appendix). Because the main objective of this work is to study the influence of firm-level variables on stock return prediction, only firm-level variables are collected in our experiment. The collected variables mainly come from company's Income statement, Balance sheet and Cash Flow. The data set is organized by year. All the data comes from http://moneycentral.msn.com/ and the Osiris database.

Data Preparation for the Top-Down Part

We consider stock return as the class variable and other variables as the candidate input variables for the HONN model. For computing the output information and the information credits, the real valued stock return needs to be discretized first. For each pattern in the data set, the log of the ratio between the stock return values corresponding to the current pattern and the pattern which belong to the same stock and one-year prior to the current one is computed. If the log value is larger than zero which means the stock return rose up at that period, we replace the stock return value corresponding to current pattern with 1. If the log value is zero which means the stock return kept unchanged at that period, we replace the stock return value with zero. If the log value is smaller than zero which means the stock return fell down at that period, we replace the stock return value with -1. These operations focus on the relative changes to the stock return, and eliminate the magnitude of the stock return itself. The data set should be divided into a training data set and a testing data set for the HONN model.

Data Preparation for the Bottom-Up Part

Because the learning algorithms of BN only can deal with discrete variables, not only the stock return, but also all the candidate financial variables should be discretized in this part. The discretization technique used to discretize the stock return in the top-down part will be applied to all the candidate variables in this part. The Hill-Climbing based learning algorithm will then run on the generated discrete data set.

Computational Results

Results of the Top-Down Part

In this part, our HONN model runs on all the candidate financial variables to select five possible predictor variables with different configurations. For comparison, the original algorithm based on ordinary first order neural networks proposed by Sindhwani et al. (2004) also runs on the same data set. Table 1 shows the results of our computation.

Both Sindhwani et al.'s algorithm (2004) and our algorithm run with two different configurations: 5000 training instances and 9000 training instances. From Table 1 we can read that high validation rates (defined as the ratio between the number of the selected possible predictor variables in the validation set to the total number of the selected possible predictor variables) are always obtained when the number of training instances is large. With the same configuration (same number of training instances), our algorithm (based on second order neural network) always performs better than Sindhwani et al.'s algorithm (based on ordinary first order neural network) according to the validation rate, but the iteration number of our algorithm is much larger than the one of Sindhwani et al.'s algorithm. Speeding up the convergence of our algorithm may be our future work.

Sindhwani et al. have shown that their algorithm selected more powerful features than some other feature selection algorithms according to the model accuracy (Sindhwani et al., 2004). For the main purpose of this chapter is applying HONN model to the selection of reasonable financial predictor variables, the results of our algorithm and that of Sindhwani et al.'s algorithm will be compared according to some financial theories.

Table 1 shows that our selection procedure selects basic EPS and diluted EPS related predictor variables (27, 28, 29, 30, 31), extraordinary income related predictor variables (65), total common shares outstanding (58) and some other commonly used predictor variables for stock return prediction (69, 85, 88). All of these variables are closely relevant to the prediction of the stock return (such as variable 58, which has gained a common acceptance as a direct predictor variable for the stock return), and some of them have in fact been picked manually by other researchers to successfully predict stock return (Blume, 1980; Keim, 1985; Naranjo, Nimalendran, & Ryngaert, 1998). All of this evidence proves that our top-down part based on the HONN model can deliver meaningful possible predictor variables for stock return prediction. However, Sindhwani et al.'s algorithm, which employs ordinary first order neural networks, mainly selects liabilities and debt related financial variables (47, 48, 57, 83) and some other financial variables as the predictor variables for stock return prediction. Although some of these variables may also be relevant to the stock return (41, 57), till now most of them are seldom considered when financial experts predict the stock return.

Generally speaking, though Sindhwani et al.'s algorithm can select exact features to enhance the model accuracy, our algorithm outperforms it when applied to financial predictor variable selection problem. Unfortunately, because of the noise in the data set and information loss in the selection procedure, there may be still some errors in our results. Some validation techniques are

Table 1. The selected possible predictor variables

Network Order	Training Number	Hidden Number	Iteration Number	Predictor Variables	Validation Rate
1	5000 Ins.	7	180	39,41,47,48,89	0%
1	9000 Ins.	7	184	1,37,57,76,83	20%
2	5000 Ins.	17	2736	27,29,30,69,88	20%
2	9000 Ins.	17	2285	28,31,58,65,85	60%

needed to validate the possible predictor variables selected in this part.

Results of the Bottom-Up Part

We run the Hill-Climbing based learning algorithm described in Algorithm 3 directly on all the financial variables in this part, and part of the generated direct acyclic graph is shown in Figure 2.

The black node (node 92) in the graph represents the stock return. Figure 2 mainly demonstrates those nodes which are close to the stock return in the graph and the arcs between these nodes and the stock return. Some other nodes and arcs are omitted in Figure 2. According to the definition of validation set, the validation set containing the nodes shown in the following table (only demonstrating a part of the nodes in the validation set) can be deduced:

According to the obtained validation set, validation rate can be calculated for each situation demonstrated in Table 2. A 60% validation rate is reached when using 9000 instances to train our HONN model. Unfortunately, ordinary first order neural network model (Sindhwani et al.'s algorithm) and HONN model with 5000 training instances obtain quite a low validation rate. In this case, other non-predictor variables which are in the validation set and have highest information credit values defined by equation (6), if they are considered reasonable by financial experts, can be used to replace those selected possible predictor variables not in the validation set to enhance the validation rate and the prediction accuracy.

The above experiments show that if the selected possible predictor variables are really relevant to the prediction of the stock return, our technique will recognize them as the true predictor variables. Otherwise, if some errors occur because of data

Figure 2. Sub-graph of the result Bayesian Network structure

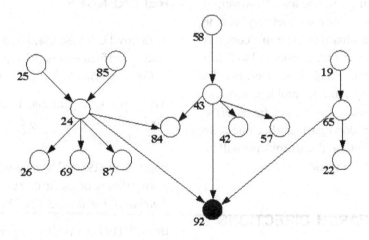

Table 2. The validation set deduced from the generated directed acyclic graph

	Parent Nodes	Child Nodes
the stock return (92)	24, 43, 65	Null
Node 24	25,85	26,69,84,87(Except the stock return 92)
Node 43	58	42,57,86(Except the stock return 92)
Node 65	19	22 (Except the stock return 92)

noise and information loss, our technique will overcome them using the validation set and find the true predictor variables. We believe that our technique consisting of the top-down part and the bottom-up part will provide researchers with a new effective and efficient way of selecting predictor variables for the prediction of stock return.

CONCLUSION

In this chapter, a novel technique consisting of a top-down part using an HONN model and a bottom-up part based on a BN model has been developed to select predictor variables for stock return prediction from a large number of financial variables (typically, over 100 variables or more) automatically. Experimental results show that our technique can deliver the true predictor variables for stock return prediction and has a powerful capability for processing data with errors.

The validation set proposed in our study effectively overcomes the selection errors caused by data noise and information loss. However, in some special cases, the validation set may become quite large. In such situations, a simple compact version of the validation set is proposed to fulfill the validation tasks, which may decrease the validation capability. Another problem with our technique is that the convergence of the selection procedure in the top-down part may become quite slow. Finding solutions to these problems will be the focus of our future work.

FUTURE RESEARCH DIRECTIONS

The combination of HONN and BN presented in our technique has been demonstrated to be a powerful tool in analyzing the relationships among financial variables that have not been effectively solved in the past. In our opinion, the following two future research directions will bring us more exciting results and worthy pursuing.

Firstly, although we use both HONN and BN in our technique, they are relatively independent. We believe that there should be a point of combining the two models to generate a new advanced model. The new model will take the advantages of both HONN and BN. There is no doubt that the new model will be more powerful in selecting predictor variables for stock return prediction. Seeking methods to combine HONN and BN will be our future work.

Secondly, large noise in the data set and information loss in the selection and discretization procedure will prevent our technique from obtaining true predictor variables. A good method to solve this problem is to incorporate domain knowledge into our technique. Domain knowledge will help us to greatly reduce the search space and to resist data noise and information loss. The HONN and BN structure setup may offer a way to incorporate such expert knowledge at an earlier stage for more powerful results.

REFERENCES

Avramov, D., & Chordia, T. (2006a). Asset pricing models and financial model anomalies. *The Review of Financial Studies, 19*(3), 1001-1040.

Avramov, D., & Chordia, T. (2006b). Predicting stock returns. *Journal of Financial Economics, 82*(2), 387-415.

Banz, R. W. (1980). The relative efficiency of various portfolios: Some further evidence: Discussion. *Journal of Finance, 35*(2), 281-283.

Basu, S. (1977). Investment performance of common stocks in relation to their price-earnings ratios: A test of the efficient market hypothesis. *Journal of Finance, 32*(3), 663-682.

Blume, M. E. (1980). Stock returns and dividend yields: Some more evidence. *Journal of Financial Economics, 62*(4), 567-577.

Cheng, J., Greiner, R., Kelly, J., Bell. D., & Liu, W. (2002). Learning Bayesian networks from data: An information-theory based approach. *Artificial Intelligence, 137*(1-2), 43-90.

Cooper, G. F. (1989). Current research directions in the development of expert systems based on belief networks. *Applied Stochastic Models and Data Analysis, 5,* 39-52.

Cooper, G. F., & Herskovits, E. (1992). A Bayesian method for the induction of probabilistic networks from data. *Machine Learning, 9*(4), 309-347.

Ding, C., & Peng, H. C. (2003). *Minimum redundancy feature selection from microarry gene expression data.* Paper presented at the second IEEE Computational Systems Bioinformatics Conference, CA.

Dunis, C. L., Laws, J., & Evans, B. (2006a). *Trading futures spread portfolios: Applications of higher order and recurrent networks* (Working Paper). Liverpool, England: Liverpool John Moores University, Centre for International Banking, Economics and Finance.

Dunis, C. L., Laws, J., & Evans, B. (2006b). *Modeling and trading the soybean crush spread with recurrent and higher order networks: A comparative analysis* (Working Paper). Liverpool, England: Liverpool John Moores University, Centre for International Banking, Economics and Finance.

Fama, E. F., & French, K. R. (1989). Business conditions and expected returns on stocks and bounds. *Journal of Financial Economics, 25,* 23-49.

Fama, E. F., & French, K. R. (1992). The cross-section of expected stock returns. *Journal of Finance, 47*(2), 427-465.

Ge, S. S., Hang, C. C., Lee, T. H., & Zhang, T. (2001). *Stable adaptive neural network control.* Norwell, MA: Kluwer Academic.

Giles, L., & Maxwell, T. (1987). Learning invariance and generalization in high-order neural networks. *Applied Optics, 26*(23), 4972-4978.

Horvitz, E. J., Breese, J. S., & Henrion, M. (1988). Decision theory in expert systems and artificial intelligence. *International Journal of Approximate Reasoning, 2,* 247-302.

Huang, W., Nakamori, Y., & Wang, S. Y. (2005). Forecasting stock market movement direction with support vector machine. *Computers & Operations Research, 32*(10), 2513-2522.

Jegadeesh, N. (1990). Evidence of predictable behavior in security returns. *Journal of Finance, 45*(3), 881-898.

Jegadeesh, N., & Titman, S. (1993). Returns to buying winners and selling losers: Implications for stock market efficiency. *Journal of Finance, 48*(1), 65-91.

Kandel, S., & Stambaugh, R. F. (1996). On the predictability of stock returns: An asset allocation perspective. *Journal of Finance, 51*(2), 385-424.

Keim, D. B. (1985). Dividend yields and stock returns: Implications of abnormal january returns. *Journal of Financial Economics, 14*(3), 473-489.

Keim, D. B., & Stambaugh, R. F. (1986). Predicting returns in the stock and the bound markets. *Journal of Financial Economics, 17,* 357-390.

Knowles, A., Hussain, A., Deredy, W. E., Lisboa, P., & Dunis, C. L. (2005) *Higher-order neural networks with bayesian confidence measure for prediction of EUR/USD exchange rate* (Working Paper). Liverpool, England: Liverpool John Moores University, Centre for International Banking, Economics and Finance.

Kutsurelis, J. E. (1998). *Forecasting financial markets using neural networks: An analysis of methods and accuracy.* Unpublished master dissertation, Naval Postgraduate School, California.

Lauritzen, S. L., & Spiegelhalter, D. J. (1988). Local computations with probabilities on graphical structures and their application to expert systems. *Journal of the Royal Statistical Society (Series B), 50*(2), 157-224.

Lettau, M., & Ludvigson, S. (2001). Resurrecting the (C)CAPM: A cross-sectional test when risk premia are time-varying. *Journal of Political Economy, 109*(6), 1238-1287.

Ludvigson, S. C., & Ng, S. (2007). The empirical risk-return relation: A factor analysis approach. *Journal of Financial Economics, 83*(1), 171-222.

Moore, A., & Wong, W. K. (2003). *Optimal reinsertion: A new search operator for accelerated and more accurate bayesian network structure learning*. Paper presented at the Twentieth International Conference on Machine Learning, Washington, DC.

Naranjo, A., Nimalendran, M., & Ryngaert, M. (1998). Stock returns, dividend yields and taxed. *Journal of Finance, 53*(6), 2029-2057.

Neapolitan, R. E. (1990). *Probabilistic reasoning in expert systems: Theory and algorithms*. New York, PA: John Wiley & Sons.

Neapolitan, R. E. (2004). *Learning Bayesian networks*. Upper Saddle River, NJ: Prentice Hall.

Pearl, J. (1986). Fusion, propagation and structuring in belief networks. *Artificial Intelligence, 29*(3), 241-288.

Pearl, J. (1988). *Probabilistic reasoning in intelligent systems*. San Mateo, CA: Morgan Kaufmann.

Peng, H. C., Long, F. H., & Ding, C. (2005). Feature selection based on mutual information: Criteria of max-dependency, max-relevance, and min-redundancy. *Pattern Analysis and Machine Intelligence, 27*(8), 1226-1238.

Saad, E. W., Prokhorov, D. V., & Wunsch, D. C. II. (1996). *Advanced neural-network training methods for low false alarm stock trend prediction*. Paper presented at IEEE International Conference on Neural Networks, Washington, DC.

Saad, E. W., Prokhorov, D. V., & Wunsch, D. C. II. (1998). Comparative study of stock trend prediction using time delay recurrent and probabilistic neural networks. *IEEE Transactions on Neural Networks, 9*(6), 1456-1470.

Shachter, R. D. (1988). Probabilistic inference and influence diagrams. *Operational Research, 36*(4), 589-605.

Sindhwani, V., Rakshit, S., Deodhare, D., Erdogmus, D., Principe, J. C., & Niyogi, P. (2004). Feature selection in MLPs and SVMs based on maximum output. *IEEE Transactions on Neural Networks, 15*(4), 937-948.

Teyssier, M., & Koller, D. (2005). *Ordering-based search: A simple and effective algorithm for learning bayesian networks*. Paper presented at the Twenty-first Conference on Uncertainty in Artificial Intelligence. Edinburgh, Scotland: University of Edinburgh.

Werbos, P. J. (1994). *The roots of backpropagation*. New York, PA: John Wiley & Sons.

Zhang, J., Ge, S. S., & Lee, T. H. (2005). Output feedback control of a class of discrete MIMO nonlinear systems with triangular form inputs. *IEEE Transactions on Neural Networks, 16*(6), 1491-1503.

Zirilli, J. S. (1997). *Financial prediction using neural network*. London: International Thompson Computer Press.

ADDITIONAL READING

Books

Azoff, A. (1994). *Neural network time series forecasting of financial markets*. New York: John Wiley & Sons.

Barac, M. A., & Refenes, A. (1997). *Handbook of neural computation*. Oxford: Oxford University Press.

Hall, J. W. (1994). Adaptive selection of US stocks with neural nets. In G. J. Deboeck (Ed.), *Trading on the edge: Neural, genetic, and fuzzy systems for chaotic financial markets* (pp. 45-65). New York: John Wiley & Sons.

Trippi, R., & Turbon, E. (1996). *Neural networks in financial and investing*. Chicago, IL: Irwin Professional Publishing.

Vemuri, V., & Rogers, R. (1994). *Artificial neural networks: Forecasting time series*. Piscataway, NJ: IEEE Computer Society Press.

Articles

Abu-Mostafa, Y. S., & Atiya, A. F. (1996). Introduction to financial forecasting. *Applied Intelligence, 6*(3), 205-213.

Avramov, D. (2002). Stock return predictability and model uncertainty. *Journal of Financial Economics, 64*(3), 423-458.

Avramov, D. (2004). Stock return predictability and asset pricing models. *The Review of Financial Studies, 17*(3), 699-738.

Barberis, N. (2000). Investing for the long run when returns are predictable. *Journal of Finance, 55*(1), 225-264.

Bossaerts, P., & Hillion, P. (1999). Implementing statistical criteria to select return forecasting models: What do we learn? *Review of Financial Studies, 12*(2), 405-428.

Chan, K. C., & Chen, N. F. (1988). An unconditional asset pricing test and the role of firm size as an instrumental variable for risk. *Journal of Finance, 43*(2), 309-325.

Chen, T., & Chen, H. (1993). Approximations of continuous functionals by neural networks with application to dynamic systems. *IEEE Transactions on Neural Network, 6*(4), 910-918.

Chordia, T., & Shivakumar, L. (2002). Momentum, business cycle and time-varying expected returns. *Journal of Finance, 57*(2), 985-1019.

Cooper, M., Gutierrez, R. C., & Marcum, W. (2001). *On the predictability of stock returns in real time* (Working Paper). West Lafayette, Indiana, USA: Purdue University.

Ge, S. S., Lee, T. H., Li, G. Y., & Zhang, J. (2003). Adaptive NN control for a class of discrete-time non-linear systems. *International Journal of Control, 76*(4), 334-354.

Ge, S. S., Li, G. Y., Zhang, J., & Lee, T. H. (2004). Direct adaptive control for a class of MIMO nonlinear systems using neural networks. *IEEE Transactions on Automatic Control, 49*(11), 2001-2006.

Ge, S. S., Zhang, J., & Lee, T. H. (2004). Adaptive neural network control for a class of MIMO nonlinear systems with disturbances in discrete-time. *IEEE Transactions on Systems, Man, and Cybernetics-Part B: Cybernetics, 34*(4), 1630-1644.

Goyal, A., & Welch, I. (2003). Predicting the equity premium with dividend ratios. *Management Science, 49*(5), 639-654.

Jensen, M. C. (1969). Risk, the pricing of capital assets, and the evaluation of investment portfolios. *Journal of Business, 42*(2), 167-247.

Lo, A. W., & MacKinlay, A. C. (1988). Stock market prices do not follow random walks: Evidence from a simple specification test. *Review of Financial Studies, 1*(1), 41-66.

McCulloch, R., & Rossi, P. E. (1990). Posterior, predictive, and utility-based approaches to testing the arbitrage pricing theory. *Journal of Financial Economics, 28*(1-2), 7-38.

Modigliani, F., & Cohn, R. A. (1979). Inflation, rational valuation and the market. *Financial Analyst Journal, 35*(2), 24-44.

Redding, N., Kowalczyk, A., & Downs, T. (1993). Constructive high-order network algorithm that is polynomial time. *Neural Networks, 6*(7), 997-1010.

Stambaugh, R. (1999). Predictive regressions. *Journal of Financial Economics, 54*(3), 375-421.

Xu, S., & Zhang, M. (1999a). *MASFinance, a model auto-selection financial data simulation software using NANNs*. Paper presented at International Joint Conference on Neural Networks, Washington, DC.

Xu, S., & Zhang, M. (1999b). *Adaptive higher order neural networks*. Paper presented at International Joint Conference on Neural Networks, Washington, DC.

Zhang, M., Xu, S. X., & Fulcher, J. (2002). Neuron-adaptive higher order neural-network models for automated financial data modeling. *IEEE Transactions on Neural Networks, 13*(1), 188-204.

Zellner, A., & Chetty, V. K. (1965). Prediction and decision problem in regression models from the Bayesian point of view. *Journal of the American Statistical Association, 60*(310), 608-616.

APPENDIX A

These are the 92 candidate financial variables (not including the stock return) from the company's Income Statement, Balance Sheet and Cash Flow as numbered sequentially in three tables tabulated below.

Table 3. Financial variables from the company's Income Statement

0	Sales
1	Cost of Sales
2	Gross Operating Profit
3	Selling, General & Admin. Expense
4	Other Taxes
5	EBITDA
6	Depreciation & Amortization
7	EBIT
8	Other Income, Net
9	Total Income Avail for Interest Exp.
10	Interest Expense
11	Minority Interest
12	Pre-tax Income
13	Income Taxes
14	Special Income/Charges
15	Net Income from Cont. Operations
16	Net Income from Discont. Opers.
17	Net Income from Total Operations
18	Normalized Income
19	Extraordinary Income
20	Income from Cum. Eff. of Acct. Chg.
21	Income from Tax Loss Carryforward
22	Other Gains (Losses)
23	Total Net Income
24	Dividends Paid per Share
25	Preferred Dividends
26	Basic EPS from Cont. Operations
27	Basic EPS from Discont. Operations
28	Basic EPS from Total Operations
29	Diluted EPS from Cont. Operations
30	Diluted EPS from Discont. Operations
31	Diluted EPS from Total Operations

Table 4. Financial variables from the company's Balance Sheet

32	Cash and Equivalents
33	Receivables
34	Inventories
35	Other Current Assets
36	Total Current Assets
37	Property, Plant & Equipment, Gross
38	Accum. Depreciation & Depletion
39	Property, Plant & Equipment, Net
40	Intangibles
41	Other Non-Current Assets
42	Total Non-Current Assets
43	Total Assets
44	Accounts Payable
45	Short Term Debt
46	Other Current Liabilities
47	Total Current Liabilities
48	Long Term Debt
49	Deferred Income Taxes
50	Other Non-Current Liabilities
51	Minority Interest
52	Total Non-Current Liabilities
53	Total Liabilities
54	Preferred Stock Equity
55	Common Stock Equity
56	Total Equity
57	Total Liabilities & Stock Equity
58	Total Common Shares Outstanding
59	Preferred Shares
60	Treasury Shares

Table 5. Financial variables from the company's Cash Flow

61	Net Income (Loss)
62	Depreciation and Amortization
63	Deferred Income Taxes
64	Operating (Gains) Losses
65	Extraordinary (Gains) Losses
66	(Increase) Decr. in Receivables
67	(Increase) Decr. in Inventories
68	(Increase) Decr. in Other Curr. Assets
69	(Decrease) Incr. in Payables
70	(Decrease) Incr. in Other Curr. Liabs.
71	Other Non-Cash Items
72	Net Cash from Cont. Operations
73	Net Cash from Discont. Operations
74	Net Cash from Operating Activities
75	Sale of Property, Plant, Equipment
76	Sale of Short Term Investments
77	Purchase of Property, Plant, Equipmt.
78	Purchase of Short Term Investments
79	Other Investing Changes Net
80	Net Cash from Investing Activities
81	Issuance of Debt
82	Issuance of Capital Stock
83	Repayment of Debt
84	Repurchase of Capital Stock
85	Payment of Cash Dividends
86	Other Financing Charges, Net
87	Net Cash from Financing Activities
88	Effect of Exchange Rate Changes
89	Net Change in Cash & Cash Equivalents
90	Cash at Beginning of Period
91	Free Cash Flow

Chapter IV
Higher Order Neural Network Architectures for Agent–Based Computational Economics and Finance

John Seiffertt
Missouri University of Science and Technology, USA

Donald C. Wunsch II
Missouri University of Science and Technology, USA

ABSTRACT

As the study of agent-based computational economics and finance grows, so does the need for appropriate techniques for the modeling of complex dynamic systems and the intelligence of the constructive agent. These methods are important where the classic equilibrium analytics fail to provide sufficiently satisfactory understanding. In particular, one area of computational intelligence, Approximate Dynamic Programming, holds much promise for applications in this field and demonstrate the capacity for artificial Higher Order Neural Networks to add value in the social sciences and business. This chapter provides an overview of this area, introduces the relevant agent-based computational modeling systems, and suggests practical methods for their incorporation into the current research. A novel application of HONN to ADP specifically for the purpose of studying agent-based financial systems is presented.

INTRODUCTION

Economists have long recognized their inability to run controlled experiments a la their physicist and biologist peers. As a result, while much real science can be done using natural experiments, analytic mathematical modeling, and statistical analysis, a certain class of discoveries regarding the governing dynamics of economic and financial systems has remained beyond the grasp of such research. However, recent advances in computing show promise to change all that by gifting economists with the power to model large scale agent-based environments in such a way that interesting insight into the underlying properties of such systems can be obtained. It is becoming increasingly evident that engineering tools from the area of computational intelligence can be used in this effort.

Agent-based methods are enjoying increased attention from researchers working in economics as well as in pure and applied computation. The central focus of this still nascent field involves the generation of populations of interacting agents and the observation of the resulting dynamics as compared to some optimality criterion, analytically or otherwise obtained. Typically, some sort of learning algorithm, such as a simple feed forward multi-layer perceptron neural network, will be implemented in the model. Often other techniques of computational intelligence, such as genetic algorithms, will be used to evolve the population, showing the promise that gains in this area of computation have for social science investigation.

This chapter proposes taking a step forward in terms of the efficacy of algorithms applied to this agent-based computational study. We discuss the framework of Approximate Dynamic Programming (ADP), an approach to computational learning used successfully in applications ranging from aircraft control to power plant control. In particular, we investigate the artificial Higher Order Neural Network Adaptive Critic Design approach to solving ADP problems and how the use of these techniques can allow economics researchers to use more robust formulations of their problems that may admit richer results.

Typically, a multi-layered perceptron neural network architecture is utilized when implementing ADP techniques. We propose and discuss using HONNs instead. A HONN is a multi-layer neural network which acts on higher orders of the input variables (see Zhang 2002 for details)

Many chapters in this volume present tutorials as to the use of these HONNs. This chapter is devoted to discussing ADP and proposing our novel approach of using a HONN engine to power ADP techniques specifically for applications in the study of agent-based financial systems.

The objective of this chapter is to introduce these frameworks, to discuss the computational economics problem types which can enjoy their benefits, and to discuss opportunities for novel applications.

BACKGROUND

The fundamental Agent-Based Computational Economics framework structure is overviewed in Testafasion (2006) and will be reviewed here. The particular formulation of the agent problem proposed in this chapter is based on the presentation in Chiarella (2003) and will be discussed following the general overview. Finally, other supporting literature will be surveyed to help solidify the main ideas of this section and to guide the reader in other directions of possible research interest.

Agent-Based Computational Economics

A standard course of study in economics grounds the reader in a host of equilibrium models: the consumer preference theory of microeconomics (Binger 1998), the wage determination cycle of labor economics (Ehrenberg 2003), the concept of purchasing power parity in international finance (Melvin 2000), and the Walrasian Auctioneer (Leijonhufud 1967) of macroeconomics. In all of these approaches to describing economic phenomena, the student is presented with top-down analytic treatments of the dynamics of an entire economy's worth of individual interacting agents. While the local scale behavior informs the higher level dynamics, it is only the global portion that enjoys specific elucidation. Exactly how the lives of the agents respond to an economic shock in order to return the system to the long-run equilibrium is not considered. Furthermore, it is often the case that the level of simplifying assumptions necessary to achieve clear and acceptable results from an analytical model, via some fixed-point theorem, serves to cast a significant measure of doubt over the entire affair. Importantly, this problem is not a fixture of economics alone; these models and the chase for mathematically provable periodicity results permeates other areas of science, notably population biology (Bohner 2006). Also, many proof-theoretic approaches require overly restrictive and wholly unrealistic linearity assumptions to arrive at a tractable model, denying insight that claims the answer to an economic question may have more than one root cause (Judd 2006.)

The discipline of Agent-Based Computational Economics (ACE) analyzes an economy from another point of view, one termed "constructive" due to the focus on the fundamental elements of the system as opposed to the global dynamics. Instead of specifying long-run equilibrium behavior, the ACE researcher takes care to capture in his or her equations the salient behaviors of the individual agents. Any emergent dynamics or long run convergence will reveal itself as a result of the collection of individual choices. In this way, equilibrium models can be tested in a manner akin to a controlled experiment in the physical sciences. The population of computational agents can be constrained in a certain way, and the resulting dynamics explored via simulation. Such studies can work to confirm theoretical fixed point long term equilibrium results or serve as evidence that such hallowed equations may be missing something quite vital about the system's reality.

For example, Hayward (2005) finds that standard analytic models for price forecasting and trading strategies in international financial markets fail to be supported by computational experimental modeling. He finds, in contradiction to the notion that a trader's success is a function of risk aversion instead of proficiency in accurate forecasting, that the agents with short time horizons in an environment with recurrent shocks emerge as dominant, as they adapt to and learn about the nature of the economic system in which they operate. His work incorporates genetic algorithms and multi-layer perceptron neural networks which, along with swarm intelligence and fuzzy logic methods, are core areas of the computational intelligence field (Engelbrecht 2002).

ACE models begin by specifying attributes and modes of interaction among the agents. One way to implement this specification is through an object-oriented programming approach, wherein the agents could be considered objects, the attributes private data members, and modes of interaction publicly-accessible methods. The books by Johnsonbaugh (2000) and Horstmann (2004) include details on object oriented programming, the specifics of which are not integral to our current discussion. Another tool accessible to a researcher conducting an ACE investigation is one of the standardized modeling frameworks, such as the one published by Meyer (2003). Finally, analytic equation models can be found in the literature, such as early work of Lettau (1997). It should be noted that these models, while analytic in nature, still conform to the constructive ACE philosophy in that they are employed in the characterization of the salient features of the agents. The equations are not being used to set the dynamics of the system a priori, or to launch a search for a periodic equilibrium solution.

Whatever agent representation a researcher chooses, it is important that the computational intelligence technique used to model the agent's ability to adapt to a complex environment be sufficiently robust to generate accurate and substantive results. It may be the case that an experiment that seemingly shows a population of agents unable to learn to converge to an analytic equilibrium is not really unearthing a new economic truth; instead, it could be an indication that the particular computational learning algorithm employed in the simulation is insufficient for the complexity of the task. Furthermore, care must be taken to appropriately read the output of an ACE simulation. Unlike standard econometric approaches (Greene 2003 and Kennedy 2001), it is often difficult to calculate a level of statistical confidence to accompany the conclusions of an ACE model. It should be noted here that the computational techniques falling under the banners of Adaptive Resonance architectures and Partially Observable Markov Decision Processes, discussed later in this chapter, have the advantage that they come equipped with readily available confidence level information, thus assuaging this objection to numerical investigation of economic phenomena. In any case, an increase in knowledge of advanced computational techniques, such as the artificial Higher Order Neural Network formulations discussed herein, will go a long way towards overcoming the inertial present naturally in any community in the face of change in paradigm, as better communication and pedagogy will help to ward off the feeling among many that these algorithms are simply "black boxes" akin to a foul sorcerer's magic that should not be trusted.

While Hayward (2005) used a multi-layer perceptron architecture to model how the agents learned to project financial information, more robust results may be gained by using sophisticated time series prediction techniques (Cai 2004, Hu 2004)) or the artificial Higher Order Neural Network techniques overviewed later in this chapter.

Other Readings

What follows is a brief survey of papers in computational economics and finance that significantly utilize the tools of computational intelligence. The interested reader may wish to consult the survey of early work in computational finance by LeBaron (2000) for more information on the following and other research.

One of the first papers in the field (Lettau 1997) addresses the problem of choice of purchasing a certain amount of a risky or risk-free asset with the price of the risky asset provided exogenously. Agents are fielded with fixed risk aversion preferences given by a utility function of the form $U(w) = E(-e^{-\gamma w})$, where $w = s(d-p)$, p is the price of the risky asset, d is a random dividend paid by the risky asset in the next time period, s is the number of shares purchased, and the task of the agent is to maximize this utility measure. In this simple simulation, it is possible to calculate an analytic solution for the optimal policy for each agent. The importance of the work, then, is to investigate whether a collection of bottom-up constructive economic agents will arrive at the same long term equilibrium point described by the top-down theoretical model. The paper uses the economic agents to, in effect, solve for the system equilibrium. Approaches to these sorts of problems have gained in computational complexity in the decade since this work was published, but the core premise of using a population of agents to evolve systemic rules remains a vital component of the modern research directions. As is common in this field, genetic algorithms are used in this work as function optimizers and continue to be used to evolve the agent populations. Other methods of function optimization from the computational intelligence toolbox, such as particle swarm optimization (Kennnedy 1995), have yet to see wide application in this field.

Arifovic (1994, 1996) studied the foreign exchange markets using computational learning techniques to investigate the economy's tendency to stabilize to a given equilibrium within the constraints of a classic overlapping generations model. The agents are let loose to, in effect, solve for the optimal solution of the analytic model. The only way for the agents to save from one period to the next is through holding amounts of currency, with the exchange rate given exogenously by the ratio of prices in each market. A similar approach tried with human agents resulted in failed convergence, demonstrating the failings of the human brain to successfully mastermind to perfection the long-run dynamics calculated so precisely through the analytic modeling.

The Santa Fe Stock Market is an artificial securities trading environment studied in Arthur (1994, 1997). This work combines well-defined economic structure with inductive learning. Agents choose between a risky and risk-free asset. The novelty is that the agents's expectations are formed not from maximization of a utility function as in Lattau (1997), but through the use of a computational classifier method for predicting the future state of the economy given current parameters. This approach ties in well with the artificial Higher Order Neural Network Adaptive Resonance classifier detailed later in this chapter. Current economic environmental parameters are listed by type in a bit string and input to a genetic algorithm to evolve the policy.

APPROXIMATE DYNAMIC PROGRAMMING

A widely used and increasingly effective approach to solving problems of adaptation and learning in applied problems in engineering, science, and operations research is that of Approximate Dynamic Programming (ADP) (Si 2004, Bertsekas 1996). ADP techniques have been used successfully in applications ranging from helicopter flight control (Enns 2003), to automotive engine resource management (Javeherian 2004), to linear discrete-time game theory, a topic near and dear to the heart of many an economist (Al-Tamimi 2007). As ADP techniques continue to enjoy favor as the approach of choice for large-scale, nonlinear, dynamic control problems under uncertainty, it becomes important for the computational economist to be aware of them. Approximate Dynamic Programming is a field grounded in mathematical rigor and full of social and biological inspiration that is

being used as a unification tool among researchers in many fields.

This section overviews the structure of ADP. Markov Decision Processes are discussed first, to introduce the core structural terminology of the field. Next, the Bellman Equation of Dynamic Programming, the true heart of ADP, is explained. The section ends with a more detailed discussion of the Reinforcement Learning problem as well as a type of solution method suggested in this chapter.

Markov Decision Processes

First, some terminology. The *state* of a system is all the salient details needed by the model. For an agent deciding how much of an asset to buy or sell, the modeler may set the state space to be a count of the current number of shares the agent is holding along with the current, stochastically generated dividend payment for the next time period. In the computational modeling of games such as Chess or Go the relevant state would be the position of all the pieces currently on the board, and possibly the number of captured stones (for Go.) At each state, the agent has a choice of *actions*. (In a control application, where the agent is a power plant or some other complex operation to be optimally managed, the actions are called *controls*.) Our economic trading agent may buy or sell a certain number of shares, the totality of which entirely enumerate its possible actions. For the game example, the entire range of legal moves constitute the action set for a given board configuration, or state. Each state nets the agent a level of *reward*. States that lead to desirable outcomes, as measured by some reasonable criteria, are assigned positive reward, while states that should be avoided are given negative reward. For example, the state arrived at after choosing the action that moves a Chess piece such that the opponent can place one's king in checkmate would generate a highly negative reward, while a winning Tic-tac-toe move would evolve the system to a state with high reward. The manner in which the agent proceeds from state to state through the choice of action is called the *evolution* of the system, and is governed stochastically through *transition probabilities.* The agent, upon buying a number of shares of a risky asset, finds itself in a new state. Part of the state structure, the size of the agent's holdings, is under deterministic control. The stochastic dividend payment, however, evolves according to a statistical rule unknown to the agent. Therefore, the agent cannot know for certain to which state it will advance upon taking a certain action. Instead, the next states constitute a probability distribution described by the transition probability matrix. To contrast, the evolution is completely deterministic in Chess or Go, as no randomness is involved.

The way we have defined the state, as embodying all necessary information to calculate the future system evolution, allows the use of a mathematical Markov chain to model the system dynamics. Any such system, said to satisfy the Markov Property, can be analyzed with the following techniques. In practice, systems of interest often have a degree of error in the state representation, or some other influx of imperfect information, and therefore do not technically fulfill the Markov Property. However, approximation techniques for these situations abound and the careful researcher can still make appropriate use of Markov chain modeling in many cases. For a more thorough analysis of such cases, see Sutton and Barto (1998).

A Markov Decision Process (MDP) model is one where Markov chains are used to analyze an agent's sequential decision making ability. In MDP terminology, the agent calculates a *policy*, an assignment of an action to every possible state. The goal is to find an optimal policy, given some reasonable criterion for optimality. An MDP consists of the components previously defined: states, actions, rewards, and transition probabilities. The time scale under consideration is also important. Discrete MDPs typically evolve along the positive

integers while continuous MDPs are defined on the non-negative real numbers. Other time scales are feasible for constructing MDPs. See the book by Bohner and Peterson (2001) for a more rigorous mathematical presentation of time scales.

MDP's have been extensively studied and applied in such areas as inventory management (Arrow 1958), behavioral biology (Kelly 1993), and medical diagnostic tests (Fakih 2006). Standard solution techniques are available and well understood (Puterman 1994). Solutions consist of an optimal policy for the agent to follow in order to maximize some measure of utility, typically infinite horizon expected reward.

It is not always the case that a system can be adequately expressed as a standard MDP. When the state information is not fully available to the agent, then the model must be supplemented with a probabilistic description of the current state, called a *belief space.* An MDP under this addition becomes a Partially Observable Markov Decision Process (POMDP). A classic POMDP example involves an agent deciding which of two doors to open. Behind one is a tiger, and behind the other is a lovely prince or princess ready to sweep the agent off its feet. In a straight MDP, the agent would have access to the transition probabilities for the two states, and would be able to calculate which door is most likely to contain the desired result. In the POMDP formulation, however, the agent does not have access to such information. Instead, the agent receives *observations*, such as hearing the tiger growl or feeling the sweet heartbeat of an awaiting lover. These observations combine to form a Bayesian approach to solving the optimal policy. POMDPs have demonstrated an ability to model a richer set of systems than the pure MDP formulation. For example, POMDPs have been used in dynamic price modeling when the exact demand faced by the vendor is unknown (Aviv 2005). When the demand at each period is known, an MDP can be used to calculate the best policy under expected reward criteria. But, when faced with an unknown state element, the agent must refer to observations such as historical marketing data to help make its decision.

Standard solution methods for POMDPs work only on specific frameworks and require significant computational capability to implement. To avoid these problems, it is common to use a technique such as a Bayesian Filter to transform a POMDP into an MDP once the observations key the agent's belief space to a sufficient degree. The solution techniques for MDPs can then be applied to the POMDP and the optimal policy calculated.

The next section provides the mathematical formulation of the task of the economic agent—the maximization of a particular optimality criterion.

The Bellman Equation

Consider an economic agent modeled with a finite set of states *s*, actions *a*, rewards *r(s)*, and transition probabilities *P(s, a)* in a discrete time scale defined to be the positive integers. In order to calculate the agent's optimal policy, some utility function needs to be maximized. In the core Approximate Dynamic Programming paradigm, the function to be maximized is the Bellman Equation:

$$J(s) = r(s) + \gamma \sum_{s'} P(s', a) J(s', a)$$

(3.2.1)

This is the discounted expected reward optimality criterion. In this equation, J(s) represents the current value of a given state, s' signifies the next-states, and a discount factor γ is applied to the future rewards. This equation is to be maximized over all actions.

In words, the Bellman equation is stating that the current value of a state is equal to the immediate reward of taking an action plus the discounted future reward that accrues from that state. Other optimality criteria are possible to account for infinite horizon or nondiscounted models. The task of ADP is to solve this equation.

One standard solution algorithm is that of backwards induction. Other approaches include value and policy iteration. The interested reader is directed to a text such as Puterman (1994) for further details on these and other optimization techniques. The solution method to be discussed in this chapter is found in the next section.

Reinforcement Learning

The computational literature calls the class of problems that include the MDPs discussed above "Reinforcement Learning" problems. Many fields, from animal learning theory to educational psychology, make use of this term to mean a great variety of things. Here we refer to a very specific mathematical definition of a problem type presented in 1.

Some form of the Bellman equation is applied here to represent the agent's optimality criterion. It is important to understand that this literature hinges vitally on the notion of the agent as a maximizer of some utility function. In that way, there is much in the fields of economics and operations research that can usefully inform ADP theory (Werbos 2004).

Figure 1 Basic Reinforcement Learning model framework. Actions a(t), rewards r(t), and states s(t) are generated by the environment model and the agent controller.

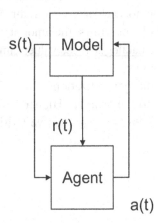

Figure 2. Q-learning algorithm for Reinforcement Learning problems. Q(s,a) is the valuation of each state-action pair, t is the iteration number, π is some method of calculating the next action (typically an e-greedy policy), γ and δ are learning rates, a' is the set of next actions, and s' is the next state.

Q-Learning Algorithm
1. Initialize $Q(s,a)$
2. Set $t = 1$
3. Initialize s
4. Set $a = \pi(s)$, calculate s'
5. Update $Q(s,a) = Q(s,a) + \gamma[r(s') + \delta\max_{a'}Q(s',a') - Q(s,a)]$
6. Set $s = s'$
7. If s is not terminal, goto 4.
8. Increment t
9. If t is not equal to the maximum number of iterations, goto 3.

Barto and Sutton (1998) discuss a wide variety of solution methods for these problems. In particular, this chapter will focus on one solution method, a member of the TD-λ family of optimization algorithms (Sutton 1995), called Q-learning (Watkins 1989).

The Q-learning algorithm is presented in Figure 2.

Note that the Q-learning algorithm iteratively updates the value of each state-action pair. The appropriate modification is calculated based on the difference between the current and realized valuations, when maximized over all possible next actions. This is a key fact that sets up the more advanced techniques discussed in the next section.

This algorithm utilizes a lookup table to store the Q-values for each state-action pair. As the scale of the simulation grows, the amount of memory required to catalogue these values can grow at a staggering rate.

Next, the generalization of the Q-learning algorithm to the artificial Higher Order Neural Network technique of Adaptive Critics is covered.

Heuristic Dynamic Programming

Q-learning is robust and has been shown to work quite well in a large number of problem domains, including being the base of the TD-λ approach at the center of a computational agent which, without any exogenously provided understanding of the rules of Backgammon, learned to perform at the master level and which was able to teach new strategies to arguably the world's oldest game to champion-level players (Tesauro 1994). However, its reliance on a lookup table to store values is a severe limitation. Generalizations of Q-learning, falling under the heading of Heuristic Dynamic Programming (HDP), replace the Q-table with a multi-layer neural network function approximator. Another generalization of Q-learning, dubbed Z-learning, involving a variable transformation to linearize the underlying MDP formulation, has been introduced and shows promise (Todorov 2007.)

The diagram for HDP, the simplest of the class of artificial Higher Order Neural Network architectures broadly known as Adaptive Critic Designs (Werbos 1992, Prokhorov 1997), is presented in Figure 3.

The Adaptive Critic architecture, in essence, translates a reinforcement learning problem into a supervised learning problem. This is a positive

Figure 3. Basic Adaptive Critic Design. J(t) is the value function being approximated, r(t) is the reward, and a(t) is the action control signal. The critic evaluates the agent's choice, modifying its adaptive weights in response to the chosen actions.

HDP Critic Network

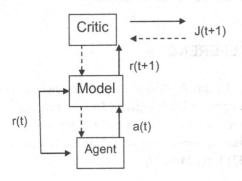

because much is known about solving supervised learning problems. The critic network learns the value function, and error between the current J-function value and the J-function value in the next time step is backpropagated through the network (Werbos 1990.)

Adaptive Critic architectures have found many application areas, including missile control (Han 2002 and Chuan-Kai 2005), fed-batch biochemical process optimization (Iyer 2001), intelligent engine control (Kulkarni 2003), multimachine power system neurocontrol (Mohagheghi 2007), and even the management of a beaver population to prevent nuisance to humans (Padhi 2006.) The promise of finding rewarding application of these techniques in the fields of computational economics and finance is too alluring to ignore.

APPLICATION TO ECONOMIC SYSTEMS

Computational economic agents must think. Their entire raison d'etre is to provide researchers

with guidance in addressing questions about the governing laws of dynamic systems. To extract the most value from the ACE approach, the most advanced computational tools available should be considered.

It is critical that the computational agent be able to effectively process information within the environment. Consider the formulation of Chiarella (2003.) They construct a population of agents engaged in the decision of whether to buy or sell a particular share of an asset. The economy consists of two assets: a risky asset with price Pt and dividend dt, and a risk-free asset with known rate of return r for every epoch t. The agents model using a benefit function V_{it} encapsulating their understanding of the market at a given point in time. This study involves heterogeneous agents, so one group of agents uses a market signal to calculate this V_{it} and another group pays a cost c_t for access to the theoretical fundamental solution:

$$F_t = \sum_{i=1}^{\infty} (1+r)^{-1} E_t(d_t)$$

which is the summation of discounted future expected dividends. An approach to this problem type using ADP and Adaptive Critics is a natural extension of the existing work. Furthermore, these techniques will allow investigation into more complex, higher scale systems. In particular, it is important to consider HONN techniques when faced with a highly nonlinear complex system such as a large-scale economy or financial market.

Following the work of Duffy (2006) on comparison to controlled economic experiments using human subjects, researchers have the need to accurately model the agent's cognitive processes as they apply to economic activity. The ART family of neural network architectures (Carpenter and Grossberg 1991) is ideally suited to such a task, given its roots in the mathematical modeling of the operation of the human brain.

It is an exciting time to be involved in computational economics and finance. The advances in computational intelligence techniques, particularly in the two areas of artificial Higher Order Neural Network research highlighted in this chapter, bring quite a bit of promise to the investigation of some major basic problems of emergent system dynamics.

FUTURE RESEARCH DIRECTIONS

There is much work to be done in expanding ADP techniques to other application areas, particularly in an operations research setting, where the tremendous scale of industrial scale logistics problems pushes the limits of current computational power. Theoretical developments need to be chased that can address this problem, as it is not sufficient to wait for the computer architects to design next generation processor capability. The scaling issue that these algorithms face as the dimensionality of the problem increases is a major stumbling block.

As pointed out in Young (2006), agent-based methods are important for studying many sorts of emergent social phenomena, including the emergence of money as the outcome of an iterated coordination game. Other social dynamics can be studied and progress made towards their understanding using these techniques. This level of human discernment can have a great positive impact on all our lives, beyond the realm of a financial market environment or mathematical psychology.

While researchers currently employ techniques such as genetic algorithms and multi-layer perceptron neural networks, there is considerable room for growth by using more advanced approaches. As these techniques become more widely understood, they may shed their image as a "black box" (LeBaron 2006). Approximate Dynamic Programming, influenced so heavily by the economic strategic risk assessment literature,

is particularly well-suited for widespread application as the computational force behind agent thinking processes.

Finally, these are research technologies capable of bringing together communities of researchers from seemingly disparate fields to approach a wide range of important problems. Much good can come from such a globalized approach to collaborative investigation.

REFERENCES

Al-Timini, A., Abu-Khala, M., & Lewis, F. (2007) Adaptive critic designs for discrete-time zero-sum games with application to H-infinity control. *IEEE Transactions on Systems, Man, and Cybernetics.* (37) 1, pp 240-247.

Arifovic, J. (1994). Genetic algorithm learning and the cobweb model. *Journal of Economic Dynamics and Control, 18*, 3-28.

Arifovic, J. (1996). The behavior of the exchange rate in the genetic algorithm and experimental economies. *Journal of Political Economy, 104*, 510-541.

Arrow, K.J. (1958). Historical background. In Arrow, K., Karlin, S., & Scarf, H. (Eds.) *Studies in the Mathematical Theory of Inventory and Production.* Stanford University Press. Stanford, CA.

Arthur, W. B. (1994), Inductive reasoning and bounded rationality. *American Economic Review, 84*, 406–411.

Arthur, W. B., Holland, J., LeBaron, B., Palmer, R. & Tayler, P. (1997), Asset pricing under endogenous expectations in an artificial stock market, in W. B. Arthur, S. Durlauf & D. Lane (Eds.), *The economy as an evolving complex system II*, pp. 15–44. Reading, MA: Addison-Wesley.

Aviv, Y., & Pazgal, A. (2005). A partially observable Markov decision process for dynamic pricing. *Management Science, 51*(9) 1400-1416.

Beltratti, A., Margarita, S., & Terna, P. (1996). *Neural networks for economic and financial modeling.* London: International Thomson Computer Press.

Bertsekas, D., & Tsitsiklis, J. (1996) *Neuro-dynamic programming.* AthenaScientific.

Binger, B., & Hoffman, E. (1998). *Microeconomics with calculus.* Addison-Wesley.

Bohner, M., & Peterson, A. (2001) *Dynamic equations on time scales: an introduction with applications.* Boston: Birkhauser.

Bohner, M., Fan., M., & Zhang, J. (2006) Existence of periodic solutions in predator-prey and competition dynamic systems. *Nonlinear Analysis: Real World Applications, 7.* 1193-1204.

Brannon, N., Conrad, G., Draelos, T., Seiffertt, J. & Wunsch. D. (2006) Information fusion and situation awareness using ARTMAP and partially observable Markov decision processes. *Proceedings of the IEEE International Joint Conference on Neural Networks.* 2023-2030.

Cai, X., Zang, N., Venayagamoorthy, G., & Wunsch, D. (2004.) Time series prediction with recurrent neural networks using a hybrid PSO-EA algorithm. *Proceedings of the International Conference on Neural Networks.* Vol. 2, 1647-1652.

Carpenter, G., Grossberg, S. (Eds) (1991) *Pattern recognition by self-organizing neural networks.* Cambridge, MA: The MIT Press.

Carpenter, G., Grossberg, S., & Reynolds, J. (1991) ARTMAP: Supervised real-time learning and classification of nonstationary data by a self-organizing neural network. *Neural Networks, 4,* 565-588.

Carpenter, G., Grossberg, S., & Rosen, D. (1991). Fuzzy ART: Fast stable learning and categorization of analog patterns by an adaptive resonance system. *Neural Networks, 4,* 759-771.

Carpenter, G., & Markuzon, N. (1998) ARTMAP-IC and medical diagnosis: Instance counting and inconsistent cases. *Neural Networks,* 11, 323-336.

Castro, J., Georgiopoulos, M., Secretan, R., DeMara, R., Anagnostopoulos, G., & Gonzalez, J. (2005) Parallelization of fuzzy ARTMAP to improve its convergence speed. *Nonlinear Analysis: Theory, Methods, and Applications, 60*(8).

Chiarella, C., Gallegati, M., Leombruni, R., & Palestrini, A. (2003). Asset price dynamics among heterogeneous interacting agents. *Computational Economics, 22*(Oct-Dec), 213-223.

Duffy, J. (2006) Agent-based models and human subject experiments. In Testafasion, L & Judd, K (Eds), *Handbook of Computational Economics Volume 2,* (pp 949-1012). Elsevier.

Ehrenberg, R.G., & Smith, R.S. (2003). *Modern labor economics. Theory and public policy.* Addison-Wesley.

Englebrecht, A. (2002) *Computational intelligence: An introduction.* John Wiley.

Enns, R., & Si, J. (2003) Helicopter trimming and tracking control using direct neural dynamic programming. *IEEE Transactions on Neural Networks, 14*(4), 929-939.

Fakih,S., & Das, T. (2006) LEAD: A methodology for learning efficient approaches to medical diagnostics. *IEEE Transactions on Information Technology in Biomedicine, 55*(1), 158-170.

Greene, W. (2003) *Econometric analysis.* Upper Saddle River, NJ: Prentice Hall.

Grossberg, S. (1976). Adaptive pattern classification and universal recoding. *Biological Cybernetics, 23,* 187-202.

Han, D., & Balakrishnan, S. (2002) State-constrained angile missile control with adaptive-critic based neural networks. *IEEE Transactions on Control Systems Technology, 10*(4), 481-489.

Hortsmann, C. (2004) *Object-oriented design and patterns.* Wiley.

Hu, X. & Wunsch, D. (2004) Time series prediction with a weighted bidirectional multi-stream extended Kalman filter. *Proceedings of the IEEE International Joint Conference on Neural Networks.* Vol. 2, pp 1641-1645.

Iyer, M., & Wunsch, D. (2001) Dynamic re-optimization of a fed-batch fermentorusing adaptive critic designs. *IEEE Transactions on Neural Networks, 12*(6), 1433-1444.

Javaherian, H., Liu, D., Zhang, Yi., & Kovalenko, O. (2003) Adaptive critic learning techniques for automotive engine control. *Proceedings of the American Control Conference.* Vol. 5, pp. 4066-4071.

Johnsonbaugh, R., & Kalin, M. (2000) *Object-oriented programming in C++.* Prentice Hall.

Judd, K. (2006) Computationally intensive analysis in economics. In Testafasion, L & Judd, K (Eds), *Handbook of Computational Economics Volume 2,* (pp 882-893). Elsevier.

Kelly, E., & Kennedy, P. (1993). A dynamic stochastic model of mate desertion. *Ecology,* (74), 351-366.

Kennedy, J., & Eberhart, R. (1995) Particle swarm optimization. *Proceedings of the IEEE International Conference on Neural Networks,* 1942-1948.

Kennedy, P. (2001) *A guide to econometrics.* MIT Press. Cambridge, MA.

Kulkarni, N., & Krishna, K. (2003) Intelligent engine control using an adaptive critic. *IEEE Transactions on Control Systems Technology, 11*(2), 164-173.

LeBaron, B. (2000) Agent-based computational finance: Suggested readings and early research. *Journal of Economic Dynamics and Control, 24,* 679-702.

LeBaron, B. (2006) Agent based computational finance. In Testafasion, L & Judd, K (Eds), *Handbook of Computational Economics, Volume 2,* (pp 1187-1235). Elsevier.

Leijonhufud, A. (1967). Keynes and the Keynesians: A suggested interperatation. *American Economic Review, 57*(2), 401-410.

Lettau, M. (1997). Explaining the facts with adaptive agents: The case of mutual fund flows. *Journal of Economic Dynamics and Control,* (21), 1117-1148.

Lin, C. (2005) Adaptive critic autopilot design of bank-to-turn missiles using fuzzy basis function networks. *IEEE Transactions on Systems, Man, and Cybernetics, 35*(2), 197-207.

Melvin, M. (2000). *International money and finance.* Addison-Wesley.

Meyer, D., Karatzoglou, A., Leisch, F., Buchta, C., & Hornik, K. (2003). A simulation framework for heterogeneous agents. *Computational Economics.* Oct-Dec, (22).

Mohagheghi, S., del Valle, V., Venayagamoorthy, G., & Harley, R. (2007) A proportional-integrator type adaptive critic design-based neurocontroller for a static compensator in a multimachine power system. *IEEE Transactions on Industrial Electronics, 54*(1), 86-96.

Moore, B. (1989). ART 1 and pattern clustering. In Touretzky, D., Hinton, G., & Sejnowski, T. (Eds.), *Proceedings of the 1988 Connectionist Models Summer School.* San Manteo, CA: Morgan Kauffman.

Muchoney, D. & Williamson, J. (2001) A Gaussian adaptive resonance theory neural network classification algorithm applied to supervised land cover mapping using multitemporal vegetation index data. *IEEE Transactions on Geoscience and Remote Sensing, 39*(9), 1969-1977.

Padhi, R., & Balakrishnan, S. (2006) Optimal management of beaver population using a reduced-order distributed parameter model and single network adaptive critics. *IEEE Transactions on Control Systems Technology, 14*(4), 628-640.

Prokhorov, D., & Wunsch, D. (1997) Adaptive critic designs. *IEEE Transactions on Neural Networks, 8*(5) 997-1007.

Puterman, M. (1994). *Markov decision processes: Discrete stochastic dynamic programming.* Wiley Series in Probability and Mathematical Statistics.

Routledge, B. (2001). Genetic algorithm learning to choose and use information. *Macroeconomic Dynamics, 5,* 303-325.

Seiffertt, J., & Wunsch, D. (2007). A single-ART architecture for unsupervised, supervised, and reinforcement learning. *Proceedings of the International Conference on Cognitive and Neural Systems.* Boston, MA.

Serrano-Gotarredona, T., & Linares-Barranco, B. (2006) A low-power current mode fuzzy-ART cell. *IEEE Transactions on Neural Networks, 17*(6), 1666-1673.

Si, J., Barto, A., Powell, W., & Wunsch, D. (2004). *Handbook of learning and approximate dynamic programming.* IEEE Press Series on Computational Intelligence. 2004.

Sutton, R. (1995). TD models: Modeling the world at a mixture of time scales. In Prieditis, A., & Russell, S. (Eds) *Proceedings of the Twelfth International Conference on Machine Learning,* pp 531-539. San Francisco: Morgan Kaufmann.

Sutton, R., & Barto, A. (1998). *Reinforcement learning.* Cambridge, MA: MIT Press.

Tesauro, G. (1994) TD-Gammon, a self-teaching backgammon program, achieves master-level play. *Neural Computation, 6*(2), 215-219.

Testafasion, L. (2006) Agent-based computational economics: A constructive approach to economic theory. In Testafasion, L & Judd, K (Eds), *Handbook of Computational Economics Volume 2,* (pp 831 – 894). Elsevier.

Todorov, E. (2007) Linearly solvable Markov decision problems. *Proceedings of NIPS.*

Vasilic, S., & Kezunovic, M. (2005) Fuzzy ART neural network algorithm for classifying the power system faults. *IEEE Transactions on Power Delivery, 20*(2), 1306-1314.

Watkins, C. (1989) *Learning from delayed rewards.* PhD thesis. Cambridge University.

Werbos, P. (1990) Backpropagation through time: What it does and how to do it. *Proceedings of the IEEE, 78*(10).

Werbos, P. (1992) Neural networks and the human mind: new mathematics fits humanistic insight. *Proceedings of the IEEE International Conference on Systems, Man, and Cybernetics,* 1, 78-83.

Werbos, P. (2004) ADP: Goals, Opportunities, and Principles. In Si, J., Barto, A., Powell, W., & Wunsch, D. (Eds) *Handbook of Learning and Approximate Dynamic Programming.* Piscataway, NJ. IEEE Press.

Williamson, J. (1996) Gaussian ARTMAP: A neural network for fast incremental learning of noisy multidimensional maps. *Neural Networks, 9*(5), 881-897.

Wunsch, D., Caudell, T., Capps, C., Marks, R., & Falk, R. (1993) An optoelectronic implementation of the adaptive resonance neural network. *IEEE Transactions on Neural Networks, 4*(4), 673-684.

Xu, R., Anagnostopoulos, G., & Wunsch. D. (2007) Multiclass cancer classification using semisupervised ellipsoid ARTMAP and particle swarm optimization with gene expression data.

IEEE/ACM Transactions on Computational Biology and Bioinformatics, 4(1), 65-77.

Young, H. (2006) Social dynamics: Theory and applications. In Testafasion, L & Judd, K (Eds), *Handbook of Computational Economics, Volume 2,* (pp 1082-1107). Elsevier.

Zadeh, L. (1965) Fuzzy sets. *Information and Control, 8*, 338-353.

Zhang, M., Xu, S., and Fulcher, J. (2002) Neuron-adaptive higher order neural-network models for automated financial data modeling. *IEEE Transactions on Neural Networks, 13*(1).

ADDITIONAL READING

The following sources should provide the interested reader with more breadth and depth of information on the computational intelligence as well as economic topics touched upon in this chapter.

Ahrens, R., & Reitz, S. (2005) Heterogeneous expectations in the foreign exchange market: Evidence from daily DM/US dollar exchange rates. *Journal of Evolutionary Economics, 15*, 65-82.

Anthony, M, & Bartlett, P. (1999) *Neural network learning: Theoretical foundations.* Cambridge, UK: Cambridge University Press.

Barrett, L., Dunbar, R., & Lycett, J. (2002) *Human evolutionary psychology.* Princeton, NJ: Princeton University Press.

Bertsekas, D. (2000). *Dynamic programming and optimal control, second edition, Vols 1 and 2.* Belmont, MA: Athena Scientific.

Bullard, J., & Duffy, J. (2001) Learning and excess volatility. *Macroeconomic Dynamics, 5,* 272-302.

Camerer, C. (2003) *Behavioral game theory.* Princeton, NJ. Princeton University Press.

Carpenter, G., Milenova, B., & Noeske, B. (1998) Distributed ARTMAP: A neural network for fast distributed supervised learning. *Neural Networks, 11*(5), 793-813.

Evans, G., Honkapohja, S. (2001) *Learning and expectations in macroeconomics.* Princeton, NJ: Princeton University Press.

Fogel, D. (2000). *Evolutionary computation: Toward a new philosophy of machine intelligence.* Piscataway, NJ: IEEE Press.

Gintis, H. (2000) *Game theory evolving: A problem-centered introduction to modeling strategic interaction.* Princeton, NJ: Princeton University Press.

Grossberg, S. (1988) *How does the brain build a cognitive code?* Cambridge, MA: MIT Press.

Haykin, S. (1999). *Neural networks: A comprehensive foundation.* Upper Saddle River, NJ: Prentice Hall.

LeBaron, B. (2001) Empirical regularities from interacting long and short memory investors in an agent based stock market. *IEEE Transactions on Evolutionary Computation, 5,* 442-455.

Neely, C., Weller, P., & Dittmer, R. (1997) Is technical analysis in the foreign exchange market profitable? A genetic programming approach. *Journal of Financial and Quantitative Analysis, 32,* 405-426.

North, D. (1981) *Structure and change in economic history.* New York: WW Norton and Company.

Pearl, J. (1988) *Probabalistic reasoning in intelligent systems: Networks of plausible inference.* San Francisco, CA: Morgan Kaufmann.

Prokhorov, D. (1997) *Adaptive critic designs and their applications.* Doctoral dissertation. University of Missouri-Rolla.

Sennott, L. (1999) *Stochastic dynamic programming and the control of queueing systems.* New York: Wiley Inter Science.

Shapiro, A., & Jain, L. (Eds) (2003) *Intelligent and other computational techniques in insurance: Theory and applications.* River Edge, NJ: World Scientific Publishing.

Sutton, R. (1988) Learning to predict by the methods of temporal differences. *Machine Learning, 3,* 9-44.

Testafasion, L., & Judd, K. (2006) *Handbook of computational economics: Agent based computational economics.* Amsterdam, The Netherlands: North-Holland.

Weibull, J. (1995) *Evolutionary game theory.* Cambridge, MA: MIT Press.

Werbos, P. (1994) *The Roots of backpropagation: From ordered derivatives to neural networks and political forecasting.* New York: Wiley.

White, D., & Sofage, D. (Eds.) *The Handbook of intelligent control: Neural, fuzzy, and adaptive approaches.* New York: Van Nostrand Reinhold.

White, L. (1999) *The theory of monetary institutions.* Malden, MA: Blackwell.

Widrow, B., & Stearns, S. (1985) *Adaptive signal processing.* Englewood Cliffs, NJ: Prentice-Hall.

Xu, R., & Wunsch, D. (2005) A survey of clustering algorithms. *IEEE Transactions on Neural Networks, 16*(3), 645-678.

Chapter V
Foreign Exchange Rate Forecasting Using Higher Order Flexible Neural Tree

Yuehui Chen
University of Jinan, China

Peng Wu
University of Jinan, China

Qiang Wu
University of Jinan, China

ABSTRACT

Forecasting exchange rates is an important financial problem that is receiving increasing attention especially because of its difficulty and practical applications. In this chapter, we apply Higher Order Flexible Neural Trees (HOFNTs), which are capable of designing flexible Artificial Neural Network (ANN) architectures automatically, to forecast the foreign exchange rates. To demonstrate the efficiency of HOFNTs, we consider three different datasets in our forecast performance analysis. The data sets used are daily foreign exchange rates obtained from the Pacific Exchange Rate Service. The data comprises of the US dollar exchange rate against Euro, Great Britain Pound (GBP) and Japanese Yen (JPY). Under the HOFNT framework, we consider the Gene Expression Programming (GEP) approach and the Grammar Guided Genetic Programming (GGGP) approach to evolve the structure of HOFNT. The particle swarm optimization algorithm is employed to optimize the free parameters of the two different HOFNT models. This chapter briefly explains how the two different learning paradigms could be formulated using various methods and then investigates whether they can provide a reliable forecast model for foreign exchange rates. Simulation results showed the effectiveness of the proposed methods.

INTRODUCTION

Foreign exchange rates are amongst the most important economic indices in the international monetary markets. Since 1973, with the abandonment of fixed foreign exchange rates and the implementations of the floating exchange rates system by industrialized countries, researchers have been striving for an explanation of the movement of exchange rates (J. T. Yao & C. L. Tan, 2000). Exchange rates are affected by many highly correlated factors. These factors could be economic, political and even psychological. The interaction of these factors is very complex. Therefore, forecasting changes of foreign exchange rates is generally very difficult. In the past decades, various kinds of forecasting methods have been developed by many researchers and experts. Technical and fundamental analysis are the basic and major forecasting methodologies popular use in financial forecasting. Like many other economic time series, a foreign exchange rate has its own trend, cycle, season, and irregularity. Thus to identify, model, extrapolate and recombine these patterns and to realize foreign *exchange rate forecasting* is a major challenge. Thus much research effort has been devoted to exploring the nonlinearity of exchange rate data and to developing specific nonlinear models to improve *exchange rate forecasting* including the autoregressive random variance (ARV) model, auto regressive conditional heteroscedasticity (ARCH), self-exciting threshold autoregressive models, There has been growing interest in the adoption of *neural networks* (Zhang, G.P., Berardi, V.L, 2001), fuzzy inference systems and statistical approaches for *exchange rate forecasting*, such as the traditional multi-layer feed-forward network (MLFN) model, the adaptive smoothing *neural network* (ASNN) model (Yu, L., Wang, S. & Lai, K.K., 2000), etc..

The major problems in designing an artificial *neural network* (ANN) for a given problem are how to design a satisfactory ANN architecture and which kind of learning algorithms can be effectively used for training the ANN. Weights and biases of ANNs can be learned by many methods, i.e. the back-propagation algorithm (Rumelhart, D.E. et al., 1986), genetic algorithm (D. Whitley et al., 1990; G. F. Miller et al., 1989); evolutionary programming (D. B. et al., 1990; N. Saravanan et al., 1995; J. R. McDonnell et al., 1994), random search algorithm (J. Hu, et al., 1998) and so on. Usually, a *neural network's* performance is highly dependent on its structure. The interaction allowed between the various nodes of the network is specified using the structure only. There may different ANN structures with different performance for a given problem, and therefore it is possible to introduce different ways to define the structure corresponding to the problem. Depending on the problem, it may be appropriate to have more than one hidden layer, feed-forward or feedback connections, and different activation functions for different units, or in some cases, direct connections between the input and output layer. In the past decades, there has been increasing interest in optimizing ANN architecture and parameters simultaneously.

There have been a number of attempts in automatically designing ANN architectures. The early methods of architecture learning include constructive and pruning algorithms (S. E. Fahlman et al., 1990; J. P. Nadal, 1989; R. Setiono et al., 1995). The main problem with these methods is that the topological subsets rather than the complete class of ANN's architecture are searched in the search space by structural hill climbing methods (J. Angeline et al., 1994). Recently, a tendency for optimizing architecture and weights of ANNs by evolutionary algorithm has become an active research area. Xin Yao, et al. (Yao X. et al., 1997, 1999), proposed a new evolutionary system called EPNet for evolving the architecture and weights of ANNs simultaneously. EPNet is a kind of hybrid technique. Here architectures are modified by mutation operators that add or delete nodes/connections. Weights are trained by a modified back-propagation algorithm with an additive learning rate and by a simulated annealing algorithm. A more recent attempt for structure optimization of ANNs was the neuroevolution of augmenting topologies (NEAT) (K. O. Stanley & R. Miikkulainen, 2002), which aims at the evolution of topologies and allows the evolution procedure to evolve an adaptive *neural network* with plastic synapses by designating which connections should be adaptive and in what ways. Byoung-Tak Zhang et al. proposed a method called evolutionary induction of the sparse neural trees (B. T. Zhang et al., 1997). Based on the representation of the neural tree, the architecture and the weights of higher order sigma-pi *neural networks* are evolved by using genetic programming and breeder genetic algorithm, respectively.

In this chapter, the HOFNT is proposed. Based on predefined instruction/operator sets, the HOFNT can be created and evolved, in which over-layer connections, different activation functions for different nodes/neurons are allowed. Therefore, the HOFNT model can be viewed as a kind of irregular multi-layer flexible *neural network*. We employ the *grammar guided genetic programming* (GGGP) algorithm to evolve the structure of HOFNT and the Particles Swarm Optimization algorithm (PSO) (Eberhart, R & Shi. Y, 2001; Kennedy, J. et al., 1995) to optimize the parameters encoded in the HOFNT model.

HIGHER ORDER FLEXIBLE NEURAL TREE

The first order *Flexible Neural Tree* (FNT) is a *tree-structure* based encoding method with specific instruction set is selected for representing a flexible *neural network*; it can be seen as a flexible multi-layer feed-forward *neural network* with over-layer connections and free parameters in the activation functions. The first order FNT has been successfully employed in many Economics and Business fields, such as stock index predic-

tion (Yuehui Chen, Lizhi Peng & Ajith Abraham, 2006; Yuehui Chen & Ajith Abraham, 2006). The encoding and evaluation of a FNT will be given in this section. Due to its *tree-structure* based encoding method, a lot of *tree-structure* based algorithms could be used to evolve a FNT, such as genetic programming (GP), ant programming (AP), probabilistic incremental program evolution (PIPE) and so on. To find the optimal parameters set (weights and activation function parameters) of a FNT model, a number of global and local search algorithms namely genetic algorithm, evolutionary programming, gradient based learning method etc. can be employed.

Higher Order Neural Networks (HONNs) are the extensions of ordinary first order neural networks. More recent research involving *higher order neural networks* shows that they have stronger approximation properties, faster convergence rates, greater storage capacity, and higher fault tolerance than traditional first order *neural networks* (Dembo A, Farotimi O. & Kailath T., 1991). From the above, we know the FNT can be seen as a flexible multi-layer feed-forward *neural network* with over-layer connections and free parameters in the activation functions. For the superior performance of HONNs on representative financial time series, we apply the idea of applying HONN approaches to FNT. This results in *Higher Order Flexible Neural Tree* (HOFNT).

Flexible Neuron Instructor and HOFNT Model

A function set F and terminal instruction set T used for generating a HOFNT model are described as follows:

$$S = F \bigcup T = \{+_2, +_3, \cdots, +_n\} \bigcup \{x_1, x_2, \cdots, x_n\}$$
(1)

where $+_i$ ($i = 2, 3, \ldots, N$) denote non-leaf nodes instructions which take i arguments. $x_1, x_2, \ldots, x_n$ are leaf nodes instructions which take no other arguments. The output of a non-leaf node is calculated as a flexible neuron model (see Figure 1). From this point of view, the instruction $+_i$ is also called a flexible neuron operator with i inputs.

In the creation process of the neural tree, if a non-terminal instruction, i.e., $+_i$ (i =2, 3, …, N) is selected, i real values are randomly generated and used for representing the connection strength between the node $+_i$ and its children. In addition, two adjustable parameters a_i and b_i are randomly created as flexible activation function parameters. For developing the HOFNT model, the flexible activation function used is as follows:

$$f(a_i, b_i, x) = e^{-(\frac{x-a_i}{b_i})^2} \qquad (2)$$

The total excitation of $+_n$ is:

$$net_n = \sum_{j}^{n} w_j * x_j + \sum_{j}^{n} \sum_{k}^{m} w_{jk} * x_j * x_k \qquad (3)$$

where x_j (j = 1, 2, …, n) are the inputs to node $+_n$, and x_k are the *higher order* inputs variables, which can be calculated by many methods, e.g. outer-product, link function etc. The output of the node +n is then calculated by:

$$out_n = f(a_n, b_n, net_n) = e^{-(\frac{net_n-a_n}{b_n})^2} \qquad (4)$$

The overall output of *flexible neural tree* can be computed from left to right by depth-first method, recursively.

A flexible neuron operator and a typical representation of the HOFNT with function set $F =$ $\{+_2, +_3, …, +_6\}$, and terminal instruction set $T =$ $\{x_1, x_2, x_3, x_1*x_1, x_1*x_2, x_1*x_3, x_2*x_2, x_2*x_3, x_3*x_3\}$ were as Figure 1. The symbol * is supposed to mean multiply.

A fitness function maps HOFNT to scalar, real-valued fitness values that reflect the HOFNT's performances on a given task. Firstly the fitness functions should be seen as several error measures, i.e., Root Mean Squared Error (RMSE), Correlation Coefficient (CC), Maximum Absolute Percentage Error (MAP) and Mean Absolute Percentage Error (MAPE). A secondary non-user-defined objective for the algorithm always optimizes HOFNTs, the size of HOFNT usually being measured by number of nodes. Among HOFNTs having equal fitness values smaller HOFNTs are always preferred. The most common measure to evaluate how closely the model is capable of predicting future rate is measured by Normalized Mean-Square Error (NMSE). The other measure important to the trader is correct prediction of movement. In this work, we used two other measures, which are: Mean Absolute Error (MAE), Directional Symmetry (DS). These criteria are given as follows, in Equations (5)-(7),

Figure 1. A flexible neuron operator(left) and a typical representation of HOFNT(right)

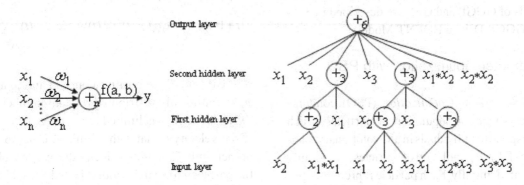

Equation (5).

$$NMSE = \frac{\sum_{i=1}^{N}(P_{actual,i} - P_{predicted,i})^2}{\sum_{i=1}^{N}(P_{actual,i} - \bar{P}_{actual})^2} = \frac{1}{\sigma^2 N}\sum_{i=1}^{N}(P_{actual,i} - P_{predicted,i})^2$$

Equation (6).

$$MAE = \frac{1}{N}\sum_{i=1}^{N}\left|P_{actual,i} - P_{predicted,i}\right|$$

Equation (7).

$$DS = \frac{100}{N}\sum_{i=1}^{N}d_i, \quad d_i = \begin{cases} 1 & \text{if}(P_{actual,i} - P_{actual,i-1})(P_{predicted,i} - P_{predicted,i-1}) \geq 0 \\ 0 & \text{otherwise} \end{cases}$$

where $P_{actual,i}$ is the actual exchange rate value on day i, $P_{predicted,i}$ is the forecast value of the exchange rate on that day and N = total number of days. The task is to have minimal values of NMSE and MAE, and a maximum value for DS.

Optimization of the HOFNT Model

Evolving the Architecture of HOFNT

Due to its *tree-structure* based encoding method, a number of *tree-structure* based algorithms could be used to evolve a FNT, such as GP, AP, PIPE etc. In this chapter, we focus on *grammar guided genetic programming* (GGGP) and the *gene express programming* (GEP) algorithm for structure optimization of the HOFNT mode(more details of GGGP and GEP are described in Section GGGP-Driven HOFNT Model).

Parameter Optimization with PSO

Particle Swarm Optimization (PSO) conducts searches using a population of particles which correspond to individuals in an evolutionary algorithm (EA). A population of particles is randomly generated initially. Each particle represents a po-

tential solution and has a position represented by a position vector x_i. A swarm of particles moves through the problem space, with the moving velocity of each particle represented by a velocity vector v_i. At each time step, a function f_i representing a quality measure is calculated by using x_i as input. Each particle keeps track of its own best position, which is associated with the best fitness it has achieved so far in a vector p_i. Furthermore, the best position among all the particles obtained so far in the population is kept track of as p_g. In addition to this global version, another version of PSO keeps track of the best position among all the topological neighbors of a particle. At each time step t, by using the individual best position, p_i, and the global best position, $p_{g(t)}$, a new velocity for particle i is updated by:

$$v_i(t+1) = v_i(t) + c_1\varphi_1(p_i(t) - x_i(t)) + c_2\varphi_2(p_g(t) - x_i(t)) \tag{8}$$

where c_1 and c_2 are positive constant and φ_1 and φ_2 are uniformly distributed random number in [0,1]. The term v_i is limited to the range of $\pm_{vmax}$. If the velocity violates this limit, it is set to its proper limit. Changing velocity this way enables the particle i to search around its individual best position, p_i, and global best position, p_g. Based on the updated velocities, each particle changes its position according to the following equation:

$$x_i(t+1) = x_i(t) + v_i(t+1) \qquad (9)$$

More precisely, PSO works as follows:

- **Step 0:** *Generation of initial condition of each agent.* Initial searching points (s_i^0) and velocity (v_i^0) of each agent are usually generated randomly within the allowable range. Note that the dimension of search space is consists of all the parameters used in the HOFNT model. The current searching point is set to p_{best} for each agent. The best-evaluated value of p_{best} is set to g_{best} and the agent number with the best value is stored.
- **Step 1:** *Evaluation of searching points of each agent.* The objective function value is calculated for each agent. If the value is better than the current p_{best} of the agent, the p_{best} value is replaced by the current value. If the best value of p_{best} is better than the current g_{best}, g_{best} is replaced by the best value and s is stored.
- **Step 2:** *Modification of each searching.* The current searching point of each agent is changed using (8) and (9).
- **Step 3:** *Checking the exit condition.* If the current iteration number reaches the predetermined maximum iteration number, then exit. Otherwise, go to *Step 1.*

GGGP-DRIVEN HOFNT MODEL

A brief overview of the GGGP algorithm and how it works is given in this section; we then discuss how the GGGP can be used for evolving the structure of a HOFNT model. The formal hybrid evolving algorithm for constructing a FNT model is discussed in this section also.

GP and GGGP

Genetic Programming (GP) (Gramer, 1985; Schmidhuber, 1987; Koza, 1992) is an Evolutionary Computation approach. GP can be most readily understood by comparison with Genetic Algorithms (Holland, 1975; Goldberg, 1989). The basic algorithm of GP can be described as follows:

- **Step 0:** Generate a population P randomly.
- **Step 1:** Select a set of fitter individuals G from population P.
- **Step 2:** Apply genetic operators on the set of selected individuals G to obtain a set of children G'.
- **Step 3:** Incorporate the children G' into population P.

Rather than evolving a linear string as a GA does, GP evolves computer programs, which are usually tree structures. The fitness of an individual may be several error measures (e.g. RMSE), the result of an objective function, etc. There are three basic genetic operators in GP: selection, crossover and mutation. They can be described as follows:

- **Selection.** A number of selection methods can be applied to select the parents for the next generation, e.g. truncation selection, fitness proportionate selection, and tournament selection, etc. For details of these selection methods, please refer to Koza (1992).
- **Crossover.** Crossover combines the genetic material of two parents by swapping certain parts from both parents, given two parents which are obtained by some selection method, then select randomly a sub-tree in each parent and swap them.
- **Mutation.** Mutation acts on only one individual. It introduces a certain amount of randomness, to encourage exploration.

Given one parent obtained by some selection method, the mutation performs three steps: select randomly a sub-tree in the parent; remove the selected sub-tree; generate randomly a new sub-tree to replace the removed sub-tree.

The GGGP (Whigham, 1995; Hoai N. X., Shan Y. & McKay R. I., 2002; Shan Y, McKay R. I., Abbas H. A. & Essam D. L., 2004) algorithm is an important extension of genetic programming (GP), i.e. it is a genetic programming system with a grammar constraint. A number of grammars can be used to describe the constraint, such as Context-free Grammars (CFG) and Stochastic Context-free Grammars (SCFG). In this chapter, we focus on CFG, the formal definition of CFG based GGGP will be given in next subsection. GGGP provides a systematic way to handle typing. In this aspect, it has a more formal theoretical basis than strongly typed GP. Essentially, GGGP has the same components and operations as in GP; however, there are a number of significant differences between the two systems. In GGGP, a program is represented as its derivation tree in the context free grammar. Crossover between two programs is carried out by swapping two sub-derivation trees with roots labeled by the same non-terminal symbol. In mutation, a sub-derivation tree is replaced by a new randomly generated sub-derivation tree rooted at the same non-terminal symbol. More importantly, GGGP can constrain the search space so that only grammatically correct individuals can be generated.

CFG Based GGGP

Context-free Grammars (CFG) were first investigated by Gruan (Gruan, 1996) and Whigham (Whigham, 1995). We called the hybrid scheme combining GP and context free grammars, CFG based GGGP, which allows for expressing and enforcing syntactic constraints on the GP solutions. A context-free grammar describes the

admissible constructs of a language by a four tuple $\{S, N, T, R\}$, where S is the start symbol, N is the set of non-terminal symbols, T is the set of terminal symbols, and R a set of productions or rules. The productions are of the form $X \rightarrow \lambda$, where $X \in N$ and $\lambda \in (N \cup T)$. X is called the left-hand side of the production, where λ is the right-hand side. Any expression is iteratively built up from the start symbol by rewriting non-terminal symbols into one of their derivations, as given by the production rules, until the expression contains terminals only. A simple example of a CFG can be found in Figure 2. As can be seen, in CFG, it is possible that one non-terminal can be rewritten in different ways. For example, non-terminal "exp" can be rewritten using either rule 1, 2, 3. In CFG, all of these rules have equal probabilities to be chosen and therefore there is no bias.

The Hybrid Learning Algorithm of GGGP-Driven HOFNT Model

The general learning procedure for constructing the GGGP-Driven HOFNT model can be described as follows:

- **Step 0:** Create an initial population randomly (HOFNT tree and its corresponding parameters).
- **Step 1:** Structure optimization is achieved by CFG based GGGP as described in the above subsections.
- **Step 2:** If a better structure is found, then go to *Step 3*, otherwise go to *Step 1*.
- **Step 3:** Parameter optimization is achieved by the PSO algorithm as described in subsection 2.2. In this stage, the architecture of the HOFNT model is fixed, and is the best tree developed during the run of the structure search run. The parameters (weights and flexible activation function parameters) encoded in the best tree formulate a particle.
- **Step 4:** If the maximum number of local searches is reached, or no better parameter

Figure 2. Example of Grammar Guided Genetic Programming

$s \to exp$	0
$exp \to exp\ op\ exp$	1
$exp \to pre\ exp$	2
$exp \to var$	3
$pre \to sin$	4
$pre \to cos$	5
$op \to +$	6
$op \to -$	7
$var \to x$	8

(a) context-free grammar

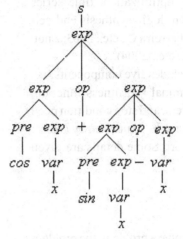

(b) derivation tree of expression of
$sin(x)+cos(x)-x$

vector is found for a significantly long time (say 100 steps) then go to *Step 5*; otherwise go to *Step 3*;

- **Step 5:** If a satisfactory solution is found, then the algorithm is stopped; otherwise go to *Step 1*.

GEP-DRIVEN HOFNT MODEL

In this section, *Gene Expression Programming* (GEP) is employed to evolve the structure of the HOFNT. We will discuss how GEP can be used to evolve the structure of the HOFNT model, and give the hybrid learning algorithm for evolving a HOFNT model.

Gene Expression Programming

The GEP algorithm is a new evolutionary algorithm that evolves computer programs; it was first introduced by Candida Ferreira (Ferreira C., 2001). GEP is, like genetic algorithm (GA) and genetic programming (GP), a genetic algorithm as it uses populations of individuals, selects them according

to fitness, and introduces genetic variation using one or more genetic operators. The fundamental difference between the three algorithms resides in the nature of the individuals: in GA the individuals are linear strings of fixed length (chromosomes); in GP the individuals are nonlinear entities of different sizes and shapes (parse trees); and in GEP the individuals are encoded as linear strings of fixed length (the genome or chromosomes) which are afterwards expressed as nonlinear entities of different sizes and shapes (i.e., simple diagram representations or expression trees). There are two important advantages of a system like GEP First, the chromosomes are simple entities: linear, compact, relatively small, easy to manipulate genetically (replicate, mutate, recombine, transpose, etc.). Second, the expression trees are exclusively the expression of their respective chromosomes; they are the entities upon which selection acts and, according to fitness, they are selected to reproduce with modification. During reproduction it is the chromosomes of the individuals, not the expression trees, which are reproduced with modification and transmitted to the next generation. GEP methods have performed well

101

for solving a large variety of problems, including symbolic regression, optimization, time series analysis, classification, logic synthesis and cellular automata, etc. (Ferreira C., etc., 2003; Zhou C., etc., 2003; Xie C., etc., 2004).

GEP generally includes five components, i.e. the function set, terminal set, fitness function, GEP control parameters, and stop condition need to be specified. GEP can be expressed by *GEP* = {*F*, *T*, *E*, *P*, *S*} for short. Some details are given as follows.

Encoding

When using GEP to solve a problem, the problem should be encoded to genotype, which is also called chromosome. Each chromosome in GEP is a character string of fixed-length, which can be composed of any element from the function set or the terminal set. For example, if the predefined function set and terminal set is *F* = {+, -, *, /, *sin*} and *T* = {*x, y, z*}, the following is an example GEP chromosome of length eight:

$$sin+**xxxy \qquad (10)$$

Where *sin* denotes the sine function; *x, y* are input variables. The above representation is referred to as Karva notation, or K-expression (Ferreira C., 2001). A K-expression can be

Figure 3. The Expression Tree corresponds to sin+**xxxy

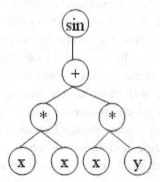

mapped into the ET stops growing when the last node in this branch is a terminal. For example, the ET shown in Figure 3 corresponds to the sample chromosome, and can be interpreted in mathematical form as (13).

The conversion of an ET into a K-expression is also very straightforward, and can be accomplished by recording the nodes from left to right in each layer of the ET in a top-down fashion to form the string. Each chromosome string in GEP is fixed-length, which is composed by K-expression in the head and complementary part in the tail, and moreover in order to guarantee the only legal expression trees are generated, some validity test methods are applied:

$$sin(x^2 + x * y) \qquad (11)$$

Description of the GEP Algorithm

The general procedure of the GEP can be described as follows:

- **Step 0:** Generate a population *P* randomly, i.e. randomly generate linear fixed-length chromosomes for individuals of the initial population.
- **Step 1:** Select a set of fitter individuals *G* from population *P*, i.e. evaluate the fitness of each individual based on a predefined fitness function; the individuals are then selected by fitness.
- **Step 2:** Apply genetic operators on the set of selected individuals *G* to obtain a set of children *G*. In this stage, the individuals of the selected new generation are, in their turn, subject to the same developmental process, i.e. expression as chromosomes, confrontation in the selection environment, and reproduction with modification.
- **Step 3:** Incorporate the children *G'* into population *P*.
- **Step 4:** If a pre-specified number of generations is reached, or a solution has been

found, stop the algorithm, otherwise jump to *Step 1*.

The Hybrid Learning Algorithm of GEP-Driven HOFNT Model

The general learning procedure for constructing the GEP-Driven HOFNT model can be described as follows:

- **Step 0:** Create an initial population randomly (HOFNT tree and its corresponding parameters);
- **Step 1:** Structure optimization is achieved by GEP as described in section 4.1.
- **Step 2:** If a better structure is found, then go to *Step 3*, otherwise go to *Step 1*.
- **Step 3:** Parameter optimization is achieved by the PSO algorithm as described in subsection 2.2. In this stage, the architecture of the HOFNT model is fixed, and it is the best tree developed during the end of run of the structure search. The parameters (weights and flexible activation function parameters) encoded in the best tree formulate a particle.
- **Step 4:** If the maximum number of local searching is reached, or no better parameter vector is found for a significantly long time then go to *Step 5*; otherwise go to *Step 3*;
- **Step 5:** If satisfactory solution is found, then the algorithm is stopped; otherwise go to *Step 1*.

EXPERIMENT SETUP AND RESULT

Some experiments for foreign exchange rates are established for evaluating the performance of the proposed methods. Two different models discussed above, are separately used to forecast foreign exchange rate. The data used are daily foreign exchange rates obtained from the Pacific Exchange Rate Service, provided by Professor

Werner Antweiler, University of British Columbia, Vancouver, Canada. The data comprises the US dollar exchange rate against Euro, Great Britain Pound (GBP) and Japanese Yen (JPY). We used the daily data from 1 January 2000 to 31 December 2001 as training data set, and the data from 1 January 2002 to 31 December 2002 as evaluation test set or out-of-sample datasets (partial data sets excluding holidays), which are used to evaluate the performance of the predictions, based on evaluation measurements.

For comparison purposes, the HOFNT model which is based Gene Expression Programming (GEP) and PSO algorithm are also established for foreign exchange rates forecasting, and we also designed an Artificial *Neural Network* model (ANN) to forecast the same data set. The ANN trained using the PSO algorithm with flexible bipolar sigmoid activation functions at hidden layer was constructed for the foreign exchange data. It has three layers; there are ten nodes in the hidden layer and one node in the output layer and five input variables. At last, we compare results for the three different models.

Experiments were carried out on a Pentium IV, 2.8 GHz Machine with 512 MB RAM and the programs implemented in C/C++. Test data was presented to the trained connectionist models, and the outputs from the network compared with the actual exchange rates in the time series.

Parameter Settings

GGGP-Driven HOFNT Parameter Settings

Parameters used by GGGP-Driven HOFNT in these experiments are presented in Table 1. The HOFNT models were trained with five inputs representing the five technical indicators and an output unit to predict the exchange rate. The values for the other parameter are adapted from Table 1. Population size was considered 100 for both test data. The actual daily exchange rates and the pre-

Table 1. Values of parameters used by GGGP-Driven HOFNT

Parameter	Value
Population size	100
Number of iteration	2000
Crossover Probability	0.9
Mutation Probability	0.01
Maximum Tree Depth	5
Function set	s, exp, $op2$, $op3$, var
Terminal set	$+_2$, $+_3$, x_1, x_2, x_3, x_4, x_5

The grammars used for modeling the data are as follows:

$s \rightarrow exp$
$exp \rightarrow op2\ exp\ exp$
$exp \rightarrow op3\ exp\ exp\ exp$
$exp \rightarrow var$
$op2 \rightarrow +_2$
$op3 \rightarrow +_3$
$var \rightarrow x_1\ |\ x_2\ |\ x_3\ |\ x_4\ |\ x_5$

Figure 4. The actual exchange rate and predicted ones for training and testing data set of Euro (Obtain by GGGP-Driven HOFNT and ANN)

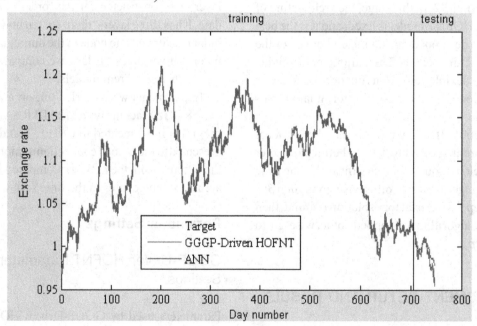

dicted ones obtained by GGGP-Driven HOFNT and ANN for three major internationally traded currencies are shown in Figure 4 through 6.

GEP-Driven HOFNT Parameter Settings

Parameters values used by GEP-Driven HOFNT for these test data are presented in Table 2. The actual daily exchange rates and the predicted ones

Figure 5. The actual exchange rate and predicted ones for training and testing data set of British pounds (Obtain by GGGP-Driven HOFNT and ANN)

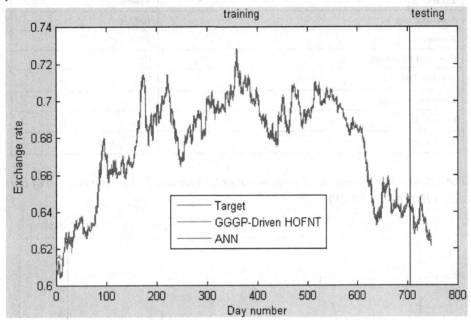

Figure 6. The actual exchange rate and predicted ones for training and testing data set of Japanese yen (Obtain by GGGP-Driven HOFNT and ANN)

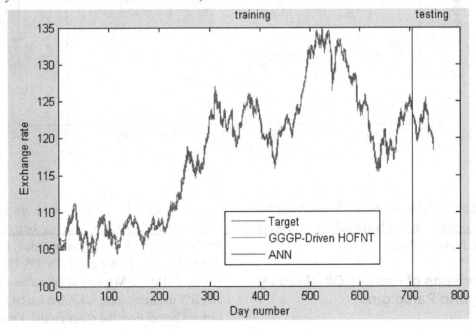

Table 2. Values of parameters used by GEP-Driven HOFNT

Parameter	Value
Population size	100
Number of iteration	2000
Crossover Probability	0.9
Mutation Probability	0.01
Chromosome length	15
Function set	$+_2, +_3,$
Terminal set	x_1, x_2, x_3, x_4, x_5

Figure 7. The actual exchange rate and predicted ones for training and testing data set of Euro (Obtain by GEP-Driven HOFNT and ANN)

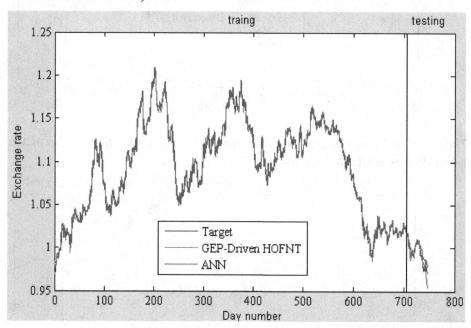

obtained by GEP-Driven HOFNT and ANN for three major internationally traded currencies are shown in Figure 7 through 9.

Comparisons of Results Obtained by Two Hybrid Paradigms

Table 3 summarizes the best results achieved for the foreign exchange rates using the two hybrid paradigms (GGGP-Driven HOFNT and GEP-Driven HOFNT).

As depicted in Table 3, for Euro test data, GGGP-Driven HOFNT gives better results for NMSE (0.144491), lower value for MAE (0.016014), and better result for DS (78.5%). In terms of NMSE, MAE, and DS values, for GBP and JPY exchange rate, GEP-Driven HOFNT performed better than the other model. From Figure 5 through Figure 9, we can see HOFNT forecasting models are better then ANN models for three major internationally traded currencies.

Figure 8. The actual exchange rate and predicted ones for training and testing data set of British pounds (Obtain by GEP-Driven HOFNT and ANN)

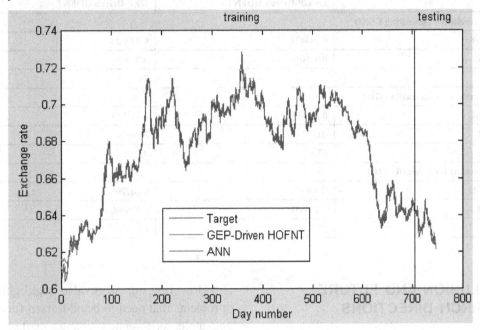

Figure 9. The actual exchange rate and predicted ones for training and testing data set of Japanese yen (Obtain by GEP-Driven HOFNT and ANN)

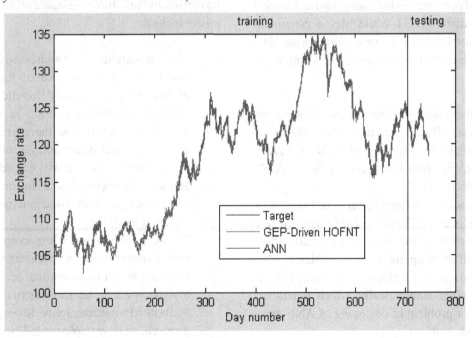

Table 3. Results obtained by two hybrid paradigms for tree foreign exchange rates

	GGGP-Driven HOFNT	**GEP-Driven HOFNT**
Test results for forecasting EURO		
NMSE	0.144491	0.230724
MAE	0.016014	0.019764
DS	78.5	74.5
Test results for forecasting GBP		
NMSE	0.259496	0.241954
MAE	0.021147	0.020703
DS	67.7	70
Test results for forecasting JPY		
NMSE	0.260479	0.207296
MAE	0.020832	0.018446
DS	52.5	57.75

CONCLUSION AND FUTURE RESEARCH DIRECTIONS

In this chapter, we presented two techniques for modeling foreign exchange rates. The performances of presented techniques (empirical results) indicate that HOFNT could play a prominent role for foreign *exchange rate forecasting*. The HOFNT models have a number of advantages, namely:

- Suitable architectures can be designed automatically. As we know, one of the major problems in designing an ANN for a given problem is how to design a satisfactory ANN architecture.
- The activation functions attached in the neurons of the ANN are flexible (have some free parameters), which can be adjusted to adapt to different approximation problems.
- It can realize the selection of important inputs variables automatically, which is another major problem in designing of ANN for a given problem.

However, our work also highlights some problems that need to be addressed further. For example, as foreign exchange markets constitute a very complex system, more factors that influence the exchange rate movement should be considered in future research. Future research issues include:

- Many researchers have addressed the problem of neural network-based forecasting of foreign exchange rates (Refenes, Barac, Chen, & Karoussos , 1992; Tenti, 1996; Yao, et al., 2000), and there are various advantages and disadvantages of the different techniques. We will consider using an ensemble approach so as to complement the advantages and disadvantages of the different methods.
- The key problem for finding an appropriate neural tree to model a nonlinear system at hand is how to find an optimal or near-optimal solution in the neural tree structure space and related parameter space. In our previous research, we have implemented Probabilistic Incremental Program evolution (PIPE), Ant Programming (AP), and et al. to evolve the

structure of the neural tree. Variants GP and Estimation of distribution of tree form solutions, i.e. EDAGP, have been an active research area in recent years. We will try to use such *tree-structure* based evolutionary algorithms to evolve the architecture of HOFNT so as to enhance its performance of HOFNT.

ACKNOWLEDGMENT

This research was supported by the NSFC under grant No. 60573065 and the Key Subject Research Foundation of Shandong Province.

REFERENCES

Angeline, P.J., Saunders, G.M., & Pollack, J.B. (1994). An evolutionary algorithm that constructs recurrent neural networks. *IEEE Trans. on Neural Networks, 5*, 54-65.

Chen, A.S., & Leung, M.T. (2004). Regression neural network for error correction in foreign exchange forecasting and trading. *Computers and Operations Research, 31*, 1049-1068.

Chen, Y.H., Peng, L.Z., & Ajith, A. (2006). Exchange rate forecasting using flexible neural trees. *Lecture Notes on Computer Science, 3973*, 518-523.

Chen, Y.H., Yang, B. & Dong, J.W. (2004). Evolving flexible neural networks using ant programming and PSO algorithm. *International Symposium on Neural Networks (ISNN'04), 3173*, 211-216.

Chen, Y.H., Peng, L.Z., & Ajith, A. (2006). Stock index modeling using hierarchical rbf networks. *10th International Conference on Knowledge-Based & Intelligent Information & Engineering Systems (KES'06), 4253*, 398-405.

Chen, Y.H., & Abraham, A. (2006). Hybrid-learning methods for stock index modeling, artificial neural networks in finance, health and manufacturing: Potential and challenges. In J. Kamruzzaman, R. K. Begg and R. A. Sarker (Eds.), *Idea Group Inc. Publishers, USA, 4*,3-79.

Dembo, A., Farotimi, O., Kailath, T. (1991). High-order absolutely stable neural networks. *IEEE Trans Circ System, 38*(1), 57–65.

Eberhart, R.C., & Shi, Y. (2001). Particle swarms optimization: Developments, applications and resource. In *Proc Congress on Evolutionary Computation, Vol 1,* (pp.81-86). NJ: IEEE Press.

Fahlman, S.E. & Lebiere, C. (1990). The cascade-correlation learning architecture. *Advances in Neural InformationProcessing Systems, 2*, 524-532.

Ferreira, C. (2001). Gene expression programming: A new adaptive algorithm for solving problems. *Complex Systems, 13*(2), 87-129.

Ferreira, C. (2003). Function finding and the creation of numerical constants in gene expression programming. *Advances in Soft Computing Engineering Design and Manufacturing*, 257-266.

Fogel, D.B., Fogel, L.J., & Porto, V.W. (1990). Evolving neural networks. *Biological Cybernetics, 63*(2), 487-493.

Gruan, F. (1996). On using syntactic constraints with genetic programming. In P.J. Angeline, & K.E, Kinnear Jr., (eds.), *Advance in Genetic Programming*, (pp. 377-394). Cambridge, MA: MIT Press.

Hoai, N.X., Shan, Y., McKay, R.I., & Essam, D. (2002). Is ambiguity useful or problematic for grammar guided genetic programming? A case study. *4th Asia-Pacific Conference on Simulated Evolution and Learning (SEAL'02)*. NJ: IEEE Press.

Hu, J., Hirasawa, K., & Murata, J. (1998). Random search for neural network training. *Journal of Advanced Computational Intelligence, 2*, 134-141.

Kennedy, J., & Eberhart, R.C. (1995). Particle Swarm optimization. *Proc. of IEEE International Conference on Neural Networks, 4*, 1942-1948.

Koza, J. R. (1992). *Genetic programming: On the programming of computers by means of natural selection.* Cambridge, MA: MIT Press.

McDonnell, J.R., & Waagen, D. (1994). Evolving recurrent perceptions for time-series modeling. *IEEE Trans on Neural Networks, 5*, 24-38.

Millar, G.F., Todd, P.M., & Hegde, S.U. (1989). Designing neural networks using genetic algorithms, In *Proc. 3rd Int. Conf. Genetic Algorithm and Their Applications,* (pp. 379-384). San Mateo: Morgan Kaufmann.

Nadal, J.P. (1989). Study of a growth algorithm for a feed-forward network. *Int. J. Neural Systems, 1*, 55-59.

Ratle, A., & Sebag, M. (2001). Avoiding the bloat with probabilistic grammar guided genetic programming. In *Artificial Evolution 5th International Conference, Evolution Artificielle* (pp.255-266). Creusot, France.

Refenes, A.N., Barac, M.A., Chen, L., & Karoussos, A.S. (1992). Currency exchange rate prediction and nerual network design strategies. *Neural Computing and Applications, 1*, 46-58.

Rumelhart, D.E. Hinton, G.E, & Williams, R.J. (1986). Learning internal representation by error propagation. *Parallel Distributed Processing, 1*, 318-362.

Saravanan, N.D., & , B. (1995). Evolving neural control systems. *Int. J. Intelligent Systems, 10*, 23-27.

Setiono, R., & Hui, L.C. (1995), Use of a quasi-newton method in a feedforward neural network construction algorithm. *IEEE Trans. on Neural Networks, 6*, 273-277.

Shan, Y., McKay R.I., Abbas, H.A, & Essam, D.L. (2004, December). Program distribution estimation with grammar models. In *The 8th Asia Pacific Symposium on Intelligent and Evolutionary Systems,* Cairns, Australia.

Stanley, K.O., & Miikkulainen, R. (2002). Evolving neural networks through augmenting topologies. *Evolutionary Computation, 10*, 99-127.

Tenti, P. (1996). Forecasting foreign exchange rates using recurrent neural networks. *Applied Artificial Intelligence, 10*, 567-581.

Whittley, D., Starkweather, T., Bogart, C. (1990). Genetic algorithms and neural networks: Optimizing connections and connectivity. *Parallel Computing, 14*, 347-361.

Whigham, P.A. (1995). Inductive bias and genetic programming. *In IEEE Conference publications, 414*, 461-466.

Whigham, P.A. (1995). Grammatically based genetic programming. In Rosca, J. P., (Ed.), *Proceedings of the Workshop on Genetic Programming: From Theory to Real World Applications,* (pp.395-432). Tahoe City, California.

Xie, Z., Li, X., Eugenio, B. D., Xiao, W., Tirpak, T. M. & Nelson, P. C. (2004). Using gene expression programming to construct sentence ranking functions for text summarization. In *Proceedings of the 20th International Conference on Computational Linguistics (COLING-2004).* Geneva, Switzerland.

Yao, J.T., & Tan, C.L. (2000). A case study on using neural networks to perform technical forecasting of forex. *Neurocomputing, 34*, 79-98.

Yao, X., & Liu, Y. (1997). A new evolutionary system for evolving artificial neural networks. *IEEE Trans. on Neural Networks, 8*, 694-713.

Yao, X. (1999). Evolving artificial neural networks. *Proc. See IEEE, 87,* 1423-1447.

Yao, X., Liu, Y., & Lin, G. (1999). Evolutionary programming made faster. *IEEE transactions on Evolutionary Computation, 3,* 82-102.

Yao, J., Li, Y., & Tan, C.L. (2000). Option price forecasting using neural networks. *OMEGA: International Journal of Management Science, 28,* 455-466.

Yao, J., & Tan, C.L.(2000). A case study on using neural networks to perform technical forecasting of forex. *Neurocomputing, 34,* 79-98.

Yu, L., Wang, S. & Lai, K.K. (2000). Adaptive smoothing neural networks in foreign exchange rate forecasting. *Lecture Notes in Computer Science, 3516,* 523-530.

Zhang, G.P., & Berardi, V.L. (2001). Time series forecasting with neural network ensembles: an application for exchange rate prediction. *Journal of the Operational Research Society, 52,* 652-664.

Zhang, B.T., Ohm, P., & Muhlenbein, H. (1997). Evolutionary induction of sparse neural trees. *Evolutionary Computation, 5,* 213-236.

Zhou, C., Xiao, W., Nelson, P.C., & Tirpak, T.M. (2003). Evolving accurate and compact classification rules with gene expression programming. *IEEE Transactions on Evolutionary Computation, 7,* 519-531.

ADDITIONAL READING

Brooks, C. (1997). Linear and nonlinear (non-) forecastability of high frequency exchange rates. *Journal of Forecasting, 16,* 125-145.

Ferreira, C. (2001, September). Gene expression programming in problem solving. In *Invited Tutorial of the 6th Online World Conference on Soft Computing in Industrial Applications,* 10-24.

Ferreira, C. (2002). Mutation, transposition, and recombination: An analysis of the evolutionary dynamics. *4th International Workshop on Frontiers in Evolutionary Algorithms,* 614-617.

Giles, C., & Maxwell, T. (1987). Learing, invariance, and generalization in high-order neural networks. *Applied Optics, 26*(23)*,* 4972-4978.

Larrañaga, P., & Lozano, J. A. (2001). *Estimation of distribution algorithms: A new tool for evolutionary computation.* Nederland: Kluwer Academic Publishers.

Leung, M.T., Chen, A.S., & Daouk, H. (2000). Forecasting exchange rates using general regression neural networks. *Computers and Operations Research, 27,* 1093-1110.

Maxwell, T., & Giles, C. (1986). Transformation invariance using high order correlations in neural network architectures. *IEEE International Congress on Syst. Man Cybern, 8,* 627-632.

Ratle, A., & Sebag, M. (2001). Avoiding the bloat with probabilistic grammar guided genetic programming. In Collet, P., Fonlupt, C., Hao, J.K., Lutton, E., and Schoenauer, M., (Eds.), *Artificial Evolution 5th International Conference, Evolution Artificielle, EA 2001, 2310,* 255–266.

Yanai, K., & Iba, H. (2003). Estimation of distribution programming based on bayesian network. In *Proceedings of Congress on Evolutionary Computation,* Canberra, Australia (pp.1618–1625).

Zhang, G.P., & Berardi, V.L. (2001). Time series forecasting with neural network ensembles: An application for exchange rate prediction. *Journal of the Operational Research Society, 52,* 652-664.

Zhang, M. (2003, May 13-15). Financial data simulation using PL-HONN Model. In *Proceedings IASTED International Conference on Modelling and Simulation,* Marina del Rey, CA (pp.229-233).

Zhang, M., & Lu, B. (2001, July). Financial data simulation using M-PHONN model. In *Proceedings of the International Joint Conference on Neural Networks*, Washington, DC (pp.1828-1832).

Chapter VI
Higher Order Neural Networks for Stock Index Modeling

Yuehui Chen
University of Jinan, China

Peng Wu
University of Jinan, China

Qiang Wu
University of Jinan, China

ABSTRACT

Artificial Neural Networks (ANNs) have become very important in making stock market predictions. Much research on the applications of ANNs has proven their advantages over statistical and other methods. In order to identify the main benefits and limitations of previous methods in ANNs applications, a comparative analysis of selected applications is conducted. It can be concluded from analysis that ANNs and HONNs are most implemented in forecasting stock prices and stock modeling. The aim of this chapter is to study higher order artificial neural networks for stock index modeling problems. New network architectures and their corresponding training algorithms are discussed. These structures demonstrate their processing capabilities over traditional ANNs architectures with a reduction in the number of processing elements. In this chapter, the performance of classical neural networks and higher order neural networks for stock index forecasting is evaluated. We will highlight a novel slide-window method for data forecasting. With each slide of the observed data, the model can adjusts the variable dynamically. Simulation results show the feasibility and effectiveness of the proposed methods.

INTRODUCTION

Stock index forecasting is an integral part of everyday life. Current methods of forecasting require some elements of human judgment and are subject to error. Stock indices are a sequence of data points, measured typically at uniform time intervals. The analysis of *time series* may include many statistical methods that aim to understand such data by constructing a model. Such as:

1. Exponential smoothing methods
2. Regression methods
3. Autoregressive moving average (ARMA) methods
4. Threshold methods
5. Generalized autoregressive conditionally heteroskedastic (GARCH) methods

ARMA processing has shown to be the most effective tool to model a wide range of *time series*. The models of order (n, m) can be viewed as linear filters from the point of view of digital signal processing. The time structure of these filters is shown in Equation (1), where *y(k)* is the variable to be predicted using previous samples of the *time series*, *e(i)* is a sequence of independent and identically distributed terms which have zero mean, and *C* is a constant.

However, these models do not work properly when there are elements of the *time series* that show a nonlinear behavior. In this case, other models, such as time processing *neural networks*, must be applied.

Several *Evolutionary Computation* (EC) studies have a full insight of the dynamic system to describe (Back T, 1996; Robert R. & Trippi, 1993). For instance, some have used Artificial *Neural networks* (ANNs) (Davide & Francesco, 1993;

Edward Gately, 1996), Genetic Programming (GP) (Edward Gately, 1996; Santini & Tattamanzi 2001) and Flexible Neural Tree (FNT) (Yuehui Chen & Bo Yang, 2005) for stock index prediction, among others, recently have used a hybrid algorithm such as Gene Expression Programming (GEP) (Ferreira.C., 2002; Heitor S.Lopes & Wagner R.Weinert, 2004) and Immune Programming (IP) Algorithm (Musilek & Adriel, 2006) for predicting stock index.

Artificial *neural networks* (ANNs) represent one widely technique for stock market forecasting. Apparently, White (1988) first used *Neural Networks* for market forecasting. In other work, Chiang, Urban, and Baldridge (1996) have used ANNs to forecast the end-of-year net asset value of mutual funds. Trafalis (1999) used feed-forward ANNs to forecast the change in the S&P (500) index. Typically the predicted variable is continuous, so that stock market prediction is usually a specialized form of regression. Any type of neural network can be used for stock index prediction (the network type must, however, be appropriate for regression or classification, depending on the problem type). The network can also have any number of input and output variables (Hecht-Nielsen R, 1987). In addition to stock index prediction, *neural networks* have been trained to perform a variety of financial related tasks. There are experimental and commercial systems used for tracking commodity markets and futures, foreign exchange trading, financial planning, company stability, and bankruptcy prediction. Banks use *neural networks* to scan credit and loan applications to estimate bankruptcy probabilities, while money managers can use *neural networks* to plan and construct profitable portfolios in real-time. As the application of *neural networks* in the

Equation (1).

$$y(k) = a_1 * y(k-1) + \cdots + a_n * y(k-n) + e(k) + b_1 * e(k-1) + \cdots + b_{m-1} * e(k-m+1) + C$$

financial area is so vast, we will focus on stock market prediction.

However, most commonly there is a single variable that is both the input and the output. Despite the wide spread use of ANNs, there are significant problems to be addressed. ANNs are data-driven model, and consequently, the underlying rules in the data are not always apparent. Also, the buried noise and complex dimensionality of the stock market data make it difficult to learn or re-estimate the ANNs parameters. It is also difficult to come up with ANNs architecture that can be used for all domains. In addition, ANNs occasionally suffer from the overfitting problem.

STOCK INDICES FORECASTING

There are several motivations for trying to predict stock market prices. The most basic of these is financial gain. Any system that can consistently pick winners and losers in the dynamic market place would make the owner of the system very wealthy. Thus, many individuals including researchers, investment professionals, and average investors are continually looking for this superior system which will yield them high returns; there is a second motivation in the research and financial communities. It has been proposed in the Efficient Market Hypothesis (EMH) (Robert R. & L. Lee. 1996; Robert R. Trippi.1993; G. Tsibouris & M. Zeidenberg, 1995) that markets are efficient in that opportunities for profit are discovered so quickly that they cease to be opportunities. The EMH effectively states that no system can continually beat the market because if this system becomes public, everyone will use it, thus negating its potential gain. There has been no consensus on the EMH's validity, but many market observers tend to believe in its weaker forms, and thus are often unwilling to share proprietary investment systems (Apostolos & A.D. Zapranis.1995; Manfred & Wittkemper, 1995). Detecting trends of stock data is a decision support process. Although the

Random Walk Theory (Burton G, 1996) claims that price changes are serially independent, traders and certain academics have observed that there is no efficient market. The movements of market price are not random and predictable.

The stock indices modeling problem can be formulated as follows: Given values of an observed series, find the appropriate p and $F(\cdot)$. In words, the objective is to find a suitable mathematical model that can roughly explain the behavior of the dynamic system. The system can be seen as in Equation (2):

$$x(t) = F\left[x(t-1), x(t-2), \cdots, x(t-p)\right]$$

(2)

The function $F(\cdot)$ and the constant p are the "center of the storm". As shown above, several studies have a full insight of the dynamic system to describe F. *Evolutionary computation* models have been used in the past, mainly for chaotic, nonlinear and empirical *time series*. Statistical methods and *neural networks* are commonly used for stock indices prediction. Empirical results have shown that *neural networks* outperform linear regression (Marquez & Tim Hill, 1991). Although stock markets are complex, nonlinear, dynamic and chaotic, *neural networks* are reliable for modeling nonlinear, dynamic market signals (White H, 1988). *Neural networks* make very few assumptions as opposed to normality assumptions commonly found in statistical methods. It can perform prediction after learning the underlying relationship between the input variables and outputs. From a statistician's point of view, *neural networks* are analogous to nonparametric, nonlinear regression models.

ARTIFICIAL NEURAL NETWORKS (ANNS)

Typical *neural network* consist of layers. In a single layered network there is an input layer of source nodes and an output layer of neurons. A multi-layer network has in addition one or more hidden layers of hidden neurons. This type of networks is displayed in Figure 1. The hidden neurons raise the network's ability to extract higher order statistics from input data (Wood & Dasgupta, 1996; Robert J. & Van Eyden, 1996). This is a crucial quality, especially if there is a large input layer. Furthermore a network is said to be fully connected if every node in each layer of the network is connected to every other node in the adjacent forward layer. In a partially connected structure at least one synaptic connection is missing.

Neural Networks can be formulated as follows:

$$Y_j^2 = f(w_0 + \sum_{i=1}^{n} Y_i^1 * w_{ij}), j = 1,2,..,n$$

$$Y_k^3 = f(w_0 + \sum_{j=1}^{p} Y_j^2 * w_{jk}), k = 1,2,..,m$$

where Y_j^1=an N-element input vector, Y_j^2=output of hidden layer, Y_j^3=output of NNs, w=adaptable weights from different layers, and f=neuron threshold function (e.g. sigmoid function).

Classical network adopts first order steepest descent technique as learning algorithm (Eitan Michael, 1993; T. Kimoto & Asakawa, 1990). Weights are modified in a direction that corresponds to the negative gradient of the error surface. Gradient is an extremely local pointer and does not point to global minimum (Apostolos-Paul & A.D. Zapranis, 1995). This hill-climbing search is in zigzag motion and may move towards a wrong direction, getting stuck in a local minimum. The direction may be spoiled by subsequent directions, leading to slow convergence. In addition, classical back propagation is sensitive to the parameters such as learning rate and momentum rate. For examples, the value of learning rate is critical in the sense that too small value will make have slow convergence and too large value will make the search direction jump wildly and never converge. The optimal values of the parameters are difficult to find and often obtained empirically.

However, *stock market prediction* networks have also been implemented using Genetic Algorithms (Back B, Laitinen & Ser, 1996; Michael & Atam, 1993), recurrent networks (Kamijo & Tanigawa, 1993), modular networks (Klimasauskas, 1993; Kimoto & Asakawa, 1990). Recurrent network architectures are the second most commonly implemented architecture. The motivation behind using recurrence is that pricing patterns may repeat in time. A network which remembers previous inputs or feedbacks previous outputs may have greater success in determining these time dependent patterns. There are a variety of such networks which may have recurrent connections between layers, or remember previous outputs and use them as new inputs to the system (increases input space dimensionality).The performance of these networks are quite good. A self-organizing system was also developed by Wilson (Wilson, 1994) to predict stock prices. The self-organizing network was designed to construct a nonlinear chaotic model of stock prices from volume and price data. Features in the data were automatically extracted and classified by the system. The benefit in using a self-organizing neural network is it reduces the number of features (hidden nodes) required for pattern classification, and the network organization is developed automatically during

Figure 1. A fully connected feed-forward network with one hidden layer and one output layer

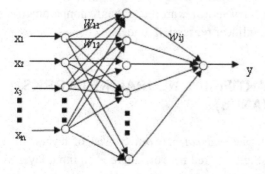

training. Wilson used two self-organizing *neural networks* in tandem; one selected and detected features of the data, while the other performed pattern classification. Overfitting and difficulties in training were still problems in this organization.

However, there is no one correct network organization (Eitan, 1993; Emad &Saad, 1996). Each of network architecture has its own benefits and drawbacks. Back propagation networks are common because they offer good performance, but are often difficult to train and configure. Recurrent networks offer some benefits over back propagation networks because their "memory feature" can be used to extract time dependencies in the data, and thus enhance prediction. More complicated models may be useful to reduce error or network configuration problems, but are often more complex to train and analyze.

Business is a diverted field with several general areas of specialization such as accounting or financial analysis. Almost any neural network application would fit into one business area or financial analysis. There is some potential for using *neural networks* for business purposes, including resource allocation and scheduling. There is also a strong potential for using *neural networks* for data mining, which is, searching for patterns implicit within the explicitly stored information in databases. Most of the funded work in this area is classified as proprietary. Thus, it is not possible to report on the full extent of the work going on. Most work is applying *neural networks*, such as the Hopfield-Tank network for optimization and scheduling.

The ultimate goal is for *neural networks* to outperform the market or index averages. The Tokyo stock trading systems (Kimoto & Asakawa, 1990) outperformed the buy-and-hold strategy and the Tokyo index. As well, most of these systems process large amounts of data on many different stocks much faster than human operators. Thus, a neural network can examine more market positions or charts than experienced traders.

Using *neural networks* to forecast stock market prices will be a continuing area of research as researchers and investors strive to outperform the market, with the ultimate goal of bettering their returns. It is unlikely that new theoretical ideas will come out of this applied work. However, interesting results and validation of theories will occur as *neural networks* are applied to more complicated problems. For example, network pruning and training optimization are two very important research topics which impact the implementation of financial *neural networks*. Financial *neural networks* must be trained to learn the data and generalize, while being prevented from over-training and memorizing the data. Also, due to their large number of inputs, network pruning is important to remove redundant input nodes and speed-up training and recall.

As shown above, the major research thrust in this area should be determining better network architectures. The commonly used back propagation network offers good performance, but this performance could be improved by using recurrence or reusing past inputs and outputs (Eiatn, 1993). *Neural networks* appear to be the best modeling method currently available as they capture nonlinearities in the system without human intervention. Continued work on improving neural network performance may lead to more insights in the chaotic nature of the systems they model. However, it is unlikely a neural network will ever be the perfect prediction device that is desired because the factors in a large dynamic system, like the stock market, are too complex to be understood for a long time.

HIGHER ORDER NEURAL NETWORKS (HONNS)

Background on HONNs

Standard ANNs models suffer from some limitations. They do not always perform well because of the complexity (higher frequency components and higher order nonlinearity) of the economic data being simulated, and the *neural networks* function as "black boxes" and are thus unable to provide explanations for their behavior, although some recent successes have been reported with rule extraction from trained ANNs (Burns, 1986; Craven & Shavlik, 1997). This latter feature is viewed as a disadvantage by users, who would rather be given a rationale for the simulation at hand.

In an effort to overcome the limitations of conventional ANNs, some researchers have turned their attention to *higher order neural networks* (HONNs) models (LU & Setiono, 1995; Hu & Shao, 1992). HONNs models are able to provide some rationale for the simulations they produce, and thus can be regarded as "open box" rather than "black box". Moreover, HONNs are able to simulate higher frequency, higher order non-linear data. Polynomials or linear combinations of trigonometric functions are often used in the modeling of financial data. Using HONNs models for financial simulation and/or modeling would lead to open box solutions, and hence be more readily accepted by target users (i.e., financial experts).

Higher order neural networks have been shown to have impressive computational, storage, and learning capabilities. Early in the history of neural network research it was known that nonlinearly separable subsets of pattern space can be dichotomized by nonlinear discriminate functions (Psaltis & Park, 1986).

Attempts to adaptively generate useful discriminate functions led to the study of Threshold Logic Units (TLUs). The most famous TLU is the perceptron (Minsky & Papert, 1969), which in its original form was constructed from randomly generated functions of arbitrarily high order. Minsky and Papert, studied TLUs of all orders, and came to the conclusions that higher order TLUs were impractical due to the combinatorial explosion of higher order terms, and that first-order TLUs

were too limited to be of much interest. Minsky and Papert also showed that single feed-forward slabs of first-order TLUs can implement only linearly separable mappings. Since most problems of interest are not linearly separable, this is a very serious limitation. One alternative is to cascade slabs of first-order TLUs. The units embedded in the cascade (hidden units) can then combine the outputs of previous units and generate nonlinear maps. However, training in cascades is very difficult because there is no simple way to provide the hidden units with a training signal. Multislab learning rules require thousands of iterations to converge, and sometimes do not converge at all, due to the local minimum problem.

These problems can be overcome by using single slabs of higher order TLUs. The higher order terms are equivalent to previously specified hidden units, so that a single higher order slab can now take the place of many slabs of first order units. Since there are no hidden units to be trained, the extremely fast and reliable single-slab learning rules can be used.

More recent research involving higher order correlations includes optical implementations(D. Psaltis & Hong,1986; Psaltis & Park, 1986; Athale & Szu, 1986; Owechko & G.J. Dunning, 1987; Griffin & Giles,1987), higher order conjunctive connections(Hinton, 1981; Feldman, 1982; Ballard, 1986), sigma-pi units, associative memories(Chen & Lee,1986; Lee & Doolen,1986; Peretto & Niez,1986), and a higher order extension of the Boltzmann machine(Sejnowski, 1986).

The addition of a layer of hidden units dramatically increase the power of layered feed forward networks, indeed, networks with a single hidden layer using arbitrary squashing functions are capable of approximating any measurable function from one finite dimensional space to another to any desired degree of accuracy, provided sufficiently many hidden units are available. In particular, the multilayered perception (MLP)using the "back propagation" learning algorithm has been successfully applied to many applications involving function approximation, pattern recognition, prediction and adaptive control. However, the training speeds for MLP are typically much slower than those for feed forward networks comprising of a single layer of linear threshold units due to back propagation of error induces by multilayering.

HONNs Structures

A higher order neuron can be defined Threshold Logic Unit (HOTLU) which includes terms contributed by various higher order weights. Usually, but not necessarily, the output of a HOTLU is (0, 1) or (-1, +1). A *higher order neural networks* slab is defined as a collection of higher order logic unit (HOTLU). A simple HOTLU slab can be described by Equation (3)

$$y_i = S\big[net(i)\big] = S\big[T_0(i) + T_1(i) + T_2(i) + T_3(i) + \cdots + T_k(i)\big]$$
(3)

where y_i is the output of the ith high-order neuron unit, and S is a sigmoid function. $T_i(i)$ is the nth order term for the ith unit, and k is the order of the unit. The zeroth-order term is an adjustable threshold, denoted by $T_0(i)$. The nth order term is a linear weighted sum over nth order products of inputs, examples of which are:

$$T_1(i) = \sum_j w_1(i,j)x(j)$$

$$T_2(i) = \sum_j \sum_k w_2(i,j,k)x(j)x(k)$$

where $x(j)$ is the jth input to the ith high-order neuron, and $w_n(i,j,\ldots)$ is an adjustable weight which captures the nth order correlation between an nth order product of inputs and the output of the unit.

The authors have developed several different HONNs models during the past decade or so. Several slabs can be cascaded to produce multislab networks by feeding the output of one slab to another slab as input. The sigma-pi *neural networks*

are multilevel networks which can have higher order terms at each level. As such, most of the *neural networks* described here can be considered as a special case of the sigma-pi units. A learning algorithm for these networks is generalized back-propagation. However, the sigma-pi units as originally formulated did not have invariant weight terms, though it is quite simple to incorporate such invariance in these units.

We now present a HONNs model derived from traditional first order *neural networks*. First order *neural networks* can be formulated as follows, assuming simple McCullough-and-pitts-type neurals (Giles & Maxwell, 1987):

$$Y_j^2 = f(w_0 + \sum_{i=1}^n Y_i^1 * w_{ij}), j = 1,2,..,n$$

$$Y_k^3 = f(w_0 + \sum_{j=1}^p Y_j^2 * w_{jk}), k = 1,2,..,m$$

where Y_j^1 = N-element input vector, w=adaptable weights from different layers, and f=neuron threshold function (e.g. sigmoid). Higher order correlations in the training data require more complex structure, characterized as follows:

$$Y_j^2 = f\left[w_0(i) + \sum_j x(j) * w_1 + \sum_j \sum_k x(j)x(k) * w_2 + \cdots\right]$$

$$Y_k^3 = f(w_0 + \sum_j^m Y_j^2 * w_{jk}) \qquad k = 1,2,\ldots m$$

where $x(j)$ is the jth input to the nth high-order neuron, and w is an adjustable weight between layers, f is neuron threshold function(e.g. sigmoid). Figure 2 shows the structure of the HONNs model.

HONNs applications

The use of HONNs as basic modules in the construction of dynamic system identifiers and of controllers for highly uncertain system, has already been established. One of the difficulties

Figure 2. A structure of HONNs model

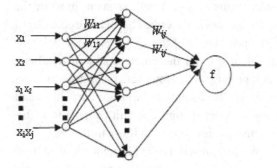

encountered in the application of recurrent *neural networks* is the derivation of efficient learning algorithms that also guarantee stability of the overall system. However in recurrent *higher order neural networks* the dynamic components are distributed throughout the network in the form of dynamic neurons. It is known that if enough higher order connections are allowed then this network is capable of approximating arbitrary dynamical systems.

The application of *higher order neural networks* (HONNs) for image recognition and image enhancement of digitized images has been used in many fields. A key property of *neural networks* is their ability to recognize invariance and extract essential parameters from complex high dimensional data. The most significant advantage of the HONNs over first-order networks is that invariance to geometric transformations can be incorporated into the network and need not be learned through iterative weight updates. A third order HONNs can be used to achieve translation, scale, and rotation invariant recognition with a significant reduction in training time over other neural net paradigms such as the multilayer perceptron.

Also the ability of *Higher Order Neural Networks* as forecasting tools to predict the future trends of financial *time series* data has been proved.

Learning Process of HONNs

The learning process involves implementing a specified mapping in a neural network by means of an iterative adaptation of the weights based on a particular learning rule and the network's response to a training set. The mapping to be learned is represented by a set of examples consisting of a possible input vector paired with a desired output. The training set is a subset of the set of all possible examples of the mapping. The implementation of the learning process involves sequentially presenting to the network examples of the mapping, taken from the training set, as input-output pairs. Following each presentation, the weights of the network are adjusted so that they capture the correlative structure of the mapping. A typical single-slab learning rule is the perceptron rule, which for the second order update rule can be expressed as:

$$w_2'(i,j,k) = w_2(i,j,k) + \left[t(i) - y(i) \right] x(j) x(k)$$

Here $t(i)$ is the target output and $y(i)$ is the actual output of the *i*th unit for input vector x. Similar learning rules exist for the other w_i terms. If the network yields the correct output for each example input in the training set, we say that the network has converged, or learned the training set. If, after learning the training set, the network gives the correct output on a set of examples in the training set that it has not yet seen, we say that the network has generalized properly.

Tabu Search

Tabu Search is a powerful approach that has been applied with great success to many difficult combinatorial problems. A particularly nice feature of TS is that, like all approaches based on local search, it can quite easily handle the "dirty" complicating constraints that are typically found in real-life applications. It is thus a really practical approach. *Tabu Search* allows the search to explore solutions that do not decrease the objective function value only in those cases where these solutions are not forbidden (Glover & Taillard, 1993). This is usually obtained by keeping track of the last solutions in term of the action used to transform one solution to the next. A solution is forbidden if it is obtained by applying a Tabu action to the current solution. In this algorithm, in order to improve the efficiency of the exploration process, some historical information related to the evolution of the search is kept (basically the itinerary through the solutions visited). Such information will be used to guide the movement from one solution to the next one avoiding cycling. This is one of the most important features of this algorithm (Franze & Speciale, 2001). The flowchart of basic TS is presented in Figure 3 as follows.

In the initialisation unit, a random feasible solution $X_{initial} \in X$ for the problem is generated,

and the Tabu list and other parameters are initialized. In the neighbour production unit, a feasible set of solutions is produced from the present solution according to the Tabu list and aspiration criteria. The evaluation unit evaluates each solution X^* produced from the present X_{now} one. After the next solution X_{next} is determined by the selection unit, in the last unit the history record of the search is modified. If the next solution determined is better than the best solution found so far X_{best}, the next solution is replaced with the present best solution.

PSO Algorithm

In the *PSO* (Kennedy & Eberhart, 1995) algorithm each individual is called a "particle", and is subject to a movement in a multidimensional space that represents the belief space. Particles have memory, thus retaining part of their previous state. There is no restriction for particles to share the same point in belief space, but in any case their individuality is preserved. Each particle's movement is the composition of an initial random velocity and two randomly weighted influences: individuality, the tendency to return to the particle's best previous position, and sociality, the tendency to move towards the neighborhood's best previous position. Each particle keeps track of its coordinates in the problem space which are associated with the best solution (fitness) it has achieved so far. The fitness value is also stored. This value is called pbest. When a particle takes all the population as its topological neighbors, the best value is a global best and is called gbest.

Figure 3. Flowchart of a basic Tabu search

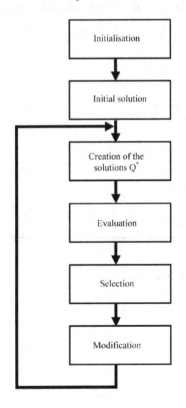

$$v = v + c1*rand()*(pbest\text{-}present) + c2*rand()* (gbest\text{-}present) \qquad (a)$$

$$present = present + v \qquad (b)$$

Flow of the algorithm is shown in Box 1.

PSO algorithms are especially useful for parameter optimization in continuous, multi-dimensional search spaces. PSO is mainly inspired by social behaviour patterns of organisms that live and interact within large groups. In particular, PSO incorporates swarming behaviour observed in flocks of birds, schools of fish, or swarms of bees.

A Dynamic Decision Model of HONNs

As expounded previously, designating the correct size for the analysis window is critical to the success of any forecasting model (Lee & Chang, 1997; Leigh & Purvis, 2002). Automatic discovery of this size is indispensable when the forecasting concern is not well understood. With each slide of the window, the model adjusts its size dynamically.

This is accomplished in the following way:

1. Select two initial window sizes, one of size n and one of size n + i or n - i, where n and i are positive integers.

2. Run dynamic generations at the beginning of the *time series* data with window size n and n + i, use the best solution for each of these two independent runs to predict the future data points, and measure their predictive accuracy.

3. Select another two window sizes based on which window size had better accuracy. For example if the smaller of the two window sizes (size n) predicted more accurately, then choose the current window sizes, one of size n and one of size n + i ;If the larger of the two window sizes (size n + i) predicted more accurately, then choose new window sizes n + i and n + 2i.

4. Slide the analysis window to include the next *time series* observation. Use the two selected window sizes to run another two dynamic generations, predict future data, and measure their prediction accuracy.

Box 1.

For each particle
_____Initialize particle
END
Do
_____For each particle
_____Calculate fitness value
_____If the fitness value is better than the best fitness value (pBest) in history
_____set current value as the new pBest
_____End
_____Choose the particle with the best fitness value of all the particles as the gBest
_____For each particle
_____Calculate particle velocity according equation (a)
_____Update particle position according equation (b)
_____End
While maximum iterations or minimum error criteria is not attained

5. Repeat the previous two steps until the analysis window reaches the end of historical data.

Thus, at each slide of the analysis window, predictive accuracy is used to determine the direction in which to adjust the window sizes (Wanger & Michalewicz, 2005). Consider the following example. Suppose the *time series* followed is to be analyzed and forecast:

{22, 33, 30, 27, 24, 20, 21, 20, 23, 26, 29, 30, 28, 29, 30, 31}

The *dynamic decision* model starts by selecting two initial window sizes, one larger than the other. Then, two separate dynamic generations are run at the beginning of data, each with its own window size. After each dynamic generation, the best solution is used to predict the future data and the accuracy of this prediction is measured.

Figure 4 illustrates these steps. In the initial step, if win2's prediction accuracy is better, two new window sizes for win1 and win2 are selected with sizes of 3 and 4, respectively. Then the analysis window slides to include the next *time series* value, two new dynamic generations are run, and the best solutions for each are used to predict future data. As shown in Figure 5, win1 and win2 now include the next *time series* value, 27, and pred has shifted one value to the right (above); if the win1s prediction accuracy is better, win1 and win2 with the current window sizes just slide to the next value 27(below).

These processes of selecting two new window sizes, sliding the analysis window, running two new dynamic generations, and predicting future data is repeated until the analysis window reaches the end of *time series* data.

Figure 4. Initial steps, win1 and win2 represent data analysis windows of size 2 and 3, respectively, and pred represents the future data predicted.

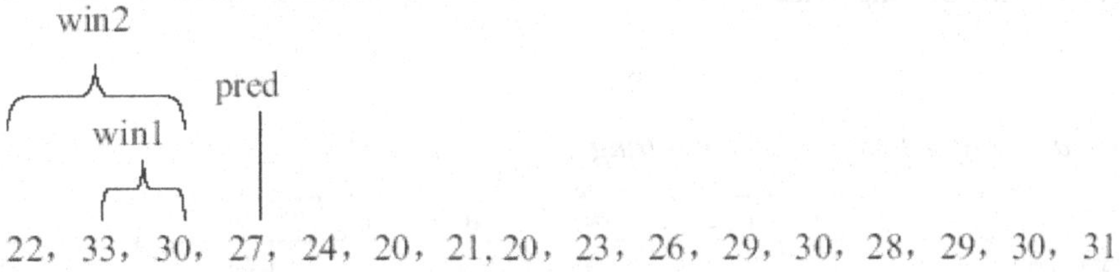

22, 33, 30, 27, 24, 20, 21, 20, 23, 26, 29, 30, 28, 29, 30, 31

Figure 5. Data analysis windows slide to new value

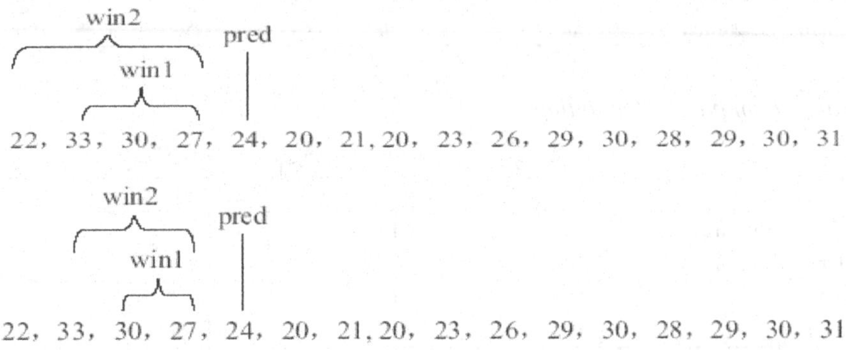

22, 33, 30, 27, 24, 20, 21, 20, 23, 26, 29, 30, 28, 29, 30, 31

22, 33, 30, 27, 24, 20, 21, 20, 23, 26, 29, 30, 28, 29, 30, 31

APPLICATION OF HONNS TO FINANCIAL TIME SERIES DATA

To test the efficacy of the proposed method we have used stock prices in the IT sector: the daily stock price of Apple Computer Inc., International Business Machines Corporation (IBM) and Dell Inc (Hassan. & Baikunth,2006), collected from www.finance.yahoo.com. Also, the experiments for foreign exchange rates are established for evaluating the performance of the proposed methods. The data used are daily foreign exchange rates obtained from the Pacific Exchange Rate Service, provided by Professor Werner Antweiler, University of British Columbia, Vancouver, Canada. The data is US dollar exchange rate against Euros (the daily data from 1 January 2000 to 31 December 2001 as training data set, and the data from 1 January 2002 to 31 December 2002 as evaluation test set or out-of-sample datasets, which are used to evaluate the good or bad performance of the predictions, based on evaluation measurements). As shown above, we don't need all of the stock data as the previous study but we just use the close price from the daily stock market. The forecast variable here is also the closing price.

The following formula was used to scale the data to within the range 0 to 1, in order to meet constraints:

$$input = \frac{current\_value - \min\_value}{\max\_value - \min\_value}$$

This equation was applied to each separate entry of a given set of simulation data—in other words, the *current_value*. The smallest entry in the data set serves as the min_*value*, and the largest entry as the max_*value*.

The performance of the method is measured in terms of Root Means Square Error(RMSE) :

$$RMSE = \sqrt{\frac{1}{n}\sum_{i=1}^{n}(y_i - p_i)^2}$$

where:

n : total number of test data sequences
y_i: actual stock price on day i
p_i: forecast stock price on day i.

The *dynamic decision model* requires that a number of parameters be specified before a run. Some of these are general parameters commonly

Table 1. Tabu search algorithm parameter setting

	Apple Inc	IBM Corp	Dell Inc
Population size	20	20	20
Window slide increment	1	1	1
Start windowsizes	2	2	2
Number of length	5	5	5
Training generation	500	500	500

Table 2. PSO algorithm parameter setting

	Apple Inc	IBM Corp	Dell Inc
Agent	20	20	20
Window slide increment	1	1	1
Start windowsize	2	2	2
Maxv	1	1	1
Training generation	500	500	500

found in application and Some are special parameters only used by the *dynamic decision model*. Table 1 and Table 2 give the parameter values used by the models.

For a set of runs, forecasting performance is measured by calculating RMSE value over all runs. Table 3 lists the observed results for the three daily stock prices, respectively comparing with static prediction model by traditional NNs structure (as shown in Figure 1) and HONNs structure.

Comparing the different models by traditional NN structure (above) and second order structure (below), the *dynamic decision model* simulation results is better than static model. Predicting IBM stock indices, Tabu search algorithm results are shown in Figure 6.

As an example of additional *time series*, we compare with traditional NNs architectures by the exchange rates, Tabu search algorithm is also used to optimize parameters.

The NNs and HONNs are commonly used for stock indices prediction. Because of their ability to deal with uncertain, fuzzy, or insufficient data which fluctuate rapidly in very short periods of time, *neural networks* (NNs) have become very important method for stock market predictions (Schoeneburg,1990). Numerous research and applications of NNs in solving business problems has proven their advantage. According to Wong,

Bodnovich and Selvi (Wong, B.K., 1997), the most frequent areas of NNs applications in past 10 years are production/operations (53.5%) and finance (25.4%). NNs in finance have their most frequent applications in stock performance and stock selection predictions.

CONCLUSION

We have introduced the concepts of typical artificial *neural networks* and higher order artificial *neural networks*. In this study the dynamic decision *time series* model is developed and tested for forecasting efficacy on real *time series*. Results show that the dynamic decision model outperforms traditional models for all experiments. These findings affirm the potential as an adaptive, non-linear model for real-world forecasting applications and suggest further investigations. The dynamic decision model presents an attractive forecasting alternative:

1. The dynamic model is an automatically self-adjusting model. Thus, in a changing environment, it may be able to adapt and predict accurately without human intervention.
2. It can take advantage of a large amount of historical data. Conventional forecasting

Table 3. The performance improvement of the dynamic decision model (RMSE)

Traditional NNs structure					
Dynamic			Static		
App	IBM	Dell	App	IBM	Dell
TS	0.127681	0.026690	0.051267	0.245945	0.032381	0.097973
PSO	0.059310	0.027413	0.032584	0.073416	0.032786	0.038484

Second order NNs					
Dynamic			Static		
App	IBM	Dell	App	IBM	Dell
TS	0.365000	0.025522	0.085153	0.409234	0.033616	0.143801
PSO	0.120930	0.029089	0.055579	0.552091	0.322913	0.379449

Figure 6. Forecasting accuracy comparison by two methods

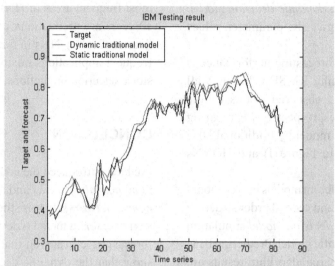

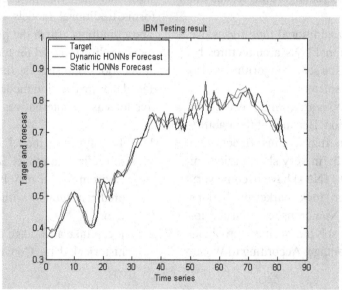

Table 4. The comparison with traditional ANNs architectures

US dollar exchange rate against Euros			
HONNs structure		Traditional NNs structure	
Dynamic model	Static model	Dynamic model	Static model
0.026479	0.030750	0.020562	0.031089

Figure 7. Forecasting accuracy comparison

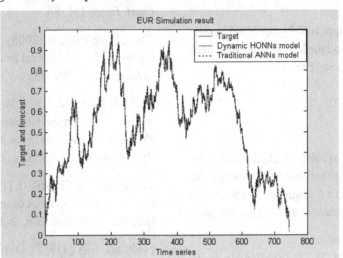

models require that the number of historical data to be analyzed be set a priori. In many cases, this means that a large number of historical data is considered to be too old to represent the current data generating process and is, thus, disregarded. This older data, however, may contain information (e.g., patterns) that can be used during analysis to better capture the current process. This model is designed to analyze all historical data, save knowledge of past processes, and exploit this learned knowledge to capture the current process.

The direction for dynamic model development is in the area of forecast combination. It is necessary to make multiple runs and use some method to combine the multiple forecasts produced into a single, out-of-sample forecast. The method utilized in this study is a simple one that ranks each dynamic run based on the accuracy of its most recent past forecast, selects the top one to run. It is reasonable to expect that a more sophisticated forecast combining method would result in performance improvements. One interesting method is the following. Suppose the combination model of the equation (redisplayed here) is considered:

$$F = \alpha_1 f_1 + \alpha_2 f_2 + \cdots + \alpha_n f_n$$

In this model, F is the combined forecast, $f_1, f_2, ..., f_n$ are the single forecasts to be combined, and $\alpha_1, \alpha_2, ..., \alpha_n$ are corresponding weights subject to the condition that their sum is one. Using all past forecasts produced by a set of n dynamic runs as training data, Genetic Algorithm or *PSO Algorithm* could be employed to evolve optimal weights for this model.

Future experiments are also planned in which the dynamic model is applied to other well-known economic *time series* as well as *time series* important to other fields such as weather-related series, seismic activity, and series arising from biological/medical processes.

All in all, the dynamic model is an effective model for real world forecasting applications and may prove to stimulate new advances in the area of *time series* forecasting.

ACKNOWLEDGMENT

This research was supported by the NSFC under grant No. 60573065 and the Key Subject Research Foundation of Shandong Province.

REFERENCES

Apostolos-Paul, R., Zapranis, A.D., & Francis, G. (1995).Modelling stock returns in the framework of APT: A comparative study with regression models. In *Neural Networks in the Capital Markets*, pp. 101–126.

Athale, R. A., Szu, H. H., & Friedlander, C. B. (1986). Optical implementation of associative memory with controlled nonlinearity in the correlation domain, *Optics Letters, 11*(7), 482.

Azoff, E. M. (1993). Reducing error in neural network time series forecasting. *Neural Computing & Applications*, pp.240-247.

Back, B., Laitinen, T., & Sere, K. (1996): Neural networks and genetic algorithms for bankruptcy predictions. *Expert Systems with Applications, 11*, 407-413.

Back, T. (1996). *Evolutionary algorithms in theory and practice: Evolution strategies, evolutionary programming, and genetic algorithms.* Oxford University Press

Ballard, D. H. (1986). Cortical connections and parallel processing: Structure and function. *Behav. Brain Sci. 9, 67*.

Burns, T. (1986). The interpretation and use of economic predictions. In *Proc. Roy. Soc. A,* pp. 103–125.

Burton, G. (1996). *A random walk down Wall Street.* W.W. Norton & Company

Chen, H. H., Lee, Y. C., Maxwell, T., Sun, G. Z., Lee, H. Y., & Giles, C. L. (1986). High order correlation model for associative memory. *AIP Conf. Proc.* 151, 86.

Chen, Y., & Yang, B. (2005). Time-series forecasting using flexible neural tree model. *Information Sciences, 174,* 219–235

Chinetti, D., Gardin, F., & Rossignoli, C. (1993). A neural network model for stock market prediction. *Proc. Int'l Conference on Artificial Intelligence Applications on Wall Street.*

Craven, M., & Shavlik, J. (1997). Understanding time series networks: A case study in rule extraction. *Int. J. Neural Syst., 8*(4), 373–384.

Feldman, J. A., (1982). Dynamic connections in neural networks. *Biol. Cybern. 46,* 27.

Ferreira, C. (2002). *Gene expression programming: Mathematical modeling by an artificial intelligence.* Angra do Heroismo, Portugal

Franze, F., & Speciale, N. (2001). A Tabu-search-based algorithm for continuous multiminima problems. *International Journal for Numerical Engineering, 50,* 665–680.

Gately, E. (1996). *Neural networks for financial forecasting.* Wiley

Glover, F., Taillard, E., & Werra, D. (1993). A user's guide to Tabu search. *Annals of Operations Research, 41, 3–28.*

Griffin, R. D., Giles, C. L., Lee, J. N., Maxwell, T., & Pursel, F. P. (1987). *Optical higher order neural networks for invariant pattern recognition.* Paper presented at Optical Society of America Annual Meeting.

Hassan, M. R., Nath, B., & Kirley, M. (2006). A fusion model of HMM, ANN and GA for stock market forecasting. *Expert Systems with Applications*

Hecht-Nielsen, R. (1987). Kolmogorov's mapping neural network existence theorem. *Proc. 1st IEEE Int'l Joint Conf. Neural Network.*

Hedar, A., & Fukushima, M. (2004). Heuristic pattern search and its hybridization with simulated annealing for nonlinear global optimization. *Optimization Methods and Software, 19,* 291–308.

Hinton, G. E. (1981). A parallel computation that assigns canonical object-based frames of reference. In A. Drina (Ed.), *Proceedings of 7th International Joint Conference on Artificial Intelligence,* (p. 683).

Kamijo, K., & Tanigawa, T. (1993). Stock price pattern recognition: A recurrent neural network approach. In *Neural networks in finance and investing,* (pp. 357–370). Probus Publishing Company

Kennedy, J., & Eberhart, R.C. (1995). Particle swarm optimization. *Proceedings of IEEE International Conference on Neural Networks,* Piscataway, NJ.

Kimoto, T., Asakawa, K., Yoda, M., & Takeoka, M. (1990). Stock market prediction system with modular neural networks. In *Proceedings of the International Joint Conference on Neural Networks,* Vol 1, pp. 1–6.

Klimasauskas, C. (1993). Applying neural networks. In *Neural networks in finance and investing,* (pp. 47–72). Probus Publishing Company.

Lee, Y. C., Doolen, G., Chen, H. H., Sun, G. Z., Maxwell, T., Lee, H. Y., & Giles, C. L. (1986). Machine learning using a higher order correlation network. *Physica D, 22,* 276.

Lopes, H. S., & Weinert, W. R. (2004, 10-12 November). A gene expression programming system for time series modeling. *Proceedings of XXV Iberian Latin American Congress on Computational Methods in Engineering(CILAMCE),* Recife, Brazil.

Lu, H., Setiono, R., & Liu, H. (1995). Neuro rule: A connectionist approach to data mining. In *Proc. Very Large Databases VLDB'95,* San Francisco, CA, pp. 478–489.

Marquez, L., Hill, T., Worthley, R., & Remus, W. (1991). Neural network models as an alternate to regression. *Proc. of IEEE 24th Annual Hawaii Int'l Conference on System Sciences, pp.129-135, Vol VI*

McInerney, M., Atam, P., & Hawan, D. (1993).Use of Genetic algorithms with back-propagation in training of feed-forward neural networks. *Proc. of IEEE Int'l Joint Conference on Neural Networks,* Vol. 1, pp. 203-208

Minsky, M. L., & Papert, S. (1969). *Perceptrons.* Cambridge, MA: MIT Press.

Musilek, P., Lau, A., & Reformart, M. (2006): Immune programming. *Information Sciences, 176,* 972-1002

Neal, W., Michalewicz, Z., & Khouja, M. (2005). Time series forecasting for dynamic environments: The DyFor genetic program model. *IEEE Transactions on Evolutionary Computation.*

Nilsson, N. J., (1965). *Learning machines.* New York: McGraw-Hill.

Owechko, Y., Dunning, G. J., & Maron, E. (1987). Holographic associative memory with nonlinearities in the correlation domain. *Applied Optics, 26*(10), 1900.

Peretto, P., & Niez, J. J. (1986). Long term memory storage capacity of multiconnected neural networks. *Biological Cybernetics, 54,* 53.

Psaltis, D., & Park, C. H. (1986). Nonlinear discriminant functions and associative memories, *AIP Conf. Proc. 151,* 370.

Psaltis, D., Hong, J., & Venkatesh, S. (1986). Shift invariance in optical associative memories. *Proc. Soc. Photo-Opt. Instrum. Eng. 625,* 189.

Robert, J., & Eyden, V. (1996). *The application of neural networks in the forecasting of share prices.* Finance and Technology Publishing.

Robert, R., & Trippi, J. (1993). *Neural networks in finance and investing.* Probus Publishing Company, 1993.

Robert, R., Trippi, J., & Lee, L. (1996). *Artificial intelligence in finance & investing*, Ch 10. IRWIN

Rosenblatt, F. (1962). *Principles of neurodynamics.* New York: Spartan.

Saad, Emad W., Danil V.P., & Donald C.W. (1996). Advanced neural network training methods for low false alarm stock trend prediction, *Proc. of World Congress on Neural Networks, Washington D.C.*

Santini, M., & Tattamanzi. A. (2001). Genetic programming for financial time series prediction. *Proceedings of EuroGP'2001, LNCS,* Vol. 2038, pp. 361-370. Berlin: Springer-Verlag.

Sejnowski, T. J. (1986). Higher-order Boltzmann machines. *AIP Conf. Proc. 151,* 398.

Steiner, Manfred, Hans-Georg & Wittkemper (1995). Neural networks as an alternative stock market model. In *Neural Networks in the Capital Markets*, pp. 137–148.

Tsibouris, G., & Zeidenberg, M. (1995). Testing the efficient markets hypothesis with gradient descent algorithms. In *Neural Networks in the Capital Markets*, pp. 127–136.

White, H. (1988). Economic prediction using neural networks: The case of IBM daily stock returns. *Proc. of IEEE Int'l Conference on Neural Networks.*

Wilson, C. L. (1994). Self-organizing neural network system for trading common stocks. In *Proc. ICNN'94, Int. Conf. on Neural Networks,* pages 3651–3654, Piscataway, NJ, IEEE Service Center.

Wood, D., & Dasgupta, B. (1996). Classifying trend movements in the MSCI USA capital market index: A comparison of regression, ARIMA and neural network methods. *Computer and Operations Research, 23*(6), 611.

ADDITIONAL READING

Blum, E., & Li, K.(1991). Approximation theory and feedforward networks. *Neural Networks, 4, 511–515.*

Brockwell, P.J., & Davis, R.A. (2002). *Introduction to time series and forecasting*, 2nd edition. New York: Springer.

De, J. E., Watson, R., & Pollack, J. (2001). Reducing bloat and promoting diversity using multi-objective methods. *Proceedings of the Genetic and Evolutionary Computation Conference (GECCO 2001)*, vol. 1, pp. 11-18.

Hedar, A., & Fukushima, M. (2002). Hybrid simulated annealing and direct search method for nonlinear unconstrained global optimization. *Optimization Methods and Software, 17,* 891–912.

Hu, S., & Yan, P. (1992). Level-by-level learning for artificial neural groups. *ACTA Electronica SINICA, 20*(10), 39–43.

Hu, Z., & Shao, H. (1992). The study of neural network adaptive control systems. *Contr. Decision, 7, 361–366.*

Iba, H., & Nikolaev, N. (2000). Genetic programming polynomial models of financial data series. *Proceedings of the 2000 Congress of Evolutionary Computation, vol. 1,* pp. 1459-1466.

Karayiannis, N., & Venetsanopoulos, A. (1993). Artificial neural networks: Learning algorithms. In *Performance Evaluation and Applications.* Boston, MA: Kluwer.

Langdon, W., & Poli, R. (1997). Fitness causes bloat. *Soft Computing in Engineering Design and Manufacturing, 1,* 13-22.

Langdon, W. (1998). The evolution of size in variable length representations. *IEEE International Conference of Evolutionary Computation, vol. 1*, pg. 633-638.

Lee, D., Lee, B., & Chang S.(1997). Genetic programming model for long term forecasting of electric power demand. *Electric Power Systems Research, 40, 17-22.*

Leigh, W., Purvis R., & Ragusa, J. (2002) Forecasting the NYSE composite index with technical analysis, pattern recognizer, neural network, and genetic algorithm: A case study in romantic decision support. *Decision Support Systems, 32,* 361-377.

McCluskey, P. G. (1993). Feedforward and recurrent neural networks and genetic programs for stock market and time series forecasting. *Technical Report CS-93-36*, Brown University, September.

McMillan, D. G. (2001). Nonlinear predictability of stock market returns: Evidence from nonparametric and threshold models. *International Review of Economics and Finance, 10,* 353-368.

Mulloy, B., Riolo R., & Savit, R. (1996). Dynamics of genetic programming and chaotic time series prediction. *Genetic Programming 1996: Proceedings of the First Annual Conference, vol. 1,* pp. 166-174.

Redding, N., Kowalczyk, A., & Downs, T. (1993). Constructive high-order network algorithm that is polynomial time, *Neural Networks, vol. 6, pp.997–1010.*

Referenes, A. P., Zapranis A., & Francis, G. (1994). Stock performance modeling using neural networks: A comparative study with regression models, *Neural Networks, 7(2),* 375-388.

Rumelhart, D.E., Hinton, G.E., & Williams, R.J. (1986). *Learning internal representations by error propagation, parallel distributed processing: Explorations the microstructure of cognition. Volume 1: Foundations.* MIT Press.

Schoeneburg, E. (1990). Stock price prediction using neural networks: A project report. *Neurocomputing, 2,* 17-27.

Stock, J. & Watson, M. (2003). Forecasting output and inflation: The role of asset prices. *Journal of Economic Literature, 41,* 788-829.

Trippi , R., & Turban, E. (1996). Neural networks in finance and investing: Using artificial intelligence to improve real-world performance. *Irwin Professional Pub.,*

Tsang, E., & Li, J. (2002). EDDIE for financial forecasting. In *Genetic algorithms and programming in computational finance*, pp. 161-174. Kluwer Series in Computational Finance.

Wong, B.K., Bonovich, T.A., & Selvi, Y., (1997). Neural network applications in business: A review and analysis of the literature (1988-95). *Decision Support Systems, 19,* 301-320

Zhang, M., Murugesan, S., & Sadeghi, M. (1995). Polynomial higher order neural network for economic data simulation. In *Proc. Int. Conf. Neural Inform. Processing,* Beijing, China, pp. 493–496.

Section II
Artificial Higher Order Neural Networks for Time Series Data

Chapter VII
Ultra High Frequency Trigonometric Higher Order Neural Networks for Time Series Data Analysis

Ming Zhang
Christopher Newport University, USA

ABSTRACT

This chapter develops a new nonlinear model, Ultra high frequency Trigonometric Higher Order Neural Networks (UTHONN), for time series data analysis. Results show that UTHONN models are 3 to 12% better than Equilibrium Real Exchange Rates (ERER) model, and 4 – 9% better than other Polynomial Higher Order Neural Network (PHONN) and Trigonometric Higher Order Neural Network (THONN) models. This study also uses UTHONN models to simulate foreign exchange rates and consumer price index with error approaching 0.0000%.

INTRODUCTION

Time series models are the most studied models in macroeconomics as well as in financial economics. Nobel Prize in Economic in 2003 rewards two contributions: nonstationarity and time-varying volatility. These contributions have greatly deepened our understanding of two central properties of many economic time series (Vetenskapsakademien, 2003). Nonstationarity is a property common to many macroeconomic and financial time series models. It means that a variable has no clear tendency to return to a constant value or a linear trend. Examples include the value of the US dollar expressed in Japanese yen and consumer price indices of the US and Japan. Granger (1981) changes the way of empirical models in macroeconomic relationships by introducing the concept of cointegrated variables. Granger and Bates (1969) research the combination of forecasts. Granger and Weiss (1983) show the importance of cointegration in the modeling of nonstationary economic series. Granger and Lee (1990) studied multicointegration. Granger and Swanson (1996) further develop multicointegration in studying of cointegrated variables. The first motivation of this chapter is to develop a new nonstationary data analysis system by using new generation computer techniques that will improve the accuracy of the analysis.

After Meese and Rogof's (1983A, and 1983B) pioneering study on exchange rate predictability, the goal of using economic models to beat naïve random walk forecasts still remains questionable (Taylor, 1995). One possibility is that the standard economic models of exchange rate determination are inadequate, which is a common response of many professional exchange rate forecasters (Kiliam and Taylor, 2003; Cheung and Chinn, 1999). Another possibility is that linear forecasting models fail to consider important nonlinear properties in the data. Recent studies document various nonlinearities in deviations of the spot exchange rate from economic fundamentals (Balke and Fomby, 1997; Taylor and Peel, 2000; Taylor et al., 2001). Gardeazabal and Regulez (1992) study monetary model of exchange rates and cointegration for estimating, testing and predicting long run and short run nominal exchange rates. MacDonald and Marsh (1999) provide a cointegration and VAR (Vector Autoregressive) modeling for high frequency exchange rates. Estimating the equilibrium exchange rates has been rigorously studied (Williamson 1994). Ibrahima A. Elbradawi (1994) provided a model for estimating long-run equilibrium real exchange rates. Based on Elbradawi's study, the average error percentage (error percentage = |error|/rate; average error percentage = total error percentage/n years) of long-run equilibrium real exchange rate is 14.22% for Chile (1968-1990), 20.06% for Ghana (1967-1990) and 4.73% for India (1967-1988). The second motivation for this chapter is to simulate actual exchange rate by developing new neural network models for improving prediction accuracy.

Barron, Gilstrap, and Shrier (1987) use polynomial neural networks for the analogies and engineering applications. Blum and Li (1991) and Hornik (1993) study approximation by feedforward networks. Chakraborty et al. (1992), and Gorr (1994) study the forecasting behavior of multivariate time series using neural networks. Azoff (1994) presents neural network time series forecasting of financial markets. Chen and Chen, (1993, 1995) provide the results of approximations of continuous functions by neural networks with application to dynamic systems. Chen and Chang (1996) study feedforward neural network with function shape auto-tuning. Scarselli and Tsoi (1998) conduct a survey of the existing methods for universal approximation using feed-forward neural networks. Granger (1995) studies modeling nonlinear relationships between extended-memory variables and briefly considered neural networks for building nonlinear models. Bierens and Ploberger (1997) derive the asymptotic distribution of the test statistic of a generalized version of the integrated conditional moment (ICM) test, which includes neural network tests. Chen and Shen (1998) give convergence rates for nonparametric regression via neural networks, splines, and wavelets. Hans and Draisma (1997) study a graphical method based on the artificial neural network model to investigate how and when seasonal patterns in macroeconomic time series change over time. Chang and Park (2003) use a simple neural network model to analyze index models with integrated time series. Shintani and Linton (2004) derive the asymptotic distribution of the nonparametric neural network estimation of Lyapunov exponents in a noisy system. However, all of the studies mentioned above use traditional artificial neural network models - black box models that do not provide users with a function that describes the relationship between the input and output. The third motivation of this chapter is to develop nonlinear "open box" neural network models that will provide rationale for network's decisions, also provide better results.

Traditional Artificial Neural Networks (ANNs) by default, employ the Standard BackPropagation (SBP) learning algorithm (Rumelhart, Hinton, and Williams,1986; Werbos, 1994), which despite being guaranteed to converge, can take a long time to converge to a solution. In the recent years, numerous modifications to SBP have been proposed in order to speed up the convergence process. Fahlman (1988) assumes the error surface is locally quadratic in order to approximate second-order (i.e. gradient) changes. Zell (1995) uses only the sign of the derivative to affect weight changes.

In addition to long convergence time, ANNs also suffer from several other well known limitations. First, ANNs can often become stuck in local, rather than global minima. Second, ANNs are unable to handle high frequency, non-linear, discontinuous data. Third, since ANNs function as "black boxes", they are incapable of providing explanations for their behavior. Researchers working in the economics and business area would rather have a rationale for the network's decisions. To overcome these limitations, research has focused on using Higher Order Neural Network (HONN) models for simulation and modeling (Redding, Kowalczyk, and Downs, 1993). HONN models are able to provide information concerning the basis of the data they are simulating and prediction, and therefore can be considered as 'open box' rather than 'black box' solutions. The forth motivation of this chapter is to develop new HONN models for nonstationary time series data analysis with more accuracy.

Psaltis, Park, and Hong (1988) study higher order associative memories and their optical implementations. Redding, Kowalczyk, Downs (1993) develop constructive high-order network algorithm. Zhang, Murugesan, and Sadeghi (1995) develop a Polynomial Higher Order Neural Network (PHONN) model for data simulation. The idea first extends to PHONN Group models for data simulation (Zhang, Fulcher, and Scofield, 1996), then to Trigonometric Higher Order Neural

Network (THONN) models for data simulation and prediction (Zhang, Zhang, and Keen, 1999). Zhang, Zhang, and Fulcher (2000) study HONN group model for data simulation. By utilizing adaptive neuron activation functions, Zhang, Xu, and Fulcher (2002) develop a new HONN neural network model. Furthermore, HONN models are also capable of simulating higher frequency and higher order nonlinear data, thus producing superior data simulations, compared with those derived from ANN-based models. Zhang and Fulcher (2004) publish a book chapter to provided detail mathematics for THONN models, which are used for high frequency, nonlinear data simulation. However, THONN models may have around 10% simulation error if the data are ultra high frequency. The fifth motivation of this chapter is to develop new HONN models, which are suitable for ultra high frequency data simulation but with more accuracy.

The contributions of this chapter will be:

- Introduce the background of HONNs with the applications of HONNs
- Develop a new HONN model called UTHONN for ultra high frequency data simulation
- Provide the UTHOHH learning algorithm and weight update formulae
- Compare UTHONN with SAS NLIN and prove HONNs can do better than SAS NLIN models
- Applications of UTHONN model for data simulation

This chapter is organized as follows: Section 1 gives the background knowledge of HONNs. Section 2 introduces UTHONN structure and different modes of the UTHONN model. Section 3 provides the UTHONN model update formula, learning algorithms, and convergence theories of HONN. Section 4 describes UTHONN computer software system and testing results. Section 5 compares UTHONN with other HONN models.

Section 6 shows the results for UTHONN and equilibrium real exchange rates (ERER). Section 7 includes three applications of UTHONN in the time series analysis area. Conclusions are presented in Section 8. Appendix will give detail steps to show how find the weight update formulae.

UTHONN MODELS

Nyquist Rule says that a sampling rate must be at least twice as fast as the fastest frequency (Synder 2006). In simulating and predicting time series data, the new nonlinear models of UTHONN should have twice as high frequency as that of

the ultra high frequency of the time series data. To achieve this purpose, a new model should be developed to enforce high frequency of HONN in order to make the simulation and prediction error close to zero. The new HONN model, Ultra High Frequency Trigonometric Higher Order Neural Network (UTHONN), includes three different models base on the different neuron functions. Ultra high frequency Cosine and Sine Trigonometric Higher Order Neural Network (UCSHONN) has neurons with cosine and sine functions. Ultra high frequency Cosine and Cosine Trigonometric Higher Order Neural Network (UCCHONN) has neurons with cosine functions. Similarly, Ultra high frequency Sine and Sine Trigonometric Higher Order Neural Network (USSHONN) has

Figure 1a. UCSHONN architecture

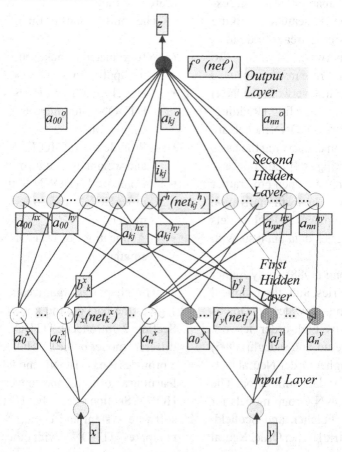

neurons with sine functions. Except for the functions in the neuron all other parts of these three models are the same. The following section will discuss the UCSHONN in detail.

UCSHONN Model

UCSHONN Model Structure can be seen in Figure 1 A and B.

The different types of UCSHONN models are shown as follows. Formula (1) (2) and (3) are for UCSHONN model 1b, 1 and 0 respectively. Model 1b has three layers of weights changeable, Model 1 has two layers of weights changeable, and model 0 has one layer of weights changeable. For models 1b, 1 and 0, Z is the output while x and

y are the inputs of UCSHONN. $a_{kj}{}^o$ is the weight for the output layer, $a_{kj}{}^{hx}$ and $a_{kj}{}^{hy}$ are the weights for the second hidden layer, and $a_k{}^x$ and $a_j{}^y$ are the weights for the first hidden layer. Functions cosine and sine are the first and second hidden layer nodes of UCSHONN. The output layer node of UCSHONN is a linear function of $f^o(net^o)=net^o$, where net^o equals the input of output layer node. UCSHONN is an open neural network model, each weight of HONN has its corresponding coefficient in the model formula, and each node of UCSHONN has its corresponding function in the model formula. The structure of UCSHONN is built by a nonlinear formula. It means, after training, there is rationale for each component of UCSHONN in the nonlinear formula.

Figure 1b. UCSHONN architecture

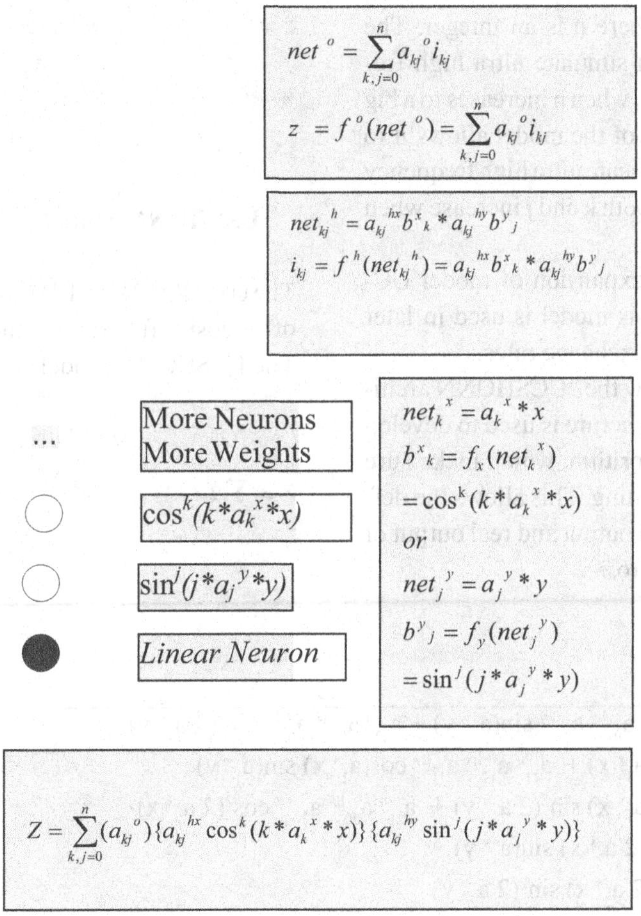

$$net^o = \sum_{k,j=0}^n a_{kj}{}^o i_{kj}$$
$$z = f^o(net^o) = \sum_{k,j=0}^n a_{kj}{}^o i_{kj}$$

$$net_{kj}{}^h = a_{kj}{}^{hx} b^x{}_k * a_{kj}{}^{hy} b^y{}_j$$
$$i_{kj} = f^h(net_{kj}{}^h) = a_{kj}{}^{hx} b^x{}_k * a_{kj}{}^{hy} b^y{}_j$$

More Neurons More Weights

$\cos^k(k*a_k{}^x*x)$

$\sin^j(j*a_j{}^y*y)$

Linear Neuron

$$net_k{}^x = a_k{}^x * x$$
$$b^x{}_k = f_x(net_k{}^x)$$
$$= \cos^k(k*a_k{}^x*x)$$
or
$$net_j{}^y = a_j{}^y * y$$
$$b^y{}_j = f_y(net_j{}^y)$$
$$= \sin^j(j*a_j{}^y*y)$$

$$Z = \sum_{k,j=0}^n (a_{kj}{}^o)\{a_{kj}{}^{hx}\cos^k(k*a_k{}^x*x)\}\{a_{kj}{}^{hy}\sin^j(j*a_j{}^y*y)\}$$

UCSHONN   Model   1b :

$$Z = \sum_{k,j=0}^{n} (a_{kj}{}^{o})\{a_{kj}{}^{hx} \cos^k (k * a_k{}^x x)\} \{a_{kj}{}^{hy} \sin^j (j * a_j{}^y y)\}$$

$$(1)$$

UCSHONN   Model   1 :

$$z = \sum_{k,j=0}^{n} a_{kj}{}^{o} \cos^k (k * a_k{}^x x) \sin^j (j * a_j{}^y y)$$

$$where: \qquad (a_{kj}{}^{hx}) = (a_{kj}{}^{hy}) = 1 \qquad (2)$$

UCSHONN   Model   0 :

$$z = \sum_{k,j=0}^{n} a_{kj}{}^{o} \cos^k (k * x) \sin^j (j * y)$$

$$where: \qquad (a_{kj}{}^{hx}) = (a_{kj}{}^{hy}) = 1$$

$$and \qquad a_k{}^x = a_j{}^y = 1 \qquad (3)$$

For equations 1, 2, and 3, values of k and j ranges from 0 to n, where n is an integer. The UCSHONN model can simulate ultra high frequency time series data, when n increases to a big number. This property of the model allows it to easily simulate and predicate ultra high frequency time series data, since both k and j increase when there is an increase in n.

Equation (4) is an expansion of model UC-SHONN order two. This model is used in later sections to predict the exchange rates.

Figure 1 a and b show the "UCSHONN architecture." This model structure is used to develop the model learning algorithm, which make sure the convergence of learning. This allows the deference between desired output and real output of UCSHONN close to zero.

UCCHONN Model

The UCCHONN models replace the sine functions from UCSHONN with cosine functions models, and the UCCHONN models are defined as follows:

UCCHONN   Model   1b :

$$Z = \sum_{k,j=0}^{n} (a_{kj}{}^{o})\{a_{kj}{}^{hx} \cos^k (k * a_k{}^x x)\} \{a_{kj}{}^{hy} \cos^j (j * a_j{}^y y)\}$$

$$(5)$$

UCCHONN   Model   1 :

$$z = \sum_{k,j=0}^{n} a_{kj}{}^{o} \cos^k (k * a_k{}^x x) \cos^j (j * a_j{}^y y)$$

$$where: \qquad (a_{kj}{}^{hx}) = (a_{kj}{}^{hy}) = 1 \qquad (6)$$

UCCHONN   Model   0 :

$$z = \sum_{k,j=0}^{n} a_{kj}{}^{o} \cos^k (k * x) \cos^j (j * y)$$

$$where: \qquad (a_{kj}{}^{hx}) = (a_{kj}{}^{hy}) = 1$$

$$and \qquad a_k{}^x = a_j{}^y = 1 \qquad (7)$$

USSHONN Model

The USSHONN models use sine functions instead of the cosine functions in the UCSHONN models. The USSHONN models are defined as follows:

USSHONN   Model   1b :

$$Z = \sum_{k,j=0}^{n} (a_{kj}{}^{o})\{a_{kj}{}^{hx} \sin^k (k * a_k{}^x x)\} \{a_{kj}{}^{hy} \sin^j (j * a_j{}^y y)\}$$

$$(8)$$

Equation (4).

$$z = a_{00}{}^{o} a_{00}{}^{hx} a_{00}{}^{hy} + a_{01}{}^{o} a_{01}{}^{hx} a_{01}{}^{hy} \sin(a_1{}^y y) + a_{02}{}^{o} a_{02}{}^{hx} a_{02}{}^{hy} \sin^2(2 a_2{}^y y)$$
$$+ a_{10}{}^{o} a_{10}{}^{hx} a_{10}{}^{hy} \cos(a_1{}^x x) + a_{11}{}^{o} a_{11}{}^{hx} a_{11}{}^{hy} \cos(a_1{}^x x) \sin(a_1{}^y y)$$
$$+ a_{12}{}^{o} a_{12}{}^{hx} a_{12}{}^{hy} \cos(a_1{}^x x) \sin^2(2 a_2{}^y y) + a_{20}{}^{o} a_{20}{}^{hx} a_{20}{}^{hy} \cos^2(2 a_2{}^x x)$$
$$+ a_{21}{}^{o} a_{21}{}^{hx} a_{21}{}^{hy} \cos^2(2 a_2{}^x x) \sin(a_1{}^y y)$$
$$+ a_{22}{}^{o} a_{22}{}^{hx} a_{22}{}^{hy} \cos^2(2 a_2{}^x x) \sin^2(2 a_2{}^y y)$$

USSHONN   Model   1:

$$z = \sum_{k,j=0}^{n} a_{kj}^{\ o}\ \sin^k(k*a_k^{\ x}x)\sin^j(j*a_j^{\ y}y)$$

where: $(a_{kj}^{\ hx}) = (a_{kj}^{\ hy}) = 1$ (9)

USSHONN   Model   0:

$$z = \sum_{k,j=0}^{n} a_{kj}^{\ o}\ \sin^k(k*x)\sin^j(j*y)$$

where: $(a_{kj}^{\ hx}) = (a_{kj}^{\ hy}) = 1$

  and $a_k^{\ x} = a_j^{\ y} = 1$ (10)

LEARNING ALGORITHM OF UTHONN MODELS

Learning Algorithm of UCSHONN Model

Weight update formulae for the output neurons and second-hidden layer neurons are the same as the formulae developed in the Chapter for Artificial Higher Order Neural Networks for Economics and Business –SAS NLIN or HONNs? For Learning Algorithm and convergence theory also refer to the above chapter.

The 1st hidden layer weights are updated according to:

$$a_k^{\ x}(t+1) = a_k^{\ x}(t) - \eta(\partial E_p / \partial a_k^{\ x})$$ (11)

where:
  η = learning rate (positive & usually < 1)
  k = kth neuron of first hidden layer
  E = error
  t = training time
  $a_k^{\ x}$ = 1st hidden layer weight for input x

The learning algorithm of the first hidden layer weights will be based on Equations (12) and (13). The detail derivation can be seen in the Appendix.

Learning Algorithm of UCCHONN Model

The learning formula for the output layer weights in UCCHONN models (model 0, 1, and 1b) is the same as that of the UCSHONN models. The learning formula for the second-hidden layer weights in the UCCHONN model (Model 1b) is the same as that of the UCSHONN model.

The first hidden layer neurons in UCCHONN (Model 1 and Model 1b) use cosine functions.

Equations (14)-(16) updated learning formulae are for UCCHINN (Model 1 and Model 1b).

Equation (12).

$$a_k^{\ x}(t+1) = a_k^{\ x}(t) - \eta(\partial E_p / \partial a_k^{\ x})$$

$$= a_k^{\ x}(t) + \eta(d-z)f^{o}{}'(net^o)a_{kj}^{\ o} * f^{h}{}'(net_{kj}^{\ h})\delta_{kj}^{\ hx}a_{kj}^{\ hx}f_x{}'(net_k^{\ x})x$$

$$= a_k^{\ x}(t) + \eta*\delta^{\ ol}*a_{kj}^{\ o}*\delta^{\ hx}*a_{kj}^{\ hx}*(-k^2)\cos^{k-1}(k*net_k^{\ x})\sin(k*net_k^{\ x})*x$$

$$= a_k^{\ x}(t) + \eta*\delta^{\ ol}*a_{kj}^{\ o}*\delta^{\ hx}*a_{kj}^{\ hx}*\delta^{\ x}*x$$

where:

  $\delta^{\ ol} = (d-z)f^{o}{}'(net^o) = d-z$ *(linear   neuron)*

  $\delta^{\ hx} = f^{h}{}'(net_{kj}^{\ h})a_{kj}^{\ hy}b^y{}_j = a_{kj}^{\ hy}b_j$ *(linear   neuron)*

  $\delta^{\ x} = f_x{}'(net_k^{\ x}) = (-k^2)\cos^{k-1}(k*net_k^{\ x})\sin(k*net_k^{\ x})$

Equation (13). (using Equation (12))

$$a_j^{\ y}(t+1) = a_j^{\ y}(t) - \eta(\partial E_p / \partial a_j^{\ y})$$

$$= a_j^{\ y}(t) + \eta(d-z)f^{o\ '}(net^{\ o})a_{kj}^{\ o} * f^{h\ '}(net_{kj}^{\ h})\delta_{kj}^{\ hy}a_{kj}^{\ hy}f_y^{\ '}(net_j^{\ y})y$$

$$= a_j^{\ y}(t) + \eta * \delta^{\ ol} * a_{kj}^{\ o} * \delta^{\ hy} * a_{kj}^{\ hy} * (j^2)\sin^{j-1}(j*net_j^{\ y})\cos(j*net_j^{\ y}) * y$$

$$= a_j^{\ y}(t) + \eta * \delta^{\ ol} * a_{kj}^{\ o} * \delta^{\ hy} * a_{kj}^{\ hy} * \delta^{\ y} * y$$

$where$:

$$\delta^{\ ol} = (d-z)f^{o\ '}(net^{\ o}) = d - z \qquad (linear \qquad neuron)$$

$$\delta^{\ hy} = f^{h\ '}(net_{kj}^{\ hy})a_{kj}^{\ hx}b_k^{\ x} \quad = a_{kj}^{\ hx}b_k^{\ x} \qquad (linear \qquad neuron)$$

$$\delta^{\ y} = f_y^{\ '}(net_j^{\ y}) = (j^2)\sin^{j-1}(j*net_k^{\ y})\cos(j*net_k^{\ y})$$

Equation (14).

$$b_k^{\ x} = f_k(net_k^{\ x}) = \cos^k(k*net_k^{\ x})$$

$$f_k^{\ '}(net_k^{\ x}) = \partial b_k^{\ x} / \partial(net_k^{\ x})$$

$$= \partial(\cos^k(k*net_k^{\ x})) / \partial(net_k^{\ x})$$

$$= k\cos^{k-1}(k*net_k^{\ x}) * (-\sin(k*net_k^{\ x})) * k$$

$$= -k^2 \cos^{k-1}(k*net_k^{\ x})\sin(k*net_k^{\ x})$$

$$b_j^{\ y} = f_j(net_j^{\ y}) = \cos^j(j*net_j^{\ y})$$

$$f_j^{\ '}(net_j^{\ y}) = \partial b_j^{\ y} / \partial(net_j^{\ y})$$

$$= \partial(\cos^j(j*net_j^{\ y})) / \partial(net_j^{\ y})$$

$$= j\cos^{j-1}(j*net_j^{\ y}) * (-\sin(j*net_j^{\ y})) * j$$

$$= -j^2 \cos^{j-1}(j*net_j^{\ y})\sin(j*net_j^{\ y})$$

Equation (15).

$$a_k^{\ x}(t+1) = a_k^{\ x}(t) - \eta(\partial E_p / \partial a_k^{\ x})$$

$$= a_k^{\ x}(t) + \eta(d-z)f^{o\ '}(net^{\ o})a_{kj}^{\ o} * f^{h\ '}(net_{kj}^{\ h})\delta_{kj}^{\ hx}a_{kj}^{\ hx}f_x^{\ '}(net_k^{\ x})x$$

$$= a_k^{\ x}(t) + \eta * \delta^{\ ol} * a_{kj}^{\ o} * \delta^{\ hx} * a_{kj}^{\ hx} * (-k^2)\cos^{k-1}(k*net_k^{\ x})\sin(k*net_k^{\ x}) * x$$

$$= a_k^{\ x}(t) + \eta * \delta^{\ ol} * a_{kj}^{\ o} * \delta^{\ hx} * a_{kj}^{\ hx} * \delta^{\ x} * x$$

$where$:

$$\delta^{\ ol} = (d-z)f^{o\ '}(net^{\ o}) = d - z \qquad (linear \qquad neuron)$$

$$\delta^{\ hx} = f^{h\ '}(net_{kj}^{\ h})a_{kj}^{\ hy}b_j^{\ y} \quad = a_{kj}^{\ hy}b_j \qquad (linear \qquad neuron)$$

$$\delta^{\ x} = f_x^{\ '}(net_k^{\ x}) = (-k^2)\cos^{k-1}(k*net_k^{\ x})\sin(k*net_k^{\ x})$$

Equation (16). (using Equation (15))

$$a_j^y(t+1) = a_j^y(t) - \eta(\partial E_p / \partial a_j^y)$$

$$= a_j^y(t) + \eta(d-z)f^o{}'(net^o)a_{kj}^o * f^h{}'(net_{kj}^h)\delta_{kj}^{hy}a_{kj}^{hy}f_y{}'(net_j^y)y$$

$$= a_j^y(t) + \eta * \delta^{ol} * a_{kj}^o * \delta^{hy} * a_{kj}^{hy} * (-j^2)\cos^{j-1}(j * net_j^y)\sin(j * net_j^y) * y$$

$$= a_j^y(t) + \eta * \delta^{ol} * a_{kj}^o * \delta^{hy} * a_{kj}^{hy} * \delta^y * y$$

where :

$$\delta^{ol} = (d-z)f^o{}'(net^o) = d-z \qquad (linear \qquad neuron)$$

$$\delta^{hy} = f^h{}'(net_{kj}^{hy})a_{kj}^{hx}b_k^x \qquad = a_{kj}^{hx}b_k^x \qquad (linear \qquad neuron)$$

$$\delta^y = f_y{}'(net_j^y) = (-j^2)\cos^{j-1}(j * net_k^y)\sin(j * net_k^y)$$

Equation (17).

$$b_k^x = f_k(net_k^x) = \sin^k(k * net_k^x)$$

$$f_k{}'(net_k^x) = \partial b_k^x / \partial(net_k^x)$$

$$= \partial(\sin^k(k * net_k^x)) / \partial(net_k^x)$$

$$= k\sin^{k-1}(k * net_k^x) * \cos(k * net_k^x) * k$$

$$= k^2\sin^{k-1}(k * net_k^x)\cos(k * net_k^x)$$

$$b_j^y = f_j(net_j^y) = \sin^j(j * net_j^y)$$

$$f_j{}'(net_j^y) = \partial b_j^y / \partial(net_j^y)$$

$$= \partial(\sin^j(j * net_j^y)) / \partial(net_j^y)$$

$$= j\sin^{j-1}(j * net_j^y) * \cos(j * net_j^y) * j$$

$$= j^2\sin^{j-1}(j * net_j^y)\cos(j * net_j^y)$$

Therefore, Equation (16) shows the learning equation for UCCHONN, which is required for developing the learning algorithm used in later simulations for the exchange rates, and consumer index.

Learning Algorithm of USSHONN Model

The learning formula for the output layer weights in USSHONN models (model 0, 1, and 1b) is same as the formula in UCSHONN models. The learning formulae for the second-hidden layer weights in USSHONN model (Model 1b) are the same as the formulae in UCSHONN model.

The first hidden layer neurons in USSHONN models (Model 1 and Model 1b) use sine functions.

Equations (17)-(19) are the updated formulae for USSHONN models.

Equation (18).

$$a_k^{\ x}(t+1) = a_k^{\ x}(t) - \eta(\partial E_p / \partial a_k^{\ x})$$

$$= a_k^{\ x}(t) + \eta(d-z)f^{o}{}'(net^{o})a_{kj}^{\ o} * f^{h}{}'(net_{kj}^{\ h})\delta_{kj}^{\ hx}a_{kj}^{\ hx}f_x{}'(net_k^{\ x})x$$

$$= a_k^{\ x}(t) + \eta * \delta^{ol} * a_{kj}^{\ o} * \delta^{hx} * a_{kj}^{\ hx} * (k^2)\sin^{k-1}(k*net_k^{\ x})\cos(k*net_k^{\ x}) * x$$

$$= a_k^{\ x}(t) + \eta * \delta^{ol} * a_{kj}^{\ o} * \delta^{hx} * a_{kj}^{\ hx} * \delta^{x} * x$$

$where:$

$$\delta^{ol} = (d-z)f^{o}{}'(net^{o}) = d - z \qquad (linear \qquad neuron)$$

$$\delta^{hx} = f^{h}{}'(net_{kj}^{\ h})a_{kj}^{\ hy}b^{y}{}_j \quad = a_{kj}^{\ hy}b_j \qquad (linear \qquad neuron)$$

$$\delta^{x} = f_x{}'(net_k^{\ x}) = (k^2)\sin^{k-1}(k*net_k^{\ x})\cos(k*net_k^{\ x})$$

Equation (19). (using Equation (18))

$$a_j^{\ y}(t+1) = a_j^{\ y}(t) - \eta(\partial E_p / \partial a_j^{\ y})$$

$$= a_j^{\ y}(t) + \eta(d-z)f^{o}{}'(net^{o})a_{kj}^{\ o} * f^{h}{}'(net_{kj}^{\ h})\delta_{kj}^{\ hy}a_{kj}^{\ hy}f_y{}'(net_j^{\ y})y$$

$$= a_j^{\ y}(t) + \eta * \delta^{ol} * a_{kj}^{\ o} * \delta^{hy} * a_{kj}^{\ hy} * (j^2)\sin^{j-1}(j*net_j^{\ y})\cos(j*net_j^{\ y}) * y$$

$$= a_j^{\ y}(t) + \eta * \delta^{ol} * a_{kj}^{\ o} * \delta^{hy} * a_{kj}^{\ hy} * \delta^{y} * y$$

$where:$

$$\delta^{ol} = (d-z)f^{o}{}'(net^{o}) = d - z \qquad (linear \qquad neuron)$$

$$\delta^{hy} = f^{h}{}'(net_{kj}^{\ hy})a_{kj}^{\ hx}b^{x}{}_k \quad = a_{kj}^{\ hx}b^{x}{}_k \qquad (linear \qquad neuron)$$

$$\delta^{y} = f_y{}'(net_j^{\ y}) = (j^2)\sin^{j-1}(j*net_k^{\ y})\cos(j*net_k^{\ y})$$

Therefore, Equation (19) shows the learning equation for USSHONN, which is required for developing the learning algorithm.

UTHONN TESTING

This chapter uses the monthly Australian and USA dollar exchange rate from Nov. 2003 to Dec. 2004 (See Table 1a) as the test data for UC-SHONN models. Input 1, R_{t-2} is the data at time t-2. Input 2, R_{t-1} is data at time t-1. While, the output, R_t is the data for the current month. The values of R_{t-2}, R_{t-1}, and R_t are converted to a range from 0 to 1 and then used as inputs and output

in the UCSHONN model. Using data from Table 1 A, the error of UCSHONN model 1b, order 2, epochs 100 is 9.4596%, (not shown in table) while the error is only 1.9457% (not shown in table) for model UCSHONN 1b Order 6 Epochs 100. This shows a decrease in error when there is increase in the order of the model.

Table 1b uses the Australian and USA dollar Exchange rate as the test data for UCSHONN model 0, model 1, and model 1b. The orders from 2 to 6 for using epochs are shown. The errors are 0.0197% (model 0), 3.2635% (Model 1), and 4.1619% (Model 1b). Table 1C shows the results for 100,000 epochs using the same test data. From Table 1b it is clear that for order 6,

Table 1. Testing UCSHONN system

Australian Dollars Vs. US Dollars							
Date	Rate 1 AU$ = ? US$	Two monthes before input 1	One month before input 2	Prediction Simulation output	UTHONN input 1	UTHONN input 2	UTHONN Desired Output
11/28/2003	0.7236						
12/31/2003	0.7520						
1/30/2004	0.7625	0.7236	0.7520	0.7625	0.3712	0.7367	0.7890
2/27/2004	0.7717	0.7520	0.7625	0.7717	0.7425	0.8729	0.8968
3/31/2004	0.7620	0.7625	0.7717	0.7620	0.8797	0.9922	0.7831
4/30/2004	0.7210	0.7717	0.7620	0.7210	1.0000	0.8664	0.3025
5/28/2004	0.7138	0.7620	0.7210	0.7138	0.8732	0.3346	0.2181
6/30/2004	0.6952	0.7210	0.7138	0.6952	0.3373	0.2412	0.0000
7/30/2004	0.7035	0.7138	0.6952	0.7035	0.2431	0.0000	0.0973
8/31/2004	0.7071	0.6952	0.7035	0.7071	0.0000	0.1077	0.1395
9/30/2004	0.7244	0.7035	0.7071	0.7244	0.1085	0.1543	0.3423
10/29/2004	0.7468	0.7071	0.7244	0.7468	0.1556	0.3787	0.6049
11/30/2004	0.7723	0.7244	0.7468	0.7723	0.3817	0.6693	0.9039
12/31/2004	0.7805	0.7468	0.7723	0.7805	0.6745	1.0000	1.0000

(a) Australia Dollars Vs US Dollars and Data for UTHONN Simulator

Error	Order 2	Order 3	Order 4	Order 5	Order 6
UCS Model 0	8.5493%	6.3269%	2.4368%	0.4486%	0.0197%
UCS Model 1	9.3254%	8.5509%	5.0727%	1.7119%	3.2635%
UCS Model 1b	12.5573%	8.8673%	8.5555%	4.9947%	4.1619%

(b) 2004 AU$ /US$ Exchange Rate Prediction Simulation Error (Epochs: 10,000)

Error	Order 2	Order 3	Order 4	Order 5	Order 6
UCS Model 0	6.2852%	4.1944%	0.0781%	0.0000%	0.0000%
UCS Model 1	11.3713%	6.2309%	0.0409%	1.8470%	0.0000%
UCS Model 1b	15.5525%	4.0699%	4.8051%	0.0000%	0.0000%

(c) 2004 AU$/US$ Exchange Rate Prediction Simulation Error (Epochs: 100,000)

all of the UCSHONN models have reached an error percentage of 0.0000%. This shows that UCSHONN models can successfully simulate Table 1a data with 0.000% error.

COMPARISON OF THONN WITH OTHER HIGHER ORDER NEURAL NETWORKS

Currency Exchange Rate model by using THONN model 0 (Zhang and Fulcher, 2004) as follows.

Currency Exchange Rate Model Using THONN Model 0:

$$R_t = a_{00} + a_{01} \sin(R_{t-1}) + a_{10} \cos(R_{t-2}) + \sum_{j=2}^{n} a_{0j} \sin^j(R_{t-1})$$

$$+ \sum_{k=2}^{n} a_{k0} \cos^k(R_{t-2}) + \sum_{k=1, j=1}^{n} a_{kj} \cos^k(R_{t-2}) \sin^j(R_{t-1})$$

(20)

Currency Exchange Rate model by using PHONN model 0 (Zhang and Fulcher, 2004) as follows:

Currency Exchange Rate Model Using PHONN Model 0:

$$R_t = a_{00} + a_{01}R_{t-1} + a_{10}R_{t-2} + \sum_{j=2}^{n} a_{0j} \ (R_{t-1})^j$$

$$+ \sum_{k=2}^{n} a_{k0} \ (R_{t-2})^k + \sum_{k=1, j=1}^{n} a_{kj} \ (R_{t-2})^k (R_{t-1})^j$$

$$(21)$$

Table 2a shows the results for Model 0 of UC-SHONN, PHONN and THONN. After 1000 epochs, the three models UCSHONN, PHONN, and THONN have reached errors of 2.3485%, 8.7080% and 10.0366%. This shows that UCSHONN can reach a smaller error in the same time frame. After 100,000 epochs, error for UCSHONN error is close to 0.0000%, but error for PHONN and THONN are still 4.4457% and 4.5712%, respectively. This result shows that UCSHONN can simulate ultra high frequency, and is more accurate than PHONN and THONN. Table 2b and Table 2c compare the

results for Model 1 and Model 1B of UCSHONN, PHONN and THONN. After 100,000 epochs, all of the UCSHONN models have reached an error close to 0.000%, while errors for PHONN and THONN are still around 6% to 9% (similar results are generated for 1,000,000 epochs for PHONN and THONN models) Therefore, the UCSHONN model is more superior for data analysis than any other HONN models.

COMPARISONS WITH UTHONN AND EQUILIBRIUM REAL EXCHANGE RATES

Chile Exchange Rate Estimation

One of the central issues in the international monetary debate is the feasibility of calculating the fundamental equilibrium exchange rates (John Williamson, 1994). Elbradawi (1994) provides a

Table 2. Comparison of HTHONN with PHONN and THONN

Error	1,000 Epochs	10,000 Epochs	100,000 Epochs
UCSHONN Model 0	2.3485%	0.0197%	0.0000%
PHONN Model 0	8.7080%	7.1142%	4.4457%
THONN Model 0	10.0366%	9.2834%	4.5712%

(a) 2004 AU\$/US\$ Exchange Rate Prediction Simulation Error – Model 0 and Order 6

Error	1,000 Epochs	10,000 Epochs	100,000 Epochs
UCSHONN Model 1	4.0094%	3.2635%	0.0000%
PHONN Model 1	9.5274%	8.3484%	7.8234%
THONN Model 1	10.8966%	7.3811%	7.3468%

(b) 2004 AU\$/US\$ Exchange Rate Prediction Simulation Error - Model 1 and Order 6

Error	1,000 Epochs	10,000 Epochs	100,000 Epochs
UCSHONN Model 1b	5.0633%	4.1619%	0.0000%
PHONN Model 1b	14.8800%	9.1474%	9.0276%
THONN Model 1b	10.560%	10.1914%	6.7119%

(c) 2004 AU\$/US\$ Dollar Exchange Rate Prediction Simulation Error – Model 1B and Order 6

formula to calculate Equilibrium Real Exchange Rates (ERER) as follows:

$$\log \tilde{e}_t = \frac{1}{1-\lambda}\delta\,'\tilde{F}_t + \eta_t \qquad (22)$$

where:

$\tilde{e}_t$: Equilibrium Real Exchange Rate

$\dfrac{1}{1-\lambda}$: The co-integration vector; δ ': Parameter vector

$\tilde{F}_t$: Vector pf fundamentals; η_t : Stationary disturbance term

Table 3 compares the UCSHONN with ERER. It shows the actual real exchange rates for Chile, misalignment from equilibrium rate (actual 1980 = 100), and estimations from the UCSHONN model. The average absolute difference of Elbradawi's ERER is 20.5%. Using the actual real exchange rates, UCSHONN predicts the next period ac-

Table 3. Comparison of UCSHONN and ERER – Chile

		Elbradawi ERRA			UCSHONN		
Year	Rate	Equilibrium (Elbradawi)	Absolute Difference	Absolute Percentage	UCSHONN Estimation	Absolute Difference	Absolute Percentage
1965	294.3						
1966	275.4						
1967	261.7						
1968	244	238.8	5.2	2.13	245.8875	1.9	0.77
1969	234.1	239	4.9	2.09	231.7034	2.4	1.02
1970	223.2	236.4	13.2	5.91	226.8309	3.6	1.63
1971	242.7	261.1	18.4	7.58	241.2088	1.5	0.61
1972	254.2	285.7	31.5	12.39	254.8970	0.7	0.27
1973	398.2	259.4	138.8	34.86	396.8596	1.3	0.34
1974	136.1	196.8	60.7	44.60	136.0834	0.0	0.01
1975	103.7	172.7	69.0	66.54	103.7502	0.1	0.05
1976	99	115.7	16.7	16.87	98.3935	0.6	0.61
1977	106.4	109.7	3.3	3.10	93.8473	12.6	11.80
1978	88.4	100.3	11.9	13.46	97.4030	9.0	10.18
1979	87.4	105.9	18.5	21.17	88.9480	1.5	1.77
1980	100	104.5	4.5	4.50	88.1116	11.9	11.89
1981	118.1	96.5	21.6	18.29	111.5722	6.5	5.53
1982	109.5	98.5	11.0	10.05	108.3879	1.1	1.02
1983	87.7	96.9	9.2	10.49	86.8537	0.8	0.96
1984	87	87	0.0	0.00	90.9335	3.9	4.52
1985	70.4	81.7	11.3	16.05	88.0505	17.7	25.07
1986	63.3	73	9.7	15.32	59.7513	3.5	5.61
1987	60.2	65.4	5.2	8.64	59.4128	0.8	1.31
1988	54.7	56.8	2.1	3.84	58.8049	4.1	7.50
1989	52.8	57.5	4.7	8.90	51.6882	1.1	2.11
1990	51.4	51.6	0.2	0.39	49.9417	1.5	2.84
Average			20.5	14.22		3.8	4.24

Chile : Actual Real Exchange Rates from equilibrium rate and UCSHONN model Real Exchange Rate Actual 1980 = 100

tual real exchange rates by using the rates from t − 1 to t − 2. The average absolute difference of UCSHONN is 3.8% and the absolute error of UCSHONN is only 4.24%. However, the absolute average error of Elbradawi's ERER is 14.22%, using the formula of (absolute difference)/(current rate)*100. From Table 3, it is clear that UCSHONN model can reach a smaller error percentage than Elbradawi's ERER model.

Ghana Exchange Rate

Table 4 shows the actual real exchange rates for Ghana and the misalignment from equilibrium. The average absolute difference of Elbradawi's ERER model is 35.25%. Using data from Table 4, the average absolute difference for UCSHONN is 5.6, and the absolute error of UCSHONN is 8.89%, while the absolute average error for Elbradawi's ERER is 20.08%. Clearly, UCSHONN model can

Table 4. Comparison of UCSHONN and ERER – Ghana

		Elbradawi's ERER			UCSHONN		
Year	Rate	Equilibrium (Elbradawi)	Absolute Difference	Absolute percentage	UCSHONN Estimation	Absolute Difference	Absolute Percentage
1965	72.8						
1966	79.9						
1967	60.4	65.8	5.4	8.94	90.1	29.7	49.16
1968	56.8	62.1	5.3	9.33	44.1	12.7	22.30
1969	59.2	59.1	0.1	0.17	57.8	1.4	2.36
1970	57.8	57.4	0.4	0.69	65.1	7.3	12.67
1971	57.6	60.1	2.5	4.34	60.5	2.9	5.01
1972	44.4	55.5	11.1	25.00	61.3	16.9	38.16
1973	50.8	55.6	4.8	9.45	47.2	3.6	7.17
1974	51.3	60.2	8.9	17.35	56.2	4.9	9.62
1975	58.9	68.3	9.4	15.96	55.8	3.1	5.26
1976	90.7	91.6	0.9	0.99	68.3	22.4	24.71
1977	177.2	112.4	64.8	36.57	162.9	14.3	8.06
1978	167.9	138.3	29.6	17.63	167.6	0.3	0.18
1979	144.7	186.2	41.5	28.68	144.8	0.1	0.05
1980	189.3	261.4	72.1	38.09	188.8	0.5	0.27
1981	432.3	292.7	139.6	32.29	431.5	0.8	0.19
1982	549	316.4	232.6	42.37	548.6	0.4	0.08
1983	388.8	308.7	80.1	20.60	388.5	0.3	0.07
1984	134.6	202	67.4	50.07	134.4	0.2	0.12
1985	100.1	117.1	17	16.98	99.9	0.2	0.17
1986	67.4	78.5	11.1	16.47	68.5	1.1	1.63
1987	49.3	55.4	6.1	12.37	44.4	4.9	9.85
1988	45.6	13.6	32	70.18	45.2	0.4	0.98
1989	44.2	44.4	0.2	0.45	45.2	1.0	2.16
1990	44	47.1	3.1	7.05	49.8	5.8	13.08
Average			35.25	20.08		5.6	8.89

reach a smaller error percentage than Elbradawi's ERER model.

India Exchange Rate

Similar to Table 3 and 4, Table 5 compares the UCSHONN with ERER model using the exchange rates for India. Table 5 shows the actual real exchange rates for India, misalignment from equilibrium rate (actual 1980 = 100), and estimations from the UCSHONN model. The average absolute difference of Elbradawi's ERER is 6.56, and the average absolute difference of UCSHONN is only 0.78. Also, Table 5 shows that the absolute average error of Elbradawi's ERER is 4.73%, while the absolute error of UCSHONN is 0.71%.

Again, UCSHONN outperforms the Elbradawi's ERER model.

APPLICATIONS

Exchange rates for Japanese Yen vs. US Dollars (2000 and 2004), US Consumer Price Index (1992-2004), and Japan Consumer Price Index (1992-2004) are selected as applications for UTHONN models. There are two reasons why these applications have been selected. The first reason is that all selected applications are high frequency data. The second reason is that these applications are used as contributing examples for

Table 5. Comparison of UCSHONN and ERER – India

		India : Actual Real Exchange Rates with ERER and HCSHONN models Real Change Rate Actual 1980 = 100					
		Elbradawi's ERER			USCHONN		
Year	Rate	Equilibrium (Elbradawi)	Absolute Difference	Absolute percentage	USCHONN Estimation	Absolute Difference	Absolute Percentage
1965	275.5	236.9					
1966	239.6	222.7					
1967	212.8	215.8	3.00	1.41	212.8	0.00	0.00
1968	218.8	206.3	12.50	5.71	218.8	0.02	0.01
1969	215	205.5	9.50	4.42	214.6	0.38	0.17
1970	218.2	205.8	12.40	5.68	217.9	0.30	0.14
1971	206.7	200.5	6.20	3.00	207.2	0.50	0.24
1972	197	187.8	9.20	4.67	197.1	0.10	0.05
1973	180	170.9	9.10	5.06	180.0	0.02	0.01
1974	149.6	152.5	2.90	1.94	149.6	0.00	0.00
1975	143.2	136.7	6.50	4.54	143.2	0.02	0.01
1976	119.5	127	7.50	6.28	119.5	0.01	0.01
1977	121.2	119.1	2.10	1.73	121.3	0.14	0.11
1978	118.9	113.7	5.20	4.37	119.2	0.32	0.27
1979	106.8	110.2	3.40	3.18	106.0	0.75	0.71
1980	100	106.7	6.70	6.70	100.0	0.02	0.02
1981	99.6	103.2	3.60	3.61	101.7	2.05	2.06
1982	101.1	100.7	0.40	0.40	103.2	2.12	2.09
1983	109.5	100.8	8.70	7.95	105.9	3.59	3.28
1984	107.9	101.8	6.10	5.65	108.4	0.46	0.43
1985	105.4	101.6	3.80	3.61	105.2	0.18	0.17
1986	110.2	99.6	10.60	9.62	106.9	3.30	3.00
1987	104.5	98.4	6.10	5.84	106.0	1.55	1.48
1988	103.6	94.7	8.90	8.59	104.9	1.31	1.27
Average			6.56	4.73		0.78	0.71

the Nobel Prize in Economics in 2003. (Vetens-kapsakademien, 2003).

Exchange Rate Predication Simulation

Currency Exchange Rate Models

Let:

$z = R_t$

$x = R_{t-2}$

$y = R_{t-1}$

$a_{kj}^{\ 0} = a_{kj}$

$n = 6$

UCSHONN Model 0 becomes:

Currency   Exchange   Rate   Model

Using   UCSHONN   Model   0:

$$R_t = \sum_{k,j=0}^{n} a_{kj} \ \cos^k(k * R_{t-2}) \sin^j(j * R_{t-1})$$

where: $(a_{kj}^{\ hx}) = (a_{kj}^{\ hy}) = 1$

and $a_k^{\ x} = a_j^{\ y} = 1$

$$\text{(23)}$$

Since

$$\cos^0(0 * R_{t-2}) = \sin^0(0 * R_{t-1}) = 1 \qquad (24)$$

Currency Exchange Rate model by using UCSHONN model 0:

Currency   Exchange   Rate

Model   Using   UCSHONN   Model   0:

$$R_t = a_{00} + a_{01} \sin(R_{t-1}) + a_{10} \cos(R_{t-2})$$

$$+ \sum_{j=2}^{6} a_{0j} \ \sin^j(j * R_{t-1})$$

$$+ \sum_{k=2}^{6} a_{k0} \ \cos^k(k * R_{t-2})$$

$$+ \sum_{k=1,j=1}^{6} a_{kj} \ \cos^k(k * R_{t-2}) \sin^j(j * R_{t-1})$$

$$\text{(25)}$$

Before using UCSHONN models, the raw data are converted by the following formula to scale the data to range from 0 to 1 in order to meet constraints:

$$individual\_data - lowest\_data \Big/ (highest\_data - lowest\_data)$$

$$\text{(26)}$$

This formula is applied to each separate entry of a given set of data. Each entry serves as the individual_data in the formula. The lowest entry of the data set serves as the lowest_data and the highest entry is the highest_data in the formula. The converted data are shown as R_{t-2}, R_{t-1}, and R_t (see Tables 6 and 7). The values of R_{t-2}, R_{t-1}, and R_t are used as UCSHONN input and desired output.

The exchange rates for Japanese Yen vs. US Dollars in both 2000 and 2004 are used as test data for UCSHONN. After 20,000 epochs, the simulation error reaches 0.0000% for the Yen/Dollars exchange rate in 2000. Details are in Table 6. Table 7 shows that after 60,000 epochs, the simulation error is 0.0000% for the Yen/Dollars exchange rate in 2004. Also, both Table 6 and 7, show the coefficients for the exchange rate models. Based on the output from UCSHONN, the exchange rate model for Japanese Yen Vs US dollars in 2000 can be written as Equation (27).

US Consumer Price Index Analysis

Let:

$z = C_t$

$x = C_{t-2}$

$y = C_{t-1}$

$a_{kj}^{\ 0} = a_{kj}$

USA Consumer Price Index model by using UCSHONN model 0 is defined as follows:

Table 6. Japanese Yen vs. US Dollar Exchange Rate Analysis (2000)

Date	Japanese Yen/ US Dollars	Data before convert to R_{t-2}	R_{t-2}	Data before convert to R_{t-1}	R_{t-1}	Data before convert to R_t	R_t
Nov-99	104.65						
Dec-99	102.58						
Jan-00	105.30	104.65	0.3040	102.58	0.0000	105.30	0.0000
Feb-00	109.39	102.58	0.0000	105.30	0.3994	109.39	0.5919
Mar-00	106.31	105.30	0.3994	109.39	1.0000	106.31	0.1462
Apr-00	105.63	109.39	1.0000	106.31	0.5477	105.63	0.0478
May-00	108.32	106.31	0.5477	105.63	0.4479	108.32	0.4370
Jun-00	106.13	105.63	0.4479	108.32	0.8429	106.13	0.1201
Jul-00	108.21	108.32	0.8429	106.13	0.5213	108.21	0.4211
Aug-00	108.08	106.13	0.5213	108.21	0.8267	108.08	0.4023
Sep-00	106.84	108.21	0.8267	108.08	0.8076	106.84	0.2229
Oct-00	108.44	108.08	0.8076	106.84	0.6256	108.44	0.4544
Nov-00	109.01	106.84	0.6256	108.44	0.8605	109.01	0.5369
Dec-00	112.21	108.44	0.8605	109.01	0.9442	112.21	1.0000

R_{t-2}	R_{t-1}	R_t					
x=input 0	y=input 1	Z=output	$R_t = \sum_{k=0,j=0}^{6} a_{kj}\ \cos^k(k*R_{t-2})\sin^j(j*R_{t-1})$				
0.4479	0.8429	0.1201					
a_{kj}	k=0	k=1	k=2	k=3	k=4	k=5	k=6
j=0	0.6971	-0.3790	-0.4455	-0.1089	-0.7142	-0.1167	0.3644
j=1	0.2311	0.3925	-0.6079	-0.5677	0.6576	0.0344	-1.0445
j=2	0.1096	0.0486	-0.0078	-0.1606	-0.2579	0.0833	-0.4352
j=3	-0.5196	-0.1491	-0.5827	0.1983	0.5528	-0.4081	0.0343
j=4	-0.5659	1.4019	-0.4672	0.2546	-0.0376	0.6464	0.5250
j=5	-0.3698	0.4701	0.8380	0.7653	0.6454	-0.3509	-0.3028
j=6	0.3440	-0.2593	0.0850	-0.1246	-0.8161	-1.0314	0.3107
Sub Σ	1.3099	-0.4406	-0.5463	-0.0130	-0.0029	0.0566	-0.2436

Equation (27).

$$R_t = 0.6971 + 0.2311 * \sin(R_{t-1}) - 0.3790 * \cos(R_{t-2})$$
$$+0.1096\sin^2(2R_{t-1}) - 0.5196\sin^3(3R_{t-1}) - 0.5659\sin^4(4R_{t-1}) - 0.3698\sin^5(5R_{t-1}) + 0.3440\sin^6(6R_{t-1})$$
$$-0.4455\cos^2(2R_{t-2}) - 0.1089\cos^3(3R_{t-2}) - 0.7142\cos^4(4R_{t-2}) - 0.1167\cos^5(5R_{t-2}) + 0.3644\cos^6(6R_{t-2})$$
$$+ \sum_{k=1,j=1}^{6} a_{kj}\ \cos^k(k*R_{t-2})\sin^j(j*R_{t-1})$$

Table 7. Japanese Yen vs. US Dollar Exchange Rate Analysis (2004)

Japanese Yen vs. US Dollar Exchange Rate Analysis (2004)							
Date	Japanese Yen/ US Dollars	Data before convert to R_{t-2}	R_{t-2}	Data before convert to R_{t-1}	R_{t-1}	Data before convert to R_t	R_t
Nov-03	109.18						
Dec-03	107.74						
Jan-04	106.27	109.18	0.4907	107.74	0.4053	106.27	0.2932
Feb-04	106.71	107.74	0.2479	106.27	0.2093	106.71	0.3456
Mar-04	108.52	106.27	0.0000	106.71	0.2680	108.52	0.5614
Apr-04	107.66	106.71	0.0742	108.52	0.5093	107.66	0.4589
May-04	112.20	108.52	0.3794	107.66	0.3947	112.20	1.0000
Jun-04	109.43	107.66	0.2344	112.20	1.0000	109.43	0.6698
Jul-04	109.49	112.20	1.0000	109.43	0.6307	109.49	0.6770
Aug-04	110.23	109.43	0.5329	109.49	0.6387	110.23	0.7652
Sep-04	110.09	109.49	0.5430	110.23	0.7373	110.09	0.7485
Oct-04	108.78	110.23	0.6678	110.09	0.7187	108.78	0.5924
Nov-04	104.70	110.09	0.6442	108.78	0.5440	104.70	0.1061
Dec-04	103.81	108.78	0.4233	104.70	0.0000	103.81	0.0000

R_{t-2}	R_{t-1}	R_t	
x=input 0	y=input 1	Z=output	$$R_t = \sum_{k=0,\,j=0}^{6} a_{kj}\ \cos^k(k*R_{t-2})\sin^j(j*R_{t-1})$$
0.0000	0.2680	0.5614	

a_{kj}	k=0	k=1	k=2	k=3	k=4	k=5	k=6
j=0	0.0005	0.4346	-0.5648	0.6230	0.5479	0.7872	-0.4324
j=1	0.5773	0.7995	0.8272	-0.4217	-0.0067	-0.5834	0.0070
j=2	-0.5283	0.4781	0.3663	-0.2656	-1.1565	-0.8809	0.6540
j=3	0.4060	-0.2691	-0.6332	-0.2581	0.0737	0.4867	-0.4085
j=4	-0.4227	-0.0263	0.3667	-0.9254	0.3035	0.7627	-0.0051
j=5	0.2559	0.9138	0.0368	0.2523	-0.6093	-0.2594	-0.1121
j=6	-0.3610	-0.5928	0.2382	-0.4285	0.2153	-0.1543	0.0497
Sub $\sum$	-0.2199	0.8634	0.0008	-0.4108	0.1342	0.6579	-0.4641

USA Consumer Price Index Model Using
UCS Model 0 :

$$C_t = a_{00} + a_{01}\sin(C_{t-1}) + a_{10}\cos(C_{t-2})$$

$$+ \sum_{j=2}^{n} a_{0j}\ \sin^j(j*C_{t-1})$$

$$+ \sum_{k=2}^{n} a_{k0}\ \cos^k(k*C_{t-2})$$

$$+ \sum_{k=1,j=1}^{n} a_{kj}\ \cos^k(k*C_{t-2})\sin^j(j*C_{t-1})$$

$$(28)$$

US Consumer Price Index (1992-2004) is the test data in this section. After 100,000 epochs, the simulation error reaches 0.0000% for the 1992-2004 US Consumer Price Index. Table 8 provides the coefficients for US consumer Price Index (1992-2004) model. The model can be written as seen in Equation (29).

Japan Consumer Price Index Prediction Simulation

Let:
$$z = J_t$$

$$x = J_{t-2}$$
$$y = J_{t-1}$$
$$a_{kj}^{\ 0} = a_{kj}$$

Japan Consumer Price Index model by using UCSHOON model 0 is:

Japan Consumer Price Index Model
Using UCS Model 0 :

$$J_t = a_{00} + a_{01}\sin(J_{t-1}) + a_{10}\cos(J_{t-2})$$

$$+ \sum_{j=2}^{n} a_{0j}\ \sin^j(j*J_{t-1})$$

$$+ \sum_{k=2}^{n} a_{k0}\ \cos^k(k*J_{t-2})$$

$$+ \sum_{k=1,j=1}^{n} a_{kj}\ \cos^k(k*J_{t-2})\sin^j(j*J_{t-1})$$

$$(30)$$

Japan Consumer Price Index (1992-2004) is the test data for USCHONN. After 200,000 epochs, the simulation error is 0.0000% for the 1992-2004 Japan Consumer Price Index. Table 9 shows the coefficients for Japan Consumer

Equation (29).

$$C_t = 1.0579 + 0.2936*\sin(C_{t-1}) - 0.8893*\cos(C_{t-2})$$
$$-0.6608\sin^2(2C_{t-1}) + 0.2960\sin^3(3C_{t-1}) - 0.5318\sin^4(4C_{t-1}) - 0.5792\sin^5(5C_{t-1}) - 0.3132\sin^6(6C_{t-1})$$
$$+0.5705\cos^2(2C_{t-2}) - 0.7049\cos^3(3C_{t-2}) - 0.2269\cos^4(4C_{t-2}) + 0.1620\cos^5(5C_{t-2}) + 0.0307\cos^6(6C_{t-2})$$
$$+ \sum_{k=1,j=1}^{6} a_{kj}\ \cos^k(k*C_{t-2})\sin^j(j*C_{t-1})$$

Equation (31).

$$J_t = -0.1275 - 0.9274*\sin(J_{t-1}) + 0.6917*\cos(J_{t-2})$$
$$-0.8318\sin^2(2J_{t-1}) + 0.9529\sin^3(3J_{t-1}) + 0.1854\sin^4(4J_{t-1}) - 0.8606\sin^5(5J_{t-1}) + 0.7017\sin^6(6J_{t-1})$$
$$+1.3996\cos^2(2J_{t-2}) + 0.4697\cos^3(3J_{t-2}) - 0.2287\cos^4(4J_{t-2}) - 1.0493\cos^5(5J_{t-2}) - 1.1555\cos^6(6J_{t-2})$$
$$+ \sum_{k=1,j=1}^{6} a_{kj}\ \cos^k(k*J_{t-2})\sin^j(j*J_{t-1})$$

Table 8. US Consumer Price Index Analysis (1992-2004)

US Consumer Price Index Analysis (1992-2004)							
Date	US CPI	Data before convert to C_{t-2}	C_{t-2}	Data before convert to C_{t-1}	C_{t-1}	Data before convert to C_t	C_t
1990	130.7						
1991	136.2						
1992	140.3	130.7	0.0000	136.2	0.0000	140.3	0.0000
1993	144.5	136.2	0.1118	140.3	0.0858	144.5	0.0864
1994	148.2	140.3	0.1951	144.5	0.1736	148.2	0.1626
1995	152.4	144.5	0.2805	148.2	0.2510	152.4	0.2490
1996	156.9	148.2	0.3557	152.4	0.3389	156.9	0.3416
1997	160.5	152.4	0.4411	156.9	0.4331	160.5	0.4156
1998	163.0	156.9	0.5325	160.5	0.5084	163.0	0.4671
1999	166.6	160.5	0.6057	163.0	0.5607	166.6	0.5412
2000	172.2	163.0	0.6565	166.6	0.6360	172.2	0.6564
2001	177.1	166.6	0.7297	172.2	0.7531	177.1	0.7572
2002	179.9	172.2	0.8435	177.1	0.8556	179.9	0.8148
2003	184.0	177.1	0.9431	179.9	0.9142	184.0	0.8992
2004	188.9	179.9	1.0000	184.0	1.0000	188.9	1.0000
C_{t-2}	C_{t-1}	C_t					
x=input 0	y=input 1	Z=output	$C_t = \displaystyle\sum_{k=0,j=0}^{6} a_{kj} \cos^k (k*C_{t-2}) \sin^j (j*C_{t-1})$				
0.0000	0.0000	0.0000					
a_{kj}	k=0	k=1	k=2	k=3	k=4	k=5	k=6
j=0	1.0579	-0.8893	0.5705	-0.7049	-0.2269	0.1620	0.0307
j=1	0.2936	0.7221	-0.3522	-0.0652	0.7003	-1.2471	-0.1326
j=2	-0.6608	-0.9835	0.8478	0.3926	0.2648	0.4667	-0.3908
j=3	0.2960	0.6595	-0.1415	0.8827	-0.0713	-0.1142	0.3791
j=4	-0.5318	0.4256	0.2436	-0.4823	-0.5585	0.4195	-0.2299
j=5	-0.5792	-0.4201	0.8837	-0.5358	0.1797	-0.9943	-0.6201
j=6	-0.3132	0.4875	-0.0767	-0.4164	-0.1399	-0.5029	0.1857
Sub$\sum$	1.0579	-0.8893	0.5705	-0.7049	-0.2269	0.1620	0.0307

Price Index (1992-2004). The1992-2004 Japan Consumer Price Index model can be written as Equation (31).

CONCLUSION

Three nonlinear neural network models, UC-SHONN, UCCHONN, and USSHONN, that are part of the Ultra High Frequency Trigonometric

Table 9. Japan Consumer Price Index Analysis (1992-2004)

Date	Japan CPI	Data before convert to J_{t-2}	J_{t-2}	Data before convert to J_{t-1}	J_{t-1}	Data before convert to J_t	J_t
1990	93.10						
1991	96.10						
1992	97.70	93.10	0.0000	96.10	0.0000	97.70	0.0000
1993	98.80	96.10	0.3659	97.70	0.3077	98.80	0.3056
1994	99.30	97.70	0.5610	98.80	0.5192	99.30	0.4444
1995	99.00	98.80	0.6951	99.30	0.6154	99.00	0.3611
1996	99.00	99.30	0.7561	99.00	0.5577	99.00	0.3611
1997	100.60	99.00	0.7195	99.00	0.5577	100.60	0.8056
1998	101.30	99.00	0.7195	100.60	0.8654	101.30	1.0000
1999	100.90	100.60	0.9146	101.30	1.0000	100.90	0.8889
2000	100.00	101.30	1.0000	100.90	0.9231	100.00	0.6389
2001	99.10	100.90	0.9512	100.00	0.7500	99.10	0.3889
2002	98.00	100.00	0.8415	99.10	0.5769	98.00	0.0833
2003	97.70	99.10	0.7317	98.00	0.3654	97.70	0.0000
2004	97.70	98.00	0.5976	97.70	0.3077	97.70	0.0000

J_{t-2}	J_{t-1}	J_t	
x=input 0	y=input 1	Z=output	$J_t = \displaystyle\sum_{k=0,j=0}^{6} a_{kj} \cos^k(k*J_{t-2})\sin^j(j*J_{t-1})$
0.9146	1.0000	0.8889	

a_{kj}	k=0	k=1	k=2	k=3	k=4	k=5	k=6
j=0	-0.1275	0.6917	1.3996	0.4697	-0.2287	-1.0493	-1.1555
j=1	-0.9274	0.6106	0.6374	0.0933	0.3337	0.3734	0.1258
j=2	-0.8318	0.3397	0.0496	-1.2872	-1.3823	0.3479	0.1871
j=3	0.9529	-0.7762	0.7556	-0.8851	0.2710	-0.3120	-0.7980
j=4	0.1854	0.7115	-0.6467	0.6516	0.1924	-2.0840	-0.9574
j=5	-0.8606	-1.3979	0.4677	0.5297	-0.2723	0.8944	0.8357
j=6	0.7071	-0.2297	-0.0614	-0.0172	0.0925	0.2005	-0.3268
Sub∑	-0.8340	1.7394	0.0906	0.5754	-0.4605	0.0001	-0.2220

Higher Order Neural Networks (UTHONN), are developed. Based on the structures of UTHONN, this chapter provides three model learning algorithm formulae. This chapter tests the UCSHONN model using ultra high frequency data and the running results are compared with THONN, PHONN, and ERER models. Experimental results show that UTHONN models are 4 – 9% better than other Polynomial Higher Order Neural Network (PHONN) and Trigonometric Higher

Order Neural Network (THONN) models. The results also show that the UTHONN model is 3 - 12% better than exchange equilibrium (ERER) models. Using the UTHONN models, models are developed for Yen vs. US dollar exchange rate, US consumer price index, and Japan consumer price index with an error reaching 0.0000%.

One of the topics for future research is to continue building models using UTHONN for different data series. The coefficients of the higher order models will be studied not only using artificial neural network techniques, but also statistical methods. Using nonlinear functions to model and analyze time series data will be a major goal in the future.

FUTHER RESEARCH DIRECTIONS

One of the topics for future research is to continue building models using Higher Order artificial Neural Networks (HONNs) for different data series. The coefficients of the higher order models will be studied not only using artificial neural network techniques, but also statistical methods. Using nonlinear functions to model and analyze time series data will be a major goal in the future. The future research direction aims at the construction of an automatic model selection simulation and prediction systems based on HONNs. There are many kinds of data, for example nonlinear, discontinuous, unsmooth, which are difficult to simulate and predict. One unsolved issue in HONNs is that there is no single higher order neural network, which can accurately simulate piecewise and discontinuous functions. Future research in this area can develop new functional-neuron multilayer feed-forward HONN models to approximate any continuous, unsmooth, piecewise continuous, and discontinuous special functions to any degree of accuracy. Traditional methods of forecasting are highly inaccurate. Artificial HONNs have strong pattern finding ability and better accuracy in nonlinear simulation and prediction. However,

currently the solution to automate the choice of the optimal HONN models for simulation and prediction is still not available. A model auto-selection prediction system will be studied in the future based on the adaptive HONNs. This study has a good chance of finding the solutions to automate the choice of the optimal HONN models for simulation and prediction.

ACKNOWLEDGMENT

I would like to acknowledge the financial assistance of the following organizations in the development of Higher-Order Neural Networks: Fujitsu Research Laboratories, Japan (1995-1996), Australian Research Council (1997-1998), the US National Research Council (1999-2000), and the Applied Research Centers and Dean's Office Grants of Christopher Newport University (2001-2007).

REFERENCES

Azoff, E. (1994). *Neural network time series: Forecasting of financial markets*. New York: Wiley.

Balke, N. S., & Fomby, T. B. (1997). Threshold cointegration. *International Economic Review*, *38*, 627-645.

Barron, R., Gilstrap, L. & Shrier, S. (1987). Polynomial and neural networks: Analogies and engineering applications. *Proceedings of International Conference of Neural Networks, Vol. II.* (pp. 431-439). New York.

Bierens, H. J., & Ploberger, W. (1997). Asymptotic theory of integrated conditional moment tests. *Econometrica. 65*(5), 1129-1151.

Blum, E., & Li, K. (1991). Approximation theory and feed-forward networks, *Neural Networks, 4*, 511-515.

Box, G. E. P., & Jenkins, G. M. (1976). *time series analysis: Forecasting and control*. San Fransisco: Holden-Day.

Chakraborty, K., Mehrotra ,K., Mohan, C., & Ranka, S. (1992). Forecasting the behavior of multivariate time series using neural networks. *Neural Networks, 5*, 961-970.

Chang, Y., & Park, J. Y. (2003). Index models with integrated time series. *Journal of Econometrics, 114*(1), 73-106.

Chen, C. T., & Chang, W. D. (1996). A feed-forward neural network with function shape autotuning. *Neural Networks, 9*(4), 627-641.

Chen, T., & Chen, H. (1993). Approximations of continuous functional by neural networks with application to dynamic systems. *IEEE Trans on Neural Networks, 4*(6), 910-918.

Chen, T., & Chen, H. (1995). Approximation capability to functions of several variables, non-linear functionals, and operators by radial basis function neural networks. *IEEE Trans on Neural Networks, 6*(4), 904-910.

Chen, X., & Shen, X. (1998). Sieve extremum estimates for weakly dependent data. *Econometrica, 66*(2), 289-314.

Chenug, Y. W., & Chinn, M. D. (1999). *Macro-economic implications of the beliefs and behavior of foreign exchange traders*. NBER, Working paper no. 7414.

Elbradawi, I. A. (1994). Estimating long-run equilibrium real exchange rates. In John Williamson (Ed.), *Estimating equilibrium exchange rates* (pp. 93-131). Institute for International Economics.

Fahlman, S. (1988). Faster-learning variations on back-propagation: An empirical study. *Proceedings of 1988 Connectionist Models Summer School*.

Gardeazabal, J., & Regulez, M. (1992). *The monetary model of exchange rates and cointegration*. New York: Springer-Verlag.

Gorr, W. L. (1994). Research prospective on neural network forecasting. *International Journal of Forecasting, 10*(1), 1-4.

Granger, C. W. J. & Weiss, A. A. (1983). Time series analysis of error-correction models. In S. Karlin, T. Amemiya, & L. A. Goodman (Eds), *Studies in econometrics, time series and multivariate statistics* (pp. 255-278). In Honor of T. W. Anderson. San Diego: Academic Press.

Granger, C. W. J. & Bates, J. (1969). The combination of forecasts. *Operations Research Quarterly, 20*, 451-468.

Granger, C. W. J., & Lee, T. H. (1990). Multicointegration. In G. F. Rhodes, Jr and T. B. Fomby (Eds.), *Advances in econometrics: Cointegration, spurious regressions and unit roots* (pp.17-84). New York: JAI Press.

Granger, C. W. J. & Swanson, N. R. (1996). Further developments in study of cointegrated variables. *Oxford Bulletin of Economics and Statistics, 58*, 374-386.

Granger, C. W. J., & Newbold, P. (1974). Spurious regressions in econometrics. *Journal of Econometrics, 2*, 111-120.

Granger, C. W. J. (1995). Modeling nonlinear relationships between extended-memory variables, *Econometrica, 63*(2), 265-279.

Granger, C. W. J. (2001). Spurious regressions in econometrics. In B. H. Baltagi (Ed.), *A companion to theoretical econometrics* (pp.557-561). Blackwell: Oxford.

Granger, C. W. J. (1981). Some properties of time series data and their use in econometric model specification. *Journal of Econometrics, 16*, 121-130.

Hans, P., & Draisma, G. (1997). Recognizing changing seasonal patterns using artificial neural networks. *Journal of Econometrics, 81*(1), 273-280.

Hornik, K. (1993). Some new results on neural network approximation. *Neural Networks, 6,* 1069-1072.

Kilian, L., & Taylor, M. P. (2003). Why is it so difficult to beat the random walk forecast of exchange rate? *Journal of International Economics, 60,* 85-107.

MacDonald, R., & Marsh, I. (1999). *Exchange rate modeling* (pp. 145 – 171). Boston: Kluwer Academic Publishers.

Meese, R., & Rogoff, K. (1983A). Empirical exchange rate models of the seventies: Do they fit out of sample. *Journal of International Economics, 14,* 3-24.

Meese, R., & Rogoff, K. (1983B). The out-of-samples failure of empirical exchange rate models: sampling error or misspecification. In Frenkel, J. A., (Ed.), *Exchange rate and international macroeconomics.* Chicago and Boston: Chicago University Press and National Bureau of Economic Research.

Psaltis, D., Park, C., & Hong, J. (1988). Higher order associative memories and their optical implementations. *Neural Networks, 1,* 149-163.

Redding, N., Kowalczyk, A., & Downs, T. (1993). Constructive high-order network algorithm that is polynomial time. *Neural Networks, 6,* 997-1010.

Rumelhart, D.G., Hinton, G., and Williams, R. (1986).Learning representations by back-propagating errors. In Rumelhart, D., & McClelland, J. (Eds.), *Parallel distributed processing: Explorations in the microstructure of cognition, Vol.1,* (Chapter 8). Cambridge, MA: MIT Press.

Scarselli, F., & Tsoi, A. C. (1998). Universal approximation using feed-forward neural networks: A survey of some existing methods, and some new results. *Neural Networks, 11*(1),15-37.

Shintani, M., & Linton, O. (2004). Nonparametric neural network estimation of Lyapunov exponents and direct test for chaos. *Journal of Econometrics, 120*(1), 1-33.

Synder, L. (2006). *Fluency with information technology.* Boston, MA: Addison Wesley.

Taylor, M. P. (1995). The economics of exchange rates. *Journal of Economic Literature, 33,* 13-47.

Taylor, M. P., & Peel, D. A. (2000). Nonlinear adjustment, long run equilibrium and exchange rate fundamentals. *Journal of International Money and Finance, 19,* 33-53.

Taylor, M. P., Peel, D. A., & Sarno, L. (2001). Nonlinear adjustments in real exchange rate: towards a solution to the purchasing power parity puzzles. *International Economic Review, 42,* 1015-1042.

Vetenskapsakademien, K. (2003). Time-series econometrics: Co-integration and autoregressive conditional heteroskedasticity. *Advanced information on the Bank of Sweden Prize in Economic Sciences in Memory of Alfred Nobel,* 8 October, 2003.

Werbos, P. (1994). *The roots of backpropagation: From ordered derivatives to neural networks and political forecasting.* New York: Wiley.

Williamson, J. (1994). *Estimating equilibrium exchange rates.* Institute for International Economics.

Zell, A. (1995). *Stuttgart neural network simulator V4.1.* University of Stuttgart, Institute for Parallel & Distributed High Performance Systems. Can be found at ftp.informatik.uni-stuttgart.de

Zhang, M., Zhang, J. C., and Keen, S. (1999) Using THONN system for higher frequency nonlinear data simulation & prediction. *Proceedings of IASTED International Conference on Artificial Intelligence and Soft Computing* (pp. 320-323). Honolulu, Hawaii, USA.

Zhang, M., Zhang, J. C., & Fulcher, J. (2000) Higher order neural network group models for data approximation. *International Journal of Neural Systems, 10*(2), 123-142.

Zhang, M., Fulcher, J., & Scofield, R. A. (1996) Neural network group models for estimating rainfall from satellite images. *Proceedings of World Congress on Neural Networks* (pp. 897-900). San Diego, CA.

Zhang, M., & Fulcher J. (2004). Higher order neural networks for satellite weather prediction. In J. Fulcher, & L. C. Jain (Eds.), *Applied intelligent systems* (Vol. 153, pp.17-57). Springer.

Zhang, M., Murugesan, S., & Sadeghi, M. (1995). Polynomial higher order neural network for economic data simulation. *Proceedings of International Conference on Neural Information Processing* (pp. 493-496). Beijing, China.

Zhang, M., Xu, S., & Fulcher, J. (2002). Neuron-adaptive higher order neural network models for automated financial data modeling. *IEEE Transactions on Neural Networks, 13*(1), 188-204.

ADDITIONAL READING

Bengtsson, M. (1990). *Higher order artificial neural networks*. Diano Pub Co.

Bouzerdoum, A. (1999). A new class of high-order neural networks with nonlinear decision boundaries. *Proceedings of ICONIP'99 6th International Conference on Neural Information Processing* (Vol. 3, pp.1004-1009). 16-20 November 1999, Perth, Australia.

Chang, C. H, Lin, J. L., & Cheung. J. Y. (1993). Polynomial and standard higher order neural network. *Proceedings of IEEE International Conference on Neural Networks* (Vol.2, pp.989 – 994). 28 March – 1 April, 1993, San Francisco, CA.

Chen, Y., Jiang, Y. & Xu, J. (2003). Dynamic properties and a new learning mechanism in higher order neural networks. *Neurocomputing, 50*(Jan 2003), 17-30.

Crane, J., & Zhang, M. (2005).Data simulation using SINCHONN model. *Proceedings of IASTED International Conference on Computational Intelligence* (pp. 50-55).Calgary, Canada.

Dunis, C. L., Laws, J., & Evans, B. (2006, forthcoming). *Modeling and trading the gasoline crack spread: A non-linear story*. Working paper, and paper accepted by Journal of Derivatives Use, Trading and Regulation. Retrieved from http://www.ljmu.ac.uk/AFE/CIBEF/67756.htm

Estevez, P. A., & Okabe, Y. (1991). Training the piecewise linear-high order neural network through error back propagation *Proceedings of IEEE International Joint Conference on Neural Networks*, (Vol. 1, pp.711 -716). 18-21 November, 1991.

Fulcher, J., Zhang, M. & Xu, S. (2006). The application of higher-order neural networks to financial time series. In J. Kamruzzaman (Ed.), *Artificial neural networks in finance, health and manufacturing: Potential and challenges* (pp. 80-108). Hershey, PA: IGI-Global.

Ghazali, R. (2005). Higher order neural network for financial time series prediction. *Annual Postgraduate Research Conference*, March 16-17, 2005, School of Computing and Mathematical Sciences, Liverpool John Moores University, UK. Retrieved from http://www.cms.livjm.ac.uk/research/doc/ConfReport2005.doc

Giles, L., & Maxwell, T. (1987). Learning, invariance and generalization in high-order neural networks. *Applied Optics, 26*(23), 4972-4978.

Giles, L., Griffin, R., & Maxwell, T. (1988). Encoding geometric invariances in high-order neural networks. *Proceedings Neural Information Processing Systems*, (pp. 301-309).

He, Z., & and Siyal, M. Y. (1999). Improvement on higher-order neural networks for invariant object recognition. *Neural Processing Letters*, *10*(1), 49-55.

Hornik, K. (1991). Approximation capabilities of multilayer feedforward networks. *Neural Networks*, *4*, 251-257.

Hu, S., & Yan, P. (1992). Level-by-level learning for artificial neural groups. Electronica Sinica, *20*(10), 39-43.

Jeffries, C. (1989). High order neural networks. *Proceedings of IJCNN International Joint Conference on Neural Networks,* (Vol.2., pp.59). 18-22 June, 1989, Washington DC, USA.

Kanaoka, T., Chellappa, R., Yoshitaka M., & Tomita, S. (1992). A higher-order neural network for distortion unvariant pattern recognition. *Pattern Recognition Letters*, *13*(12), 837-841.

Karayiannis, N. B., & Venetsanopoulos, A. N. (1995). On the training and performance of high-order neural networks. *Mathematical Biosciences*, *129*(2), 143-168.

Karayiannis, N., & Venetsanopoulos, A. (1993). *Artificial neural networks: Learning algorithms, performance evaluation and applications.* Boston, MA: Kluwer.

Knowles, A., Hussain, A., Deredy, W. E., Lisboa, P. G. J., & Dunis, C. (2005). Higher-order neural network with Bayesian confidence measure for prediction of EUR/USD exchange rate. *Forecasting Financial Markets Conference*, 1-3 June, 2005, Marseilles, France.

Lee, M., Lee, S. Y., & Park, C. H. (1992). Neural controller of nonlinear dynamic systems using higher order neural networks. *Electronics Letters*, *28*(3), 276-277.

Leshno, M., Lin, V., Pinkus, A., & Schoken, S. (1993). Multi-layer feedforward networks with a non-polynomial activation can approximate any function. *Neural Networks*, 6, 861-867.

Li, D., Hirasawa K., & Hu, J. (2003). A new strategy for constructing higher order neural networks with multiplication units. *SICS 2003 Annual Conference*, (Vol. 3, pp.2342-2347).

Lisboa, P., & Perantonis, S. (1991). Invariant pattern recognition using third-order networks and zernlike moments. *Proceedings of the IEEE International Joint Conference on Neural Networks,* (Vol. II, pp. 1421-1425) .Singapore.

Lu, B., Qi, H., Zhang, M., & Scofield, R. A. (2000). Using PT-HONN models for multi-polynomial function simulation. *Proceedings of IASTED International Conference on Neural Networks* (pp.1-5). Pittsburg, USA.

Manykin, E. A., & Belov, M. N. (1991). Higher-order neural networks and photo-echo effect. *Neural Networks*, *4*(3), 417-420.

Park, S., Smith, M. J. T., & Mersereau, R. M. (2000). Target recognition based on directional filter banks and higher-order neural network. *Digital Signal Processing*, *10*(4), 297-308.

Shin, Y. (1991). The Pi-Sigma network: An efficient higher-order neural network for pattern classification and function approximation. *Proceedings of the International Joint Conference on Neural Networks,* (Vol. I, pp.13-18). Seattle, WA.

Spirkovska L., & Reid, M. B. (1994). Higher-order neural networks applied to 2D and 3D object recognition. *Machine Learning*, *15*(2), 169-199(31).

Spirkovska, L., & Reid, M. B. (1992). Robust position, scale, and rotation invariant object recognition using higher-order neural networks. *Pattern Recognition*, *25*(9), 975-985.

Tai, H., & Jong, T. (1990). Information storage in high-order neural networks with unequal neural activity. *Journal of the Franklin Institute*, *327*(1), 129-141.

Venkatesh, S. S., & Baldi, P. (1991). Programmed interactions in higher-order neural networks: Maximal capacity. *Journal of Complexity, 7*(3), 316-337.

Wilcox, C. (1991). Understanding hierarchical neural network behavior: A renormalization group approach. *Journal of . Physics A, 24,* 2644-2655.

Xu, S., & Zhang, M. (1999). Approximation to continuous functions and operators using adaptive higher order neural networks. *Proceedings of International Joint Conference on Neural Networks '99,* Washington, D.C., USA.

Zhang, J. (2005). Polynomial full naïve estimated misclassification cost models for financial distress prediction using higher order neural network. *14th Annual Research Work Shop on Artificial Intelligence and Emerging Technologies in Accounting, Auditing, and Ta.* San Francisco, CA.

Zhang, J. (2006). *Linear and nonlinear models for the power of chief elected officials and debt.* Pittsburgh, PA: Mid-Atlantic Region American Accounting Association.

Zhang, J. C., Zhang, M., & Fulcher, J. (1997). Financial prediction using higher order trigonometric polynomial neural network group models. *Proceedings of ICNN/IEEE International Conference on Neural Networks* (pp. 2231-2234). Houston, TX.

Zhang, M., Fulcher, J., & Scofield, R. (1997). Rainfalll estimation using artificial neural network group. *International Journal of Neuralcomputing, 16*(2), 97-115.

Zhang, M. (2001). Financial data simulation using A-PHONN model. *International Joint Conference on Neural Networks '01* (pp.1823 – 1827). Washington DC, USA.

Zhang, M. (2002) Financial data simulation using PL-HONN model, *Proceeding of IASTED International Conference on Modeling and Simulation (NS2002).* Marina del Rey, CA.

Zhang, M., & Lu, B. (2001).Financial data simulation using M-PHONN model. *International Joint Conference on Neural Networks '01* (pp. 1828 – 1832). Washington DC, USA.

Zhang, M. (2005). A data simulation system using sinx/x and sinx polynomial higher order neural networks. *Proceedings of IASTED International Conference on Computational Intelligence* (pp.56 – 61). Calgary, Canada.

Zhang, M. (2006). A data simulation system using CSINC polynomial higher order neural networks. *Proceedings of The 2006 International Conference on Artificial Intelligence* (Vol. I, pp. 91-97). Las Vegas, USA.

APPENDIX

First Hidden Layer Neurons in UCS (Model 1 and Model 1b)

The 1st hidden layer weights are updated according to:

$$a_k^{\ x}(t+1) = a_k^{\ x}(t) - \eta(\partial E_p / \partial a_k^{\ x}) \tag{C.1}$$

where:

$a_k^{\ x}$ = 1st hidden layer weight for input x; k = kth neuron of first hidden layer
η = learning rate (positive & usually < 1)
E = error
t = training time

The equations for the kth or jth node in the first hidden layer are:

$$net_k^{\ x} = a_k^{\ x} * x$$
$$b_k^x = f_x(net_k^{\ x})$$
or
$$net_j^{\ y} = a_j^{\ y} * y$$
$$b_j^y = f_y(net_j^{\ y}) \tag{C.2}$$

where:

i_{kj} = output from 2nd hidden layer (= input to the output neuron)
b_k^x and b_j^y = output from the 1st hidden layer neuron (= input to 2nd hidden layer neuron)
fx and f_y = 1st hidden layer neuron activation function
x and y = input to 1st hidden layer

The total error is the sum of the squared errors across all hidden units, namely:

$$E_p = 0.5 * \delta^2 = 0.5 * (d - z)^2$$
$$= 0.5 * (d - f^o(net^o))^2$$
$$= 0.5 * (d - f^o(\sum_j a_{kj}^{\ o} i_{kj}))^2 \tag{C.3}$$

For a cosine function (and similarly for sine):

$$b^x_k = f_x \, (net_k^{\,x}) = \cos^k (k * net_k^{\,x})$$

$$f_x \,'(net_k^{\,x}) = \partial b^x_{\,k} / \partial(net_k^{\,x})$$

$$= \partial(\cos^k (k * net_k^{\,x})) / \partial(net_k^{\,x})$$

$$= k \cos^{k-1} (k * net_k^{\,x}) * (-\sin(k * net_k^{\,x})) * k$$

$$= -k^2 \cos^{k-1} (k * net_k^{\,x}) \sin(k * net_k^{\,x})$$

$$b^y_{\,j} = f_y \, (net_j^{\,y}) = \sin^j (j * net_j^{\,y})$$

$$f_y \,'(net_j^{\,y}) = \partial b^y_{\,j} / \partial(net_j^{\,y})$$

$$= \partial(\sin^j (j * net_j^{\,y})) / \partial(net_j^{\,y})$$

$$= j \sin^{j-1} (j * net_j^{\,y}) * \cos(j * net_j^{\,y}) * j$$

$$= j^2 \sin^{j-1} (j * net_j^{\,y}) \cos(j * net_j^{\,y}) \tag{C.4}$$

The gradient $(\partial E_p / \partial a_k^{\,x})$ is given by:

$$\partial E_p / \partial a_k^{\,x} = \partial(0.5 * (d - z)^2) / \partial a_k^{\,x}$$

$$= (\partial(0.5 * (d - z)^2) / \partial z)(\partial z / \partial(net^{\,o}))$$

$$(\partial(net^{\,o}) / \partial i_{kj})(\partial i_{kj} / \partial(net_{kj}^{\,h}))(\partial(net_{kj}^{\,h}) / \partial b^x_{\,k})$$

$$(\partial b^x_{\,k} / \partial(net_k^{\,x}))(\partial(net_k^{\,x}) / \partial a_k^{\,x}) \tag{C.5}$$

$$\partial(0.5 * (d - z)^2 / \partial z = -(d - z) \tag{C.6}$$

$$\partial z / \partial(net^{\,o}) = \partial f^{\,o} / \partial(net^{\,o}) = f^{\,o} \,'(net^{\,o}) \tag{C.7}$$

$$\partial(net^{\,o}) / \partial i_{kj} = \partial(\sum_{k,j=1}^{L} (a_{kj}^{\,o} i_{kj})) / \partial i_{kj} = a_{kj}^{\,o} \tag{C.8}$$

$$\partial i_{kj} / \partial(net_{kj}^{\,h}) = \partial(f^{\,h} (net_{kj}^{\,h})) / \partial(net_{kj}^{\,h}) = f^{\,h} \,'(net_{kj}^{\,h}) \tag{C.9}$$

$$\partial net_{kj}^{\,h} / \partial b^x_{\,k} = \partial((a_{kj}^{\,hx} * b^x_{\,k}) * (a_{kj}^{\,hy} * b^y_{\,j})) / \partial b^x_{\,k} = a_{kj}^{\,hx} * a_{kj}^{\,hy} * b^y_{\,j}$$

$$= \delta_{kj}^{\,hx} a_{kj}^{\,hx}$$

$$where : \delta_{kj}^{\,hx} = a_{kj}^{\,hy} * b^y_{\,j} \tag{C.10}$$

$$\partial b^x_{\,k} / \partial(net_k^{\,x}) = f_x \,'(net_k^{\,x}) \tag{C.11}$$

$$\partial(net_k^{\,x}) / \partial a_k^{\,x} = \partial(a_k^{\,x} * x) / \partial a_k^{\,x} = x \tag{C.12}$$

Combining Formulae C.5 through C.12 the negative gradient is:

$$-\partial E_p / \partial a_k^{\,x} = (d-z)f^{\,o}{}'(net^{\,o})a_{kj}^{\,o} * f^{\,h}{}'(net_{kj}^{\,h})\delta_{kj}^{\,hx}a_{kj}^{\,hx}f_x{}'(net_k^{\,x})x \tag{C.13}$$

The weight update equations are calculated as follows. For linear output neurons:

$$f^{o}{}' \, (net^{o}) = 1$$

$$\delta^{ol} = (d - z)\,f^{o}{}'(net^{o}) = (d - z) \tag{C.14}$$

For linear neurons of second hidden layer:

$$f^{\,h}{}'(net_{kj}^{\,h}) = 1 \tag{C.15}$$

The negative gradient is:

$$-\partial E_p / \partial a_k^{\,x} = (d-z)f^{\,o}{}'(net^{\,o})a_{kj}^{\,o} * f^{\,h}{}'(net_{kj}^{\,h})\delta_{kj}^{\,hx}a_{kj}^{\,hx}f_x{}'(net_k^{\,x})x$$

$$= \delta^{\,ol} * a_{kj}^{\,o} * \delta_{kj}^{\,hx} * a_{kj}^{\,hx} * (-k^2)\cos^{k-1}(k*net_k^{\,x})\sin(k*net_k^{\,x}) * x \tag{C.16}$$

In the case of sigmoid output neurons, and by combining Formulae C.1, C.4, and C.16, for a linear 1st hidden layer neuron:

$$a_k^{\,x}(t+1) = a_k^{\,x}(t) - \eta(\partial E_p / \partial a_k^{\,x})$$

$$= a_k^{\,x}(t) + \eta(d-z)f^{\,o}{}'(net^{\,o})a_{kj}^{\,o} * f^{\,h}{}'(net_{kj}^{\,h})\delta_{kj}^{\,hx}a_{kj}^{\,hx}f_x{}'(net_k^{\,x})x$$

$$= a_k^{\,x}(t) + \eta * \delta^{\,ol} * a_{kj}^{\,o} * \delta^{\,hx} * a_{kj}^{\,hx} * (-k^2)\cos^{k-1}(k*net_k^{\,x})\sin(k*net_k^{\,x}) * x$$

$$= a_k^{\,x}(t) + \eta * \delta^{\,ol} * a_{kj}^{\,o} * \delta^{\,hx} * a_{kj}^{\,hx} * \delta^{\,x} * x$$

$$where:$$

$$\delta^{\,ol} = (d-z)f^{\,o}{}'(net^{\,o}) = d - z \qquad (linear \qquad neuron)$$

$$\delta^{\,hx} = f^{\,h}{}'(net_{kj}^{\,h})a_{kj}^{\,hy}b^{\,y}{}_j \qquad = a_{kj}^{\,hy}b_j \qquad (linear \qquad neuron)$$

$$\delta^{\,x} = f_x{}'(net_k^{\,x}) = (-k^2)\cos^{k-1}(k*net_k^{\,x})\sin(k*net_k^{\,x}) \tag{C.17}$$

Using the above procedure:

$$a_j^{\ y}(t+1) = a_j^{\ y}(t) - \eta(\partial E_p / \partial a_j^{\ y})$$

$$= a_j^{\ y}(t) + \eta(d-z)f^{o}{}'(net^{o})a_{kj}^{\ o} * f^{h}{}'(net_{kj}^{\ h})\delta_{kj}^{\ hy}a_{kj}^{\ hy}f_y{}'(net_j^{\ y})y$$

$$= a_j^{\ y}(t) + \eta * \delta^{ol} * a_{kj}^{\ o} * \delta^{hy} * a_{kj}^{\ hy} * (j^2)\sin^{j-1}(j*net_j^{\ y})\cos(j*net_j^{\ y}) * y$$

$$= a_j^{\ y}(t) + \eta * \delta^{ol} * a_{kj}^{\ o} * \delta^{hy} * a_{kj}^{\ hy} * \delta^{y} * y$$

where:

$$\delta^{ol} = (d-z)f^{o}{}'(net^{o}) = d-z \qquad (linear \qquad neuron)$$

$$\delta^{hy} = f^{h}{}'(net_{kj}^{\ hy})a_{kj}^{\ hx}b^x_k \qquad = a_{kj}^{\ hx}b^x_k \qquad (linear \qquad neuron)$$

$$\delta^{y} = f_y{}'(net_j^{\ y}) = (j^2)\sin^{j-1}(j*net_k^{\ y})\cos(j*net_k^{\ y}) \qquad\qquad\qquad (C.18)$$

Benefits of this study will be:

- This study draws together the skills and expertise of researchers from disciplines including information science, computer science, business, and economics.
- This study can be further developed for other financial simulation and prediction such as forecasting stock market and currency futures.

Immediate outcomes will be the construction of new higher order neural network models, and the construction of innovative forecasting techniques which will be able to manipulate both normal situations and changing situations. Long term outcomes will be the development of a practical simulation and prediction system in real world conditions based on new HONN models and techniques.

Chapter VIII

Artificial Higher Order Pipeline Recurrent Neural Networks for Financial Time Series Prediction

Panos Liatsis
City University, London, UK

Abir Hussain
John Moores University, UK

Efstathios Milonidis
City University, London, UK

ABSTRACT

The research described in this chapter is concerned with the development of a novel artificial higher order neural networks architecture called the second-order pipeline recurrent neural network. The proposed artificial neural network consists of a linear and a nonlinear section, extracting relevant features from the input signal. The structuring unit of the proposed neural network is the second-order recurrent neural network. The architecture consists of a series of second-order recurrent neural networks, which are concatenated with each other. Simulation results in one-step ahead predictions of the foreign currency exchange rates demonstrate the superior performance of the proposed pipeline architecture as compared to other feed-forward and recurrent structures.

INTRODUCTION

The problem of predicting financial time-series data is an issue of a much interest to both economic and academic communities. Decisions regard-ing investments and trading by large companies and the economic policy of governments rely on computer modelling forecasts. The foreign currency exchange rates (or FX rates as they are more commonly known) are very important in this respect, with FX market worth an estimated daily trading volume of 1 trillion US Dollars (Huang et al., 2004).

Most financial data is non-stationary by default, this means that the statistical properties of the data change over time. These changes are caused as a result of various business and economic cycles (e.g. demand for air travel is higher in the summer months, this can have a knock-on effect of exchange rates, fuel prices, etc) (Magdon-Ismail et al., 1998). While this information should be taken into account in the current closing price of a stock, share or exchange rate it still means that long term study of the behaviour of a given variable is not always the best indicator of its future behaviour. An example of how this problem manifests itself is in the volatility (standard deviation) of stocks and shares. The probabilistic distribution of financial data can change greatly over time; during a period of time, it appears calm with only small changes, and during another period of time, it shows large changes (both positive and negative). It is for this reason that the volatility itself often becomes the central focus of financial time series prediction by the economic forecasting community, where it is assumed that a stable stock or exchange rate is a safer investment (Pham, 1995).

The Efficient Market Hypothesis states that a stock price at a given time reflects all the information available such as news events, other stock prices, and exchange rates at that time period. The hypothesis states that the future information is random and it is unknown in the present time. This indicates that it is impossible to produce above average returns based on historical share prices or other financial data. In reality, the markets reaction to new information is not always immediate due to various factors such as the psychological factors and reactions of various human actors. Therefore, the prediction of financial data is possible (Jensen, 1978).

There has been a considerable evidence to prove that markets are not fully efficient. Many researchers provide evidence showed that stock market returns are predictable by various means such as time-series data on financial and economic variables (Fama & Schwert, 1977; Fama & French, 1988)

There are two main approaches to financial time series forecasting, based on univariate, and multivariate analyses. In univariate approaches, the input variables are restricted to the signal being predicted. In multivariate approaches, any indication whether or not it is directly related to the output can be incorporated as the input variable (Cao & Tay, 2001). Financial time series have a number of properties, which make the prediction changeling, these include:

1. Nonstationary, since the statistical properties of the data change over time. The main cause of this is the effect of various business and economic cycles.
2. Nonlinearity, which makes linear parameter models information difficult to use.
3. High level of noise in the form of random day-to-day variations in financial time series.

Conventional statistical techniques such as autoregressive integrated moving average (ARIMA) and exponential smoothing (Brown, 1963; Hanke & Reitsch 1989) have been extensively used for financial forecasting as univariate models. However, since these models are linear, they fail to capture the nonlinear characteristics of financial time series signals.

There are lot of efforts and researches to explore the nonlinearity of the exchange rate time series and to develop nonlinear models which are capable of improving the forecasting of FX time series. These include the autoregressive random variance (ARV) (So, Lam, & Li, 1999), the autoregressive conditional heteroskedasticity (ARCH) (Hsieh, 1989), chaotic dynamic (Peel & Yadav, 1995) and self-exciting threshold autoregressive (Chappel, Padmore, Mistry & Ellis, 1996) models. These models may show good prediction for particular applications and perform badly for other applications. The problem associated with these models is that the pre-specification of the models restricts their usefulness since there could be lot of input patterns that can be considered (Huang, Lai, Nakamori, & Wang, 2004).

The use of neural network models for the prediction of financial time series as multivariate models has shown significant improvements in terms of prediction and financial metrics (Abecasis & Lapenta, 1996). This is not surprising since these models utilise more information such as inter market indicators, fundamental indicators and technical indicators. Furthermore, neural networks are capable of describing the dynamics of nonstationary time series due to their non-parametric, adaptive and noise tolerant properties (Cao & Tay, 2001).

There are several features of the artificial neural networks which make them attractive to financial time series prediction. First, artificial neural networks are data driven in that there is no need to make prior assumptions about the model under study. This means that neural network are well suited to problems where their solutions requires some knowledge that is difficult to specify however there enough data or observations (Zhang, Patuwo, & Hu, 1998). Second, neural network can generalise. This means that after the training, they often can produce good results even if the training data contains unseen input patterns. Third, it has been shown that artificial neural networks are universal approximator. This means that neural networks can approximate any continuous function to any desire accuracy (Irie, Miyake, 1988). Finally, neural networks are nonlinear. In contrast to the nonlinear statistical models which require hypothesized explicit relationship for the data series at hand, artificial neural networks are data driven models which are capable of performing nonlinear modelling without a prior knowledge about the relationship between the inputs and the outputs of the problem at hand.

However, despite the encouraging results of using artificial neural networks (ANN) for financial time series prediction compared to linear statistical models, the robustness of these findings has been questioned (Versace, Bhatt, Hinds & Shiffer, 2004), due to a number of well known problems with neural models such as:

1. Different neural networks algorithms can produce different results when trained and tested on the same data set. This is because there are different classes of decision boundaries that different ANN prefers.

2. For any given type of neural network, the network is sensitive to the network size and the size of the data set. Neural networks suffer from overfitting and as a result network architecture, learning parameters and training data have to be selected carefully in order to achieve good generalisation, which is critical when using the network for financial time series prediction.

3. The inherent nonlinearity of financial time series can prevent a single neural network from being able to accurately forecast an extended trading period even if it could forecast changes in the testing data.

In this chapter, we propose a new type of artificial higher-order pipeline recurrent neural network, which incorporates second-order terms, which is used in the one-step ahead prediction of the daily exchange rates between the US dollar and the British pound, the Canadian dollar, the Japanese yen and the Swiss franc.

The significance of the proposed network is that it enjoys adaptive online training; this means that it will track sudden changes in the financial data. This is a significantly different compared with offline neural networks models such as the MLP networks. In offline network, the objective of the network is to minimize the error over all the dataset, while for online network, the learning is concentrated on the local properties of the signal and the aim of the network is to adapt to the local properties of the observed signal. Thus the online networks have a more detailed mapping of the underlying structure within the data and are able to respond more readily to any greater changes or regime shifts which are common in non-stationary financial data.

The remainder of the chapter is organised as follows: Section 2 provides an overview of artificial neural networks, in terms of their structure, transfer functions and types of connections. Next, section 3 introduces the various types of artificial higher-order neural networks, drawing upon neurophysiological evidence for the existence of higher-order connections in biological systems. Section 4 is concerned with the topic of pipeline neural networks, which were originally proposed by Haykin and Li (1993), discussing their architecture and learning rule, before introducing the second-order pipeline recurrent neural network. Section 5 presents the simulation results of the pipeline networks in the prediction of financial time series together with a comparison with other feed-forward and feedback neural models. Finally, sections 6 and 7 provide the conclusions of this work and future research directions.

OVERVIEW OF NEURAL NETWORKS

Artificial neural networks also known as neuro-computers, parallel distributed processors, connectionist models or simply neural networks are devices that process information. Usually, they are implemented using electronic components or simulated in software. The main purpose of neural networks is to improve the capability of computers to make decisions in a way similar to the human brain and in which standard computers are unsuitable (Abe, 1997). Neural networks typically consist of a large number of processing elements called neurons or nodes. The processing elements are connected to each other by direct links known as synaptic weights. One of the most

important features of artificial neural networks is their capability to adapt to different environments by changing the values of their links.

On the other hand, the human brain contains a high number of interconnected sets of 10^{10} to 10^{11} biological neurons of nerve cells, which help us in breathing, reading, motion, and thinking (Hertz, Krogh & Palmer, 1991). At the early stages of life, some of the neural structures are developed through learning, while others are wasted away (Hagan, Demuth & Beale, 1995). Figure 1 shows a simplified schematic structure of a biological neuron. There are three main components to the biological neuron. The soma or cell body performs the logical operations of the biological neuron. It sums and thresholds the incoming signals. The axon is a nerve fibre connected to the cell body. It carries the signal from the cell body to other biological neurons. The dendrites are highly branching trees of fibres, connected to the cell body and carry electrical signals to it. The axon of the biological neuron is connected to dendrites of other cells through the synapses. The strengths of the synapses and the arrangement of the neurons determine the function of the neural network (Cichocki & Unbehauen, 1993).

As mentioned before, artificial neural networks consist of a number of simple artificial neurons.

Figure 1. Structure of a biological neuron

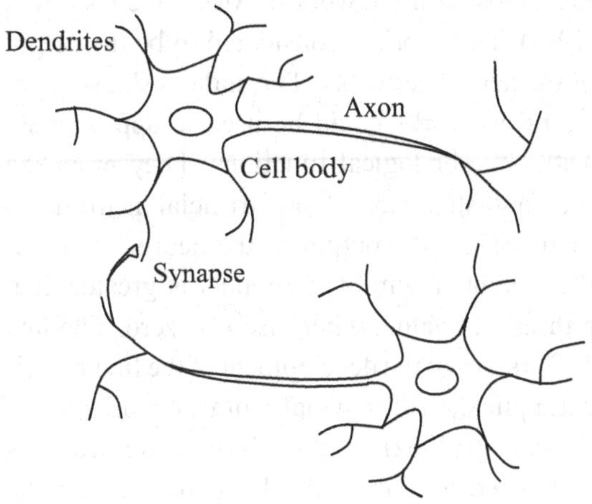

The sum of the weighted inputs of the neuron is usually passed through a nonlinear function to give the output of the neuron.

In comparing the biological neuron with the basic structure of an artificial neuron, we can notice that the cell body is replaced by the summation unit and the transfer function. The signal on the axon is represented by the output of the neuron and the weights of the artificial neuron are related to the strengths of the synapses.

Neural networks can provide many important features. They consist of a number of interconnected neurons with nonlinear transfer functions. Therefore, neural networks can carry out nonlinear mappings. This feature is very important particularly in discovering complex patterns in high dimensional data, such as images. They are powerful computational devices due to their massively parallel structure. Another important feature of neural networks is their ability to learn and generalise. The weights of the neural network can be trained either using supervised or unsupervised learning algorithms with part of the data called the training set. The trained weights of the network can be used to predict values not included in the training set. In most cases, the trained weights can provide acceptable generalisation. All these features make researchers interested to study and implement neural networks on digital computers.

The interest in neural networks dates back to the 1940s with the work of McCulloch & Pitts (1943). This work is considered to be the origin of the neural networks. The authors showed that neural networks could be used to approximate arithmetic or logical functions. They proposed the first structure of an artificial neuron. In their design, the output of the neuron is one if the weighted sum of the inputs is greater than a threshold value, otherwise it is zero. The late 1950s showed the development of the first practical application of artificial neural networks, when Rosenblatt (1962) invented the perceptron and its associated learning rule. He demonstrated the

ability of the network to perform simple pattern recognition tasks. In his work, the neuron model of McCulloch and Pitts was organised in layers and the learning algorithm to update the weights connected to the output layer of the network was developed. The perceptron opened the door to many researches and neural networks started to emerge widely until the work of Minsky & Papert (1969). In their book *Perceptrons*, they showed that perceptrons cannot solve any logical problem unless it is linearly separable. They demonstrated mathematically that the XOR is one of the logical problems that perceptrons are incapable of solving. This work effectively contributed to the shrinking of neural networks research over the next decade or so.

During the 1970s, Kohonen (1972) and Anderson (1972) independently and separately invented new neural network architectures that could act as memories. The most important developments in the field of neural networks came in the 1980s. In this period, personal computers and powerful workstations were becoming widely available. In the 1980s, Hopfield (1982) proposed a recurrent neural network with mutual connections and the idea of an energy function that decreases as time elapses. This type of recurrent network is known as the Hopfield network. In addition, the discovery of the backpropagation learning algorithm (Rumelhart & McClelland, 1986) for the training of multilayer perceptron networks by many researchers independently and separately has widened the applicability of neural networks.

Nowadays artificial neural networks are being applied to an increasing number of real-world problems of considerable complexity. They offer ideal solutions to a variety of classification problems such as speech and signal recognition. Neural networks can be used in function prediction and system modelling, where the physical processes are highly complex. They may also be applied to control problems, where the input variables and measurements are used to drive an output actuator, and the neural network are used as a general structure for an adaptive nonlinear controller (Lightbody, Wu & Irwin, 1992).

Neuron Structure

As mentioned before, the neuron is the basic structure of an artificial neural network. It is the information-processing unit also known as a node. There are three basic components to the neuron. The first is a set of synaptic weights, which represent the strength or the connection of the neuron. They are trainable and can either be positive if the associated synapse is excitatory or negative if the synapse is inhibitory. The summing unit is the second component of the neuron, which adds the weighted inputs and passes the results to a usually nonlinear transfer function.

Figure 2 illustrates a graphical description of the neuron. As well as, the set of inputs x_1, x_2, ..., x_p, the set of weights w_{k1}, w_{k2}, ..., w_{kp} and the activation function F, the model includes a bias value b_k added to the net input of the neuron. Thus, the output of the kth neuron is determined by:

$$y_k = f(n_k + b_k)$$

$$n_k = \sum_{i=1}^{p} w_{ki} x_i \qquad (1)$$

The bias can be included as a direct input to the neuron by adding an extra input line of value one. Both the weights and bias of the neuron are adjustable scalar parameters.

Figure 2. Model of an artificial neuron

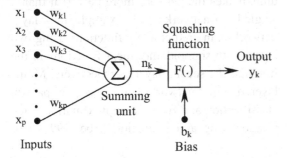

Activation Functions

The activation or squashing function is usually a nonlinear function that suppresses the range of the output of the neuron to a range of values. There are three basic types of activation functions. The first one is the hard limit or the threshold function. In this case, the output of the neuron can be one if the sum of the weighted inputs and the bias is greater than (or equal to) zero. Otherwise, the output of the neuron is zero. Therefore:

$$y_k = \begin{cases} 1, & \text{if} \quad W^T X + b_k \geq 0 \\ 0, & \text{if} \quad W^T X + b_k < 0 \end{cases} \qquad (2)$$

where W is the vector of the weight values and X is a vector of the inputs.

The piecewise linear function is another type of activation function. The output of this function is zero if the net sum of the weighted inputs is less than -0.5, or one if the net sum of the weighted inputs is greater than 0.5, and linear in the range -0.5 and 0.5. Therefore, the output of the neuron is determined according to the following equation:

$$y_k = \begin{cases} 1, & \text{if } W^T X + b_k \geq 0.5 \\ W^T X + b_k, & \text{if } -0.5 < W^T X + b_k < 0.5 \\ 0, & \text{if } W^T X + b_k \leq -0.5 \end{cases} \qquad (3)$$

Another basic type of the activation functions is the logistic sigmoid function. It is one of the most popular functions used in the construction of neural networks because of its nonlinearity and differentiability. The output of the neuron is given by:

$$y_k = \frac{1}{1 + e^{-a \cdot n_k}} \qquad (4)$$

where a is the slope parameter of the sigmoid function and n_k is the net sum of the weighted inputs and bias. The output of the neuron is in the range of 0 and 1.

The threshold, piecewise linear and sigmoid functions all have their outputs in the range of 0 and 1. However, it is sometimes desirable to have negative values in the output. Therefore, the signum and the hyperbolic transfer functions have their outputs in the range –1 and 1, and are defined as follows:

$$y_k = \begin{cases} 1, & \text{if } W^T X + b_k > 0 \\ 0, & \text{if } W^T X + b_k = 0 \\ -1, & \text{if } W^T X + b_k < 0 \end{cases} \qquad (5)$$

and

$$y_k = \frac{1 - e^{-(n_k + b_k)}}{1 + e^{-(n_k + b_k)}} \qquad (6)$$

respectively.

Network Architectures

A single neuron by itself usually cannot predict functions or manage to process different types of information. This is because a neural network gains its power from its massively parallel structure and interconnected weights. As a result, many neural network architectures have been proposed.

Figure 3. A single layer neural network

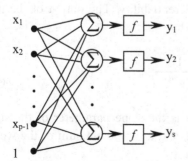

Single Layers Of Neurons

Figure 3 shows the structure of a single layer of neurons. The network has P inputs and S neurons. Each neuron can have its own transfer function, i.e., it is not necessary to have the same activation function for all the neurons. The weights in this case are organised in a S x P matrix. The row indices of the weight matrix correspond to the neuron location and the column indices correspond to the input location. Therefore, the weight value w_{ij} represents the weight that connects the jth input to the ith neuron.

The perceptron networks and the adaptive linear elements are examples of single layers of neurons structures.

Multiple Layers Of Neurons

An example of multiple layers of neurons is shown in Figure 4. As it can be noticed from this figure, the network consists of three main layers. The output layer corresponds to the final output of the neural network. The external inputs are presented to the network through the input neurons. Since no mathematical operations are performed by these neurons, we will not consider them as a separate layer. Each layer has its own weights, biases and transfer functions. The weight matrix of the ith layer is represented by W^i. Suppose that the network has P external inputs and S neurons in the first layer, then the weight matrix of the first layer is represented by $W^1_{S \times P}$. The outputs of the hidden layer are the inputs to the following layer.

The use of more than one layers of nonlinear units makes the network more powerful than a single layer network. As an example, multilayer networks can predict many functions using two layers with sigmoid and linear functions in the first and the second layers, respectively. Multi-layered neural networks can be used for pattern classification and function approximation, such as modelling and prediction (Abe, 1997). An

Figure 4. An example of a multilayer network

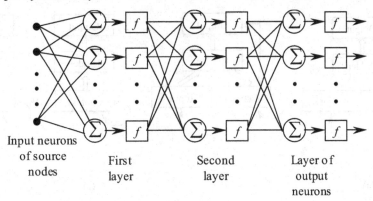

Input neurons
of source
nodes

First
layer

Second
layer

Layer of
output
neurons

example of multilayer neural network structures is the multilayer perceptron.

Recurrent Neural Networks

The single and multilayer neural networks presented so far are called feed-forward neural networks mainly because all the connections either go from the input layer to the output layer, from the input layer to the hidden layer, or from the hidden layer to the output layer. In the case of recurrent neural networks, in addition to the feed-forward connections there are also feedback connections that propagate in the opposite direction, which allow them to have capabilities not found in feed-forward networks such as storing information for latter use and attractor dynamics (Draye, Pavisic, Cheron & Libert, 1996).

When using feed-forward neural networks as dynamical systems, tapped-delay-line is usually employed to provide them with memory. The aim of the tapped-delay-line is to turn the temporal sequences into spatial sequences. The utilisation of the tapped-delay-line involves several problems such as large number of delay units has to be selected in advance, which can cause slow computation. In addition, the input should be forwarded to the tapped-delay-line at the proper time and with the correct rate. While recurrent neural networks have feedback connections that

allow them to have memory and hence avoid the problems of utilising tapped-delay-lines.

Recurrent neural network can be classified into two categories with respect to their connectivity, i.e., fully and partially recurrent. Fully recurrent neural networks have feed-forward and feedback connections in any order, all of them are trainable.

Partially recurrent neural networks have special units called context units where the outputs from the hidden or the output layers are fed back. The feed-forward connections are trainable, while the feedback connections are fixed. Figure 5 shows various partially recurrent neural networks architectures.

Figure 5 (a) shows the basic structure of the Elman network (Elman, 1990). It consists of two layers, the hidden layer with nonlinear transfer functions and the output layer with linear transfer functions. The input units hold copy of the values of the external inputs, while the context units hold copy of the values of feedback outputs of the hidden units. The initial weights are randomly selected and the network is trained using the backpropagation learning algorithm.

The Elman network can be used to represent the time implicitly, rather than explicitly. To illustrate this point, consider solving the XOR problem using an Elman network with one input, two context units, two hidden units, and one output. The input

Figure 5. Various structures of partially recurrent neural networks

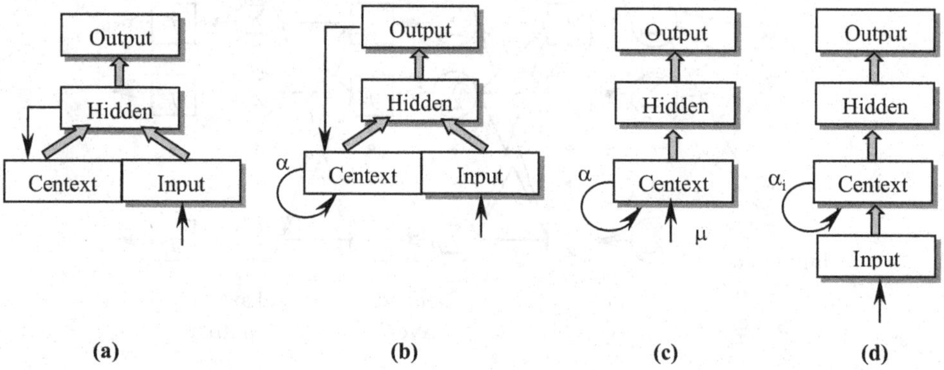

(a)   (b)   (c)   (d)

sequence consists of two bits representing the XOR input values, followed by the target value and the network is trained to produce the correct output value. Hence, if the input sequence is (000 011 101 110) the output of the networks is (000 010 010 00?). The simulation result indicated that the network managed to give good prediction and learn the temporal sequence.

Jordan (1986) has further improve the Elman network by utilising self-feedback connections at the context units, which provide them with inertia and increase the memory of the network as illustrated in Figure 5(b). The network consists of two layers, the output and the hidden layers. The outputs of the network are fed back to the context units, which hold a copy of the previous values of the context units themselves. The value of the context unit is determined according the following equation:

$$x_i^c(t+1) = \alpha x_i^c(t) + y_i(t)$$

$$= \sum_{t'=0}^{t} \alpha^{t-t'} y_i(t'), \qquad (7)$$

where $x_i^c(t+1)$ is the output of the context unit i at time t+1, α is the strength of the self-connections, and $y_i(t)$ is the ith output of network at time t. The network was trained using the standard backpropagation learning algorithm and utilised

in various applications such as the prediction of the speech signal.

Stornetta, Hogg & Huberman (1987) developed different partially recurrent neural network architecture shown in Figure 5(c) and which was used for pattern recognition. The input is forwarded to the network through the context units, which hold a copy of the previous values of the context units themselves. The output of the context units is determined according to the following equation:

$$x_i^c(t+1) = \alpha x_i^c(t) + \mu x_i(t+1) \qquad (8)$$

where $x_i^c(t+1)$ is the ith output of the context unit at time t+1, $x_i(t)$ is the ith input of the network at time t, α is the decay rate and μ is the input amplitude.

Figure 5(d) shows another structure of a partially recurrent neural network, which was developed by Mozer (1989). It consists of three layers, which are the context unit, the hidden, and the output layers. The network calculates the weighted inputs and passes the results to the context units. The context units forward the weighted inputs to nonlinear transfer function and update its output values as follows:

$$x_i^c(t+1) = \alpha_i x_i^c(t) + f(net_i(t)) \qquad (9)$$

where $x_i^c(t+1)$ is the ith output of the context unit at time t+1, α_i is a decay weight associated with the unit i, f is a nonlinear transfer function, and $net_i(t)$ is the net input sum to the context unit i.

The adjustable weights from the input units to the context units allow the context units to be flexible and appropriate to solve various problems. The self-connections provide the context units with inertia, and since they are trainable then they allow the decay values to match the time scales of the inputs.

Because of the feedback connections, recurrent neural networks have capabilities not found in feed-forward networks such as storing information for latter use and attractor dynamics. Therefore, they can be applied to highly nonlinear dynamic system identification. Since they can settled to a fixed stable state, they can be applied as associative memories, for pattern completion and pattern recovery and they are potentially useful for time varying behaviour.

Figure 6 shows a type of fully recurrent network with self-feedback loops. We consider that a recurrent neural network has self-feedback loops if the output of a neuron is fed back to its input. Furthermore, the network has hidden output neurons. A recurrent network has hidden output neurons if one or more of its output neurons have no target values. The feedback connections result in nonlinear dynamical behaviour because of the nonlinear nature of the neuron. Such behaviour provides recurrent neural networks with storage capabilities.

The feedback connections have great influence on the learning capability of the network. There are different types of learning algorithms that have been proposed to train recurrent neural networks. The backpropagation through time or unfolding of time (Werbos, 1990) is one of those algorithms that have been used for training recurrent neural networks. The main idea of the algorithm is to unfold the recurrent network into an equivalent feed-forward network and hence the name unfolding of time. Williams & Zipser (1989) proposed another learning algorithm for fully recurrent neural networks. The online version of this algorithm is called real time recurrent learning algorithm (RTRL), where the synaptic weights are updated for each presentation of the training set. As a result, there is no need to allocate memory proportional to the number of sequences.

Figure 6. Structure of a fully recurrent neural network

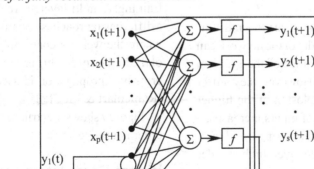

HIGHER-ORDER NEURAL NETWORKS

The abandonment of neural networks research in the 70s was partly the result of the critical work of Minsky & Papert (1969). In their investigations, summarised in their book *Perceptrons*, they showed that single-layered perceptrons could not even solve problems as elementary and simple as the exclusive OR (XOR) logical function. The answer to this question has to do with the directions that neural networks research took in the 60s, where the requirement of non-linear mappings was interpreted as a need for multiple linear decision boundaries that would allow the formation of arbitrary complex decision regions. As a direct consequence, the perceptron architecture was extended to accommodate intervening layers of neurons (hidden layers), capable of extracting higher-order features, and thereby resulting in networks that could solve reasonably well any given input-output problem (Whitley & Hanson, 1989).

Going back to our original question regarding the nature of decision boundaries, the XOR problem could be solved if the decision boundary is non-linear. In order for boundaries to have such form, the network should include non-linear combinations of its inputs. This has led to the development of artificial *higher-order neural networks* (HONNs).

HONNs demonstrate good learning and storage capabilities since the order of the network can be designed to match the order of the problem (Giles & Maxwell, 1987). However, they suffer from the combinatorial explosion of the higher order terms as the number of inputs increases.

HONNs can be classified into single and multiple layer structures. Single-layer, higher-order networks consist of a single processing layer and inputs nodes, such as the functional link network (FLN) (Pao, 1989), which functionally expands the input space, by suitable pre-processing of the inputs.

The advantages of utilising the functional link network are that the supervised and the unsupervised learning can be used to train the same network architecture. This enhancement is important in any real pattern recognition tasks (Pao, 1989).

Multilayered HONNs incorporate hidden layers, in addition to the output layer. A popular example of such structures is the sigma-pi network, which consists of layers of sigma-pi units (Rumelhart, Hinto & Williams, 1986). A sigma-pi unit consists of a summing unit connected to a number of product units, whose order is determined by the number of input connections. Another architecture that belongs to this category is the pi-sigma network (Shin & Ghosh, 1992). This consists of a layer of summing units, connected to a single product unit. The output of the product unit is usually passed through a nonlinear transfer function. The main difference between the pi-sigma and the sigma-pi networks is that the former utilise a smaller number of weights, however they are not universal approximators. To address this disadvantage, Shin & Ghosh (1991) proposed an extension to the pi-sigma network, the so-called ridge polynomial neural network (RPN), which consists of a number of increasing order pi-sigma units. Most of the above networks have one layer of trainable weights, and hence simple weights updating procedures can be used for their training. A multi-layered architecture which uses a different approach is the product units network, where the weights correspond to the exponents of the higher-order terms. Hence, an extension of error-backpropagation is used for their training (Rumelhart & McClelland, 1986).

Figure 7 shows the structures of various higher-order neural networks.

Higher-Order Interactions in Biological Networks

The assumption of first-order connections between neurons is not tenable for biological net-

Figure 7. Layer-based classification of various higher neural networks

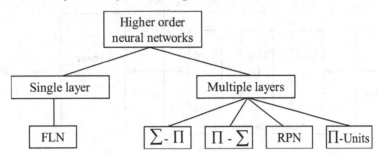

works (Kohring, 1990). In fact, biological systems have a propensity for higher-order interactions between neurons, although the reasons for this are far from clear. This section provides some examples of biological neuronal networks with built-in interactions to support the use of higher-order correlations between inputs.

Experiments in the crustacean neuromuscular junction, and the mammalian central nervous system (Solomon & Schmidt, 1990) have demonstrated the existence of axo-axonic synapses responsible for *pre-synaptic inhibition*. Pre-synaptic inhibition is very useful for information processing in neurons activated by many converging pathways, since under certain circumstances some inputs may act to suppress others selectively (Poggio & Torre, 1981).

Extensive research in the retina suggests that electrical couplings at the level of photoreceptors are responsible for amplification of small signals and their extraction from system noise (Baylor, 1981). The organisation is such that rods are coupled only to other rods, while cones are coupled only to other cones of the same spectral sensitivity.

The interaction in the cones of the turtle retina operates over a distance of several cell diameters, while in the rod system, the interaction distance is larger than 10 cell diameters. The coupling interaction computes a running average of the internal potentials of a number of receptors, smoothing fluctuations introduced by the quantum nature

of light and by intrinsic noise sources within the receptors.

Simon, Lamb & Hodgkin (1975) have found an inverse correlation between the amplitude of dark noise in a cone and the length constant of its interaction with other cells. In other words, cells with large length constants, indicative of extensive coupling, were relatively quiet in darkness, while cells with smaller length constants are noisier.

The signal averaging resulting from receptor couplings is a well established phenomenon, however its functional significance is not yet clear. It seems that although coupling reduces the level of receptor dark noise and increases the steadiness of signals evoked by dim diffuse light, it does not improve the signal-to-noise ratio for single-photon effects, and in fact it introduces spatial blurring in the receptor excitation. Further understanding of the role of coupling will require a clearer picture of the operation of chemical synapses between receptors and bipolar cells.

PIPELINED RECURRENT NEURAL NETWORKS (PRNNS)

The pipelined recurrent neural network is a relatively new type of recurrent neural network, which was introduced by Haykin & Li (1995). It was designed to adaptively predict highly nonlinear and nonstationary signals such as the speech time series.

Figure 8. The general structure of the pipelined recurrent neural network

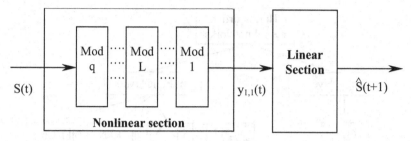

Figure 9. Structure of module i of the PRNN

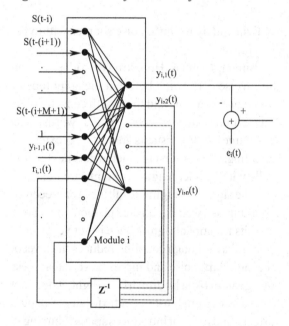

The pipelined network is based on the engineering concept of 'divide and conquer', meaning that if the problem is too big, then this problem can be more usefully solved by dividing it into a number of more manageable problems. Therefore, the aim of the network was to first solve individual small-scale problems.

The PRNN network consists of two subsections, the nonlinear and linear subsections. The former extracts the nonlinear information, while the latter extracts the linear information from the signal. The structure of the pipelined recurrent neural network is shown in Figure 8. For more information about the PRNN refer to (Haykin & Li, 1995).

The nonlinear section consists of a q number of recurrent neural networks concatenated with each other. Each recurrent neural network is called a module and consists of M external inputs and N outputs. All modules of the PRNN are partially recurrent neural networks, except the last module which is a fully recurrent network where all its outputs are fed back to the inputs. For the partially recurrent network, N-1 outputs are fed back to the inputs, while the first output is forwarded to the next module as input. The bias is included into the structure of the module by adding an extra input line of value 1. The total number of weights in each module is (M+N+1)×N and each module holds a copy of the same weight matrix W. The detailed structure of the ith module is shown in Figure 9.

In what follows, the inputs and outputs, as well as, the processing equations of the pipelined recurrent neural networks are presented.

If S(t) represent the value of the nonlinear and nonstationary signal at time t, then the external inputs presented to the ith module is defined as follows:

$$X_i(t) = [S(t-i) \; S(t-(i+1)),....., S(t-(i+M-1))]^T \qquad (10)$$

while the recurrent inputs are represented into an N×1 input vector defined as:

$$R_i(t) = [y_{i-1,1}(t), r_i(t)]^T \qquad (11)$$

where $y_{i-1,1}$ represent the first output of module i-1 and:

$$r_i(t) = [y_{i,2}(t-1),....,y_{i,N}(t-1)]^T,$$
for i = 1,2,..., (q-1) $\qquad$ (12)

Since the final module is a fully recurrent neural network, then we have:

$$R_q(t) = [y_{q,1}(t-1),\ y_{q,2}(t-1),.....,y_{q,N}(t-1)]^T \qquad (13)$$

Let $y_{i,k}$ represent the kth output of module i which is defined as follows:

$$y_{i,k}(t) = f(v_{i,k}(t)) \qquad (14)$$

where f is a nonlinear transfer function and $v_{i,k}$ is the net internal activation of module i, determined according to the following equation:

$$v_{i,k}(t) = \sum_{l=1}^{M+N+1} w_{kl} z_{i,k}(t) \qquad (15)$$

where $z_{i,k}$ is the kth input to module i.

The linear section of the PRNN is a taped delay network where the L previous values of the first output of the first module of the nonlinear subsection are weighted and linearly summed to give the final output of the pipelined recurrent network.

Real Time Recurrent Learning Algorithm Of The PRNN

The PRNN was trained using the RTRL algorithm. Since the same weights are used for all the modules of the network, the learning algorithm starts by initialising the weights of one of the network module to small random values. Then, the RTRL algorithm is used to train the weights of one module. The trained weights are copied for the whole modules and used as the initial weights for the PRNN.

The PRNN is trained adaptively in which the errors produced from each module are calculated and the overall cost function of the PRNN is defined as follows:

$$\varepsilon(t) = \sum_{i=1}^{q} \lambda^{i-1} e_i^2(t) \qquad (16)$$

where λ is an exponential forgetting factor selected in the range (0, 1]. At each time t, the output of each module $y_i(t)$ is determined and the error $e_i(t)$ is calculated as the difference between the actual value expected from each unit i and the predicted value $y_i(t)$. The change in the weight is determined according to the following equation:

$$\Delta w_{kL}(t) = -\eta \frac{\partial \varepsilon(t)}{\partial w_{kL}} \qquad (17)$$

where η is the learning rate and:

$$\frac{\partial \varepsilon(t)}{\partial w_{kL}} = 2\sum_{i=1}^{q} \lambda^{i-1} e_i(t) \frac{\partial e_i(t)}{\partial w_{kL}},$$

$$= -2\sum_{i=1}^{q} \lambda^{i-1} e_i(t) \frac{\partial y_{i,1}(t)}{\partial w_{kL}} \qquad (18)$$

Let $p_{kl}^{ij}(t)$ be:

$$p_{kL}^{ij}(t) = \frac{\partial y_{i,j}(t)}{\partial w_{kL}} \qquad (19)$$

Then, the values of the p_{kl}^{ij} matrix are updated by differentiating the processing equations as follows:

$$p_{kL}^{ij}(t+1) = f'(v_{i,j}(t)) \left[\sum_{n=1}^{N} w_{jn}(t) P_{kl}^{in}(t) + \delta_{kj} z_{i,L}(t) \right] \qquad (20)$$

where f' is the derivative of the transfer function, and δ_{kj} is the Konecker's delta.

Since the initial state is assumed to be independent of the initial weights of the network, then:

$$p_{kL}^{ij}(0) = 0 \qquad (21)$$

Hence, the change of the weight is determined according to the follow equation:

$$\Delta w_{kL}(t) = 2\eta \sum_{i=1}^{q} \lambda^{i-1} e_i(t) p_{kL}^{i1}(t) \qquad (22)$$

Applications Of The Pipelined Recurrent Neural Networks

Haykin & Li (1995) used the PRNN to predict the speech time series. They utilised a pipelined network of five modules, two output neurons per module, and four external inputs to predict a male speech. The network achieved 25.14 dB for 10000 speech samples, this is an improvement of approximately 3 dB over the linear adaptive predictor which produced only 22.01 dB.

The PRNN was also used for the prediction of the traffic video signals (Chang & Hu, 1997). A "Bike" video source lasts for 5s and composed of three frames I, P and B were selected to test the performance of the network using the annealing learning rate scheme. The predicted values were

closer to the actual traffic signals and the prediction errors of the three frames were maintained within certain small values.

Second Order Pipelined Recurrent Neural Networks (SOPRNNs)

In this section, we propose a new type of higher order pipelined recurrent neural network called the second pipelined recurrent neural network. The purpose of the network is to improve the performance of the PRNN by accommodating second order terms at the inputs. Similarly to the PRNN, the nonlinear subsection of the SOPRNN consists of a number of modules concatenated with each other. Each module is a second order fully recurrent neural network. All the modules are partially recurrent neural networks, apart from the last module which is a fully RNN. Figure 10 shows the structure of the nonlinear subsection of the SOPRNN with M external inputs and N outputs for each module.

The second order fully recurrent neural network (Forcada & Carrasco, 1995) calculates the second order terms generated by the multiplica-

Figure 10. The structure of the nonlinear subsection of the SOPRNN

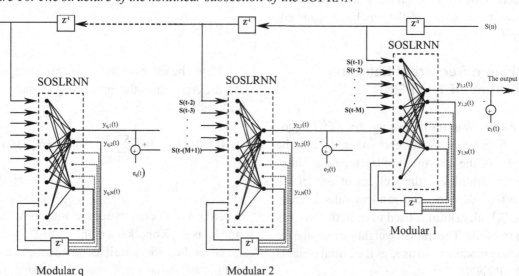

tion of the external inputs by the outputs and then passes the results to the input nodes. Figure 11 illustrates the block diagram of a second-order recurrent neural network, which contains some hidden output units.

In what follows, the processing equations of the SOPRNN are presented.

Let X_i represent the external input vector of module i, which can determined according to the following equation:

$$X_i(t) = [x_{i,1}(t) \ x_{i,2}(t), \ldots\ldots\ldots, x_{i,M}(t)]^T$$
$$[= \ S(t-i) \ S(t-(i+1)), \ldots\ldots, S(t-(i+M-1))]^T \tag{23}$$

where $\{S(t)\}$ is the nonlinear and nonstationary signal.

Let Y_i represent the output vector of module i which is defined as follows:

$$Y_i(t) = [y_{i,1}(t) \ y_{i,2}(t), \ldots\ldots\ldots, y_{i,N}(t)]^T \tag{24}$$

where $y_{i,j}$ represent the jth output of module i.

The processing equations of the SOPRNN are determined as follows:

$$y_{i,j}(t) = f(v_{i,j}(t)) \tag{25}$$

For the last module of the second order pipelined recurrent neural network, we have:

$$v_{q,j}(t) = \sum_{n=1}^{N}\sum_{m=1}^{M} w_{j(m+(n-1)M)}x_{q,m}(t)y_{q,n}(t)$$
$$= \sum_{L=1}^{MN} w_{jL}z_{q,L}(t) \tag{26}$$

where $z_{q,L}$ is the actual L^{th} input of module q.

For all other modules of the SOPRNN, we have:

$$v_{i,j}(t) = \sum_{n=2}^{N}\sum_{m=1}^{M} w_{j(m+(n-1)M)}x_{i,m}(t)y_{i,n}(t) + \sum_{m=1}^{M} w_{jm}x_{i,m}(t)y_{i-1,1}(t)$$
$$(= \sum_{L=1}^{MN} w_{jL}z_{i,L} \ t)$$
$$\tag{27}$$

where $z_{i,L}$ is the actual L^{th} input of module i (determined by the second order combinations between the inputs and outputs of the SOPRNN).

The Learning Algorithm of the SOPRNN

Similarly to the PRNN, the proposed second order pipelined recurrent neural network is trained using the real time recurrent learning algorithm. In this

Figure 11. The block diagram of a second-order single layer fully recurrent neural network

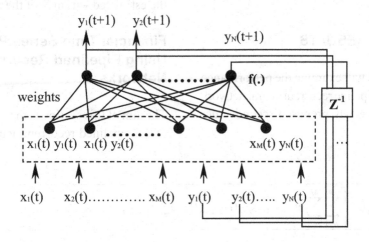

case, the change applied to the kl[th] element of the weight matrix can be determined as follows:

$$\Delta w_{kl}(t) = 2\eta \sum_{i=1}^{q} \lambda^{i-1} e_i(t) \frac{\partial y_{i,L}(t)}{\partial w_{kL}} \tag{28}$$

where η is the learning rate, q is the total number of modules, and $e_i(t)$ is the error of module i.

Let $p_{kl}^{ij}(t)$ to be:

$$p_{kL}^{ij}(t) = \frac{\partial y_{i,j}(t)}{\partial w_{kL}} \tag{29}$$

then the updated value of $p_{kl}^{ij}(t+1)$ at time t+1can be determined by differentiating the processing equations of the network:

$$p_{kl}^{ij}(t+1) = \frac{\partial}{\partial w_{kL}}(f(v_{i,j}(t))) = f'(v_{i,j}(t))\left[\frac{\partial}{\partial w_{kL}}(v_{i,j}(t))\right] \tag{30}$$

where f' is the derivative of the transfer function, and δ_{kj} is the Kronecker's delta.

Therefore, $p_{kl}^{ij}(t+1)$ is determined as shown in Equation (31).

Since it is assumed that the initial state is independent to the initial weights of the networks then:

$$p_{kL}^{ij}(0) = 0 \tag{32}$$

SIMULATION RESULTS

In this section, we will examine the performance of the traditional pipeline recurrent neural network structure and the newly proposed second-order

pipeline recurrent neural network in the one-step ahead prediction of the daily exchange rates of the US dollar and the British pound, the Canadian dollar, the Japanese yen and the Swiss franc. To facilitate comparison with other artificial neural networks, we will provide the results of one-step prediction of the multi-layer perceptron, the single layer recurrent neural network and the second-order single layer recurrent neural network. For all neural network predictors, logistic sigmoid transfer functions were used in the output layer, hence, the time series signals were normalised between 0 and 1. The performance of the various neural networks architectures was evaluated using two measures, namely the signal to noise ratio (SNR) or the prediction gain and the average relative variance (ARV). The SNR can be determined as follows:

$$SNR = 10 \log_{10}\left(\frac{\sigma^2}{\sigma_e^2}\right) dB \tag{33}$$

where σ^2 is the estimated variance of the input signal and σ_e^2 is the estimated variance of the error signal.

The ARV can be determined according to the following equation:

$$arv = \frac{1}{\sigma^2} \frac{1}{N} \sum_{i=1}^{N}(x_i - \hat{x}_i)^2 \tag{34}$$

where N is the number of data points and σ^2 is the estimated variance of the data.

Financial Time Series Prediction Using Pipelined Recurrent Neural Networks

The aim of this section is to test the performance of the pipelined recurrent neural networks with

Equation (31).

$$p_{kl}^{ij}(t+1) = f'(v_{i,j}(t))\left[\sum_{n=1}^{N}\sum_{m=1}^{M} w_{j(m+nM)} x_{i,m}(t) p_{kl}^{im}(t) + \delta_{kj} z_{i,L}(t)\right]$$

various time series. The network was implemented in C++ with the output of the pipelined recurrent network being the output of the nonlinear section. The weights of one module were randomly initialised between -0.1 and 0.1 and trained using the real time recurrent learning algorithm. The trained weights are copied for all modules of the pipelined recurrent neural networks and used as the initial weights of the network. The adaptive real time learning algorithm was used for the training of the network.

The exchange rates time series between the US dollar and the British Pound, the Canadian Dollar, the Japanese Yen and the Swiss Frank in the period between 3 September 1973 to 18 May 1983 were predicted using the pipelined recurrent neural network. The networks parameters and performances are shown in Table 1, while the actual and the predicted signals are illustrated in Figure 12.

Financial Time Series Prediction Using Second-Order Pipelined Recurrent Neural Networks

The newly proposed second order pipelined recurrent neural network was utilised to predict various time series. A C++ program was written to implement the structure of the second order pipelined network. Similarly to the pipelined recurrent neural network, the weights of one module were randomly initialised between - 0.1 and 0.1 and trained using the real time recurrent learning algorithm. The trained weights were then copied in the modules of the pipelined network. The output of the second-order pipelined network is the output of the first module of the network. A number of trials were performed to determine the appropriate network parameters.

The exchange rates time series between the US dollar and the four currencies (the British Pound, the Canadian Dollar, the Japanese Yen, the Swiss Frank) in the period between 3 September 1973 to 18 May 1983 were predicted using the second order pipelined recurrent neural network. The network gave good performance as illustrated in Figures 12 and 13. These results were confirmed by small average relative variances and high signal to noise ratio values (refer to Table 2).

Comparison with Other ANN Approaches

This section is concerned with the comparison of the simulation results obtained using various neural network architectures. The comparison is performed according to the two metrics, i.e., SNR and AVR. In our simulations, we investigated the range of values for the parameters that influence the network performance in which the results

Table 1. The parameters and performance of the pipelined recurrent neural network used in the prediction of the exchange rates time series.

Signal	US $/£	US$/ Canadian $	US$/ Yen	US$/Swiss Franc
Number of Modules	5	5	5	5
Number of Neurons	5	5	4	4
Nonlinear prediction order	5	5	5	5
Learning rate	0.5	0.5	0.5	0.4
Forgetting factor	0.1	0.7	0.5	0.4
ARV	0.0046	0.0017	0.0060	0.0043
SNR	23.3698	27.6561	22.2284	23.6241

Figure 12. Nonlinear prediction of the daily exchange using the pipelined recurrent neural network in the period between 3 September 1973 to 18 May 1983 between the US Dollar and (a) the British Pound; (b) the Canadian Dollar; (c) the Japanese Yen; (d) the Swiss Franc.

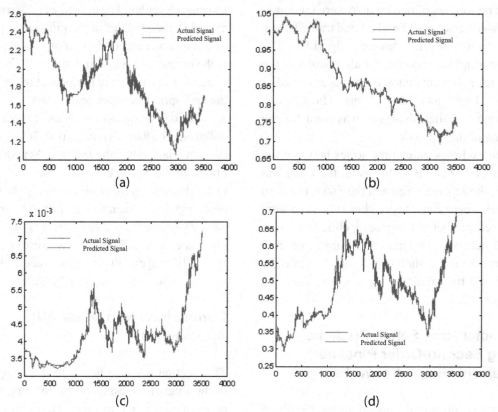

Table 2. The parameters and performance of the second-order pipelined recurrent neural network used in the prediction of the exchange rates time series.

Signal	US$/£	US$/ Canadian $	US$/ Yen	US$/Swiss Franc
Number of Modules	5	5	5	5
Number of Neurons	3	3	4	4
Nonlinear prediction order	5	5	5	5
Learning rate	0.5	0.9	0.9	0.5
Forgetting factor	0.6	0.9	0.9	0.5
ARV	0.003	0.0013	0.0074	0.0030
SNR	25.1809 dB	29.0405 dB	21.3460	25.2121

Figure 13. Nonlinear prediction of the daily exchange using the second order pipelined recurrent neural network in the period between 3 September 1973 to 18 May 1983 between the US Dollar and (a) the British Pound; (b) the Canadian Dollar; (c) the Japanese Yen; (d) the Swiss Franc.

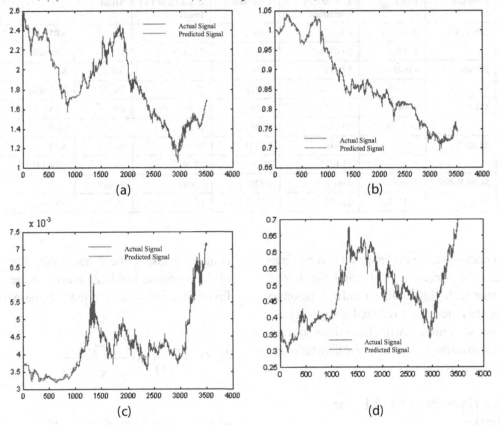

are stable. In the case of the MLP, the number of external inputs was varied between 4 and 10, while we carried out experiments with the hidden layer consisting of 5 to 10 hidden units. The size of the training set for the MLP experiments varied between 1000 and 2000 samples. The number of external inputs varied between 6 and 10 in the training of the SLRNN, while the number of output units was between 5 and 10. Half of the training set (i.e., 1500 points) was used for the training of the single layer recurrent neural network. The experimental setup for the SOSLRNN was similar to that of the SLRNN. The results showed that similar performances were sustained across different training and testing sets. The performance

of the proposed network was also compared to the multilayer perceptron (MLP), the single layer recurrent neural network (SLRNN) trained using the real time learning algorithm of Williams & Zipser (1989), and the second order single layer recurrent neural network (SOSLRNN), and the results are shown in Table 3. In summary, the SOPRNN achieves an average improvement of 0.976 dB in comparison to the PRNN, 3.475 dB in comparison MLP, 3.325 dB in comparison to the SLRNN, and 5.485 dB in comparison to the SOSLRNN. In addition, the network demonstrates a low AVR.

Table 3. The signal to noise ratio and the average relative variance in predicting the exchange rates time series using various neural networks

Network	US$/£	U S $ / Canadian$	US$/ Yen	U S $ / S w i s s Franc	Mean	
SOPRNN	0.003	0.0013	0.0074	0.003	0.0037	ARV
	25.1809	29.0405	21.346	25.2121	25.195	SNR(dB)
PRNN	0.0046	0.0017	0.006	0.0043	0.0042	ARV
	23.3698	27.6561	22.2284	23.6241	24.219	SNR(dB)
MLP	0.0045	0.0105	0.0202	0.0019	0.0093	ARV
	24.1719	19.9263	17.0533	27.2011	21.72	SNR (dB)
SLRNN	0.0057	0.0049	0.0064	0.0062	0.0114	ARV
	22.487	23.1229	22.0692	22.0468	21.87	SNR (dB)
SOSLR-NN	0.0096	0.0042	0.0207	0.0217	0.0077	ARV
	20.1712	23.776	17.9219	17.3629	19.71	SNR (dB)

In conclusion, the exchange rates time series between the American Dollar and the 4 other currencies are highly nonlinear and nonstationary signals, they are better predicted using pipelined recurrent structures, particularly since they are designed to estimate nonlinear and nonstationary signals, adaptively.

Comparison with the Linear Predictor

One of the main concerns of time series analysis is the development of parametric model, which can be used in various applications such as prediction, control and data compression (Makhoul, 1975). In this case, the signal S_n is considered the output of a system with unknown input u_n and its value is determined by the linear combinations of previous outputs and inputs according to the following equation (Makhoul, 1975):

$$S_n = -\sum_{k=1}^{P} a_k S_{n-k} + G \sum_{m=0}^{q} b_m u_{n-m}, \quad b_0 = 1 \tag{35}$$

where a_k and G are the model parameters. The above equation can be specified in the frequency

domain by taking the Z transform of both sides of the equation. Let $H(Z)$ represent the transfer function of the system in the Z domain, then:

$$H(Z) = \frac{S(Z)}{U(Z)} = G \frac{1 + \sum_{m=1}^{q} b_m z^{-m}}{1 + \sum_{k=1}^{p} a_k z^{-k}} \tag{36}$$

and the Z transform of the signal is:

$$S(Z) = \sum_{n=-\infty}^{\infty} s_n z^{-n} \tag{37}$$

In this case, the roots of the numerator and the denominator of the transfer function $H(Z)$ are the zeros and the poles of the model, respectively. When $a_k = 0$, the model is considered as all-zeros and called the moving average (MA) model, when $b_m = 0$, the model is considered as all poles and known as autoregressive (AR) model, while a model that has pole and zero values is referred to as autoregressive moving average (ARMA) model.

We utilised the MATLAB identification toolbox to implement the AR model, which was used to predict the exchange rates time series between the US dollar and the four currencies (the British Pound, the Canadian Dollar, the Japanese Yen, the Swiss Frank) in the period between 3 September 1973 to 18 May 1983.

When predicting the exchange rate time series, various experiments were performed to obtain good simulation results. The order of the AR model was varied between two and five to achieve the performance summarised in Table 4. As it can be noticed from Table 4, there are no significant differences in the performance of the AR model when the order was changed between 2 and 5.

Although linear models are simple to implement, however the SOPRNNs produced better simulation results using the SNR when used to predict the exchange rate between the US dollar and the British pounds, the US dollar and the Canadian dollar and well as the US dollar and the Swiss franc with an improvement of 0.667 dB, 8.151 dB and 2.891 dB, respectively.

CONCLUSION

In this research, we presented a novel recurrent neural networks architecture, which consists of a number of second-order recurrent neural networks, concatenated with each other. The network consists of two sections, i.e., the non-linear and the linear ones, which extract the relevant features from the input signal. All modules of the pipeline network are partially recurrent neural networks, apart from the last module, which is a fully recurrent one, i.e., all outputs are fed back to the inputs. The improvement that was introduced into the structure of the pipeline recurrent neural network by incorporating the second-order single layer recurrent neural network as the basic module of the pipeline network, provided the overall structure with higher-order terms. The performance of the proposed network was found to be superior of the first-order pipeline neural network, the multi-layer perceptron, the single-layer recurrent neural network and the second-order, single-layer recurrent neural network.

FUTURE RESEARCH DIRECTIONS

Future work will investigate the use of a mixture of feed-forward and recurrent artificial higher-order architectures in a pipeline fashion. For instance, it is envisaged that all structuring modules within the pipeline network are feed-forward higher-order structures (e.g., Pi-sigma networks), while the last module is a recurrent one. A further research direction will involve the use of genetic algorithms to determine the best

Table 4. The simulation results for predicting the exchange rate time series using various order of the AR-model

Order	US$/£	US$/ Canadian$	US$/ Yen	US$/Swiss Franc	
2	24.5139	20.8894	23.7916	22.3209	SNR(dB)
	0.0035	0.0081	0.0042	0.0059	ARV
3	24.5020	20.8566	23.7650	22.2943	SNR(dB)
	0.0035	0.0082	0.0042	0.0059	ARV
4	24.4604	20.8207	23.7571	22.2994	SNR(dB)
	0.0036	0.0083	0.0042	0.0059	ARV
5	24.4091	20.7848	23.7228	22.2497	SNR(dB)
	0.0036	0.0083	0.0042	0.006	ARV

choice of the network architecture, the number of units concatenated in the pipelined structure and the number of inputs. Furthermore, this research has focused on one-step ahead prediction. It would be interesting to evaluate the capabilities of higher-order pipelined neural networks in multi-step ahead prediction.

REFERENCES

Abe, S. (1997). *Neural networks and fuzzy systems.* Kluwer Academic Publishers.

Abecasis, S.M., & Lapenta, E.S. (1996). Modeling multivariate time series with neural networks: comparison with regression analysis. *Proceedings of the INFONOR '96: IX International Symposium in Informatics Applications.* Antofagasta, Chile, 18-22.

Baylor, D.A. (1981), Retinal specializations for the processing of small systems, In Reichardt, W.E., & Poggio, T., (Eds.), *Theoretical approaches in neurobiology.* MIT Press.

Brown, R.G. (1963). *Smoothing, forecasting and prediction of discrete time series.* Prentice Hall.

Cao, L., & Tay, F.E.H. (2001). Financial forecasting using vector machines. *Neural Computing and Applications, 10,* 184-192.

Chang, P., & Hu, J. (1997). Optimal nonlinear adaptive prediction and modeling of MPEG video in ATM networks using pipelined recurrent neural networks. *IEEE Journal on Selected Areas in Communications, 15*(6), 1087-1100.

Chappel, D., Padmore, J., Mistry, P., & Ellis, C. (1996). A threshold model for French franc/Deutsch mark exchange rate. *Journal of Forecasting, 15,* 155–164.

Chen, A.S., & Leung, M.T. (2005). Performance evaluation of neural network architectures: The case of predicting foreign exchange correlations. *Journal of Forecasting, 24*(6), 403-420.

Cheng, W., Wanger, L., & Lin, C.H. (1996). Forecasting the 30-year US treasury bond with a system of neural networks. *J. Computational Intelligence in Finance, 4,* 10-16.

Cichocki, A., & Unbehauen, R. (1993). *Neural networks for optimization and signal processing.* J. Wiley & Sons.

Draye, J.S., Pavisic, D.A., Cheron, G.A., & Libert, G.A. (1996). Dynamic recurrent neural networks: A dynamic analysis. *IEEE Transactions SMC-Part B, 26*(5), 692-706.

Elman, J.L. (1990). Finding structure in time. *Cognitive Science, 14,* 179-211.

Fama, E.F., & Schwert, W.G. (1977). Asset returns and inflation. *Journal of Financial Economics, 5,* 115–146.

Fama, E.F, & French, E.F. (1988) Dividend yields and expected stock returns. *Journal of Financial Economics, 22,* 3–25.

Forcada, M. L., & Carrasco, R. C. (1995). Learning the initial state of second-order recurrent neural network during regular language inference. *Neural Computation, 7,* 923-930.

Giles, C.L., & Maxwell, T. (1987), Learning invariance and generalization in higher-order neural networks. *Applied Optics, 26*(23), 4972-4978.

Hagan, M.T., Demuth, H.B., & Beale, M. (1995). *Neural networks design.* PWS Publishing Co.

Hanke, J.E., & Reitsch, A.G. (1989). *Business forecasting.* Allyn and Bacon.

Hertz, J., Krogh, A., & Palmer, R.G. (1991). *Introduction to the theory of neural computation.* Addison-Wesley.

Hopfield, J.J. (1982). Neural networks and physical systems with emergent collective computational abilities. *Proc. Nat. Acad. Sci., 79,* 2554-2558.

Huang, W., Lai, K. K, Nakamori, N, & Wang, S. (2004). Forecasting foreign exchange rates with artificial neural networks: A review. *International Journal of Information Technology and Decision Making*, Vol. 3, No. 1, pp. 145-165.

Hsieh, D. A., (1989). Modeling heteroscedasticity in daily foreign-exchange rates. *Journal of Business and Economic Statistics*, 7, 307–317.

Irie, B. Miyake, S., (1988). Capabilities of three-layered perceptrons. *Proceedings of the IEEE International Conference on Neural Networks*, *I*, pp. 641–648.

Jensen, M. (1978). Some anomalous evidence regarding market efficiency. *Journal of Financial Economic*, 6, 95–101.

Jordan, M.I. (1986), Attractor dynamics and parallelism in a connectionist sequential machine. *Proceedings 8th Annual Conference of the Cognitive Science Society*, pp. 531-546.

Kohonen, T. (1972). Correlation matrix memories. *IEEE Transactions on Computer*, 21, 353-359.

Kohring, G.A. (1990). Neural networks with many-neuron interactions. *J. Phys. France*, 51, 145-155.

Lightbody, G., Wu, Q.H., & Irwin, G.W. (1992), Control application for feedforward networks. In Warwick, K., Irwin, G.H., & Hunt, K.J. (Eds.), *Neural networks for control and systems* (pp. 51-71). Peter Peregrinus.

Makhoul, J. (1975). Linear prediction: A tutorial review. *Proceedings of the IEEE*, *63*(4), 561-580.

Magdon-Ismail, M., Nicholson, A., & Abu-Mustafa, Y.S. (1998). Financial markets: Very noisy information processing. *Proceedings of the IEEE*, *86*(11).

McCullock, W.S., & Pitts, W. (1943). A logical calculus of the ideas immanent in nervous activity. *Bull. Math. Biophys.*, 5, 115-133.

Minsky, M.L., & Papert, S.A. (1969). *Perceptrons*. MIT Press.

Mozer, M.C. (1989). A focused backpropagation algorithm for temporal pattern recognition. *Complex Systems*, *3*, 349-381.

Pao, Y. (1989). *Adaptive pattern recognition and neural networks*. Addison-Wesley.

Pham, D.T. (1995). *Neural networks for identification, prediction and control*. Springer-Verlag.

Peel, D. A., & Yadav, P., (1995). The time series behavior of spot exchange rates in the German hyper-inflation period: Was the process chaotic? *Empirical Economics, 20*, 455–463.

Poggio, T., & Torre, V. (1981), A theory of synaptic interactions. In Rechardt, W.E., & Poggio, T. (Eds.), *Theoretical approaches in neurobiology*. MIT Press.

Rosenblatt, F. (1962). *Principles of neurodynamics*. Spartan.

Rumelhardt, D.E., & McClelland, J.L. (1986). *Parallel distributed processing*. MIT Press.

Rumelhardt, D.E., Hinton, G.E., & Williams, R.J. (1986). Learning representation by back-propagation errors. *Nature, 323*, 533-536.

Sharda, R., & Patil, R.B. (1993). A connectionist approach to time series prediction: An empirical test. *Neural Networks in Finance Investing*, 451-464.

Shin, Y., & Ghosh, J. (1991), The Pi-sigma network: An efficient higher-order neural network for pattern classification and function approximation. *Intelligent Engineering Systems Through Artificial Neural Networks*, 2, 379-384.

Shin, Y., & Ghosh, J. (1992). Computationally efficient invariant pattern classification with higher-order pi-sigma networks. *International Journal of Neural Systems*, *3*(4), 323-350.

Simon, E.J., Lamb, T.D., & Hodgkin, A.L. (1975). Spontaneous voltage fluctuations in retinal cones and bipolar cells. *Nature, 256,* 661-662.

So, M.K.P, Lam, K., & Li, W.K., (1999). Forecasting exchange rate volatility using autoregressive random variance model. *Applied Financial Economics, 9,* 583–591.

Solomon, E.P., & Schmidt, R.R. (1990). *Human anatomy and physiology, 2nd Edition.* Saunders.

Stornetta, W.S., Hogg, T., & Huberman, B.A. (1987). A dynamical approach to temporal pattern matching. *Proceedings Neural Information Processing Systems,* 750-759.

Van, E., & Robert, J. (1997). *The application of neural networks in forecasting of share prices.* Finance and Technology Publishing.

Versace, M., Bhatt, R., Hinds, O., & Shiffer, M. (2004). Predicting the exchange traded fund DIA with a combination of genetic algorithms and neural networks. *Expert Systems with Applications, 27,* 417-425.

Werbos, P.J. (1990). Backpropagation through time: What is does and how to do it. *Proceedings of the IEEE, 78*(10), 1550-1560.

Whitley, D., & Hanson, T. (1989). Optimising NNs using faster, more accurate genetic search. *Proceedings of the 3rd ICGA.* Morgan-Kaufmann.

Williams, R.J., & Zipser, D. (1989). A learning algorithm for continually running fully recurrent neural networks. *Neural Computation, 1,* 270-280.

Zhang, G., Patuwo, B. E., & Hu, M. Y. (1998). Forecasting with artificial neural networks: The state of the art. *International Journal of Forecasting, 14,* 35-62.

ADDITIONAL READING

An-Sin, C., & Mark, T.L. (2005). Performance evaluation of neural network architectures: The case of predicting foreign exchange correlations. *Journal of Forecasting, 24,* 403-420.

Durbin, R., & Rumelhart, D. E. (1989). Product units: A computationally powerful and biologically plausible extension to back-propagation networks. *Neural Computation, 1,* 133-142.

Caruana, R., Lawrence, S., & Giles, L. (2000). Overfitting in neural nets: Backpropagation, conjugate gradient, and early stopping. *Neural Information Processing Systems,* 402-408.

Hellstrom, T., & Holmstrom, K. (1997). *Predicting the stock market.* (Technical report Series IMa-TOM-1997-07). Center of Mathematical Modeling (CMM), Department of Mathematics & Pyhsics, Malardalen University, Sweden.

Henriksson, R.D., & Merton R.C. (1981). On the market timing and investment performance of managed portfolios II: statistical procedures for evaluating forecasting skills. *Journal of Business, 54,* 513-533.

Ho, S. L., Xie, M., & Goh, T. N. (2002). A comparative study of neural network and Box-Jenkins ARIMA modeling in time series prediction. *Computers & Industrial Engineering, 42,* 371-375.

Husken, M., & Stagge, P. (2003). Recurrent neural networks for time series classification. *Neurocomputing, 50,* 223-235.

Kaastra, I, & Boyd, M. (1996). Designing a neural network for forecasting financial and economic time series. *Neurocomputing, 10,* 215-236.

Leung, M. T., Chen, A. S., & Daouk, H. (2000). Forecasting exchange rates using general regression neural networks. *Computers & Operations Research, 27,* 1093-1110.

Merton, R.C. (1981). On market timing and investment performance of managed performance I: An equilibrium theory of value for market forecasts. *Journal of Business, 5*, 363-406.

Pesaran, M. H., & Timmermann, A. (2002). Market timing and return prediction under model instability. *Journal of Empirical Finance, 9*, 495–510.

Plummer, E. A. (2000). *Time series forecasting with feed-forward neural networks: Guidelines and limitations*. Thesis for Master of Science in Computer Science, University of Wyoming, 2000. Retrieved from http://www.karlbranting.net/papers/plummer/Paper_7_12_00.htm

Robert, E.C., & David, M.M. (1987). Testing for market timing ability: A framework for forecast evaluation. *Journal of Financial Economics, 19*, 169-189.

Schmitt, M. (2001a). On the complexity of computing and learning with multiplicative neural networks. *Neural Computation, 14*, 241-301.

Schmitt, M. (2001b). Product unit neural networks with constant depth and superlinear VC dimension. *Proceedings of the International Conference on Artificial Neural Networks ICANN 2001*. Lecture Notes in Computer Science, Volume 2130, pp. 253-258. Berlin: Springer-Verlag.

Serdar, Y., Fikret, S. G., & Nesrin, O. (2005). A comparison of global, recurrent and smoothed-piecewise neural models for Istanbul stock exchange (ISE) prediction. *Pattern Recognition Letters, 26*, 2093–2103.

Sitte, R., & Sitte, J. (2000). Analysis of the predictive ability of time delay neural networks applied to the S&P 500 time series. *IEEE Transaction on Systems, Man, and Cybernetics-part., 30*(4), 568-572.

Thomason, M. (1998). The practitioner method and tools: A basic neural network-based trading system project revisited (parts 1 & 2). *Journal of Computational Intelligence in Finance, 6*(1), 43-44.

Walczal, S. (2001). An empirical analysis of data requirements for financial forecasting with neural networks. *Journal of Management Information Systems, 17*(4), 203–222.

Yao, J., & Tan, C. L. (2001). Guidelines for financial forecasting with neural networks. *Proceedings of International Conference on Neural Information Processing*, (pp. 757-761). Shanghai, China.

Yao, J., & Tan, C. L. (2000). A case study on neural networks to perform technical forecasting of forex. *Neurocomputing. 34*, 79-98.

Zekić, M. (1998). Neural network applications in stock market prediction: A methodology analysis. In Aurer, B., Logožar, R., & Varaždin (Eds.), *Proceedings of the 9th International Conference on Information and Intelligent Systems '98*, (pp. 255-263).

Chapter IX
A Novel Recurrent Polynomial Neural Network for Financial Time Series Prediction

Abir Hussain
John Moores University, UK

Panos Liatsis
City University, London, UK

ABSTRACT

The research described in this chapter is concerned with the development of a novel artificial higher-order neural networks architecture called the recurrent Pi-sigma neural network. The proposed artificial neural network combines the advantages of both higher-order architectures in terms of the multi-linear interactions between inputs, as well as the temporal dynamics of recurrent neural networks, and produces highly accurate one-step ahead predictions of the foreign currency exchange rates, as compared to other feedforward and recurrent structures.

INTRODUCTION

This research is concerned with the development of a novel artificial neural networks (ANNs) architecture, which takes advantage of higher-order correlations between the samples of a time series as well as encapsulating the temporal dynamics of the underlying mathematical model of the underlying time series.

Time series prediction involves the determination of an appropriate model, which can encapsulate the dynamics of the system, described by the sample data. Previous work has demonstrated the potential of neural networks in predicting the behaviour of complex, non-linear systems. Various ANNs were applied in the prediction of time series signals with varying degrees of success, the most popular being multi-layered perceptrons (MLPs) (Fadlalla & Lin, 2001; Bodyanskiy & Popov, 2006; Chen & Leung, 2005;). In this work, we turn our attention to artificial higher-order neural networks (HONNs).

Artificial higher-order or polynomial neural networks formulate weighted sums of products or functions of the input variables, which are then processed by the subsequent layers of the network (Fulcher & Brown, 1994; Ghosh & Shin 1992). In essence, they expand the representational space of the neural network with non-linear terms that can facilitate the process of mapping from the input to the output space.

This remaining of this chapter is organised as follows. In Section 2, we provide a brief introduction to the problem of time series prediction, describing the fundamental issues which govern the analysis of time series systems. In Section 3, we introduce the various ANNs, which will be used in our work, describing the concepts of their architectures, learning rules and issues related to their performance. Section 4 is concerned with the evaluation criteria for the performance of the artificial neural networks architectures in the problem of one-step ahead prediction of the foreign exchange rates. Section 5 presents the simulation results of the proposed neural network, i.e., recurrent Pi-sigma network, and provides a performance comparison with relevant feedforward and recurrent ANN architectures. Section 6 is concerned about the identification of the NARMAX model using the proposed recurrent Pi-Sigma neural network. Sections 7 and 8 give the conclusion of the research and provide recommendations for further development of the work, respectively.

TIME SERIES ANALYSIS

A time series is a set of observations x_t, each one being recorded at a specific time t (Anderson, 1976). A discrete time series is one where the set of times at which observations are made is a discrete set. Continuous time series are obtained by recording observations continuously over some time interval.

Analysing time series data leads to the decomposition of time series into components (Box & Jenkins, 1976). Each component is defined to be a major factor or force that can affect any time series. Three major components in time series may be identified. *Trend* refers to the long-term tendency of a time series to rise or fall. *Seasonality* refers to the periodic behaviour of a time series within a specified period or time. The fluctuation in a time series after the trend and seasonal components have been removed is termed as the *irregular* component.

If a time series can be exactly predicted from past knowledge, it is termed as *deterministic*. Otherwise, it is termed as *statistical*, where past knowledge can only indicate the probabilistic structure of future behaviour. A statistical series can be considered as a single realisation of some stochastic process. A stochastic process is a family of random variables defined on a probability space. A realisation of a stochastic process is a sample path of this process.

The prediction of time series signals is based on their past values. Therefore, it is necessary to obtain a data record. When obtaining a data record, the objective is to have data that are maximally informative and an adequate number of records for prediction purposes. Hence, future values of a time series x(t) can be predicted as a function of past values (Brockwell & Davis, 1991):

$$x(t+\tau) = f(x(t-1), x(t-2), ..., x(t-\varphi))$$

$$(1)$$

where τ refers to the number of prediction steps ahead, and φ is the number of past observations taken into consideration (also known as the order of the predictor).

In the above formulation, the problem of time series prediction becomes one of system identification (Harvey, 1981; Ljung, 1999). The unknown system to be identified is the function $f(\cdot)$, with inputs the past values of the time series. When observing a system, there is a need for a concept that defines how its variables relate to each other. The relationship between observations of a system or the knowledge of its properties is termed as the *model* of the system. The search for the most suitable model is guided by an assessment criterion of the goodness of a model. In time series prediction, the assessment of the model's goodness is based upon the prediction error of the specific model (Kantz & Schreiber, 1997). After a suitable model has been identified, it has to be validated. Model validation verifies that the chosen model indeed describes the dynamics of the underlying temporal process.

Traditional approaches to time series prediction are based on either finding the law underlying the actual physical process or on discovering some strong empirical regularities in the observation of the time series. In the first case, if the law can be discovered and analytically described, for instance, by a set of differential equations, then by solving them, we can predict the future evolution of the time series, given that the initial conditions are known. The disadvantage of this approach is that normally only partial information is known about the dynamical process. In the second case, if the time series consists of components of periodic processes, it is possible to model it by the superposition of sinusoids. In real-world problems however, regularities such as periodicity are masked by noise, and some phenomena are described by chaotic time series, where the data seem random with no apparent periodicities (Priestley, 1988).

An alternative to the above is the use of stochastic methods based on the statistical analysis of the signal were used for the prediction of financial time series (Anderson, 1976; Teodorescu, 1990). The nonlinear nature of financial data has inspired many researchers to use neural networks as a modelling approach (Hamid & Iqbal, 2004; Nag & Mitra, 2002; Oliveira & Meira, 2006; Rihani & Garg, 2006) by replacing explicit linearity-in-the-parameters dependencies with implicit semi-parametric models (Saad, Prokhorov & Wunsch, 1998).

When the networks are trained on financial data with multivariate function, they become minimum average function approximators (Hornik, Stinchcombe & White, 1989). Whilst ease of use and capability to model dynamical data are appealing features of typical neural networks, there are concerns about generalisation ability and parsimony.

ARTIFICIAL NEURAL NETWORKS ARCHITECTURES

In this section, we will present the ANN structures which have been developed for the prediction of the financial time series data. Specifically, we will introduce the single layer recurrent neural network, the second order single layer recurrent neural network, the Pi-sigma network and finally, the recurrent Pi-sigma network. The presentation of the neural networks is carried out with regards to the properties of their architectures, their learning rules and issues related to their convergence, as appropriate. The performance of the recurrent Pi-sigma network is also compared to that of the MLP. As this is a traditional neural networks system, we refer the interested reader to any of the texts describing the subject of artificial neural networks, such as (Haykin, 1994; Taylor & Lisboa, 1993; Bishop, 1997; Picton, 2000; Pao, 1989).

Single Layer Recurrent Neural Networks (SLRNNs)

A single layer recurrent neural network (Tenti, 1996; Saad, Prokhorov & Wunsch, 1998) is a fully recurrent network. As the name suggests, the SLRNN consists of a single processing layer. At the processing layer, the weighted inputs are calculated and forwarded to nonlinear transfer functions. The outputs of the processing units are then fedback to the input nodes. The weights that connect the external inputs to the processing units are called inter-weights, while the weights that connect the feedback outputs to the processing units are called the intra-weights. Figure 1 shows the structure of the single layer fully recurrent neural network, which contains some 'hidden' output units.

Consider a SLRNN with M external inputs and N outputs. If $\mathbf{y}$(t) represents the N-tuple outputs of the network at time t and $\mathbf{x}$(t) represents the M-tuple external inputs of the network at time t, then the overall inputs at time t is the concatenation of $\mathbf{x}$(t) and $\mathbf{y}$(t) and is referred to as $\mathbf{z}$(t). Let U refer to the set of indices k, where z_k represents the feedback output of a unit in the network and let I refer to the set of indices k, where z_k represents the external input of a unit in the network. Therefore, the input z_k can be represented as follows:

$$z_k(t) = \begin{cases} x_k(t) & \text{if } k \in I \\ y_k(t) & \text{if } k \in U \end{cases} \qquad (2)$$

The weights of the network are represented by the matrix W, which is of size N × (N + M). The bias can be included into the network structure by adding an extra input line of value 1.

The processing equations of the network are determined as follows:

$$s_k(t) = \sum_{l \in U \cup I} w_{kl} z_l(t)$$
$$y_k(t+1) = f_k(s_k(t)) \qquad (3)$$

where s_k(t) represents the net input of the k unit at time t, and y_k(t+1) represents the output of the same unit at time t+1. The activation function, f, is a nonlinear transfer function and usually taken to be the logistic sigmoid.

Derivation of the Learning Algorithm

Williams and Zipser (1989) proposed three types of their learning algorithms that can be used to train fully recurrent neural networks, which are the exact gradient-following, the teacher-forcing and the real time recurrent learning algorithms. In what follows, the three types of learning algorithms are presented.

Exact Gradient-Following Algorithm

The exact gradient-following learning algorithm is a general learning algorithm that can be used to train recurrent neural networks, as well as, simpler network architectures, including the feedforward network, where it is considered that some of the interconnection weights are fixed and not trainable (Williams & Zipser, 1995).

Let d_k(t) represent the desired response of neuron k at time t and let T(t) represent the set of indices k ∈ U for which neuron k has a target value. The error can be presented according to the following equation:

Figure 1. Single layer fully recurrent neural network.

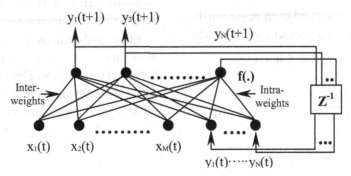

$$e_k(t) = \begin{cases} d_k(t) - y_k(t), & \text{if } k \in T(t) \\ 0, & \text{otherwise} \end{cases} \quad (4)$$

The overall network error at time t is described as follows:

$$\varepsilon(t) = \frac{1}{2} \sum_{k \in U} [e_k(t)]^2 \quad (5)$$

If the network is trained from time t_o up to t_{final}, then the total error is:

$$\varepsilon_{total}(t_o, t_{final}) = \sum_{t=t_o}^{t_{final}} J(t) \quad (6)$$

The aim of the exact gradient-following learning algorithm is to minimise the total error through a gradient descent procedure, where the weights are adjusted along the negative gradient of the total error value $\varepsilon_{total}(t_o, t_{final})$.

Since the total error is the sum of the individual errors at different time steps, then the gradient is calculated by accumulating the values of $\nabla_W \varepsilon(t)$ at each time step along the trajectory. Therefore, the total change in the weight w_{ij} is determined according to the following equation:

$$\Delta w_{ij} = \sum_{t=t_o}^{t_{final}} \Delta w_{ij}(t) \quad (7)$$

and:

$$\Delta w_{ij}(t) = -\eta \frac{\partial \varepsilon(t)}{\partial w_{ij}} + \alpha \Delta w_{ij}(t-1) \quad (8)$$

where η is a positive real number representing the learning rate and α is the momentum term. The value $\frac{\partial \varepsilon(t)}{\partial w_{ij}}$ is determined as follows:

$$\frac{\partial \varepsilon(t)}{\partial w_{ij}} = -\sum_{k \in U} e_k(t) \frac{\partial y_k(t)}{\partial w_{ij}} \quad (9)$$

In this case, $\frac{\partial y_k(t)}{\partial w_{ij}}$ is found by differentiating the network processing equations to yield:

$$\frac{\partial y_k(t+1)}{\partial w_{ij}} = f_k'(s_k(t)) \left[\sum_{l \in U} w_{kl} \frac{\partial y_l(t)}{\partial w_{ij}} + \delta_{ik} z_j(t) \right] \quad (10)$$

where δ_{ik} represents the Kronecher delta operator.

Since the initial state is assumed to be independent of the initial weights of the network, then:

$$\frac{\partial y_k(t_o)}{\partial w_{ij}} = 0 \quad (11)$$

Let $p_{ij}^k(t) = \frac{\partial y_k(t)}{\partial w_{ij}}$, then:

$$p_{ij}^k(t+1) = f_k'(s_k(t)) \left[\sum_{l \in U} w_{kl} p_{ij}^l(t) + \delta_{ik} z_j(t) \right] \quad (12)$$

and:

$$p_{ij}^k(0) = 0 \quad (13)$$

The elements of matrix p_{ij}^k, known as the impact matrix, define the importance of the connections between nodes i and j on the output value of node k. For a fully connected network, the impact matrix p_{ij}^k can be regarded as a matrix whose rows correspond to a weight in the network, while its columns correspond to a unit in the network. The total number of elements of the impact matrix is $n^3 = mn^2$, and the network always has to update all the elements of p_{ij}^k even for those values of k that have no target values. Therefore, this is a computationally demanding learning algorithm, which suffers from slow training, particularly when a large number of processing units is required.

Atiya (1988) showed that for any recurrent network to follow a unique fixed attractor, the following condition has to be satisfied:

$$\frac{1}{\|W\|^2} < \frac{1}{\left(\max|f'|\right)^2} \quad (14)$$

where $\|W\|$ represents the Euclidean norm of the full synaptic weight matrix, and f' is the derivative of the nonlinear activation function with respect to its argument. In this case, the network is assumed to have the same activation function for all its processing units. Hence, when utilising the exact gradient-following learning algorithm with a large number of processing units, this implies that the value of $\|W\|$ is increased and therefore it is more difficult to satisfy the stability condition.

Real-Time Recurrent Learning Algorithm (RTRL)

Williams and Zipser (1995) proposed a variation to their learning algorithm, which is known as real time recurrent learning. Instead of assuming that the weights are constant during the whole trajectory, this condition is relaxed and the weights are updated for each input pattern presentation. This is similar to the online training algorithm of a feedforward neural network (Haykin, 1994).

The advantage of utilising the RTRL algorithm is that the epoch boundaries are no longer required, making the implementation of the algorithm simpler, while the network is allowed to be trained for an indefinite period of time. However, the algorithm is not guaranteed to follow the negative gradient of the total error, which may cause the observed trajectory to be dependent on the variations in the weights provided by the algorithm, which can be regarded as additional feedback connections. To overcome this problem, the learning rate has to be selected sufficiently small, hence leading to a time scale of the weight changes substantially slower than the network processing.

Teacher-Forced Real-Time Recurrent Learning

A variation to the standard training algorithm is proposed by replacing the output values by their teacher values. The technique is said to force the network with the teacher signal (also known as teacher forcing). The teacher-forcing algorithm is subsequently used in temporal supervised learning tasks (Haykin, 1994) and is useful in certain training tasks such as stable oscillation (Cichocki, & Unbehauen, 1993).

Let the output and the teacher-forced values of the network at time t to be y(t) and y(t)+e(t), respectively. The input of the network is determined according to the following equation:

$$z_k(t) = \begin{cases} x_k(t) \text{ if } k \in I \\ d_k(t) \text{ if } k \in T(t) \\ y_k(t) \text{ if } k \in U\text{-}T(t) \end{cases} \quad (15)$$

The learning algorithm is determined by differentiating the processing equations of the system as follows:

$$\frac{\partial y_k(t+1)}{\partial w_{ij}} = f_k'(s_k(t)) \left[\sum_{l \in U-T(t)} w_{kl} \frac{\partial y_l(t)}{\partial w_{ij}} + \delta_{ik} z_j(t) \right] \quad (16)$$

and the values of the impact matrix p_{ij}^k can be updated according to the following equation:

$$p_{ij}^k(t+1) = f_k'(s_k(t)) \left[\sum_{l \in U-T(t)} w_{kl} p_{ij}^l(t) + \delta_{ik} z_j(t) \right] \quad (17)$$

In summary, the teacher-forcing algorithm is similar to the RTRL except that the output values of the networks are replaced by the desired values, whenever teacher signals are available and the impact matrix p_{ij}^k is set to zero, when the change in the weight values is computed.

Second Order Single Layer Recurrent Neural Networks (SOSLRNNs)

The second-order single layer recurrent neural network is a fully recurrent neural network, which calculates the second order terms produced through the multiplication of the external inputs by the outputs and passes the results to the input nodes. Figure 2 shows the block diagram of a second-order recurrent neural network, which contains some 'hidden' output units.

Consider a SOSLRNN with M external inputs and N inputs. The total number of inputs is N × M and the weights are represented by a two-dimensional matrix of size N × (N × M). Let $x_m(t)$ to be the mth external input, $y_n(t)$ to be the nth output, and $z_L(t)$ to be the Lth actual input to the network at time t. In this case, the input of the network can be presented according to the following equation:

$$z_L(t) = x_m(t) \cdot y_n(t) \text{ where } m \in M, n \in N, \text{ and } L \in N \times M$$

(18)

The net input to the kth unit is determined as follows:

$$s_k(t) = \sum_{j=1}^{N} \sum_{i=1}^{M} w_{k(i+(j-1)M)} x_i(t) y_j(t)$$

$$= \sum_{l=1}^{NM} w_{kl} z_l(t)$$

(19)

while the kth output of the network at time t+1 is:

$$y_k(t + 1) = f_k(s_k(t))$$

(20)

where f represents the activation function of the network. The above two equations describe the dynamics of the second order fully recurrent neural network.

Learning Algorithm of the SOSLRNN

The SOSLRNN can be trained using the RTRL algorithm in which the change in the weights is determined according to the following equation:

$$\Delta w_{ij}(t) = \eta \sum_{k \in T(t)} e_k(t) \frac{\partial y_k(t)}{\partial w_{ij}} + \alpha \Delta w_{ij}(t-1)$$

(21)

where $e_k(t)$ represents the error of the kth node at time t, η is the learning rate, α is the momentum

Figure 2. The block diagram of a second-order single layer fully recurrent neural network

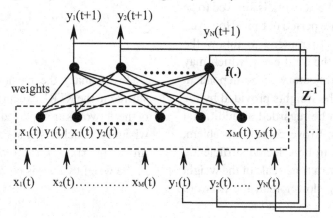

term and T(t) represents the set of indexes for all the output units that have target values.

The value $\frac{\partial y_k(t)}{\partial w_{ij}}$ can be determined by differentiating the processing equations of the network, hence giving Equation (22), where f_k' is the derivative of the nonlinear transfer function, and δ_{ik} is the Kronecker delta operator. Let $P_{ij}^k = \frac{\partial y_k(t)}{\partial w_{ij}}$, then the above equation can be written as Equation (23), with:

$$p_{ij}^k(0) = 0 \qquad\qquad (24)$$

In this case, the impact matrix p_{ij}^k is of size $N \times (N \times N \times M)$.

Clearly, for a large number of inputs, the SOSLRNN requires more computational power than the SLRNN. However, since the SOSLRNN utilises second-order terms, it may converge faster and may require a smaller number of external inputs and outputs than the SLRNN to perform the same prediction task.

The Pi-Sigma Network

The Pi-Sigma neural network (PSNN) is a multi-layer artificial higher order neural network. It was introduced by Ghosh and Shin (1992) to perform function approximation and classification tasks (Shin & Ghosh, 1991). The network aims to maintain the high learning capabilities

of HONNs, whilst addressing the problem of the combinatorial explosion of the higher-order terms (or equivalently the network's weights) as the order of the network increases.

The Pi-Sigma network consists of two layers, the product and the summing unit layers. The weights of the summing unit's layer are adjustable, while those of the product units layer as fixed to unity. At the summing unit's layer, the network processes the input data and calculates their weighted sums. At the product units layer, the network calculates the products of the outputs of the summing units. The number of the product terms depends on the order of the network. For instance, in the case of a third-order PSNN, a unit in the product layer will multiply the outputs of any three summing units. Figure 3 shows the architecture of the Pi-Sigma network with m external inputs and one additional input line for the bias input (which is set to unity).

The number of summing units corresponds to the order of the network, i.e., a second order network contains two summing units, a third order network contains three summing units and so on. This means that the network enjoys a regular structure, in contrast to artificial higher order networks, which have an irregular structure since increasing their order will increase excessively the number of interconnected weights as shown in Table 1.

Consider a pi-sigma neural network with k summing units and one output. The weight matrix

Equation (22).

$$\frac{\partial y_k(t)}{\partial w_{ij}} = f_k'(s_k(t-1)) \left[\sum_{n=1}^{N} \sum_{m=1}^{M} w_{k(m+nM)} x_m(t-1) \frac{\partial y_n(t-1)}{\partial w_{ij}} + \delta_{ik} z_j(t-1) \right]$$

Equation (23).

$$p_{ij}^k(t) = f_k'(s_k(t-1)) \left[\sum_{n=1}^{N} \sum_{m=1}^{M} w_{k(m+nM)} x_m(t-1) p_{ij}^n(t-1) + \delta_{ik} z_j(t-1) \right]$$

has a size of k×(M+1) and the processing equations are determined as follows:

$$h_L = \sum_{m=1}^{M+1} w_{Lm} x_m(t)$$

$$y = f(\prod_{L=1}^{k} h_L) \tag{25}$$

where f is a nonlinear transfer function and h_L is the output of the Lth summing unit.

Training Algorithm of the Pi-Sigma Network

The pi-sigma network is trained using the gradient descent learning algorithm on the estimated mean squared error. The weights of the pi-sigma network are updated according to the following equation:

$$\Delta w_{ij} = \eta \cdot (d^P - y^P) f'(\prod_{L=1}^{k} h_L) \prod_{L \neq i} h_L x_j \tag{26}$$

where η is the learning rate and f' is the derivative of the transfer function.

Shin and Ghosh (1991) proposed three updating rules, which are the fully synchronous, the randomised, and the asynchronous updating rules. In the fully synchronous rule, the entire weights matrix is updated, when an input pattern P is presented to the network in a synchronised order. In this case, the network may suffer from unstable convergence when the leaning rate is not selected sufficiently small. In the randomised updating rule, the weights of one summing unit are selected randomly and updated when an input pattern is presented to the network. In the asynchronous updating rule, for each iteration, all the weights of the network are updated in an asynchronous order, that is, for each input pattern a summing unit is selected randomly and its weights are updated, next, for the same input pattern, the weights of a different summing unit are updated, and so on. The drawback of the randomised and the asynchronous updating rules is that the network converges when an input pattern is repeatedly presented, which means that the network cannot converge for large training sets.

Recurrent Pi-Sigma Neural Networks (RPSNs)

In this section, we propose a new type of higher order recurrent neural network called the recurrent Pi-sigma network (RPSN). It has a similar structure to the feedforward pi-sigma neural network. The main difference is the incorporation of a recurrent link from the output to the input layer. The RPSN enjoys the benefits of both the recurrent and the higher order neural networks.

Figure 3. The feedforward Pi-sigma neural network

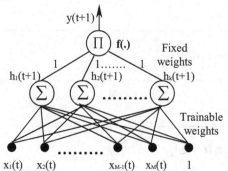

Table 1. The number of weights required for the Pi-sigma and the artificial higher order neural networks (where M is the number of inputs)

Order of network	Number of weights			
	Pi-sigma		Single layer HONN	
	M = 5	M = 10	M = 5	M = 10
2	12	22	21	66
3	18	33	56	286
4	24	44	126	901

The RPSN consists of two layers, the product and the summing unit layers. The weights between the input nodes and the summing unit layer are trainable, while the weights between the summing and the product unit layers are fixed to unity. The network calculates the product of the sum of the weighted inputs and passes the results to a nonlinear transfer function. This is in contrast to Sigma-pi neural networks, which calculate the sum of the product of the weighted inputs and as a result suffer from the combinatorial explosion of higher order terms as the number of inputs increases. The number of sigma units corresponds to the order of the network, which means that increasing the order of the RPSN is done by adding a further summing unit. Figure 4 shows the structure of the recurrent pi-sigma network.

For each increase in order, only one extra summing unit is required. The product units give the networks higher-order capabilities without suffering from the exponential increase in weights, which is a major problem in a single layer HONNs.

It has a topology of a fully connected two-layered feedforward network. Since there are *K* summing units incorporated, it is called a *K*-th order RPSN. Since the weights between the summing and the output layer are fixed to unity,

and they are not trainable. For that reason, the summing layer is not "hidden" as in the case of Multi Layer Perceptron (MLP). Such a network topology with only one layer of trainable weights drastically reduces the training time.

The structure of RPSN is highly regular in the sense that summing units can be added incrementally till an appropriate order of the network is achieved without over-fitting of the function. The order can be gradually increased until the desired low predefined error is reached. The reduction in the number of weights as compared to FLNN allows the network to enjoy fast training

Consider a RPSN with M external inputs and one output. The total number of inputs is M+2 (M external inputs, one input line is accommodated for the bias, and one input line is used to represent the recurrent link). Let the number of summing unit to be k and W to be the weight matrix of size k × (M + 2). If $x_m(t)$ represents the mth external input and y(t) represents the output of the network at time t, then the total input to the network is the concatenation of $x_j(t)$ (j=1,...,M) and y(t) and is referred to as z(t) which is determined according to the following equation:

$$z_j(t) = \begin{cases} x_j(t) & \text{if } 1 \le j \le M \\ 1 & \text{if } j = M+1 \\ y(t) & \text{if } j = M+2 \end{cases} \quad (27)$$

The processing equations of the RPSN are given as follows:

$$h_L(t+1) = \sum_{m=1}^{M+2} w_{Lm} z_m(t)$$

$$y(t+1) = f\left(\prod_{L=1}^{k} h_L(t+1)\right) \quad (28)$$

where $h_L(t+1)$ represents the net sum of the L unit at time t+1, and the output of the network is y(t+1). The unit's activation function f is a nonlinear transfer function and taken to be the logistic sigmoid transfer function.

Figure 4. The structure of the recurrent pi-sigma neural network

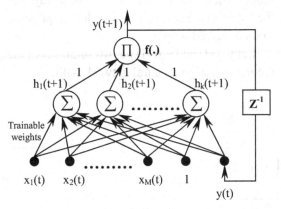

199

Learning Algorithm of the Recurrent Pi-Sigma Network

In this section, the learning algorithm of the RPSN is derived. The network is trained using dynamic backpropagation (Williams & Zipser, 1995), which is a gradient descent learning algorithm, based on the assumption that the initial state of the network is independent of the initial weights.

Let d(t+1) represent the desired response of the network at time t+1. The error of the network at time t+1 is defined as:

$$e(t+1) = d(t+1) - y(t+1) \qquad (29)$$

The cost function of the network is the squared error between the original and the predicted value, that is:

$$J(t+1) = \frac{1}{2}\left[e(t+1)\right]^2 \qquad (30)$$

The aim of the learning algorithm is to minimise the squared error by a gradient descent procedure. Therefore, the change for any specified element w_{ij} of the weight matrix is determined according to the following equation:

$$\Delta w_{ij}(t+1) = -\eta \frac{\partial J(t+1)}{\partial w_{ij}} + \alpha \Delta w_{ij}(t) \qquad (31)$$

where η is a positive real number representing the learning rate and α is the momentum term. The value $\frac{\partial J(t+1)}{\partial w_{ij}}$ is determined as:

$$\frac{\partial J(t+1)}{\partial w_{ij}} = -e(t+1)\frac{\partial y(t+1)}{\partial w_{ij}} \qquad (32)$$

In this case, $\frac{\partial y(t+1)}{\partial w_{ij}}$ is calculated by using the chain rule, where:

$$\frac{\partial y(t+1)}{\partial w_{ij}} = \frac{\partial y(t+1)}{\partial h_i(t+1)} \cdot \frac{\partial h_i(t+1)}{\partial w_{ij}} \qquad (33)$$

The value $\frac{\partial y(t+1)}{\partial h_i}$ is determined by differentiating the network processing equations (Equation (34)), and the value $\frac{\partial h_i(t+1)}{\partial w_{ij}}$ is determined as follows:

$$\frac{\partial h_i(t+1)}{\partial w_{ij}} = z_j(t) + w_{i(M+2)}\frac{\partial y(t)}{\partial w_{ij}} \qquad (35)$$

where $f'(.)$ is the derivative of the nonlinear transfer function.

Convergence of the Recurrent Pi-Sigma Neural Network

In this section, the convergence of the recurrent pi-sigma neural networks will be discussed. For a given input, it is required that after a short transition period, the recurrent neural network produces a steady and a fixed output. This means that, starting with any initial condition, the state of the network should go to equilibrium and there should be a unique equilibrium state. Therefore, the aim of the learning algorithm is to adjust the weights of the network, such that it allows the unique equilibrium state to move in a way that the output of the network goes as close as possible to the required output.

Let $y_1(t+1)$ and $y_2(t+1)$ be two solutions to the recurrent pi-sigma neural network with:

Equation (34).

$$\frac{\partial y(t+1)}{\partial h_i} = \frac{\partial}{\partial h_i}\left(f\left(\prod_{L=1}^{k} h_L(t+1)\right)\right) = f'\left(\prod_{L=1}^{k} h_L(t+1)\right)\left(\prod_{\substack{L=1 \\ L \neq i}}^{k} h_L(t+1)\right)$$

$$y_1(t+1) = f\left(\prod_{L=1}^{k} h_{1L}(t+1)\right) \qquad (36)$$

and:

$$y_2(t+1) = f\left(\prod_{L=1}^{k} h_{2L}(t+1)\right) \qquad (37)$$

where f is the nonlinear transfer function and:

$$h_{1L}(t+1) = \sum_{i=1}^{M} w_{Li}x_i + w_{L(M+1)} + w_{L(M+2)}y_1(t)$$
$$= \alpha_L + \beta_L y_1(t) \qquad (38)$$

with:

$$\alpha_L = \sum_{i=1}^{M} w_{Li}x_i + w_{L(M+1)}$$
$$\beta_L = w_{L(M+2)} \qquad (39)$$

while:

$$h_{2L}(t+1) = \sum_{i=1}^{M} w_{Li}x_i + w_{L(M+1)} + w_{L(M+2)}y_2(t)$$
$$(= \alpha_L + \beta_L y_2\ t) \qquad (40)$$

Let J(t+1) be:

$$J(t+1) = \left\| y_1(t+1) - y_2(t+1) \right\| \qquad (41)$$

where $\|\ \|$ is the norm.

Substituting the values of $y_1(t+1)$ and $y_2(t+1)$ into J(t+1), we get:

$$J(t+1) = \left\| f\left(\prod_{L=1}^{k} h_{1L}(t+1)\right) - f\left(\prod_{L=1}^{k} h_{2L}(t+1)\right) \right\| \qquad (42)$$

Using the mean value theorem, we get Equation (43). Therefore:

$$J(t+1) \le \left(\max|f'|\right)\left\| \prod_{L=1}^{k} h_{1L}(t+1) - \prod_{L=1}^{k} h_{2L}(t+1) \right\| \qquad (44)$$

Let g(y) to be:

$$g(y) = \prod_{L=1}^{k} (\alpha_L + \beta_L y) \qquad (45)$$

Hence:

$$\left\| \prod_{L=1}^{k} h_{1L}(t+1) - \prod_{L=1}^{k} h_{2L}(t+1) \right\| = \left\| g(y_1(t)) - g(y_2(t)) \right\| \qquad (46)$$

Using the mean value theorem again, we obtain:

$$J(t+1) \le \left(\max|f'|\right)\left(\max|g'|\right)\left\| y_1(t) - y_2(t) \right\| \qquad (47)$$

Let:

$$\delta = \left(\max|f'|\right)\left(\max|g'|\right) \qquad (48)$$

Then:

$$J(t+1) \le \delta J(t) \qquad (49)$$

This means that:

$$J(t) \le \delta^t J(0) \qquad (50)$$

Equation (43).

$$\left\| f\left(\prod_{L=1}^{k} h_{1L}(t+1)\right) - f\left(\prod_{L=1}^{k} h_{2L}(t+1)\right) \right\| \le \left(\max|f'|\right)\left\| \prod_{L=1}^{k} h_{1L}(t+1) - \prod_{L=1}^{k} h_{2L}(t+1) \right\|$$

Hence, the error value J(t) goes to zero, for large t ($t \rightarrow \infty$), when δ is less than or equal to unity. Therefore, we have:

$$\max\left(\left|f'\right|\right)\max\left(\left|g'\right|\right) \leq 1 \qquad (51)$$

Since $g(y) = \prod_{L=1}^{k}(\alpha_L + \beta_L y)$, then:

$$\ln\left(g(y)\right) = \sum_{L=1}^{k}\ln(\alpha_L + \beta_L y) \qquad (52)$$

hence:

$$\frac{g'(y)}{g(y)} = \sum_{L=1}^{k}\frac{\beta_L}{(\alpha_L + \beta_L y)} \qquad (53)$$

This means that:

$$g'(y) = \sum_{L=1}^{k}\beta_L \prod_{\substack{s=1\\s \neq L}}^{k}(\alpha_L + \beta_L y) \qquad (54)$$

and:

$$\left|g'(y)\right| = \left|\sum_{L=1}^{k}\beta_L\left(\sum_{\substack{s=1\\s \neq L}}^{k}\alpha_s + \beta_s y\right)\right| \qquad (55)$$

where:

$$\left|\sum_{L=1}^{k}\beta_L\left(\sum_{\substack{s=1\\s \neq L}}^{k}\alpha_s + \beta_s y\right)\right| \leq \sum_{L=1}^{k}|\beta_L|\prod_{\substack{s=1\\s \neq L}}^{k}\left(|\alpha_s| + |\beta_s|\right) \qquad (56)$$

and:

$$\left|\alpha_L\right| \leq \sum_{m=1}^{M+1}\left|w_{Lm}\right| \qquad (57)$$

This means that:

$$\left|\sum_{L=1}^{k}\beta_L\left(\sum_{\substack{s=1\\s \neq L}}^{k}\alpha_s + \beta_s y\right)\right| \leq \sum_{L=1}^{k}\left|w_{LM+2}\right|\prod_{\substack{s=1\\s \neq 1}}^{k}\sum_{m=1}^{M+2}\left|w_{sm}\right| \qquad (58)$$

and we have:

$$\left(\max\left|f'\right|\right)\max\left(\sum_{L=1}^{k}\left|w_{LM+2}\right|\prod_{\substack{s=1\\s \neq 1}}^{k}\sum_{m=1}^{M+2}\left|w_{sm}\right|\right) \leq 1 \qquad (59)$$

Therefore, the condition for the recurrent pi-sigma neural network to converge is described according to the following equation:

$$\max\left(\sum_{L=1}^{k}\left|w_{LM+2}\right|\prod_{\substack{s=1\\s \neq 1}}^{k}\sum_{m=1}^{M+2}\left|w_{sm}\right|\right) \leq \frac{1}{\left(\max\left|f'\right|\right)} \qquad (60)$$

which means that as the order of the network increases, it is more difficult to satisfy the stability criteria.

PERFORMANCE METRICS

The performance of the various neural networks architectures is evaluated using two measures. The first measure is the signal to noise ratio (SNR) or the prediction gain which is defined as follows:

$$SNR = 10\log_{10}\left(\frac{\sigma^2}{\sigma_e^2}\right)\text{dB} \qquad (61)$$

where σ^2 is the estimated variance of the input signal and σ_e^2 is the estimated variance of the error signal.

The second measure is the average relative variance (ARV) or the relative mean squares error defined according to the following equation (Taylor & Lisboa, 1993):

$$arv = \frac{1}{\sigma^2}\frac{1}{N}\sum_{i=1}^{N}(x_i - \hat{x}_i)^2 \qquad (62)$$

where N is the number of data points and σ^2 is the estimated variance of the data.

For all neural network predictors, logistic sigmoid transfer functions were used in the output layer. As a result, the signals were normalised between 0 and 1 as follows:

$$x\_new_i = \frac{x\_old_i - Min}{abs(Max - Min)} \qquad (63)$$

where x_new_i is the new value of the signal, x_old_i is the old value of the signal, Min and Max are the minimum and the maximum values of the original signal respectively, and abs is the absolute value.

The sample autocorrelation coefficient is a significant factor to measure the properties and the correlation between observations taken at different positions of the time series (Priestley, 1988). The autocorrelation coefficient allows us to get some knowledge about the probability model that forms the data. Consider a discrete time series of N data points and x_i is the ith element of the signal. The correlation between observation i and i+k is determined according to the following equation (Kantz & Schreiber, 1997):

$$r_k = \frac{\sum_{i=1}^{N-k}(x_i - \overline{x})(x_{i+k} - \overline{x})}{\sum_{i=1}^{N}(x_i - \overline{x})^2} \qquad (64)$$

where $\overline{x}$ is the mean value of the signal and r_k is called the autocorrelation coefficient at lag k.

The plot of the autocorrelation coefficient versus the lag is called the correlogram. For a completely random time series, the autocorrelation coefficient is zero for all non-zero values of the lag. For a nonstationary signal, which is defined as a signal containing a trend (long term change in the mean), the autocorrelation coefficient will not drop to zero but only for large values of the lag. On the other hand, stationary signals show short term correlations, for instance, r_1 has a very large value, while r_2 and r_3 have values greater than zero, however, significantly smaller than r_1.

For large values of the lag, the autocorrelation coefficient tends to zero.

SIMULATION RESULTS

We carried out extensive simulations to evaluate the performance of the RPSN in the prediction of the daily exchange rates between the US Dollar and various foreign currencies (British Pound, Canadian Dollar, Japanese Yen, Swiss Franc) in the period between 3 September 1973 to 18 May 1983.

Figures 5-8 show the various exchange rates time series and their corresponding correlograms.

When using the recurrent Pi-sigma neural network to predict the daily exchange rates between the US Dollar and the various foreign currencies (British Pound, Canadian Dollar, Japanese Yen, Swiss Franc), the corresponding networks were trained for 4000 epochs and the weights were initialised between -0.1 and 0.1. The learning rate and the momentum term were set to 0.05 and 0.5, respectively. The number of input units and the order of the networks, which are required to obtain the necessary mapping accuracy, were determined experimentally.

The data sets used in this work were segregated in time order. In other words earlier period of data are used for training, and the data of the later period are used for testing. The main purpose of sorting them into this order is to discover the underlying structure or trend of the mechanism generating the data, that is to understand the relationship exist between the past, present and future data. The data were partitioned into two categories: the training and the out-of-sample data, with a distribution of 25% and 75%, respectively.

Figure 9 displays the performance of the recurrent pi-sigma neural networks when used to predict the various exchange rates and Table 2 summarises the corresponding network param-

Figure 5. Exchange rate US Dollar vs British Pound (a)time series, (b) Correlogram

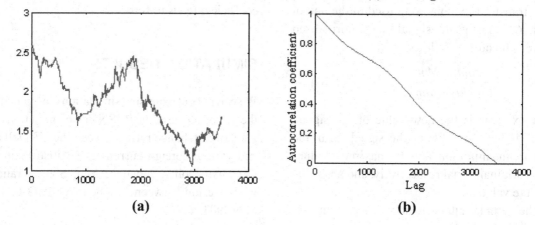

(a)   **(b)**

Figure 6. Exchange rate US Dollar vs Canadian Dollar (a) time series, (b) Correlogram

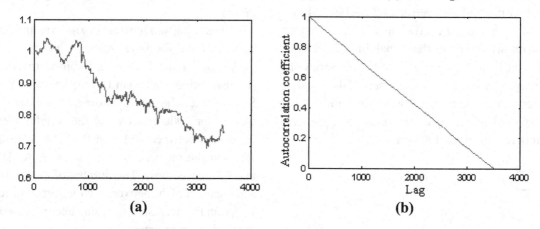

(a)   **(b)**

Figure 7. Exchange rate US Dollar vs Japanese Yen (a)time series, (b) Correlogram

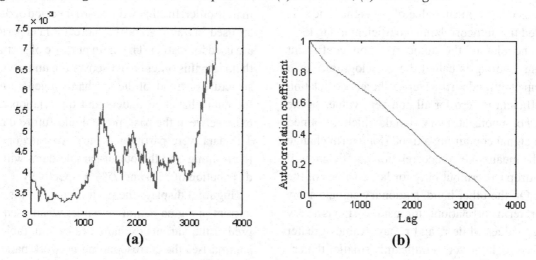

(a)   **(b)**

Figure 8. Exchange rate US Dollar vs Swiss Franc (a)time series, (b) Correlogram

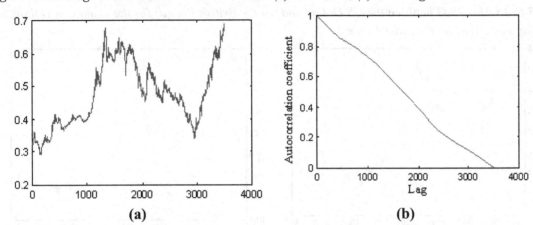

(a) (b)

Table 2. RPSNs parameters and performance in prediction of the exchange rates

Signal	US $/£	US$/Canadian $	US $/ Yen	US $/Swiss Franc
Training Set Size	400	600	650	550
External Inputs	4	4	4	4
Network Order	3	3	2	2
ARV	0.0045	0.0034	0.0094	0.0051
SNR	23.49 dB	25.44 dB	20.29 dB	22.95 dB

eters, the signal to noise ratios and the average relative variances.

In our simulations, we investigated the range of values for the parameters that influence the network performance in which the results are stable. The results showed that similar performances were sustained across different training and testing sets. The performance of the proposed network was also compared to the pi-sigma network, the multilayer perceptron (MLP), the single layer recurrent neural network (SLRNN) trained using the real time learning algorithm of Williams and Zipser (1989), and the second order single layer recurrent neural network (SOSLRNN), and the results are shown in Table 3. In terms of the PSN, the number of external inputs varied between 4 and 6, while the appropriate order of the network was between 2 and 4, while on average 1000 samples were used for the training of the network. In the

case of the MLP, the number of external inputs was varied between 4 and 10, while we carried out experiments with the hidden layer consisting of 5 to 10 hidden units. The size of the training set for the MLP experiments varied between 1000 and 2000 samples. The number of external inputs varied between 6 and 10 in the training of the SLRNN, while the number of output units was between 5 and 10. Half of the training set (i.e., 1500 points) was used for the training of the single layer recurrent neural network. The experimental setup for the SOSLRNN was similar to that of the SLRNN. In summary, the RPSN achieves an average improvement of 4.185 dB in comparison to the PSN, 1.323 dB in comparison MLP, 1.173 dB in comparison to the SLRNN, and 3.333 dB in comparison to the SOSLRNN. In addition, the network demonstrates a low AVR. Because the RPSN enjoys both the benefits of higher order

Figure 9. Prediction of the daily exchange rates using the RPSN in the period between 3 September 1973 to 18 May 1983 between the US Dollar and (a) the British Pound; (b) the Canadian Dollar; (c) the Japanese Yen; (d) the Swiss Franc

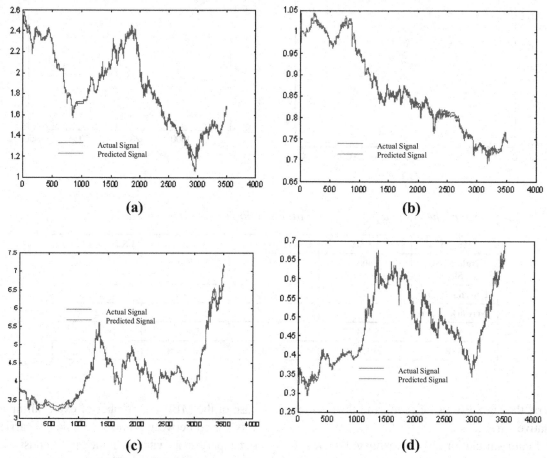

Table 3. Signal to noise ratio and average relative variance in predicting the exchange rates time series using various neural networks

Network	US$/£	US$/Canadian$	US$/ Yen	US$/Swiss Franc	Mean	
RPSN	0.0045	0.0034	0.0094	0.0051	0.0056	**ARV**
	23.49	25.44	20.29	22.95	23.043	**SNR (dB)**
PSN	0.0194	0.0067	0.0316	0.0057	0.0168	**ARV**
	17.1151	21.7898	15.8048	22.6024	18.858	**SNR (dB)**
MLP	0.0045	0.0105	0.0202	0.0019	0.0093	**ARV**
	24.1719	19.9263	17.0533	27.2011	21.72	**SNR (dB)**
SLRNN	0.0057	0.0049	0.0064	0.0062	0.0114	**ARV**
	22.487	23.1229	22.0692	22.0468	21.87	**SNR (dB)**
SOSLR-NN	0.0096	0.0042	0.0207	0.0217	0.0077	**ARV**
	20.1712	23.776	17.9219	17.3629	19.71	**SNR (dB)**

and recurrent networks, better performance was achieved than the PSN and the MLP.

In contrast to the MLP, the SLRNN and the SOSLRNN, the recurrent pi-sigma neural network demonstrated the advantage that a small size training set was required. Furthermore, the average order and the average number of inputs used to predict the exchange rates time series were three and four, respectively. This means that the network utilised on average 18 weights for forecasting the time series and achieved fast training and convergence in comparison to other feedforward and recurrent neural networks.

A different set of experiments were carried out for the prediction of the exchange rates time series using the radial basis function (RBF) (Lee & Haykin, 1999). Our simulation results indicated that the RBF failed to produce a good ARV and SNR values. In the case of RBFs, the networks are trained only once on a large example set taken from the signal such that the dynamics of the underlying system can be captured. Therefore, the networks produce sequential outputs in response for newly arriving data. This means that such a system can be used when the dynamics of the time series does not change considerably over time, a condition which is usually contravened in practice (Lee & Haykin, 1999).

IDENTIFICATION OF NARMAX MODEL USING THE RECURRENT PI-SIGMA NEURAL NETWORK

In this section, the learning and the modelling capability of the recurrent pi-sigma neural network as Nonlinear Autoregressive Moving Average with exogenous inputs (NARMAX) is explained from the mathematical point of view.

Let us consider a simple second order RPSN with one input as shown in Figure 10.

Let us consider the hyperbolic tangent function as the activation function of the network which can be determined as follows:

$$f(u(t)) = \frac{e^{u(t)} - e^{-u(t)}}{e^{u(t)} + e^{-u(t)}}$$

$$= u(t) - \frac{1}{3}u(t)^3 + \frac{2}{15}u(t)^5 + \dots \quad (65)$$

The input-output relationship for the RPSN is determined as follows:

$$y(t) = f\left(\prod_{L=1}^{2} \left(w_{L1}x(t) + w_{L2} + w_{L3}y(t-1) \right) \right) \quad (66)$$

By substituting Equation (66) into Equation (65) and rearranging the terms, this can give the following representation:

$$y(t) = a_0 + a_1 u(t-1) + a_2 y(t-1) + a_3 u(t-1)^2 + a_4 y(t-1)^2$$
$$+ a_5 u(t-)y(t-1) + a_6 u(t-1)^3 + a_7 y(t-1)^3$$
$$+ a_8 u(t-)^2 y(t-1) + a_9 u(t-1)y(t-1)^2 + \dots \quad (67)$$

In this case, the parameters a_s are function of the weight values w_{LS}.

As it can be noticed from Equation (67), the RPSN is the general polynomial type of the NARMAX model. The learning capability is stored in the parameters. The quality of the identified network can be measured using the normalized root-mean-square-error (rmse) value (Huang & Loh, 2001).

Figure 10. A simple second order RPSN with one input

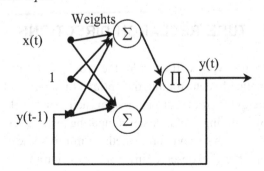

It is worth to mention that Billings et al. (1992) showed that the neural network does not generate components of higher order lagged system inputs and outputs that are not specified in the inputs nodes and that if insufficiently and inappropriately lagged values for the inputs u(t) and the previous outputs y(t) are assigned as input signals, the network cannot generate the missing dynamic terms. This means that the network does not "learn" the system behaviour completely and it will not be a general model of the system, and network performance will be limited. For the RPSN, this can be achieved by utilising sufficient higher order terms.

CONCLUSION

This work described a new recurrent neural network architecture, the recurrent Pi-sigma neural network, and its application to the one-step prediction of the exchange rate time-series. The proposed artificial neural network has a small structure and enjoys fast training and rapid convergence. It combines the properties of artificial higher-order neural networks and recurrent neural networks, and as a result, encouraging prediction results were obtained. Simulation results for the predicted financial signals using the recurrent Pi-sigma predictor have shown an improvement in the SNR over the feedforward pi-sigma network, multilayer perceptron, the single layer fully recurrent neural network and the second order single layer recurrent neural networks.

FUTURE RESEARCH DIRECTIONS

Future work will consider the problem of automatically determining the optimal topology and weights of the recurrent Pi-sigma neural network, by applying evolutionary computing techniques. Evolutionary computing methods mimic some of the processes observed in natural evolution and are based on the Darwinian principle of the survival of the fittest. For instance in (Nag & Mitra, 2002), a framework for the determination of polynomial higher-order architectures as applied to time series prediction was proposed.

Another avenue of research involves the transformation of data into a five-day relative difference in percentage. This allows the distribution of the transformed data to become more symmetrical and closer to normal distribution. This modification to the trend of the data will have the implication of improving the prediction of the neural networks. As a further extension of this work, we will consider the appropriateness of confidence metrics in order to establish suitable trading strategies (see for instance, Oliveira & Meira, 2006). Dunis and Williams (2002) proposed the use of neural networks attached to a simple trading strategy to assess its profitability: if the return forecast is an increase, then a buy signal is produced, otherwise a signal is sent to sell. In addition, a third option called "don't know" could be introduced, when the model does not send either a buy or sell signal, effectively opting out of making any transaction.

REFERENCES

Anderson, O.D. (1976). *Time series analysis and forecasting*. Butterworths.

Atiya, A. (1988). Learning on a general network. In D. Anderson, (Ed.) *Neural information processing systems (NIPS)*. New York: American Institute of Physics.

Billings S.A, Jamaluddin, H. B., & Chen, S. (1992). Properties of neural networks with applications to modeling non-linear dynamical systems. *International Journal of Control, 55*, 193–224.

Bishop, C.M. (1997). *Neural networks for pattern recognition*. Clarendon Press.

Bodyanskiy, Y., & Popov, S. (2006). Neural network approach to forecasting of quasiperiodic financial time series. *European Journal of Operational Research, 175*(3), 1357-1366.

Box, G.E.P., & Jenkins, G.M. (1976). *Time series analysis: Forecasting and control.* Holden-Day.

Brockwell, P.J. & Davis, R.A. (1991). *Time series: Theory and methods, 2nd Edition.* Springer.

Chen, A.S., & Leung, M.T. (2005). Performance evaluation of neural network architectures: The case of predicting foreign exchange correlations. *Journal of Forecasting, 24*(6), 403-420.

Cichocki, A., & Unbehauen, R. (1993). *Neural networks for optimization and signal processing.* J. Wiley & Sons.

Coa, L., & Tay, F.E.H. (2001). Financial forecasting using support vector machines. *Neural Computing and Applications, 10,* 184-192.

Dunis, C.L. & Williams, M. (2002). Modelling and trading the EUR/USD exchange rate: Do neural network models perform better? *Derivatives Use, Trading and Regulation, 8*(3), 211-239.

Fadlalla, A., & Lin, C.H. (2001). An analysis of the applications of neural networks in finance. *Interfaces, 31*(4), 112-122.

Fulcher, G.E., & Brown, D.E. (1994). A polynomial neural network for predicting temperature distributions. *IEEE Transactions on Neural Networks, 5*(3), 372-379.

Ghosh, J., & Shin, Y. (1992). Efficient higher-order neural networks for classification and function approximation. *International Journal of Neural Systems, 3*(4), 323-350.

Hamid, S.A., & Iqbal, Z. (2004). Using neural networks for forecasting volatility of S&P 500 Index future prices. *Journal of Business Research, 57*(10), 1116-1125.

Harvey, A.C. (1981). *Time series models.* Philip Allan.

Haykin, S.S. (1994). *Neural networks: A comprehensive foundation.* Maxwell Macmillan.

Hornik, K., Stinchcombe, M., & White, H. (1989). Multilayer feedforward networks are universal approximators. *Neural Networks, 2*(5), 359-366.

Huang C., & Loh, C. (2001). Nonlinear identification of dynamic systems using neural networks. *Computer-Aided Civil and Infrastructure Engineering, 16,* 28–41

Kantz, H., & Schreiber, T. (1997). *Nonlinear time series analysis.* Cambridge University Press.

Kuan, M. (1989). *Estimation of neural networks models.* PhD thesis, University of California, San Diego.

Lee, P. and Haykin, S. (1999). A dynamic regularised radial basis function network for nonlinear, nonstationary time series prediction. *IEEE Transactions on Signal processing, 47*(9), 2503- 2521.

Ljung, L. (1999). *System identification: Theory for the user, 2nd Edition.* Prentice-Hall.

Nag, A.K., & Mitra, A. (2002). Forecasting daily foreign exchange rates using genetically optimized neural networks. *Journal of Forecasting, 21*(7), 501-511.

Oliveira, A.L.I., & Meira, S.R.L. (2006). Detecting novelties in time series through neural networks forecasting with robust confidence intervals. *Neurocomputing, 70*(1-3), 79-92.

Pao, Y. (1989). *Adaptive pattern recognition and neural networks.* Addison-Wesley.

Picton, P.D. (2000). *Neural networks, 2nd Edition.* Palgrave.

Priestley, M.B. (1988). *Non-linear and non-stationary time series analysis.* Academic Press.

Rihani, V., & Garg, S.K. (2006). Neural networks for the prediction of the stock market. *IETE Technical Review, 23*(2), 113-117.

Saad, E.W., Prokhorov, D.V., & Wunsch, D.C. (1998). Comparative study of stock trend prediction using time delay, recurrent and probabilistic neural networks. *IEEE Transactions on Neural Networks, 9*(6), 1456-1470.

Shin, Y., & Ghosh, J. (1991). The pi-sigma network: An efficient higher-order neural network for pattern classification and function approximation. *IEEE Transactions on Neural Networks, 1*(1), 13-18.

Taylor M., & Lisboa, P. (1993). *Techniques and applications of neural networks.* Ellis Horwood.

Teodorescu, D. (1990). Time series: Information and prediction. *Biological Cybernetics, 63*(6), 477-485.

Tenti, P. (1996). Forecasting foreign exchange rates using recurrent neural networks. *Applied Artificial Intelligence, 10*(6), 567-581.

Vapnik, V.N., Golowish, S.E., & Smola, A.J. (1991). Support vector method for function approximation, regression and signal processing. *Advances in Neural Information Systems, 9,* 281-287.

Vellido, A., Lisboa, P.J.G., & Vaughan, J. (1999). Neural networks in business: A survey of applications (1992-1998). *Expert Systems with Applications, 17*(1), 51-70.

Williams, R.J., & Zipser, D. (1989). A learning algorithm for continually running fully recurrent neural networks. *Neural Computation, 1,* 270-280.

Williams, R.J., & Zipser, D. (1995). Gradient-based learning algorithms for recurrent neural networks. In Chauvin, Y., & Rumelhart, D.E. (Eds.), *Backpropagation theory, architecture and applications* (pp. 433-486). Lawrence Erlbaurn Association.

ADDITIONAL READING

An-Sin, C., & Mark, T.L. (2005). Performance evaluation of neural network architectures: The case of predicting foreign exchange correlations. *Journal of Forecasting, 24,* 403-420.

Durbin, R., & Rumelhart, D. E. (1989). Product units: A computationally powerful and biologically plausible extension to back-propagation networks. *Neural Computation, 1,* 133-142.

Caruana, R., Lawrence, S., & Giles, L. (2000). Overfitting in neural nets: Backpropagation, conjugate gradient, and early stopping. *Neural Information Processing Systems,* 402-408.

Hellstrom, T., & Holmstrom, K. (1997). *Predicting the stock market.* Technical report Series IMa-TOM-1997-07. Center of Mathematical Modeling (CMM), Department of Mathematics & Pyhsics, Malardalen University, Sweden.

Henriksson, R.D., & Merton R.C. (1981). On the market timing and investment performance of managed portfolios II: Statistical procedures for evaluating forecasting skills. *Journal of Business, 54,* 513-533.

Ho, S. L., Xie, M., & Goh, T. N. (2002). A comparative study of neural network and Box-Jenkins ARIMA modeling in time series prediction. *Computers & Industrial Engineering, 42,* 371-375.

Husken, M., & Stagge, P. (2003). Recurrent neural networks for time series classification. *Neurocomputing, 50,* 223-235.

Kaastra, I., & Boyd, M. (1996). Designing a neural network for forecasting financial and economic time series. *Neurocomputing, 10,* 215-236.

Leung, M. T., Chen, A. S., & Daouk, H. (2000). Forecasting exchange rates using general regression neural networks. *Computers & Operations Research, 27,* 1093-1110.

Merton, R.C. (1981). On market timing and investment performance of managed performance I: An equilibrium theory of value for market forecasts. *Journal of Business*, *5*, 363-406.

Pesaran, M. H., & Timmermann, A. (2002). Market timing and return prediction under model instability. *Journal of Empirical Finance*, *9*, 495– 510.

Plummer, E. A. (2000). *Time series forecasting with feed-forward neural networks: Guidelines and limitations*. Thesis for Master of science in computer science, University of Wyoming, 2000. Retrieved from: http://www.karlbranting.net/papers/plummer/Paper_7_12_00.htm

Robert, E.C., & David, M.M. (1987). Testing for market timing ability: A framework for forecast evaluation. *Journal of Financial Economics*, *19*, 169-189.

Schmitt, M (2001a). On the complexity of computing and learning with multiplicative neural networks. *Neural Computation*, *14*, 241-301.

Schmitt, M. (2001b). Product unit neural networks with constant depth and superlinear VC dimension. *Proceedings of the International Conference on Artificial Neural Networks ICANN 2001*. Lecture Notes in Computer Science, volume 2130, pp. 253-258. Berlin: Springer-Verlag.

Serdar, Y, Fikret, S. G., & Nesrin, O. (2005). A comparison of global, recurrent and smoothed-piecewise neural models for Istanbul stock exchange (ISE) prediction. *Pattern Recognition Letters, 26*, 2093–2103.

Sitte R. & Sitte, J. (2000). Analysis of the predictive ability of time delay neural networks applied to the S&P 500 time series. *IEEE Transaction on Systems, Man, and Cybernetics-part. 30*(4), 568-572.

Thomason, M. (1998). The practitioner method and tools: A basic neural network-based trading system project revisited (parts 1 & 2). *Journal of Computational Intelligence in Finance*, *6*(1), 43-44.

Walczal, S. (2001). An empirical analysis of data requirements for financial forecasting with neural networks. *Journal of Management Information Systems, 17*(4), 203–222.

Yao, J., & Tan, C. L. (2001). Guidelines for financial forecasting with neural networks. *Proceedings of International Conference on Neural Information Processing* (pp. 757-761). Shanghai, China.

Yao, J., & Tan, C. L. (2000). A case study on neural networks to perform technical forecasting of forex. *Neurocomputing, 34*, 79-98.

Zekić, M. (1998). Neural network applications in stock market predictions: A methodology analysis. In Aurer, B., Logožar, & R.,Varaždin (Eds.), *Proceedings of the 9th International Conference on Information and Intelligent Systems '98* (pp. 255-263).

Chapter X
Generalized Correlation Higher Order Neural Networks for Financial Time Series Prediction

David R. Selviah
University College London, UK

Janti Shawash
University College London, UK

ABSTRACT

Generalized correlation higher order neural network designs are developed. Their performance is compared with that of first order networks, conventional higher order neural network designs, and higher order linear regression networks for financial time series prediction. The correlation higher order neural network design is shown to give the highest accuracy for prediction of stock market share prices and share indices. The simulations compare the performance for three different training algorithms, stationary versus non-stationary input data, different numbers of neurons in the hidden layer and several generalized correlation higher order neural network designs. Generalized correlation higher order linear regression networks are also introduced and two designs are shown by simulation to give good correct direction prediction and higher prediction accuracies, particularly for long-term predictions, than other linear regression networks for the prediction of inter-bank lending risk Libor and Swap interest rate yield curves. The simulations compare the performance for different input data sample lag lengths.

INTRODUCTION

Neural networks are usually trained by means of a training algorithm, which calculates the values of the interconnection weights and threshold biases.

After training, it is difficult to understand how the final weights encapsulate the trends and patterns in the training data. If the network does not perform sufficiently well, it is difficult to understand how to modify or redesign the network or the training algorithm to give better performance. The correlation model (Selviah, 1989; Midwinter, 1989; Midwinter, 2003; Twaij, 1992) of first order neural networks provides a conceptual framework, which gives an insight into the behavior of neural networks (Selviah, 1989) and has enabled improved network structures (Selviah, 1989; Selviah, 1989) and training algorithms to be developed (Selviah, 1996; Stamos, 1998; Selviah, 2002). Instead of dealing with individual weights, the model considers the network to store two sets of vectors or patterns, each formed by various combinations of the weights. One layer in a first order neural network is equivalent to two cascaded arrays of inner product correlators, each array storing one set of vectors, as in Figure 1. The inner product correlation, or dot product, of the input vector and each of the first set of stored vectors yields a number of correlation magnitudes. The inner product correlation operation is particularly useful for comparing patterns and for recognizing any similarities between them, provided the patterns are in alignment with each other. The inner product correlation magnitudes are passed to the second set of vectors with which they multiply. This weighted second set of vectors is then summed

and thresholded. By expanding the neurons non-linear threshold function as a power series, (Selviah, 1989) weighted higher order products of the second set of stored vectors are formed generating high order terms in an otherwise "first order" neural network.

Higher order neural networks offer improved performance over first order networks as the higher order cross products between elements of the input vector highlight inter-element relationships. Apart from the use of the non-linear threshold, the higher order cross products may be formed in additional pre-processing layers or by multiplier unit neurons. However, the number of such cross products increases exponentially as the input vector lengthens, resulting in many interconnection weights, long training times, insufficient simulating computer memory and convergence to one of the many shallow local minima (Leshno, 1993) in the neural networks energy surface instead of one of the few deep global minima, which give high accuracy. The challenge is to find new higher order neural network designs having fewer network variables, but which still give the same high accuracy.

Figure 1. Correlator model of one neural network layer

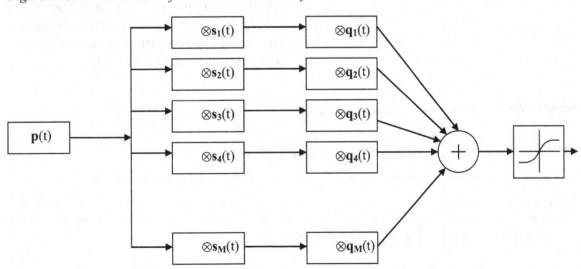

In this chapter, we review the correlation model and explore how it might be extended to model higher order neural networks and to design improved higher order neural networks. The chapter begins by extending the correlation model to include both inner and outer product correlations. The outer products allow time lag correlations to be identified. The network reduces to a first order neural network if only the inner product correlations are considered and the second correlator acts simply as a multiplier unit. The extended correlation model is explored mathematically for certain choices of stored vectors and is shown to operate as if the input vector elements consisted of linear weighted sums of inner and outer product correlations. We refer to this design of higher order neural network as one of a class of "generalized correlation" higher order neural networks. These networks are then simulated for the prediction of two types of financial time series. The first simulations predict the values of stock market shares and share indices and the second predict inter-bank lending interest rates and yield curves, which are considered more difficult to predict (Risk, 2007). In both cases, designs from the class of generalized correlator higher order neural networks outperform conventional higher order neural networks giving better prediction accuracies.

EXTENDED CORRELATION MODEL OF NEURAL NETWORKS

The theoretical derivation below is carried out using continuous functions and integrals, for convenience, and then digitized into numerical form with summations although it could also be all carried out in digital form.

In the correlator model, Figure 1, the input vector $\mathbf{p}(t)$ is correlated in two dimensions with several vectors, $\mathbf{s}_k(t)$, previously stored during training. The stored vectors are stored in the weights of the interconnections. Each correlator channel consists, in general, of *two* correlators, each having a, generally, different stored vector. Let the first vector be $\mathbf{s}$, and the second vector be $\mathbf{q}$. Therefore, one correlation channel performs two correlations. The first correlation, $\otimes$, is given by:

$$\mathbf{p}(t) \otimes \mathbf{s}(t) = \int_{t_0=-\infty}^{+\infty} \mathbf{p}(t_0)\mathbf{s}^*(t+t_0)dt_0 \qquad (1)$$

where t_0 is a dummy variable inside the integral representing the sliding of one vector across the other vector in t to all possible positions of overlap. This is then correlated with the second vector, $\mathbf{q}$, giving Equation (2), where t_1, is a dummy variable over which the second integration take place. Firstly, remove the brackets to get Equation (3).

Next is the key step in which the integrations are moved and the variables reassociated within new brackets to give Equation (4).

Equation (2).

$$\left(\mathbf{p}(t) \otimes \mathbf{s}(t)\right) \otimes \mathbf{q}(t) = \int_{t_1=-\infty}^{+\infty} \left(\int_{t_0=-\infty}^{+\infty} \mathbf{p}(t_0)\mathbf{s}^*(t_1+t_0)dt_0 \right) \mathbf{q}^*(t+t_1)dt_1$$

Equation (3).

$$\left(\mathbf{p}(t) \otimes \mathbf{s}(t)\right) \otimes \mathbf{q}(t) = \int_{t_1=-\infty}^{+\infty} \int_{t_0=-\infty}^{+\infty} \mathbf{p}(t_0)\mathbf{s}^*(t_1+t_0)dt_0\mathbf{q}^*(t+t_1)dt_1$$

Equation (4).

$$(\mathbf{p}(t) \otimes \mathbf{s}(t)) \otimes \mathbf{q}(t) = \int\limits_{t_0=-\infty}^{+\infty} \mathbf{p}(t_0) \left(\int\limits_{t_1=-\infty}^{+\infty} \mathbf{s}^*(t_1+t_0)\mathbf{q}^*(t+t_1)dt_1 \right) dt_0$$

Now let us define the weight matrix to be:

$$\boldsymbol{\omega}(t_0,t) = \int\limits_{t_1=-\infty}^{+\infty} \mathbf{s}^*(t_1+t_0)\mathbf{q}^*(t+t_1)dt_1 \qquad (5)$$

Substituting this into the double correlation equation gives:

$$(\mathbf{p}(t) \otimes \mathbf{s}(t)) \otimes \mathbf{q}(t) = \int\limits_{t_0=-\infty}^{+\infty} \mathbf{p}(t_0)\boldsymbol{\omega}(t_0,t)dt_0 \qquad (6)$$

Now we must remember that this is only the output of one double correlation channel. A number of parallel correlation channel vector outputs must then be summed together in alignment. This is expressed as:

$$\sum_{k=1}^{M}(\mathbf{p}(t) \otimes \mathbf{s}_k(t)) \otimes \mathbf{q}_k(t) = \sum_{k=1}^{M} \int\limits_{t_0=-\infty}^{+\infty} \mathbf{p}(t_0)\boldsymbol{\omega}_k(t_0,t)dt_0 \qquad (7)$$

$$\boldsymbol{\omega}_k(t_0,t) = \int\limits_{t_1=-\infty}^{+\infty} \mathbf{s}_k^*(t_1+t_0)\mathbf{q}_k^*(t+t_1)dt_1 \qquad (8)$$

if we assume that there are *M* parallel correlator channels. Now moving the summation inside the integral:

$$\sum_{k=1}^{M}(\mathbf{p}(t) \otimes \mathbf{s}_k(t)) \otimes \mathbf{q}_k(t) = \int\limits_{t_0=-\infty}^{+\infty} \mathbf{p}(t_0) \left(\sum_{k=1}^{M} \boldsymbol{\omega}_k(t_0,t) \right) dt_0 \qquad (9)$$

and redefining the weight matrix we obtain:

$$\sum_{k=1}^{M}(\mathbf{p}(t) \otimes \mathbf{s}_k(t)) \otimes \mathbf{q}_k(t) = \int\limits_{t_0=-\infty}^{+\infty} \mathbf{p}(t_0)\mathbf{w}(t_0,t)dt_0 \qquad (10)$$

$$\mathbf{w}(t_0,t) = \sum_{k=1}^{M} \boldsymbol{\omega}_k(t_0,t) = \sum_{k=1}^{M} \int\limits_{t_1=-\infty}^{+\infty} \mathbf{s}_k^*(t_1+t_0)\mathbf{q}_k^*(t+t_1)dt_1 \qquad (11)$$

These are the two most general equations but in order to understand them it is easier to examine some special cases in which they are simplified.

In a correlation, there are two types of term: The terms arising, when the two vectors are exactly in alignment, are known as *inner products* and those when they are misaligned or offset so that they only partially overlap known as *outer products*. Let us firstly examine the behavior when the correlation only consists of inner product terms.

Correlation Model of First Order Neural Network

In order to only consider the inner product terms of a correlation it is necessary to set *t*=0 in the earlier equation so that there is no relative offset of the vectors giving in the definition:

$$[\mathbf{p}(t) \otimes \mathbf{s}(t)]_{t=0} = \int\limits_{t_0=-\infty}^{+\infty} \mathbf{p}(t_0)\mathbf{s}^*(t_0)dt_0 \qquad (12)$$

This results in a single real value for the inner product and not a vector. This value is equivalent to setting all of the outer product values to zero in the equations of the previous section, which for continuous non-pixelated vectors is a centered spatial delta function. So, when this correlates with the second vector the subsequent equation becomes Equation (13) and (14).

The second correlation just reduces to a multiplication. Continuing as before moving the integrals and reassociating variables inside brackets gives:

$$\left[\mathbf{p}(t) \otimes \mathbf{s}(t)\right]_{t=0} \otimes \mathbf{q}(t) = \int\limits_{t_0=-\infty}^{+\infty} \mathbf{p}(t_0)\left(\mathbf{s}^*(t_0)\mathbf{q}^*(t)\right)dt_0$$

(15)

Let the weight matrix be:

$$\boldsymbol{\omega}(t_0,t) = \mathbf{s}^*(t_0)\mathbf{q}^*(t)$$

(16)

Substituting in we obtain:

$$\left[\mathbf{p}(t) \otimes \mathbf{s}(t)\right]_{t=0} \otimes \mathbf{q}(t) = \int\limits_{t_0=-\infty}^{+\infty} \mathbf{p}(t_0)\boldsymbol{\omega}(t_0,t)dt_0$$

(17)

Then summing over all of the M correlation channels gives:

$$\sum_{k=1}^{M}\left[\mathbf{p}(t) \otimes \mathbf{s}(t)\right]_{t=0} \otimes \mathbf{q}_k(t) = \sum_{k=1}^{M} \int\limits_{t_0=-\infty}^{+\infty} \mathbf{p}(t_0)\boldsymbol{\omega}_k(t_0,t)dt_0$$

(18)

$$\boldsymbol{\omega}_k(t_0,t) = \mathbf{s}_k^*(t_0)q_k^*(t)$$

(19)

Moving the summation into the integral:

$$\sum_{k=1}^{M}\left[\mathbf{p}(t) \otimes \mathbf{s}(t)\right]_{t=0} \otimes \mathbf{q}_k(t) = \int\limits_{t_0=-\infty}^{+\infty} \mathbf{p}(t_0)\left(\sum_{k=1}^{M}\boldsymbol{\omega}_k(t_0,t)\right)dt_0$$

(20)

and redefining the weight matrix gives:

$$\sum_{k=1}^{M}\left[\mathbf{p}(t) \otimes \mathbf{s}(t)\right]_{t=0} \otimes \mathbf{q}_k(t) = \int\limits_{t_0=-\infty}^{+\infty} \mathbf{p}(t_0)\mathbf{w}(t_0,t)dt_0$$

(21)

$$\mathbf{w}(t_0,t) = \sum_{k=1}^{M}\boldsymbol{\omega}_k(t_0,t) = \sum_{k=1}^{M}\mathbf{s}_k^*(t_0)\mathbf{q}_k^*(t)$$

(22)

Now digitizing the input vector, changing the integral to a summation, replacing, t_0 by the integer index, i, setting the number of elements in the input vector to be, N, and replacing, t by the integer index, j, gives:

$$\sum_{k=1}^{M}\left[\mathbf{p}(t) \otimes \mathbf{s}(t)\right]_{t=0} \otimes \mathbf{q}_k(t) = \sum_{i=1}^{N}\mathbf{p}_i\mathbf{w}_{ij}$$

(23)

$$\mathbf{w}_{ij} = \sum_{k=1}^{M}\boldsymbol{\omega}_{kij} = \sum_{k=1}^{M}\mathbf{s}_{ki}^*\mathbf{q}_{kj}^*$$

(24)

The right hand side of this equation is the usual vector-matrix multiplication. This proves that the output, when an input vector passes

Equation (13).

$$\left[\mathbf{p}(t) \otimes \mathbf{s}(t)\right]_{t=0} \otimes \mathbf{q}(t) = \int\limits_{t_1=-\infty}^{+\infty}\left(\int\limits_{t_0=-\infty}^{+\infty} \mathbf{p}(t_0)\mathbf{s}^*(t_0)dt_0\right)\delta(t_1)\mathbf{q}^*(t+t_1,)dt_1$$

Equation (14).

$$\left[\mathbf{p}(t) \otimes \mathbf{s}(t)\right]_{t=0} \otimes \mathbf{q}(t) = \left(\int\limits_{t_0=-\infty}^{+\infty} \mathbf{p}(t_0)\mathbf{s}^*(t_0)dt_0\right)\mathbf{q}^*(t)$$

through a weighted interconnection layer is the same as that one would obtain, if the input vector were correlated firstly with one set of stored vectors and correlated secondly with a second set of stored vectors. Moreover, we have derived the relationship required between the two sets of stored vectors, **s** and **q** and the weights **w**, in the conventional model. The relationship states that the ith component of the first stored vector, **s**, is multiplied by the jth component of the second stored vector, **q**, in that channel and then summed over all such channels. The complex conjugation operations may normally be neglected when dealing with real valued time-series.

Correlation Model of Higher Order Neural Networks

If we do not make the simplification of the last section in which we only considered inner product correlations, the correlation model for higher order neural networks can be derived, which also includes outer product correlations. We begin by rewriting Equation (3) to make Equation (25), which is the output of one of the double correlation

channels. Although it is unnecessarily restrictive, let us firstly consider the special case when each of the second set of stored vectors, $\mathbf{q}_k$, is the same as input vector, **p**, as this will reveal the underlying behavior. Substituting and summing over all channels we obtain Equation (26). Rearranging gives Equation (27).

Defining the weight matrix in a different way to before gives:

$$\mathbf{w}(t_0 + t_1) = \sum_{k=1}^{M} \mathbf{s}_k^*(t_1 + t_0)$$

(28)

in which the values of **w** are not independently related to t_0, nor t_1 but instead are related to their sum; the implications of this are discussed in the next section. Substituting back into Equation (27) gives Equation (29).

Now digitizing the input vector, changing the integral to a summation, replacing, t_0 by the integer index, i, setting the number of elements in the input vector to be, N, replacing, $(t+t_1)$ by the integer index, j, and replacing, t by the integer index, n, so the integer indices are defined differently from the last section, gives:

Equation (25).

$$\left(\mathbf{p}(t) \otimes \mathbf{s}(t)\right) \otimes \mathbf{q}(t) = \int_{t_1=-\infty}^{+\infty} \int_{t_0=-\infty}^{+\infty} \mathbf{p}(t_0)\mathbf{s}^*(t_1+t_0)dt_0 \mathbf{q}^*(t+t_1)dt_1$$

Equation (26).

$$\sum_{k=1}^{M}\left(\mathbf{p}(t) \otimes \mathbf{s}_k(t)\right) \otimes \mathbf{p}(t) = \sum_{k=1}^{M} \int_{t_1=-\infty}^{+\infty} \int_{t_0=-\infty}^{+\infty} \mathbf{p}(t_0)\mathbf{s}_k^*(t_1+t_0)dt_0 \mathbf{p}^*(t+t_1)dt_1$$

Equation (27).

$$\sum_{k=1}^{M}\left(\mathbf{p}(t) \otimes \mathbf{s}_k(t)\right) \otimes \mathbf{p}(t) = \int_{t_1=-\infty}^{+\infty} \int_{t_0=-\infty}^{+\infty} \mathbf{p}(t_0)\mathbf{p}^*(t+t_1)\left(\sum_{k=1}^{M}\mathbf{s}_k^*(t_1+t_0)\right)dt_0 dt_1$$

Equation (29).

$$\sum_{k=1}^{M}\left(\mathbf{p}(t) \otimes \mathbf{s}_k(t)\right) \otimes \mathbf{p}(t) = \int_{t_1=-\infty}^{+\infty} \int_{t_0=-\infty}^{+\infty} \mathbf{p}(t_0)\mathbf{p}^*(t+t_1)\mathbf{w}(t_0+t_1)dt_0 dt_1$$

$$\sum_{k=1}^{M} \left(\mathbf{p}_n \otimes \mathbf{s}_{kn}\right) \otimes \mathbf{p}_n = \sum_{i}^{N} \sum_{j}^{N} \mathbf{p}_i \mathbf{p}_j^* \mathbf{w}_{i+j-n} \quad (30)$$

Let us secondly, consider another special case when each of the first set of stored vectors, **s**, is the same as the input vector, **p**. In this case the equation corresponding to Equation (27) becomes Equation (31). Defining the weight in a different way to before gives Equation (32) and:

$$\mathbf{w}(t + t_1) = \sum_{k=1}^{M} \mathbf{q}_k^*(t + t_1) \quad (33)$$

Now digitizing the input vector, changing the integral to a summation, replacing, t_0 by the integer index, i, setting the number of elements in the input vector to be, N, replacing, $(t_1 + t_0)$ by the integer index, j, and replacing, t by the integer index, n, so the integer indices are defined differently from above, gives

$$\sum_{k=1}^{M} \left(\mathbf{p}_n \otimes \mathbf{p}_n\right) \otimes \mathbf{q}_{kn} = \sum_{i=1}^{N} \sum_{j=1}^{N} \mathbf{p}_i \mathbf{p}_j^* \mathbf{w}_{j-i+n} \quad (34)$$

Equations (30) and (34) both have a form similar to that of a second order higher order neural network, which outputs a vector, $\mathbf{z}_n$, after the first interconnection layer, before passing through the neuron non-linear threshold:

$$\mathbf{z}_n = \sum_{i=1}^{N} \sum_{j=1}^{N} \mathbf{p}_i \mathbf{p}_j \mathbf{w}_{nij} \quad (35)$$

DESIGN OF GENERALIZED CORRELATION HIGHER ORDER NEURAL NETWORKS

We begin by discussing the final Equations (30) and (34) derived in the previous section and through this analysis design a higher order neural network. In the previous sections, the correlation model for a first order neural network was extended by including both inner and outer product correlations and then was reduced in two special cases to equations resembling that for a second order neural network but having some differences. In the derived equations, the term $\mathbf{p}_i \mathbf{p}_j$ may be considered one element of the covariance matrix, $\mathbf{p}^T \mathbf{p}$, having j columns and i rows. The complex conjugation operations may be neglected if the time-series consists of real valued elements.

The main difference between the two derived equations (30) and (34) and the second order neural network equation (35) is that the weight matrix is replaced by a longer weight vector as seen in equations (28) and (33). Alternatively, this vector can be considered the usual weight matrix in which many of the elements are the same. Let us consider a 4-element vector to show the behavior. For the nth element of the output vector, the weight matrix *subscripts* would be for an $N = 4$ element

Equation (31).

$$\sum_{k=1}^{M} \left(\mathbf{p}(t) \otimes \mathbf{p}(t)\right) \otimes \mathbf{q}_k(t) = \int_{t_1=-\infty}^{+\infty} \int_{t_0=-\infty}^{+\infty} \mathbf{p}(t_0)\mathbf{p}^*(t_1 + t_0)\left(\sum_{k=1}^{M} \mathbf{q}_k^*(t + t_1)\right) dt_0 dt_1$$

Equation (32).

$$\sum_{k=1}^{M} \left(\mathbf{p}(t) \otimes \mathbf{p}(t)\right) \otimes \mathbf{q}_k(t) = \int_{t_1=-\infty}^{+\infty} \int_{t_0=-\infty}^{+\infty} \mathbf{p}(t_0)\mathbf{p}^*(t_1 + t_0)\mathbf{w}(t + t_1) dt_0 dt_1$$

input vector with $j=1..4$ columns and $i=1..4$ rows (see Equation (36)).

By considering the weight matrix subscripts to overlay the covariance matrix terms which are to be multiplied by the weights we see that all of the terms along the same diagonal have the same weight values although the magnitude of the weight values differ for each term, n, in the output vector. If the input vector were moved along its length, since the diagonal element weights are all the same the result is translation invariant (Kaita, 2002). In effect, the terms along each diagonal, separately, of the covariance matrix could be summed to form a composite term, which could then be weighted and summed to form a linear combination. In fact, these composite terms are the inner product correlation for the main diagonal of the covariance matrix and the outer product correlations for the other diagonals of the covariance matrix. Therefore, each term in the output vector consists of a differently weighted linear sum of the inner and outer products. This could be considered a new type of higher order neural network design in which the inputs to a first order neural network are formed by differently weighted linear combinations of the inner and outer product correlations.

The formation of the inner and outer products reduces the number of input terms to N since the covariance matrix is symmetric and so we only need to consider an upper triangular section including the main diagonal. This reduces the training time and the memory requirements of the simulating computer. However, are we losing some important variables by not allowing each of the diagonal elements to have its own weight?

In order to investigate this question, we could directly simulate this new design of higher order neural network. However, instead of making an input vector from weighted linear combinations of inner and outer products it is simpler and more instructive to make an input vector directly from the inner and outer product correlations. Several further correlation higher order neural network designs can be envisaged in which the input vector only consists of the inner product, or only the outer products (Bandyopadhyay, 1996) or both the inner and outer products. We can also generalize this further by considering another type of sum of elements of the covariance matrix such as the sum of the elements along the same row rather than the same diagonal. We refer to all of these designs as falling within the class of generalized correlation higher order neural networks, and the one having an input vector consisting of the inner and outer product correlations as being the correlation higher order neural network.

GENERALIZED CORRELATION HIGHER ORDER NEURAL NETWORK DESIGNS FOR SIMULATION

Four of the generalized correlation higher order neural network designs were simulated and compared to a first order neural network, a conventional higher order neural network and to

Equation (36).

1	2	3	4		2	3	4	5		3	4	5	6		4	5	6	7
0	1	2	3		1	2	3	4		2	3	4	5		3	4	5	6
−1	0	1	2		0	1	2	3		1	2	3	4		2	3	4	5
−2	−1	0	1		−1	0	1	2		0	1	2	3		1	2	3	4
	for n = 1					*for n = 2*					*for n = 3*					*for n = 4*		

higher order linear regression neural networks. The networks were given the following labels: First Order, Full Cross Product, Inner Product, Outer Product, Sum of Diagonals, and Sum of Horizontals.

For example if the input vector is $\mathbf{p}$ = {1, 2, 3, 4}, all of the cross products can be obtained from $\mathbf{p}$ by finding the covariance matrix:

$$\mathbf{p^T p} = \begin{Bmatrix} 1 & 2 & 3 & 4 \\ 2 & 4 & 6 & 8 \\ 3 & 6 & 9 & 12 \\ 4 & 8 & 12 & 16 \end{Bmatrix} \quad (37)$$

The Full Cross Product network, which is the conventional higher order neural network, uses only the matrix elements in the upper triangular section of the covariance matrix, due to its symmetry:

$$Full\ Cross\ Products = \begin{Bmatrix} 1 & 2 & 3 & 4 \\ & 4 & 6 & 8 \\ & & 9 & 12 \\ & & & 16 \end{Bmatrix} \quad (38)$$

The Sum of Diagonals input vector is found by taking the sum of the main diagonal of the covariance matrix and the sum of diagonals off the main diagonal (see Equation (39)).

The Sum of Horizontals input vector is found by taking the sum of the rows of the covariance matrix:

$$Sum\ of\ Horizontals = \begin{Bmatrix} 1 & 2 & 3 & 4 \\ 2 & 4 & 6 & 8 \\ 3 & 6 & 9 & 12 \\ 4 & 8 & 12 & 16 \end{Bmatrix} \begin{matrix} \sum \to \\ \sum \to \\ \sum \to \\ \sum \to \end{matrix} \begin{Bmatrix} 10 \\ 20 \\ 30 \\ 40 \end{Bmatrix}$$

$$(40)$$

The inner product network uses only the main diagonal sum of the covariance matrix as input. The outer product matrix uses only the sum of the other diagonals off the main diagonal of the covariance matrix as input. In the first set of simulations, the sum of horizontals network was omitted.

It is important to point out that for all networks, in addition to the higher order elements of the input vector described above, the original input vector elements are also input. Every network had a first layer of neurons having linear thresholds, into which the input higher order and first order elements were input. Every network also had a final layer of neurons having linear thresholds, which output the predicted vector values. We compared networks having an intermediate layer of hidden neurons having logistic function thresholds with those without. This allowed higher order neural networks having non-linear thresholds to be compared with higher order linear regression 4 layer networks. The hidden layer neural networks could be considered to be 5 layer feed forward neural networks having linear 1st, 3rd and 5th layer neurons, a 2nd layer of multiplier unit neurons with binary monopolar [0,1] weights specified by the design chosen in the first two interconnection

Equation (39).

$$Sum\ of\ Diagonals = \begin{Bmatrix} 1 & 2 & 3 & 4 \\ 2 & 4 & 6 & 8 \\ 3 & 6 & 9 & 12 \\ 4 & 8 & 12 & 16 \end{Bmatrix} \begin{matrix} \sum \\ \sum \searrow \\ \sum \searrow \\ \sum \searrow \\ \searrow \end{matrix} \begin{Bmatrix} 4 \\ 11 \\ 20 \\ 30 \end{Bmatrix} \begin{matrix} \\ \} \ Outer\ product\ correlations \\ \\ \} \ Inner\ product\ correlation \end{matrix}$$

layers and the remaining interconnection weights trained by the training algorithm.

SIMULATIONS PREDICTING STOCK MARKET SHARE PRICE AND SHARE INDEX

We found it very convenient to carry out the simulations by writing programs in MATLAB 2006a code making use of the MATLAB Neural Network Toolbox although it did not have any pre-programmed Higher Order Neural Networks. All of the simulations were carried out on a laptop 2.16 GHz dual core Centrino processor, with 2 Gbytes of RAM running under Windows XP.

Financial Time-Series Stock Market Data

The stock market share price and share index time-series data for training the neural networks

is publicly available online (Yahoo!, 2007) from which we selected the individual share price time series for five companies and also four share indices which combine the share prices for several top performing companies in different world regions. The data for each share time-series spans a different length of time and so, as the data consists of daily values, there are a different number of sample points in each dataset. To give generally applicable results we use these datasets as they stand (Table 1) rather than taking into account the number of sample points (Walzcak, 2001) which would further improve the results we obtained. The labels in the first column will be used hereafter in the text, for convenience.

Data Scaling

Before the raw data was presented to any Neural Network for training or simulation it was first scaled to an appropriate range so that it would experience the non-linearity and slope of the neuron

Table 1. Share price and share index time-series training data details

Company or Index Label	Duration	Number of sample points	Company Shares or Share Index Full Name
AAPL	7/9/1984~3/5/2007	5716	Apple Inc.
GOOG	19/8/2004~3/5/2007	681	Google Inc.
IBM	2/1/1962~3/5/2007	11412	IBM Corp.
MSFT	13/3/1986~3/5/2007	5333	Microsoft Corp.
SNE	6/4/1983~3/5/2007	6069	Sony Corp.
FTSE 100	2/4/1984~23/4/2007	5825	Financial Times Stock Exchange aggregated share index of the top 100 performing company shares
FTSE 350	4/1/2000~20/4/2007	1883	Financial Times Stock Exchange aggregated share index of the top 350 performing company shares
NASDAQ	5/2/1971~3/5/2007	9144	National Association of Securities Dealers Automated Quotations US aggregated share index
NIKKEI	4/1/1984~2/5/2007	5742	Japan Aggregated share index

non-linear threshold functions. If this were not done and if the data had large values compared to the threshold, the data would swing between the saturation limits of the threshold function running it into positive and negative saturation and so converting the data into a binary form, which would lose much of the information in it. If the data magnitudes were too small, they would only experience the linear portion at the center of the threshold function. In the simulations, the data was rescaled to the range {–5,5} to suit the range of the MATLAB non-linear Logistic function (Figure 2):

Stationary Versus Non-Stationary Data

Data is often non-stationary, so the variance is not constant throughout the duration of the signal and it is important to have a constant variance for best results. Figure 3 shows a histogram of the number of occurrences of different data values for the AAPL share before scaling. This plot shows that the most common value is 10 and that lower values occur more often than very large values. Since the data is monopolar it does not suit the bipolar input expected for the Logistic Function so half of the threshold function would not be used.

Figure 2. Logistic Function F(x) = 1/(1 + e⁻ˣ)

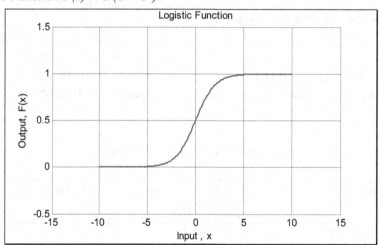

Figure 3 Histogram of the non-stationary AAPL closing share value

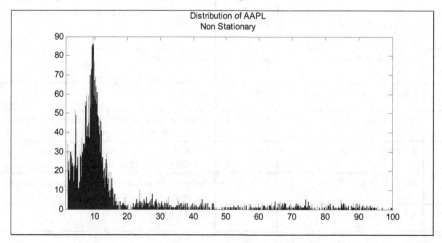

In addition, the large values in the data would run into the saturation of the threshold function and so would not be distinguishable.

The data can be converted into a stationary form in many ways. We used the method described by McNelis (2005) and Masters (1995) in which a new time-series is formed from the difference between the logarithms of adjacent points using the following equation:

$$\mathbf{p}_{stat}(t) = \ln(\mathbf{p}_{nonstat}(t)) - \ln(\mathbf{p}_{nonstat}(t-1)) \tag{42}$$

where $\mathbf{p}_{nonstat}(t)$ is the original non-stationary closing price of the share, and $\mathbf{p}_{stat}(t)$ is the stationary time-series obtained after the transformation. This creates a new time-series consisting of the natural logarithm of ratios of adjacent points in the original time-series. The signs of the terms in the new series are the slopes, or direction changes, in the original series. Figure 4 shows how the original non-stationary AAPL share price magnitude histogram changes into a stationary histogram having a greater degree of symmetry and few high and low values. This is more suited to the Logistic function threshold response but

must still be rescaled to experience the non-linear curvature of the function as otherwise the values in Figure 4 would mainly experience the linear slope near the origin of the function. After prediction, this transformation can be undone by multiplying a known point by the ratio terms in the new time-series in turn. However, this was not done in the simulations in this chapter, so the errors given are those for the prediction of a stationary value time-series.

Sample Window Lag Length

The Neural Network was trained by taking a contiguous set of data from the time-series in a sampling "window", or vector, and using this as input data. A second output "window", or vector, also consisted of contiguous data, immediately followed the first sampling window in time, and so represented the predicted values. The data in the output window was used as target data during training being supplied to the output of the neural network. The network was trained using the data vectors from the two contiguous windows and then the two windows were slid forwards in time by one time step, or day, and the training

Figure 4. Histogram of the stationary AAPL closing share value

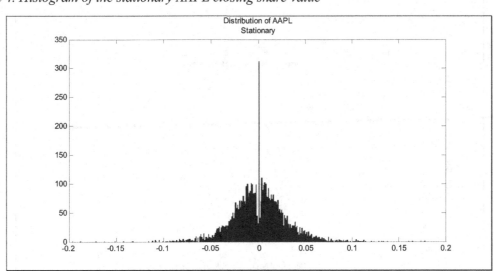

repeated a large number of times. This gave a large number of training samples. The number of elements in the input data vector, or lag length, was chosen to be 12 while the output vector was chosen to have 10 samples of target data. The same length data vector was used for all of the time-series for consistency, as this determines the number of variables in the neural network. An input vector of 12 samples means each of the samples represents a different sequential day in a time-series sequence and the output target vector of 10 samples means that the network will predict the next 10 elements in the time-series.

Initialization

The initial neural network interconnection weights and biases were set using the Nguyen-Widrow

method to obtain the fastest convergence and accuracy when training the networks (Nguyen, 1990). No special account was taken of cyclic seasonal changes such as the marking of time periods of 5 working days plus 2 weekend days, 4 weeks in a month or 12 months in a year or marking Christmas, Easter and Summer holidays periods as it would have introduced more data variables and we aimed to minimize the number of variables.

Hidden Layer with Variable Number of Neurons Versus No Hidden Layer

Simulations were run both with no hidden layer and with a hidden layer having various numbers of neurons. The first graph in Figure 5 shows the normalized Mean Square Error of all of the time-

Figure 5. Normalized mean square error and training time versus number of neurons in hidden layer

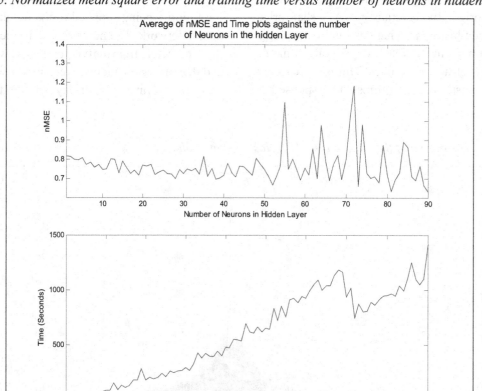

series predictions and the second graph shows the training time with both graphs being a function of the number of neurons in the hidden layer. The normalized Mean Square Error (nMSE) is defined to be:

$$nMSE = \frac{\frac{1}{N}\sum_i \left(Actual_i - Predicted_i\right)^2}{Mean\left(Predicted\right) \times Mean\left(Actual\right)}$$

(43)

The normalized Mean Square Error appears to decrease to a level of about 0.75 at about 25 neurons before it begins to fluctuate markedly after about 50 neurons. As the number of neurons increases the number of variables in the net, that is the weights and threshold offsets, increases and so requires a longer training time as is shown in the second graph in Figure 5 by the exponential increase. The reason for the sudden drop in training time at 70 neurons is that the memory capacity of the computer was reached at this point and so subsequent calculations for higher numbers of neurons were incorrect. Therefore, the choice of the optimum number of neurons in the hidden layer is a trade-off of minimizing the normalized Mean Square Error, lying in a stable region where the error does not fluctuate, at the same time as minimizing the training time by minimizing the number of neurons in the hidden layer.

Table 2 compares numerical values for six different hidden layer sizes and shows the relative changes in error and changes in training times compared to a hidden layer with 14 neurons. The table shows the same trends as Figure 5 with a decreasing nMSE error and an increasing training time as the number of neurons in the hidden layer increases. 19 neurons coincided with a small peak in the graph of training time and so gave a longer training time than 28 neurons. As a result, we chose a hidden layer having 14 neurons for these simulations as a trade-off compromise.

Neural Network Independent Variables

The number of independent variables, consisting of the weights and threshold biases that must be trained is important as it determines the training time. If there are too many variables, the network performance can be degraded. If there are too few variables there will be insufficient to represent fully the training data. An increased number of network variables may cause convergence to a local minimum in the energy surface rather than the global minimum (Leshno, 1993). The networks simulated are shown in Figure 6 and the number of network variables is shown in Table 3 for our chosen values of a 12 element time-series vector, a 10 element target time-series vector and, in the case of a hidden layer, a hidden layer having 14 neurons. The number of elements in the input vector, N, varied depending on the network structure. The first order neural network had an input vector made up of the 12 element input time-series vector. The "inner product"

Table 2. Comparison of Error and Training Time as a function of number of neurons

Number of Neurons in Hidden Layer	5	10	**14**	19	28	52
nMSE	0.8066	0.7452	**0.7277**	0.7175	0.6695	0.6657
Time (seconds)	26.55	83.17	**131.9**	278.6	261.4	832.3
nMSE improvement	-1.11%	-1.02%	**0%**	1.42%	4.03%	9.32%
Time increase	x 0.22	x 0.63	**x 1**	x 2.1117	x 1.9815	x 6.3081

Table 3. Number of independent variables for the different networks simulated

	Network	Weights	Biases	Total Parameters
Without Hidden layer	First Order	12*10	10	130
	Inner Product	13*10	10	140
	Outer Products	23*10	10	240
	Full cross Product	90*10	10	910
	Sum of Diagonals	24*10	10	250
With Hidden Layer	First Order	12*14 + 14*10	14+10	332
	Inner Product	13*14 + 14*10	14+10	346
	Outer Products	23*14 + 14*10	14+10	486
	Full cross Product	90*14 + 14*10	14+10	1424
	Sum of Diagonals	24*14 + 14*10	14+10	476

Figure 6. Structure of neural networks with and without a hidden layer

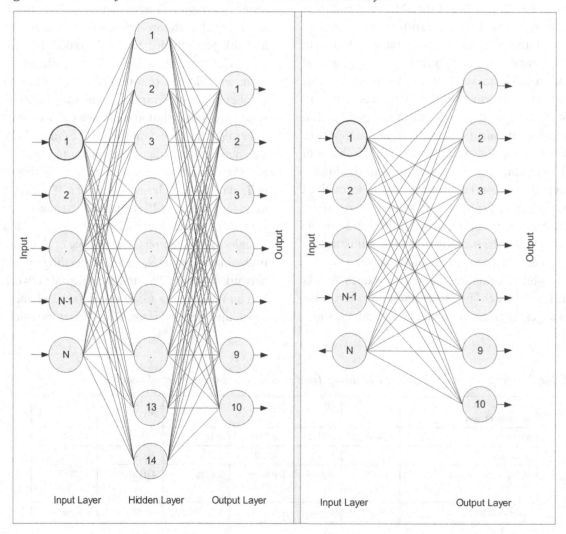

neural network had an input vector made up of the inner product formed from the sum of the main diagonal elements of the covariance matrix *and* the 12 element time-series vector which made an effective vector of 13 elements. The "outer product" network had an input vector made up of the 11 outer products formed by summing the diagonals apart from the main diagonal *and* the 12 element time-series vector which made an effective vector of 23 elements. The "Full Cross Product" network had an input vector made up of all 66 of the off-diagonal independent elements in the top half of the covariance matrix *and* the 12 on-diagonal elements of the covariance matrix *and* the 12 element time-series vector which made an effective vector of 90 elements. The "Sum of Diagonals" Network had an input vector made up of the 1 inner product and the 11 outer products formed by summing the diagonal elements of the covariance matrix *and* the 12 element time-series vector which made an effective vector of 24 elements.

Training Algorithms

The neural networks were trained using three different training algorithms to be sure that the results were not specific to one training algorithm and to find the best training algorithm. The training algorithms used were the Levenberg-Marquardt (Marquardt, 1963), Quasi-Newton (Edwin, 2001) and Scaled Conjugate Gradient (Moller, 1993) training algorithms. 60% of the dataset was used as training data, 20% used as validation data to prevent overfitting by stopping the training when the validation error becomes more than the training error and, 20% used for testing.

Simulation Results

Tables 4 to 9 present the results of the simulations for the three training methods, Levenberg-Marquardt, Quasi-Newton and Scaled Conjugate Gradient, with Stationary and Non Stationary data inputs for three layer and two layer neural networks formats for each of the 5 designs of neural network. The histograms show the average error for the 9 different financial time-series. The total error, which is the sum of the nMSE errors over the 10 output, time interval predictions, for each of the designs of higher order neural network is tabulated with the lowest in each set being marked in bold.

Simulation Analysis

The simulations may be analyzed by considering the total error, however, this hides a lower error for short-term predictions and larger errors for long-term predictions and vice versa, so we will analyze the results for each of these cases. All of the histograms show that the error increases with time ahead of the prediction as we might expect and we note that this increase is almost linear with time.

The share data having the fewest number of data points (GOOG, FTSE350) gave the highest error but this does not affect the comparison of the performance of different networks. In terms of the total error, for each algorithm, the stationary data yields clearly lower errors than the non-stationary data, although this was not converted back to the original non-stationary time-series form, so we will only concentrate on the stationary data results. For the Levenberg-Marquardt training the hidden layer error is lower that without the hidden layer except for the full cross product. For the Quasi-Newton training and for the scaled Conjugate Gradient training the total error is always lower for the network without a hidden layer so these two differ from the former training method. In terms of the magnitude of the total error, the total errors for the Levenberg- Marquardt training are often lower than for the other two training methods and far lower in the case of the network with a hidden layer for the first order, inner product, outer product and sum of diagonals networks. The lowest total error occurs for stationary data, for a network with a hidden layer trained by the

Table 4. Neural networks trained using the Levenberg-Marquardt Training Algorithm (Non-Stationary Data)

Neural Networks Trained using the Levenberg-Marquardt Training Algorithm (*Non-Stationary Data*)

	Total Error				
	Sum of Diagonals	Full Cross Product	Outer Product	Inner Product	First Order
With Hidden Layer	0.102767	0.111999	**0.080811**	0.080966	0.080966
Without a Hidden Layer	0.090146	**0.087978**	0.090101	0.090968	0.090967

(Charts: With Hidden Layer and Without a Hidden Layer, each plotting First Order, Inner Product, Outer Product, Full Cross Product, Sum of Diagonals across time intervals 1–10.)

Levenberg- Marquardt training algorithm for the sum of diagonals network design, which is the new correlation higher order neural network with a hidden layer.

For short-term predictions of one time interval, again we concentrate on the stationary data results since they give the lowest short-term prediction errors. It is clear that the neural networks without a hidden layer always give lower errors than those with hidden layers although we note that for the networks with a hidden layer the sum of diagonals network again performs best. The conclusion is that for short-term predictions the choice of training method and the design of network make little difference except that a network having no hidden layer is best.

For long-term predictions of 10 time intervals, the error is far less for the stationary data so we will concentrate on these results. The nMSE errors are at about the same level of 0.122 except for the networks trained using the Levenberg-Marquardt training algorithm. For this algorithm when there is no hidden layer the lowest error occurs for Full cross product conventional higher order, neural network and the outer product and sum of diagonal networks also perform well. However, the improvements are most marked in the case of the higher order neural networks with a hidden

Table 5. Neural networks trained using the Levenberg-Marquardt Training Algorithm (Stationary Data)

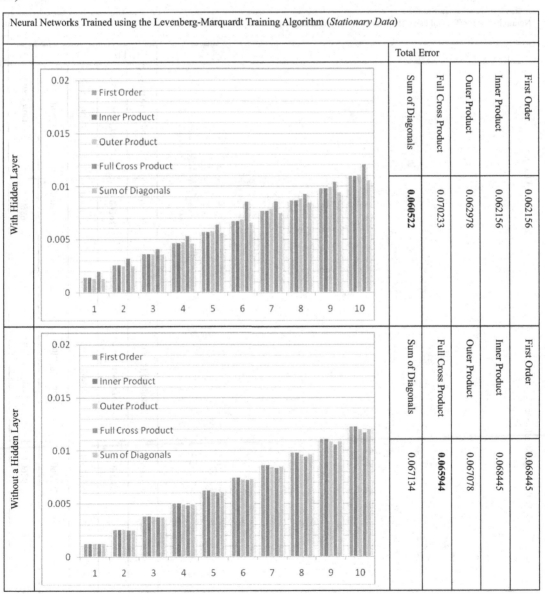

Neural Networks Trained using the Levenberg-Marquardt Training Algorithm (*Stationary Data*)					
		Total Error			
		Sum of Diagonals	Full Cross Product	Outer Product	Inner Product	First Order
With Hidden Layer		**0.060522**	0.070233	0.062978	0.062156	0.062156
		Sum of Diagonals	Full Cross Product	Outer Product	Inner Product	First Order
Without a Hidden Layer		0.067134	**0.065944**	0.067078	0.068445	0.068445

layer trained by the same Levenberg- Marquardt training algorithm for 4 networks: first order, inner product, outer product and sum of diagonals. In this case, the conventional higher order neural network did not perform even as well as the first order. The clearly lowest error was obtained for the Sum of Diagonals network design, which is the

correlation higher order neural network, proposed in this chapter, with a hidden layer trained by the Levenberg- Marquardt training algorithm.

Table 6. Neural networks trained using the Quasi-Newton Training Algorithm (Non-Stationary Data)

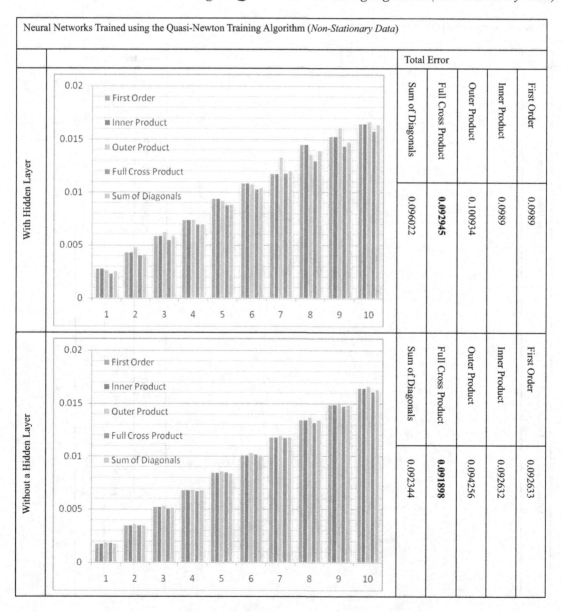

Neural Networks Trained using the Quasi-Newton Training Algorithm (*Non-Stationary Data*)		Total Error				
		Sum of Diagonals	Full Cross Product	Outer Product	Inner Product	First Order
With Hidden Layer		0.096022	**0.092945**	0.100934	0.0989	0.0989
Without a Hidden Layer		0.092344	**0.091898**	0.094256	0.092632	0.092633

Table 7. Neural networks trained using the Quasi-Newton Training Algorithm (Stationary Data)

Neural Networks Trained using the Quasi-Newton Training Algorithm (*Stationary Data*)		Total Error				
		Sum of Diagonals	Full Cross Product	Outer Product	Inner Product	First Order
With Hidden Layer		0.072043	**0.071311**	0.073112	0.075867	0.075867
Without a Hidden Layer		0.068744	0.068967	0.068877	0.068623	**0.068622**

Conclusion of Simulations Predicting Stock Market Share Price and Share Index

The simulation nMSE error results were averaged over all of the 9 Share price and share index time-series and so represent general conclusions, although specific results for individual financial time-series may differ. We have different conclusions for short term and long-term predictions. For short-term predictions, the choice of training method and the design of network make little difference and the best choice of network is that having no hidden layer. It would be best

Table 8. Neural networks trained using the Scaled Conjugate Gradient Training Algorithm (Non-Stationary Data)

Neural Networks Trained using the Scaled Conjugate Gradient Training Algorithm (*Non-Stationary Data*)					
		Total Error			
		Sum of Diagonals	Full Cross Product	Outer Product	Inner Product	First Order

With Hidden Layer

		Sum of Diagonals	Full Cross Product	Outer Product	Inner Product	First Order
		0.097056	0.112878	0.104877	0.100656	0.100656

Without a Hidden Layer

		Sum of Diagonals	Full Cross Product	Outer Product	Inner Product	First Order
		0.090965	0.091622	0.091488	0.091278	0.091278

to choose the first order neural network as it has the least, 130 variables and so could be trained the most quickly. For long-term predictions the most accurate predictions were obtained for the Sum of Diagonals network design which is the correlation higher order neural network proposed in this chapter, with a hidden layer, trained by

the Levenberg- Marquardt training algorithm, using stationary data. If accurate predictions are required across a range of short, medium and long-term periods then the best network to choose is again the sum of diagonals network design. This is the correlation higher order neural network, with a hidden layer, trained by the Levenberg-

Marquardt training algorithm, using stationary data as it gave the lowest total nMSE error of 0.061 averaged over all time-series and summed for all 10 predictions. This network had 476 independent variables, which is one third of those in a conventional higher order neural network. Therefore, the interesting conclusion is that for short term predictions higher order neural networks have no advantage. However, for long term, predictions higher order neural networks offer an advantage and the Sum of Diagonals correlation higher order network proposed in this chapter is the best and also exceeds the performance of higher order linear regression networks, which are those simulated having no hidden layer. The prediction of increases or falls in the share prices, known as

Table 9. Networks trained using Scaled Conjugate Gradient (Stationary Data)

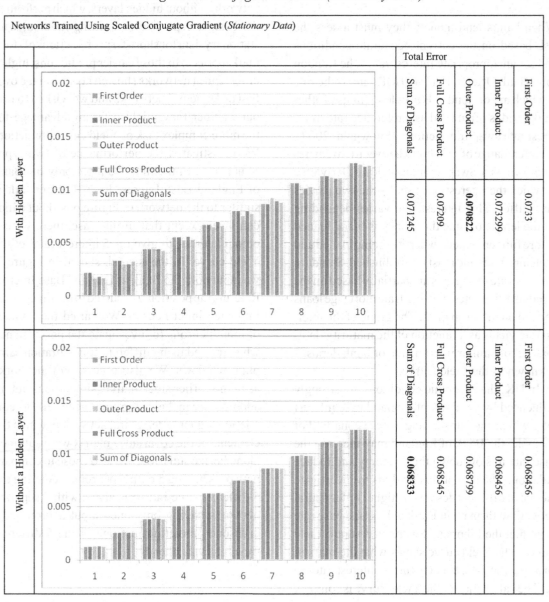

Networks Trained Using Scaled Conjugate Gradient (*Stationary Data*)		Total Error				
		Sum of Diagonals	Full Cross Product	Outer Product	Inner Product	First Order
With Hidden Layer		0.071245	0.07209	**0.070822**	0.073299	0.0733
Without a Hidden Layer		**0.068333**	0.068545	0.068799	0.068456	0.068456

the correct directional prediction, equation (45), occurred on average correctly for 48.4% with the non-stationary data and 48.9% with the stationary data. In the next section, it is shown how this can be improved significantly by also inputting the date along with the data.

SIMULATIONS PREDICTING INTER-BANK LENDING RISK INTEREST RATE YIELD CURVES

When banks lend money, they must assess the risk based on the current economic conditions and set an appropriate interest rate. The London Inter Bank Offered Rate (LIBOR rate) is the rate at which major London Banks lend funds to other banks and is often used as a reference rate in interest rate swap transactions. (Snowgold, 2007). An interchange of cash flows between two parties is known as a Swap or Interest Rate Derivative in which the interest rates set by the two parties may differ. This interest rate varies depending on the length of time the money is being loaned before full repayment, when it is being loaned and exchange rates and must be established. Standard variable rate mortgages are partially based on the 3-month Libor rates, and fixed rate mortgage loans depend on the swap rates. The graph of the interest rate yields as a function of the maturity dates for a set of similar instruments or bank deposits is known as the Yield Curve.

In UK, the economic conditions are strongly influenced by the Bank of England base interest rate, which the bank changes occasionally. For example, the Bank of England may increase the base rate to slow down the economy and reduce inflation. The aim of this study is to investigate the use of different designs of higher order neural network with an input Bank of England base rate to predict the Libor and Swap interest rate Yield Curve. The Yield curve shows what the market, on a specific date, expects future interest rates to be. The calculation of the Yield Curve is complex and has an important effect on setting the price for options and interest rate derivatives. The random fluctuations of the Yield curve are considered harder to predict than the movements of a specific stock or a stock index price as the whole curve is being predicted over a period rather than a single value at a future point in time (Risk, 2007).

Network Design

In this research, we limited ourselves to use neural networks without hidden layers, which performed the best, irrespective of training method, with stationary data for short-term predictions of stock market prices. In those earlier predictions, higher order neural networks showed no advantage over first order neural networks and we wished to find out whether they might offer an advantage for the more complex task of Yield curve prediction. We investigated the performance of two types of network. In the first, we input only the Bank of England Base Interest Rate. The network is similar to the network in Figure 6 without a hidden layer except that in this case, there were 5 output neurons to give the 5 interest rates of the Yield curve. In the second, shown in Figure 7, we input both the Bank of England Base Interest Rate and the position it occurred in the time-series into each input neuron. We varied the number of input neurons to investigate the performance when trained using different time duration sampling windows. We also used several networks as in the earlier stock market simulations but, in addition, we included the new "generalized" correlation higher order neural network in which the elements of the covariance matrix were summed along horizontal rows. We also chose to compare networks having 5 output neurons predicting the 5 different time intervals ahead with 5 separate networks having only one output neuron each, each one predicting just one of the 5 different time intervals ahead.

Figure 7. Neural Network model used to predict Libor and Swap interest rate Yield Curve

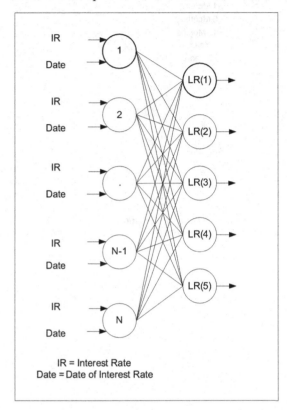

Network Training

We also limited ourselves to use the Levenberg-Marquardt training algorithm, which generally gave the lowest errors in the earlier simulations. We obtained a time-series of the Bank of England Base Rate, Figure 8, from Bank of England (2007). We obtained five daily time-series for 3 month Libor rate, 6 month Libor rate, 12 month Libor rate, 5 year Swap rate, 10 year Swap rate,

Figure 8, from Mao (2007) for the period from 3rd January 2006 to 15th June 2007. The Yield curve is plotted in Figure 9 for just the last day from the time-series to give the reader an idea of the shape of the curve. In these simulations, the data was not transformed to stationary data form but was used raw.

Choice of Optimum Sample Window Lag Length

The choice of window lag structure (Huang, 2006) plays an important part in the performance of the neural network. We used the Hannan Quinn InFormation, HQIF, criterion (Hannan, 1979) over window duration from 1 to 100 days, to find the optimum sample window lag length. The Hannan Quinn InFormation, HQIF, criterion is calculated from Equation (44), where, N, is the number of elements in the input vector and represents the total time duration, or lag length, of the sample window. We chose a value of $m=2$ arbitrarily, since it is just a scaling factor, to plot Figures 10 and 11.

The Network, Net 1, in Figure 10, which predicts all 5 of the Yield curve interest rates, shows a HQIF value that generally reduces as the window duration lag length increases but which also fluctuates. The Network, Net 2, in Figure 11 shows a clearly decreasing HQIF value with increasing window duration, lag length until about 46 time samples after which it fluctuates wildly although still has a decreasing trend. It is interesting to note that for the stock market simulations in which we predicted all 10 times ahead together, we found that when the number

Equation (44).

$$HQIF = \ln\left\{\frac{1}{N}\sum_{t=1}^{N}\left(Actual_t - \text{Pr}edicted_t\right)^2\right\} + \frac{m}{N}\left(\ln\left[\ln\left\{N\right\}\right]\right)$$

Figure 8. Bank of England base interest rate and the Libor Rates and Swap Rates

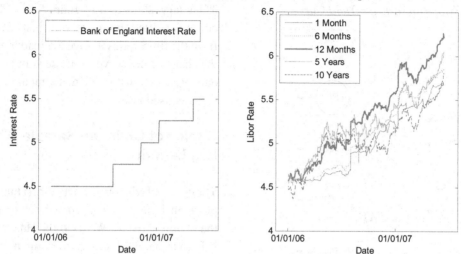

Figure 9. Yield Curve for the last day in the data set

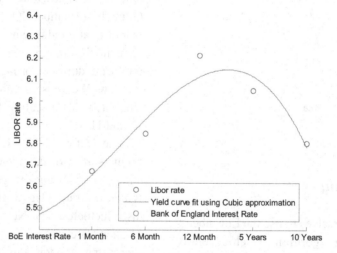

of neurons in the hidden layer exceeded about 46 we also saw fluctuations in the error although the training dataset was quite different.

For the best sample window duration lag length we need to choose the lowest value of HQIF which can reliably be obtained to minimize the error and also need to choose the smallest window length to minimize the number of input neurons and so the number of network variables and training time. The errors in Net 1 and Net 2 are similar below about 50 lag length, so it makes little dif-

ference whether five nets predicting one or one net predicting five different time predictions are used so in the remaining simulations, Net 1 was used to predict 5 values. A window duration, lag length of 46 appears to give the best results but for comparison purposes, we also simulated windows of length, 18 and 9.

Figure 12 shows the HQIF for a network having one hidden layer neuron which gives worse values of HQIF than in Figures 10 and 11, for the same input window lag lengths so the following

Figure 10. Hannan Quinn InFormation criterion, HQIF, in a network predicting all 5 interest rate points in the Yield curve, Net 1

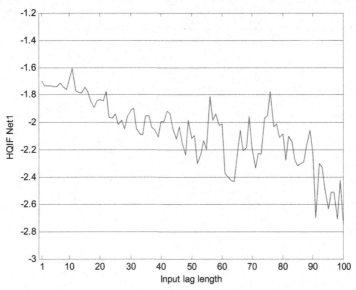

Figure 11. Hannan Quinn InFormation criterion, HQIF, predicting just one of the interest rate points in the Yield curve, Net 2

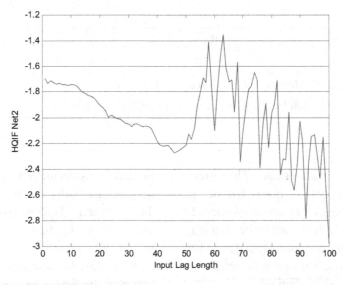

Performance Metrics

simulations only used the higher order neural networks, without a hidden layer, as they gave a lower error.

As for the stock market prediction simulations, we calculated the normalized Mean Square Error, nMSE. In addition, we calculated the direction in which the changes were occurring, up or down;

Figure 12. Hannan Quinn InFormation criterion, HQIF of a Neural Network having 1 hidden layer neuron with a non-linear Logistic function predicting just one of the interest rate points in the Yield curve, Net 2

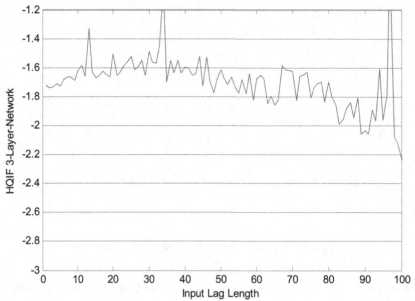

Equation (45).

$$Correct\ Directional\ Prediction,\ DS = \frac{100}{N}\sum_{i=1}^{N}d_i$$

$$d_i = \begin{cases} 1 & when\ \left(Actual_i - Actual_{i-1}\right)\left(Predicted_i - Predicted_{i-1}\right) \geq 0 \\ 0 & when\ \left(Actual_i - Actual_{i-1}\right)\left(Predicted_i - Predicted_{i-1}\right) < 0 \end{cases}$$

buy or sell; positive or negative slopes. The correct directional prediction, or Directional Symmetry, DS, was calculated using Equation (45) (Walczak, 2001), where $Actual_i$ is the actual value on day i, $Predicted_i$ is the forecast value on that day and N = total number of days. The aim is to maximize the Correct Directional Prediction.

Simulation Results

Figure 13 compares the nMSE and Correct Direction Prediction simulation results averaged over all of the 5 Libor and Swap rates for a two and a three layer first order neural network for a range of input data lag lengths from 1 to 100. The detailed

numerical results for each Libor and Swap rate for several lag lengths, 46, 18, 9, 3, 1 are tabulated in Table 10 for a 3-layer network and Table 11 for a 2-layer network. The upper two plots in Figure 13 are for the network which only had the Bank of England Base Interest Rate input while the lower two plots are for the network which also had the position in the time-series sequence, or date, as input. The position in the time series was provided by an integer, which increased in daily increments of unity from 1 on Jan 1st 2000 and so, was in the range 2195 to 2722 for our data.

In Figure 13 the two-layer network curves are similar to the three layer network curves except that the latter fluctuate a lot and give a lower

Figure 13. Comparison of nMSE error and Correct Direction Prediction for two layer and three layer neural network having only interest rate as input, and another having both interest rate and position in time-series as inputs

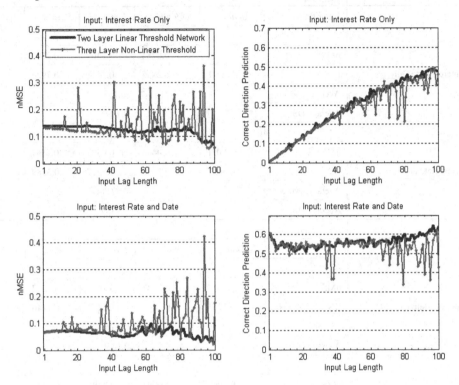

nMSE error when only the Bank of interest rate is entered in the top left graph. The results in Figure 13 top graphs for just the Bank of England Base Rate input confirm the results of the Hannan Quinn InFormation criterion, HQIF, used earlier for the two-layer network in that the nMSE reduces to an input window duration lag length of about 46 after which it fluctuates. However, the top plot of the Correct Direction Prediction has a strongly increasing value from zero with increasing window duration although the magnitude of this metric is rather small and less than about 0.45. Again, fluctuations are seen beyond about a window length of 46 although the upward trend continues. In the case of the lower curves for networks also having the input of the date and the Bank of England Interest Rate the results are quite different. The error is much lower

for shorter window lengths. However, the most marked differences occur in the Correct Direction Prediction, which has a more constant value of 53-62% although there are fluctuations. These values for the Correct Direction Prediction are similar in magnitude to those obtained by (Walczak, 2001) and occur at the same time as the lowest values of nMSE error for the fewest number of input neurons. This is an exciting finding as it means that networks into which both Bank of England Base rate and date are entered as input, having few input neurons corresponding to very short input sample window, lag lengths can be used which will be quick to train and will give good results. It also suggests that very short-term patterns in the data are most important for prediction.

Considering both minimum error and maximum directivity, Tables 10 and 11 show that the

Table 10. nMSE errors and Directional Symmetry for predictions of the 5 interest rates in the Yield Curves using a three layer network with best values in bold

	Lag Length	46				
	Libor Rate	*1 Month*	*6 Month*	*1 Year*	*5 Years*	*10 Years*
Interest Rate Only	nMSe	0.066	0.0784	0.1408	0.2308	0.2765
	DS	0.2648	0.2835	0.3458	0.3925	0.3115
	Average nMSe	0.1585				
	Average DS	0.31962				
Interest Rate and Date	nMSe	0.011	0.0446	0.0507	0.1161	**0.1333**
	DS	0.5607	0.5296	0.5327	0.5389	0.5327
	Average nMSe	0.07114				
	Average DS	0.53892				
	Lag Length	18				
		1 Month	*6 Month*	*1 Year*	*5 Years*	*10 Years*
Interest Rate Only	nMSe	0.017	0.0507	0.1066	0.2017	0.2882
	DS	0.1261	0.2607	0.1117	0.1146	0.1203
	Average nMSe	0.13284				
	Average DS	0.14668				
Interest Rate and Date	nMSe	**0.0097**	0.0092	**0.0197**	0.1318	0.2293
	DS	0.5158	0.5272	0.5731	0.5559	**0.5759**
	Average nMSe	0.07994				
	Average DS	0.54958				
	Lag Length	9				
		1 Month	*6 Month*	*1 Year*	*5 Years*	*10 Years*
Interest Rate Only	nMSe	0.0178	0.0272	0.1005	0.213	0.312
	DS	0.0615	0.0726	0.0587	0.0559	0.0615
	Average nMSe	0.1341				
	Average DS	0.06204				
Interest Rate and Date	nMSe	0.1396	**0.01**	0.025	0.1131	0.1934
	DS	0.0838	0.5559	0.581	**0.5698**	0.5335
	Average nMSe	0.09622				
	Average DS	0.4648				

continued on the following page

Table 10. (continued)

	Lag Length	3				
		1 Month	*6 Month*	*1 Year*	*5 Years*	*10 Years*
Interest Rate Only	nMSe	0.0182	0.0283	0.076	0.2175	0.3178
	DS	0.0275	0.0302	0.0165	0.0165	0.0165
	Average nMSe	0.13156				
	Average DS	0.02144				
Interest Rate and Date	nMSe	0.0106	**0.01**	0.0212	0.1098	0.1927
	DS	0.5632	0.5907	**0.5989**	0.5165	0.5247
	Average nMSe	0.06886				
	Average DS	0.5588				
	Lag Length	1				
		1 Month	*6 Month*	*1 Year*	*5 Years*	*10 Years*
Interest Rate Only	nMSe	0.0199	0.0297	0.0776	0.2198	0.3192
	DS	0.0082	0.0109	0.0082	0.0082	0.0055
	Average nMSe	0.13324				
	Average DS	0.0082				
Interest Rate and Date	nMSe	0.0112	0.0104	0.021	**0.1059**	0.1854
	DS	**0.6284**	**0.6749**	0.5929	0.5656	0.571
	Average nMSe	**0.06678**				
	Average DS	**0.60656**				

Table 11. nMSE errors and Directional Symmetry for predictions of the 5 interest rates in the Yield Curves using a two layer linear threshold network with best values in bold

	Lag Length	46				
	Libor Rate	*1 Month*	*6 Month*	*1 Year*	*5 Years*	*10 Years*
Interest Rate Only	nMSe	0.0226	0.0323	0.0655	0.1867	0.3009
	DS	0.2804	0.243	0.2617	0.3022	0.2617
	Average nMSe	0.1216				
	Average DS	0.2698				
Interest Rate and Date	nMSe	**0.0091**	**0.0097**	**0.0168**	**0.0697**	**0.1405**
	DS	0.5514	0.5358	**0.6137**	0.5763	**0.6106**
	Average nMSe	**0.04916**				
	Average DS	0.57756				

continued on the following page

Table 11. (continued)

	Lag Length	18				
		1 Month	*6 Month*	*1 Year*	*5 Years*	*10 Years*
Interest Rate Only	nMSe	0.021	0.034	0.0782	0.2144	0.3377
	DS	0.1261	0.1232	0.1175	0.1318	0.0917
	Average nMSe	0.13706				
	Average DS	0.11806				
Interest Rate and Date	nMSe	0.0104	0.0102	0.0204	0.1121	0.2008
	DS	0.4585	0.5129	0.5759	**0.5788**	0.4957
	Average nMSe	0.07078				
	Average DS	0.52436				
	Lag Length	9				
		1 Month	*6 Month*	*1 Year*	*5 Years*	*10 Years*
Interest Rate Only	nMSe	0.0217	0.0351	0.0818	0.2179	0.3381
	DS	0.0587	0.067	0.0531	0.067	0.0559
	Average nMSe	0.13892				
	Average DS	0.06034				
Interest Rate and Date	nMSe	0.0108	0.0112	0.0221	0.1129	0.1993
	DS	0.5531	0.6006	0.5391	0.4804	0.4916
	Average nMSe	0.07126				
	Average DS	0.53296				
	Lag Length	3				
		1 Month	*6 Month*	*1 Year*	*5 Years*	*10 Years*
Interest Rate Only	nMSe	0.0219	0.0355	0.0834	0.2213	0.3378
	DS	0.0275	0.0302	0.0165	0.022	0.0165
	Average nMSe	0.13998				
	Average DS	0.02254				
Interest Rate and Date	nMSe	0.0117	0.0117	0.0218	0.1085	0.1914
	DS	0.6209	0.5907	0.5989	0.5192	0.533
	Average nMSe	0.06902				
	Average DS	0.57254				

continued on the following page

Table 11. (continued)

	Lag Length	*1*				
		1 Month	*6 Month*	*1 Year*	*5 Years*	*10 Years*
Interest Rate Only	nMSe	0.0234	0.0369	0.0852	0.2224	0.3355
	DS	0.0082	0.0109	0.0082	0.0082	0.0055
	Average nMSe	0.14068				
	Average DS	0.0082				
Interest Rate and Date	nMSe	0.0124	0.0123	0.0211	0.106	0.1866
	DS	**0.6284**	**0.6749**	0.5929	0.5656	0.571
	Average nMSe	0.06768				
	Average DS	**0.60656**				

best results are obtained for inputting both the interest rate and the date. In three layer neural networks the best results are for the shorter lag lengths. The averaged lowest error across all of the yield curve points occurs at the shortest lag length of 1. However, when considering correct direction prediction, for short term predictions, the first two points, the shortest lag length of 1 is best, for the mid-term 3rd point a lag length of 3 is best, for the 4th point a lag length of 9 and for the long –term 5 point a lag length of 18. Therefore, for three layer nets the lag length needs to be increased in line with the time ahead of the prediction.

For two layer neural networks the best results occur for longest and shortest lag lengths. The lowest error always occurs at the longest lag length of 46. However, when considering correct direction prediction, for short-term predictions, the first two points, the shortest lag length of 1 is best, while for mid and long term predictions the longest lag lengths are best, 46 for 3rd and 5th points and 18 for the 4th point.

The best correction direction prediction was 67.49% and occurred for both two layer and three layer networks for the second point with the shortest lag length. The best average correct

direction prediction of 60.656% was achieved across the full yield curve for both two layer and three layer networks for the shortest lag length of 1. However, the lowest error of 0.04916 averaged, across the yield curve, occurred for the two-layer network at a lag length of 46.

In Figure 14 the average nMSE error and the Directional Symmetry of the 5 points in the predicted Yield curve are shown for six different neural network designs for an input window lag length of 46. Figures 15, 16, 17 and 18 show the same but for input window lag lengths of 18, 9, 3, 1 respectively. For clarity, the errors are also tabulated in Table 12 for each of the window duration and each of the interest rates in the Yield curve. The lowest errors in the table for each point predicted are in bold font.

Analysis of Simulation Results for Yield Curve Interest Rate Prediction

In Figures 14, 15, 16, 17 and 18 the nMSE errors increase with the time ahead of the prediction but unlike in the stock market predictions, where it increased linearly with point, here it increases exponentially with point. However, it must be remembered that the spacing between the points

Figure 14. nMSE error and Directional Symmetry when input sample window duration lag length is 46

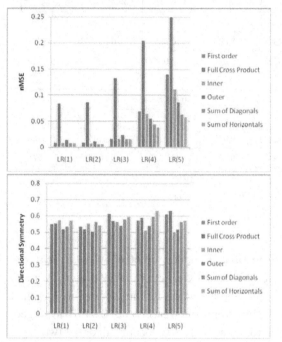

Figure 15. nMSE error and Directional Symmetry when the input window duration lag length is 18

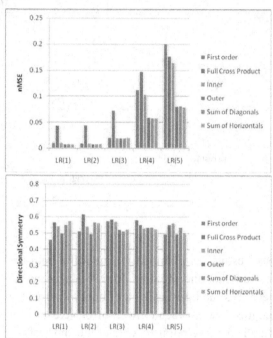

Figure 16. nMSE error and Directional Symmetry when the input window duration lag length is 9

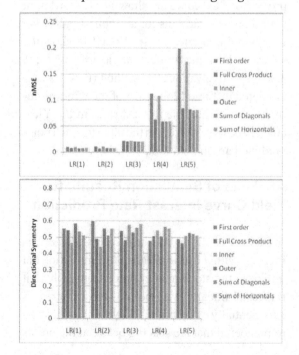

Figure 17. nMSE error and Directional Symmetry when the input window duration lag length is 3

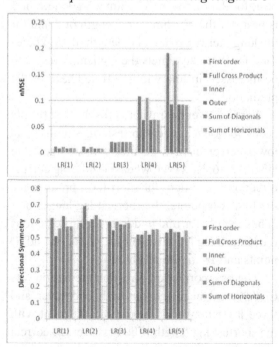

Figure 18. nMSE error and Directional Symmetry when the input window duration lag length is 1

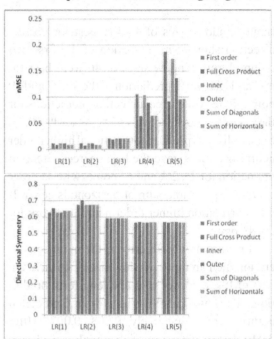

here increases exponentially in time so the error may increase linearly in time. The largest errors are about 0.25, which is far larger than in the stock market predictions, which may be due to the much longer time scales over which the interest rates are being predicted than in the stock market case.

There are some very large differences in the accuracy of the prediction between the different types of networks. In Figure 14 for the longest input data window of 46 the lowest errors for all times ahead being predicted were obtained for the Sum of Diagonals Correlation Higher Order Neural Network and for the Sum of Horizontals Generalized Correlation Higher Order Neural Network with the latter network giving the lowest errors. In Figure 15 and Table 12 for the input data window of 18 the lowest error for the long-term prediction of the 2 points furthest away in time were obtained for the Sum of Horizontals. For

Table 12. nMSE errors of prediction of the 5 interest rates in Yield Curves for lag lengths of 46, 18 and 9

Lag	Network Type	One Month Libor Rate	3 Months Libor Rate	12 Months Libor Rate	5 Year Swap Rate	10 Year Swap Rate
46	First order	0.0091	0.0097	0.0168	0.0697	0.1405
	Full Cross Product	0.0842	0.0865	0.1329	0.2047	0.2514
	Inner	0.0091	0.0076	0.0167	0.0652	0.1117
	Outer	0.015	0.0122	0.0247	0.0562	0.0863
	Sum of Diagonals	0.0084	**0.0065**	**0.0164**	**0.045**	**0.0638**
	Sum of Horizontals	0.0085	**0.0067**	**0.0164**	**0.0395**	**0.0584**
18	First order	0.0104	0.0102	0.0204	0.1121	0.2008
	Full Cross Product	0.0439	0.0449	0.0725	0.1468	0.1761
	Inner	0.0105	0.0101	0.0198	0.1034	0.1644
	Outer	**0.0077**	0.0081	0.0196	0.0592	0.0801
	Sum of Diagonals	**0.0077**	0.008	0.0195	0.058	0.0811
	Sum of Horizontals	0.008	0.0085	0.0204	0.0577	0.0794
9	First order	0.0108	0.0112	0.0221	0.1129	0.1993
	Full Cross Product	0.0086	0.008	0.0213	0.0634	0.0852
	Inner	0.0107	0.0115	0.0227	0.1085	0.1743
	Outer	0.0081	0.0087	0.0213	0.0602	0.083
	Sum of Diagonals	0.0082	0.0086	0.0212	0.06	0.0808
	Sum of Horizontals	0.0095	0.0086	0.0211	0.0602	0.0817

the mid term, 2nd and 3rd points the lowest error was for the sum of diagonals. For the short term, prediction of the first point the outer product and sum of diagonals gave the best results.

In Figure 16 and Table 12 for the input data window of 9 the lowest errors for the long term prediction of the two points furthest away in time being predicted were obtained for the sum of diagonals network. For the mid-term, 3rd point the sum of horizontals is best while for the mid term 2nd point both the sum of diagonals and the sum of horizontals give the lowest errors. For the short term, prediction of the first point the outer product network gives the lowest errors. In Figure 17 Outer Product, Sum of Diagonals and Sum of Horizontals networks gave the lowest errors. In Figure 18 for the 1st point the sum of diagonals and sum of horizontals networks gave the lowest errors while for the long-term predictions the full cross product was slightly better than the sum of diagonals and sum of horizontals networks.

When we examine Table 12 to find the lowest errors for each point in bold we find that for the short-term prediction of the first point a window of 18 gives the best results equally well for the outer product and sum of diagonals networks. For all of the remaining points in mid and long term the sum of diagonals and sum of horizontals both give the lowest errors with the sum of diagonals being best for the 2nd points and the sum of horizontals being the best for the last two points.

The best correct direction prediction, 70% occurred for full cross product network for a lag length of 1 for the second point. The second best correct direction prediction, 65%, was for the 1st point for the same cross product network with the same lag length of 1. The best correct direction predictions for the 3rd, 4th and 5th points were for lag lengths of 46 and for the networks, first order, 61%, sum of horizontals, 63%, and full cross product, 63%, respectively.

Conclusion of Yield Curve Prediction Simulations

Input window sizes of 1 were best for correct direction short-term prediction of the first two points. Input window sizes of 46 were best for mid and long-term prediction of the 3rd, 4th and 5th points. The best correct detection predictions for the points were, respectively 65%, 70%, 61%, 63%, 63%. Full cross product conventional higher order neural networks gave the best correct direction prediction for 1st, 2nd, and 5th points with 1st order for the 3rd point and sum of horizontals generalized correlation higher order neural network for the 4th point.

If minimum nMSE error is the main consideration then an input window size of 46 gave the best nMSE error for mid and long-term predictions. The lowest nMSE errors for the 5 predicted points were, respectively, 0.008, 0.007, 0.016, 0.040, 0.058. The sum of diagonals correlation higher order neural network gave excellent low error predictions for all times ahead. The outer product correlation network gave equally good predictions as the sum of diagonals correlation higher order neural network for the first short term prediction. The sum of horizontals generalized correlation higher order neural network and the sum of diagonals correlation neural network gave the lowest errors for the long-term predictions for the 4th and 5th points in the yield curve.

FUTURE RESEARCH DIRECTIONS

The simulations in this chapter prove that the outer product, sum of diagonals correlation and sum of horizontals generalized correlation higher order neural networks simulated in this chapter are beneficial for time-series prediction as they give the lowest errors. Other weighted linear combinations of covariance matrix cross product elements in different groupings should be investigated to see if they give lower errors or better directionality.

Cyclic seasonal changes should be included as input data. In the stock market predictions, the predictions made on stationary data should be converted back into non-stationary form to assess the level of error. Linearly weighted combinations of inner and outer product correlation higher order neural networks, derived in equations (30), (34) and (36), should be simulated and investigated.

REFERENCES

Bandyopadhyay, S., Datta, AK. (1996). A novel neural hetero-associative memory model for pattern recognition. *Pattern Recognition, 29*(5), 789-795.

Bank of England (2007). Retrieved June 7, 2007. from http://www.bankofengland.co.uk/

Chong, E.K.P., & Zak, S.H. (2001). *An introduction to optimization,* 2nd ed. John Wiley & Sons Pte. Ltd.

Hannan, E.J., & Quinn, B.G. (1979). The determination of the order of an autoregression. *Journal of the Royal Statistical Society B, 41*, 190-195.

Huang, W., Wang, S. Y., Yu, L., Bao, Y. K. & Wang, L. (2006). A new computation method of input selection for stock marker forecasting with neural networks. *Computational Science Proceedings, ICCS 2006*, Part 4, 3994, 308-315

Leshno, M., Lin, V., Pinkus, A., & Schoken, S. (1993). Multi-layer feedforward networks with a non-polynomial activation can approximate any function. *Neural Networks, 6*, 861-867.

Mao, Z. Q. (2007). *Abbey Bank part of Santander Group, Abbey National plc.* Registered Number 2294747. Registered in England. www.abbey.com

Marquardt, D. (1963). An algorithm for least-squares estimation of nonlinear parameters. *SIAM J. Appl. Math. 11*, 431-441.

Masters, T. (1995). *Neural, novel & hybrid algorithms for time series prediction*. New York: Wiley.

McNelis, P. (2005). *Neural networks in finance: Gaining predictive edge in the market*. San Diego: Elsevier.

Midwinter, J.E., & Selviah, D.R. (1989). Digital neural networks, matched filters and optical implementations. In Aleksander, I. (Ed.) *Neural Computing Architectures* (pp. 258-278). Kogan Page, North Oxford Academic Publishers Ltd.

Moller. (1993) A scaled conjugate gradient algorithm for fast supervised learning. *Neural Networks, 6*(4), pp.525-533.

Nguyen B., & Widrow, B. (1990) Neural network for self-learning control systems. *IEEE Control Systems Magazine*, 18-23.

Risk Waters Group (2000). Retrieved 6th Sept 2007 from http://www.financewise.com/public/edit/riskm/interestrate/interestrisk00-models.htm

Selviah, D. R., Midwinter, J. E., Rivers, A. W., & Lung, K. W. (1989). Correlating matched filter model for analysis and optimisation of neural networks. *IEE Proceedings, Part F Radar and Signal Processing, 136*(3), 143-148.

Selviah, D.R, & Midwinter, J.E. (1989). Extension of the Hamming neural network to a multilayer architecture for optical implementation. *First IEE international Conference on Artificial Neural Networks, IEE, 313*, 280-283

Selviah, D.R, & Midwinter, J.E. (1989). Matched filter model for design of neural networks. In Taylor, J.G., & Mannion, C.L.T. (Eds.), *Institute of Physics Conference New Developments in Neural Computing*, IOP, 141-148.

Selviah, D. R., & Midwinter, J. E. (1989). Memory Capacity of a novel optical neural net architecture. *ONERA-CERT Optics in Computing International*

Symposium (pp. 195-201). Toulouse: ONERA-CERT.

Selviah, D. R., Twaij, A. H. A. A., & Stamos, E. (1996). Invited author: Development of a feature enhancement encoding algorithm for holographic memories. *International Symposium on Holographic Memories*. Athens.

Selviah, D. R., & Stamos, E. (2002). Invited paper: Similarity suppression algorithm for designing pattern discrimination filters. *Asian Journal of Physics, 11*(3), 367-389.

Stamos, E., & Selviah, D. R. (1998). Feature enhancement and similarity suppression algorithm for noisy pattern recognition. In D. P. Casasent, & T. H. Chao (Eds.), *Optical Pattern Recognition IX* (pp 182-189). Orlando, USA: SPIE.

Twaij, A. H., Selviah, D. R., & Midwinter, J. E. (1992). An introduction to the optical implementation of the Hopfield Network via the matched filter formalism. *University of London Centre for Neural Networks Newsletter* (3).

Snowgold (2007). Accessed 6th Sept 2007, http://www.snowgold.com/financial/fingloss.html

Walczak S. (2001). An empirical analysis of data requirements for financial forecasting with neural networks. *Journal of Management Information Systems, 17*(3), 203-222.

Walczak, S., & Cerpa, N. (1999) Heuristic principles for the design of artificial neural networks. *Information and Software Technology, 41*(2), 109-119.

Yahoo! (2007). *Finance*. Retrieved May 3, 2007, from http://finance.yahoo.com

ADDITIONAL READING

Bishop, C. M. (1995). Neural networks for pattern recognition. In *Higher-order networks*, 133-134.

Dayhoff, J.E., & DeLeo J.M. (2001). Artificial neural networks: Opening the black box. *Cancer, 91*, 1615-1635.

Giles, C. L., & Maxwell, T. (1987). Learning, invariance, and generalization in high-order neural networks. *Applied Optics, 26*(23), 4972-4978

Giles, C. L., Griffin, R. D., & Maxwell, T. (1988). Encoding geometric invariances in higher-order neural networks. *Neural information processing systems: Proceedings of the First IEEE Conference* (301-309). Denver, CO.

Hussain, A. (1997). A new neural network structure for temporal signal processing. *IEEE International Conference on Acoustics, Speech, and Signal Processing (ICASSP'97), 4*, 3341

Kaita, T., Tomita, S., & Yamanaka, J. (2002, June). On a higher-order neural network for distortion invariant pattern recognition. *Pattern Recognition Letters, 23*(8), 977 – 984.

Karayiannis, N., & Venetsanopoulos, A. (1999, July). On the dynamics of neural networks realizing associative memories of first and higher order. *Network: Computation in Neural Systems, 1*(3), 345-364.

Keeler, J. D., Pichler, E. E., & Ross, J. (1989, March). Noise in neural networks: Thresholds, hysteresis, and neuromodulation of signal-to-noise. *Proceedings of the National Academy of Sciences of the United States of America, 86*(5), 1712-1716.

Lee, Y. C. et al. (1986). Machine learning using a higher order correlation network. *Physica, 22D*, 276-306.

Luo, F. and Unbehauen, R. (1997) *Applied neural networks in signal processing*. New York: Cambridge University Press.

Manykin, E. A. (1993, October). Neural network architecture based on nonlinear interaction of ultrashort optical pulses with matter. *Proceed-*

ings of 1993 International Joint Conference on Neural Networks, IJCNN '93, Nagoya, 1(25-29), 837 - 840.

Mendel, J.M. (1991) Tutorial on higher-order statistics (spectra) in signal processing and system theory: Theoretical results and some applications, *Proceedings of the IEEE, 79*(3), 278-305.

Pao, Y. H., & Khatibi, F. (1990, December). *Neural network with non-linear transformations.* Patent Number 4979126, Filed March 30th 1988.

Perantonis, S. J., & Lisboa, P. J. G. (1992). Translation, rotation, and scale invariant pattern recognition by high-order neural networks and moment classifiers. *IEEE Transactions on Neural Networks, 3*(2), 241-251.

Reid, M. B., Spirkovska, L. & Ochoa, E., (1989). Rapid training of higher-order neural networks for invariant pattern recognition. *International Joint Conference on Neural Networks*, Vol.1, 689-692. Washington, DC, USA,

Schmitt, M. (2002, February). On the complexity of computing and learning with multiplicative neural networks. *Neural Computation, 14*(2), 241 – 301.

Shin, Y., & Ghosh, J. (1991). The pi-sigma network: an efficient higher-order neural network for pattern classification and function approximation. *Seattle International Joint Conference on Neural Networks*, Vol. 1, 13-18. Seattle, WA, USA.

Spirkovska, L., & Reid, M. B. (1992). Robust position, scale, and rotation invariant object recognition using higher-order neural networks. *Pattern Recognition, 25*(9), 975-985.

Spirkovska, L., & Reid, M. B. (1993). Coarse-coded higher-order neural networks for PSRI object recognition. *IEEE Transactions on Neural Networks, 4*(2), 276-283.

Spirkovska, L., & Reid, M. B., (1990). Connectivity strategies for higher-order neural networks applied to pattern recognition. *IJCNN International Joint Conference on Neural Networks, 1*, 21-26. San Diego, CA, USA.

Twaij, A.H., Selviah, D.R., & Midwinter, J.E. (1992). Optical implementation of hopfield network using the matched filter formalism tool. *Second Conference on Information Technology and its Applications ITA'92.* Leicester, UK: Markfield Conference Centre.

Twaij, A. H., Selviah, D. R., & Midwinter, J. E. (1992, June). Feature Refinement learning algorithm for opto-electronic neural networks. Paper presented at *Institute of Physics conference on Opto-electronic Neural Networks,* Sharp Laboratories of Europe, Oxford Science Park

Venkatesh, S. S., & Baldi, P. (1991). Programmed interactions in higher-order neural networks: The outer-product algorithm. *Journal of Complexity, 7*(4), 443-479

Wang, J. H., Wu, K. H., & Chang, F. C. (2004, November). Scale equalization higher-order neural networks. *Proceedings of the 2004 IEEE International Conference on Information Reuse and Integration, 2004, 8*(10), 612 – 617.

Zhang, M., Zhang, J.C., & Fulcher, J. (1997). Financial prediction system using higher order trigonometric polynomial neural network group model. *Proceedings of the IEEE International Conference on Neural Networks* (pp. 2231-2234). Houston, TX.

Chapter XI
Artificial Higher Order Neural Networks in Time Series Prediction

Godfrey C. Onwubolu
University of the South Pacific, Fiji

ABSTRACT

Real world problems are described by nonlinear and chaotic processes, which makes them hard to model and predict. This chapter first compares the neural network (NN) and the artificial higher order neural network (HONN) and then presents commonly known neural network architectures and a number of HONN architectures. The time series prediction problem is formulated as a system identification problem, where the input to the system is the past values of a time series, and its desired output is the future values of a time series. The polynomial neural network (PNN) is then chosen as the HONN for application to the time series prediction problem. This chapter presents the application of HONN model to the nonlinear time series prediction problems of three major international currency exchange rates, as well as two key U.S. interest rates—the Federal funds rate and the yield on the 5-year U.S. Treasury note. Empirical results indicate that the proposed method is competitive with other approaches for the exchange rate problem, and can be used as a feasible solution for interest rate forecasting problem. This implies that the HONN model can be used as a feasible solution for exchange rate forecasting as well as for interest rate forecasting.

BACKGROUND

Exchange Rates Time Series

Forecasting exchange rates is an important financial problem that is receiving increasing attention especially because of its difficulty and practical applications. Exchange rates are affected by many highly correlated economic, political and even psychological factors. These factors interact in a very complex fashion. Exchange rate series exhibit high volatility, complexity and noise that result from an elusive market mechanism generating daily observations (Theodossiou, 1994).

Much research effort has been devoted to exploring the nonlinearity of exchange rate data and to developing specific nonlinear models to improve exchange rate forecasting, i.e., the autoregressive random variance (ARV) model (So *et al.*, 1999), autoregressive conditional heteroscedasticity [ARCH] (Hsieh, 1989), self-exciting threshold autoregressive models (Chappel *et al.*, 1996). There has been growing interest in the adoption of neural networks, fuzzy inference systems and statistical approaches for exchange rate forecasting problem (Refenes, 1993a; Refenes *et al.*, 1993b; Yu *et al.*, 2005a; Yu *et al.*, 2005b). A recent review of neural networks based exchange rate forecasting is found in (Wang *et al.*, 2004).

The input dimension (i.e. the number of delayed values for prediction) and the time delay (i.e. the time interval between two time series data) are two critical factors that affect the performance of neural networks. The selection of dimension and time delay has great significance in time series prediction.

Flexible Neural Tree [FNT] (Chen *et al.*, 2004; Chen *et al.*, 2005) has been used for time-series forecasting. The FNT framework, combined with an evolutionary technique, was proposed for forecasting exchange rates (Chen *et al.*, 2006). Based on the pre-defined instruction/operator sets, a flexible neural tree model can be created and evolved. FNT allows input variables selection, over-layer connections and different activation functions for different nodes. The hierarchical structure is evolved using the Extended Compact Genetic Programming (ECGP), a tree-structure based evolutionary algorithm (Sastry and Goldberg, 2003). The fine tuning of the parameters encoded in the structure is accomplished using particle swarm optimization (PSO). In summary, they used FNT model for selecting the important inputs and/or time delays and for forecasting foreign exchange rates. Some other previous work done in predicting exchange rates include Abraham et al. 2001; Abraham et al. 2002; Onwubolu et al. 2007

Interest Rates Time Series

The time series under study here are two of the key interest rates in the U.S. financial system, although they are by no means of exclusive importance. Forecasting interest rates is an important financial problem that is receiving increasing attention especially because of its difficulty and practical applications. Some elements of the institutional and theoretical backgrounds of these rates are explained in this section as presented by Ohasi in detail in Farlow (pp.199—214, 1984). In particular, the federal funds rate will be discussed in greater length, because it is a more specialized rate and also because more of the forecasting effort was concentrated on this rate

The Federal Funds

The federal funds market is one of the pivotal markets in the U. S. financial system. More than 14,000 commercial banks and other participants trade immediately available funds, mostly on an overnight basis. The Federal funds rate is the interest rate charged in such an overnight transaction. The original need for the market arose from the reserve requirements imposed by the Federal Reserve System on various financial institutions. Required reserves (i.e., certain percentages of deposit liabilities specified by Regulation D) must be held in a combination of vault cash and non-interest bearing reserve balances at a Federal Reserve Bank. Since reserves do not earn any interest, banks try to minimize their holding of excess reserves (i.e., reserves in excess of what is required by the Federal Reserve Bank). Although banks only need to meet the requirements on a weekly average basis, unexpected changes in assets or liabilities can easily create some shortfall or excess every week during operations. This gives rise to a market in which the excess funds are purchased by banks with reserve deficiencies.

However, this function of smoothing out the reserve funds distribution alone does not justify all the attention that this market receives. The special importance of the federal funds market is attributable to two other factors. First, the central bank constantly applies a varying degree of pressure on this market to implement its monetary policy objectives. Second, many large banks have come to rely on overnight money as a more permanent source of their funds, and consequently made the federal funds availability a particularly effective tool of monetary policy.

The 5-Year Treasury Note

U.S. Treasury notes are the interest-bearing obligations of the U.S. government. They are issued for initial maturities of 2 years to 30 years. Together with the 3-month to 12-month Treasury bills, which are issued at a discount instead of having semiannual interest payments, the Treasury notes are used to finance shortfalls in government revenue. Although the yield for any maturity is important, the 5-year yield is one of the most important, because the financial market considers it the representative intermediate rate and the issue in that maturity range is actively traded in the bond market. Unlike very short-term interest rates, which may be influenced heavily by technical and temporary factors in the financial markets, intermediate term to long-term rates are presumably determined by the long-run cost of credit and the long-term expectations about inflation, and are therefore less volatile than shorter maturity rates.

Theoretical Basis for Selecting Explanatory Variables

Interest rates are the prices paid to obtain liquidity (or money) on various terms in regard to the length of time for which liquidity is made available and the risk involved. They are determined in the general process through which an economy as a whole attains a state of equilibrium. The mechanism of this process has been a subject of much controversy in economics. Broadly speaking, however, there is little doubt that some variables play essential roles in this general equilibrium system. The level of economic activity, money supply, inflation, and investment demand, in addition to the interest rates, are considered to constitute the basic elements of the system in the classical tradition of economics. Economic activities and investment demand influence the demand for liquidity. Money supply interacts with the demand for liquidity to determine interest rates. Inflation affects the real (or inflation-adjusted) demand for liquidity. For intermediate- and long-term rates, the expected inflation rate influences the nominal interest rate, as the latter is considered to be the total of the real interest rate and the expected rate of inflation. Exchange rates may be important as well, for foreign capital markets are closely linked to the U.S. counterpart through foreign exchange markets.

COMPARISON OF NEURAL NETWORK (NN) AND ARTIFICIAL HIGHER ORDER NEURAL NETWORK (HONN)

Neural networks (NNs) have been widely used for modeling nonlinear systems. The approximation capability of NNs also has been investigated by many researchers. NNs provide an excellent flexibility in mapping complex 'input-output dependencies. The use of NNs has, however, some disadvantages compared with the artificial Higher Order Neural Network (HONN). In particular, the equations built during NNs training are opaque, and NNs do not distinguish inputs by their significance, leaving the responsibility to select significant inputs to a user. Also, the number of nodes and layers of the NNs are fixed by the user, and while there are many factors contributing to the flexibility of the NNs such as training tolerance, hidden neurons, initial weight distribution, and two gradients of activation functions, the factors contributing to the flexibility of the HONN are developed through the modeling process. The training of NNs is a kind of statistical estimation often using algorithms that are slow. If noise is considerable in a data sample, the generated models tend to be over fitted in order to achieve good results, whereas the HONN model creates an optimal complex model systematically and autonomously. The optimal complex model is a model that optimally balances model quality on a given data set and its generalization power on new, not previously seen, data with respect to the data's noise level and the task of modeling (prediction). It thus solves the basic problems of experimental systems analysis, systematically avoiding "over fitted" models based on the data's information only. This makes the HONN method a most automated, fast, and very efficient supplement and alternative to the predictions of time series prediction methods.

Neural Networks (NNs)

Different neural network architectures can be and have been used in time series prediction. The learning process of a neural network can be regarded as producing a multi-dimensional surface composed of a set of simpler non-linear functions that fit the data in some best sense. The advantage of using neural network models is that they can approximate or reconstruct any non-linear continuous function. The following subsections summarize multi-layer perceptron, radial basis function networks, sigma-pi/pi-sigma networks, and ridge polynomial network (Foka, 1999).

Multi-Layer Perceptron (MLP)

In multi-layer perceptron network, the past values of the time series are applied to the input of the network. The hidden layer of the MLP network (see Figure 1) performs the weighting summation of the inputs and the non-linear transformation is performed by the sigmoid function. The log-sigmoid function is:

$$f(x) = \frac{1}{1 + \exp(-x)} \qquad (1)$$

and the tan-sigmoid function is:

$$f(x) = \frac{\exp(x) - \exp(-x)}{\exp(x) + \exp(-x)} \qquad (2)$$

The output layer of the network performs a linear weighting summation of the outputs of all the hidden units, producing the predicted value of the time series as (Cichocki & Unbehauen, 1993):

Figure 1. The multi-layer perceptron

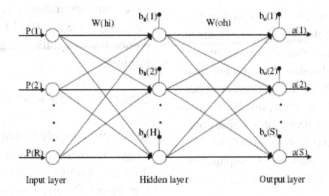

$$\hat{x}(t) = w_0 + \sum_{j=1}^{h} w_j f_j \left(\sum_{i=1}^{n} w_{ji} x(k-i) + w_{j0} \right)$$

(3)

where h is the number of hidden units, n is the number of input units, w_{ji} are the weights between the input and hidden layer, w_j are weights between the hidden and output layer and $f_j(.)$ is the sigmoid activation function at the jth hidden unit. The weights are adjustable and are determined during the training of the network.

The number of hidden layers and hidden units has to be determined before the training of the network is performed. It has been suggested that for a training set with p samples, a network with one hidden layer with $(p\text{-}1)$ hidden units can exactly implement the training set (Cichocki & Unbehauen, 1993). However, this is only guidance and the number of hidden layers and units is problem specific. In addition, according to the problem, other activation functions than the sigmoid can be used. A two-layer MLP can exactly represent any Boolean function. A two-layer MLP with log-sigmoid in the hidden layer and linear functions in the output layer can approximate with arbitrarily small error any continuous function. A three-layer MLP with the same transfer functions as before, can approximate non-linear functions to arbitrary accuracy.

Artificial Higher Order Neural Networks (HONNs)

Artificial Higher Order Neural Networks (HONNs) have an architecture that is similar to feed-forward neural networks whose neurons are replaced by polynomial nodes. The output of each node in the HONN is obtained using several types of polynomials such as a linear, quadratic, and modified quadratic of input variables. These polynomials are called partial descriptions (PDs). The HONN has fewer nodes than a back-propagation neural network, but the nodes are more flexible. In

this chapter, a number of HONNs are reviewed, and then, the polynomial neural network (PNN) (Kim and Park, 2003), which is one of the useful approximator techniques, is applied to model a time series prediction problem (TSPP).

Radial Basis Function Networks

The radial basis function (RBF) networks are two-layered structures (Figure 2). RBF networks have only one hidden layer with radial basis activation functions, and linear activation functions at the output layer. Typical choices for radial basis functions $\varphi(x) = \Phi(\|x - c\|)$ are:

- *Piecewise linear approximations:* $\Phi(r) = r$
- *Cubic approximation:* $\Phi(r) = r^3$
- *Gaussian function:* $\Phi(r) = \exp(-r^2/\sigma^2)$
- *Thin plate splines:* $\Phi(r) = r^2 \log(r)$
- *Multi-quadratic function:* $\Phi(r) = \sqrt{r^2 + \sigma^2}$
- *Inverse multi-quadratic function:*
  $\Phi(r) = 1/\sqrt{r^2 + \sigma^2}$, where σ is a parameter termed as the width or scaling parameter.

The output of the network is a linear combination of the radial basis functions (Cichocki & Unbehauen, 1993), and is given by

$$x(t) = w_0 + \sum_{j=1}^{h} w_i \Phi(\|x(t) - c_i\|)$$

(4)

where $\mathbf{x}(t) = [x(t-1), x(t-2),..., x(t-n)]^{\mathrm{T}}$.

RBF networks have the advantage that they have a simpler architecture than MLPs. In addition, they have localized basis functions, which reduce the possibility of getting stuck to local minima.

Sigma-Pi and Pi-Sigma Networks

Higher order or polynomial neural networks send weighted sums of products or functions of inputs through the transfer functions of the output layer. The aim of HONNs is to replace the hidden neurons

Figure 2. The Radial Basis Function network

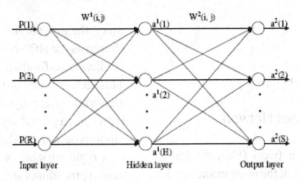

Figure 3. (a) The sigma-pi network, (b) The pi-sigma network.

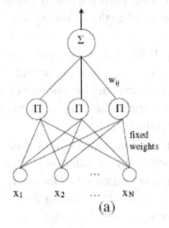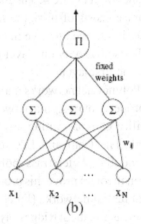

(a)   (b)

found with first order neural networks and thus reduce the complexity of their structure.

The sigma-pi network (Figure 3a) is a feed-forward network with a single *hidden* layer. The output of the *hidden* layer is the product of the input terms and the output of the network is the sum of these products. They have only one layer of adaptive weights which results in fast training. The output of the network is given by:

$$\hat{x}(t) = w_0 + \sum_{j=1}^{h} w_i \varphi_i(v_i) \tag{5}$$

where:

$$v_i = \prod_{j=1}^{n} a_{ij} x_j \tag{6}$$

φ_i is the activation function at the *hidden* layer, a_{ij} are the fixed weights (usually set to 1) and w_i are the adjustable weights.

The pi-sigma network (Figure 3b) has a very similar structure to the sigma-pi network. Their difference is that the output of the hidden layer is the sum of the input terms and the output of the network is the product of these terms. They also have a single layer of adaptive weights, but in these networks the adaptive weights are in the first layer. The output of the network is:

$$\hat{x}(t) = w_0 + \prod_{j=1}^{h} a_i \varphi_i(v_i) \tag{7}$$

where:

$$v_i = \sum_{j=1}^{n} w_{ij} x_j \qquad (8)$$

in the same notation as before.

The Ridge Polynomial Network

The Ridge Polynomial network (Shin & Ghosh, 1995) is a generalization of the pi-sigma network. It uses pi-sigma networks as basic building blocks as shown in Figure 4. The hidden layer of the network consists of pi-sigma networks and their output is summed to give the output of the network. It also has only one layer of adjustable weights in the first layer.

Ridge Polynomial networks maintain the fast learning property of pi-sigma networks and have the capability of representing any multivariate polynomial. The Chui and Li's representation theorem and the Weierstrass polynomial approximation theorem prove this property of ridge polynomial neural networks (Fulcher & Brown, 1994). More details about Ridge Polynomial Neural Networks can be found in (Fulcher & Brown, 1994) and (Shin & Ghosh, 1995).

Figure 4. The Ridge Polynomial network

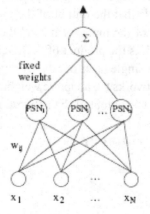

POLYNOMIAL NEURAL NETWORK

Since the polynomial neural network (PNN) is chosen as the HONN to be applied to time series prediction, its fundamentals are briefly explained. This section explains the PNN architecture and its algorithm. Each polynomial in the PNN algorithm represents a partial description (PD), and the best model is determined by selecting the most significant input variables and polynomial order. The design procedures are detailed in (Oh *et al.*, 2000; Kim and Park, 2003). Here, the architecture and algorithm of the PNN are briefly explained. The PNN is operated in the following steps:

- **Step 1:** We define the input variables such as $x_{1i}, x_{2i},..., x_{Ni}$ related to output variable y_i, where N and i are the number of the entire input variables and input-output data sets, respectively.

- **Step 2:** The input-output data sets are separated into training (n_{tr}) data sets and testing (n_{te}) data sets. Obviously, we have $n = n_{tr} + n_{te}$. The training data set is used to construct a PNN model. And the testing data set is used to evaluate the constructed PNN model.

- **Step 3:** The structure of the PNN is strongly dependent on the number of input variables and the order of PD in each layer. Two kinds of PNN structures, namely, the basic PNN structure and the modified PNN structure, can be available. Each of them comes with two cases.

  a. Basic PNN structure: The number of input variables of the PDs is the same in every layer.

  b. Modified PNN structure: The number of input variables of the PDs varies from layer to layer.

      Case 1: The polynomial order of the PDs is the same in each layer of the network.

Case 2: The polynomial order of the PDs in the 2nd or higher layer is different from the one in the 1st layer.

- **Step 4:** We determine arbitrarily the number of input variables and type of polynomial in the PDs. The polynomials differ according to the number of input variables and the polynomial order. Several types of polynomials are shown in Table 1. Because the outputs of the nodes of the preceding layer become the input variables for the current layer, the total number of PDs located at the current layer is determined by the number of selected input variables (r) from the nodes of the preceding layer. The total number of PDs in the current layer is equal to the combination, $^{N}C_r$, that is, $\dfrac{N!}{r!(N-r)!}$, where N is the number of nodes in the preceding layer. For an example, the specific forms of a PD in the case of two inputs are given as:

  o Bilinear $= c_0 + c_1 x_1 + c_2 x_2$ (9)
  o Biquadratic $=$
   $c_0 + c_1 x_1 + c_2 x_2 + c_3 x_1^2 + c_4 x_2^2 + c_5 x_1 x_2$
   (10)
  o Modified biquadratic $=$
   $c_0 + c_1 x_1 + c_2 x_2 + c_3 x_1 x_2$ (11)
   where c_i is the regression coefficient.

- **Step 5:** The vector of the coefficients of the PDs is determined using a standard mean squared error by minimizing the following index:

$$E_k = \frac{1}{n_{tr}} \sum_{i=1}^{n_{tr}} \left(y_i - z_{ki} \right)^2$$

$$k = 1, 2, \dots, \frac{N!}{r!(N-r)!}$$

where z_{ki} denotes the output of the k-th node with respect to the i-th data, and n_{tr} is the number of training data subsets. This step is completed repeatedly for all the nodes in the current layer.

- **Step 6:** The predictive capability of each PD is evaluated by a performance index using the testing data set. We then choose w PDs among $^{N}C_r$ PDs in due order from the best predictive capability (the lowest value of the performance index). Here, w (30) is the pre-defined number of PDs that must be preserved to the next layer. The outputs of the chosen PDs serve as inputs to the next layer.

- **Step 7:** The PNN algorithm terminates when the number of layers predetermined by the designer is reached. Here, the number of total layers was limited to 5.

- **Step 8:** If the stopping criterion is not satisfied, the next layer is constructed by repeating steps 4 through 8.

Figure 5 shows a PNN architecture. In the figure, four input variables $(x_1, x_2, \dots x_4)$, three layers, and a PD processing example are considered. z_i^{j-1} indicates the output of the i-th node in the $(j-1)$th layer, which is employed as a new input of the j-th layer. The black nodes have influence on the best node (output node), and these networks represent the ultimate PNN model. Meanwhile, the solid line nodes have no influence over the output node. In

Table 1. Different types of the polynomial in PDs

No. of inputs	1	2	3
Order of the polynomial			
1 (Type 1)	Linear	Bilinear	Trilinear
2 (Type 2)	Quadratic	Biquadratic	Triquadratic
2 (Type 3)	Modified quadratic	Modified biquadratic	Modified triquadratic

Figure 5. Overall-architecture of the PNN

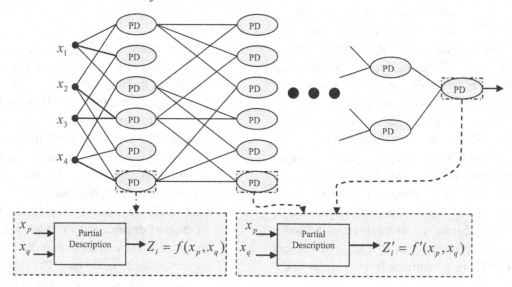

addition, owing to poor performance, the dotted line nodes are excluded when choosing the PDs with the best predictive performance in the corresponding layer. Therefore, the solid line nodes and dotted line nodes should not be present in the final PNN model.

APPLICATIONS OF THE POLYNOMIAL NEURAL NETWORK

The PNNs presented in this chapter are applied to two types of problems: (1) prediction of exchange rates of three international currencies; and (2) prediction of two key U.S. interest rates—the federal funds rate and the yield on the 5-year U.S. Treasury note.

Exchange Rates Prediction Using PNN Paradigms

The Data Set

In our experimentation, we used three different datasets (Euros, Great Britain Pound and Japanese Yen) in our forecast performance analysis. The data used are daily Forex exchange rates obtained from the Pacific Exchange Rate Service (2007). The data comprises the US dollar exchange rate against Euros, Great Britain Pound (GBP) and Japanese Yen (JPY). The length of the data is January 1, 2000 to December 31, 2002 (partial data sets excluding holidays). Half of the data set was used as training data set, and half as evaluation test set or out-of-sample datasets, which are used to evaluate the good or bad performance of the predictions, based on evaluation measurements. The forecasting evaluation criteria used is the mean squared error (MSE).

Experimental Results

For simulation, the five-day-ahead data sets are prepared for constructing PNN models. A PNN model was constructed using the training data and then the model was used on the test data set. The actual daily exchange rates and the predicted ones for three major internationally traded currencies are shown in Figures 8, 11 and 14.

Analysis for EURO

Figure 7 shows that the fitness function steadily increases with number of layers. Since fitness function used is inversely proportional to the objective function, it implies that the objective function decreases with number of layers. Figure 8 shows the PNN prediction and absolute difference error for the EURO exchange rate problem; here there is a good match between the measured and predicted values, showing that the proposed PNN model can be used as a feasible solution for exchange rate forecasting. From Figure 9 the absolute difference error is found be within the range of ±1. The grand final outputs for the PNN is designated as {1 4 0.000049 0.000056} as shown in Table 2.

Analysis for GBP

Figure 10 shows that the fitness function steadily increases with number of layers. Since fitness function used is inversely proportional to the objective function, it implies that the objective function decreases with number of layers. Figure 11 shows the PNN prediction and absolute difference error for the GBP exchange rate problem; here there is a good match between the measured and predicted values, showing that the proposed PNN model can be used as a feasible solution for exchange rate forecasting. From Figure 12, the absolute difference error is found be within the range of ±1. The grand final outputs for the PNN is designated as {1 3 0.000011 0.000011} as shown in Table 3.

Table 2. Input signals, training error (PI), and testing error (EPI)

1	2	0.000049	0.000057
1	3	0.000050	0.000056
1	4	0.000049	0.000056
2	3	0.000097	0.000118
2	4	0.000096	0.000118
3	4	0.000154	0.000160

Figures 7. Fitness functions variations with number of layers

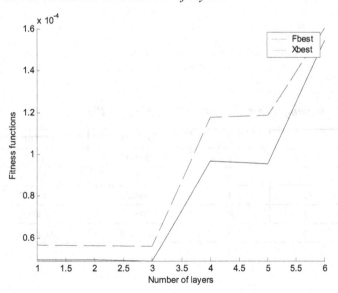

Figure 8. Predicted and tested results for the EURO exchange rate problem

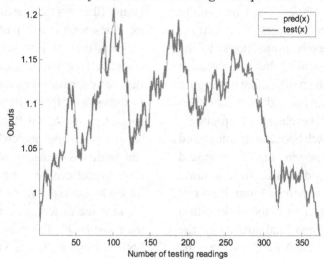

Figure 9. Absolute difference error for the EURO exchange rate problem

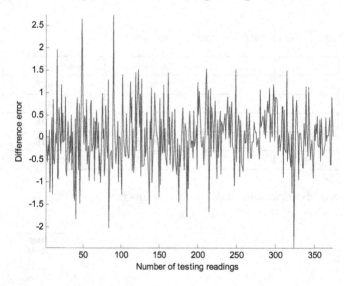

Table 3. Input signals, training error (PI), and testing error (EPI)

1	2	0.000011	0.000011
1	3	0.000011	0.000011
1	4	0.000011	0.000011
2	3	0.000022	0.000022
2	4	0.000022	0.000022
3	4	0.000032	0.000033

Figure 10. Fitness functions variations with number of layers

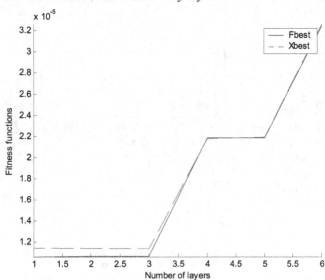

Figure 11. Predicted and tested results for the GBP exchange rate problem

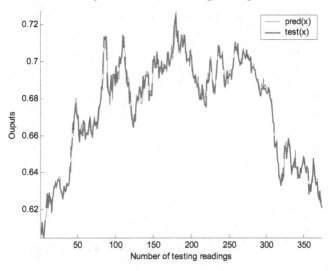

Analysis for YEN

Figure 13 shows that the fitness function steadily increases with number of layers. Since fitness function used is inversely proportional to the objective function, it implies that the objective function decreases with number of layers. Figure 14 shows the PNN prediction and absolute difference error for the YEN exchange rate problem; here there is a good match between the measured

and predicted values, showing that the proposed PNN model can be used as a feasible solution for exchange rate forecasting. From Figure 15 the absolute difference error is found be within the range of ±1. The grand final outputs for the PNN is designated as {1 3 0.483756 0.623222} as shown in Table 4.

Figure 12. Absolute difference error for the GBP exchange rate problem

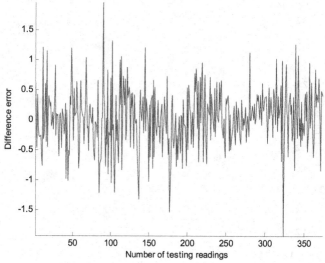

Figures 13. Fitness functions variations with number of layers

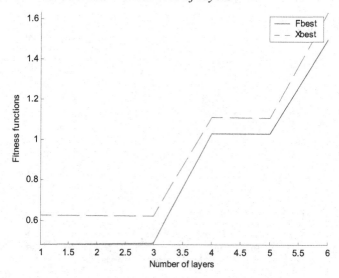

Table 4. Input signals, training error (PI), and testing error (EPI)

1	2	0.478256	0.626213
1	3	0.483756	0.623222
1	4	0.486561	0.623235
2	3	1.031326	1.113781
2	4	1.031385	1.109121
3	4	1.500447	1.635893

Figure 14. Predicted and tested results for the YEN exchange rate problem

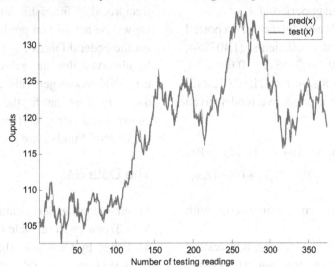

Figure 15. Absolute difference error for the YEN exchange rate problem

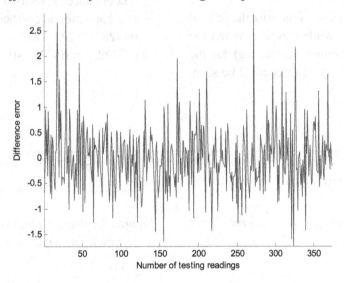

Interest Rates Prediction Using Enhanced PNN Paradigms

Forecasting interest rates is an important financial problem that is receiving increasing attention especially because of its difficulty and practical applications. This chapter presents the experiment using enhanced PNN model for forecasting two key U.S. interest rates; the Federal funds rate and the yield on the 5-year U.S. Treasury note. For these examples, we use enhanced PNN, which is a preferred HONN for this class of problem.

The Data Set

In our first experimentation, we used the US Federal Funds Rate (%), monthly average published by

Ohashi of the Washington World Bank in (Farlow, pp208, 1984) and a delay period of 3.

The enhanced PNN used for the work reported in this chapter found coefficients {1.407984, 2.724110, -0.404710, -1.215819, -0.000000, -0.000000, -0.000000, -0.105411, 0.012242, 0.080376}, leading to a predictive model given as:

$$FFR = 1.408 + 2.724x_1 - 0.404x_2 - 1.215x_3 - 0x_1^2$$
$$-0x_2^2 - 0x_3^2 - 0.105x_1x_2 + 0.012x_1x_3 + 0.080x_2x_3$$

Interpreting this in terms of time series with lags, leads to Box 1.

The weighted average training and testing error is 9.515511, average training error (PI) is 8.505876, while the average testing error (E_PI) is 2.869034.

Figure 16 shows the best fitness for the Federal Funds Rate problem, while Figure 17 shows the fitness functions (training and testing) for the Federal Funds Rate problem. As could be seen,

the best fitness is minimal while the best function (reciprocal of fitness) is a maximum. Figure 18 shows the actual and predicted (testing) figures for the Federal Funds Rate problem and it could be observed that the enhanced PNN, which is a HONN model generalizes well for the tested data set except that for the third data. Figure 19 shows the difference error (testing) figures for the Federal Funds Rate problem

The Data Set

In our second experimentation, we used the 5-Year Treasury Note Yield (%), monthly average published by Ohashi of the Washington World Bank in (Farlow, pp209, 1984) and a delay period of 3.

The enhanced PNN used for the work reported in this chapter found coefficients to be as follows: {-209.128325, 29.918832, -11.271954, 20.865937, -0.627108, -5.319332, -0.533701, 5.963975, -

Box 1.

$$FFR(t) = 1.408 + 2.724x(t-1) - 0.404x(t-2) - 1.215(t-3) - 0.105x(t-1)x(t-2)$$
$$+ 0.012x(t-1)x(t-3) + 0.080x(t-2)x(t-3)$$

Figure 16. Best fitness for the Federal Funds Rate problem

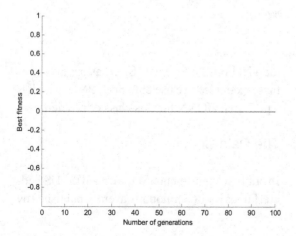

Figure 17. Fitness functions (training and testing) for the Federal Funds Rate problem

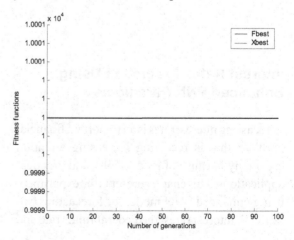

Figure 18. Actual and predicted (testing) figures for the Federal Funds Rate problem

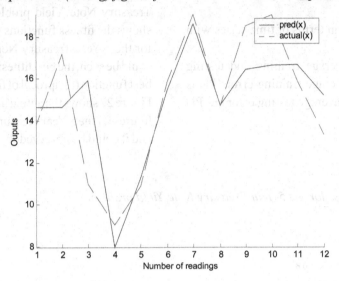

Figure 19. Percentage difference error (testing) figures for the Federal Funds Rate problem

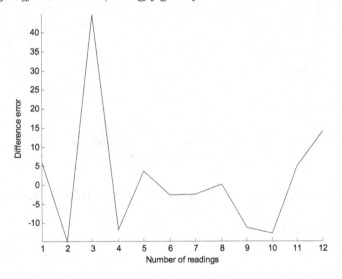

Box 2.

$$TNY\_5(t) = -209.128 + 29.918x_1 - 11.271x_2 + 20.865x_3$$
$$-0.627x_1^2 - 5.319x_2^2 - 0.533x_3^2 + 5.964x_1x_2 - 7.528x_1x_3 + 6.264x_2x_3$$

Box 3.

$$TNY\_5(t) = -209.128 + 29.918x(t-1) - 11.271x(t-2) + 20.865x(t-3) - 0.627x(t-1)^2 - 5.319x(t-2)^2$$
$$-0.533x(t-3)^2 + 5.964x(t-1)x(t-2) - 7.528x(t-1)x(t-3) + 6.264x(t-2)x(t-3)$$

7.528610, 6.264164}, leading to a predictive model given as Box 2.

Interpreting this in terms of time series with lags, leads to Box 3.

The weighted average training and testing error is 1.794888, average training error (PI) is 1.624866, while the average testing error (E_PI) is 0.404930.

Figure 20 shows the best fitness for the 5-Year Treasury Note Yield problem, while Figure 21 shows the fitness functions (training and testing) for the 5-Year Treasury Note Yield problem. As could be seen, the best fitness is minimal while the best function (reciprocal of fitness) is a maximum. Figure 22 shows the actual and predicted (testing) figures for the 5-Year Treasury Note Yield problem and it could be observed that the enhanced PNN,

Figure 20. Best fitness for the 5-Year Treasury Note Yield problem

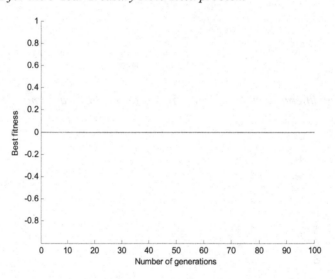

Figure 21. Fitness functions (training and testing) for the 5-Year Treasury Note Yield problem

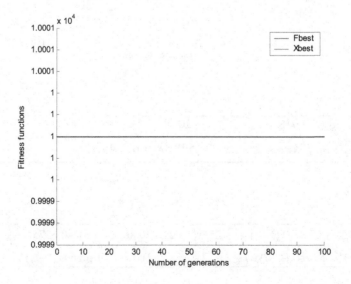

Figure 22. Actual and predicted (testing) figures for the 5-Year Treasury Note Yield problem

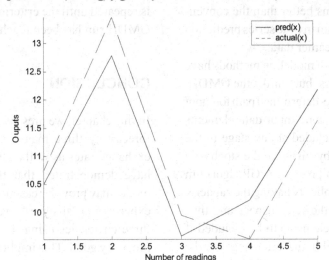

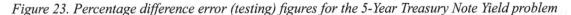

Figure 23. Percentage difference error (testing) figures for the 5-Year Treasury Note Yield problem

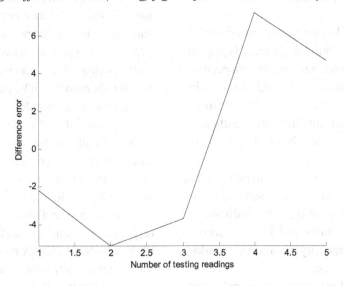

which is a HONN model generalizes well for the tested data set. Figure 23 shows the difference error (testing) figures for the 5-Year Treasury Note Yield problem.

FUTURE RESEARCH DIRECTIONS

The HONN and evolutionary approach (EP) are two popular non-linear methods of mathematical modeling. It is generally accepted that the future trend for realizing more robust HONN architectures is to hybridize HONNs-like architectures with evolutionary approaches (EAs) such as genetic programming (GP), genetic algorithm (GA), etc. Hiassat *et al* (2003; 2004) introduced the GP-GMDH algorithm, which uses genetic programming to find the best function that maps the input to the output in each layer of the group method of data handling (GMDH) algorithm, and showed that it performs better than the conventional GMDH algorithm in time series prediction using financial and weather data.

It is evident that both modeling methods have many common features, but, unlike the GMDH, GP does not follow a pre-determined path for input data generation. The same input data elements can be included or excluded at any stage in the evolutionary process by virtue of the stochastic nature of the selection process. A GP algorithm can thus be seen as implicitly having the capacity to learn and adapt in the search space and thus allow previously bad elements to be included if they become beneficial in the latter stages of the search process. The standard GMDH algorithm is more deterministic and would thus discard any underperforming elements as soon as they are realized.

Using GP in the selection process of the GMDH algorithm, the model building process is free to explore a more complex universe of data permutations. This selection procedure has three main advantages over the standard selection method. Firstly, it allows unfit individuals from early layers to be incorporated at an advanced layer where they generate fitter solutions.

Secondly, it also allows those unfit individuals to survive the selection process if their combinations with one or more of the other individuals produce new fit individuals, and thirdly, it allows more implicit non-linearity by allowing multi-layer variable interaction.

The new GMDH algorithm that is proposed in this chapter is constructed in exactly the same manner as the standard GMDH algorithm except for the selection process. In order to select the individuals that are allowed to pass to the next layer, all the outputs of the GMDH algorithm at the current layer are entered as inputs in the GP algorithm where they are allowed to evolve, mutate, crossover and combine with other individuals in order to prove their fitness. The selected fit individuals are then entered in the GMDH algorithm

as inputs at the next layer. The whole procedure is repeated until the criterion for terminating the GMDH run has been reached.

CONCLUSION

In this chapter, we presented the PNN model for forecasting three major international currency exchange rates as well as two interest rates. We have demonstrated that the PNN forecasting model may provide reasonably good results. Our experimental analyses reveal that the MSE for three currencies using the PNN model are appreciably good. This implies that the PNN model can be used as a feasible solution for exchange rate forecasting.

Figures 8, 11, and 14 show the PNN prediction and absolute difference error for the euro, GBP, and yen exchange rate problems, respectively. In each, there is a good match between the measured and predicted values, showing that the PNN, which is a HONN model, can be used as a feasible solution for exchange rate forecasting.

Since the interest rate problem seems to bee more difficult to solve, an enhanced PNN architecture was employed for solving this problem. Figures 18 and 22 show the actual and predicted (testing) figures for the Federal Funds Rate problem and the 5-year Treasury note yield problem, respectively. It can be observed that the enhanced PNN, which is a HONN model, generalizes well for the tested data sets except that for the third data set with the federal funds rate problem.

REFERENCES

Abraham, A., Nath, B., & Mahanti, P.K. (2001). Hybrid intelligent systems for stock market analysis. In Vassil N. Alexandrov et al. (Eds.), *Computational Science* (pp. 337-345). Springer-Verlag.

Abraham, A., Philip, N.S., & Saratchandran, P. (2003). Modeling chaotic behavior of stock indices using intelligent paradigms. *International Journal of Neural, Parallel and Scientific Computations*, *11*(1-2), 143-160.

Chappel, D., Padmore, J., Mistry, P., & Ellis, C. (1996). A threshold model for French franc/Deutschmark exchange rate. *Journal of Forecasting*, *15*, 155-164.

Chen, Y., Yang, Y., & Dong, J., (2004). Nonlinear system modeling via optimal design of neural trees. *International Journal of Neural Systems*, *14*(2), 125-137.

Chen, Y., Yang, Y., & Dong, J., & Abraham, A. (2005). Time-series forecasting using flexible neural tree model. *Information Science*, *174*(3/4), 219-235.

Chen, Y., Peng, L., & Abraham, A. (2006). Exchange rate forecasting using flexible neural tree model. In Wang, J., et al. (Eds.), *Lecture Notes Computer Science* (pp. 518-523). Springer-Verlag.

Cichocki, A., & Unbehauen, R., (1993). *Neural networks for optimization and signal processing*. Wiley.

Draper, N. R., & Smith, H. (1966). *Applied regression analysis*. Wiley.

Farlow, S. (1984). (Ed.), *Self-organizing methods in modeling: GMDH type algorithms*. Dekker.

Foka, A. (1999). *Time series prediction using evolving polynomial neural networks*. MSc Thesis, University of Manchester Institute of Science & Technology, UK.

Fulcher, G. E., & Brown, D. E. (1994). A polynomial neural network for predicting temperature distributions. *IEEE Transactions on Neural Networks*, *5*(3), 372-379.

Hiassat, M., Abbod, M., & Mort, N. (2003). using genetic programming to improve the GMDH in time series prediction. In Bozdogan, H. (Ed.), *Statistical data mining and knowledge discovery* (pp. 257-268). Chapman & Hall CRC.

Hiassat, M., & Mort, N. (2004). *An evolutionary method for term selection in the group method of data handling*. Retrieved from http://www.maths.leeds.ac.uk/Statistics/workshop/lasr2004/Proceedings/hiassat.pdf

Hsieh, D. A. (1989). Modeling heteroscedasticity in daily foreign-exchange rates. *Journal of Business and Economic Statistics*, 7:307C317.

Kim, D.W., & Park, G. T. (2003). Optimization of polynomial neural networks: An evolutionary approach. *Trans. Transaction, Korean Institute of Electrical Engineers*, *52D*(7), 424-433.

Oh, S. K., Kim, D. W., & Park, B. J. (2000). A study on the optimal design of polynomial neural networks structure. *Transaction, Korean Institute of Electrical Engineers*, *49D*, 145-156.

Ohashi, K. (1984). GMDH forecasting using U.S. interest rates. In Farlow, S. J. (Ed.), *Self-organizing methods in modeling: GMDH type algorithms* (pp. 199-214). New York: Marcel Dekker, Inc.

Onwubolu, G. C., Buryan, P., & Abraham, A. (2007). Self organizing data mining using enhanced group method data handling approach. *Proceedings of the First European Conference on Data Mining* (pp. 170-175). Lisbon, Portugal.

Pacific Exchange Rate Service (2007). Retrieved from http://fx.sauder.ubc.ca/

Refenes, A. N. (1993a). Constructive learning and its application to currency exchange rate forecasting. In Trippi, R. R., & Turban, E. (Eds.), *Neural networks in finance and investing: Using artificial intelligence to improve real-world performance* (pp. 777-805). Chicago: Probus Publishing Company.

Refenes, A. N., Azema-Barac, M., Chen, L., & Karoussos, S. A. (1993b). Currency exchange rate prediction and neural network design strategies. *Neural Computing and Application, 1*, 46-58.

Sastry, K., & Goldberg. D. E. (2003). Probabilistic model building and competent genetic programming. In Riolo, R. L. & Worzel, B. (Eds.), *Genetic programming theory and practice* (pp. 205-220). Kluwer.

Shin, Y., & Ghosh, J. (1995). Ridge polynomial networks. *IEEE Transactions on Neural Networks, 6*(3), 610-622.

So, M. K. P., Lam, K., & Li, W. K. (1999). Forecasting exchange rate volatility using autoregressive random variance model. *Applied Financial Economics, 9*, 583-591.

Theodossiou, P. (1994). The stochastic properties of major Canadian exchange rates. *The Financial Review, 29*(2), 193-221.

Wang, W., Lai, K. K., Nakamori, Y., & Wang, S. (2004). Forecasting foreign exchange rates with artificial neural networks: A review. *International Journal of Information Technology & Decision Making, 3*(1), 145-165.

Yao, J.T., & Tan, C.L. (2000). A case study on using neural networks to perform technical forecasting of forex. *Neurocomputing, 34*, 79-98.

Yu, L., Wang, S., & Lai, K. K. (2005a). Adaptive smoothing neural networks in foreign exchange rate forecasting. In Sunderam, V.S. et al. (Eds.), *ICCS, Lecture Notes Computer Science, 3516*, pp. 523-530.

Yu, L., Wang, S., & Lai, K. K. (2005b). A novel nonlinear ensemble forecasting model incorporating GLAR and ANN for foreign exchange rates. *Computers & Operations Research, 32*, 2523-2541.

ADDITIONAL READING

Leigh W., Modani, N., Purvis, R., & Roberts, T. (2002). Stock market trading rule discovery using technical charting heuristics. *Expert Systems with Applications, 23*(2), 155-159.

Leigh, W., Purvis, R., & Ragusa, J. M. (2002). Forecasting the NYSE composite index with technical analysis, pattern recognizer, neural network, and genetic algorithm: A case study in romantic decision support. *Decision Support Systems, 32*(4), 361-377.

Nasdaq Stock Market (n.d.). http://www.nasdaq.com

National Stock Exchange of India, Limited. http://www.nse-india.com

Yao, J. T., & Tan, C. L. (2000). A case study on using neural networks to perform technical forecasting of forex. *Neurocomputing, 34*, 79-98.

Chen, Y., Abraham, A., Yang, J., & Yang, B. (2005). Hybrid methods for stock index modeling. *2005 International Conference on Fuzzy Systems and Knowledge Discovery (FSKD'05)*, China. Lecture Notes in Computer Science, Volume 3614, pp. 1067- 1070.

Chapter XII
Application of Pi–Sigma Neural Networks and Ridge Polynomial Neural Networks to Financial Time Series Prediction

Rozaida Ghazali
Liverpool John Moores University, UK

Dhiya Al-Jumeily
Liverpool John Moores University, UK

ABSTRACT

This chapter discusses the use of two artificial Higher Order Neural Networks (HONNs) models; the Pi-Sigma Neural Networks and the Ridge Polynomial Neural Networks, in financial time series forecasting. The networks were used to forecast the upcoming trends of three noisy financial signals; the exchange rate between the US Dollar and the Euro, the exchange rate between the Japanese Yen and the Euro, and the United States 10-year government bond. In particular, we systematically investigate a method of pre-processing the signals in order to reduce the trends in them. The performance of the networks is benchmarked against the performance of Multilayer Perceptrons. From the simulation results, the predictions clearly demonstrated that HONNs models, particularly Ridge Polynomial Neural Networks generate higher profit returns with fast convergence, therefore show considerable promise as a decision making tool. It is hoped that individual investor could benefit from the use of this forecasting tool.

INTRODUCTION

There are numerous research works being carried out in the area of neural networks, however not all of these research works can be used in real commercial applications. This is probably due to the size of the neural networks which can be large enough to prevent the problem solution from being used in real world problems. Furthermore, the large network size can slow down the training speed and its convergence.

The highly popularized Multilayer Perceptrons (MLPs) models have been successfully applied in financial time series forecasting. A review on existing literature reveals financial studies on a wide variety of subjects such as stock price forecasting (Castiglione, 2000; Chan, Wong, & Lam, 2000; Zekić, 1998), currency exchange rate forecasting (Chen & Leung, 2005; Gradojevic & Yang, 2000; Yao & Tan, 2000; Yao, Poh, & Jasic, 1996; Kuan & Liu, 1995), returns prediction (Dunis & Williams, 2002; Shachmurove & Witkowska, 2000; Franses, 1998), forecasting currency volatility (Yumlu, Gurgen, & Okay, 2005; Dunis & Huang, 2002), sign prediction (Fernandez-Rodriguez, Gonzalec-Martel, & Sosvilla-Rivero, 2000). Since MLPs structure is multilayered and the Backpropagation algorithm involves high computational complexity, this structure requires excessive training time for learning. Further, the number of weights and in turn the training time increases as the number of layers and the nodes in a layer increases (Patra & Pal, 1995; Chen & Leung, 2004).

Concerned with the slow learning problems of MLPs, this chapter investigates the use of artificial Higher Order Neural Networks (HONNs) which have a fast learning properties and powerful mapping of single layer **trainable weights** networks in financial time series prediction. Higher Order Neural Networks distinguish themselves from ordinary feedforward networks by the presence of **higher order terms** in the network. In a great variety of Neural Networks models, neural inputs are combined using the summing operation. HONNs in contrast contain not only summing unit, but also units that multiply their inputs which referred to **higher order terms** or product units.

Although most neural network models share a common goal in performing functional mapping, different network architectures may vary significantly in their ability to handle different types of problems. For some tasks, higher order combinations of some of the inputs or activations may be appropriate to help form good representation for input-output mapping. Two types of HONNs; the Pi-Sigma Neural Networks and the Ridge Polynomial Neural Networks were used as nonlinear predictor to capture the underlying movement in financial time series signals and to predict the future trend in the financial market.

ARTIFICIAL HIGHER ORDER NEURAL NETWORKS (HONNS)

Neurons in an ordinary feedforward network is just a first order neuron, also called a 'linear neuron' since it only uses a linear sum of its inputs for decision. This linearity, providing a hyperplane for decision limits the capability of the neuron to solve only linear discriminate problems (Guler & Sahin, 1994). Since Minsky and Papert's results (1969), it is well known that usual feedforward neural networks with first-order units can implement only linear separability mappings. One possibility to drop this limitation is to use multilayer networks where so-called hidden units can combine the outputs of previous units and so give rise to nonlinear mappings (Hornik, Stinchcombe, & White, 1989). MLP is of type 1st order neural network which can effectively carry out inner products which are then weighted and summed before passing through the non-linear threshold function. The other way to overcome the restriction to linear maps is to introduce higher order units to model nonlinear dependences (Giles & Maxwell, 1987; Giles, Griffin, & Maxwell, 1998).

HONNs are type of feedforward neural networks which provide nonlinear decision boundaries, therefore offering a better classification capability than the linear neuron (Guler & Sahin, 1994). The nonlinearity is introduced into the HONNs by having multi-linear interactions between their inputs or neurons which enable them to expand the input space into higher dimensional space. This lead to an easy separation of nonlinear separability classes where linear separability is possible or a reduction in the dimension of the nonlinearity is achieved. For example, the XOR problem could not be solved with a network without a hidden layer or by a single layer of first-order units, as it is not linear separability. However the same problem is easily solved if the patterns are represented in three dimension in terms of an enhanced representation (Pao, 1989), by just using a single layer network with second-order terms.

The presence of **higher order terms** in HONNs allowing the multiplication activity in the networks. Multiplication is an arithmetic operation that, when used in Neural Networks, helps to increase their computational power (Schmitt, 2001). There are good reasons to explicitly apply multiplication in the network. For instance, empirical evidence is available and reported for the existence of exponential and logarithmic dendritic processes in biological neural systems, allowing multiplication and polynomial processing (Schmitt, 2001). Consequently, as argued in (Durbin & Rumelhart, 1990), in order to model biological Neural Networks, one should extend the standard MLP model with multiplicative or product units. Further, biological networks make use of non-linear activation components in the form of axo-axonic synapses performing pre-synaptic inhibition (Neville, Stonham, & Glover, 2000). The simplest way of modelling such synapses and introducing increased node complexity is to use multi-linear activation, which is the node's activation is in 'higher order' nodes form (Rumelhart, Hinton, & Williams, 1986), resulting the use of non-linear activation components.

According to (Durbin & Rumelhart, 1989), there are various ways in which product units could be used in a network. One way is for a few of them to be made available as inputs to the network in addition to the original raw inputs. Alternatively, they can be used as the output of the network itself. The other way of utilizing them

is a whole hidden layer of product units, feeding into a subsequent layer of summing units. The attraction is rather in mixing both types of units; product unit and summing unit, so that product units are mainly used in a network where they occur together with summing units.

A major advantage of HONNs is that only one layer of **trainable weights** is needed to achieve nonlinear separability, unlike the typical Multilayer Perceptron or feedforward networks (Park, Smith, & Mersereau, 2000). They are simple in their architecture and require fewer numbers of weights to learn the underlying equation when compared to ordinary feedforward networks, in order to deliver the same input-output mapping (Park et al., 2000; Leerink, Giles, Horne, & Jabri, 1995; Giles & Maxwell, 1987; Shin & Ghosh, 1995). Consequently, they can learn faster in view of the fact that each iteration of the training procedure takes less time (Cass & Radl, 1996). This makes them suitable models for complex problem solving where the ability to retrain or adapt to the new data in real time is critical (Pau & Phillips, 1995; Artyomov & Pecht, 2004). Moreover, **higher order terms** in HONNs can increase the information capacity of neural networks in comparison to neural networks that utilise summation units only. The larger capacity means that the same function or problem can be solved by network that has fewer units. As a result, the representational power of **higher order terms** can help solving complex problems with construction of significantly smaller network while maintaining fast learning capabilities (Leerink et al., 1995).

Although it is possible to implement any continuous function using two layers of such nodes as in the MLPs, the resources required in terms of hardware and time can be prohibited. Memory requirements are minimized, making the hardware requirements more feasible. The simpler characteristic of HONNs, which having a single layer of trainable weights, can offers a large saving of hardware in the implementation

(Patra & Pal, 1995). HONNs are endowed with certain unique characteristics; stronger approximation property, faster convergence rate, greater storage capacity, and higher fault tolerance than lower order neural networks (Wang, Fang, & Liu, 2006). The networks have been considered as good candidates, due to their design flexibility for given geometric transforms, robustness to noisy and/or occluded inputs, inherent fast training ability, and nonlinearly separable (Park et al., 2000).

Two types of artificial HONNs; Pi-Sigma Neural Networks, and Ridge Polynomial Neural Networks are considered in this chapter. Each one of them employs the powerful capabilities of product units with some combinations with summing units. Their architectures are varied in the way the position where the product units or **higher order terms** are used in the networks. The Pi-Sigma Neural Networks utilizes the **higher order terms** at the output layer, as the output of the network itself. On the other hand, the Ridge Polynomial Neural Networks made the **higher order terms** available as the whole hidden layer of product units feeding into a subsequent layer of summing units. With different strength and capabilities, the structure and characteristic of these networks is elaborated and discussed below, as well as their training algorithms and applications in used.

PI-SIGMA NEURAL NETWORKS (PSNNS)

The Pi-Sigma Neural Networks were first used by Shin and Ghosh (1991b) to overcome the problem of weights explosion in a single layer HONNs (Giles & Maxwell, 1987). They are feedforward networks with a single hidden layer and product units at the output layer. The networks calculate the product of sum of the input components and pass it to a nonlinear function.

The motivation was to develop a systematic method for maintaining the fast learning property and powerful mapping capability of single layer HONNs whilst avoiding the combinatorial explosion in the **number of free parameters** when the input dimension is increased. In contrast to a single layer HONNs, the **number of free parameters** in PSNNs increases linearly to the order of the network. For that reason, PSNNs can overcome the problem of weights explosion that occurs in a single layer HONNs which rise exponentially to the number of inputs. Shin and Ghosh (1991b) argued that PSNNs not only require less memory (weights and nodes), but typically need at least two orders of magnitude less number of computations as compared to MLP for similar performance level, and over a broad class of problems.

The network architecture of PSNN with a single output consists of two layers; the product layer and the summing layer, as shown in Figure 1. The input layers are connected to the summing layer by trainable weighted connections. The output from this layer is passed to the product unit (by non-trainable connections set to unity), which passes the signal through a nonlinear transfer function to produce the network output. For each increase in order, only one extra summing unit is required. The product units give the networks higher order capabilities without suffering the exponential increase in weights, which is a major problem in a single layer HONNs.

The Pi-Sigma Neural Networks has a topology of a fully connected two-layered feedforward network. Since there are K summing units incorporated, it is called a K-th order PSNN. In this case, W_{kj} from input X_k to the h_j summing units is a trainable weight (the dotted line arrows). The weights on the connections between the summing and the output layer are fixed to one (the solid black line arrows), and they are not trainable. For that reason, the summing layer is not "hidden" as in the case of Multi Layer Perceptron (MLP). Such a network topology with only one layer of **trainable weights** drastically reduces the training time.

Figure 1. Pi-Sigma Neural Network of k-th order. Bias nodes are not shown here for reason of simplicity

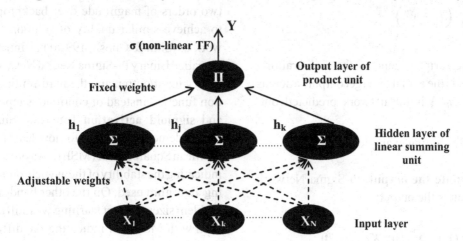

The output of the PSNN is computed as follows:

$$Y = \sigma \left(\prod_{j=1}^{K} \sum_{k=1}^{N} \left(W_{kj} Xk + W_{jo} \right) \right) \quad (1)$$

where W_{kj} are adjustable weights, W_{j0} are the biases of the summing units, X_k is the input vector, K is the number of summing unit, N is the number of input nodes, and σ is a nonlinear transfer function.

The utilization of product units in the output layer indirectly incorporates the capabilities of higher order networks while using a small number of weights and processing units (Ghosh & Shin, 1992). This also enables the network to be regular and incrementally expandable, since the order of the network can be increased by adding another summing unit and associated weight without disturbing any connection established previously. If multiple outputs are required, an independent summing layer is needed for each output. Thus, for an M-dimensional output vector y, and N-dimensional input vector x, a total of $\sum_{i=1}^{M}(N+1)K_i$ weights connections are needed, where K_i is the number of summing units for the i-th output. This allows a great flexibility since all outputs do not have to retain the same complexity.

A further advantage of PSNN is that we do not have to pre-compute the **higher order terms** in order to feed them into the network, as what one need to do in a single layer HONNs. PSNN is able to learn in a stable manner even with fairly large learning rates (Ghosh & Shin, 1992). The use of linear summing units makes the convergence analysis of the learning rules for PSNN more accurate and tractable. The price to be paid is that the PSNNs are not universal approximators. Indeed, a k-th order PSNN realizes a constraint representation of a k-th order single layer HONNs (Shin & Ghosh, 1995). Despite not being universal approximators, PSNNs demonstrated competent ability to solve many scientific and engineering problems, such image compression (Hussain & Liatsis, 2002), pattern recognition (Shin, Ghosh, & Samani, 1992), and financial time series prediction (Hussain, Knowles, Lisboa, El-Deredy, & Al-Jumeily, 2006).

Learning Algorithm of PSNN

Learning algorithm for Pi-Sigma Neural Networks introduced in this chapter is based on the gradient descent on the estimated mean squared error (MSE), which is calculated as follows:

$$E = \frac{1}{N} \sum_{p=1}^{N} \left(d^p - y^p \right)^2 \tag{2}$$

where superscript p denotes the p-th training example, d^p is the actual or target output, whereas $y^p = \sigma \left(\prod_j h_j^p \right)$ is the network predicted output.

For each training example, do:

- **Calculate the output.** Pi-Sigma Network computes the output:

$$Y = \sigma \left(\prod_{j=1}^{K} \sum_{k=1}^{N} \left(W_{kj} X_k + W_{jo} \right) \right) \tag{3}$$

- Compute the benefit β at output node:

$$\beta = (d_i - y_i) \, y_i \, (1 - y_i) \tag{4}$$

- Compute the weight changes. The delta weight is:

$$\Delta w_i = \eta \beta \left(\prod_{j \neq l}^{M} h_{ji} \right) x_k \tag{5}$$

where h_{ji} is the output of summing unit.

- Update the weight:

$$W_i = W_i + \Delta W_i \tag{6}$$

2. If current epoch > maximum epoch
   Stop the training
3. Else
   Go to step 1

PSNNs' Applications

Previous research work found that PSNNs are good models for various applications. (Shin et al., 1992) investigated the applicability of PSNNs for shift, scale and rotation invariant pattern recognition. Preliminary results for both function approximation and classification are extremely encourag-

ing, and showed a faster performance of about two orders of magnitude over backpropagation to achieve similar quality of solution. Another work of (Shin & Ghosh, 1991a) has introduced a so-called Binary Pi-Sigma Neural Networks with binary input/output and the hardlimiting activation function instead of continuous input/output and **sigmoid activation function**. Simulation results demonstrated that for low learning rates, the Mean Squared error (MSE) always decreasing, indicating the stability of the asynchronous learning algorithm used. On the other hand, for large problem sizes, perfect learning was still achieved even with MSE ≥ 1, indicating the difficulty of the underlying mapping problems.

Hussain and Liatsis (2002) proposed a new Recurrent Polynomial Networks for predictive image coding that explores both multi-linear interactions between the input pixel as well as the temporal dynamics of the image formation process. They have extended the architecture of ordinary PSNNs to include a recurrent connection from the output to the input layer. The networks do not suffer from a slow convergence rate and because of the feedback connections and the existence of **higher order terms**, they can be applied to highly nonlinear problem.

RIDGE POLYNOMIAL NEURAL NETWORKS (RPNNS)

Albeit the prevailing of Pi-Sigma Neural Networks which can provide good classification and function approximation results, the network however are not universal approximators due to their utilization of a reduced number of interconnected weights. To evade this drawback, Shin and Ghosh (1995) have formulated Ridge Polynomial Neural Networks (RPNNs); a generalization of PSNNs, and the networks are universal approximator. RPNNs have a well regulated structure which is constructed by adding gradually more complex PSNNs, therefore preserving all the advantages of PSNNs.

A ridge polynomial is a ridge function that can be represented as:

$$\sum_{i=0}^{n}\sum_{j=1}^{m} a_{ij}\left\langle X, W_{ij}\right\rangle^{i} \tag{7}$$

for some $a_{ij} \in \Re$ and $W_{ij} \in \Re$. Any multivariate polynomial can be represented in the form of a ridge polynomial and realized by RPNN (Shin & Ghosh, 1995) whose output is determined according to the following equations:

$$f(x) = \sigma\left(\sum_{i=1}^{N} P_i(x)\right)$$

$$P_i(x) = \prod_{j=1}^{i}\left(\left\langle X, W_j\right\rangle + W_{j0}\right) i = 1,.....,N. \tag{8}$$

where N is the number of PSNN blocks used, σ denotes a suitable nonlinear transfer function, typically the sigmoid transfer function, and $\left\langle X, W\right\rangle$ is the inner product of weights matrix W, and input vector X, such that:

$$\left\langle X, W\right\rangle = \sum_{i=1}^{d} x_i w_i \tag{9}$$

The details on the representation theorem to proof this theorem can be found in (Shin & Ghosh, 1995).

RPNNs can approximate any multivariate continuous functions on a compact set in multi-dimensional input space, with arbitrary degree of accuracy. In contrast to a single layer HONN which uses multivariate polynomials that causes an explosion of weights, RPNNs are efficient in a way that they utilize univariate polynomials which are easy to handle (Shin & Ghosh, 1995) as shown in Figure 2. Similar to the PSNNs, RPNNs have only a single layer of adaptive weights (the dotted line arrows). The structure of RPNNs is highly regular in the sense that Pi-Sigma units can be added incrementally until an appropriate order of the network or the desired low predefined error is achieved without **over-fitting** of the function.

RPNNs provide a natural mechanism for incremental network growth, by which the **number of free parameters** is gradually increased, if need, with the orderly architecture. Unlike other growing networks such as Self-Organizing Neural Networks (SONNs) (Tenorio & Lee, 1990) and Group Method of Data Handling (GMDH) (Ivakhnenko, 1971), in which their structure will grow to

Figure 2. The Ridge Polynomial Neural Network of k-th order. Bias nodes are not shown here for reason of simplicity

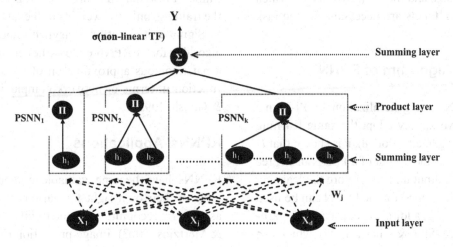

any arbitrary number of hidden layers and nodes, RPNNs have well regulated architecture.

As argued by Nikolaev and Iba (2003), the constructive polynomial networks like GMDH and SONN do not attempt to improve the weights further once the network is built. The reason is that the estimation of the network weights the near input layer is frozen when estimating the weights near the output node layers, and the estimation of weights in near output layer node layers do not influence the weights in near input layers. As a result, the network weights are not sufficiently tuned so that they are in tight interplay with respect to the concrete structure. Oh, Pedrycz, and Park (2003) claimed that GMDH have some drawbacks; it tends to generate quite complex polynomial for relatively simple system, and also tends to produce an overly complex network when it comes to highly nonlinear system.

While more efficient polynomial-based networks may be obtained through incremental growth procedures, it requires extensive pre-processing and data analysis to develop such kind of networks (Ivakhnenko, 1971). The main trade-off is that RPNN does not require extensive preprocessing using training data to come up with the desired structure. In circumstances where the complexity of the problem is not known a priori, the RPNN provides a natural mechanism for incrementally growing a network till it is of appropriate size and the networks decide which **higher order terms** are necessary for the task at hand.

Learning Algorithm of RPNN

Since RPNN is a generalization of Pi-Sigma Neural Network, they adopt the same learning rule. Referring to equation (8), it is shown that P_i is obtainable as the output of a PSNN of degree i with linear output units, therefore the learning algorithms developed for the PSNN can be used for the RPNNs, in addition to constructive learning procedure (Shin & Ghosh, 1995), which can be divided into the following steps:

1. Initialization step: RPNN's order = 1. Assign suitable values for threshold r, learning rate n, *dec_r* and *dec_n*.
2. For all training patterns, do:
   o Calculate actual network output
   o Update the weights asynchronously
3. At the end of each epoch, calculate the error for the current epoch, e_c.
4. If $e_c < e_{th}$ or $t > t_{th}$,
   o Stop the training
5. Else do
   o If $\left|(e_c - e_p)/e_p\right| < r$
     ➢ Add higher order Pi-Sigma unit
     ➢ $r = r * dec\_r$
     ➢ $n = n * dec\_n$
     ➢ $e_p = e_c$
     ➢ order = order + 1
     ➢ $t = t + 1$
     ➢ Go to step 2
   o Else do
     ➢ $t = t + 1$
     ➢ $e_p = e_c$
     ➢ Go to step 2

where e_c is the MSE for the current epoch, and e_p is the MSE for the previous epoch, e_{th} is threshold MSE for the training phase, t is number of training epoch, and t_{th} is threshold epoch to finish the training. Notice that every time a higher order Pi-Sigma unit is added, the weights of the previously trained Pi-Sigma units are kept frozen. During the training, only the weights of the latest added Pi-Sigma unit are attuned asynchronously. The algorithm for the RPNN endows the networks with a parsimonious approximation of an unknown function in terms of network complexity (Shin & Ghosh, 1995).

RPNNs' Applications

RPNNs have become valuable computational tools in their own right for various tasks such as pattern recognition (Voutriaridis, Boutalis, & Mertzios, 2003), image prediction (Liatsis &

Hussain, 1999), function approximation (Shin & Ghosh, 1995; Shin & Ghosh, 1992), time series prediction (Tawfik & Liatsis, 1997), data classification (Shin & Ghosh, 1995), and intelligent control (Karnavas & Papadopoulos, 2004). Liatsis and Hussain (1999) have presented a new 1-D predictor structure for Differential Pulse Code Modulation (DPCM) which utilizes RPNNs. They found that, in the case of 1-D image prediction, the 3rd order RPNNs can achieve high signal to noise ratio compression results. At a transmission rate of 1 bit/pixel, the 1-D RPNNs system provides on average 13 dB improvements in the signal to noise ratio over the standard linear DPCM and a 9 dB improvement when compared to single layer HONNs.

Voutriaridis et al. (2003) examined the capability of RPNNs in pattern recognition and function approximation. They used features from the image block representation of the characters and traditional invariant moments to test the ability of RPNNs as object classifiers. Meanwhile, to examine the powerful of RPNNs as approximators, they tested the networks to a number of multivariable functions. Simulation results demonstrated that RPNNs can give satisfactory results with significantly high recognition rate when used in character recognition and act as reliable approximators when used in function approximation.

The architecture of RPNNs has been tested successfully on a 4-carrier Orthogonal Frequency Division Multiplexing (OFDM) system (Tertois, 2002). The networks were placed in the receiver, and corrected the non-linearities introduced by the transmitter's high-power amplifier. RPNNs in their work have shown good results in simulations and improved the performance of OFDM systems, or keep the same performance with lower power consumption.

RPNNs have also been tested for one step prediction of the Lorenz attractor and solar spot time series (Tawfik & Liatsis, 1997). The work proved that RPNNs have a more regular structure

with a superior performance in terms of speed and efficiency, and shows good generalization capability when compared to Multilayer Perceptron.

Karnavas and Papadopoulos (2004) presented a design of an intelligent type controller using PSNNs and RPNNs concepts for excitation control of a practical power generating system. Both PSNNs and RPNNs controllers demonstrated good performance over a wide range of operating conditions. Both networks offer competitive damping effects on the generator oscillations, with respect to the Fuzzy Logic Excitation Controller (FLC). They also emphasized that the hardware implementation for the proposed PSNNs and RPNNs controllers is easier than that of FLC, and the computational time needed for real time applications is drastically reduced.

FINANCIAL TIME SERIES PREDICTION

Time series prediction is the process of predicting future values from a series of past data extending up to the present. The mapping takes an existing series of data X_{t-n}, ..., X_{t-2}, X_{t-1}, X_t and forecasts the next incoming values of the time series X_{t+1}, X_{t+2}, ... Three noisy financial time series are considered in this chapter, which were obtained from a financial information and prices database provided by Datastream®. The daily time series signals are given in Table 1.

The signals were transformed into 5-day Relative Different Price (RDP) (Thomason, 1999a). The input variables were determined from 4 lagged RDP values based on 5-day periods (RDP-5, RDP-10, RDP-15, and RDP-20) and one transformed signal of Exponential Moving Average (EMA15) which is obtained by subtracting a 15-day exponential moving average from the original signal. The advantage of this transformation is that the distribution of the transformed data will become more symmetrical and will follow more closely to normal distribution. This means that most of the

Table 1. Time series signals used

	Time Series Data	Time Periods	Total
1	US dollar to EURO exchange rate (US/EU)	03/01/2000 to 04/11/2005	1525
2	Japanese yen to EURO exchange rate (JP/EU)	03/01/2000 to 04/11/2005	1525
3	The United States 10-year government bond (CBOT-US)	01/06/1989 to 11/12/1996	1965

Table 2. Calculations for input output variables

	Indicator	Calculations
Input variables	EMA15	$p(i)$ $\overline{EMA_{15}(i)}$ $$EMA_n(i) = \frac{\alpha^0 p_i + \alpha^1 p_{i-1} + \alpha^2 p_{i-2} + ... + \alpha^{n-1} p_{i-n+1}}{\alpha^0 + \alpha^1 + \alpha^2 + ... + \alpha^{n-1}}$$
	RDP-5	$(p(i) - p(i-5))/p(i-5) * 100$
	RDP-10	$(p(i) - p(i-10))/p(i-10) * 100$
	RDP-15	$(p(i) - p(i-15))/p(i-15) * 100$
	RDP-20	$(p(i) - p(i-20))/p(i-20) * 100$
Output variable	RDP+5	$(p(i+5) - p(i))/p(i) * 100$ $$p(i) = \overline{EMA_3(i)}$$

$EMA_n(i)$ is the n-day exponential moving average of the i-th day.
$p(i)$ is the signal of the i-th day.
α is weighting factor

transformed data are close to the average value, while relatively few data tend to one extreme or the other. The calculations for the transformation of input and output variables are presented in Table 2.

As mentioned in (Thomason, 1999a), the optimal length of the moving day is not critical, but it should be longer than the forecasting horizon. Since the use of RDP to transform the original series may remove some useful information embedded in the data, EMA15 was used to retain the information contained in the original data. Smoothing both input and output data by using either simple or exponential moving average is a good approach and can generally enhance the prediction performance (Thomason, 1999b). The

weighting factor, $\alpha=[0,1]$ determines the impact of past returns on the actual volatility. Volatility here means the changeability in asset returns. The larger the value of α, the stronger the impact and the longer the memory. In our work, exponential moving average with weighting factor of $\alpha=0.85$ was experimentally selected.

From the trading aspect, the forecasting horizon should be sufficiently long such that excessive transaction cost resulted from over-trading could be avoided (Cao & Francis, 2003). Meanwhile, from the prediction aspect, the forecasting horizon should be short enough as the persistence of financial time series is of limited duration. Thomason in his work (1999a) suggested that a forecasting horizon of five days is a suitable choice for the

Table 3. Performance Metrics and their Calculations

Metrics	AR	NMSE	SNR
Calculations	$AR = 252 * \dfrac{1}{n} \sum_{i=1}^{n} R_i$ $R_i = \begin{cases} |y_i| & (y_i)(\hat{y}_i) \geq 0 \\ -|y_i| & otherwise \end{cases}$	$NMSE = \dfrac{1}{\sigma^2 n} \sum_{i=1}^{n} \left(y_i - \hat{y}_i \right)^2$ $\sigma^2 = \dfrac{1}{n-1} \sum_{i=1}^{n} (y_i - \bar{y})^2$ $\bar{y} = \sum_{i=1}^{n} y_i$	$SNR = 10 * log_{10} \left(sigma \right)$ $sigma = \dfrac{m^2 n}{SSE}$ $SSE = \sum_{i=1}^{n} (y_i - \hat{y}_i)^2$ $m = max(y_i)$

n is the total number of data patterns, y and $\hat{y}$ represent the actual and predicted output respectively.

daily data. Therefore, in this work, we consider the prediction of a relative difference in percentage of price for the next five business day. The output variable, RDP+5, was obtained by first smoothing the signal with an *n*-day exponential moving average, where *n* is less than 5. The smoothed signal is then presented as a relative difference in percentage of price for five days ahead. Because statistical information of the previous 20 trading days was used for the definition of the input vector, the original series has been transformed and is reduced by 20. The input and output series were subsequently scaled using standard minimum and maximum **normalization method** which then produces a new bounded dataset. One of the reasons for using data scaling is to process outliers, which consist of sample values that occur outside normal range.

PERFORMANCE MEASURES

The main interest in financial time series forecasting is how the networks generate profits. Therefore, it is important to consider the out-of-sample profitability, as well as its forecasting accuracy. The prediction performance of our networks was evaluated using one financial metric, where the objective is to use the networks predictions to make money, and two statistical metrics which are

used to provide accurate tracking of the signals, as shown in Table 3. In order to measure profits generated from the networks predictions, a simple trading strategy is used. If the network predicts a positive change for the next five day RDP, a 'buy' signal is sent, otherwise a 'sell' signal is sent. The ability of the networks as traders was evaluated by the Annualized Return (AR), a real trading measurement which used to test the possible monetary gains and to measure the overall profitability in a year, through the use of the 'buy' and 'sell' signals. The Normalized Mean Squared Error (NMSE) is used to measure the deviation between the actual and the predicted signals. The smaller the value of NMSE, the closer is the predicted signals to the actual signals. The Signal to Noise Ratio (SNR) provides the relative amount of useful information in a signal; as compared to the noise it carries.

RESULTS

For all neural networks, an average performance of 20 trials was used with the respective learning parameters as given in Table 4. These set of parameters were experimentally choose to yield the best performance on out of sample data. Out of sample data is the unseen data that has not yet being used during the training of the networks,

Table 4. The learning parameters used for RPNNs, PSNNs and the MLPs

Neural Networks	Initial Weights	Learning Rate (n)	dec_n	Threshold (r)	dec_r
MLP & PSNN	[-0.5,0.5]	0.1 or 0.05	-	-	-
RPNN	[-0.5,0.5]	[0.1, 0.2]	0.8 or 09	[0.005,0.6]	[0.09,0.1]

Table 5. The best average performance of all neural networks

US/EU exchange rate			
Predictor	MLP-Hidden 3	PSNN-Order 2	RPNN-Order 2
AR (%)	87.88	87.54	88.32
Std of AR	0.2173	0.1455	0.4509
NMSE	0.2375	0.2369	0.2506
SNR (dB)	23.81	23.82	23.58
JP/EU exchange rate			
Predictor	MLP-Hidden 7	PSNN -Order 5	RPNN-Order 4
AR (%)	87.05	87.06	87.48
Std of AR	0.0360	0.0163	0.2447
NMSE	0.2156	0.2133	0.2152
SNR (dB)	27.84	27.89	27.85
CBOT-US government bond			
Predictor	MLP-Hidden 7	PSNN -Order 5	RPNN-Order 5
AR (%)	86.10	86.17	86.60
Std of AR	0.7961	0.3072	0.7146
NMSE	0.2537	0.2515	0.2563
SNR (dB)	25.20	25.23	25.15

and it is reserved for the use of testing. A **sigmoid activation function** was employed and all networks were trained with a maximum of 3000 epochs. MLPs and PSNNs were trained with the incremental backpropagation algorithm (Haykin, 1999), while the RPNNs were trained with the constructive learning algorithm (Shin & Ghosh, 1995). The **higher order terms** of the PSNNs and the RPNNs were selected between 2 to 5.

As we are concerned with financial time series prediction, a primary interest is not to assess the predictive ability of the network models, but more on the profitable value contained in them. Therefore, during generalization, we focus more on how the networks generate the profits, and the neural network structure which endows the highest percentage of AR on unseen data is considered the best model.

Table 5 demonstrates the best average results of 20 simulations obtained on unseen data from all neural networks, in which the HONNS models are benchmarked against the MLPs. In each network, the best average results were chosen from all different network topologies and different learning parameters setting. As it can be noticed, both HONNs models; PSNNs and RPNNs, successfully attained higher profit (AR) compared to the MLPs on all data signals, except for PSNN

Figure 3. The average maximum epoch reached

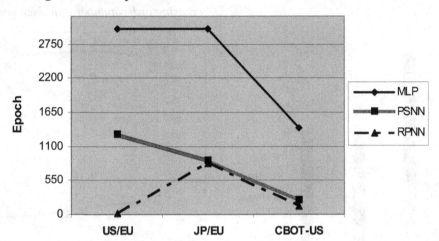

Table 6. CPU time for training the networks

Predictor	MLP	PSNN	RPNN
US/EU	190.23	261.89	7.125
JP/EU	649.61	187.66	63.625
CBOT-US	99.297	33.828	7.297

when used to predict the US/EU signal, where the profit is slightly lower than that of MLP. In terms of SNR, simulation results in each data set demonstrated that very little deviation between the highest average value and the remaining results. The PSNNs have significantly shown to track the signals better than other network models. The overall results given by all network predictors on the amount of meaningful information, with the amount of background noise in the forecast signals suggested that the data sets are highly noisy. Results shown in Table 5 also demonstrated that the NMSE produced by HONNs on average is below 0.26 which is considered to be satisfactory with respect to the high profit return generated by the networks. In general, the average simulation results given in Table 5 demonstrate that PSNNs and RPNNs of order 2 to 5 appeared to have learned the financial time series signals.

The maximum average number of epochs reached for the prediction of all data signals (using all neural network models) are shown in Figure 3. Both HONNs models; PSNNs and RPNNs have revealed to use less number of **training cycles** (epochs) to converge on all data, which is about 2 to 125 times faster than the MLPs. Following the number of epochs, Table 6 shows the results for CPU time taken by each network model during their training. Both HONNs models obviously demonstrated a very quick training when compared to the MLPs, with the exception for PSNN when used to predict the US/EU signal. Apart from attaining the highest average profit return, RPNNs also outperformed the MLPs on the best simulation results when using the annualized return by around 1.38% – 1.69% (see Figure 4). This strongly demonstrated that Ridge Polynomial Neural Networks generate higher

Figure 4. Best simulation result using the Annualized Return

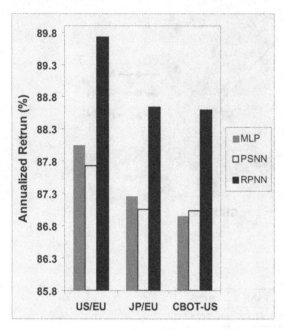

Figure 5. Performance of all networks with increasing order/number of hidden nodes

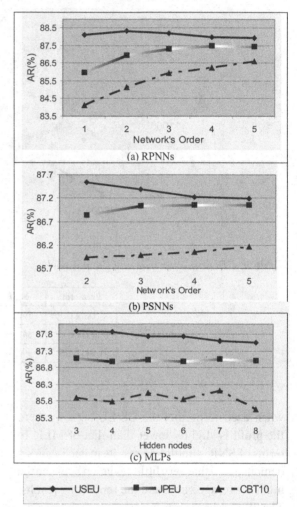

profit returns with fast convergence on various noisy financial signals.

In order to test the modelling capabilities and the stabilities of all network models, Figure 5 illustrates the percentage of Annualized Return from the best average result tested on out-of-sample data when used to predict all the signals. The performance of the networks was evaluated with the number of **higher order terms** increased from 1 to 5 (for HONNs), and number of hidden nodes increased from 3 to 8 (for MLP). The plots in Figure 5(a) and Figure 5(b) indicate that the RPNNs and the PSNNs, respectively, learned the data steadily with the AR continues to increase along with the network growth, except for the US/EU signal in which the value of AR kept decreasing for a higher degree networks. However, for the prediction of JP/EU signal using RPNN, the percentage of AR started to decrease when a 5th order PSNN unit is added to the network. This is probably due to the utilization of large **number of free parameters** for the network

of order three and more has led to unpromising generalization for the input-output mapping of that particular signal. On the other hand, the plot for MLP in Figure 5(c) shows a 'zig-zag' line for both JP/EU and CBOT-US signals, indicating that there is no clear pattern whether the profit is going up or down when we append the number of hidden nodes in the network. Meanwhile, MLP when used to predict the JP/US signal generates a continuously decreasing profit with the increment number of hidden nodes.

Figure 6. Learning curves for RPNNs

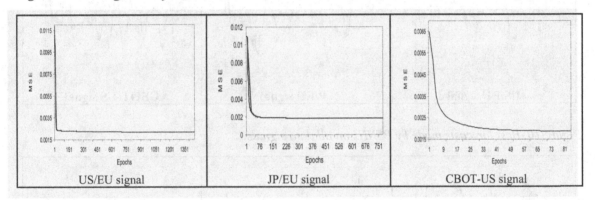

Figure 7. Learning curves for PSNNs

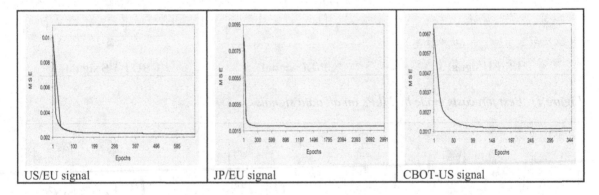

Figure 8. Learning curves for MLPs

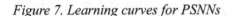

Figure 6 to 8 show the learning curves from the best simulation for the prediction of all signals using all network models. RPNNs (refer Figure 6) have apparently showed the ability to learn the signals very quickly when compared to the PSNNs. In actual fact, the fastest learning using RPNN just required 9 epochs when used to train the CBOT-US signal, and the networks learned the US/EU and JP/EU signals at 46 and 191 epochs, respectively. For all signals, the learning was quite stable and the Mean Squared Error (MSE) continuously decreased every time a Pi-Sigma unit of a higher degree is added to the RPNNs. For PSNNs, the plots in Figure 7 demonstrate that the networks fairly learned the mapping task in a moderately rapid learning, considering all the curves end up at less than 1500 epochs. The quickest learning was when training the CBOT-US signal, which finished off at 84 epochs, followed by the JP/EU and US/EU signals at 775 and 1456 epochs, respectively. In the case MLPs (refer Figure 8), the networks utilized the largest epochs when used to train two out of three signals, namely the JP/EU and CBOT-US signals. When learning the JP/EU signal, the network revealed to reach maximum number of pre-determined epoch of 3000.

Figure 9. Best forecasts made by RPNNs on all data signals

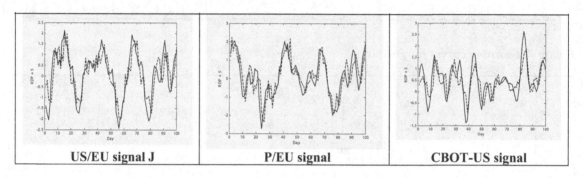

Figure 10. Best forecasts made by PSNNs on all data signals

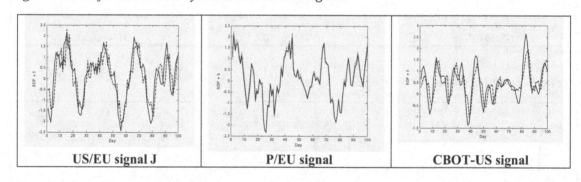

Figure 11. Best forecasts made by MLPs on all data signals

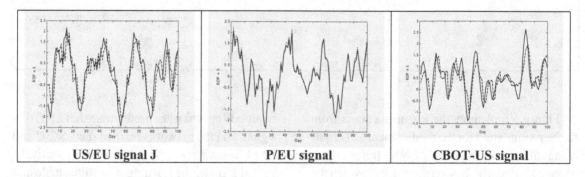

Original signal: ——— *Predicted signal:* - - - - - - -

For purpose of demonstration, the best forecast made by all neural network models on all financial signals is illustrated in Figure 9 to 11. As it can be noticed from Figure 9 to 11, all network models are capable of learning the behaviour of chaotic and highly non-linear financial time series data and they can capture the underlying movements in financial markets. Figure 12 to 14 demonstrate the histograms of the nonlinear prediction errors using all neural network models which indicate that the prediction errors may be approximately modelled as a white Gaussian process. This sug-

Figure 12. Histograms of the signals error using RPNNs

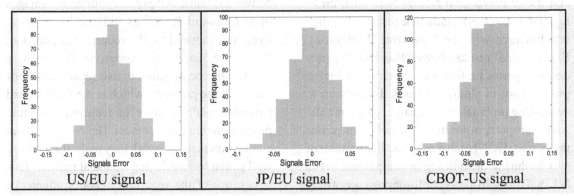

Figure 13. Histograms of the signals error using PSNNs

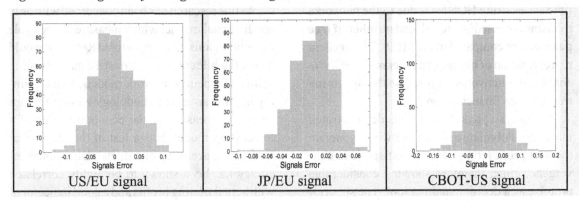

Figure 14. Histograms of the signals error using MLPs

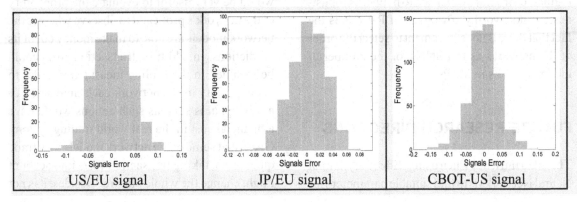

gests that the prediction errors consist of stationary independent samples.

CONCLUSION

This chapter investigates the predictive capability of two HONN models; Pi-Sigma Neural Networks and Ridge Polynomial Neural Networks, on financial time series signals. The results were then benchmarked with the Multilayer Perceptrons. Experimental results showed that HONNs produced superior performance in terms of higher profit return in almost all cases. In addition to generating profitable return value, which is a desirable property in nonlinear financial time series prediction, HONNs also used smaller number of epochs during the training in comparison to the MLPs. This is obviously due to the presence of only a single layer of adaptive weights. The enhanced performance in the prediction of the financial time series using HONNs is due to the networks robustness caused by the reduced **number of free parameters** compared to the MLPs. The prudent representation of **higher order terms** in HONNs enables the networks to forecast the upcoming trends of the financial signals.

The overall predictions results demonstrated that Ridge Polynomial Neural Networks generate the best profit returns with a vast speed in convergence time, therefore showing considerable promise as a decision making tool. The superior performance of RPNNs is attributed to the well regulated structure which led to networks robustness. A noteworthy advantage of RPNNs is the fact that there is no requirement to select the order of the networks as in PSNNs, or the number of hidden units as in MLPs.

FUTURE RESEARCH DIRECTIONS

The main intricacy when using Ridge Polynomial Neural Networks is to find suitable parameters for successively adding a new Pi-Sigma unit in the network. Future research direction could involve the use of genetic programming to automatically generating and finding appropriate parameters used in the training of RPNNs. Another avenue for research will be the investigation on the use of **recurrent links** in the RPNNs. The significant of the new Recurrent Ridge Polynomial Neural Network is that it will explore both the advantages of feedforward RPNN as well as the temporal dynamics induced by the recurrent connection. Prediction using this Recurrent RPNN may involve the construction of two separate components: (1) the predictor which is the feedforward part of the RPNN, and (2) a recurrent layer that provides the temporal context. The use of recurrent connection in the network may make the network well suited to forecasting financial market. This is because of the recurrent network adherence to non-linearity as well as the subtle regularities found in these markets.

As this research has been concerned with only one financial metric, which measure the possible monetary gains, the Annualized Return, it would be worthwhile endeavour to test the market timing ability of a neural network models. Market timing hypothesis is a methodology which provides us with a measure of the economic value of a forecasting model. It is a test of the directional forecasting accuracy of a model. Directional accuracy has been shown to be highly correlated with actual trading profits and a good indicator of the economic value of a forecasting model. This would be very useful to evaluate the probability of the network's profit and to observe whether the network models are able to make money out of its predictions. In addition, transaction costs could be included in the trading measures in order to apply penalty to the network each time a buy or a sell signal is sent, as such actions would have a financial cost in the real world trading system. Given that some of the network models may trade quite often, taking transaction costs into account might change the whole picture. Besides, it is not realistic to account for the success or otherwise of a trading system unless transactions costs are taken into account.

REFERENCES

Artyomov, E. & Pecht, O.Y. (2005) Modified high-order neural network for invariant pattern recognition. *Pattern Recognition Letters, 26,* 843-851.

Cao, L. J. & Francis E. H. T. (2003). Support vector machine with adaptive parameters in financial time series forecasting. *IEEE Transactions on Neural Networks, 14*(6), 1506-1518.

Cass, R. & Radl, B. (1996). Adaptive process optimization using functional-link networks and evolutionary algorithm. *Control Eng. Practice, 4*(11), 1579-1584.

Castiglione, F. (2000). Forecasting price increments using an artificial neural network. *Adv. Complex Systems, 1,* 1-12.

Chan, M.C., Wong, C.C., & Lam, C.C. (2000). *Financial time series forecasting by neural network using conjugate gradient learning algorithm and multiple linear regression weight initialization. department of computing.* The Hong Kong Polytechnic University, Kowloon, Hong Kong.

Chen, A.S., & Leung, M.T. (2005) Performance evaluation of neural network architectures: The case of predicting foreign exchange correlations. *Journal of Forecasting, J. Forecast. 24,* 403-420.

Chen, A.S. & Leung, M.T. (2004). Regression neural network for error correction in foreign exchange forecasting and trading. *Computers & Operations Research, 31,* 1049-1068.

Dunis, C.L. & Huang, X. (2002). Forecasting and trading currency volatility: An application of recurrent neural regression and model combination. *Journal of Forecasting, J. Forecast., 21,* 317-354.

Dunis, C. L. & Williams, M. (2002). Modeling and trading the UER/USD exchange rate: Do neural network models perform better? *Derivatives Use, Trading and Regulation, 8*(3), 211-239.

Durbin, R. & Rumelhart, D. E. (1990). Product units with trainable exponents and multilayer networks. In F. Fogelman Soulie, & J. Herault, (Eds.) *Neurocomputing: Algorithms, architecture and applications* (pp. 15-26). NATO ASI Series, vol. F68, Springer-Verlag.

Durbin, R. & Rumelhart, D. E. (1989). Product units: A computationally powerful and biologically plausible extension to back-propagation networks. *Neural Computation, 1,* 133-142.

Fernandez-Rodriguez, F., Gonzalez-Martel, C., & Sosvilla-Rivero, S. (2000). On the profitability of technical trading rules based on artificial neural networks: Evidence from the Madrid stock market. *Economics Letters, 69,* 89-94.

Franses, P. H. (1998). Forecasting exchange rates using neural networks for technical trading rules. *Studies in Nonlinear Dynamics and Econometrics, 2*(4), 109-114.

Ghosh, J. & Shin, Y. (1992). Efficient higher-order neural networks for function approximation and classification. *Int. J. Neural Systems, 3*(4), 323-350.

Giles, C. L., Griffin, R. D. & Maxwell, T. (1998). Encoding geometric invariances in HONN. *American Institute of Physics,* 310-309.

Giles, C. L. & Maxwell, T. (1987). Learning, invariance and generalization in high-order neural networks. *Applied Optics, 26*(23), 4972-4978.

Gradojevic, N. & Yang, J. (2000). *The application of artificial neural networks to exchange rate forecasting: The role of market microstructure variables.* Working Paper 2000-23. Bank of

Canada, Financial Markets Department, Bank of Canada, Ontario.

Guler, M. & Sahin, E. (1994). A new higher-order binary-input neural unit: Learning and generalizing effectively via using minimal number of monomials. *Third Turkish Symposium on Artificial Intelligence and Neural Networks Proceedings* (pp. 51-60). Middle East Technical University, Ankara, Turkey.

Haykin, S. (1999). *Neural networks: A comprehensive foundation.* Second Edition. Prentice-Hall, Inc.

Hornik, K., Stinchcombe, M. & White, H. (1989). Multilayer feedforward networks are universal approximators. *Neural networks, 2,* 359-366.

Hussain, A., Knowles, A., Lisboa, P., El-Deredy, W, & Al-Jumeily, D. (2006). Polynomial pipelined neural network and its application to financial time series prediction. *Lecture Notes in Artificial Intelligence, 4304,* 597-606.

Hussain, A. J. & Liatsis, P. (2002). Recurrent pi-sigma networks for DPCM image coding. *Neurocomputing, 55,* 363-382.

Ivakhnenko, A. G. (1971). Polynomial theory of complex systems. *IEEE transactions on Systems, Man, and Cybernetics, SMC-1*(4), 364-378.

Karnavas, Y.L. & Papadopoulos, D.P. (2004). Excitation control of a synchronous machine using polynomial neural networks. *Journal of Electrical Engineering, 55*(7-8), 169-179.

Kuan, C. M. & Liu, T. (1995). Forecasting exchange rates using feedforward and recurrent neural networks. *Journal of Applied Economics, 10,* 347-364.

Leerink, L. R., Giles, C. L., Horne, B. G. & Jabri, M. A. (1995). Learning with product units. In G. Tesaro, D. Touretzky, & T. Leen (Eds.), *Advances in Neural Information Processing Systems 7* (pp. 537-544). Cambridge, MA: MIT Press.

Liatsis P., & Hussain A. J. (1999). Nonlinear one-dimensional DPCM image prediction using polynomial neural networks. *In Proc. SPIE: Applications of Artificial Neural Networks in Image Processing IV* (pp. 58-68). San Jose, California.

Minsky, M. & Papert, S. (1969). *Perceptrons.* MIT Press.

Neville, R.S., Stonham, T.J., & Glover, R.J.(2000). Partially pre-calculated weights for the backpropagation learning regime and high accuracy function mapping using continuous input RAM-based sigma-pi nets. *Neural Networks, 13,* 91-110.

Nikolaev N. Y., & Iba, H. (2003). Learning polynomial feedforward neural networks by genetic programming and backpropagation. *IEEE Transactions on Neural Networks, 14*(2), 337-350.

Oh, S. K., Pedrycz, W., & Park, B. J. (2003). Polynomial neural networks architecture: Analysis and design. *Computer and Electrical Engineering, 29,* 703-725.

Pao, Y.H. (1989). *Adaptive pattern recognition and neural networks.* Addison-Wesley, USA.

Park, S., Smith, M.J.T., & Mersereau, R.M. (2000). Target recognition based on directional filter banks and higher-order neural networks. *Digital Signal Processing, 10,* 297-308.

Patra, J.C. & Pal, R.N. (1995). A functional link artificial neural network for adaptive channel equalization. *Signal Processing, 43,* 181-195.

Pau, Y. H & Phillips S. M. (1995). The Functional Link Net and learning optimal control. *Neurocomputing, 9,* 149-164.

Rumelhart, D.E., Hinton, G.E., & Williams, G.E. (1986). Learning internal representations by error propagation. In D. E. Rumelhart & J. L. McClelland (Eds.), *Parallel distributed processing,* vol.1 (pp. 318-362). The MIT Press.

Shachmurove, Y. & Witkowska, D. (2000). *Utilizing artificial neural network model to predict stock markets.* (CARESS Working Paper, Series No. 00-11). University of Pennsylvania, Center for Analytic Research in Economics and the Social Sciences.

Schmitt, M (2001). On the complexity of computing and learning with multiplicative neural networks. *Neural Computation, 14*, 241-301.

Shin, Y. & Ghosh, J. (1995). Ridge Polynomial Networks. *IEEE Transactions on Neural Networks, 6*(3), 610-622.

Shin, Y. & Ghosh, J. (1991a). Realization of boolean functions using binary pi-sigma networks. In Kumara & Shin, (Eds.), *Intelligent engineering systems through artificial neural networks, Dagli* (pp. 205-210). ASME Press.

Shin, Y. & Ghosh, J. (1991b). The pi-sigma networks: an efficient higher-order neural network for pattern classification and function approximation. *Proceedings of International Joint Conference on Neural Networks*, Vol.1, 13-18. Seattle, Washington.

Shin, Y., Ghosh, J. & Samani, D. (1992). Computationally efficient invariant pattern classification with higher-order pi-sigma networks. In Burke and Shin, (Eds.), *Intelligent engineering systems through artificial neural networks-II* (pp. 379-384). ASME Press.

Tawfik, H, & Liatsis, P. (1997). Prediction of non-linear time-series using higher-order neural networks. *Proceeding IWSSIP'97 Conference.* Poznan, Poland.

Tenorio, M.F. & Lee, W.T. (1990). Self-organizing network for optimum supervised learning. *IEEE Transactions on Neural Networks, 1*(1), 100-110.

Tertois, S.,Glaunec, A.L., & Vaucher, G. (2002). Compensating the non linear distortions of an OFDM signal using neural networks. In P. Liatsis (Ed.) *Recent Trends in Multimedia Information*

Processing, Proceedings of IWSSIP'02 (pp. 484-488). World Scientific.

Thomason, M. (1999a). The practitioner method and tools. *Journal of Computational Intelligence in Finance, 7*(3), 36-45.

Thomason, M. (1999b). The practitioner method and tools. *Journal of Computational Intelligence in Finance, 7*(4), 35-45.

Voutriaridis, C., Boutalis, Y. S. & Mertzios, G. (2003). Ridge polynomial networks in pattern recognition. *EC-VIP-MC 2003, 4th EURASIP Conference focused on Video / Image Processing and Multimedia Communications* (pp. 519-524). Croatia.

Wang, Z., Fang, J., & Liu, X. (2006). Global stability of stochastic high-order neural networks with discrete and distributed delays. *Chaos, Solutions and Fractals.* doi:10.1016/j.chaos.2006.06.063

Yao, J., Poh, H. & Jasic, T. (1996). Foreign exchange rates forecasting with neural networks. National University of Singapore Working Paper, in *Proceedings of the International Conference on Neural Information Processing.* Hong Kong.

Yao, J. & Tan, C. L. (2000). A case study on neural networks to perform technical forecasting of forex. *Neurocomputing, 34*, 79-98.

Yumlu, S., Gurgen, F.S., & Okay, N. (2005). A comparison of global, recurrent and smoothed-piecewise neural models for Istanbul stock exchange (ISE) prediction. *Pattern Recognition Letters 26,* 2093-2103.

Zekić, M. (1998). Neural network applications in stock market predictions: A methodology analysis. In Aurer, B., Logažar, R.,& Varaždin (Eds.) *Proceedings of the 9th International Conference on Information and Intelligent Systems '98,* (pp. 255-263).

ADDITIONAL READING

An-Sin, C., & Mark, T.L. (2005). Performance evaluation of neural network architectures: The case of predicting foreign exchange correlations. *Journal of Forecasting, 24*, 403-420.

Atiya, A. (1988). Learning on a general network. In Dana Anderson (Ed.) *Neural information processing systems NIP*S. New York: American Institute of Physics.

Caruana, R.,Lawrence, S. & Giles, L. (2000). Overfitting in neural nets: Backpropagation, conjugate gradient, and early stopping. *Neural Information Processing Systems* (pp. 402-408). Denver, Colorado.

Hellstrom, T. & Holmstrom, K. (1997). *Predicting the stock market.* (Technical report Series IMa-TOM-1997-07). Center of Mathematical Modeling (CMM), Department of Mathematics & Pyhsics, Malardalen University, Sweden.

Henriksson, R.D. & Merton R.C. (1981). On the market timing and investment performance of managed portfolios II: Statistical procedures for evaluating forecasting skills. *Journal of Business, 54*, 513-533.

Ho, S. L., Xie, M. & Goh, T. N. (2002). A comparative study of neural network and Box-Jenkins ARIMA modelling in time series prediction. *Computers & Industrial Engineering, 42*, 371-375.

Husken, M. & Stagge, P. (2003). Recurrent neural networks for time series classification. *Neurocomputing, 50*, 223-235.

Kaastra, I, & Boyd, M. (1996). Designing a neural network for forecasting financial and economic time series. *Neurocomputing, 10*, 215-236.

Kuan, C.M. (1989). *Estimation of neural network models.* PhD Thesis, University of California, San Diego.

Leung, M. T., Chen, A. S., & Daouk, H. (2000). Forecasting exchange rates using general regression neural networks. *Computers & Operations Research, 27*, 1093-1110.

Merton, R.C. (1981). On market timing and investment performance of managed performance I: An equilibrium theory of value for market forecasts. *Journal of Business, 5*, 363-406.

Pesaran, M. H., & Timmermann, A. (2002). Market timing and return prediction under model instability. *Journal of Empirical Finance 9*, 495– 510.

Plummer, E. A. (2000). *Time series forecasting with feed-forward neural networks: Guidelines and limitations.* Master of Science in Computer Science, University of Wyoming. Retrieved March 17, 2006, from http://www.karlbranting. net/papers/plummer/Paper_7_12_00.htm

Robert, E.C., & David, M.M. (1987). Testing for market timing ability: A framework for forecast evaluation. *Journal of Financial Economics, 19*, 169-189.

Schmitt, M. (2001). Product unit neural networks with constant depth and superlinear VC dimension. *Proceedings of the International Conference on Artificial Neural Networks ICANN 2001, Lecture Notes in Computer Science*, vol. 2130, 253-258. Springer-Verlag.

Serdar, Y, Fikret, S. G., & Nesrin, O. (2005). A comparison of global, recurrent and smoothed-piecewise neural models for Istanbul stock exchange (ISE) prediction. *Pattern Recognition Letters, 26*, 2093–2103.

Sitte R. & Sitte, J. (2000). Analysis of the predictive ability of time delay neural networks applied to the S&P 500 time series. *IEEE Transaction on Systems, Man, and Cybernetics-part., 30*(4), 568-572.

Thomason, M. (1998). The practitioner method and tools: A basic neural network-based trading system project revisited (parts 1 & 2). *Journal of Computational Intelligence in Finance*, *6*(1), 43-44.

Walczal, S. (2001). An empirical analysis of data requirements for financial forecasting with neural networks. *Journal of Management Information Systems, Spring, 17*(4), 203–222.

Williams, R.J., & Zipser, D. (1989). A learning algorithm for continually running fully recurrent neural networks. *Neural Computation, 1*, 270-280.

Yao, J. and Tan, C. L. (2000). A case study on neural networks to perform technical forecasting of forex. *Neurocomputing, 34*, 79-98.

Yao, J. & Tan, C. L. (2001). Guidelines for financial forecasting with neural networks. *Proceedings of International Conference on Neural Information Processing* (pp. 757-761). Shanghai, China.

Section III
Artificial Higher Order Neural Networks for Business

Chapter XIII
Electric Load Demand and Electricity Prices Forecasting Using Higher Order Neural Networks Trained by Kalman Filtering

Edgar N. Sanchez
CINVESTAV, Unidad Guadalajara, Mexico

Alma Y. Alanis
CINVESTAV, Unidad Guadalajara, Mexico

Jesús Rico
Universidad Michoacana de San Nicolas de Hidalgo, Mexico

ABSTRACT

In this chapter, we propose the use of Higher Order Neural Networks (HONNs) trained with an extended Kalman filter based algorithm to predict the electric load demand as well as the electricity prices, with beyond a horizon of 24 hours. Due to the chaotic behavior of the electrical markets, it is not advisable to apply the traditional forecasting techniques used for time series; the results presented here confirm that HONNs can very well capture the complexity underlying electric load demand and electricity prices. The proposed neural network model produces very accurate next day predictions and also, prognosticates with very good accuracy, a week-ahead demand and price forecasts.

INTRODUCTION

For most of the twentieth century, when consumers wanted to buy electrical energy, they had no choice. They had to buy it from the utility that held the monopoly for the supply of electricity in the area where these consumers were located. Some of these utilities were vertically integrated, which means that they generated the electrical energy, transmitted it from the power plants to the load centers and distributed it to individual consumers. In other cases, the utility from which consumers purchased electricity was responsible only for its sale and distribution in a local area. This distribution utility in turn had to purchase electrical energy from a generation and transmission utility that had a monopoly over a wider geographical area. In some parts of the world, these utilities were regulated private companies, while in others they were public companies or government agencies. Irrespective of ownership and the level of vertical integration, geographical monopolies were the norm. Thus, for many years, economists thought the electricity industry was a "natural monopoly," because of the great expense of creating transmission networks (Joskow, 1998).

However, during the last two decades, the electric power industry around the world has been undergoing an extensive restructuring process. The critical changes began in 1982, when Chile formalized an electric power reorganization (Rudnick, 1996) followed, several years later, by the United Kingdom (Green & Newbery, 1992), New Zealand, Sweden (Anderson & Bregman, 1995) Norway (Amundsen, Bjorndalen & Rasmussen, 1994), Australia (Brennan & Melanie, 1998) and some important United States jurisdictions such as New York (NYSO) and California (CISO). Before these changes, it was noticed that the industry could be reconstituted into a more competitive framework (Stoft, 2002) because of technological changes in generation. New technologies allowed that small size plants were as efficient as larger plants. Thus, many economists and engineers thought that the distribution and transmission of electrical power may be a natural monopoly because of scale economies but its generation was not.

In this new engineering world, the basic economic characteristics of the electricity chain have been reconceptualized, with differing implications for generation, transmission, and distribution. Some of these activities have been restructured to give rise to new participants such as retailers, system operators and market operators, all with new functions and motivations. To optimize benefits derived from the new markets, the participants must have tools to take the best decisions. One of these tools is no doubt a technique to forecast electricity demand and pricing. Electricity demand forecasting is a task that power systems operators have used for many years since it provides critical information for the operation and planning of the system. In fact, the ability to forecast the long-term demand for electricity is a fundamental prerequisite for the development of a secure and economic power system. Also, demand forecast is used as a basis for system development, and for determining electricity tariffs. More and more, accurate forecasting models of electricity demand are a prerequisite in modern power systems operating in competitive markets. Over estimation of demand may lead to unnecessary investment in transmission and generation assets. In an open and competitive market excess generation will tend to force electricity prices down. However unnecessary infrastructure will impose additional costs on all customers. Under estimation of demand may lead to shortages of supply and infrastructure. In open markets, energy prices would most likely rise in this scenario, while system security would be below standard. Both extremes are undesirable for the electricity industry and the economy of any country as a whole. Thus, it is essential to select an appropriate model which will produce as accurate, robust and understandable a forecast as possible. The method proposed in this chapter has shown to have these characteristics as shown in numerical experiments.

With the opening of electricity markets system and market operators have started to use forecasting not only for electricity demand but also for electricity prices. Forecasting electricity prices has its own challenges; fortunately, the model presented in this chapter has also proven satisfactory for this task. There are many incentives to forecast electricity prices, below some key activities that will benefit from it are described.

The electricity exchanges are a rather new development to provide a platform, on which electricity companies and traders can buy and sell current or future blocs of electricity, in order to correct overproduction or shortage, exploit market imperfections by arbitrage trading, hedge against future changes of electricity prices, and speculate to gain profit from future price changes. Two important opportunities arise from an accurate forecast of electricity market prices: An electricity company can optimize its power production and the state or some infrastructure maintenance company can monitor the electricity price development in order to predict and pre-empt threats to the power supply (Xu, Hsieh, Lu, Bock & Pao, 2004).

Forecasts of electricity demand and prices are of great value for the main electrical market agents: generation companies, consumers and retailers. Generation companies may optimize their benefits if accurate forecast are available. The best mixture of generation fuels can be dispatched when electrical demand is known in advanced. Also, consumers whose peak demand is at least a few hundred kilowatts may be able to save significant amounts of money by employing specialized personnel to forecast their demand and trade in the electricity markets to obtain lower prices. Such consumers can be expected to participate directly and actively in the markets. On the other hand, such active trading is not worthwhile for smaller consumers. These smaller consumers usually prefer purchasing on a tariff, that is, at a constant price per kilowatt-hour that is adjusted at most a few times per year. Electricity retailers are in business to bridge the gap between the wholesale market and these smaller consumers. The challenge for them is that they have to buy energy at a variable price on the wholesale market and sell it at a fixed price at the retail level. A retailer will typically lose money during periods of high prices because the price it has to pay for energy is higher than the price at which it resells this energy. On the other hand, during periods of low prices it makes a profit because its selling price is higher than its purchase price. To stay in business, the quantity-weighted average price at which a retailer purchases electrical energy should therefore be lower than the rate it charges its customers. This is not always easy to achieve because the retailer does not have direct control over the amount of energy that its customers consume.

To reduce its exposure to financial risk associated with the unpredictability of the spot market prices, a retailer therefore tries to forecast as accurately as possible the demand of its customers. It then purchases energy on the various markets to match this forecast. A retailer thus has a strong incentive to understand the consumption patterns of its customers. This is in fact, the use that the authors of this chapter have tried to promote for *higher order recurrent neural networks*.

As has been mentioned before, generation is recognized as the one part of the chain where there are no economies of scale: since small power plants can produce energy at about the same costs as large ones, competition can be introduced. But electrical power is different from other commodities. It cannot appreciably be stored and system stability requires constant balance between supply and demand. This need to produce electric energy on demand entails a form of coordination of the physical operation. This has been the main motivation for the creation of electric pools in competitive, unrestricted generation markets and different frameworks to enable physical bilateral contracts.

BACKGROUND

Power pools are designed e-marketplaces where producers and consumers meet to decide on the price of their product. With this in mind, electric power system is now thought of as the electricity market, and the consumer as the customer. The basic regulatory philosophy no longer is "protection for public utilities that provide an electric service with determined costs," but rather, "competition among firms that offer a commodity with resultant prices." In short, economic and business matters can take priority over technical ones.

In the pool, the power exchange (PX), power producers (GENCOs) submit generation bids and their corresponding bidding prices, and cosumers (consumption companies CONCOs) do the same with consumption bids. The market operator (MO) uses a market clearing tool to then clear the market. The tool is normally based on single round auctions (Sheblé, 1999), and considers the hours of the market horizon (24 hours) one at a time. Therefore, one of the many ramifications resulting from this change has been an increase in the importance of modeling and forecasting electricity prices. An accurate price forecast for an electricity spot market has a definitive impact on the bidding strategies by producers or costumers, or in the negotiation of a bilateral contract. A precursor for reliable valuation of electricity contracts is an accurate description of the underlying price process.

Under regulation, electricity prices are set by state public utility commissions (PUC's) in order to curb market power and ensure the solvency of the firm. Price variation is minimal and under the strict control of regulators, who determine prices largely on the basis of average costs. This setting focuses the utility industry's attention on demand forecasting, as prices are held constant between PUC hearings. Market entry is barred and investment in new generation by incumbent firms is largely based on demand forecasts. In addition, there is little need for hedging electricity

price risk because of the deterministic nature of prices. Therefore, developing predictive models for electrical markets is a relatively new area of application for the forecasting profession. This task has become particularly relevant with the beginning of deregulation.

The facts that electricity is an instantaneous product and that most users of electricity are, on short time scales, unaware or indifferent to its price drive extreme price volatility and make electricity price forecasting a very challenging task. The stochastic properties of power prices are now becoming well recognized as spiky, mean-reverting with extraordinary volatilities (Davison, Anderson, Marcus & Anderson, 2002). Conventional models from financial econometrics, therefore, are generally unsatisfactory in capturing the characteristics of spot prices. Dynamical characteristics such as those mentioned before are absent in load demand, where a significant amount of literature has emerged. Models widely used for load forecasting must be carefully evaluated before they are utilized for price prediction.

Hence, the question of how best to model spot electricity prices remains open (EPRI, 2005). Several models have been put forward for electricity price forecasting, Auto Regressive Integrated Moving Average (ARIMA) have been used with good result (Contreras, Espinola, Nogales & Conejo, 2003). Simpler autoregressive models (ARMA models) have been also used elsewhere (Fosso, Gjelvik & Haugstad, 1999) and in (Nogales, Contreras, Conejo & Espinola, 2002) approaches based on time series analysis are successfully applied in next day price forecasts. In addition stochastic models of price, as in (Skantze, Ilic & Capman, 2000), are also competing in order to predict daily or average weekly prices.

Techniques based on Artificial *Neural Networks* (ANN) are specifically effective in the solution of high complexity problems for which traditional mathematical models are difficult to build. For instance, it is well established that feedforward neural networks can approximate nonlinear functions to a desired accuracy. This attribute has made many researchers use them to model dynamic systems. Problems of electricity price forecasting also fall into this category. ANNs have already been used to solve problems of load forecasting (Sanchez, Alanis & Rico, 2004) and they are now being used for price prediction, in particular (Szkuta, Sanabria and Dillon, 1999) used a three-layered ANN paradigm with back-propagation. However, static neural networks such as this suffer from many limitations (Gupta & Rao, 1994).

This chapter focuses on the electric load demand and price forecast of a daily electricity market using HONNs. Such neural networks are known as dynamic or recurrent and offer computational advantages over purely static neural networks; for instance, a lower number of units are required to approximate functions with the similar accuracy provided by static neural networks. In this chapter, HONNs accurately forecast for electric load demand and prices in the electricity markets of Spain (OMEL, 1999), Australia (NEMCO, 2000) and California (CISO, 2000).

Due to their nonlinear modeling characteristics, neural networks have been successfully applied in pattern classification, pattern recognition, and *time series forecasting* problems. In this chapter, we will introduce HONNs to forecasting problems. There are many works that use artificial *neural networks* to predict time series in electric markets (EPRI, 2004; Nogales, et al., 2002; Sanchez, et al., 2004), for one hour ahead or half an hour ahead, but with the HONNs proposed here is possible to expand the horizon of forecasting.

The best-known training approach for RNN is backpropagation through time learning (Werbos, 1990). However, it is merely a first-order gradient descent method and hence its learning speed is very slow. Recently, some *extended Kalman filter* (EKF) based algorithms have been introduced to the *training* of neural networks (Singhal & Wu, 1989). With an EKF-based algorithm, the learning convergence can be improved. Over the

past decade, the EKF-based training of *neural networks*, both feedforward and recurrent ones, has proved to be reliable and practical for many applications (Williams & Zipser, 1989).

In this chapter, we propose the use of HONNs trained with an EKF-based algorithm to predict the next day electric load demand as well the electricity prices with an horizon of 24 hours, at least. The results presented here confirm that HONNs can very well capture the complexity underlying electricity prices. The model may produce very accurate next day prediction, and also supports, with very good accuracy, a week-ahead demand and price forecasts.

MAIN THRUST OF THE CHAPTER

Issues, Controversies, Problems

Time series prediction in electric markets is a relatively new procedure. Market clearing prices and electric load demand are public information that have made available only until recently by some market operators in the internet. Not until substantial historical data has been accumulated will the salient features of these time series are becoming to be understood. In this work public information from the day-ahead pool of main land Spain (OMEL), (OMEL, 1990) and from the California Independent System Operator (CISO), (CISO, 2000) was used. Time series exhibit similar qualitative behavior in these markets.

Most spot markets for electricity are defined on hourly intervals and some are defined on half-hourly such as the British market or the Australian market, (NEMCO, 2000). It is clear that throughout the day and throughout the year, the time series in electricity markets are different at different times. Furthermore, when one looks at a comparison of demand and electricity price time series it is possible to see that price series exhibit much greater complexity than might initially be expected from activity of scheduling different plant to meet fluctuations in demand. In Figure 1, a typical demand evolution is shown for 24 hours (CISO, 2000) and this should be compared with atypical electricity prices (OMEL, 1999). It is clear that electricity spot prices display a rich structure and the much more complicated than a simple functional scaling of demand to reflect the marginal costs of generation. Tools for predicting time series in electricity markets must take into account these differences and the underlying properties that caused them.

The crucial feature of this time series formation in wholesale electricity spot markets is the instantaneous nature of the product. The physical laws that determine the delivery of power across a transmission grid require a synchronized energy balance between the injection of power at generating points and the off take at demand points plus some allowance of transmission and distribution losses. Across the electric network, production and consumption are perfectly synchronized without any significant capability for electricity storage. If the two get out of balance, even for a moment, both frequency and voltage will fluctuate with serious consequences for the power system and their users. Furthermore, end users treat the product electricity as a service at their convenience; this will cause very little

short term elasticity of demand to price. Under this scenario, the task of the grid operator is to be continuously monitoring the demand process and to call on those generators who have technically capability and capacity to respond quickly to the fluctuations in demand at almost any price.

A salient feature of this time series that has been highlighted by some commentators (Gupta & Rao, 1994) is the presence of *chaotic behavior*. Chaotic behavior in electricity time series has very important consequences. The hallmark of a chaotic process is sensitivity to initial conditions, which means that if the starting point of motion is perturbed by a very small increment, the deviation in the resulting waveform, compared to the original waveform, increases exponentially with time. Consequently, unlike an ordinary deterministic process, a chaotic process is predictable only in the short term. Long term forecasting is impossible because the phase space trajectories that initially have nearly identical states separate from each other at an exponentially fast rate. This fact, in principle, explains the rather modest performance achieved by conventional econometric models; linear time series prediction techniques lack predictive power in this case. Commonly, dynamical systems such as *neural networks* with

Figure 1. Typical demand and prices evolution for 24 hours

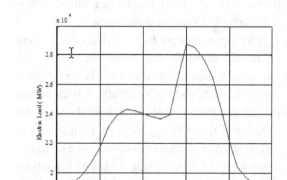
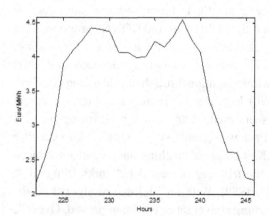

feedback structures are used to model chaotic systems (OMEL, 1999).

The distinction between ordered and chaotic motion in dynamical systems is fundamental in many areas of applied sciences. In the prediction of electricity time series, detection of *chaotic behavior* determines selection of the predicting tools. However, this distinction is particularly difficult in systems with many degrees of freedom, basically because it is not feasible to visualize their phase space. Many methods have been developed over the years trying to give an answer to this problem. The inspection of the successive intersections of an orbit with a Poincaré surface of section (PSS) (Joskow, 1998) has been used mainly for 2 dimensional (2d) maps and Hamiltonian systems. One of the most common methods of chaos detection is computation of the maximal Lyapunov Characteristic Number (Werbos, 1990). Chaos Data Analyzer (CDA) is a software package that provides different methods to detect chaos in time series. Computation of Lyapunov exponents is one of the main features of CDA that was utilized, in this work, for chaos detection in electricity spot prices. Positive Lyapunov exponents were detected in both electric power and electricity spot prices which confirmed the presence of *chaotic behavior* in electricity markets. With the use of CDA, it was also possible to confirm richer structure in prices than in electric power time series. Larger Lyapunov exponents were calculated for electricity time series.

The goal of *time series prediction* or forecasting can be stated succinctly as follows: given a sequence $y(1),...,y(N)$ up to time N, find the continuation $y(N+1),...,y(N+M)$ up to time M. The series may arise from sampling of a continuous time system and be either stochastic or deterministic in origin.

The standard prediction approach involves constructing an underlying model which gives rise to the observed sequence. In the conventional and most studied method, which dates back to

(Yule, 1927), a linear autoregression (AR) is fit to the data:

$$y(k) = \sum_{n=1}^{T} a(n)y(k-n) + e(k) = \hat{y}(k) + e(k)$$

$$(1)$$

This AR model forms $y(k)$ as a weighted sum of past values of the sequence. The single step prediction for $y(k)$ is given by $\hat{y}(k)$. The error term $e(k) = y(k) - \hat{y}(k)$ is often assumed to be white noise process for analysis in a stochastic framework.

More modern techniques employ nonlinear prediction schemes. In this chapter, a specialized neural network is used to extend the linear model in Equation (1). The basic form $y(k) = \hat{y}(k) + e(k)$ is retained; however, the estimate $\hat{y}(k)$ is taken as the output $\mathbb{N}$ of a neural network driven by past values of the sequence. This is written as:

$$y(k) = \hat{y}(k) + e(k) = \mathbb{N}(\hat{y}(k-1),...,\hat{y}(k-T)) + e(k)$$

$$(2)$$

Notice that model in Equation (2) is applicable for both scalar and vector sequences.

In contrast to linear regression, the use of nonlinear regression is motivated by Takens' Theorem (Skantze, et al., 2000). When Takens' Theorem holds, there is a diffeomorphism (one-to-one differential mapping) between the delay reconstruction:

$$[y(k-1),y(k-2),...,y(k-T)] \qquad (3)$$

and the underlying state space of the dynamic system which give rise to the time series. Thus, there exists, in theory, a nonlinear autoregression of the form:

$$\hat{y}(k) = g[\hat{y}(k-1), \hat{y}(k-2),...,\hat{y}(k-T)] \qquad (4)$$

which models the series exactly in absence of noise. In this context, *neural networks* are used to approximate the ideal function $g(\cdot)$. Furthermore, it is very well known that any neural network $\mathbb{N}$ with an arbitrary number of neurons is capable of approximating any uniformly continuous function (Hornik, 1991). These arguments provide the basic motivation for the use of neural networks for electricity prices and load demand.

Solutions and Recommendations

Due to their nonlinear modeling characteristics, neural networks have been successfully applied in pattern classification, pattern recognition, and *time series forecasting* problems. In this section, we will introduce an ANN to forecasting problems. There are many works that use ANN to predict prices and load demand for one hour ahead or half an hour ahead, but with the ANN proposed here is possible to expand the horizon of forecasting, even to five days.

Architecture

As it has been mentioned before, application *of neural networks* to time series representing electricity time series is not new. In this chapter, however, we focus on a special structure, the HONNs, which widens the focus to also include black-box modeling of nonlinear dynamic systems. The problem of selecting model structures becomes increasingly difficult. The most used *neural networks* structures are: *Feedforward* and *Recurrent*. The latter offers a better suited tool to model and control nonlinear systems. Since the seminal paper (Narendra & Parthasarathy, 1990) there has been continuously increasing interest in applying neural

networks to identification and control of nonlinear systems, specially *higher order neural networks* due to their excellent approximation capabilities, using few units, compared to first order ones which makes them flexible and robust when faced with new and/or noisy data patterns (Gosh & Shin, 1992). Besides, *Higher Order Neural Networks* perform better than the Multilayer First Order ones using a small number of free parameters (Rovitakis & Chistodoulou, 1990). Furthermore, several authors have demonstrated the feasibility of using these *architectures* in applications such as system identification and control (Rovitakis & Chistodoulou, 1990; Sanchez & Ricalde, 2003 and references therein); therefore, it is natural to bring up HONNs. By making this choice, model structure selection is basically reduced to: (1) Selecting the inputs to the network and (2) Selecting an internal network *architecture* (i.e. number of hidden units, number of *higher order terms*).

A common practice is to use the structures from the linear models while letting the internal *architecture* be an ANN. Depending on the choice of regression vector, different nonlinear model structures emerge. In this case the model structure uses is named NNOE as the acronym for Neural Network OE, because the input vector for the ANN is selected like the regression vector of an Output Error linear model structure (OE) or parallel (Sanchez, Alanis & Rico, 2004). This structure allows us to find the continuation $\hat{y}(N+1), \ldots, \hat{y}(N+M)$ up to time M after *training* with the sequence $\hat{y}(1), \ldots, \hat{y}(N)$ up to time N; where $\hat{y}(\cdot)$ is the prediction of the real value of $y(\cdot)$. The network, used in this work contains *higher order units* only in the hidden layer; the output layer

Equation (5).

$$\sigma_j(x) = S\left[w_j^{(0)} + \sum_{i_1=1}^{d} w_{ji_1}^{(1)} x_{i_1} + \sum_{i_1=1}^{d}\sum_{i_2=1}^{d} w_{ji_1i_2}^{(2)} x_{i_1} x_{i_2} + \sum_{i_1=1}^{d}\sum_{i_2=1}^{d}\sum_{i_3=1}^{d} w_{ji_1i_2i_3}^{(3)} x_{i_1} x_{i_2} x_{i_3} + \cdots \right]$$

$$\hat{y}(x) = \sum_{j=0}^{m} w_j \sigma_j(x)$$

contains linear units. Thus for *d* input variables, we could consider a *higher order polynomial neural network*, which can be represented by Equation (5), where *m* is the number of hidden units, $\sigma_0(x) = 1$ and $S(\bullet)$ is a sigmoid function. The higher-order *weights* capture higher-order correlations. A unit which includes terms up to and including degree *l* will be called a *l*-th order unit (Bishop, 2000).

The input vector for the HONN depicted in Figure 2 is constructed as in (6) and this vector is the regression vector of a linear model structure OE, because of the name of NNOE.

$$\phi = \left[\hat{y}(k-1), \cdots, \hat{y}(k-d), u_i(k), \cdots, u_p(k) \right]^T \tag{6}$$

The use of the structure (5) has several attractive advantage, for example: (1) It is a natural extension of the well-known linear model structures; (2) The internal *architecture* can be expanded gradually as higher flexibility is need to model

more complex nonlinear relationships; and (3) the structural decisions required by the user are reduced to a level that is reasonable to handle.

Training

In this chapter we propose a *Kalman Filter*-based method to update the *connecting weights* during *training*. With the two kind of *weights*: hidden and output, we construct a weight vector *w*. Kalman filtering (KF) estimates the state of a linear system with additive state and output white noise. Before using the Kalman filter *training*, it is necessary to consider the equations which serve as the basis for the derivation of the EKF *training* algorithm. A neural network behavior can be described by the following nonlinear discrete-time system:

$$w(k + 1) = w(k) + \omega(k) \tag{7}$$

$$y(k) = h\big(w(k), u(k), v(k), k\big) + v(k) \tag{8}$$

Figure 2. Neural network structure

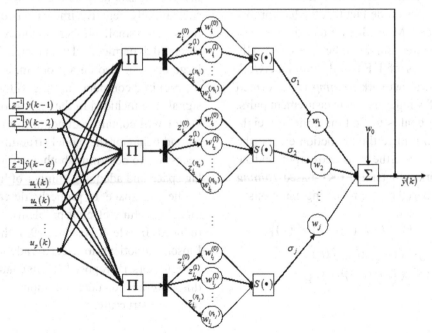

Equation (7) is known as the process equation; it only specifies that the state of the ideal neural network is characterized as a linear process corrupted by process noise $\omega(k)$, where the state of the system is given by the neural network *weights* $w(k)$. On the other hand, equation (8) is known as the observation or measurement equation, representing the network desired response $y(k)$ as a nonlinear function of the input vector $u(k)$, the weight parameter vector $w(k)$ and, for recurrent networks, the recurrent node activations $v(k)$; this equation is augmented by random measurement noise $v(k)$. The measurement noise $v(k)$ is typically characterized as zero-mean, white noise with covariance given by $E\left[v(k)v^T(l)\right]=\delta_{k,l}R(k)$. Similarly, the process noise $\omega(k)$ is also characterized as zero-mean, white noise with covariance given by $E\left[\omega(k)\omega^T(l)\right]=\delta_{k,l}Q(k)$ (Haykin, 2001).

For KF-based neural network *training*, the network *weights* become the states to be estimated, with the error between the neural network and the desired output being considered as additive white noise. Due to the fact that the neural network mapping is nonlinear, an EKF-type of algorithm is required.

Interest in using a KF-based neural network *training* emerges of the fact that the backpropagation, the least-Mean-Square and the steepest descent methods, among others, are actually particular forms of KF-based neural network *training*. Neural network *training* is performed using a set of N input-output measurement pairs. The *training* goal is to find the optimal weight values that minimize the prediction errors (the differences between the measured outputs and the neural network outputs). The EKF-based *training* algorithm is based on the following equations:

$$K(k)=P(k)H^T(k)\left[R+H(k)P(k)H^T(k)\right]^{-1}$$
$$w(k+1)=w(k)+K(k)\left[y(k)-\hat{y}(k)\right]$$
$$P(k+1)=P(k)-K(k)H(k)P(k)+Q \qquad (9)$$

where $P\in\Re^{LxL}$ and $P(k+1)\in\Re^{LxL}$ are the prediction error covariance matrices at steps k and $k+1$, respectively; $w\in\Re^L$ is the weight (state) vector; L is the total number of neural network *weights*; $y\in\Re^m$ is the measured output vector; $\hat{y}\in\Re^m$ is the network output; m is the total number of outputs, $K\in\Re^{Lxm}$ is the Kalman gain matrix; $Q\in\Re^{LxL}$ is the state noise covariance matrix; $R\in\Re^{mxm}$ is the measurement noise covariance matrix; $H\in\Re^{mxL}$ is a matrix, in which each entry is the derivative of one of the neural network output, $(\hat{y}_i)$, with respect to one neural network weight, (w_j), as follows:

$$H_{ij}(k)=\left[\frac{\partial\hat{y}_i(k)}{\partial w_j(k)}\right]_{w(k)=\hat{w}(K+1)} , i=1\cdots m,\ j=1\cdots L$$
$$(10)$$

Usually P, Q and R are initialized as diagonal matrices, with entries P_0, Q_0 and R_0, respectively.

Data Treatment

A wrong choice of lag space, i.e., the number of delayed signals used as regressors, may have a substantially negative impact on some applications. A too small number obviously implies that essential dynamics will not be modeled but a too large one can also be a problem, especially for the required computation time. If too many past signals are included in the regression vector the vector will contain redundant information. For a good behavior the model structure selected is necessary to determine both a sufficiently large lag space and adequate number of hidden units. If the lag space is properly determined, the model structure selection problem is substantially reduced. In (He & Asada, 1993), the use of the Lipschitz quotients to select the adequate number of regressors, is proposed. In this chapter we adopt this criterion for determination of the optimal regressor structure.

Time series in electric power systems are characterized by the presence of some cycles. In particular, a daily cycle and a weekly cycle (He & Asada, 1993), as a result of people's rhythm of life and economical periodical changes. In light of that we propose the introduction of two external inputs that represents these two characteristics, in order to improve the performance of the network.

RESULTS OF SIMULATION

In this section we present the results of using the HONN depicted in Figure 2 with the algorithm presented above to predict electrical load demand and electrical power spot prices, respectively. As study cases in this chapter, HONNs accurate *forecast time series* in the electricity markets of California and Spain, respectively.

Application for Electricity Load Demand

The goal of this section is to implement a neural network predictor for electricity load demand, on the basis of *Kalman filter training*. This predictor is developed using data from the State of California, USA (CISO, 2000). Figure 3 presents the

Figure 3. State of California electric load demand

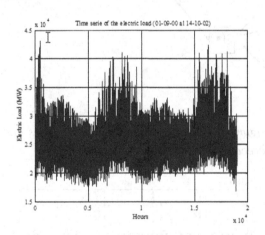

Figure 4. Electric load demand for a typical day

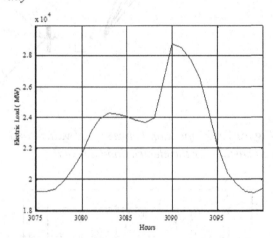

Figure 5. Electric load demand for a typical week

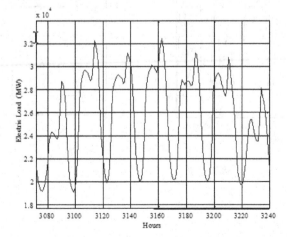

Figure 6. Neural network structure used to predict electric load demand.

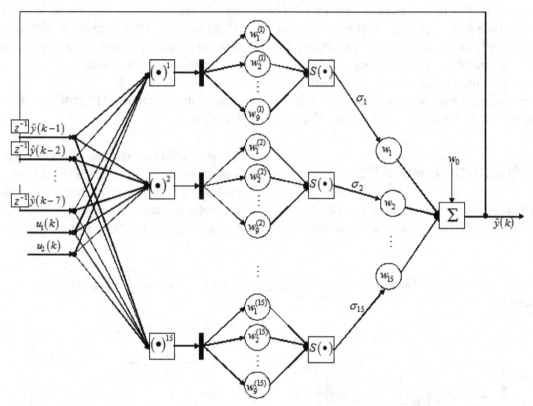

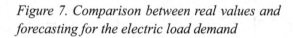

Figure 7. Comparison between real values and forecasting for the electric load demand

Figure 8. Comparison between real values and forecasting for the electric load demand

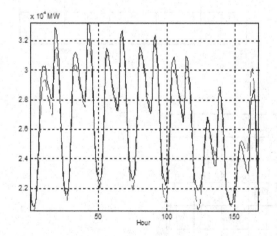

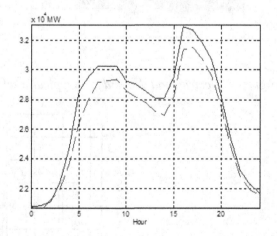

data corresponding to a time lapse of 26 months; Figure 4 and Figure 5 display a typical day and a typical week, respectively.

The neural network used is a HONN, whose structure is presented in Figure 6; the hidden layer has 15 *higher order units*, with logistic activation functions, and the output layer is composed of just one neuron, with a linear activation function. The initial values for the covariance matrices (R, Q, P) are $R_0 = Q_0 = P_0 = 10000$. The length of the regression vector is 7 because that is the order of the system, which was found with an algorithm based on the Lipschitz quotient, and is necessary to add two external signals corresponding to the day and the hour ($u_1(k)$, $u_2(k)$).

The *training* is performed off-line, using a series-parallel configuration; for this case the delayed outputs are taken from the electric load demand. The specified target prediction error is 1×10^{-5}. Once the neural network is trained, its prediction capabilities are tested, with fixed *weights*, using a parallel configuration, with delayed output taken from the neural network output.

The results are presented in Figure 7, Figure 8 and Figure 9, for a week prediction, a prediction of 24 hours and the LMS error, respectively. It is important to remark that the prediction data are different from the *training* data.

Application for Electricity Price

The goal of this section is to implement a neural network predictor for electricity prices, on the basis of *Kalman filter training*. This predictor is developed using data from the Spanish market (OMEL, 1999). Figure 10 presents the data corresponding to September 1999; Figure 11 and Figure 12 display a typical day and a typical week, respectively.

The neural network used is a HONN, whose structure is presented in Figure 13; the hidden layer has 25 *higher order units*, with logistic activation functions, and the output layer is composed of just one neuron, with a linear activation function. The initial values for the covariance matrices (R, Q, P) are $R_0 = Q_0 = P_0 = 10000$. The length of the regression vector is 10 because that is the order of the system, which was found with an algorithm based on the Lipschitz quotient, and is necessary to add two external signals, corresponding to the day and the hour ($u_1(k)$, $u_2(k)$).

The *training* is performed off-line, using a series-parallel configuration; for this case the

Figure 9. Performance of the LMS during the training

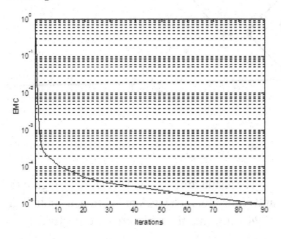

Figure 10. Electricity prices in the Spanish market

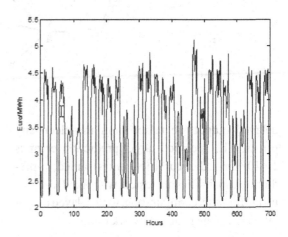

Figure 11. Electricity prices for a typical day

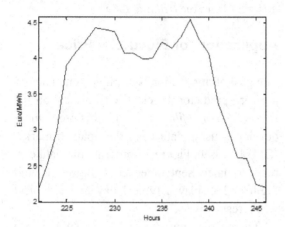

Figure 12. Electricity prices for a typical week

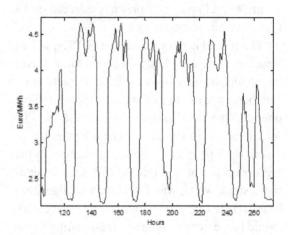

Figure 13. Neural network structure used to predict electricity prices

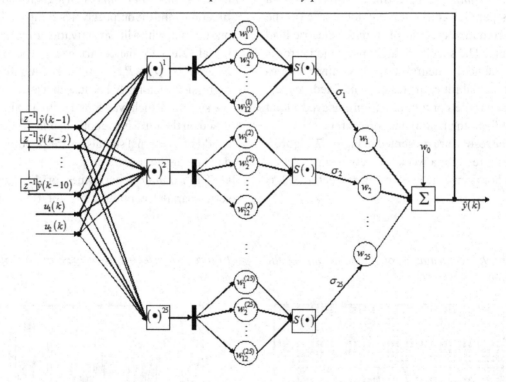

delayed output are taken from the electricity prices. The specified target prediction error is 1×10^{-5}. Once the neural network is trained, its prediction capabilities are tested, with fixed *weights*; using a parallel configuration, with delayed output taken from the neural network output.

The results are presented in Figure 14, Figure 15 and Figure 16, for a week prediction, a prediction of 24 hours and the LMS error, respectively.

Figure 14. Comparison between real values and forecasting electricity price.

Figure 15. Comparison between real price and forecasting price

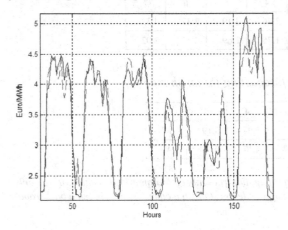

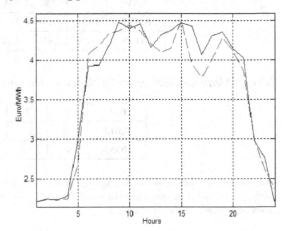

Figure 16. Performance of the LMS during the training

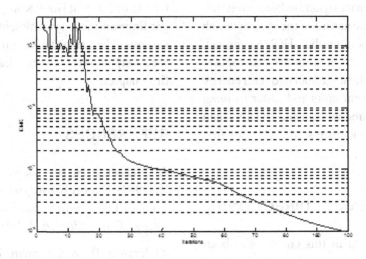

Comparative Analysis

In a previous work (Sanchez, et al., 2004) the same study cases were analyzed, using a Recurrent Multilayer Perceptron RMLP, with the same number of neurons, trained using the same learning algorithm. There, the prediction error reached was 1×10^{-4} in 100 and 125 iterations respectively for electricity load demand and prices; with similar number of iterations, it is possible to reach a prediction error of 1×10^{-5} and as it can be seen

in Table 1 and Table 2, the mean absolute error is significant is reduced.

CONCLUSION

This chapter proposes the use of HONNs to predict hourly prices and load demand in electricity markets under deregulation with good results as shown by the daily mean errors. Daily mean errors are well below 5%, a value that compares very well with approaches found in the literature.

Table 1. Mean absolute error for the load demand forecasting (Californian market)

DAY	1	2	3	4	5	6	7
RMLP	3.10	3.28	3.67	3.46	3.19	3.47	4.32
HONN	1.51	1.97	1.34	1.75	2.69	2.47	3.02

Table 2. Mean absolute error for the electricity price forecasting (Spanish market)

DAY	1	2	3	4	5	6
RMLP	2.80	2.83	2.92	2.97	3.19	2.87
HONN	1.56	2.19	1.77	4.17	2.34	2.41

When training the neural network, proposed above, with a backpropagation (Levenberg-Marquardt) algorithm, it was only possible to predict three hours in advance at the most. Thus, it is impossible to establish a comparison between a backpropagation algorithm and the proposed one.

With more compact structure but taking into account the dynamic nature of the system which behavior one wants to predict, HONNs proved, in our experiments, to be a model that capture very well the complexity associated with energy markets. Fewer neural units and faster *training* processes are required when using HONNs than in applications considering static ANN, or first order ones.

FUTURE RESEARCH DIRECTIONS

The model presented in this chapter has been validated on important electricity markets and will be, in the future, used to predict prices for different electricity industries such as that of Mexico.

Another future research direction is to include a state space model for the time series in electricity markets.

ACKNOWLEDGMENT

The authors thank the support of CONACYT, Mexico, on project 39866Y. They also thank the useful discussions with Professor Guanrong Chen, City University of Hong Kong, P. R. of China, regarding nonlinear dynamics, in particular chaotic systems. They also thank the useful comments of the anonymous reviewers, which help to improve this chapter.

REFERENCES

Amundsen, E. S., Bjorndalen, J., & Rasmussen, H. (1994). Export Norwegian hydropower under common European regime of environmental taxes. *Energy Economics, 16*, 271-280.

Andersson, B., & Bregman, L. (1995). Market structure and the price of electricity: An ex ante analysis of the deregulated Swedish electricity market. *Energy Journal, 16*, 97-105.

Bishop, C. M. (2000). *Neural network for pattern recognition*. Oxford, University Press.

Brennan, D., & Melanie, J. (1998). Market powering the Australian power market. *Energy Economics, 20*, 121-133.

California Independent System Operator (2000). From http://www.caliso.com, 2000.

Contreras, J., Espínola, R., Nogales, F. J., & Conejo, A. J. (2003). ARIMA models to predict next-day electricity prices. *IEEE Transactions on Power Systems, 18*(3), 1014-1020.

Davison, M., Anderson, C. L., Marcus, B., & Anderson, K. (2002). Development of a hybrid model for electricity power spot prices. *IEEE Transactions on Power Systems, 17*(2), 257-264.

EPRI destinations (2004). From http://www.epri.com/destinations/d5foc.aspx

Fosso, O. B., Gjelvik, A., Haugstad, A., Birger, M., & Wangensteen, I. (1999). Generation scheduling in a deregulated system: The Norwegian case. *IEEE Transactions on Power Systems, 14*(1), 75-81.

Ghosh, J., & Shin, Y. (1992). Efficient high-order neural networks for classification and function approximation. *International Journal of Neural Systems, 3*(4), 323-350.

Green, R. J., & Newbery, D.M. (1992). Competition in the British electricity spot market. *Journal of Political Economics, 100*, 929-953.

Gupta, M. M., & Rao, D. H. (1994). *Neuro-control systems: Theory and applications*. IEEE Press.

Haykin, S. (2001). *Kalman filtering and neural networks*. New Jersey, USA: Wiley.

He, X., & Asada, H. (1993). *A new method for identifying orders of input-output models for nonlinear dynamical systems*. Paper presented at the IEEE American Control Conference, San Francisco, California, USA.

Hornik, K. (1991). Approximation capabilities of multilayer feedforward networks. *Neural Networks, 4*(2), 251-257.

Joskow, P. J. (1998). Electricity sectors in transition. *Energy Journal, 19*, 25-52.

Rudnick, H. (1996). Pioneering electricity reform in South America. *IEEE Spectrum, 33*, 38-44.

Narendra, K. S., & Parthasarathy, K. (1990). Identification and control of dynamical systems using neural networks. *IEEE Transactions on Neural Networks, 1*(2), 4-27.

National electricity market management (2000). From http://www.nemco.com.au

New York Independent System Operator (2000). From http://www.nyiso.com

Nogales, F. J., Contreras, J., Conejo, A., & Espínola, R. (2002). Forecasting next day electricity prices by time series models. *IEEE Transactions on Power Systems, 17*(2), 342-348.

Operador del Mercado Eléctrico (1999). From http://www.omel.es

Rovithakis, G. A., & Chistodoulou, M. A. (2000). Adaptive control with recurrent high-order neural networks. New York: Springer Verlag.

Sanchez, E. N., Alanis, A. Y., & Rico, J. J., (2004). *Electric load demand prediction using neural networks trained by Kalman filtering*. Paper presented at the IEEE International Joint Conference on Neural Networks, Budapest, Hungray.

Sanchez, E. N., & Ricalde, L. J. (2003). *Trajectory tracking via adaptive recurrent neural control with input saturation*. Paper presented at the International Joint Conference on Neural Networks. Portland, Oregon, USA.

Sheblé, G. B. (1999). *Computational auction mechanisms for restructured power industry operation*. Norwell, MA: Kluwer.

Singhal, S., & Wu, L. (1989). Training multilayer perceptrons with the extended Kalman algorithm. In D. S. Touretzky (Eds.), *Advances in neural information processing systems* (pp.133-140). San Mateo, CA: Morgan Kaufmann.

Skantze, P., Ilic, M., & Chapman, J. (2000). Stochastic modeling of electric power prices in a multi-market environment. *IEEE Power Engineering Society Winter Meeting, 2*, 1109-1114.

Stoft, S. (2002). *Power system economics*. Wiley Interscience and IEEE Press.

Szkuta, B. R., Sanabria, L. A., & Dillon, T. S. (1999). Electricity price short-term forecasting using artificial neural networks. *IEEE Transactions on Power Systems, 14*(3), 851-857.

Werbos, P. J. (1990). Backpropagation through time: What it does and how to do it. *Proceedings of the IEEE, 78*(10), 1550 - 1560.

Williams, R. J., & Zipser, D. (1989). A learning algorithm for continually running fully recurrent neural networks. *Neural Computation, 1,* 270-280.

Xu, Y.Y., Hsieh, R., Lu, Y.L., Bock, C., & Pao, H. T. (2004). *Forecasting electricity market prices: A neural network based approach*. Paper presented at the IEEE International Joint Conference on Neural Networks, Budapest, Hungray.

Yule, G. U. (1927). On a method of investigating periodicities in disturbed series, with special reference to Wolfer's sunspot numbers. *Philosophical Transactions of the Royal Society of London: Series A. 226,* 267-298.

ADDITIONAL READING

Arroyo J. M., & Conejo A. J. (2000). Optimal response of a thermal unit to an electricity spot market. *IEEE Transactions on Power Systems, 15*(3), 1098–1104.

Bunn, D. W. (2000). Forecasting loads and prices in competitive power markets. *Proceedings of the IEEE, 88*(2), 163–169.

Bushnell, J. B., & Mansur, E. T. (2001). The impact of retail rate deregulation on electricity consumption in San Diego. *Working Paper PWP-082, Program on Workable Energy Regulation.* University of Californian Energy Institute, from http://www.ucei.org

Chen G., & Dong, X. (1998). *From chaos to order: Methodologies, perspectives and applications.* Singapore: World Scientific.

Feldkamp, L. A., Feldkamp, T. M., & Prokhorov, D. V. (2001). *Neural network training with the nprKF.* Paper presented at the IEEE International Joint Conference on Neural Networks, Washington, USA.

Haykin, S. (1999). *Neural Networks: A comprehensive foundation.* (2nd ed.). New Jersey: Prentice Hall.

Joya, G., García-Lagos, F., Atencia, M., & Sandoval, F. (2004). Artificial neural networks for energy management system: Applicability and limitations of the main paradigms. *European Journal of Economic and Social Systems, 17*(1), 11-28.

Kirschen, D., & Strbac, G. (2004). *Fundamentals of power system economics.* West Sussex, England: John Wiley and Sons, Ltd.

Koritarov, V. S. (2004). Real-world market representation with agents. *IEEE Power and Energy, 2*(4), 39-46.

Norgaard, M., Ravn, O., Poulsen, N. K., & Hansen, L. K. (2000). *Neural networks for modelling and control of dynamic systems.* Springer-Verlag.

Olsina, F., Garces, F., & Haubrich, H.J. (2006). Modeling long-term dynamics of electricity markets. *Energy Policy, 34*(12), 1411-1433.

Poznyak, A. S., Sanchez, E. N., & Yu, W. (2001). *Differential neural networks for robust nonlinear control.* Singapore: World Scientific.

Principe, J., Wang, L., & Kuo, J. (1997). *Nonlinear dynamic modeling with neural networks.* Paper presented at the first European Conference on Signal Analysis and Prediction, Prague, Czech Republic.

Ruck, D. W., Rogers, S. K., Kabrisky, M., Maybeck, P. S., & Oxley, M. E. (1992). Comparative analysis of backpropagation and the extended Kalman filter for training multilayer perceptrons. *IEEE transactions on Pattern Analysis and Machine Intelligence, 14*(6), 686-691.

Rudnick, H., Barroso, L.A., Skerk, C., & Blanco, A. (2005). South American reform lessons: Twenty years of restructuring and reform in Argentina, Brazil, and Chile. *IEEE Power & Energy Magazine, 3*(4), 49-59.

Sanchez, E. N., & Alanis, A. Y. (2006). *Neural Networks: Concepts and applications to automatic control.* Madrid: Pearson eduacación (*in Spanish*).

Sanchez, E. N., Alanis, A. Y., & Chen, G.R. (2007). Recurrent neural networks trained with Kalman filtering for discrete chaos reconstruction. *Dynamics of Continuous, Discrete and Impulsive Systems: Part B, 13*(c), 1-18.

Sanchez, E. N., Alanis, A. Y., & Rico, J. (2004). *Electric load demand prediction using neural networks trained by Kalman filtering.* Paper presented at the Latin American congress of Automatic Control (*in Spanish*), La Habana, Cuba.

Sumila, C. C. (2001). *Extraction of temporary patterns in data base of time series.* Unpublished master dissertation (*in Spanish*), University of San Nicolás de Hidalgo, Michoacan, Mexico.

Chapter XIV
Adaptive Higher Order Neural Network Models and Their Applications in Business

Shuxiang Xu
University of Tasmania, Australia

ABSTRACT

Business is a diversified field with general areas of specialisation such as accounting, taxation, stock market, and other financial analysis. Artificial Neural Networks (ANNs) have been widely used in applications such as bankruptcy prediction, predicting costs, forecasting revenue, forecasting share prices and exchange rates, processing documents and many more. This chapter introduces an Adaptive Higher Order Neural Network (HONN) model and applies the adaptive model in business applications such as simulating and forecasting share prices. This adaptive HONN model offers significant advantages over traditional Standard ANN models such as much reduced network size, faster training, as well as much improved simulation and forecasting errors, due to their ability to better approximate complex, non-smooth, often discontinuous training data sets. The generalisation ability of this HONN model is explored and discussed.

INTRODUCTION

Business is a diversified field with several general areas of specialisation such as accounting or financial analysis. Artificial Neural networks (ANNs) provide significant benefits in business applications. They have been actively used for applications such as bankruptcy prediction, predicting costs, forecast revenue, processing documents and more (Kurbel et al, 1998; Atiya et al, 2001; Baesens et al, 2003). Almost any neural network model would fit into at least one business area or financial analysis. Traditional statistical methods have been used for business applications with many limitations (Azema-Barac et al, 1997; Blum et al, 1991; Park et al, 1993).

Human financial experts usually use charts of financial data and even intuition to navigate through the massive amounts of financial information available in the financial markets. Some of them study those companies that appear to be good for long-term investments. Others try to predict the future economy such as share prices based on their experiences, but with the large number of factors involved, this seems to be an overwhelming task. Consider this scenario: how can a human financial expert handle years of data for 30 factors, 500 shares, and other factors such as keeping track of the current values simulataneously? This is why some researchers insists that massive systems such as the economy of a country or the weather are not predictable due to the effects of chaos. But ANNs can be used to help automate such tasks (Zhang et al, 2002).

ANNs can be used to process subjective information as well as statistical data and are not limited to particular financial principle. They can learn from experience (existing financial data set) but they do not have to follow specific equations or rules. They can be asked to consider hundreds of different factors, which is a lot more than what human experts can digest. They won't be overwhelmed by decades of financial data, as long as the required computational power has been met. ANNs can be used together with traditional statistical methods and they do not conflict with each other (Dayhoff, 1990).

Using ANNs for financial advice means that you don't have to analyse complex financial charts in order to find a trend (of, eg, a share). The ANN architecture determines which factors correlate to each other (each factor corresponds with an input to the ANN). If patterns exist in a financial dataset, an ANN can filter out the noise and pick up the overall trends. You as the ANN program user decide what you want the ANN to learn and what kind of information it needs to be given, in order to fulfill a financial task.

ANN programs are a new computing tool which simulate the structure and operation of the human brain. They simulate many of the human brain's most powerful abilities such as sound and image recognition, association, and more importantly the ability to generalize by observing examples (eg, forecasting based on existing situation). ANNs establish their own model of a problem based on a training process (with a training algorithm), so no programming is required because existing traning programs are readily available.

Some large financial institutions have used ANNs to improve performance in such areas as bond rating, credit scoring, target marketing and evaluating loan applications. These ANN systems are typically only a few percentage points more accurate than their predecessors, but because of the amounts of money involved, these ANNs are very profitable. ANNs are now used to analyze credit card transactions to detect likely instances of fraud (Kay et al, 2006).

While conventional ANN models have been bringing huge profits to many financial institutions, they suffer from several drawbacks. First, conventional ANNs can not handle discontinuities in the input training data set (Zhang et al, 2002). Next, they do not perform well on complicated business data with high frequency components and high order nonlinearity, and finally, they are considered as 'black boxes' which can not explain their behaviour (Blum et al, 1991; Zhang et al, 2002 ; Burns, 1986).

To overcome these limitations some researchers have proposed the use of Higher Order Neural Networks (HONNs) (Redding et al, 1993 ; Zhang et al, 1999 ; Zhang et al, 2000). HONNs are able to provide some explanation for the simulation they produce and thus can be considered as 'open box' rather than 'black box'. HONNs can simulate high frequency and high order nonlinear business data, and can handle discontinuities in the input traning data set (Zhang et al, 2002). Section 3 of this chapter offers more information about HONNs.

The idea of setting a few free parameters in the neuron activation function (or transfer function) of an ANN is relatively new. ANNs with such activation function seem to provide better fitting properties than classical architectures with fixed activation functions (such as sigmoid function). Such activation functions are usually called adaptive activation functions because the free parameters can be adjusted (in the same way as connection weights) to adapt to different applications. In (Vecci et al, 1998), a Feedforward Neural Network (FNN) was able to adapt its activation function by varying the control points of a Catmull-Rom cubic spline. First, this FNN can be seen as a sub-optimal realization of the additive spline based model obtained by the regularization theory. Next, simulations confirm that the special learning mechanism allows one to use the network's free parameters in a very effective way, keeping their total number at lower values than in networks with traditional fixed neuron activation functions such as the sigmoid activation function. Other notable properties are a shorter training time and a reduced hardware complexity. Based on regularization theory, the authors derived an architecture which embodies some regularity characteristics in its own activation function much better than the traditional FNN can do. Simulations on simple two-dimensional functions, on a more complex non-linear system and on a pattern recognition problem exposed the good generalization ability expected according to the theory, as well as other advantages, including the ability of tuning the activation function to determine the reduction of the number of hidden units.

Campolucci et al (1996) proposed an adaptive activation function built as a piecewise approximation with suitable cubic splines that can have arbitrary shape and allows them to reduce the overall size of the neural networks, trading connection complexity with activation function complexity. The authors developed a generalized sigmoid neural network with the adaptive activation function and a learning algorithm to operate on the identification of a non-linear dynamic system. The experimental result confirmed the computational capabilities of the proposed approach and the attainable network size reductions.

In (Chen et al, 1996), real variables a (gain) and b (slope) in the generalised sigmoid activation function were adjusted during learning process. A comparison with classical FNNs to model static and dynamical systems was reported, showing that an adaptive sigmoid (ie, a sigmoid with free parameters) leads to an improved data modelling. Based on the steepest descent method, an auto-tuning algorithm was derived to enable the proposed FNN to automatically adjust free parameters as well as connection weights between neurons. Due to the ability of auto-tuning, the flexibility and non-linearity of the FNN was increased significantly. Furthermore, the novel feature prevented the non-linear neurons from saturation, and therefore, the scaling procedure, which is usually unavoidable for traditional neuron-fixed FNNs, became unnecessary. Simulations with one and two dimensional functions approximation indicated that the proposed FNN with adaptive sigmoid activation function gave better agreement than the traditional fixed neuron FNN, even though fewer processing nodes were used. Moreover, the convergence properties were superior.

There have been limited studies with emphasis on setting free parameters in the neuron activation function before Chen and Chang (1996). To increase the flexibility and learning ability of neural networks, Kawato's group (Kawato et al, 1987) determined the near-optimal activation functions empirically. Arai et al (1991) proposed an auto-tuning method for adjusting the only free parameter in their activation function and confirmed it to be useful for image compression. Next, based on using the steepest descent method, Yamada & Yabuta (1992a,b) proposed an auto-tuning method for determining an optimal nonlinear activation function. Still, only a single parameter that governs the shape of the nonlinear function was tuned, and their single parameter tuning method may restrict the structure of the possible optimum shape of the nonlinear activation function. Finally, Hu and Shao (1992) constructed a learning algorithm based on introducing a generalized S-shape activation function.

This chapter is organized as follows. Section 2 is a breif introduction to ANN architecture and its learning process (this section can be skipped by users who have some basic knowledge about ANN). Section 3 is a brief introduction to HONNs. Section 4 presents several Adaptive HONN models. Section 5 gives several examples to demonstrate how Adaptive HONN models can be used in business, and finally, Section 6 concludes this chapter.

ANN STRUCTURE AND LEARNING PROCESS (Dayhoff, 1990; Haykin, 1994; Picton, 2000)

One of the most intriguing things about humans is how we use our brains to think, analyse, and make predictions. Our brain is composed of hundreds of billions of neurons which are massively connected with each other. Recently some biologists have discovered that it is the way the neurons are connected which gives us our intelligence, rather than what are in the neurons themselves. ANNs simulate the structure and processing abilities of the human brain's neurons and connections.

An ANN works by creating connections between different processing elements (artificial neurons), each analogous to a single neuron in a biological brain. These neurons may be physically constructed or simulated by a computer program. Each neuron takes many input signals, then, based on an internal weighting mechanism, produces a single output signal that's typically sent as input to another neuron.

The neurons are interconnected and organized into different layers. The input layer receives the input, the output layer produces the final output. Usually one or more hidden layers are set between the two.

An ANN is taught about a specific financial problem, such as predicting a share's price, using a technique called training. Training an ANN is largely like teaching small children to remember and then recognize the letters of the English alphabet. You show a child the letter "A" and tell him what letter he's looking at. You do this a couple of times, and then ask him if he can recognise it, and if he can, you go on to the next letter. If he doesn't remember it then you tell him again that he is looking at an "A". Next, you show him a "B" and repeat the process. You would do this for all the letters of the alphabet, then start over. Eventually he will learn to recognize all of the letters of the English alphabet correctly. Later we will see that the well-known backpropagation traning algorithm (supervised training) is based on this mechanism.

An ANN is fed with some financial data and it guesses what the result should be. At first the guesses would be garbage. When the trained ANN does not produce a correct guess, it is corrected. The next time it sees that data, it will guess more accurately. The network is shown lots of data (thousands of training pairs, sometimes), over and over until is learns all the data and results. Like a person, a trained ANN can generalize, which means it makes a reasonable guess when the given data have not been seen before. You decide what information to provide and the ANN finds (after learning) the patterns, trends, and hidden relationships.

The learning process involves updating the connections (usually called weights) between the neurons. The connections allow the neurons to communicate with each other and produce forecasts. When the ANN makes a wrong guess, an adjustment is made to some weights, thus it is able to learn.

ANN learning process typically begins with randomizing connection weights between the neurons. Just like biological brains, ANNs can not do anything without learning from existing knowledge. Typically, there are two major methods for training an ANN, depending on the problem it has to solve.

A self-organizing ANN is exposed to large amounts of data and tends to discover patterns and relationships in that large data set (data mining). Researchers often use this type of training to analyze experimental data (such as economic data).

A back-propagation supervised ANN, conversely, is exposed to input-output training pairs so that a specific relationship could be learned. During the training period, the target values in the training pairs are used to evaluate whether the ANN's output is correct. If it's correct, the neural weightings that produced that output are reinforced; if the output is incorrect, those responsible weightings are diminished. This method has been extensively used by many institutions for specific problem-solving applications.

Implemented on a single computer, an ANN is usually slower than a more traditional algorithm (especially when the training set is large). The ANN's parallel nature, however, allows it to be built using multiple processors, giving it a great speed advantage at very little development cost. The parallel architecture also allows ANNs to process very large amounts of data very efficiently.

There are a few steps involved in designing a financial neural network. First of all, you need to decide what result you want the ANN to produce for you (ie, the outputs) and what information the ANN will use to arrive at the result (ie., inputs). As an example, if you want to create an ANN to predict the price of the Dow Jones Industrial Average (DOW) on a month to month average basis, one month in advance, then the inputs to the ANN would include the Consumer Price Index (CPI), the price of crude oil, the inflation rate, the prime interest rate, and others. Once these factors have been determined you then know how many input neurons should be set for the ANN. In this

example, the number of output neurons would be one because you only want to predict the price for next month. Theorectically an ANN with only one hidden layer is able to model any practical problem. The number of hidden layer neurons can not be determined based on any universal rules but generally speaking this number should be less than N/d, where N is the number of training data sets and d is the number of input neurons (Barron, 1994).

It's usually good to give the ANN lots of information. If you are unsure if a factor is related to the output, the neural network will determine if the factor is important and will learn to ignore anything irrelevant. Sometimes a possibly irrelevant piece of information can allow the ANN to make distinctions which we are not aware of (which is the essence of data mining). If there's no correlation, the ANN will just ignore the factor.

HONNs

HONNs (Higher Order Neural Networks) (Lee et al, 1986) are networks in which the net input to a computational neuron is a weighted sum of products of its inputs. Such neuron is called a Higher-order Processing Unit (HPU) (Lippman, 1989). It was known that HONN's can implement invariant pattern recognition (Psaltis et al, 1988 ; Reid et al, 1989 ; Wood et al, 1996). Giles in (Giles et al, 1987) showed that HONN's have impressive computational, storage and learning capabilities. In (Redding et al, 1993), HONN's were proved to be at least as powerful as any other FNN architecture when the orders of the networks are the same. Kosmatopoulos et al (1995) studied the approximation and learning properties of one class of recurrent HONNs and applied these architectures to the identification of dynamical systems. Thimm et al (1997) proposed a suitable initialization method for HONN's and compared this method to weight initialization techniques for FNNs. A large number of experiments were performed which leaded to the proposal of a suitable initialization approach for HONNs.

Giles et al (1987) showed that HONN's have impressive computational, storage and learning capabilities. The authors believed that the order or structure of a HONN could be tailored to the order or structure of a particular problem, and thus a HONN designed for a particular class of problems becomes specialized and efficient in solving these problems. Furthermore, a priori knowledge could be encoded in a HONN.

In Redding et al (1993), HONN's were proved to be at least as powerful as any other FNN architecture when the order of the networks are the same. A detailed theoretical development of a constructive, polynomial-time algorithm that would determine an exact HONN realization with minimal order for an arbitrary binary or bipolar mapping problem was created to deal with the two-or-more clumps problem, demonstrating that the algorithm performed well when compared with the Tiling and Upstart algorithms.

Kosmatopoulos et al (1995) studied the approximation and learning properties of one class of recurrent HONN's and applied these architectures to the identification of dynamical systems. In recurrent HONN's the dynamic components are distributed throughout the network in the form of dynamic neurons. It was shown that if enough higher order connections were allowed, then this network was capable of approximating arbitrary dynamical systems. Identification schemes based on higher order network architectures were designed and analyzed.

Thimm et al (1997) proposed a suitable initialization method for HONN's and compared this method to weight initialization techniques for FNN's. As proper initialization is one of the most important prerequisites for fast convergence of FNN's, the authors aimed at determining the optimal variance (or range) for the initial weights and biases, the principal parameters of random initialization methods. A large number of experiments were performed which led to the proposal of a suitable initialization approach for HONN's. The conclusions were justified by sufficiently small confidence intervals of the mean convergence times.

ADAPTIVE HONN MODELS

Adaptive HONNs are HONNs with adaptive activation functions. The network structure of an Adaptive HONN is the same as that of a multi-layer FNN. That is, it consists of an input layer with some input units, an output layer with some output units, and at least one hidden layer consisting of intermediate processing units. Usually there is no activation function for neurons in the input layer and the output neurons are summing units (linear activation), and the activation function in the hidden units is an adaptive one.

In (Zhang et al, 2002) a one-dimensional Adaptive HONN was defined as follows.

Suppose that:

i = The ith neuron in layer-k

k = The kth layer of the neural network

h = The hth term in the *NAF* (Neural network Activation Function)

s = The maximum number of terms in the *NAF*

x = First neural network input

y = Second neural network input

$net_{i,k}$ = The input or internal state of the ith neuron in the kth layer

$w_{i,j,k}$ = The weight that connects the jth neuron in layer $k-1$ with the ith neuron in layer k

$o_{i,k}$ = The value of the output from the ith neuron in layer - k

The one-dimension adaptive HONN activation function is defined as:

$$NAF: \Psi_{i,k}\left(net_{i,k}\right) = o_{i,k}\left(net_{i,k}\right) = \sum_{h=1}^{s} f_{i,k,h}(net_{i,k})$$

(1)

In case of s = 4:

$$f_{i,k,1}(net_{i,k}) = a1_{i,k} \cdot \sin^{c1_{i,k}}\left(b1_{i,k} \cdot (net_{i,k})\right)$$

$$f_{i,k,2}(net_{i,k}) = a2_{i,k} \cdot e^{-b2_{i,k} \cdot (net_{i,k})}$$

$$f_{i,k,3}(net_{i,k}) = a3_{i,k} \cdot \frac{1}{1 + e^{-b3_{i,k} \cdot (net_{i,k})}}$$

$$f_{i,k,4}(net_{i,k}) = a4_{i,k} \cdot (net_{i,k})^{b4_{i,k}}$$

(2)

The one-dimensional Adaptive HONN activation function then becomes Equation (3), where $a1_{i,k}, b1_{i,k}, c1_{i,k}, a2_{i,k}, b2_{i,k}, a3_{i,k}, a4_{i,k}, b4_{i,k}$ are free parameters which can be adjusted (as well as weights) during training.

In this chapter, we will only discuss the following special case of the above adaptive activation function: $a1_{i,k} = b1_{i,k} = 0$, $a4_{i,k} = b4_{i,k} = 0$.

So the adaptive activation function we are interested in is Equation (4).

The learning algorithm for Adaptive HONN with activation function (4) can be found in the Appendix section.

ADAPTIVE HONN MODEL APPLICATIONS IN BUSINESS

In this section, the Adaptive HONN model as defined in Section 4 has been used in several finanical applications. The results are given and discussed.

Simulating and Forecasting Total Taxation Revenues of Australia

The Adaptive HONN model has been used to simulate and forecast the Total Taxation Revenues of Australia as shown in Figure 5.1. The financial data were downloaded from the Australian Taxation Office (ATO) web site. For this experiment monthly data between Jan 1994 and Dec 1999 were used. The detailed comparison between the adaptive HONN and traditional standard ANN for this example is illustrated in Table 5.1.

After the Adaptive HONN (with only 4 hidden units) has been well trained over the training data pairs, it was used to forecast the taxation revenues for each month of the year 2000. Then the forecasted revenues were compared with the real revenues for the period and the overall RMS error reached 2.55%. To demonstrate the advatages of the Adaptive HONN, the above-trained Standard ANN (with 18 hidden units) was also used for the same forecasting task which resulted in an overall RMS error of 5.63%.

Next, some cross-validation approach was used to improve the performance of the Adaptive HONN. Cross-validation is the statistical practice of dividing a sample of data into subsets so that the experiment is initially performed on a single

Equation (3).

$$\Psi_{i,k}\left(net_{i,k}\right) = \sum_{h=1}^{4} f_{i,k,h}(net_{i,k})$$

$$= a1_{i,k} \cdot \sin^{c1_{i,k}}\left(b1_{i,k} \cdot (net_{i,k})\right) + a2_{i,k} \cdot e^{-b2_{i,k} \cdot (net_{i,k})2} + a3_{i,k} \cdot \frac{1}{1 + e^{-b3_{i,k} \cdot (net_{i,k})}} + a4_{i,k} \cdot (net_{i,k})^{b4_{i,k}}$$

Equation (4).

$$\Psi_{i,k}\left(net_{i,k}\right) = \sum_{h=1}^{2} f_{i,k,h}(net_{i,k}) = a2_{i,k} \cdot e^{-b2_{i,k} \cdot (net_{i,k})2} + a3_{i,k} \cdot \frac{1}{1 + e^{-b3_{i,k} \cdot (net_{i,k})}}$$

Figure 5.1. Total taxation revenues of Australia ($ million) (Jan 1994 To Dec 1999)

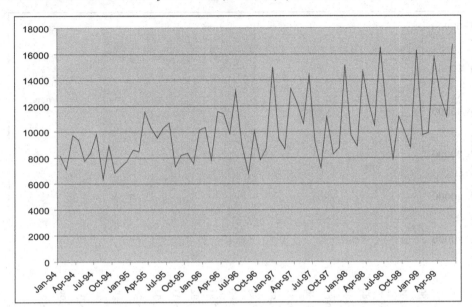

Table 5.1. Adaptive HONN with NAF and standard ANN to simulate taxation revenues

Neural Network	No. HL	HL Nodes	Epoch	RMS Error
Adaptive HONN	1	4	5,000	0.025468
Standard ANN	1	4	12,000	0.965874
Standard ANN	1	10	12,000	0.856654
Standard ANN	1	14	12,000	0.087996
Standard ANN	1	18	12,000	0.056345

(HL: Hidden Layer. RMS: Root-Mean-Square)

subset, while the other subset(s) are retained for subsequent use in confirming and validating the initial analysis. The initial subset of data is usually called the training set, and the other subset(s) are called validation or testing sets. Cross-validation is one of several approaches for estimating how well the ANN you've just trained from some training data is going to perform on future as-yet-unseen data. Cross-validation can be used to estimate the generalization error of a given ANN model. It can also be used for model selection by choosing one of several models that has the smallest estimated generalization error.

For this example, the traning data set was divided into a traning set made 70% of the original training set and a validation set made of 30% of the original training set. The training (training time and number of epochs) was optimized based on evaluation over the validation set. Then the well-trained Adaptive HONN was used to forecast the taxation revenues for each month of the year 2000, and the forecasted taxation revenues were compared with the real prices for the period. The overall RMS error reached 2.05%. The same mechanism was applied to using a Standard ANN, which resulted in an RMS error of 4.77%.

Figure 5.2. Reserve Bank Of Australia Assets ($ million) (Jan 1980 To Dec 2000)

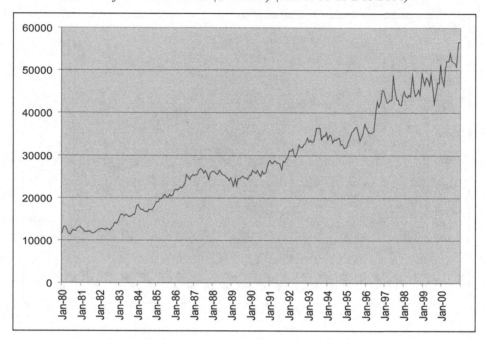

Table 5.2. Adaptive HONN with NAF and standard ANN to simulate Reserve Bank Of Australia Assets ($ million)

Neural Network	No. HL	HL Nodes	Epoch	RMS Error
Adaptive HONN	1	3	5,000	0.019654
Standard ANN	1	3	12,000	0.912354
Standard ANN	1	9	12,000	0.798652
Standard ANN	1	16	12,000	0.065487
Standard ANN	1	22	12,000	0.053321

(HL: Hidden Layer. RMS: Root-Mean-Square)

Simulating and Forecasting Reserve Bank Of Australia Assets

The Adaptive HONN model has also been used to simulate and forecast the Reserve Bank Of Australia Assets as shown in Figure 5.2. The financial data were obtained from the Reserve Bank Of Australia. For this experiment monthly data between Jan 1980 and Dec 2000 were used. The detailed comparison between the adaptive HONN and traditional standard ANN for this example is illustrated in Table 5.2.

After the Adaptive HONN (with only 3 hidden units) has been well trained over the training data pairs, it was used to forecast the Reserve Bank Of Australia Assets for each month of the year 2001. Then the forecasted assets were compared with the real assets for the period and the overall RMS error reached 1.96%. To demonstrate the advatages of the Adaptive HONN, the above-trained Standard ANN (with 22 hidden units) was also used for the same forecasting task which resulted in an overall RMS error of 5.33%.

Again, some cross-validation approach was used to improve the performance of the Adaptive

HONN. For this time, the traning data set was divided into a traning set made 75% of the original training set and a validation set made of 25% of the original training set. The training (training time and number of epochs) was optimized based on evaluation over the validation set. Then the well-trained Adaptive HONN was used to predict the assets for each month of the year 2001, and the forecasted assets were compared with the real assets for the period. The overall RMS error reached 1.80%. The same mechanism was applied to using a Standard ANN, which resulted in an RMS error of 5.02%.

Simulating and Forecasting Fuel Economy

In the next expriment a dataset containing information of different cars built in the US, Europe, and Japan was trained using the Adaptive HONN to determine car fuel economy (MPG - Miles Per Gallon) for each vehicle. There were a total of 392 samples in this data set with 9 input variables and 1 output. The dataset was from UCI Machine Learning Repository (2007). The output was the fuel economy in MPG, and the input variables were:

- Number of cylinders
- Displacement
- Horsepower
- Weight
- Acceleration
- Model year
- Made in US? (0,1)
- Made in Europe? (0,1)
- Made in Japan? (0,1)

To compare the performance of Adaptive HONN and Standard ANN the dataset was divided into a set containing 353 samples for training, and a set containing 39 samples for forecasting (or generalization). This time, a cross-validation mechanism was adopted directly which split the

training set into 2 sections to train both an Adaptive HONN and a Standard ANN. After both neural networks were well-trained, the forecasting RMS error (over the 39 samples) from the Adaptive HONN reached 6.03%, while the forecasting error from the Standard ANN (over the 39 samples) reached 13.55%.

CONCLUSION

In this chapter an Adaptive HONN model was introduced and applied in business applications such as simulating and forecasting government taxation revenues. Such models offer significant advantages over traditional Standard ANN models such as much reduced network size, faster training, as well as much improved simulation and forecasting errors, due to their ability to better approximate complex, non-smooth, often discontinuous training data sets. Compared with some existing approaches on applying ANN models in business applications, although there are more free parameters in the Adaptive HONN model, training speed is increased due to a significant decrease of network size. What is more, simulation and forecasting accuracy is greatly improved, which has to be one of the main concerns in the business world.

The method described in this chapter relies on using cross-validation to improve generalisation ability of the Adaptive HONN model. As part of the future research, some current cross-validation approaches would be improved so that the forecasting errors could be reduced further down to a more satisfactory level. More factors which can help improve the generalisation ability would be considered.

ACKNOWLEDGMENT

The author wishes to thank Prof Ming Zhang for his valuable advice on this chapter.

REFERENCES

Arai, M., Kohon, R., & Imai, H. (1991). Adaptive control of a neural network with a variable function of a unit and its application, *Transactions on Inst. Electronic Information Communication Engineering, J74-A*, 551-559.

Atiya, A.F. (2001). Bankruptcy prediction for credit risk using neural networks: A survey and new results. *IEEE Transactions on Neural Networks, 12*(4), 929-935.

Azema-Barac, M., & Refenes, A. (1997). Neural networks for financial applications. In Fiesler, E., & Beale, R. (Eds.), *Handbook of Neural Computation*. Oxford University Press (G6:3:1-7).

Baesens, B., Setiono, R., Mues, C., & Vanthienen, J. (2003). Using neural network rule extraction and decision tables for credit-risk evaluation. *Management Science, 49*(3).

Barron, A. R. (1994), Approximation and estimation bounds for artificial neural networks. *Machine Learning, (14)*, 115-133.

Blum, E., & Li, K. (1991). Approximation theory and feed-forward networks. *Neural Networks, 4*, 511-515.

Burns, T. (1986). The interpretation and use of economic predictions. *Proc. Royal Society A*, pp. 103-125.

Campolucci, P., Capparelli, F., Guarnieri, S., Piazza, F., & Uncini, A. (1996). Neural networks with adaptive spline activation function. *Proceedings of IEEE MELECON 96* (pp. 1442-1445). Bari, Italy.

Chen, C.T., & Chang, W.D. (1996). A feedforward neural network with function shape autotuning. *Neural Networks, 9*(4), 627-641

Dayhoff, J. E. (1990). *Neural network architectures : An introduction*. New York: Van Nostrand Reinhold.

Gallant, A. R., & White, H. (1988). There exists a neural network that does not make avoidable mistakes. *IEEE Second International Conference on Neural Networks, I*, 657-664. San Diego: SOS Printing,

Giles, C.L., & Maxwell, T. (1987). Learning, invariance, and generalization in higher order neural networks. *Applied Optics, 26*(23), 4972-4978.

Grossberg, S. (1986). Some nonlinear networks capable of learning a spatial pattern of arbitrary complexity. *Proc. National Academy of Sciences, 59*, 368-372.

Hammadi, N. C., & Ito, H. (1998). On the activation function and fault tolerance in feedforward neural networks. *IEICE Transactions on Information & Systems, E81D*(1), 66 – 72.

Hansen, J.V., & Nelson, R.D. (1997). Neural networks and traditional time series methods: A synergistic combination in state economic forecasts. *IEEE Transactions on Neural Networks, 8*(4), 863-873.

Hinton, G. E. (1989). Connectionist learning procedure, *Artificial Intelligence, 40*, 251 – 257.

Holden, S.B., & Rayer, P.J.W. (1995). Generalisation and PAC learning: some new results for the class of generalised single-layer networks. *IEEE Transactions on Neural Networks, 6*(2), 368 – 380.

Haykin, S. S, (1994). *Neural networks : A comprehensive foundation*. New York : Macmillan.

Hu, Z., & Shao, H. (1992). The study of neural network adaptive control systems. *Control and Decision, 7*, 361-366.

Kawato, M., Uno, Y., Isobe, M., & Suzuki, R. (1987) A hierarchical model for voluntary movement and its application to robotics. *Proc. IEEE Int. Conf. Network, IV*, 573-582.

Kay, A. (2006). Artificial neural networks. *Computerworld*. Retrieved on 27 November 2006 from http://www.computerworld.com/softwaretopics/software/appdev/story/0,10801,57545,00.html

Kosmatopoulos, E.B., Polycarpou, M.M., Christodoulou, M.A., & Ioannou, P.A. (1995). High-order neural network structures for identification of dynamical systems. *IEEE Transactions on Neural Networks, 6*(2), 422-431.

Kurbel, K., Singh, K., & Teuteberg, F. (1998). Search and classification of interesting business applications in the World Wide Web using a neural network approach. *Proceedings of the 1998 IACIS Conference*. Cancun, Mexico.

Lee, Y.C., Doolen, G., Chen, H., Sun, G., Maxwell, T., Lee, H., & Giles, C.L. (1986). Machine learning using a higher order correlation network. *Physica D: Nonlinear Phenomena, 22*, 276-306.

Lippman, R.P. (1989). Pattern classification using neural networks. *IEEE Commun. Mag., 27*, 47-64.

Park, J., & Sandberg, I.W. (1993). Approximation and radial-basis-function networks. *Neural Computation, 5*, 305-316.

Picton, P. (2000). *Neural networks*. Basingstoke: Palgrave.

Psaltis, D., Park, C.H., & Hong, J. (1988). Higher order associative memories and their optical implementations. *Neural Networks, 1*, 149-163.

Redding, N., Kowalczyk, A., & Downs, T. (1993). Constructive high-order network algorithm that is polynomial time. *Neural Networks, 6*, 997-1010.

Redding, N.J., Kowalczyk, A., & Downs, T. (1993). Constructive higher-order network algorithm that is polynomial time. *Neural Networks, 6*, 997-1010.

Reid, M.B., Spirkovska, L., & Ochoa, E. (1989). Simultaneous position, scale, rotation invariant pattern classification using third-order neural networks. *Int. J. Neural Networks, 1*, 154-159.

Rumelhart, D.E., & McClelland, J.L. (1986). *Parallel distributed computing: Exploration in the microstructure of cognition*. Cambridge, MA: MIT Press.

Thimm, G., & Fiesler, E. (1997). High-order and multilayer perceptron initialization. *IEEE Transactions on Neural Networks, 8*(2), 349-359.

UCI Machine Learning Repository (2007). Retrieved April 2007 from ftp://ftp.ics.uci.edu/pub/machine-learning-databases/auto-mpg/auto-mpg.data

Vecci, L., Piazza, F., & Uncini, A. (1998). Learning and approximation capabilities of adaptive spline activation function neural networks. *Neural Networks, 11*, 259-270.

Wood, J., & Shawe-Taylor, J. (1996). A unifying framework for invariant pattern recognition. *Pattern Recognition Letters. 17*, 1415-1422.

Yamada, T., & Yabuta, T. (1992). Remarks on a neural network controller which uses an autotuning method for nonlinear functions. *IJCNN, 2*, 775-780.

Zhang, M., Xu, S., & Lu B. (1999). Neuron-adaptive higher order neural network group models. *Proc. Intl. Joint Conf. Neural Networks - IJCNN'99*, Washington, DC, USA, (Paper # 71).

Zhang, M., Xu, S., & Fulcher, J. (2002). Neuron-adaptive higher order neural-network models for automated financial data modeling. *IEEE Transactions on Neural Networks, 13*(1).

Zhang, M., Zhang, J. & Fulcher, J. (2000). Higher order neural network group models for financial simulation. *Intl. J. Neural Systems, 12*(2), 123–142.

ADDITIONAL READING

Baptista-Filho, B. D., Cabral, E. L. L., & Soares, A. J. (1999). A new approach to artificial neural networks. *IEEE Transactions on Neural Networks*, *9*(6), 1167 – 1179.

Barron, A. (1993). Universal approximation bounds for superposition of a sigmoidal function. *IEEE Transactions on Information Theory*, *3*, 930-945.

Brent, R. P. (1991). Fast training algorithm for multilayer neural networks. *IEEE Transactions on Neural Networks*, *2*, 346 – 354.

Carroll, S., & Dickinson, B. (1989). Construction of neural networks using the radon transform. *IEEE International Conference on Neural Networks*, Vol. 1, pp. 607 – 611. Washington DC.

Cichocki, A., & Unbehauen, R. (1993). *Neural networks for optimization and signal processing*. New York: Wiley.

Clemen, R.T. (1989). Combining forecasts: A review and annotated bibliography. *International Journal of Forecasting*, *5*, 559 – 583.

Day, S., & Davenport, M. (1993). Continuous-time temporal backpropagation with adaptive time delays. *IEEE Transactions on Neural Networks*, *4*, 348 – 354.

Durbin, R., & Rumelhart, D. E. (1989). Product units: a computationally powerful and biologically plausible extension to backpropagation networks, *Neural Computation*, *1*, 133 – 142.

Finnoff, W., Hergent, F., & Zimmermann, H.G. (1993). Improving model selection by nonconvergent methods, *Neural Networks*, *6*, 771 - 783.

Fogel, D.B. (1991). *System identification through simulated evolution: A machine learning approach to modelling*. Needham Heights, MA: Ginn.

Gallant, S.I. (1993). *Neural Network Learning and Expert Systems*. Cambridge, MA: MIT Press.

Geva, S., & Sitte, J. (1992). A constructive method for multivariate function approximation by multilayered perceptrons. *IEEE Transactions on Neural Networks*, *3*(4), 621-623.

Girosi, F., Jones, M., & Poggio, T. (1995). Regularisation theory and neural networks architecture. *Neural Computation*, *7*, 219 – 269.

Gorr, W.L. (1994). Research prospective on neural network forecasting. *International Journal of Forecasting*, *10*(1), 1-4.

Grossberg, S. (1976). Adaptive pattern classification and universal recording. I: Parallel development and coding of neural detectors. *Biological Cybernetics*, *23*, 121-134.

Harp, S., Samad, T., & Guuha, A. (1989). Toward the genetic synthesis of neural networks. In D. Shaffer (Ed.), *Proceedings of 3rd International Conference on Genetic Algorithms*. San Mateo, CA: Morgan Kaufmann.

Hill, T., Marquez, L., O'Connor, M., & Remus, W. (1994). Artificial neural network models for forecasting and decision making. *International Journal of Forecasting*, *10*, 5 – 15.

Hill, T., O'Connor, M., & Remus, W. (1996). Neural network models for time series forecasting. *Management Science*, *42*, 1082 – 1092.

APPENDIX

We use the following notations:

$I_{i,k}(u)$ the input or internal state of the *i* h neuron in the *k*th layer

$w_{i,j,k}$ the weight that connects the *j*th neuron in layer $k-1$ and the *i*th neuron in layer *k*

$O_{i,k}(u)$ the value of output from the *i* h neuron in layer *k*

$A1, B1, A2, B2$

     adjustable variables in activation function

$\theta_{i,k}$ the threshold value of the *i* h neuron in the *k* h layer

$d_j(u)$ the *j*th desired output value

β learning rate

m total number of output layer neurons

l total number of network layers

r the iteration number

η momentum

First of all, the input-output relation of the *i*th neuron in the *k*th layer can be described by:

$$I_{i,k}(u) = \sum_{j}\left[w_{i,j,k}O_{j,k-1}(u) \right] - \theta_{i,k} \tag{A.1}$$

where *j* is the number of neurons in layer *k-1*, and:

$$O_{i,k}(u) = \Psi\left(I_{i,k}(u)\right) = A1_{i,k} \cdot e^{-B1_{i,k} \cdot I_{i,k}(u)} + \frac{A2_{i,k}}{1 + e^{-B2_{i,k} \cdot I_{i,k}(u)}} \tag{A.2}$$

To train our neural network an energy function:

$$E = \frac{1}{2}\sum_{j=1}^{m}\left(d_j(u) - O_{j,l}(u)\right)^2 \tag{A.3}$$

is adopted, which is the sum of the squared errors between the actual network output and the desired output for all input patterns. In (A.3), *m* is the total number of output layer neurons, *l* is the total number of constructed network layers (here *l* = 3). The aim of learning is undoubtedly to minimize the energy function by adjusting the weights associated with various interconnections, and the variables in the activation function. This can be fulfilled by using a variation of the steepest descent gradient rule (Rumelhart et al, 1986) expressed as follows:

$$w_{i,j,k}^{(r)} = \eta \, w_{i,j,k}^{(r-1)} + \beta \, \frac{\partial E}{\partial w_{i,j,k}}$$

(A.4)

$$\theta_{i,k}^{(r)} = \eta \, \theta_{i,k}^{(r-1)} + \beta \, \frac{\partial E}{\partial \theta_{i,k}}$$

(A.5)

$$A1_{i,k}^{(r)} = \eta \, A1_{i,k}^{(r-1)} + \beta \, \frac{\partial E}{\partial A1_{i,k}}$$

(A.6)

$$B1_{i,k}^{(r)} = \eta \, B1_{i,k}^{(r-1)} + \beta \, \frac{\partial E}{\partial B1_{i,k}}$$

(A.7)

$$A2_{i,k}^{(r)} = \eta \, A2_{i,k}^{(r-1)} + \beta \, \frac{\partial E}{\partial A2_{i,k}}$$

(A.8)

$$B2_{i,k}^{(r)} = \eta \, B2_{i,k}^{(r-1)} + \beta \, \frac{\partial E}{\partial B2_{i,k}}$$

(A.9)

To derive the gradient information of E with respect to each adjustable parameter in equations (A.4)-(A.9), we define:

$$\frac{\partial E}{\partial I_{i,k}(u)} = \zeta_{i,k}$$

(A.10)

$$\frac{\partial E}{\partial O_{i,k}(u)} = \xi_{i,k}$$

(A.11)

Now, from equations (A.2), (A.3), (A.10) and (A.11), we have the partial derivatives of E with respect to adjustable parameters as follows:

$$\frac{\partial E}{\partial w_{i,j,k}} = \frac{\partial E}{\partial I_{i,k}(u)} \frac{\partial I_{i,k}(u)}{\partial w_{i,j,k}} = \zeta_{i,k} O_{j,k-1}(u)$$

(A.12)

$$\frac{\partial E}{\partial \theta_{i,k}} = \frac{\partial E}{\partial I_{i,k}(u)} \frac{\partial I_{i,k}(u)}{\partial \theta_{i,k}} = -\zeta_{i,k}$$

(A.13)

$$\frac{\partial E}{\partial A1_{i,k}} = \frac{\partial E}{\partial O_{i,k}} \frac{\partial O_{i,k}}{\partial A1_{i,k}} = \xi_{i,k} e^{-B1_{i,k} \cdot I_{i,k}}$$

(A.14)

$$\frac{\partial E}{\partial B1_{i,k}} = \frac{\partial E}{\partial O_{i,k}} \frac{\partial O_{i,k}}{\partial B1_{i,k}}$$
$$= -\xi_{i,k} \cdot A1_{i,k} \cdot I_{i,k} \cdot e^{-B1_{i,k} \cdot I_{i,k}}$$

(A.15)

$$\frac{\partial E}{\partial A2_{i,k}} = \frac{\partial E}{\partial O_{i,k}} \frac{\partial O_{i,k}}{\partial A2_{i,k}} = \xi_{i,k} \cdot \frac{1}{1 + e^{-B2_{i,k} \cdot I_{i,k}}}$$

(A.16)

$$\frac{\partial E}{\partial B2_{i,k}} = \frac{\partial E}{\partial O_{i,k}(u)} \frac{\partial O_{i,k}(u)}{\partial B2_{i,k}} = \xi_{i,k} \cdot \frac{A2_{i,k} \cdot I_{i,k}(u) \cdot e^{-B2_{i,k} \cdot I_{i,k}(u)}}{\left(1 + e^{-B2_{i,k} \cdot I_{i,k}(u)}\right)^2}$$

(A.17)

And for (A.10) and (A.11) the following equations can be computed:

$$\zeta_{i,k} = \frac{\partial E}{\partial I_{i,k}} = \frac{\partial E}{\partial O_{i,k}} \frac{\partial O_{i,k}}{\partial I_{i,k}} = \xi_{i,k} \cdot \frac{\partial O_{i,k}}{\partial I_{i,k}}$$

(A.18)

while:

$$\frac{\partial O_{i,k}(u)}{\partial I_{i,k}(u)} = A1_{i,k} \cdot B1_{i,k} \cdot e^{-B1_{i,k} \cdot I_{i,k}(u)} + \frac{A2_{i,k} \cdot B2_{i,k} \cdot e^{-B2_{i,k} \cdot I_{i,k}(u)}}{\left(1 + e^{-B2_{i,k} \cdot I_{i,k}(u)}\right)^2}$$

(A.19)

and:

$$\xi_{i,k} = \begin{cases} \sum_j \zeta_{j,k+1} w_{j,i,k+1}, & \text{if } 1 \le k < l; \\ O_{i,l} - d_i, & \text{if } k = l. \end{cases}$$

(A.20)

All the training examples are presented cyclically until all parameters are stabilized, i.e., until the energy function *E* for the entire training set is acceptably low and the network converges.

Chapter XV
CEO Tenure and Debt:
An Artificial Higher Order Neural Network Approach

Jean X. Zhang
George Washington University, USA

ABSTRACT

This chapter proposes nonlinear models using artificial neural network models to study the relationship between chief elected official (CEO) tenure and debt. Using Higher Order Neural Network (HONN) simulator, this study analyzes debt of the municipalities as a function of population and CEO tenure, and compares the results with that from SAS. The linear models show that CEO tenure and the amount of debt vary inversely. Specifically, a longer length of CEO tenure leads to a decrease in debt, while a shorter tenure leads to an increase in debt. This chapter shows nonlinear model generated from HONN out performs linear models by 1%. The results from both models reveal that CEO tenure is negatively associated with the level of debt in local governments.

INTRODUCTION

Reducing debt costs through investment in financial control systems is important to the municipalities. Several theoretical and empirical studies examine the determinants of borrowing costs on tax-exempt bond issues (Benson 1979; Benson, Marks, and Raman 1991). In the early eighties and nineties of the last century, some early studies examine state imposed disclosure requirements. For example, Ingram and Copeland (1982), Benson, Mark, and Raman (1984), and Fairchild and Kock (1998) consider state imposed disclosure requirements in the context of municipal debt costs. Benson, Mark, and Raman (1991) estimate the magnitude of the interest cost savings on general obligation bonds as a potential benefit from differential GAAP compliance. Their study suggests that bond prices incorporate the effects of differential GAAP compliance.

More recently, Downing and Zhang (2004) posit municipal bond markets are less liquid. In addition, Harris and Piwowar (2004) show higher transaction costs are associated with municipal bond markets. Most recently, Baber and Gore (2005) compare municipal debt costs in states that mandate the adoption of GAAP disclosure with debt costs in states that do not regulate municipal accounting methods. The result shows that municipal debt costs in states that impose GAAP are lower by 15 basis points.

Several studies examine the effect of audit variables and accounting variables on the borrowing costs on new bond issues for local governments. Wallace (1981) suggests that lower interest costs and higher bond ratings are associated with compliance with GAAFR, hiring a national auditor, and having a clean audit report. Employing a national sample, Wilson and Howard (1984) find poorer financial operating performance and substandard reporting practices are associated with lower bond ratings and higher borrowing costs. Most existing studies in the government sector examine the determinants of cost of debt, determinants other than CEO tenure; an important goal for this chapter is to extend the current literature and shed light on the issue of debt in the nonprofit area.

Debt is studied extensively in the private sector. According to prior research, debt is associated with accounting methods and accounting conservatism (Beatty and Weber 2003; Ahmed et al. 2002). Beatty and Weber (2003) show that borrowers with bank debt contracts that allow accounting method changes to affect contract calculations are more likely to make income-increasing rather than income-decreasing changes. On the other side, accounting conservatism plays an important role in reducing firms' debt costs. Ahmed et al. (2002) provide the evidence that accounting conservatism is associated with a lower cost of debt after controlling for other determinants of firms' debt costs.

Prior studies have also examined complex relationships between debt and other factors. For example, Trigeorgis (1991) provides an explanation that cost-reimbursed not-for-profits (NFP) tend to use debt financing when purchasing capital assets.

Schmukler and Vesperoni (2006) examine how financial globalization affects debt structure in emerging economies. Frank and Goyal (2003) find that financing deficit is less important in explaining net debt issues over time for firms of all sizes. In addition, they also find that net equity issues can track financing deficit more closely than net debt issues do. Lang, Ofek, and Stulz (1996) show that at the firm level or at the business segment level for diversified firms, there is a negative relation between future growth and leverage. Corporate borrowing is shown to be inversely related to the proportion of market value accounted for by real options (Myers 1997). Jung, Kim and Stulz (1996) investigate firms' decisions on whether to issue debt or equity, the stock price reaction to their decisions, and their actions afterward using the pecking-order model, the agency model, and the timing model. The evidence shows that for certain firms, agency costs of managerial discretion can lead to issue equity when debt issuance would have better consequences for firm value.

Corporate governance and capital structure are studied rigorously in the current literature. On corporate governance, Shleifer and Vishny (1997) focus on the legal protection of investors and of ownership concentration in corporate governance systems. On capital structure, Rajan and Zingales (1995) investigate relevant determinants by analyzing the financing decisions of public firms in the major industrialized countries. To examine whether capital structure decisions are in part motivated by managerial self-interest, Friend and Lang (1988) show that the debt ratio is inversely related to management's shareholding.

To analyze the impact of managerial discretion and corporate control mechanisms on leverage and firm value, Morellec (2004) apply a contingent claims model where the manager derives perquisites from investment. The model shows that manager-shareholder conflicts explain the low debt levels observed in practice. Moreover, Defond and Hung (2004) examine whether measures of investor protection are associated with identifying and terminating poorly performing CEOs. They show that institutions with strong law enforcement significantly improve the association between CEO turnover and poor performance. Jensen and Meckling (1976) indicate that managers may not act in the best interests of the shareholders, therefore it is possible that managers may not choose the optimal leverage as a result of agency costs. This suggests that managers may act in their interest and reduce the firm's leverage to a level below that of value maximization.

Entrenched managers prefer less debt in their capital structure. Garvey and Hanka (1999)'s results indicate that the threat of hostile take-over motivates managers to take on more debt. Analyzing the relationship between managerial entrenchment and firms' capital structure, Berger, Ofek, and Yermak (1997) suggest that entrenched CEOs avoid debt. They find firms whose CEOs have several entrenchment characteristics lead to a lower leverage. One of the characteristics is long tenure in office. This study extends the current research on debt in the government area. Specifically, it determines the relation between municipal debt and CEO tenure.

In many of the above studies, linear models are used. Many researchers also use nonlinear models in their studies (Kaplan and Welam 1974, Brock and Sayers 1988, Lee and Wu 1988), as nonlinear models can usually provide less simulation and prediction error. Schipper (1991) find that the usual regression approach in evaluating the earnings-share price relation implies a linear loss function, which may not be descriptive. Free-man and Tse (1992) provide the evidence that a nonlinear approach results in both significantly higher explanatory power and richer explanation for differences between ERCs and price-earnings ratio. In this study we use both linear and nonlinear models to explore the relationship between debt and CEO tenure.

The artificial neural network is used as a tool in economics and finance (Ijiri and Sunder 1990; Kryzanowski, Galler, and Wright 1993; Bansal

and Viswanathan 1993; Hutchinson, Lo, and Poggio 1994; Brown, Goetzmann, and Kumar 1998). Using neural network models, Lee, White, and Granger (1993) test neglected nonlinearity in time series models. Their results suggest that neural network model plays an important role in evaluating model adequacy. Employing a feed-forward neural model, Garcia and Gençay (2000) estimate a generalized option pricing formula. The functional shape of this formula is similar to the usual Black-Scholes formula. Franses and Draisma (1997) use an artificial neural network model to investigate the changes of seasonal patterns in macroeconomic time series. This chapter employs artificial neural network techniques to develop nonlinear models for the relationship between debt and CEO tenure and compares the performance of both linear and nonlinear models.

This chapter uses HONN models rather than the standard Artificial Neural Network (ANN) models. Most of the current research uses the standard ANN models. However, ANN models are unable to provide explanations for their be-havior. On the contrary, HONN models (Redding, Kowalczyk, and Downs 1993; Zhang, Zhang, and Fulcher 2000) provide some rationale for the simu-lations they produce, and are regarded as 'open box' rather than 'black box.' Moreover, HONNs are capable of simulating higher frequency and higher order nonlinear data, hence, providing superior results as compared to those from stan-dard ANN models. Therefore, this chapter uses HONN models to develop a nonlinear model that shows the relation between debt and CEO tenure controlling for population. Polynomial functions are often used in the modeling of financial data. More specifically, this study uses Polynomial HONN (PHONN) to model the relationship be-tween debt and CEO tenure.

This study considers the following types of debt: Long Term Debt Beginning Outstanding, NEC (19X), Long Term Debt Issue, Unspecified –Other NEC (29X), Long Term Debt Outstanding Full Faith & Credit -Other NEC (41X), and Long

Term Debt Outstanding Nonguaranteed –Other NEC (44X). Evidence shows that length of CEO tenure is associated with the amount of debt for local governments. Moreover, this chapter compares and analyzes the performance of the linear and nonlinear models.

The remainder of the article is organized as follows. Section II introduces Polynomial Higher Order Neural Networks. The hypotheses are presented in section III. Section IV describes data and methodology. T-test results and analysis are reported in section V. The regression results and linear models are introduced in section VI. Section VII presents the HONN simulating results and nonlinear models. Conclusions are presented in section VIII.

POLYNOMIAL HIGHER ORDER NEURAL NETWORKS

Due to the limitations of the traditional statistical approaches, alternative approaches, i.e. ANNs, have been considered in modeling and predicting financial data (Azoff 1994). In overcoming the limitations of the standard ANNs, researchers have developed Higher Order Neural Network (HONN) models (Karayiannis and Venetsanopoulos, 1993; Redding et al., 1993; and Zhang et al., 2000).

Polynomial curve fitting is an example of nonlinear mapping from input space to output space. By minimizing an error function, polynomial curve fitting aims to fit a polynomial to a set of n data points (Zhang et al., 2000). The function f(x, y) is determined by the values of the parameters a_{k1k2}, which is equivalent to ANN weights w0, w1, w2 ... etc. The PHONN model utilizes a combination of linear, power and multiplicative neurons. In addition, the training of this ANN uses the standard Back Propagation. The PHONN Model is able to extract coefficients a_{k1k2} of the general nth-order polynomial form as follows:

$$z = \sum_{k1,k2=0}^{n} a_{k1k2} x^{k1} y^{k2} \quad (1)$$

PHONN simulation system is written in C language. The system runs under X-Windows on a SUN workstation and incorporates a user-friendly Graphical User Interface (GUI). All steps, data and calculations can be viewed and modified dynamically in different windows.

HYPOTHESES

As aforementioned, Berger et al. (1997) find a significantly lower leverage in firms whose CEOs have a long tenure in office. Furthermore, Defond and Hung (2004) find that CEO turnover is negatively associated with firm performance in countries with strong law enforcement.

This chapter extends the current studies in the private sector to the municipalities by examining whether there is an association between the length of CEO tenure in the governmental setting and long-term debt. In particular, the following items are considered: Long Term Debt Beginning Outstanding, NEC (19X), Long Term Debt Issue, Unspecified –Other NEC (29X), Long Term Debt Outstanding Full Faith & Credit -Other NEC (41X), and Long Term Debt Outstanding Nonguaranteed –Other NEC (44X).

The first hypothesis considers the effect of CEO tenure and population on Long Term Debt Beginning Outstanding, NEC (19X):

Hypothesis 1: Population, CEO tenure and Long Term Debt Beginning Outstanding, NEC (19X) are unrelated.

My second hypothesis considers the effect of the length of CEO tenure and population on Long Term Debt Issue, Unspecified – Other NEC (29X):

Hypothesis 2: Population, CEO tenure and Long Term Debt Issue, unspecified –other NEC (29X) are unrelated.

Applying the same logic, the hypotheses 3 and 4 for Long Term Debt Outstanding Full Faith & Credit - Other NEC (41X) and Long Term Debt Outstanding Nonguaranteed - Other NEC (44X) are as follows:

Hypothesis 3: Population, CEO tenure and Long Term Debt Outstanding Full Faith & Credit -Other NEC (41X) are unrelated.

Hypothesis 4: Population, CEO tenure and Long Term Debt Outstanding Nonguaranteed –Other NEC (44X) are unrelated.

METHODOLOGY

This study uses two data sets: 2002 Census of Governments and 2001 Municipal Form of Government survey. The 2002 Census of Governments is downloaded from www.census.gov. The Census data are for individual government fiscal years ended between July 1, 2001 and June 30, 2002. The 2002 Census, similar to those taken since 1957, covers the entire range of government financial activities (revenue, expenditure, debt, and assets). The 2001 Municipal Form of

Government surveys are mailed in summer 2001 and winter 2002 to the municipal clerks in municipalities with populations 2,500 and over and to those municipalities under 2,500 in population that are in ICMA's database. There are a total of 4245 observations from the ICMA data. This study uses SAS to generate the results for the t-tests and linear models, and uses Polynomial Higher Order Neural Network (PHONN) to build nonlinear models.

T-TEST RESULTS AND ANALYSIS

This study examine whether the average amount of Long Term Debt Beginning Outstanding, NEC (19X) where CEO tenure is 1 to 2 years differ from the average amount of Long Term Debt Beginning Outstanding, NEC where CEO tenure is 3 years or more. Specifically, the following hypothesis is examined:

$H_0 : \mu_{year1,2} = \mu_{year3,4,5}$
$H_a : Not (\mu_{year1,2} = \mu_{year3,4,5})$

There are a total of 1479 observations for 19X where CEO tenure equals 1 or 2 years and 1517 observations for 19X where CEO tenure is greater than 3 years. Table 1 presents the results. The p-value of 0.0011 is significant at the 0.05 level. The tests for Long Term Debt Issue, Unspecified

Table 1. T-test Results for Long Term Debt, NEC ($H_0 : \mu_{year1,2} = \mu_{year3,4,5}$)

Code	Name	Number of Observations	Test Value	P-value
19X	Long Term Debt Beginning Outstanding, NEC	1479(1, 2 years) 1512(3, 4, 5 years)	3.26	0.0011
29X	Long Term Debt Issue, Unspecified –Other, NEC	740(1, 2 years) 727(3, 4, 5 years)	3.17	0.015
41X	Long Term Debt Outstanding – Full Faith & Credit –Other, NEC	1234(1, 2 years) 1186(3, 4, 5 years)	2.38	0.0174
44X	Long Term Debt Outstanding Non-guaranteed –Other, NEC	817(1, 2 years) 918(3, 4, 5 years)	3.76	0.0002

–Other NEC (29X), Long Term Debt Outstanding Full Faith & Credit -Other NEC (41X), and Long Term Debt Outstanding Nonguaranteed –Other NEC (44X) show significant p-values. The evidence suggests that the mean average amount of debt is different when the length of CEO tenure is less than three years than when it is three years or more.

Table 2 shows the results for another t-test for 19X, 29X, 41X and 44X to determine if the average amount where the length of CEO tenure is equal to 1 year is different from the average amount where CEO tenure is 4 years or more. Specifically, the following hypothesis is examined:

$$H_0 : \mu_{year1} = \mu_{year>4}$$
$$H_a : \text{Not } (\mu_{year1} = \mu_{year>4})$$

The results suggest that the mean average amount is different when CEO tenure is 1 year

than when it is 4 years or more. However, results are mixed for Tables 3 and 4. From Table 3, the p-values for 19X and 29X are significant and the p-values for 41X and 44X are non-significant. On the other hand, Table 4 shows that none of the p-values are significant. These findings are reasonable due to the closeness of the length of CEO tenure.

LINEAR MODELS

I estimate a variety of regression models for different types of debt, using population and length of CEO tenure as regressors. The following regression formula is used in Table 5:

$$AmountLog = b0 + b1 \; PopulationLog + b2 \; Length$$

Table 2. T-test results of long term debt, NEC (H_0: $\mu_{year1} = \mu_{year4}$)

Code	Name	Number of Observations	Test Value	P-value
19X	Long Term Debt Beginning Outstanding, NEC	430 (1 year) 1286 (4 years)	2.02	0.04
29X	Long Term Debt Issue, Unspecified –Other, NEC	216(1 year) 605(4 yeas)	2.54	0.01
41X	Long Term Debt Outstanding – Full Faith & Credit –Other, NEC	345(1 year) 981(4 years)	2.61	0.01
44X	Long Term Debt Outstanding Non-guaranteed –Other, NEC	203(1 year) 828(4 years)	2.35	0.02

Table 3. T-test results for long term debt, NEC (H_0: $\mu_{year2} = \mu_{year3}$)

Code	Name	Number of Observations	Test Value	P-value
19X	Long Term Debt Beginning Outstanding, NEC	1049 (2 years) 139(3 years)	2.02	0.04
29X	Long Term Debt Issue, Unspecified –Other, NEC	524(2 years) 110(3 years)	2.03	0.04
41X	Long Term Debt Outstanding – Full Faith & Credit –Other, NEC	889(2 years) 172(3 years)	0.61	0.54
44X	Long Term Debt Outstanding Non-guaranteed –Other, NEC	614(2 years) 80(3 years)	1.52	0.13

where:

AmountLog = Log(Amount)*0.075
PopulationLog = Log(Population)*0.065
Length = length of CEO tenure *0.1

The long-term debt amounts, population and CEO tenure are scaled using the above formula so that the data range between 0 to 1. This conversion allows the results from the linear model to be comparable to that of the nonlinear model. Since this study uses PHONN simulator to build nonlinear models, the converted data generates more accurate simulating results.

In Table 5, the coefficients for population are positive for 19X, 29X, 41X, and 44X. For 19X, the

coefficient for PopulationLog is 1.12987, and for 29X the coefficient is 1.0577. This is reasonable since the increase in population increases the amount for long-term debt. There is a negative relationship between CEO tenure and the following long-term debt amounts: Long Term Debt Issue, Unspecified –Other NEC (29X), Long Term Debt Outstanding – Full Faith & Credit –Other, NEC (41X) and Long Term Debt Outstanding Non-Guaranteed –Other, NEC (44X). Specifically the coefficient for 29X is –0.02421, and the coefficient for 41X is -0.05714.

Chart 1 (for all Charts, please see Appendix) shows the linear model for Long-term Debt Beginning Outstanding, NEC (AmountLog = -0.13872 +

Table 4. T-test results for long term debt, NEC (H_0: $\mu_{year1} = \mu_{year2}$)

Code	Name	Number of Observations	Test Value	P-value
19X	Long Term Debt Beginning outstanding, NEC	430(1 year) 1049(2 years)	0.18	0.86
29X	Long Term Debt Issue, Unspecified –Other, NEC	216(1 year) 524(2 years)	0.64	0.53
41X	Long Term Debt Outstanding – Full Faith & Credit –Other, NEC	345(1 years) 889(2 years)	1.68	0.09
44X	Long Term Debt Outstanding Non-guaranteed –Other, NEC	203(1 year) 614(2 years)	-0.44	0.66

Table 5. Regression results for long term debt, NEC (AmountLog = b_0 + b_1 PopulationLog + b_2 Length)

Code	Name	Coefficients	T-statistic	P-value	Root MSE	R²
19X	Long Term Debt Beginning Outstanding, NEC	-0.14 1.30 0.03	-9.89 58.13 -2.34	<0.01 <0.01 0.02	0.09	0.53
29X	Long Term Debt Issue, Unspecified –Other, NEC	-0.08 1.06 -0.02	-3.29 27.05 -0.91	<0.01 <0.01 0.36	0.12	0.33
41X	Long Term Debt Outstanding – Full Faith & Credit –Other, NEC	-0.12 1.25 -0.06	-7.63 48.11 -3.26	<0.01 <0.01 <0.01	0.10	0.49
44X	Long Term Debt Outstanding Non-Guaranteed –Other, NEC	-0.05 1.11 -0.07	-2.5 33.22 -2.80	0.01 <0.01 <0.01	0.11	0.39

1.29872*PopulationLog + 0.03475*Length). From this chart, it is clear that AmountLog positively associated with CEO tenure.

However, there is a different trend in Chart 2, which shows the linear model for Long-Term Debt Issue, Unspecified – Other, NEC. The amount issued is inversely related to the length of CEO tenure. Specifically, the amount issued increases when the length of CEO tenure decreases. The linear model for 29X is:

AmountLog = -0.08157 + 1.05771*PopulationLog – 0.02421*Length

Chart 3 presents the linear model for Long Term Debt Outstanding – Full Faith & Credit – Other, NEC. Similar to Chart 2, Chart 3 also shows that the amount is inversely related to CEO tenure. Specifically, the amount issued increases when the length of CEO tenure decreases. The following shows the linear model for 41X:

AmountLog = -0.12331 + 1.24819*PopulationLog – 0.05714*Length

Chart 4 shows the linear model of Long Term Debt Outstanding – Non-guaranteed – Other, NEC. Similar to Chart 2 and Chart 3, Chart 4 shows that the amount outstanding is inversely related to CEO tenure. Specifically, the amount issued increases when the length of CEO tenure decreases.

The linear model for 44X is as follows:

AmountLog = -0.05379 + 1.11248*PopulationLog – 0.06770*Length

Chart 5 shows the amounts for 19X, 29X, 41X, and 44X when CEO tenure is equal to one year. When PopulationLog is small, there is a similar behavior for items 29X, 41X and 44X. However, as the PopulationLog increases, the amount for those three items start to diverge. The following

linear models are shown in Chart 5, where CEO tenure equals to one year.

19X(Length = 1 year): AmountLog = -0.13872 + 1.29872*PopulationLog + 0.03475*Length

29X(Length = 1 year): AmountLog = -0.08157 + 1.05771*PopulationLog – 0.02421*Length

41X(Length = 1 year): AmountLog = -0.12331 + 1.24819*PopulationLog – 0.05714*Length

44X(Length = 1 year): AmountLog = -0.05379 + 1.11248*PopulationLog – 0.06770*Length

where Length=0.1.

Chart 6 shows the amounts for 19X, 29X, 41X, and 44X when CEO tenure is equal to two years. When population is small, the amount for 29X is greater than that for 41X and 44X. However, when population increases, the amount for 41X is more than 29X and 44X. The following models are graphed in Chart 6, where the CEO tenure is two years:

19X(Length = 2 years): AmountLog = -0.13872 + 1.29872*PopulationLog + 0.03475*Length

29X(Length = 2 years): AmountLog = -0.08157 + 1.05771*PopulationLog – 0.02421*Length

41X(Length = 2 years): AmountLog = -0.12331 + 1.24819*PopulationLog – 0.05714*Length

44X(Length = 2 years): AmountLog = -0.05379 + 1.11248*PopulationLog – 0.06770*Length

where Length = 0.2.

Chart 7 presents the amounts for 19X, 29X, 41X, and 44X when the CEO tenure is equal to three years. The amount for 29X is greater than 41X and 44X when the population is small. However, when the population increases, the amount for 41X and 29X are greater than that for 44X. The following models are graphed in Chart 7, where CEO tenure equals three years:

19X(Length = 3 years): AmountLog = -0.13872 + 1.29872*PopulationLog + 0.03475*Length

29X(Length = 3 years): AmountLog = -0.08157 + 1.05771*PopulationLog – 0.02421*Length

41X(Length = 3 years): AmountLog = -0.12331 + 1.24819*PopulationLog – 0.05714*Length

44X(Length = 3 years): AmountLog = -0.05379 + 1.11248*PopulationLog – 0.06770*Length

Similarly, Chart 8 shows all items 19X, 29X, 41X, and 44X when the length of CEO tenure is equal to 4 years. When PopulationLog is small, 41X is similar to 44X and when PopulationLog is large, 41X is similar to 29X. The following models are used for Chart 8:

19X(Length = 4 years): AmountLog = -0.13872 + 1.29872*PopulationLog + 0.03475*Length

29X(Length = 4 years): AmountLog = -0.08157 + 1.05771*PopulationLog – 0.02421*Length

41X(Length = 4 years): AmountLog = -0.12331 + 1.24819*PopulationLog – 0.05714*Length

44X(Length = 4 years): AmountLog = -0.05379 + 1.11248*PopulationLog – 0.06770*Length

NONLINEAR MODEL BY USING HONNs

Results from both the linear and nonlinear models are shown on Table 6 and Chart 9. Table 6 compares the results for the linear model and the nonlinear model for Long Term Debt Issue,

Unspecified - Other NEC, Kansas. For the linear model, the following formula is used.

AmountLog = b0 + b1* PopulationLog +b2* Length

where:
   AmountLog = Log(Amount)*0.075
   PopulationLog=Log(Population)*0.065
   Length = length of CEO tenure *0.1

CEO tenure is converted to a number that ranges from 0 to 1, this ensures better simulation results for the HONN model. For example, if CEO tenure is 1 then Length equals 0.1. The following linear model is employed in Table 6.

AmountLog = -0.1724 + 1.28693*PopulationLog – 0.04516*Length

The following nonlinear model for 29X (Kansas) is generated by HONN:

AmountLog = 0.0219+1.1571* PopulationLog -0.3802* PopulationLog^2

-0.2416* Length -0.4921* Length * PopulationLog +2.2599* Length * PopulationLog^2

-1.8606* Length^2 +4.1006* Length^2 * PopulationLog -3.6252* Length^2 * PopulationLog^2

The Root MSE is calculated for the linear model generated from SAS and for the nonlinear model from PHONN to determine which model provides better results. The evidence shows that the linear model has a Root MSE of 0.063008, and the nonlinear model has a Root MSE of 0.062370. This suggests that the nonlinear model, generated by PHONN, is about 1.00% better than the linear model, since the nonlinear model has a smaller Root MSE.

Chart 9 shows the linear model for Long Term Debt Outstanding – Full Faith & Credit – Other,

Table 6. Linear and nonlinear models. Long term debt issue, unspecified - Other NEC for Kansas, USA.

Observation	PopulationLog	Length	AmountLog Actual Data	Linear Model Results	HONN Results	Linear Model Squared Error	HONN Model Squared Error
1	0.527935	0.30	0.406208	0.493478	0.508009	0.007616	0.010364
2	0.572622	0.40	0.596129	0.546471	0.530620	0.002466	0.004291
3	0.587517	0.40	0.588611	0.565641	0.555725	0.000528	0.001082
4	0.610831	0.20	0.616207	0.604677	0.618828	0.000133	0.000007
5	0.528473	0.20	0.531756	0.498686	0.524390	0.001094	0.000054
6	0.547687	0.40	0.338314	0.514382	0.506209	0.031000	0.028189
7	0.562294	0.10	0.544907	0.546728	0.566210	0.000003	0.000454
8	0.610322	0.10	0.618226	0.608538	0.608775	0.000094	0.000089
9	0.611629	0.10	0.682940	0.610220	0.605821	0.005288	0.005947
10	0.641219	0.10	0.660773	0.648300	0.635964	0.000156	0.000615
11	0.510181	0.10	0.522168	0.479661	0.515253	0.001807	0.000048
12	0.666636	0.10	0.590377	0.681011	0.664930	0.008215	0.005558
13	0.610094	0.10	0.561201	0.608244	0.612279	0.002213	0.002609
14	0.640001	0.10	0.579234	0.646734	0.640120	0.004556	0.003707
15	0.633885	0.10	0.672525	0.638863	0.628118	0.001133	0.001972
16	0.664794	0.40	0.685333	0.665092	0.676669	0.000410	0.000075
17	0.689167	0.40	0.779784	0.696459	0.710487	0.006943	0.004802
18	0.743596	0.20	0.812792	0.775540	0.764889	0.001388	0.002295
19	0.774295	0.40	0.837269	0.806016	0.845849	0.000977	0.000074
Observation	PopulationLog	Length	AmountLog Actual Data	Linear Model Results	HONN Results	Linear Model Squared Error	HONN Model Squared Error
20	0.700627	0.40	0.695499	0.711208	0.734774	0.000247	0.001543
21	0.528300	0.10	0.488603	0.502980	0.535806	0.000207	0.002228
22	0.680877	0.10	0.671900	0.699339	0.673138	0.000753	0.000002
23	0.662653	0.10	0.657888	0.675885	0.656716	0.000324	0.000001
24	0.503734	0.20	0.417051	0.466848	0.501655	0.002480	0.007158
25	0.510837	0.40	0.349047	0.466957	0.444391	0.013903	0.009091
26	0.594726	0.10	0.658640	0.588467	0.590858	0.004924	0.004594
27	0.501396	0.20	0.555549	0.463840	0.487767	0.008411	0.004594
28	0.697411	0.10	0.643864	0.720617	0.690583	0.005891	0.002183
29	0.486593	0.20	0.518082	0.444789	0.474048	0.005372	0.001939
30	0.489621	0.40	0.467581	0.439653	0.401383	0.000780	0.004382
31	0.555602	0.40	0.491331	0.524568	0.509314	0.001105	0.000323
32	0.552078	0.40	0.622874	0.520033	0.494882	0.010576	0.016382
33	0.761466	0.40	0.786647	0.789505	0.828246	0.000008	0.001730
Root MSE						0.063008	0.062370

AmountLog = -0.17240 + 1.28695* PopulationLog -0.04516* Length
where: AmountLog = Log(Amount)*0.075; PopulationLog=Log(Population)*0.065

NEC for Kansas. Similar to Chart 3, Chart 9 also shows that the amount issued is inversely related to CEO tenure. Specifically, the amount issued decreases when CEO tenure increases.

Chart 10 shows the nonlinear model of Long Term Debt Issue, Unspecified – Other, NEC, for Kansas. The results show that the amount issued is inversely related to CEO tenure when population is small. However, there is an opposite effect when the population is large. Specifically, the amount issued decreases as the length of CEO tenure increases when the population is small, and the amount issued and CEO tenure both increase when population is large.

CONCLUSION

This research employs linear and nonlinear models to study the relationship between CEO tenure and debt. Using t-test, this chapter finds significant relation between CEO tenure and the Long Term Debt Beginning Outstanding, NEC (19X), Long Term Debt Issue, Unspecified – Other NEC (29X), Long Term Debt Outstanding Full Faith & Credit -Other NEC (41X), and Long Term Debt Outstanding Non-guaranteed –Other NEC (44X). From the linear models, this study find that the longer the CEO tenure the lesser the amount of debt in Long Term Debt Issue Unspecified –Other NEC (29X), Long Term Debt Outstanding Full Faith & Credit -Other NEC (41X), and Long Term Debt Outstanding Non-guaranteed–Other NEC (44X). This study employs HONN simulator in building the nonlinear model. The results show that the nonlinear model is about 1.00% more accurate than linear model in simulating Long Term Debt Unspecified –Other NEC (29X), Kansas.

Future research in this area can consider not only using PHONN simulator, but also other HONN simulators to model the relationship between CEO tenure and short-term debt.

FUTURE RESEARCH DIRECTIONS

This chapter shows that nonlinear models generated by the HONN simulator can outperform linear models. As mentioned above, future research can examine the relation between CEO tenure and different types of debt using the HONN simulator. Another direction is to examine the above relation in the private sector. References of this new direction are included in the 'Additional Reading' section.

REFERENCES

Azoff, E. (1994). *Neural network time series forecasting of financial markets.* New York: Wiley.

Ahmed, A., Billings, B., Morton, R., & Stanford-Harris, M. (2002). The role of accounting conservatism in mitigating bondholder-shareholder conflicts over dividend policy and in reducing debt costs. *The Accounting Review, 77*(4), 867-890.

Baber, W., & Gore, A. (2005). *Consequences of GAAP reporting requirements evidence from municipal debt issues.* Unpublished working paper. George Washington University and University of Oregon.

Bansal, R., & Viswanathan, S. (1993). No arbitrage and arbitrage pricing: A new approach. *The Journal of Finance, 48*(4), 1231-1263.

Beatty, A., & Weber, J. (2003). The effects of debt contracting on voluntary accounting method changes. *The Accounting Review, 78*(1), 119-143.

Benson, E. (1979). The search for information by underwriters and its impact on municipal interest cost. *Journal of Finance, 34*, 871-884.

Benson, E., Marks, B., & Raman, K. (1984). State regulation of accounting practices and municipal borrowing costs. *Journal of Accounting and Public Policy, 3*(2), 107-122.

Benson, E., Marks B., & Raman, K. (1991). The effect of voluntary GAAP compliance and financial disclosure on governmental borrowing costs. *Journal of Accounting, Auditing & Finance, 6*(3), 303-319.

Berger, P., Ofek, E., & Yermack, D.(1997). Managerial entrenchment and capital structure decisions *The Journal of Finance, 52*(4), 1411-1439

Brock, W., & Sayers, C. (1988). Is the business cycle characterized by deterministic chaos? *Journal of Monetary Economics, 22*(1), 71-91.

Brown, S., Goetzmann, W., & Kumar, A. (1998). The Dow theory: William Peter Hamilton's track record reconsidered. *The Journal of Finance, 53*(4), 1311-1334.

Defond, M., & Hung, M. (2004). Investor protection and corporate governance: Evidence from worldwide CEO turnover. *Journal of Accounting Research, 42*(2), 269-312.

Downing, C., & Zhang, F. (2004). Trading activity and price volatility in the municipal bond market. *Journal of Finance, 59*(2), 899-931.

Fairchild, L., & Kock, T. (1998). The impact of state disclosure requirements on municipal yields. *National Tax Journal, 51*(4), 733-753.

Frank, M., & Goyal, V. (2003). Testing the pecking order theory of capital structure. *Journal of Financial Economics, 67*(2), 217-248.

Franses, P., & Draisma, G. (1997). Recognizing changing seasonal patterns using artificial neural networks. *Journal of Econometrics, 81*(1), 273-280.

Freeman, R., & Tse, S. (1992). A non-linear model of security price responses to unexpected earnings. *Journal of Accounting Research, Autumn*, 85-109.

Friend, I., & Lang, L. (1988). An empirical test of the impact of managerial self-interest on corporate capital structure. *The Journal of Finance, 43*(2), 271-281.

Garcia, R., & Gençay, R. (2000). Pricing and hedging derivative securities with neural networks and a homogeneity hint. *Journal of Econometrics, 94*, 93-115.

Garvey, G., & Hanka, G. (1999). Capital structure and corporate control: The effect of antitakeover statutes on firm leverage. *The Journal of Finance, 54*(2), 519-548.

Harris, L., & Piwowar, M. (2004). *Municipal bond liquidity.* Unpublished working paper, University of Southern California.

Hutchinson, J., Lo, A., & Poggio, T. (1994). A nonparametric approach to pricing and hedging derivative securities via learning networks. *The Journal of Finance, 49*(3), 851-890.

Ijiri, Y., & Sunder, S. (1990). Information technologies and organizations. *The Accounting Review, 65*(3), 658-668.

Ingram, R., & Copeland, R. (1982). Municipal market measures and reporting practices: An extension. *Journal of Accounting Research, 20*(2), 766-772.

Jensen, M., & Meckling, W. (1976). Theory of the firm: Managerial behavior, agency costs and ownership structure. *Journal of financial Economics, 3*, 305-360.

Jung, K., Kim, Y., & Stulz, R. (1996). Timing, investment opportunities, managerial discretion, and the security issue decision. *Journal of Financial Economics, 42*, 159-186.

Kaplan, R., & Welam, U. (1974). Overhead allocation with imperfect markets and nonlinear technology. *The Accounting Review, 49*(3), 477–484.

Karayiannis, N., & A. Venetsanopoulos. (1993). *Artificial neural networks: Learning algorithms, performance evaluation and applications.* Kluwer.

Kryzanowski, L., Galler, M., & Wright, D. (1993). Using artificial neural networks to pick stock. *Financial Analysts Journal, 49*(4), 21-28.

Lang, L., Ofek, E., & Stulz, R. (1996). Leverage, investment, and firm growth. *Journal of Financial Economics, 40*(1) 3-29.

Lee, T., White, H., & Granger, C. (1993). Testing for neglected nonlinearity in time series models: A comparison of neural network methods and alternative tests. *Journal of Economics, 56*(3), 269-290.

Lee, C., & Wu, C. (1988). Expectation formation and financial ratio adjustment process. *The Accounting Review, 63*(2), 292-307.

Morellec, E. (2004). Can managerial discretion explain observed leverage ratios? *Review of Financial Studies, 17*(1), 257-294.

Myers, S. (1977). Determinants of corporate borrowing. *Journal of Financial Economics, 5,* 147-175.

Rajan, R., & Zingales, L. (1995). What do we know about capital structure? some evidence from international data. *The Journal of Finance, 50*(5), 1421-1460.

Redding, N., Kowalczyk, A., & Downs, T. (1993). Constructive high-order network algorithm that is polynomial time. *Neural Networks, 6,* 997-1010.

Schipper, K. (1991). Commentary on analysts' forecasts. *Accounting Horizons, 5*(4), 105-119.

Schmukler, S., & Vesperoni, E. (2006). Financial globalization and debt maturity in emerging economies. *Journal of Development Economics, 79,* 183– 207.

Shleifer, A., & Vishny, R. (1997). A survey of corporate governance. *The Journal of Finance, 52*(2), 737-783.

Trigeorgis, L. (1991). Why cost-reimbursed not-for-profits use debt financing despite the absence of tax incentives. *Financial Accountability & Management, 7*(4), 229-238.

Wallace, W. A. (1981). Internal control reporting practices in the municipal sector. *The Accounting Review, 56*(3), 666-689.

Wilson, E. R., & Howard, T. P. (1984). The association between municipal market measures and selected financial reporting practices: Additional evidence. *Journal of Accounting Research, 22*(1), 207-224.

Zhang, M., Zhang, J. C., & Fulcher, J. (2000). Higher order neural network group models for data approximation. *International Journal of Neural Systems, 10*(2), 123-142.

ADDITIONAL READING

Allayannis, G., Brown, G., & Klapper, L. (2003). Capital structure and financial risk: Evidence from foreign debt use in East Asia. *The Journal of Finance, 58*(6), 2667–2710.

Baber, W., Kang, S., & Liang, L. (2006). *Strong boards, management entrenchment, and accounting restatements.* Unpublished working paper. George Washington University.

Berkovitch, E., & Israel, R. (1996). The design of internal control and capital structure. *The Review of Financial Studies, 9*(1), 209-240.

Booth, L., Aivazian, V., Demirguc-Kunt, A., & Maksimovic, V. (2001). Capital structures in developing countries. *Journal of Finance, 56,* 87–120.

Datta, S., Iskandar-datta, M., & Raman, K. (2005). Managerial stock ownership and the maturity structure of corporate debt. *The Journal of Finance, 60*(5), 2333–2350.

Eichenseher, J., & Shields, D. (1985). Corporate director liability and monitoring preferences. *Journal of Accounting and Public Policy, 4*, 13-31.

Fama, E. (1980). Agency problems and the theory of the firm. *Journal of Political Economy, 88*(2), 288-307.

Graham, J., & Harvey, C. (2001). The theory and practice of corporate finance: Evidence from the field. *Journal of Financial Economics, 60*, 187–243.

Leland, H. (1998). Agency costs, risk management, and capital structure. *Journal of Finance, 53*, 1213–1243.

Myers, S. (1977), The determinants of corporate borrowing, *Journal of Financial Economics, 5*, 147–175.

APPENDIX

Chart 1. Linear model for long term debt beginning outstanding, NEC

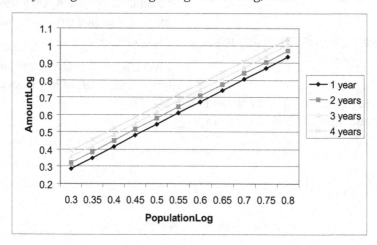

Chart 2. Linear models for long term debt issue, unspecified – Other, NEC

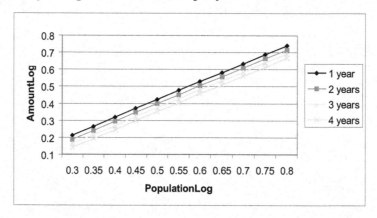

Chart 3. Linear models for long term debt outstanding – Full Faith & Credit – Other, NEC

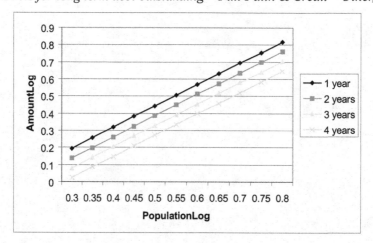

Chart 4. Linear models for long term debt outstanding – non-guaranteed – Other, NEC

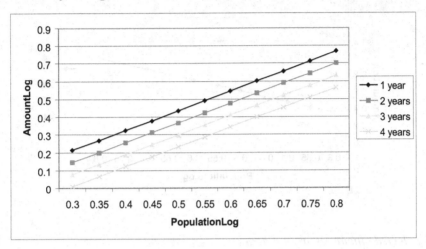

Chart 5. Chief elected official tenure = 1 Year

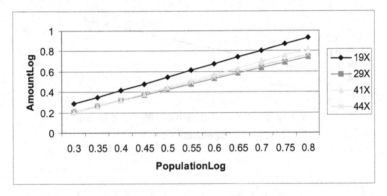

Chart 6. Chief elected official tenure = 2 Years

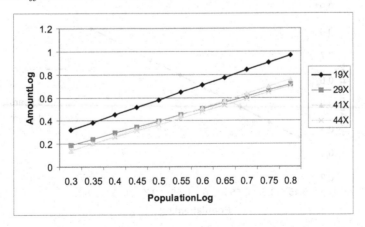

Chart 7. Chief elected official tenure = 3 Years

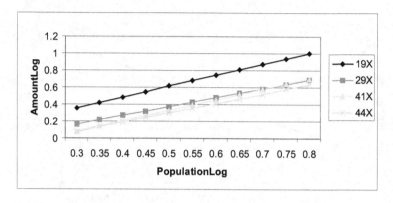

Chart 8. Chief elected official tenure = 4 Years

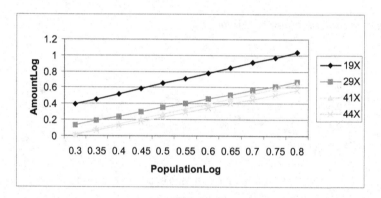

Chart 9. Linear models of long term debt issue, unspecified – Other, NEC, Kansas

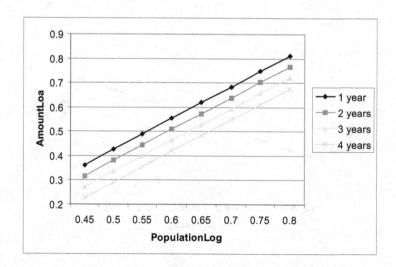

Chart 10. Nonlinear models of long term debt issue, unspecified – Other, NEC, Kansas

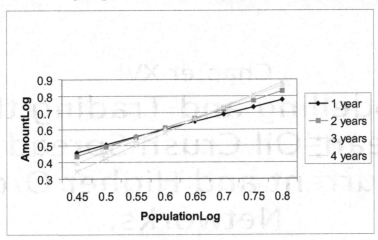

Chapter XVI
Modelling and Trading the Soybean–Oil Crush Spread with Recurrent and Higher Order Networks:
A Comparative Analysis

Christian L. Dunis
CIBEF, and Liverpool John Moores University, UK

Jason Laws
CIBEF, and Liverpool John Moores University, UK

Ben Evans
CIBEF, and Dresdner-Kleinwort-Investment Bank in Frankfurt, Germany

ABSTRACT

This chapter investigates the soybean-oil "crush" spread, that is the profit margin gained by process-ing soybeans into soyoil. Soybeans form a large proportion (over 1/5th) of the agricultural output of US farmers and the profit margins gained will therefore have a wide impact on the US economy in general. The chapter uses a number of techniques to forecast and trade the soybean crush spread. A traditional regression analysis is used as a benchmark against more sophisticated models such as a MultiLayer Perceptron (MLP), Recurrent Neural Networks and Higher Order Neural Networks. These are then used to trade the spread, the implementation of a number of filtering techniques as used in the literature are utilised to further refine the trading statistics of the models. The results show that the best model before transactions costs both in- and out-of-sample is the Recurrent Network generating a superior risk ad-justed return to all other models investigated. However in the case of most of the models investigated the cost of trading the spread all but eliminates any profit potential.

INTRODUCTION

Motivation for this chapter is taken from Dunis *et al.* (2005) who discover that trading the Gasoline Crack spread can lead to abnormal out-of-sample returns especially when traded using the neural network architectures described here. Further it is discovered that the application of a filter can further refine the trading statistics achieved. The Soybean Crush Spread can be interpreted as the profit margin gained by processing soybeans into soybean oil and soybean meal. It is simply the monetary difference between 1 bushel of soybeans on the one side and 1 bushel's worth of soybean oil and 1 bushel's worth of soybean meal on the other, all three of which have futures contracts that are traded on the Chicago Board of Trade (CBOT). The focus of this chapter will be the spread between soybeans and soybean oil henceforth called "soybean-oil spread."

Although large scale production of soybeans occurred only after the 2nd World War soybeans are now very important to US agriculture. In 2004 around 23% of all crops (by acre) planted in the US were soybeans. Approximately 400,000 farmers harvest 3.1 billion bushels of soybeans annually. Approximately 39 million tons of soymeal and about 18,800 million pounds of soybean oil was manufactured in the US.[1] It is easy to underestimate the impact soybean prices have on the US economy, and in particular the agricultural economy.

Soybeans can be processed into two main products, soymeal and soyoil. Soymeal is used extensively in livestock feeds, mainly for poultry, swine and cattle. However livestock feed is a very substitutional good and therefore demand for soymeal is influenced by the demand for livestock and the relative prices of other protein meals (such as canola, rapeseed or cottonseed meal). The demand for soymeal can therefore have an influence on the price of soybeans.

Soyoil is the most widely consumed oil in the US, in fact it forms 75% of all oils consumed as vegetable oils and fats.[1] High vegetable oil prices in the late 1990s spurred a global expansion in the production of soyoil. An increase in crushing activity led to an oversupply of soymeal and a collapse in the price of soymeal, along with protein meals in general. Uses of soyoil are extensive for example, soybean oil can be used in paints, waterproof cements, alkyd resins, soaps, shaving creams, greases and lubricants, enamels, varnishes, leather dressing, caulking compounds, grain-dust suppressant and as an alternative fuel (biodiesel). With the increase in petroleum prices this latter use of soyoil is starting to become of particular interest.

In fact soy-biodiesel may well prove to be quite a breakthrough in sustainable energy resources. In small quantities (~2% soyoil and 98% traditional diesel fuel) biodiesel can provide both economic and lubrication benefits over straight diesel fuel. In larger quantities (~20% soyoil and 80% traditional diesel fuel) it can provide significant emissions benefits to cut air pollution. In the extreme case (~100% soyoil) it could provide a fully sustainable replacement for traditional diesel fuels.[2]

The calculation of the soybean-oil spread is not a straight forward one, since the pricing of both contracts is in different units. Soybeans are priced in cents per bushel and soyoil is priced in cents per pound. From one bushel of soybeans, on average 11 pounds of oil[3] can be extracted. The spread should therefore be calculated as shown in equation 1 below:

$$S_t = P_{SB} - (11 \times P_{SO}) \tag{1}$$

where:

S_t = Price of spread at time t (in cents per bushel)

P_{SB} = Price of soybean contract at time t (in cents per bushel)

P_{SO} = Price of soyoil contract at time t (in cents per pound)

The manufacture of soybeans is subsidised heavily, one processor of soybeans Archer Daniels Midland (ADM) is a case in point. In fact "Archer, Daniels Midland has been the most prominent recipient of corporate welfare in recent U.S. history" (Bovard, 1995, page 1). As an example of the level of subsidies that ADM enjoy "every $1 of profits earned by ADM's corn sweetener operation costs consumers $10…at least 43% of ADM's annual profits are from products heavily subsidised or protected by the American government" (Bovard, 1995, page 1). The case of whether this market is efficient is pertinent, particularly in light of the cost to the US taxpayer.

The spread time series for the in-sample period (01/01/1995 - 25/04/2003) is shown in Figure 1.

From Figure 1 it is clear that the spread is mean reverting only in the final 2/3rd of the in-sample period with large degree of market trending characterising the first 1/3rd of the sample period. This is due to the fact that although the spread is representative of a profit margin and as the margin increases this tempts suppliers to increase output. The delay between planting soybeans and increasing output is too long to address short-term fluctuations in demand. Therefore mean-reversion is not a consistent characteristic of this spread.

The reason that this relationship can show large and sustained deviations from fair value is because "the amount of [soy]meal and [soy]oil and the quality of the [soy]oil produced by a bushel of soybeans varies according to growing conditions" (Simon, 1999, page 247), it is accepted that in extreme cases this could have some effect on the calculations of the spread, although since the models used all trade futures contracts the standard 1-11 conversion given by CBOT has been used for the entire time series in this chapter. It is further noted "the results…indicate that the degree of mean-reversion during the sample period would have been adequate to give rise to profitable trading strategies" (Simon, 1999, page 288). This

Figure 1. Soybean-oil Crush Spread price 01/01/1995 – 25/04/2003

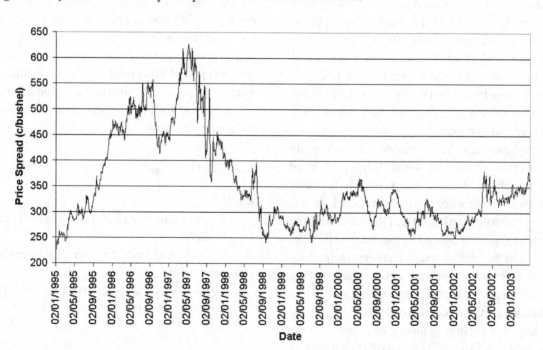

finding stimulates this chapter. If it is possible to gain profits from a simple mean reverting model, such as a fair value model investigated in Evans *et al.* (2006), would more sophisticated models, such as traditional regression analysis or neural networks, enable a trader to generate larger out-of-sample risk-adjusted returns?

This chapter extends the literature in two ways: firstly the soybean-oil spread is traded using a traditional regression analysis approach, which is used as a benchmark for more advanced regression models, a MultiLayer Perceptron (MLP), a Recurrent Neural Network (RNN) and a Higher Order Neural Network (HONN). The models are used to forecast ΔS_t, the daily change in the spread.

Secondly the correlation filter of Evans *et al.* (2006) is investigated and is benchmarked against a more traditional threshold filter. The exact specifications of these filters are included in section 5. Using these filters it may be possible to further refine the trading statistics of the models described above.

The remainder of this chapter is set out as follows: Section 2 details some of the relevant literature; section 3 explains the data and methodology; section 4 defines the trading models used; section 5 defines the filters that have been employed; sections 6 and 7 give the results and conclusions respectively.

LITERATURE REVIEW

Many researchers have extolled the virtues of soybeans, listing benefits such as the prevention of bone loss in osteoporosis sufferers (Arjmandi *et al.*, 1996), improvement in cardiovascular disease factors (Antony *et al.*, 1996), and the possession of some cancer protective compounds (Adlercreutz *et al.*, 1995). Studies such as Simon (1999) and Rechner and Poitras (1993) investigate the soybean crush spread in terms of its trading potential. Both papers indicate an ability to generate abnormal

returns with mean reverting trading rules being the most often used tool.

Simon (1999) states "the soybean crush spread reverts to a long run equilibrium that is characterised by strong seasonality and by an upward trend over the sample period" (page 288), the sample period in this case being January 1985-February 1995. The soybean spread, over the in-sample period used in this research, also seems to revert to a long run equilibrium however as shown in Figure 1 these deviations can be quite large. This will inevitably impact on the risk-adjusted return of any trading method and may result in the trader being priced out of the market.

Rechner and Poitras (1993) use a day trading strategy that has the added benefit of a short time horizon. Liquidating trades regularly may prevent the trader being out of the market. Using the trading rule "If the GPM[4] on the open is less (greater) than the previous day's close, a reverse crush (normal crush)[5] spread is placed. In all cases the position is liquidated on the close of the same day" (Rechner and Poitras, 1998, page 63). Using this rule they find that "participants in the soybean complex pits can potentially pursue profitable "naïve" day trading strategies based on the GPM. In particular the open-to-close day trading strategies examined here could be exploited by floor traders operating in those pits." (Rechner & Poitras, 1993, page 74).

Further research into soybean markets was conducted by Emery and Liu (2003), who investigated the pricing relationship between Hog, Corn and Soymeal futures. It was found that "there is a significant tendency for the spread among the three futures prices to revert to its long-run equilibrium" (Emery and Liu, 2003, page 20). Although this is not a startling insight into the dynamics of spreads, Emery and Liu (2003) go further and suggest "the spread also significantly reverts to short-run 5-day and 10-day moving averages" (Emery and Liu, 2003, page 20). Thus proving that the Hog-Corn-Soybean spread is predictable in both the short and long-run and ultimately that *ex post, ex ante* profits are achievable from these strategies.

Krishnaswamy *et al.* (2000) attempt to show the development of neural networks as modelling tools for finance. In turn they cite valuable contributions from Kryzanowski *et al.* (1993), Refenes *et al.* (1995), Bansal and Viswanathan (1993) and Zirilli (1997) in the field of stock market and individual stock prediction, proving that not only do Neural Networks (NNs) outperform linear regression models, but that NNs are "superior in dealing with structurally unstable relationships, notably stock market returns," (Krishnaswamy *et al.,* 2000, page 79). This research kick started the search for increasingly more advanced NN architectures.

Recurrent networks were first developed by Elman (1990) and possess a form of error feedback, which is further explained in section 4.3. These networks are generally better than MLP networks but as mentioned in Tenti (1996), they do suffer from long computational times. However according to Saad *et al.* (1998), compared to other architectures this should not matter a lot as "RNN has the capability to dynamically incorporate past experience due to internal recurrence, and it is the most powerful network of the three in this respect... but its minor disadvantage is the implementation complexity," (Saad *et al.*, 1998, page 1468).

HONNs were first introduced by Giles and Maxwell (1987) and were called "Tensor Networks". Although the extent of their use in finance is limited, Knowles *et al.* (2005) show that despite shorter computational times and limited input variables on the EUR/USD time series "the best HONN models show a profit increase over the MLP of around 8%", (Knowles *et al.*, 2005, page 7). A significant advantage of HONNs is detailed in Zhang and Fulcher (2002) "HONN models are able to provide some rationale for the simulations they produce and thus can be regarded as "open box" rather then "black box." Moreover, HONNs are able to simulate higher frequency, higher

order non-linear data, and consequently provide superior simulations compared to those produced by ANNs (Artificial Neural Networks)," (Zhang and Fulcher, 2002, page 188).

This chapter investigates the use of traditional regression analysis, which is used as a benchmark for the MLP, RNN and HONN models. These models are described more fully in sections 4.2, 4.3 and 4.4 respectively.

DATA AND METHODOLOGY

Data

The data set used is daily closing price data of the Chicago Board of Trade (CBOT) Soybean futures and CBOT Soyoil futures. With both markets trading on the same exchange and closing at identical times we avoid the problem of non-simultaneous pricing. Figure 1 above shows the in-sample pricing series of soybeans and soybean oil. The spread between the two pricing series is calculated as shown in equation 1 above. The histogram and statistics of the in-sample returns are shown in appendix figure 1.

Following the methodology from Butterworth and Holmes (2002), Dunis *et al.* (2005) and Evans *et al.* (2006) the returns of the spread are calculated as follows:

$$\Delta S_t = \left[\frac{(P_{SB(t)} - P_{SB(t-1)})}{(P_{SB(t-1)})} - \frac{(P_{SO(t)} - P_{SO(t-1)})}{(P_{SO(t-1)})} \right]$$

(2)

where:

ΔS_t = Percentage return of spread at time t.

$P_{SB(t)}$ is the price of soybeans at time t (in cents per bushel)

$P_{SB(t-1)}$ is the price of soybeans at time t-1 (in cents per bushel)

$P_{SO(t)}$ is the price of soybeans at time t (in cents per bushel)[6]

$P_{SO(t-1)}$ is the price of soybeans at time t-1 (in cents per bushel)

Forming the returns series in this way means that it is possible to present results with more conventional % return/risk profiles.

The dataset has been split into 2 sets, the in-sample and out-of-sample. They are shown in Table 1.

In the case of the neural network models the in-sample dataset was further divided into two periods. They are shown in Table 2.

The reason for the further segmentation of the in-sample dataset is to avoid overfitting. As described in section 4.5 the networks are trained to fit the training dataset and stopped when returns on the test dataset are maximised.

Rollovers

Using an aggregated timeseries brings a unique problem, since any long-term study will require a continuous series. If a trader takes a position on a futures contract, which subsequently expires, he can take the same position on the next available contract. This is called rolling forward. The problem with rolling forward is that two contracts of different expiry but same underlying may not (and usually do not) have the same price. When the roll forward technique is applied to a futures

time series it will cause the time series to exhibit periodic blips in the pricing series.

In this study, we have rolled forward both contracts on the first day of the contract's expiry month. The cost of carry, which is the cause of the difference between the cash and futures price is determined by the cost (physical and financial) of buying the underlying in the cash market now and holding it until futures expiry. Since the cost of storage of the underlying is different (storing soybeans is different to storing soyoil), they will not offset each other completely. Therefore, the additional return that is caused by the cost of carry will have to be eliminated.

In order to eliminate the effect of the cost of carry, the return calculation is slightly modified. When a rollover is apparent the return is calculated as equation 12 but with $P_{SO(t-1)}$ and $P_{SB(t-1)}$ being the price at t-1 of the next available contract. For example, when rolling over from the February to the April contract on the first day of February, $P_{SO(t-1)}$ and $P_{SB(t-1)}$ will be prices of the April contract for the last trading day in January. This eliminates the effect of rollovers.

Transactions Costs

In order to realistically assess the returns of each model they have been assessed in the presence of transactions costs. The transactions costs are

Table 1. In-sample and out-of-sample dates

Data set	Dates	No. Observations
In-Sample	01/01/1995 – 25/04/2003	2170
Out-of-Sample	28/04/2003 - 01/01/2005	440

Table 2. Training and test period dates

Period of In-sample	Dates	No. Observations
Training	01/01/1995 – 17/08/2001	1730
Test	20/08/2001 – 25/04/2003	440

calculated from an average of five bid-ask spreads on soybeans and soybean oil (ten in total), taken from different times of the trading day. These are 0.09% for soybeans and 0.20% for soybean oil.[7] Therefore, on the spread we have a total round trip transaction cost of 0.29%. Since commission fees are relatively small they have not been considered here.

TRADING MODELS

The following section details the trading rules used, the architectures of the neural network models and the training procedure. The use of a cointegration fair value trading model, such as that used in Evans *et al.* (2006) has not been used here. The Johansen (1988) cointegration test showed no significant cointegration between the soybean and soybean oil series so any model would be mis-specified.

Traditional Regression Analysis

The benchmark trading decision model is traditional regression analysis. That is an ARMA or GARCH model. Firstly an ARMA(10,10) model was used to estimate the percentage change in the spread (since the spread is I(1)) and a restricted model was estimated using the Akaike information criterion as the optimising parameter (over the in-sample period). Autocorrelation was then tested for and removed with the addition of lags of the percentage change in the spread. If heteroskedasticity was present an alternative GARCH(1,1) model was similarly estimated. The final model arrived at is a Garch(1,1)ARMA(1,1) this model is free from heteroskedasticity and autocorrelation, with an optimised Akaike information criterion.[8] This model was then used to estimate the out-of-sample period using a "one size fits all" estimation as in Dunis and Laws (2003).

Multi-Layer Perceptron

The most basic neural network model used in this chapter is the MultiLayer Perceptron (MLP). The MLP network has three layers; they are the input layer (explanatory variables), the output layer (the model estimation of the time series) and the hidden layer. The number of nodes in the hidden layer defines the amount of complexity that the model can fit. The input and hidden layers also include a bias node (similar to the intercept for standard regression), which has a fixed value of 1, see Lindemann *et al.* (2005) and Krishnaswamy *et al.* (2000).

The network processes information as shown below:

1. The input nodes contain the values of the explanatory variables (in this case lagged values of the change in the spread).
2. These values are transmitted to the hidden layer as the weighted sum of its inputs.
3. The hidden layer passes the information through a non-linear activation function and, onto the output layer.

The connections between neurons for a single neuron in the net are shown in Figure 3, where:

$x_t^{[n]}$ ($n = 1,2,...,k + 1$) are the model inputs (including the input bias node) at time t (in this case these are lags of the spread).
$h_t^{[m]}$ ($m = 1,2,...,m + 1$) are the hidden nodes outputs (including the hidden bias node)
$\Delta \tilde{S}_t$ is the MLP model output (predicted % change in the spread at time t)
u_{jk} and w_j are the network weights
Ⓙ is the transfer sigmoid function: $S(x) = \dfrac{1}{1+e^{-x}}$
⊘ is a linear function: $F(x) = \sum_i x_i$

Figure 3. A single output, fully connected MLP model

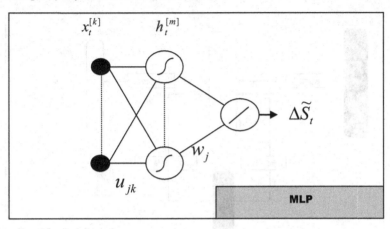

The error function to be minimised is:

$$E(u_{jk}, w_j) = \frac{1}{T} \sum (\Delta S_t - \Delta \tilde{S}_t(u_{jk}, w_j))^2$$

with ΔS_t being the target value (the actual % change of the spread at time t).

Recurrent Neural Network

While a complete explanation of the recurrent network is beyond the scope of this chapter, below is presented a brief explanation of the significant differences between RNN and MLP architectures. For an exact specification of the recurrent network, see Elman (1990).

A simple recurrent network has activation feedback, which embodies short-term memory, see for example Elman (1990). The advantages of using recurrent networks over feedforward networks, for modelling non-linear time series, has been well documented in the past, see for example Adam *et al.* (1993). However as described in Tenti (1996) "the main disadvantage of RNNs is that they require substantially more connections, and more memory in simulation, than standard backpropagation networks" (Tenti, 1996, page 569), thus resulting in a substantial increase in computational time. However having said this RNNs can yield better results in comparison

to simple MLPs due to the additional memory inputs.

Connections of a simple recurrent network are shown in Figure 4.

The state/hidden layer shown above is updated with external inputs, as in the simple MLP (section 4.2) but also with activation from previous forward propagation, shown as "Previous State" above. In short the RNN architecture can provide more accurate outputs because the inputs are (potentially) taken from all previous values.

The Elman network in this study uses the transfer sigmoid function, error function and linear function as described for the MLP architecture in section 4.2. This has been done in order to be able to draw direct comparisons between the architectures of both models.

Higher Order Neural Network

Higher Order Neural Networks (HONNs) were first introduced by Giles and Maxwell (1987) who referred to them as "Tensor networks." While they have already experienced some success in the field of pattern recognition and associative recall, they have not been used extensively in financial applications. The architecture of a three input second order HONN is shown in Figure 5, where:

Figure 4. Architecture of Elman or recurrent neural network

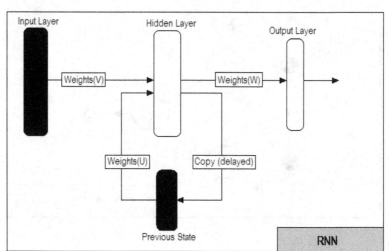

Figure 5. Left, MLP with three inputs and two hidden nodes. Right, second order HONN with three inputs

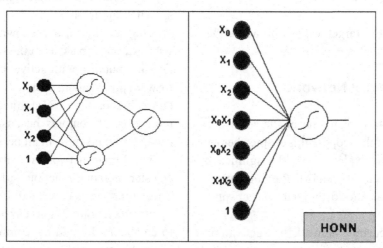

● are the model inputs

⌇ is the transfer sigmoid function:

$$S(x) = \frac{1}{1 + e^{-x}}$$

⊘ is a linear function: $F(x) = \sum_i x_i$

HONNs use joint activation functions; this technique reduces the need to establish the relationships between inputs when training. Further-

more this reduces the number of free weights and means that HONNs can be faster to train than even MLPs. However because the number of inputs can be very large for higher order architectures, orders of 4 and over are rarely used.

Another advantage of the reduction of free weights means that the problems of overfitting and local optima affecting the results can be largely avoided, Knowles *et al.* (2005). For a complete description of HONNs see Giles and Maxwell (1987).

The HONN in this study uses the transfer sigmoid function and error function as described for the MLP architecture in section 4.2. This has been done in order to be able to draw direct comparisons between the architectures of the models.

Neural Network Training Procedure

The training of the network is of utmost importance, since it is possible for the network to learn the training subset exactly (commonly referred to as overfitting). For this reason the network training must be stopped early. This is achieved by dividing the dataset into 3 different components (as shown in Table 2). Firstly a training subset is used to optimise the model, the "back propagation of errors" algorithm is used to establish optimal weights from the initial random weights. Secondly a test subset is used to stop the training subset from being overfitted. Optimisation of the training subset is stopped when the test subset is at maximum positive return. These two subsets are the equivalent of the in-sample subset for the fair value model. This technique will prevent the model from overfitting the data whilst also ensuring that any structure inherent in the spread is captured.

Finally the out-of-sample subset is used to simulate future values of the time series, which for comparison is the same as the out-of-sample subset of the fair value model.

Since the starting point for each network is a set of random weights, a committee of ten networks has been used to arrive at a trading decision (the average estimate decides on the trading position taken). This helps to overcome the problem of local minima affecting the training procedure. The trading model predicts the change in the spread from one closing price to the next, therefore the average result of all ten neural network models was used as the forecast of the change in the spread, or ΔS_t.

This training procedure is identical for all the neural networks used in this study. The inputs used in the MLP, HONN and RNN are shown in appendix tables 2, 3 and 4 respectively.

TRADING FILTERS

A number of filters have been employed to refine the trading rules, they are detailed in the following section.

Threshold Filter

With all the models in this study predicting the percentage change in the spread ($\Delta \tilde{S}_t$), the threshold filter X is as follows:

If $\Delta \tilde{S}_t > X$ then go, or stay, long the spread
If $\Delta \tilde{S}_t < -X$ then go, or stay, short the spread
If $-X < \Delta \tilde{S}_t < X$, then stay out of the spread

Where $\Delta \tilde{S}_t$ is the model's predicted spread return, X is the level of the filter (optimised in-sample).

With accurate predictions of the spread it should be possible to filter out trades that are smaller than the level of the filter, thus improving the risk/return profile of the model.

Correlation Filter

As well as the application of the threshold filter, the models are filtered in terms of correlation. The idea is to enable the trader to filter out periods of static spread movement (when the correlation between the underlying legs is increasing) and retain periods of dynamic spread movement (when the correlation of the underlying legs of the spread is decreasing). This was done in the following way.

A rolling Z-day correlation of the daily price changes of the two futures contracts is produced for the two legs of the spread. The Y-day change of this series is then calculated. From this a binary output of either 0 if the change in the correlation is above X, or 1 if the change in the correlation is below X. X being the filter level. This is then multiplied by the returns series of the trading model.

Figure 6 shows the entry and exit points of the filter with X=0. It also shows that we enter the market the day after the change in correlation is below zero (ie. $\Delta C < 0$), and exit the market the day after the change in correlation is above zero (ie. $\Delta C > 0$). In the case of figure 6 above we can maintain large moves, such as the one from \$250-\$290 but filter out moves of lower amplitude, such as those that appear from 30/03/1995 to the end of the period shown in Figure 6.

There are several optimising parameters, which can be used for this type of filter, namely the length of correlation lag (Z), period of correlation change (Y) and amount of correlation change (X). For this study we have set the correlation lag to 30-days and the period of correlation change to 1-day.[9] The only optimising parameter used was

the amount of correlation change. Formally the correlation filter, X_c can be written as:

If $\Delta C < X_c$, then take the decision of the trading rule,
If $\Delta C > X_c$, then stay out of the market.

Where ΔC is the change in correlation and, X_c is the size of the correlation filter.

RESULTS

The following section shows the results of the empirical investigation. The filters have been optimised in sample in order to maximise the Calmar ratio, as used in Dunis *et al.* (2005) and defined by Jones and Baehr (2003) as:

$$Calmar\ Ratio = \frac{Return}{|MaxDD|} \tag{5}$$

Figure 6. Operation of the correlation filter

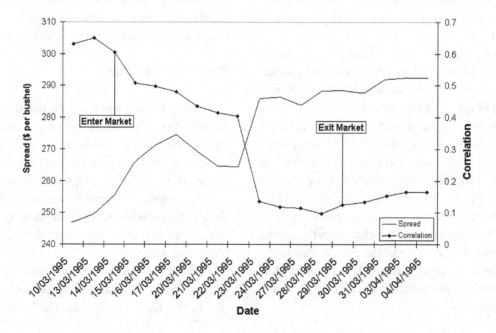

where:

Return is annualised return of trading model

MaxDD is the maximum drawdown of the trading model defined as:

$$Maximum \ drawdown = Min\left[r_t - Max(\sum_{t=1}^{n} r_t) \right]$$

(6)

Equation 5 is given a high priority since futures are naturally leveraged instruments. This statistic gives a good measure of the amount of return that can be expected for the amount of investment capital needed to finance a strategy. Furthermore, unlike the Sharpe ratio which assumes large losses and large gains are equally undesirable, the Calmar ratio defines risk as the maximum likely loss and is therefore a more realistic measure of risk adjusted return.

Traditional Regression Analysis

This section contains the results of the GARCH(1,1) ARMA(2,2) model, the trading statistics are shown in Tables 3 and 4.[10]

It is evident from Table 3 above that the GARCH(1,1) ARMA(2,2) model, while statistically satisfactory does not produce either high returns or high Calmar ratios in-sample. The threshold filter and correlation filter would have been chosen to take through to the out-of-sample

period since they both outperform the unfiltered model in terms of the in-sample Calmar ratio.

Table 4 above shows the out-of-sample trading statistics of the GARCH(1,1) ARMA(2,2) model. It is evident that the choice of threshold filter from the in-sample statistics, is vindicated as the out-of-sample Calmar ratio is larger than that of the unfiltered model. The choice of the correlation filter in this case is not vindicated leaving us with a lower out-of-sample Calmar ratio than that of the unfiltered model.

Multi-Layer Perceptron Network

This section contains the results of the Multi-Layer Perceptron Network, the trading statistics are shown in Tables 5 and 6.

From the in-sample results it is evident that the correlation filter would have been chosen. This is shown by an improvement in the in-sample Calmar ratio over and above that achieved by the unfiltered model. In this case the threshold filter fails to improve the in-sample statistics and is therefore not chosen.

It is evident from Table 6 that the correlation filter proves to be a good choice since it produces a Calmar ratio above that of the unfiltered model. Further it can be noted that out-of-sample the unfiltered MLP does not out-perform the unfiltered ARMA(2,2) GARCH(1,1) model (in terms of the out-of-sample Calmar ratio) and therefore its use cannot be justified for trading purposes. This is largely a result of high trading costs.

Table 3. In-sample results of GARCH(1,1) ARMA(2,2) model

	Unfiltered	Threshold	Correlation
RETURNS	4.36%	4.73%	9.27%
STDEV	32.17%	32.06%	31.64%
MAXDD	-62.98%	-61.26%	-50.00%
CALMAR	0.0693	0.0772	0.1853
TRADES	60.24	60.34	61.96

Table 4. Out-of-sample results of GARCH(1,1) ARMA(2,2) model

	Unfiltered	Threshold	Correlation
RETURNS	7.97%	7.97%	4.85%
STDEV	33.88%	33.88%	33.73%
MAXDD	-46.77%	-44.92%	-35.63%
CALMAR	0.1705	0.1775	0.1361
TRADES	66.95	66.95	67.45

Recurrent Neural Networks

This section contains the results of the Recurrent Neural Network, the trading statistics are shown in Tables 7 and 8.

From Table 7 both the threshold and correlation filters display improved in-sample performance over and above the unfiltered model and can therefore be selected.

From Table 8 it is evident that the threshold filter improves the out-of-sample trading results of the RNN model in terms of out-of-sample Calmar ratio. The selection of the correlation filter can be considered a bad selection as the out-of-sample Calmar ratio has dropped in relation to the unfiltered model. Conversely, the use of this modelling technique over the benchmark GARCH(1,1) ARMA(2,2) model is justified generating significantly improved Calmar ratios and annualised returns for the unfiltered models.

Higher Order Neural Networks

This section contains the results of the Higher Order Neural Network, the trading statistics are shown in Tables 9 and 10.

From Table 9 the threshold and correlation filters could both have been selected to take through to the out-of-sample dataset since they produce larger in-sample Calmar ratios than the unfiltered model.

From Tables 9 and 10 it is evident that, on the basis of the in-sample statistics, both filters would have been chosen. The out-of-sample statistics show that both filters prove to be good choices, generating Calmar ratios above that of the unfiltered model. The use of HONN architecture is encouraging, generating better in- and out-of-sample statistics for the unfiltered models than the MLP, despite being faster to train.

The results of the filters show that, of those selected there is an improvement in the out-of-sample trading statistics, over and above that

Table 5. In-Sample results of MLP architecture

	Unfiltered	Threshold	Correlation
Return	20.04%	20.04%	21.16%
STDEV	33.64%	33.64%	32.89%
MAXDD	-66.26%	-66.26%	-58.17%
Calmar	0.3025	0.3025	0.3637
Trades	92.27	92.27	92.87

Table 6. Out-of-sample results of MLP architecture

	Unfiltered	Threshold	Correlation
Return	4.99%	4.99%	8.56%
STDEV	35.77%	35.77%	35.26%
MAXDD	-73.55%	-73.55%	-64.88%
Calmar	0.0679	0.0679	0.1320
Trades	103.75	103.75	103.75

Table 7. In-sample results of RNN architecture

	Unfiltered	Threshold	Correlation
Return	23.14%	25.68%	26.56%
STDEV	33.26%	32.82%	32.49%
MAXDD	-46.17%	-46.17%	-42.92%
Calmar	0.5012	0.5561	0.6189
Trades	83.37	82.30	83.84

Table 8. Out-of-sample results of RNN architecture

	Unfiltered	Threshold	Correlation
Return	19.24%	22.36%	18.88%
STDEV	35.27%	34.58%	34.78%
MAXDD	-61.41%	-56.72%	-61.41%
Calmar	0.3132	0.3942	0.3075
Trades	81.21	80.63	82.36

Table 9. In-sample results of HONN architecture

	Unfiltered	Threshold	Correlation
Return	16.45%	16.22%	19.80%
STDEV	33.06%	32.63%	32.29%
MAXDD	-76.92%	-68.15%	-56.87%
Calmar	0.2139	0.2381	0.3481
Trades	54.75	55.22	55.58

Table 10. Out-of-sample results of HONN architecture

	Unfiltered	Threshold	Correlation
Return	14.72%	13.51%	14.36%
STDEV	35.00%	34.85%	34.52%
MAXDD	-67.35%	-61.14%	-50.41%
Calmar	0.2185	0.2210	0.2849
Trades	49.42	49.42	50.57

achieved by the unfiltered model, in 5 out of 7 cases. The threshold filter changes the out-of-sample Calmar ratio by a total of 0.09. This proves to be the same as the correlation filter for which the total improvement is also 0.09.

Finally if the choice of trading model is based on the in-sample Calmar ratio the RNN with a correlation filter would have been chosen. With hindsight this proves to be a good performer out-of-sample with a Calmar ratio of over 0.3.

CONCLUSION

If the aim is to model ΔS_t, or the change in the spread, then the best model is the RNN model, this is evidence by the largest out-of-sample annualised returns for an unfiltered model before the addition of transactions costs, indicating a superior ability to predict the direction of ΔS_t. It is also worth noting that the HONN outperformed the MLP out-of-sample (in terms of the unfiltered models) despite shorter computational times and limited variables. This finding supports the view of Knowles *et al.* (2005) and Dunis *et al.* (2005) and we feel that this justifies the further investigation of HONNs and their application to financial markets.

The effect of transactions costs is large on active models like the 3 neural networks investigated here, resulting in a high level of transactions costs, for the MLP it is 27.5%, 24.8% for the RNN and 16.4% for the HONN (indicating around 92, 83

and 55 trades per year respectively).[11] Interestingly the GARCH(1,1) ARMA(2,2) model proves no better with an average of around 60 trades per year resulting in transactions costs of 17.9%.

Finally, we conclude that trading with alternative architectures may provide an advantage in terms of added model sophistication although there is a note of caution that due to the high transactions costs, profitable strategies may be hard to come by. Further and in accordance with Dunis *et al.* (2005) we find that the trading filters investigated here may provide added value when forecasting the soybean-oil spread.

FUTURE RESEARCH DIRECTIONS

Overall, the main conclusion from this research is that HONNs can add economic value for investors and fund managers. In the circumstances, our results should go some way towards convincing a growing number of quantitative fund managers to experiment beyond the bounds of traditional regression models and technical analysis for portfolio management.

Further research remains to be done in the use of HONNs for time-series prediction: the use of joint activations and other functional-link terms in feed-forward networks is a promising area, as is the use of higher order terms in recurrent networks for prediction.

Another promising area for financial applications is the use of alternative model architectures in order to move away from the traditional level or class prediction (i.e. forecasting that , say, tomorrow's stock index is going to rise by x% or drop by y%, or that its move will be 'up' or 'down') in order to forecast the whole asset probability distribution, thus enabling one to predict moves of, say, more than α% with a probability of β%. We have included references of this exciting new approach in our 'Additional Reading' section.

ACKNOWLEDGMENT

This chapter previously appeared under the same title in *Neural Network World*, *3*(6), 193-213.

CIBEF is the Centre for International Banking, Economics and Finance, located at JMU, John Foster Building, 98 Mount Pleasant, Liverpool, L35UZ.

REFERENCES

Adam, O., Zarader, J. L., & Milgram, M. (1993). Identification and prediction of non-linear models with recurrent neural networks. *Proceedings of the International Workshop on Artificial Neural Networks*, 531-535.

Adlercreutz, C. H., Goldin, B. R., Gorbach, S. L., Hockerstedt, K. A., Watanabe, S., Hamalainen, E. K., Markkanen, M. H., Makela, T. H., Wahala, K. T., & Adlercreutz, T. (1995). Soybean phytoestrogen intake and cancer risk. *The British Journal of Nutrition*, *125*(7), 1960.

Anthony, M. S., Clarkson, T. B., Hughes, C. L. Jr., Morgan, T. M., & Burke, G. L. (1996). soybean isoflavones improve cardiovascular risk factors without affecting the reproductive system of peripubertal rhesus monkeys. *The British Journal of Nutrition*, *126*(1), 43-50.

Arjmandi, B. H., Alekel, L., Hollis, B. W., Amin, D., Stacewicz-Sapuntzakis, M., Guo, P., &

Kukreja, S. C. (1996). Dietary soybean protein prevents bone loss in an ovariectomized rat model of osteoporosis. *The British Journal of Nutrition*, *126*(1), 161-7.

Bansal, R., & Viswanathan, S. (1993). No arbitrage and arbitrage pricing: A new approach. *Journal of Finance*, *48*, 1231-1262.

Bovard, J. (1995). Archer Daniels Midland: A case study in corporate welfare. *Cato Policy Analysis*, *241*. Retrieved from http://www.cato.org/pubs/pas/pa-241.html

Butterworth, D., & Holmes, P. (2002). Intermarket spread trading: Evidence from UK index futures markets. *Applied Financial Economics*, *12*, 783-790.

Dunis, C., & Laws, L. (2003). FX volatility forecasts and the informational content of market data for liquidity. *European Journal of Finance*, *9*(3), 242-72.

Dunis, C. L., Laws, J., & Evans, B. (2005). Recurrent and higher order neural networks: A comparative analysis. *Neural Network World*, *6*, 509-523.

Elman, J. L. (1990). Finding structure in time. *Cognitive Science*, *14*, 179-211.

Emery, G. W., & Liu, Q. W. (2003). *Price relationship among hog, corn and soybean meal futures*. Financial Management Association Working Papers, 1st May 2003.

Evans, B., Dunis, C. L., & Laws, J. (2006). Trading futures spreads: Applications of threshold and correlation filters. *Applied Financial Economics* (Forthcoming).

Giles, L., & Maxwell, T. (1987). Learning invariance and generalization in high-order neural networks. *Applied Optics*, *26*(23), 4972-4978.

Johansen, S. (1988). Statistical analysis of cointegration vectors. *Journal of Economic Dynamics and Control*, *12*, 231-254.

Jones, M. A., & Baehr, M. (2003). Manager searches and performance measurement. In K. S. Phillips, & P. J. Surz (Eds.), *Hedge Funds Definitive Strategies and Techniques* (pp. 112-138). Hoboken, NJ: John Wiley & Sons.

Krishnaswamy, C. R., Gilbert, E. W., & Pashley, M. M. (2000). Neural network applications in finance. *Financial Practice and Education, Spring/Summer*, 75-84.

Kryzanowski, L., Galler, M., & Wright, D. W. (1993). Using artificial neural networks to pick stocks. *Financial Analysts Journal, 49*, 21-27.

Knowles, A., Hussein, A., Deredy, W., Lisboa, P., & Dunis, C. L. (2005). *Higher-order neural networks with bayesian confidence measure for prediction of EUR/USD exchange rate.* CIBEF Working Papers, www.cibef.com

Lindemann, A., Dunis, C., & Lisboa, P. (2005). Level estimation, classification and probability distribution architectures for trading the EUR/USD exchange rate. *Neural Computing and Applications, 14*(3), 256-271.

Rechner, D., & Poitras, G. (1993). Putting on the crush: Day trading the soybean complex spread. *Journal of Futures Markets, 13*(1), 61-75.

Refenes, A. P., Zapranis, A., & Francis, G. (1995). Modelling stock returns in the framework of APT. In A.P. Refenes (Ed.), *Neural networks in the capital markets* (pp. 101-125). Chichester, England: John Wiley & Sons.

Saad, E. W., Prokhorov, D. V., & Wunsch, D. C. (1998). Comparative study of stock trend prediction using time delay, recurrent and probabilistic neural networks. *Transactions on Neural Networks, 9*,1456-1470.

Simon, D. P. (1999). The soybean crush spread: Empirical evidence and trading strategies. *The Journal of Futures Markets, 19*(3), 271-289.

Tenti, P. (1996). Forecasting foreign exchange rates using recurrent neural networks. *Applied Artificial Intelligence, 10*, 567-581.

Working, H. (1949), The theory of price of storage. *American Economic Review, 39*, 1254-1262.

Zhang, M., Xu, S., & Fulcher, J. (2002). Neuron-adaptive higher order neural-network models for automated financial data modeling. *Transactions on Neural Networks, 13*, 188-204.

Zirilli, J. S. (1997). *Financial prediction using neural networks.* London: International Thompson Computer Press.

ADDITIONAL READING

Dunis, C., Laws, J., & Naim, P. (2003), *Applied quantitative methods for trading and investment.* John Wiley.

Dunis, C. L., & Chen, Y. X. (2005). Alternative volatility models for risk management and trading: An application to the EUR/USD and USD/JPY rates. *Derivatives Use, Trading & Regulation, 11*(2), 126-156.

Dunis, C. L, Laws, J., & Evans, B. (2005). Modelling with recurrent and higher order networks: A comparative analysis. *Neural Network World, 6*(5), 509-523.

Dunis, C. L, Laws, J., & Evans, B. (2006). Trading futures spreads: An application of correlation and threshold filters. *Applied Financial Economics, 16*, 1-12.

Dunis, C. L, Laws, J., & Evans, B. (2006). Modelling and trading the gasoline crack spread: A non-linear story. *Derivatives Use, Trading & Regulation, 12*(1-2), 126-145.

Dunis, C. L., Laws, J., & Evans, B. (2006). *Trading futures spread portfolios: Applications of higher order and recurrent networks.* Available from www.cibef.com

Dunis, C. L., & Nathani, A. (2007). *Quantitative trading of gold and silver using nonlinear models.* Available from www.cibef.com

Dunis, C. L., & Morrison, V. (2007). The economic value of advanced time series methods for modelling and trading 10-year government bonds. *European Journal of Finance*, forthcoming.

Lindemann, A., Dunis, C.L., & Lisboa, P. (2004). Probability distributions, trading strategies and leverage: An application of gaussian mixture models. *Journal of Forecasting, 23*(8), 559-585.

Lindemann, A., Dunis, C. L., & Lisboa, P. (2005). Probability distributions and leveraged trading strategies: An application of gaussian mixture models to the morgan stanley technology index tracking fund. *Quantitative Finance, 5*(5), 459-474.

Lindemann, A., Dunis, C.L., & Lisboa, P. (2005). Probability distribution architectures for trading silver. *Neural Network World, 5*(5), 437-470.

Lindemann, A., Dunis, C. L., & Lisboa, P. (2005). Level estimation, classification and probability distribution architectures for trading the EUR/USD exchange rate. *Neural Computing & Applications, 14*(3), 256-271.

ENDNOTES

[1] Source: http://www.soystats.com/2005/Default-frames.htm

[2] Source: http://www.biog-3000.com

[3] Source: http://www.asasoya.org/Statistics/Conversions.htm

[4] Gross Processing Margin =

$$GPM(t,T) = 48\frac{FM(t,T)}{2000lbs.} + 11\frac{FO(t,T)}{100lbs} - FS(t,T)$$

Where: *GPM(t,T)* is the per bushel gross processing margin observed at time *t*, *FM(t,T)* is the associated price of meal, *FO* is the price of oil and *FS(t,T)* is the price per bushel of soybeans.

[5] The crush spread is long soybeans and short soybean oil and soybean meal, conversely the reverse crush spread is short soybeans, long soybean oil and long soybean meal.

[6] $P_{so(t)} = (P_{SO}*11)$ as expressed in equation 1.

[7] These have been taken from www.sucden.co.uk.

[8] The actual output of the model can be seen in Appendix Table 1.

[9] These parameters seem to have limited effect when compared with the impact of the amount of correlation change.

[10] **UnFiltered:** Results of the unfiltered model.
Threshold: Results with the threshold filter applied to the model.
Correlation: Results with the correlation filter applied to the model.
Return: Annualised return of the model.
Stdev.: Annualised standard deviation of the model.
MaxDD: Maximum drawdown of the model, given by Equation 4.
Calmar, Calmar ratio: Equation 3, indicates the amount of return for probable capital input.
Trades: Average annualised trades.

[11] Examples of transactions costs are taken for the unfiltered model over the in-sample period.

APPENDIX

Figure 1. Histogram and statistics of in-sample spread returns

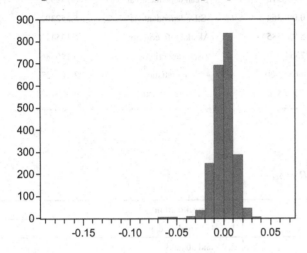

Series: DSOYBEANS_SOYOIL	
Sample 1 2170	
Observations 2169	
Mean	0.000191
Median	0.000175
Maximum	0.066406
Minimum	-0.184332
Std. Dev.	0.011783
Skewness	-2.805889
Kurtosis	42.39827
Jarque-Bera	143128.3
Probability	0.000000

Table 1. Output of GARCH(1,1)ARMA(1,1) model

Dependent Variable: D(SP)

Method: ML - ARCH

Date: 03/14/06   Time: 14:41

Sample (adjusted): 4 2170

Included observations: 2167 after adjustments

Convergence achieved after 44 iterations

MA backcast: 2 3, Variance backcast: ON

GARCH = C(6) + C(7)*RESID(-1)^2 + C(8)*GARCH(-1)

	Coefficient	Std. Error	z-Statistic	Prob.
C	0.055970	0.115942	0.482742	0.6293
AR(1)	0.907994	0.195563	4.642961	0.0000
AR(2)	-0.588402	0.174866	-3.364865	0.0008
MA(1)	-0.895456	0.189067	-4.736191	0.0000
MA(2)	0.632156	0.163806	3.859182	0.0001
	Variance Equation			
C	0.512559	0.115350	4.443518	0.0000
RESID(-1)^2	0.067188	0.008263	8.131682	0.0000
GARCH(-1)	0.917928	0.009597	95.64327	0.0000

continued on following page

Table 1. (continued)

R-squared	0.008578	Mean dependent var	0.149958
Adjusted R-squared	0.005364	S.D. dependent var	5.852302
S.E. of regression	5.836585	Akaike info criterion	6.175413
Sum squared resid	73547.89	Schwarz criterion	6.196386
Log likelihood	-6683.060	F-statistic	2.668727
Durbin-Watson stat	1.993478	Prob(F-statistic)	0.009457

Table 2. Inputs to MLP soybean-oil MLP model

Type of Input	Input Specification
Lag returns of spread	1, 2, 4, 15 and 20 days
Moving Average	5, 10 and 30 days

Table 3 - Inputs to RNN soybean-oil RNN model

Type of Input	Input Specification
Lag returns of spread	1, 2, 4, 8, 15 and 20 days
Moving Average	5, 10 and 30 days

Table 4 - Inputs to HONN soybean-oil HONN model

Type of Input	Input Specification
Lag returns of spread	1, 2, 4, 15 and 20 days
Moving Average	5 and 30 days

Section IV
Artificial Higher Order Neural Networks Fundamentals

Chapter XVII
Fundamental Theory of Artificial Higher Order Neural Networks

Madan M. Gupta
University of Saskatchewan, Canada

Noriyasu Homma
Tohoku University, Japan

Zeng-Guang Hou
The Chinese Academy of Sciences, China

Ashu M. G. Solo
Maverick Technologies America Inc., USA

Takakuni Goto
Tohoku University, Japan

ABSTRACT

In this chapter, we aim to describe fundamental principles of artificial higher order neural units (AHONUs) and networks (AHONNs). An essential core of AHONNs can be found in higher order weighted combinations or correlations between the input variables. By using some typical examples, this chapter describes how and why higher order combinations or correlations can be effective.

INTRODUCTION

The human brain has more than 10 billion neurons, which have complicated interconnections, and these neurons constitute a large-scale signal processing and memory network. Indeed, the understanding of neural mechanisms of higher functions of the brain is very complex. In the conventional neurophysiological approach, one can obtain only some fragmentary knowledge of neural processes and formulate only some mathematical models for specific applications. The mathematical study of a single neural model and its various extensions is the first step in the design of a complex neural network for solving a variety of problems in the fields of signal processing, pattern recognition, control of complex processes, neurovision systems, and other decision making processes. Neural network solutions for these problems can be directly used for business and economic applications.

A simple neural model is presented in Figure 1. In terms of information processing, an individual neuron with dendrites as multiple-input terminals and an axon as a single-output terminal may be considered a multiple-input/single-output (MISO) system. The processing functions of this MISO neural processor may be divided into the following four categories:

i. *Dendrites:* They consist of a highly branching tree of fibers and act as input points to the main body of the neuron. On average, there are 10^3 to 10^4 dendrites per neuron, which form receptive surfaces for input signals to the neurons.

ii. *Synapse:* It is a storage area of past experience (knowledge base). It provides long-term memory (LTM) to the past accumulated experience. It receives information from sensors and other neurons and provides outputs through the axons.

iii. *Soma:* The neural cell body is called the *soma*. It is the large, round central neuronal body. It receives synaptic information and performs further processing of the information. Almost all logical functions of the neuron are carried out in the soma.

iv. *Axon:* The neural output line is called the *axon*. The output appears in the form of an action potential that is transmitted to other neurons for further processing.

The electrochemical activities at the synaptic junctions of neurons exhibit a complex behavior because each neuron makes hundreds of interconnections with other neurons. Each neuron acts as a parallel processor because it receives action potentials in parallel from the neighboring neurons and then transmits pulses in parallel to other neighboring synapses. In terms of information processing, the synapse also performs a crude pulse frequency-to-voltage conversion as shown in Figure 1.

Figure 1. A simple neural model as a multiinput (dendrites) and single-output (axon) processor

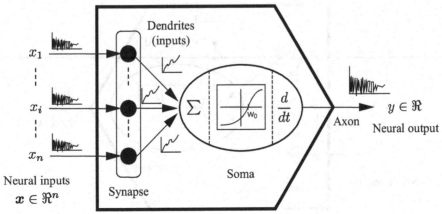

Neural Mathematical Operations

In general, it can be argued that the role played by neurons in the brain reasoning processes is analogous to the role played by a logical switching element in a digital computer. However, this analogy is too simple. A neuron contains a sensitivity threshold, adjustable signal amplification or attenuation at each synapse, and an internal structure that allows incoming nerve signals to be integrated over both space and time. From a mathematical point of view, it may be concluded that the processing of information within a neuron involves the following two distinct mathematical operations:

i.   *Synaptic operation:* The strength (weight) of the synapse is a representation of the storage of knowledge and thus the memory for previous knowledge. The synaptic operation assigns a relative weight (significance) to each incoming signal according to the past experience (knowledge) stored in the synapse.

ii. *Somatic operation:* The somatic operation provides various mathematical operations such as aggregation, thresholding, nonlinear activation, and dynamic processing to the

synaptic inputs. If the weighted aggregation of the neural inputs exceeds a certain threshold, the soma will produce an output signal to its axon.

A simplified representation of the above neural operations for a typical neuron is shown in Figure 2. A biological neuron deals with some interesting mathematical mapping properties because of its nonlinear operations combined with a threshold in the soma. If neurons were only capable of carrying out linear operations, the complex human cognition and robustness of neural systems would disappear.

Observations from both experimental and mathematical analysis have indicated that neural cells can transmit reliable information if they are sufficiently redundant in numbers. However, in general, a biological neuron is an unpredictable mechanism for processing information. Therefore, it is postulated that the collective activity generated by large numbers of locally redundant neurons is more significant than the activity generated by a single neuron.

Synaptic Operation

As shown in Figure 2, let us consider a neural memory vector of accumulated past experi-

Figure 2. Simple model of a neuron showing (a) synaptic and (b) somatic operations

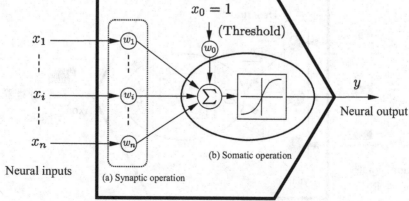

ences $\mathbf{w} = [w_1, w_2, ..., w_n]^T \in \Re^n$, which is usually called synapse weights and a neural input vector $\mathbf{x} = [x_1, x_2, ..., x_n]^T \in \Re^n$ as the current external stimuli. Through the comparison process between the neural memory $\mathbf{w}$ and the input $\mathbf{x}$, the neuron can calculate a similarity between the usual (memory base) and current stimuli and thus know the current situation (Kobayashi, 2006). According to the similarity, the neuron can then derive its internal value as the membrane potential.

A similarity measure u can be calculated as an inner product of the neural memory vector $\mathbf{w}$ and the current input vector $\mathbf{x}$ given by:

$$u = \mathbf{w} \cdot \mathbf{x} \, (= \mathbf{w}^T \mathbf{x})$$

$$= w_1 x_1 + w_2 x_2 + \cdots + w_n x_n = \sum_{i=1}^{n} w_i x_i \qquad (1)$$

The similarity implies the linear combination of the neural memory and the current input, or correlation between them. This idea can be traced back to the milestone model proposed by McCulloch and Pitts (1943). Note that the linear combination can be extended to higher order combinations. To capture the higher order nonlinear properties of the inputs, AHONNs have been proposed (Rumelhart et al., 1986; Giles and Maxwell, 1987; Softky and Kammen, 1991; Xu et al., 1992; Taylor and Commbes, 1993; Homma and Gupta, 2002).

Somatic Operation

Typical neural outputs are generated by a sigmoidal activation function of the similarity measure u of the inner product of neural memories (past experiences) and current inputs. In this case, the neural output y can be given as:

$$y = \phi(u) \in \Re^1 \qquad (2)$$

where ϕ is a neural activation function. An example of the activation function can be defined as a so-called sigmoidal function given by:

$$\phi(x) = \frac{1}{1 + \exp(-x)} \qquad (3)$$

and shown in Figure 3.

Note that the activation function is not limited to the sigmoid one. However, this type of sigmoid function has been widely used in various fields. Here if the similarity u is large—that is, the current input $\mathbf{x}$ is similar to the corresponding neural memory $\mathbf{w}$—the neural output y is also large. On the other hand, if the similarity u is small, the neural output y is also small. This is a basic characteristic of biological neural activities. Note that the neural output is not proportional to the similarity u, but a nonlinear function of u with saturation characteristics. This nonlinearity might be a key mechanism to make the neural activities more complex as brains do.

Learning from Experience

From the computational point of view, we have discussed how neurons, which are elemental computational units in the brain, produce outputs y as the results of neural information processing based on comparison of current external stimuli $\mathbf{x}$ with neural memories of past experiences $\mathbf{w}$. Consequently, the neural outputs y are strongly dependent on the neural memories $\mathbf{w}$. Thus, how

Figure 3. A sigmoidal activation function

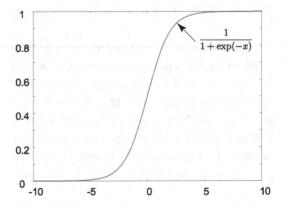

neurons can memorize past experiences is crucial for neural information processing. Indeed, one of the most remarkable features of the human brain is its ability to adaptively learn in response to knowledge, experience, and environment. The basis of this learning appears to be a network of interconnected adaptive elements by means of which transformation between inputs and outputs is performed.

Learning can be defined as the acquisition of new information. In other words, learning is a process of memorizing new information. Adaptation implies that the element can change in a systematic manner and in so doing alter the transformation between input and output. In the brain, transmission within the neural system involves coded nerve impulses and other physical chemical processes that form reflections of sensory stimuli and incipient motor behavior.

Many biological aspects are associated with such learning processes, including (Harston, 1990):

- Learning overlays hardwired connections.
- Synaptic plasticity versus stability: A crucial design dilemma.
- Synaptic modification providing a basis for observable organism behavior.

Here, we have presented the basic foundation of neural networks starting from a basic introduction to the biological foundations, neural models, and learning properties inherent in neural networks. The rest of the chapter contains the following five sections:

In section 2, as the first step to understanding artificial higher order neural networks, we will develop a general matrix form of the artificial second order neural units (ASONUs) and the learning algorithm. Using the general form, it will be shown that, from the point of view of both the neural computing process and its learning algorithm, the widely used linear combination

neural units described above are only a subset of the developed ASONUs.

In section 3, we will conduct some simulation studies to support the theoretical development of artificial second order neural networks (ASONNs). The results will show how and why ASONNs can be effective for many problems.

In section 4, AHONUs and AHONNs with a learning algorithm will be presented. Toward business and economic applications, function approximation and time series analysis problems will be considered in section 5.

Concluding remarks and future research directions will be given in section 6.

ARTIFICIAL SECOND ORDER NEURAL UNITS AND NETWORKS

Neural networks, consisting of first order neurons which provide the neural output as a nonlinear function of the weighted linear combination of neural inputs, have been successfully used in various applications such as pattern recognition/classification, system identification, adaptive control, optimization, and signal processing (Sinha et al., 1999; Gupta et al., 2003; Narendra and Parthasarathy, 1990; Cichochi and Unbehauen, 1993).

The higher order combination of the inputs and weights will yield higher neural performance. However, one of the disadvantages encountered in the previous development of AHONUs is the larger number of learning parameters (weights) required (Schmidt, 1993). To optimize the features space, a learning capability assessment method has been proposed by Villalobos and Merat (1995).

In this section, in order to reduce the number of parameters without loss of higher performance, an ASONU is presented (Homma and Gupta, 2002). Using a novel general matrix form of the second-order operation, the ASONU provides the output as a nonlinear function of the weighted second-order combination of input signals.

Formulation of the Artificial Second Order Neural Unit

A novel ASONU with n-dimensional neural inputs, $\mathbf{x}(t) \in \Re^n$, and a single neural output, $y(t) \in \Re^1$, is developed in this section (Figure 4). Let $\mathbf{x}_a = [x_0, x_1, ..., x_n]^T \in \Re^{n+1}$, $x_0 = 1$, be an augmented neural input vector. Here, a new second-order aggregating formulation is proposed by using an augmented weight matrix $\mathbf{W}_a(t) \in \Re^{(n+1) \times (n+1)}$ as:

$$u = \mathbf{x}_a^T \mathbf{W}_a \mathbf{x}_a \qquad (4)$$

Then the neural output, y, is given by a nonlinear function of the variable u as:

$$y = \phi(u) \in \Re^1 \qquad (5)$$

Because both the weights w_{ij} and w_{ji}, $i,j \in \{0,1,...,n\}$ in the augmented weight matrix $\mathbf{W}_a$ yield the same second-order term $x_i x_j$ (or $x_j x_i$), an upper triangular (or lower triangle) matrix is sufficient to use. The upper triangular matrix can give the general second-order combination as:

$$u = \mathbf{x}_a^T \mathbf{W}_a \mathbf{x}_a = \sum_{i=0}^{n} \sum_{j=i}^{n} w_{ij} x_i x_j, \quad x_0 = 1 \qquad (6)$$

Note that the conventional first-order weighted linear combination is only a special case of this second-order matrix formulation. For example, the special weight matrix (row vector), $\mathbf{W}_a \equiv Row[w_{00}, w_{01}, ..., w_{0n}] \in \Re^{(n+1) \times (n+1)}$, can produce the equivalent weighted linear combination, $u = \sum_{j=0}^{n} w_{0j} x_j$. Therefore, the proposed neural model with the second-order matrix operation is more general and, for this reason, it is called an ASONU.

Learning Algorithm for Artificial Second Order Neural Units

Here learning algorithms are developed for ASONUs. Let k denote the discrete-time steps, $k = 1, 2, ...$, and $y_d(k) \in \Re^1$ be the desired output signal corresponding to the neural input vector $\mathbf{x}(k) \in \Re^n$ at the k-th time step. A square error, $E(k)$, is defined by the error, $e(k) = y(k) - y_d(k)$, as:

$$E(k) = \frac{1}{2} e(k)^2 \qquad (7)$$

where $y(k)$ is the neural output corresponding to the neural input $\mathbf{x}(k)$ at the k-th time instant.

The purpose of the neural units is to minimize the error E by adapting the weight matrix $\mathbf{W}_a$ as:

$$\mathbf{W}_a(k + 1) = \mathbf{W}_a(k) + \Delta \mathbf{W}_a(k) \qquad (8)$$

Figure 4. An ASONU defined by Equations (4) and (5)

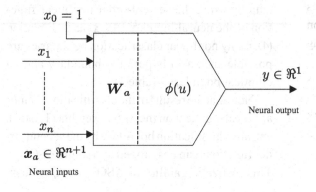

$$u = \boldsymbol{x}_a^T \boldsymbol{W}_a \boldsymbol{x}_a$$
$$y = \phi(u)$$

where,

$$\boldsymbol{x}_a = [x_0, x_1, \cdots, x_n]^T \in \Re^{n+1}, \quad x_0 = 1$$

$$\boldsymbol{W}_a = \begin{bmatrix} w_{00} & w_{01} & \cdots & w_{0n} \\ 0 & w_{11} & \cdots & w_{1n} \\ \vdots & \vdots & \ddots & \vdots \\ 0 & 0 & \cdots & w_{nn} \end{bmatrix}$$

Here $\Delta \mathbf{W}_a(k)$ denotes the change in the weight matrix, which is defined as proportional to the gradient of the error function $E(k)$:

$$\Delta \mathbf{W}_a(k) = -\eta \frac{\partial E(k)}{\partial \mathbf{W}_a(k)} \qquad (9)$$

where $\eta > 0$ is a learning coefficient. Since the derivatives, $\partial E / \partial w_{ij}, i, j \in \{1, 2, \ldots, n\}$, are calculated by the chain rule as:

$$\frac{\partial E(k)}{\partial w_{ij}(k)} = \frac{\partial E(k)}{\partial y(k)} \cdot \frac{\partial y(k)}{\partial u(k)} \cdot \frac{\partial u(k)}{\partial w_{ij}(k)}$$

$$= e(k)\phi'(u(k))x_i(k)x_j(k) \qquad (10)$$

or

$$\frac{\partial E(k)}{\partial \mathbf{W}_a(k)} = e(k)\phi'(u(k))\mathbf{x}_a(k)\mathbf{x}_a^T(k) \qquad (11)$$

The changes in the weight matrix are given by:

$$\Delta \mathbf{W}_a(k) = -\eta e(k)\phi'(u(k))\mathbf{x}_a(k)\mathbf{x}_a^T(k) \qquad (12)$$

Here $\phi'(u)$ is the slope of the nonlinear activation function used in Equation (5). For activation functions such as sigmoidal function, $\phi'(u) \geq 0$ and $\phi'(u)$ can be regarded as a gain of the changes in weights. Then:

$$\Delta \mathbf{W}_a(k) = -\gamma e(k)\mathbf{x}_a(k)\mathbf{x}_a^T(k) \qquad (13)$$

where $\gamma = \eta\phi'(u)$. Note that, taking the average of the changes for some input vectors, the changes in the weights, $\Delta w_{ij}(k)$, implies the correlation between the error $e(k)$ and the corresponding inputs term $x_i(k)x_j(k)$.

Therefore, conventional learning algorithms such as the backpropagation algorithm can easily be extended for multilayered neural network structures having the proposed ASONUs.

PERFORMANCE ASSESSMENT OF ARTIFICIAL SECOND ORDER NEURAL UNITS

To evaluate learning and generalization abilities of the proposed general ASONUs, the XOR classification problem is used. The XOR problem will provide a simple example of how well an ASONU works for the nonlinear classification problem.

XOR Problem

Since the two-input XOR function is not linearly separable, it is one of the simplest logic functions that cannot be realized by a single linear combination neural unit. Therefore, it requires a multilayered neural network structure consisting of linear combination neural units.

On the other hand, a single ASONU can solve this XOR problem by using its general second-order functions defined in Equation (6). To implement the XOR function using a single ASONU, the four learning patterns corresponding to the four combinations of two binary inputs $(x_1, x_2) \in \{(-1, -1), (-1, 1), (1, -1), (1, 1)\}$ and the desired output $y_d = x_1 \oplus x_2 \in \{-1, 1\}$ were applied to the ASONU.

For the XOR problem, the neural output, y, is defined by the signum function as $y = \phi(u) = Sgn(u)$. The correlation learning algorithm with a constant gain, $\gamma = 1$, in Equation (13) was used in this case. The learning was terminated as soon as the error converged to 0. Because the ASONU with the signum function classifies the neural input data by using the second-order nonlinear function of the neural inputs $\mathbf{x}_a^T \mathbf{W}_a \mathbf{x}_a$ as in Equation (4), many nonlinear classification boundaries are possible such as a hyperbolic boundary and an elliptical boundary (Table 1).

Note that the results of the classification boundary are dependent on the initial weights (Table 1), and any classification boundary by the second-order functions can be realized by a single ASONU. This realization ability of ASONU is obviously

Table 1. Initial weights (k = 0), final weights, and the classification boundaries for the XOR problem.

k	w_{00}	w_{01}	w_{02}	w_{11}	w_{12}	w_{22}	Boundaries
	(A hyperbolic boundary)						
0	0.323	-0.870	-0.153	0.977	0.031	-0.332	
4	-0.177	0.630	0.347	0.477	-1.469	-0.832	
	(A hyperbolic boundary)						
0	-0.773	0.818	0.748	0.793	-0.525	0.369	
4	-1.023	0.568	0.498	0.543	-0.775	0.119	
	(An elliptical boundary)						
0	0.847	0.397	0.779	-0.996	-0.961	-0.803	
3	0.947	0.497	0.679	-0.896	-1.061	-0.703	

superior to the linear combination neural unit which cannot achieve such nonlinear classification using a single neural unit. At least three linear combination neural units in a layered structure are needed to solve the XOR problem.

Secondly, the number of parameters (weights) required for solving this problem can be reduced by using the ASONU. In this simulation study, by using the upper triangular weight matrix, only six parameters including the threshold were required for the ASONU whereas at least nine parameters were required for the layered structure with three linear combination neural units.

ARTIFICIAL HIGHER ORDER NEURAL UNITS AND NETWORKS

To capture the higher order nonlinear properties of the input pattern space, extensive efforts have been made by Rumelhart et al. (1986), Giles and Maxwell (1987), Softky and Kammen (1991), Xu et al. (1992), Taylor and Commbes (1993), and Homma and Gupta (2002) toward developing architectures of neurons that are capable of capturing not only the linear correlation between components of input patterns, but also the higher order correlation between components of input patterns. AHONNs have proven to have good computational, storage, pattern recognition, and learning properties and are realizable in hardware (Taylor and Commbes, 1993). Regular polynomial networks that contain the higher-order correlations of the input components satisfy the Stone-Weierstrass theorem that is a theoretical background of universal function approximators by means of neural networks (Gupta et al., 2003), but the number of weights required to accommodate all the higher order correlations increases exponentially with the number of the inputs. AHONUs are the basic building block for such an AHONN. For such an AHONN as shown in Figure 5, the output is given by:

$$y = \phi(u) \tag{14}$$

$$u = w0 + \sum_{i_1}^{n} w_{i_1} x_{i_1} + \sum_{i_1, i_2}^{n} w_{i_1 i_2} x_{i_1} x_{i_2} + \cdots + \sum_{i_1, \ldots, i_N}^{n} w_{i_1 \cdots i_N} x_{i_1} \cdots x_{i_N} \tag{15}$$

where $\mathbf{x} = [x_1, x_2, \ldots, x_n]^T$ is a vector of neural inputs, y is an output, and $\phi(.)$ is a strictly monotonic

Figure 5. Block diagram of the AHONU, Equations (14) and (15)

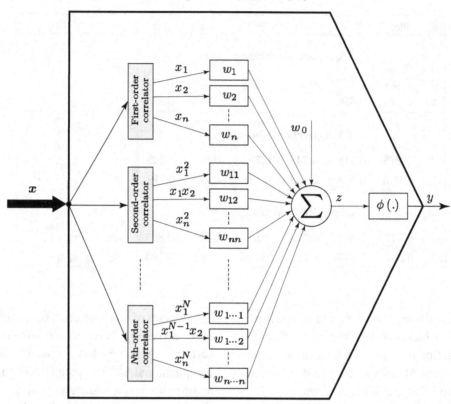

Box 1.

$$C(i_1 \cdots i_j) \equiv \{< i_1 \cdots i_j >: 1 \le i_1 \cdots i_j \le n, i_1 \le i_2 \le \cdots \le i_j\}, 1 \le j \le N$$

activation function such as a sigmoidal function whose inverse, $\phi^{-1}(.)$, exists. The summation for the kth-order correlation is taken on a set $C(i_1 \cdots i_j), (1 \le j \le N)$, which is a set of the combinations of j indices $1 \le i_1...i_j \le n$ defined by Box 1. Also, the number of the Nth-order correlation terms is given by:

$$\binom{n+j-1}{j} = \frac{(n+j-1)!}{j!(n-1)!}, \quad 1 \le j \le N$$

The introduction of the set $C(i_1...i_j)$ is to absorb the redundant terms due to the symmetry of the induced combinations. In fact, Equation (15) is a truncated Taylor series with some adjustable

coefficients. The artificial Nth-order neural unit needs a total of:

$$\sum_{j=0}^{N} \binom{n+j-1}{j} = \sum_{j=0}^{N} \frac{(n+j-1)!}{j!(n-1)!}$$

weights including the basis of all of the products up to N components.

Example 1

In this example, we consider a case of the artificial third-order ($N = 3$) neural network with two neural inputs ($n = 2$). Here:

$$C(i) = \{0,1,2\}$$
$$C(i_1 i_2) = \{11,12,22\}$$
$$C(i_1 i_2 i_3) = \{111,112,122,222\}$$

and the network equation is shown in Box 2.

The AHONUs may be used in conventional feedforward neural network structures as hidden units to form AHONNs. In this case, however, consideration of the higher correlation may improve the approximation and generalization capabilities of the neural networks. Typically, ASONNs are employed to give a tolerable number of weights as discussed in sections 2 and 3. On the other hand, if the order of the AHONU is high enough, eqns. (14) and (15) may be considered as a neural network with n inputs and a single output. This structure is capable of dealing with the problems of function approximation and pattern recognition.

To accomplish an approximation task for given input-output data $\{\mathbf{x}(k), y(k)\}$ the learning algorithm for the AHONN can easily be developed on the basis of the gradient descent method. Assume that the error function is formulated as:

$$E(k) = \frac{1}{2}[d(k) - y(k)]^2 = \frac{1}{2}e^2(k)$$

where $e(k) = d(k) - y(k)$, $d(k)$ is the desired output, and $y(k)$ is the output of the neural networks. Minimization of the error function by a standard steepest-descent technique yields the following set of learning equations:

$$w_0^{new} = w_0^{old} + \eta(d - y)\phi'(u) \tag{16}$$

$$w_{ij}^{new} = w_{ij}^{old} + \eta(d - y)\phi'(u) x_{i_1} x_{i_2} \cdots x_{i_j} \tag{17}$$

where $\phi'(u) = d\phi/du$. Like the backpropagation algorithm for a multilayered feedforward neural network (MFNN), a momentum version of the above is easily obtained.

Alternatively, because all the weights of the AHONN appear linearly in Equation (15), one may use the method for solving linear algebraic equations to carry out the preceding learning task if the number of patterns is finite. To do so, one has to introduce the following two augmented vectors:

$$\mathbf{w} \equiv \left[w_0, w_1, ..., w_n, w_{11}, w_{12}, ..., w_{nn}, ..., w_{1\cdots1}, w_{2\cdots2}, ..., w_{n\cdots n}\right]^T$$

and

$$\mathbf{u}(\mathbf{x}) \equiv \left[x_0, x_1, ..., x_n, x_1^2, x_1 x_2, ..., x_n^2, ..., x_1^N, x_1^{N-1} x_2, ..., w_n^N\right]^T$$

where $x_0 \equiv 1$, so that the network equations, eqns. (14) and (15), may be rewritten in the following compact form:

$$y = \phi(\mathbf{w}^T \mathbf{u}(\mathbf{x})) \tag{18}$$

For the given p pattern pairs $\{\mathbf{x}(k), d(k)\}$, $(1 \leq k \leq p)$, define the following vectors and matrix shown in Box 3, where $\mathbf{u}(k) = \mathbf{u}(\mathbf{x}(k))$, $1 \leq k \leq p$. Then, the learning problem becomes one of finding a solution of the following linear algebraic equation:

$$\mathbf{U}\mathbf{w} = \mathbf{d} \tag{19}$$

Box 2.

$$y = \phi\left(w0 + w_1 x_1 + w_2 x_2 + w_{11} x_1^2 + w_{12} x_1 x_2 + w_{22} x_2^2 + w_{111} x_1^3 + w_{112} x_1^2 x_2 + w_{122} x_1 x_2^2 + w_{222} x_2^3\right)$$

Box 3.

$$\mathbf{U} = \left[u^T(1), u^T(2), ..., u^T(p)\right]^T, \quad \mathbf{d} = \left[\phi^{-1}(d(1)), \phi^{-1}(d(2)), ..., \phi^{-1}(d(p))\right]^T$$

If the number of the weights is equal to the number of the data and the matrix **U** is nonsingular, then Equation (19) has a unique solution:

$$\mathbf{w} = \mathbf{U}^{-1}\mathbf{d}$$

A more interesting case occurs when the dimension of the weight vector **w** is less than the number of data p. Then the existence of the exact solution for the above linear equation is given by:

$$rank\left[\mathbf{U}\vdots\mathbf{d}\right] = rank\left[\mathbf{U}\right]$$

In case this condition is not satisfied, the pseudoinverse solution is usually an option and gives the best fit.

The following example shows how to use the AHONN presented in this section to deal with pattern recognition problems that are also typical applications in business and economic situations.

It is of interest to show that solving such problems is equivalent to finding the decision surfaces in the pattern space such that the given data patterns are located on the surfaces.

Example 2

Consider a three-variable XOR function defined as Box 4. The eight input pattern pairs and corresponding outputs are given in Table 2. This is a typical nonlinear pattern classification problem. A single linear neuron with a nonlinear activation function is unable to form a decision surface such that the patterns are separated in the pattern space. Our objective here is to find all the possible solutions using the third-order network to realize the logic function.

A third-order neural network is designed as Box 5, where $x_1, x_2, x_3 \in \{-1, 1\}$ are the binary inputs, and the network contains eight weights. To implement the above mentioned logic XOR

Box 4.

$$y = f(x_1, x_2, x_3) = (x_1 \oplus x_2) \oplus x_3 = x_1 \oplus (x_2 \oplus x_3) = (x_3 \oplus x_1) \oplus x_2 = x_1 \oplus x_2 \oplus x_3$$

Box 5.

$$y = w_0 + w_1 x_1 + w_2 x_2 + w_3 x_3 + w_{12} x_1 x_2 + w_{13} x_1 x_3 + w_{23} x_2 x_3 + w_{123} x_1 x_2 x_3$$

Table 2. Truth table of XOR function $x_1 \oplus x_2 \oplus x_3$

Pattern	Input x_1	Input x_2	Input x_3	Output y
A	−1	−1	−1	−1
B	−1	−1	1	1
C	−1	1	−1	1
D	−1	1	1	−1
E	1	−1	−1	1
F	1	−1	1	−1
G	1	1	−1	−1
H	1	1	1	1

function, one may consider the solution of the following set of linear algebraic equations:

$$\begin{cases} w_0 - w_1 - w_2 - w_3 + w_{12} + w_{13} + w_{23} - w_{123} = -1 \\ w_0 - w_1 - w_2 + w_3 + w_{12} - w_{13} - w_{23} + w_{123} = 1 \\ w_0 - w_1 + w_2 - w_3 - w_{12} + w_{13} - w_{23} + w_{123} = 1 \\ w_0 - w_1 + w_2 + w_3 - w_{12} - w_{13} + w_{23} - w_{123} = -1 \\ w_0 + w_1 - w_2 - w_3 - w_{12} - w_{13} + w_{23} + w_{123} = 1 \\ w_0 + w_1 - w_2 + w_3 - w_{12} + w_{13} - w_{23} - w_{123} = -1 \\ w_0 + w_1 + w_2 - w_3 + w_{12} - w_{13} - w_{23} - w_{123} = -1 \\ w_0 + w_1 + w_2 + w_3 + w_{12} + w_{13} + w_{23} + w_{123} = 1 \end{cases}$$

The coefficient matrix **U** is given by:

$$U = \begin{bmatrix} 1 & -1 & -1 & -1 & 1 & 1 & 1 & -1 \\ 1 & -1 & -1 & 1 & 1 & -1 & -1 & 1 \\ 1 & -1 & 1 & -1 & -1 & 1 & -1 & 1 \\ 1 & -1 & 1 & 1 & -1 & -1 & 1 & -1 \\ 1 & 1 & -1 & -1 & -1 & -1 & 1 & 1 \\ 1 & 1 & -1 & 1 & -1 & 1 & -1 & -1 \\ 1 & 1 & 1 & -1 & 1 & -1 & -1 & -1 \\ 1 & 1 & 1 & 1 & 1 & 1 & 1 & 1 \end{bmatrix}$$

which is nonsingular. The equations have a unique set of solutions:

$$w_0 = w_1 = w_2 = w_3 = w_{12} = w_{13} = w_{23} = 0, \quad w_{123} = 1$$

Therefore, the logic function is realized by the third-order polynomial $y = x_1 x_2 x_3$. This solution is unique in terms of the third-order polynomial.

Xu et al. (1992) as well as Taylor and Commbes (1993) also demonstrated that AHONNs may be effectively applied to problems using a model of a curve, surface, or hypersurface to fit a given data set. This problem, called *nonlinear surface fitting*, is often encountered in many engineering, business, and economic applications. Some learning algorithms for solving such problems may be found in their papers. Moreover, if one assumes $\phi(x) = x$ in the AHONU, the weight exhibits linearity in the networks and the learning algorithms for the

AHONNs may be characterized as a linear LS procedure. Then the well-known local minimum problems existing in many nonlinear neural learning schemes may be avoided.

Modified Polynomial Neural Networks

Sigma-Pi Neural Networks

Note that an AHONU contains all the linear and nonlinear correlation terms of the input components to the order n. A slightly generalized structure of the AHONU is a polynomial network that includes weighted sums of products of selected input components with an appropriate power. Mathematically, the input-output transfer function of this network structure is given by:

$$u_i = \prod_{j=1}^{n} x_j^{w_{ij}} \tag{20}$$

$$y = \phi\left(\sum_{i=1}^{N} w_i u_i\right) \tag{21}$$

where $w_i, w_{ij} \in \Re$, N is the order of the network and u_i is the output of the i-th hidden unit. This type of feedforward network is called a *sigma-pi network* (Rumelhart et al. 1986). It is easy to show that this network satisfies the Stone-Weierstrass theorem if $\phi(x)$ is a linear function. Moreover, a modified version of the sigma-pi network, as proposed by Hornik et al. (1989) and Cotter (1990), is:

$$u_i = \prod_{j=1}^{n} \left(p(x_j)\right)^{w_{ij}} \tag{22}$$

$$y = \phi\left(\sum_{i=1}^{N} w_i u_i\right) \tag{23}$$

where $w_i, w_{ij} \in \Re$ and $p(x_j)$ is a polynomial of x_j. It is easy to verify that this network satisfies the Stone-Weierstrass theorem, and thus, it can be an approximator for problems of functional approximations. The sigma-pi networks defined in eqns. (20) and (21) is a special case of the above network while $p(x_j)$ is assumed to be a linear function of x_j. In fact, the weights w_{ij} in both the networks given in eqns. (20) and (22) may be restricted to integer or nonnegative integer values.

Ridge Polynomial Neural Networks (RPNNs)

To obtain fast learning and powerful mapping capabilities, and to avoid the combinatorial increase in the number of weights of AHONNs, some modified polynomial network structures have been introduced. One of these is the *pi-sigma network* (Shin and Ghosh, 1991), which is a regular higher-order structure and involves a much smaller number of weights than the AHONNs. The mapping equation of a pi-sigma network can be represented as:

$$u_i = \sum_{j=1}^{n} w_{ij} x_j + \theta_i$$

$$\tag{24}$$

$$y = \phi\left(\prod_{i=1}^{N} u_i\right) = \phi\left(\prod_{i=1}^{N}\left[\sum_{j=1}^{n} w_{ij} x_j + \theta_i\right]\right)$$

$$\tag{25}$$

The total number of weights for an Nth-order pi-sigma network with n inputs is only $(n + 1)N$. Compared with the sigma-pi structure, the number of weights involved in this network is significantly reduced. Unfortunately, when $\phi(x) = x$, the pi-sigma network does not match the conditions provided by the Stone-Weierstrass theorem because the linear subspace condition is not satisfied (Gupta et al., 2003). However, some studies have shown that it is a good network model for smooth functions (Shin and Ghosh, 1991).

To modify the structure of the above mentioned pi-sigma networks such that they satisfy the Stone-Weierstrass theorem, Shin and Ghosh (1991) suggested considering the *ridge polynomial neural network* (RPNN). For the vectors $\mathbf{w}_{ij} = [w_{ij1}, w_{ij2}, ..., w_{ijn}]^T$ and $\mathbf{x} = [x_1, x_2, ..., x_n]^T$, let:

$$< \mathbf{x}, \mathbf{w}_{ij} > = \sum_{k=1}^{n} w_{ijk} x_k$$

which represents an inner product between the two vectors. A one-variable continuous function f of the form $< \mathbf{x}, \mathbf{w}_{ij} >$ is called a *ridge function*. A *ridge polynomial* is a ridge function that can be represented as:

$$\sum_{i=0}^{N} \sum_{j=0}^{M} a_{ij} < \mathbf{x}, \mathbf{w}_{ij} >^i$$

for some $a_{ij} \in \Re$ and $\mathbf{w}_{ij} \in \Re^n$. The operation equation of an RPNN is expressed as:

$$y = \phi\left(\sum_{j=1}^{N} \prod_{i=1}^{n}\left(< \mathbf{x}, \mathbf{w}_{ij} > + \theta_{ji}\right)\right)$$

where $\phi(x) = x$. The *denseness*, which is a fundamental concept for universal function approximators described in the Stone-Weierstrass theorem, of this network can be verified (Gupta et al., 2003).

The total number of weights involved in this structure is $N(N + 1)(n + 1)/2$. A comparison of the number of weights of the three types of polynomial network structures is given in Table 3. The results show that when the networks have the same higher-order terms, the weights of a RPNN are significantly less than those of an AHONN. In particular, this is a very attractive improvement offered by RPNNs.

TOWARD BUSINESS AND ECONOMIC APPLICATIONS

Function approximation problems are typical examples in many business and economic situations. The capability to approximate nonlinear complex functions can be a basis of the complex pattern classification ability as well. Furthermore, the neural network approach with high approximation ability can be used for time series analysis

Table 3. The number of weights in the polynomial networks

Order of network	Number of weights					
	Pi-sigma		RPNN		AHONN	
N	$n=5$	$n=10$	$n=5$	$n=10$	$n=5$	$n=10$
2	12	22	18	33	21	66
3	18	33	36	66	56	286
4	24	44	60	110	126	1001

Figure 6. A two-layered neural network structure with two ASONUs in the first layer and a single ASONU in the output layer for the function approximation problem

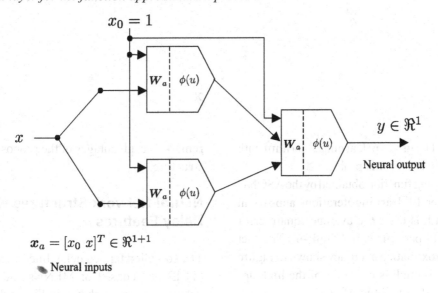

by introducing time delay features into the neural network structure. Time series analysis or estimation is one of the most important problems in business and economic applications such as stock market estimation and business strategy or economic policy evaluation. In this section, we will explain the function approximation ability of AHONNs first. Neural network structures to represent time delay features will then be introduced for time series analysis.

Function Approximation Problem

For evaluating the function approximation ability of AHONNs, an example was taken from Klas-

sen et al. (1988). The task consists of learning a representation for an unknown, one-variable nonlinear function, $F(x)$, with the only available information being the 18 sample patterns (Villalobos and Merat, 1995).

For this function approximation problem, a two layered neural network structure was composed of two ASONUs in the first layer and a single ASONU in the output layer (Figure 6). The nonlinear activation function of the ASONUs in the first layer was defined by a bipolar sigmoidal function as $\phi(u) = (1 - \exp(-u))/(1 + \exp(-u))$, but for the single output ASONU, instead of the sigmoidal function, the linear function was used:

Figure 7. Training pairs and outputs estimated by the network with ASONUs for the Klassen's function approximation problem (Klassen et al., 1988)

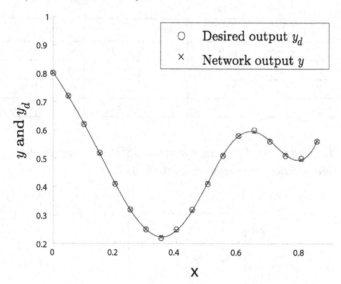

$y = \phi(u) = u$. The gradient learning algorithm with $\eta = 0.1$ was used for this problem.

The mapping function obtained by the ASONU network after 10^7 learning iterations appears in Figure 7. In this case, the average square error taken over 18 patterns was 4.566E-6. The fact that the approximation accuracy shown in Figure 7 is extremely high is evidence of the high approximation ability of the ASONN.

Five particular trigonometric functions, $\sin(\pi x)$, $\cos(\pi x)$, $\sin(2\pi x)$, $\cos(2\pi x)$ and $\sin(4\pi x)$, were used as special features of the extra neural inputs (Klassen et al., 1988). Also, it has been reported (Villalobos and Merat, 1995) that the term $\cos(\pi x)$ is not necessary to achieve a lower accuracy within the error tolerance 1.125E-4, but still four extra features were required.

On the other hand, in this study, the high approximation accuracy of the proposed ASONU network was achieved by only two ASONUs with the sigmoidal activation function in the first layer and a single ASONU with the linear activation function in the output layer, and no special features were required for high accuracy. These are

remarkable advantages of the proposed ASONN structure.

Neural Network Structures with Time Delay Features

The so-called tapped delay line neural networks (TDLNNs) consist of MFNNs and some time delay operators as shown in Figure 8. Let $y(k) \in \Re$ be an internal state variable at the time instant k. The delayed states $y(k), y(k-1), ..., y(k-n)$ are used as inputs of a TDLNN. The various type of TDLNNs can be further defined on the basis of specified applications.

For time series analysis, the q-step prediction equations of the TDLNNs, as shown in Figure 8, can be given as follows:

$$y(k+q) = F(\mathbf{w}, y(k), ..., y(k-n), u(k)) \quad (26)$$

where $F(.)$ is a continuous and differentiable function that may be obtained from the operation of the MFNN. The input components of the neural networks are the time-delayed versions of the

Figure 8. Tapped delay line neural networks (TDLNNs) for time series analysis

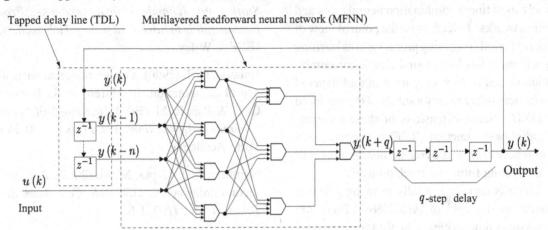

outputs of the networks. In this case, Equation (26) represents a q-step-ahead nonlinear predictor. TDLNNs consisting of AHONUs can further contribute to capture the complex nonlinear features by using the higher order combinations of inputs.

These neural network structures have the potential to represent a class of nonlinear input-output mappings of unknown nonlinear systems or communication channels without internal dynamics, and have been successfully applied to time series analysis (Matsuba, 2000). Because there are no state feedback connections in the network, the static backpropagation learning algorithm may be used to train the TDLNN so that the processes of system modeling or function approximation are carried out.

On the other hand, neural units with internal dynamics have been proposed (Gupta et al., 2003). Neural units with learning and adaptive capabilities discussed so far had only static input-output functional relationships. This implies, therefore, that for a given input pattern to such a static neural unit, an instantaneous output is obtained through a linear or nonlinear mapping procedure. Note that this is true even for TDLNNs in the neural unit level. However, a biological neuron not only contains a nonlinear mapping operation on the weighted sum of the input signals, but also has some dynamic processes such as the state signal feedback, time delays, hysteresis, and limit cycles. To emulate such a complex behavior, a number of dynamic or feedback neural units have been proposed relatively recently. As the basic building blocks of the dynamic feedback neural networks, these dynamic neural units may be used to construct a complex dynamic neural network structure through internal synaptic connections. To further use the higher order nonlinearity, the synaptic operation in AHONUs can be incorporated into the dynamic neural units.

CONCLUSION AND FUTURE RESEARCH DIRECTIONS

In this chapter, the basic foundation of neural networks, starting from a basic introduction to biological foundations, neural unit models, and learning properties, has been introduced. Then as the first step to understanding AHONNs, a general ASONU was developed. Simulation studies for both the pattern classification and function approximation problems demonstrated that the learning and generalization abilities of the proposed ASONU and neural networks having ASONUs are greatly superior to that of the widely used linear combination neural units and their networks. Indeed, from the point of view of both the neural computing process and its learning algorithm, it has been found that linear combination neural units widely used in multilayered neural networks are only a subset of the proposed ASONUs. Some extensions of these concepts to radial basis function (RBF) networks, fuzzy neural networks, and dynamic neural units will be interesting future research projects.

There is certainly rapidly growing research interest in the field of AHONNs. There are increasing complexities in applications not only in the fields of aerospace, process control, ocean exploration, manufacturing, and resource-based industry, but also in economics and business; this is the main issue of this book. This chapter deals with the theoretical foundations of AHONNs and will help readers to develop or apply the methods to their own business and economic problems. The rest of the book deals with real business and economic applications.

We hope that our efforts in this chapter will stimulate research interests, provide some new challenges to its readers, generate curiosity for learning more in the field, and arouse a desire to seek new theoretical tools and applications. We will consider our efforts successful if this chapter raises one's level of curiosity.

REFERENCES

Cichochi, A., & Unbehauen, R. (1993). *Neural networks for optimization and signal processing.* Chichester: Wiley.

Cotter, N. (1990). The Stone-Weierstrass theorem and its application to neural networks. *IEEE Trans. Neural Networks, 1*(4), 290-295.

Giles, C. L., & Maxwell, T. (1987). Learning invariance, and generalization in higher-order networks. *Appl. Optics, 26,* 4972-4978.

Gupta, M. M., Jin, L., & Homma, N. (2003). *Static and dynamic neural networks: From fundamentals to advanced theory.* Hoboken, NJ: IEEE & Wiley.

Harston, C. T. (1990). The neurological basis for neural computation. In Maren, A. J., Harston, C. T., & Pap, R. M. (Eds.), *Handbook of Neural Computing Applications, Vol. 1* (pp. 29-44). New York: Academic.

Homma, N., & Gupta, M. M. (2002). A general second order neural unit. *Bull. Coll. Med. Sci., Tohoku Univ., 11*(1), 1-6.

Hornik, K., Stinchcombe, M., & White, H. (1989). Multilayer feedforward networks are universal approximators. *Neural Networks, 2*(5), 359-366.

Klassen, M., Pao, Y., & Chen, V. (1988). Characteristics of the functional link net: A higher order delta rule net. *Proc. of IEEE 2nd Annual Int'l. Conf. Neural Networks.*

Kobayashi, S. (2006). *Sensation world made by the brain: Animals do not have sensors.* Tokyo: Corona (in Japanese).

Matsuba, I. (2000). *Nonlinear time series analysis.* Tokyo: Asakura-syoten (in Japanese).

McCulloch, W. S., & Pitts, W. H. (1943). A logical calculus of the ideas imminent in nervous activity. *Bull. Math. Biophys., 5,* 115-133.

Narendra, K., & Parthasarathy, K. (1990). Identification and control of dynamical systems using neural networks. *IEEE Trans. Neural Networks, 1,* 4-27.

Pao, Y. H. (1989). *Adaptive pattern recognition and neural networks.* Reading, MA: Addison-Wesley..

Rumelhart, D. E., Hinton, G. E., & Williams, R. J. (1986). Learning internal representations by error propagation. In Rumelhart, D. E., & McClelland, J. L. (Eds.), *Parallel distributed processing: Explorations in the microstructure of cognition, Vol. 1* (pp. 318-362). Cambridge, MA: MIT Press.

Schmidt, W., & Davis, J. (1993). Pattern recognition properties of various feature spaces for higher order neural networks. *IEEE Trans. Pattern Analysis and Machine Intelligence, 15*, 795-801.

Shin, Y., & Ghosh, J. (1991). The pi-sigma network: An efficient higher-order neural network for pattern classification and function approximation. *Proc. Int. Joint Conf. on Neural Networks* (pp. 13-18).

Sinha, N., Gupta, M. M., & Zadeh, L. (1999). *Soft computing and intelligent control systems: Theory and applications.* New York: Academic.

Softky, R. W., & Kammen, D. M. (1991). Correlations in high dimensional or asymmetrical data sets: Hebbian neuronal processing. *Neural Networks, 4*, 337-347.

Taylor, J. G., & Commbes, S. (1993). Learning higher order correlations. *Neural Networks, 6*, 423-428.

Villalobos, L., & Merat, F. (1995). Learning capability assessment and feature space optimization for higher-order neural networks. *IEEE Trans. Neural Networks, 6*, 267-272.

Xu, L., Oja, E., & Suen, C. Y. (1992). Modified hebbian learning for curve and surface fitting. *Neural Networks, 5*, 441-457.

ADDITIONAL READINGS

Biological Motivation on Neural Networks

Ding, M.-Z., & Yang, W.-M. (1997). Stability of Synchronous Chaos and On-Off Intermittency in Coupled Map Lattices. *Phys. Rev. E, 56*(4), 4009-4016.

Durbin, R. (1989). On the correspondence between network models and the nervous system. In R. Durbin, C. Miall, & G. Mitchison (Eds.), *The computing neurons.* Reading, MA: Addison-Wesley.

Engel, K., Konig, P., Kreiter, A. K., & Singer, W. (1991). Interhemispheric synchronization of oscillatory neuronal responses in cat visual cortex. *Science, 252*, 1177-1178.

Ersu, E., & Tolle, H. (1984). A new concept for learning control inspired by brain theory. *Proc. 9th World Congress IFAC* (pp. 245-250).

Forbus, K. D., & Gentner, D. (1983). Casual reasoning about quantities. *Proc. 5th Annual Conf. of the Cognitive Science Society* (pp. 196-206).

Fujita, M. (1982). Adaptive filter model of the cerebellum. *Biological Cybernetics, 45*, 195-206.

Garliaskas, A., & Gupta, M. M. (1995). A generalized model of synapse-dendrite-cell body as a complex neuron. *World Congress on Neural Networks, Vol. 1* (pp. 304-307).

Gupta, M. M. (1988). Biological basis for computer vision: Some perspective. *SPW Conf. on Intelligent Robots and Computer Vision* (pp. 811-823).

Gupta, M. M., & Knopf, G. K. (1992). A multitask visual information processor with a biologically motivated design. *J. Visual Communicat., Image Representation, 3*(3), 230-246.

Hiramoto, M., Hiromi, Y., Giniger, E., & Hotta, Y. (2000). The drosophila netrin receptor frazzled guides axons by controlling netrin distribution. *Nature, 406*(6798), 886-888.

Honma, N., Abe, K., Sato, M., & Takeda, H. (1998). Adaptive evolution of holon networks by an autonomous decentralized method. *Applied Mathematics and Computation, 9*(1), 43-61.

Kaneko, K. (1994). Relevance of dynamic clustering to biological networks. *Phys. D, 75*, 55-73.

Kohara, K., Kitamura, A., Morishima, M., & Tsumoto, T. (2001). Activity-dependent transfer of brain-derived neurotrophic factor to postsynaptic neurons. *Science, 291,* 2419-2423.

LeCun, Y., Boser, B., & Solla, S. A. (1990). Optimal brain damage. In D. Touretzky (Ed.), *Advances in neural information processing systems, Vol. 2* (pp. 598-605), Morgan Kaufmann.

Lovejoy, C. O. (1981). The origin of man. *Science, 211,* 341-350.

Maire, M. (2000). On the convergence of validity interval analysis. *IEEE Trans. on Neural Networks, 11*(3), 799-801.

[AMantere, K., Parkkinen, J., Jaasketainen, T., & Gupta, M. M. (1993). Wilson-Cowan neural network model in image processing. *J. of Mathematical Imaging and Vision, 2,* 251-259.

McCarthy, J., & Hayes, P. J. (1969). Some philosophical problems from the standpoint of artificial intelligence. In Meltzer & Michie (Eds.), *Machine intelligence, 4* (pp. 463-502). Edinburgh: Edinburgh Univ. Press.

McCulloch, W. S., & Pitts, W. H. (1943). A logical calculus of the ideas imminent in nervous activity. *Bulletin of Mathematical Biophysics, 5,* 115-133.

McDermott, D. (1982). A temporal logic for reasoning about processes and plans. *Cognitive Science, 6,* 101-155.

Melkonian, D. S. (1990). Mathematical theory of chemical synaptic transmission. *Biological Cybernetics, 62,* 539-548.

Pecht, O. Y., & Gur, M. (1995). A biologically-inspired improved MAXNET. *IEEE Trans. Neural Networks, 6,* 757-759.

Petshe, T., & Dickinson, B. W. (1990). Trellis codes, receptive fields, and fault-tolerance self-repairing neural networks. *IEEE Trans. Neural Networks, 1*(2), 154-166.

Poggio, T., & Koch, C. (1987). Synapses that compute motion. *Scientific American, May,* 46-52.

Rao, D. H., & Gupta, M. M. (1993). A generic neural model based on excitatory: Inhibitory neural population. *IJCNN-93* (pp. 1393-1396).

Rosenblatt, F. (1958). The perceptron: A probabilistic model for information storage and organization in the brain. *Psychological Review, 65, 386-408.*

Skarda, C. A., & Freeman, W. J. (1987). How brains make chaos in order to make sense of the world. *Behavioral and Brain Sciences, 10,* 161-195.

Stevens, C. F. (1968). Synaptic physiology. *Proc. IEEE, 79*(9), 916-930.

Wilson, H. R. and Cowan, J. D. (1972). Excitatory and inhibitory interactions in localized populations of model neurons. *Biophysical J, 12,* 1-24.

Neuronal Morphology: Concepts and Mathematical Models

Amari, S. (1971). Characteristics of randomly connected threshold-element networks and network systems. *Proc. IEEE, 59*(1), 35-47.

Amari, S. (1972). Characteristics of random nets of analog neuron-like elements. *IEEE Trans. Systems, Man and Cybernetics, 2,* 643-654.

Amari, S. (1972). Learning patterns and pattern sequences by self-organizing nets of threshold elements. *IEEE Trans. on Computers, 21,* 1197-1206.

Amari, S. (1977). A mathematical approach to neural systems. In J. Metzler (Ed.), *Systems neuroscience* (pp. 67-118). New York: Academic.

Amari, S. (1977). Neural theory of association and concept formation. *Biological Cybernetics, 26,* 175-185.

Amari, S. (1990). Mathematical foundations of neurocomputing. *Proc. IEEE, 78*(9), 1443-1462.

Amit, D. J., Gutfreund, G., & Sompolinsky, H. (1985). Spin-glass model of neural networks. *Physical Review A, 32,* 1007-1018.

Anagun, A. S., & Cin, I. (1998). A neural-network-based computer access security system for multiple users. *Proc. 23rd Inter. Conf. Comput. Ind. Eng., Vol.* 35 (pp. 351-354).

Anderson, J. A. (1983). Cognition and psychological computation with neural models. *IEEE Trans. System, Man and Cybernetics, 13,* 799-815.

Anninos, P. A. Beek, B., Csermel, T. J., Harth, E. E., & Pertile, G. (1970). Dynamics of neural structures. *J. of Theoretical Biological, 26,* 121-148.

Aoki, C., & Siekevltz, P. (1988). Plasticity in brain development. *Scientific American, Dec.,* 56-64,

Churchland, P. S., & Sejnowski, T. J. (1988). Perspectives on cognitive neuroscience. *Science, 242,* 741-745.

Holmes C. C., & Mallick, B. K. (1998). Bayesian radial basis functions of variable dimension. *Neural Computations, 10*(5), 1217-1233.

Hopfield, J. (1990). Artificial neural networks are coming: An interview by W. Myers. *IEEE Expert, Apr.,* 3-6.

Joshi, A., Ramakrishman, N., Houstis, E. N., & Rice, J. R. (1997). On neurobiological, neuro-fuzzy, machine learning, and statistical pattern recognition techniques. *IEEE Trans. Neural Networks, 8.*

Kaneko, K. (1994). Relevance of dynamic clustering to biological networks. *Phys. D, 75,* 55-73.

Kaneko, K. (1997). Coupled maps with growth and death: An approach to cell differentiation. *Phys. D, 103,* 505-527.

Knopf, G. K., & Gupta, M. M. (1993). Dynamics of antagonistic neural processing elements. *Inter. J. of Neural Systems, 4*(3), 291-303.

Kohonen, T. (1988). An introduction to neural computing. *Neural Networks, 1*(1), 3-16.

Kohonen, T. (1990). The self-organizing map. *Proc. of the IEEE, 78*(9), 1464-1480.

Kohonen, T. (1991). Self-organizing maps: optimization approaches. In T. Kohonen, K. Makisara, O. Simula, & J. Kangas (Eds.), *Artificial neural networks* (pp. 981-990). Amsterdam: Elsevier.

Kohonen, T. (1993). Things you haven't heard about the self-organizing map. *Proc. Inter. Conf. Neural Networks 1993* (pp. 1147-1156).

Kohonen, T. (1998). Self organization of very large document collections: State of the art. *Proc. 8th Inter. Conf. Artificial Neural Networks, Vol. 1* (pp. 65-74).

LeCun, Y., Boser, B., & Solla, S. A. (1990). Optimal brain damage. In D. Touretzky (Ed.), *Advances in neural information processing systems, Vol. 2* (pp. 598-605). Morgan Kaufmann.

Lippmann, R. P. (1987). An introduction to computing with neural networks. IEEE *Acoustics, Speech and Signal Processing Magazine, 4*(2), 4-22.

Mantere, K., Parkkinen, J., Jaasketainen, T., & Gupta, M. M. (1993). Wilson-Cowan neural network model in image processing. *J. of Mathematical Imaging and Vision, 2,* 251-259.

McCarthy, J., & Hayes, P. J. (1969). Some philosophical problems from the standpoint of artificial intelligence. In Meltzer & Michie (Eds.), *Machine Intelligence, 4* (pp. 463-502). Edinburgh: Edinburgh Univ.

McCulloch, W. S., & Pitts, W. H. (1943). A logical calculus of the ideas imminent in nervous activity. *Bulletin of Mathematical Biophysics, 5,* 115-133.

McDermott, D. (1982). A temporal logic for reasoning about processes and plans. *Cognitive Science, 6,* 101-155.

Melkonian, D. S. (1990). Mathematical theory of chemical synaptic transmission. *Biological Cybernetics, 62,* 539-548.

Petshe, T., & Dickinson, B. W. (1990). Trellis codes, receptive fields, and fault-tolerance self-repairing neural networks. *IEEE Trans. Neural Networks, 1*(2), 154-166.

Poggio, T., & Koch, C. (1987). Synapses that compute motion. *Scientific American, May,* 46-52.

Sandewall, E. (1989). Combining logic and differential equations for describing real-world systems. *Proc. 1st Inter. Conf. on Principles of Knowledge Representation and Reasoning* (pp. 412-420). Morgan Kaufmann.

Setiono, R., & Liu, H. (1996). Symbolic representation of neural networks. *Computer, 29*(3), 71-77.

Wilson, H. R., & Cowan, J. D. (1972). Excitatory and inhibitory interactions in localized populations of model neurons. *Biophysical J., 12,* 1-24.

Chapter XVIII
Dynamics in Artificial Higher Order Neural Networks with Delays

Jinde Cao
Southeast University, China

Fengli Ren
Southeast University, China

Jinling Liang
Southeast University, China

ABSTRACT

This chapter concentrates on studying the dynamics of artificial higher order neural networks (HONNs) with delays. Both stability analysis and periodic oscillation are discussed here for a class of delayed HONNs with (or without) impulses. Most of the sufficient conditions obtained in this chapter are presented in linear matrix inequalities (LMIs), and so can be easily computed and checked in practice using the Matlab LMI Toolbox. In reality, stability is a necessary feature when applying artificial neural networks. Also periodic solution plays an important role in the dynamical behavior of all solutions though other dynamics such as bifurcation and chaos do coexist. So here we mainly focus on questions of the stability and periodic solutions of artificial HONNs with (or without) impulses. Firstly, stability analysis and periodic oscillation are analyzed for higher order bidirectional associative memory (BAM) neural networks without impulses. Secondly, global exponential stability and exponential convergence are studied for a class of impulsive higher order bidirectional associative memory neural networks with time-varying delays. The main methods and tools used in this chapter are linear matrix inequalities (LMIs), Lyapunov stability theory and coincidence degree theory.

INTRODUCTION

In recent years, Hopfield neural networks and their various generalizations have attracted the attention of many scientists (e.g., mathematicians, physicists, computer scientists and so on), due to their potential for the tasks of classification, associative memory, parallel computation and their ability to solve difficult optimization problems (Hopfield, 1984; ChuaYang, 1988; Marcus and Westervelt, 1989; Cohen and Grossberg, 1983; Driessche and Zou, 1998; Cao and Tao, 2001; Cao, 2001; Cao and Wang, 2004; Cao, Wang and Liao, 2003). For the Hopfield neural network characterized by first order deferential equations, Abu-Mostafa and Jacques (1985); McEliece, Posner, Rodemich and Venkatesh (1987) and Baldi (1988) presented its intrinsic limitations. As a consequence, different architectures with higher order interactions (Personnaz, Guyon and Dreyfus, 1987; Psaltis, Park and Hong, 1988; Simpson, 1990; Peretto and Niez, 1986; Ho, Lam, Xu and Tam, 1999) have been successively introduced to design neural networks which have stronger approximation properties, faster convergence rate, greater storage capacity, and higher fault tolerance than lower order neural networks. Meanwhile stability properties of these models have been investigated in Dembo, Farotimi and Kailath (1991); Kamp and Hasler (1990); Kosmatopoulos, Polycarpou, Christodoulou and Ioannou (1995); Xu, Liu and Liao (2003); Ren and Cao (2006); Ren and Cao (2007a); Ren and Cao (2007b). In this chapter, we will give some criteria on higher order BAM neural networks.

BAM neural networks were proposed in Kosko (1988). This model generalizes the single-layer auto-associative circuit and possesses good application prospects in the areas of pattern recognition, signal and image processing. The circuit diagram and connection pattern implementing the delayed BAM networks can be found in Cao and Wang (2002). From a mathematical viewpoint, although the system in this chapter can be regarded as a network with dimension $n+m$, it produces many nice properties due to the special structure of connection weights and its practical application in storing paired patterns via both directions: forward and backward. When a neural circuit is employed as an associative memory, the existence of many equilibrium points is a necessary feature. However, when applied to parallel computation and signal processing involving the solution of optimization problems, it is required that there be a well-defined computable solution for all possible initial states. This means that the network should have a unique equilibrium point that is globally attractive. Indeed, earlier applications in optimization have suffered from the existence of a complicated set of equilibriums. Thus, the global attractiveness of systems is of great importance for both practical and theoretical reasons. For more details about BAM neural networks, see Cao (2003); Cao and Dong (2003); Liao and Yu (1998); Mohamad (2001); Chen, Cao and Huang (2004).

In this chapter, firstly, we investigate the following second order BAM neural networks with time delays, shown in Equation (1.1), where $i=1,2,\dots, n; j=1,2, \dots, m; t>0$; $u_i(t)$, $v_j(t)$ denote

Equation (1.1).

$$\begin{cases} \dfrac{du_i(t)}{dt} = -a_i u_i(t) + \sum_{j=1}^{m} b_{ij}\tilde{g}_j(v_j(t-\tau)) + \sum_{j=1}^{m}\sum_{l=1}^{m} e_{ijl}\tilde{g}_j(v_j(t-\tau))\tilde{g}_l(v_l(t-\tau)) + I_i, \\[2em] \dfrac{dv_j(t)}{dt} = -d_j v_j(t) + \sum_{i=1}^{n} c_{ji}\tilde{f}_i(u_i(t-\sigma)) + \sum_{i=1}^{n}\sum_{l=1}^{n} s_{jil}\tilde{f}_i(u_i(t-\sigma))\tilde{f}_l(u_l(t-\sigma)) + J_j; \end{cases}$$

the potential (or voltage) of cell i and j at time t; a_i, d_j are positive constants; time delays τ, σ are non-negative constants, which correspond to finite speed of axonal signal transmission; b_{ij}, c_{ji}, e_{ijl}, s_{jil} are the first and second order connection weights of the neural network, respectively; I_i, J_j denote the ith and the jth component of an external input source introduced from outside the network to cell i and j, respectively; and $\tau^* = \max\{\tau, \sigma\}$.

Secondly, we present a class of impulsive higher order BAM neural networks with time-varying delays and study the global exponential stability and exponential convergence for such systems (see Equation (1.2)), where $t > 0$; $i=1, 2, \ldots, n$; $j=1, 2, \ldots, m$; $k=1, 2, \ldots$ and $0 < t_0 < t_1 < \ldots$, $\lim_{k \to +\infty} t_k = +\infty$:

$$\Delta x_i(t_k) = x_i(t_k) - x_i(t_k^-) = x_i(t_k) - \lim_{t \to t_k^-} x_i(t),$$

$$\Delta y_j(t_k) = y_j(t_k) - y_j(t_k^-) = y_j(t_k) - \lim_{t \to t_k^-} y_j(t);$$

time delays $\tau(t)$, $\sigma(t)$ are continuous functions and $0 \le \sigma(t) \le \sigma$, $0 \le \tau(t) \le \tau$.

Definition 1.1.1: *The equilibrium point (u^*, v^*) of system (1.1) is said to be globally exponentially stable, if there exist constants $k > 0$ and $\gamma \ge 1$ such that, for $t \ge 0$:* $\|u(t) - u^*\| + \|v(t) - v^*\| \le \gamma e^{-kt}$ $\left(\sup_{s \in [-\tau^*, 0]} \|u(s) - u^*\| + \sup_{s \in [-\tau^*, 0]} \|v(s) - v^*\| \right)$

DYNAMICS OF HIGHER ORDER BAM NEURAL NETWORKS

In this section, the stability and periodic solutions of higher order bidirectional associative memory (BAM) neural networks without impulses are investigated. We begin by studying the stability for higher order BAM neural networks (1.1).

EXPONENTIAL STABILITY OF HIGHER ORDER BAM NEURAL NETWORKS WITH TIME DELAYS

As will be specified in the development, we make some assumptions for the activation functions $\tilde{f}_i(\cdot)$, $\tilde{g}_j(\cdot)$ in the system (1.1):

Equation (1.2).

$$\begin{cases} \dfrac{dx_i(t)}{dt} = -a_i x_i(t) + \sum_{j=1}^{m} b_{ij} f_j(y_j(t - \tau(t))) + \sum_{j=1}^{m} \sum_{l=1}^{m} b_{ijl} f_j(y_j(t - \tau(t))) f_l(y_l(t - \tau(t))), & t \ne t_k \\[4mm] \dfrac{dy_j(t)}{dt} = -d_j y_j(t) + \sum_{i=1}^{n} c_{ji} g_i(x_i(t - \sigma(t))) + \sum_{i=1}^{n} \sum_{l=1}^{n} c_{jil} g_i(x_i(t - \sigma(t))) g_l(x_l(t - \sigma(t))); & t \ne t_k \\[4mm] \Delta x_i(t) = e_i x_i(t^-) + \sum_{j=1}^{m} w_{ij} h_j(y_j(t^- - \tau(t))) \\[2mm] \qquad\qquad + \sum_{j=1}^{m} \sum_{l=1}^{m} w_{ijl} h_j(y_j(t^- - \tau(t))) h_l(y_l(t^- - \tau(t))), & t = t_k \\[4mm] \Delta y_j(t) = r_j y_j(t^-) + \sum_{i=1}^{n} u_{ji} s_i(x_i(t^- - \sigma(t))) \\[2mm] \qquad\qquad + \sum_{i=1}^{n} \sum_{l=1}^{n} u_{jil} s_i(x_i(t^- - \sigma(t))) s_l(x_l(t^- - \sigma(t))); & t = t_k \end{cases}$$

(H_1) There exist numbers $N_i > 0$, $M_j > 0$ such that $\left|\tilde{f}_i(x)\right| \le N_i$, $\left|\tilde{g}_j(x)\right| \le M_j$; for all $x \in R$ ($i = 1,2,\ldots, n; j=1,2,\ldots, m$).

(H_2) There exist numbers $L_i > 0$, $K_j > 0$ such that:

$$\left|\tilde{f}_i(x) - \tilde{f}_i(y)\right| \le L_i |x-y|, \quad \left|\tilde{g}_j(x) - \tilde{g}_j(y)\right| \le K_j |x-y|;$$

for all $x, y \in R$ ($i = 1,2,\ldots, n; j = 1,2, \ldots, m$).

(H'_2) There exist numbers $L_i > 0$, $K_j > 0$ such that:

$$0 \le \frac{\tilde{f}_i(x) - \tilde{f}_i(y)}{x-y} \le L_i, \quad 0 \le \frac{\tilde{g}_j(x) - \tilde{g}_j(y)}{x-y} \le K_j;$$

for all $x \ne y \in R$ ($i = 1,2,\ldots, n; j=1,2, \ldots, m$).

The initial conditions associated with (1.1) are of the form:

$$u_i(t) = \varphi_i(t)$$
$$v_j(t) = \psi_j(t)$$
$$-\tau^* \le t \le 0 \qquad (1.3)$$

in which $\varphi_i(t)$, $\psi_j(t)$ ($i = 1,2,\ldots, n; j=1,2, \ldots, m$) are continuous functions.

Under assumptions (H_1) and (H_2) (or (H'_2)), system (1.1) has an equilibrium point (u^*, v^*) (Cao, 1999), where $u^* = [u_1^*, u_2^*, \cdots, u_n^*]^T$, $v^* = [v_1^*, v_2^*, \cdots, v_m^*]^T$. Let $x_i(t) = u_i(t) - u_i^*$, $y_j(t) = v_j(t) - v_j^*$; $f_i(x_i(t)) = \tilde{f}_i(x_i(t) + u_i^*) - \tilde{f}_i(u_i^*)$, $g_j(y_j(t)) = \tilde{g}_j(y_j(t) + v_j^*) - \tilde{g}_j(v_j^*)$; and system (1.1) is transformed into Equation (1.4), where:

$$\xi_l = e_{ijl} / (e_{ijl} + e_{ilj})\tilde{g}_l(v_l(t-\tau)) + e_{ilj}/(e_{ijl} + e_{ilj})\tilde{g}_l(v_l^*)$$

when $e_{ijl} + e_{ilj} \ne 0$, it lies between $\tilde{g}_l(v_l(t-\tau))$ and $\tilde{g}_l(v_l^*)$; otherwise $\xi_l = 0$. Similarly:

$$\eta_l = s_{jil} / (s_{jil} + s_{jli})\tilde{f}_l(u_l(t-\sigma)) + s_{jli} / (s_{jil} + s_{jli})\tilde{f}_l(u_l^*)$$

Equation (1.4)

$$\begin{cases} \dfrac{dx_i(t)}{dt} = -a_i x_i(t) + \sum_{j=1}^{m} b_{ij} g_j(y_j(t-\tau)) \\[2mm] \qquad + \sum_{j=1}^{m} \sum_{l=1}^{m} e_{ijl}[g_j(y_j(t-\tau))\tilde{g}_l(v_l(t-\tau)) + g_l(y_l(t-\tau))\tilde{g}_j(v_j^*)] \\[2mm] \qquad = -a_i x_i(t) + \sum_{j=1}^{m}[b_{ij} + \sum_{l=1}^{m}(e_{ijl}\tilde{g}_l(v_l(t-\tau)) + e_{ilj}\tilde{g}_l(v_l^*))]g_j(y_j(t-\tau)) \\[2mm] \qquad = -a_i x_i(t) + \sum_{j=1}^{m}[b_{ij} + \sum_{l=1}^{m}(e_{ijl} + e_{ilj})\xi_l]g_j(y_j(t-\tau)), \\[4mm] \dfrac{dy_j(t)}{dt} = -d_j y_j(t) + \sum_{i=1}^{n} c_{ji} f_i(x_i(t-\sigma)) \\[2mm] \qquad + \sum_{i=1}^{n} \sum_{l=1}^{n} s_{jil}[f_i(x_i(t-\sigma))\tilde{f}_l(u_l(t-\sigma)) + f_l(x_l(t-\sigma))\tilde{f}_i(u_i^*)] \\[2mm] \qquad = -d_j y_j(t) + \sum_{i=1}^{n}[c_{ji} + \sum_{l=1}^{n}(s_{jil}\tilde{f}_l(u_l(t-\sigma)) + s_{jli}\tilde{f}_l(u_i^*))]f_i(x_i(t-\sigma)) \\[2mm] \qquad = -d_j y_j(t) + \sum_{i=1}^{n}[c_{ji} + \sum_{l=1}^{n}(s_{jil} + s_{jli})\eta_l]f_i(x_i(t-\sigma)), \end{cases}$$

when $s_{jil} = s_{jli} \neq 0$, it lies between $\tilde{f}_l(u_l(t - \sigma))$ and $\tilde{f}_l(u_l^*)$; otherwise $\eta_l = 0$.

If we denote what appears in Box 1, system (1.4) can be rewritten in the following vector-matrix form:

$$\begin{cases} \dfrac{dx(t)}{dt} = -Ax(t) + Bg(y(t-\tau)) + \Gamma^T \Pi g(y(t-\tau)), \\ \dfrac{dy(t)}{dt} = -Dy(t) + Cf(x(t-\sigma)) + \Theta^T \Omega f(x(t-\sigma)). \end{cases}$$

$$(1.5)$$

The global exponential stability of the origin of (1.5) is equivalent to the global exponential stability of the equilibrium point (u^*, v^*) of (1.1).

In the following:

$x_t(s) = x(t + s)$, $s \in [-\tau^*, 0]$, $t \geq 0$; $y_t(s) = y(t + s)$, $s \in [-\tau^*, 0]$, $t \geq 0$.

$M^* = \sum_{j=1}^{m} M_j^2$, $N^* = \sum_{i=1}^{n} N_i^2$. $K = \mathrm{diag}(K_1, K_2, ..., K_m)$,

$L = \mathrm{diag}(L_1, L_2, ..., L_n)$.

For $\mathbf{x} \in R^n$, its norm is defined as $\|x\| = \sqrt{x^T x}$. A^T and A^{-1} denote the transpose and inverse of the matrix A. $A > 0$ means that matrix A is real symmetric and positive definite. $\lambda_{\max}(A)$ and $\lambda_{\min}(A)$ represent the maximum and minimum eigenvalue of matrix A, respectively.

In the proof of the main results we need the following lemma which can be found in Boyd, Ghaoui, Feron and Balakrishnan (1994).

Lemma 1.2.1: (Boyd, Ghaoui, Feron and Balakrishnan, 1994)

1. Suppose W, U are any matrices, ε is a positive number and matrix $D > 0$, then:

$$W^T U + U^T W \leq \varepsilon W^T D W + \varepsilon^{-1} U^T D^{-1} U.$$

2. (Schur complement) The following LMI:

$$\begin{bmatrix} Q(x) & S(x) \\ S^T(x) & R(x) \end{bmatrix} > 0,$$

where $Q(x) = Q^T(x)$, $R(x) = R^T(x)$, and $S(x)$ depend affinely on x, is equivalent to:

$$R(x) > 0, \quad Q(x) - S(x)R^{-1}(x)S^T(x) > 0;$$

or

$$Q(x) > 0, \quad R(x) - S^T(x)Q^{-1}(x)S(x) > 0.$$

Theorem 1.2.1 Under assumptions (H_1) and (H_2), the equilibrium point (u^*, v^*) of system (1.1) is unique and globally exponentially stable if there exist positive definite matrices P, Q, Σ_1, Σ_2, positive diagonal matrices W, T and constants $\varepsilon_i > 0$ $(i = 1,2)$ such that:

$$\begin{bmatrix} AP + PA - LWL & P & PB \\ P & \dfrac{\varepsilon_1}{M^*}I_{n \times n} & 0 \\ B^T P & 0 & \Sigma_1 \end{bmatrix} > 0,$$

Box 1.

$x(t) = [x_1(t), x_2(t), ..., x_n(t)]^T$, $y(t) = [y_1(t), y_2(t), ..., y_m(t)]^T$;

$g(y(t-\tau)) = [g_1(y_1(t-\tau)), g_2(y_2(t-\tau)), ..., g_m(y_m(t-\tau))]^T$, $f(y(t-\sigma)) = [f_1(x_1(t-\sigma)),$

$f_2(x_2(t-\sigma)), ..., f_n(x_n(t-\sigma))]^T$; $A = \mathrm{diag}(a_1, a_2, ..., a_n)$, $D = \mathrm{diag}(d_1, d_2, ..., d_m)$; $B = (b_{ij})_{n \times m}$, $C = (c_{ji})_{m \times n}$;

$\Pi = (E_1 + E_1^T, E_2 + E_2^T, ..., E_n + E_n^T)^T$, where $E_i = (e_{ijl})_{m \times m}$, $\Omega = (S_1 + S_1^T, S_2 + S_2^T, ..., S_m + S_m^T)^T$,

where $S_j = (s_{jil})_{n \times n}$; $\Gamma = \mathrm{diag}(\xi, \xi, ..., \xi)_{n \times n}$, where $\xi = [\xi_1, \xi_2, ..., \xi_m]^T$; $\Theta = \mathrm{diag}(\eta, \eta, ..., \eta)_{m \times m}$,

where $\eta = [\eta_1, \eta_2, ... \eta_n]^T$.

$$\begin{bmatrix} QD + DQ - KTK & Q & QC \\ Q & \dfrac{\varepsilon_2}{N^*}I_{m\times m} & 0 \\ C^T Q & 0 & \Sigma_2 \end{bmatrix} > 0;$$

(1.6)

$$\varepsilon_1 \Pi^T \Pi + \Sigma_1 - T < 0, \ \varepsilon_2 \Omega^T \Omega + \Sigma_2 - W < 0.$$

(1.7)

Proof: From Lemma 1.2.1, we know that condition (1.6) is equivalent to Box 2. Then there exists a scalar $k > 0$ such that:

$$AP + PA - 2kP - LWL - \frac{M^*}{\varepsilon_1}P^2 - PB\Sigma_1^{-1}B^T P > 0,$$

$$QD + DQ - 2kQ - KTK - \frac{N^*}{\varepsilon_2}Q^2 - QC\Sigma_2^{-1}C^T Q > 0$$

(1.8)

$$\varepsilon_1 \Pi^T \Pi + \Sigma_1 - e^{-2k\tau}T \leq 0, \ \varepsilon_2 \Omega^T \Omega + \Sigma_2 - e^{-2k\sigma}W \leq 0$$

(1.9)

Define the Lyapunov functional as:

$$V(x_t, y_t) = e^{2kt}x(t)^T Px(t) + e^{2kt}y(t)^T Qy(t)$$

$$+ \int_{t-\sigma}^{t} e^{2ks} f^T(x(s))Wf(x(s))ds + \int_{t-\tau}^{t} e^{2ks} g^T(y(s))Tg(y(s))ds.$$

Calculate the derivative of $V(x_t, y_t)$ along the solutions of (1.5) and we obtain Equation (1.10).

By Lemma 1.2.1, we have Equations (1.11) – (1.14). It follows from:

$$\Gamma^T \Gamma = \|\xi\|^2 I_{n\times n}, \quad \|\xi\|^2 \leq \sum_{j=1}^{m} M_j^2 = M^*$$

that:

$$x^T(t)P\Gamma^T\Gamma Px(t) \leq M^* x^T(t)P^2 x(t)$$

(1.15)

Since $\Theta^T \Theta = \|\eta\|^2 I_{m\times m}$ and $\|\eta\|^2 \leq \sum_{i=1}^{n} N_i^2 = N^*$, one can obtain:

$$y^T(t)Q\Theta^T\Theta Qy(t) \leq N^* y^T(t)Q^2 y(t)$$

(1.16)

Box 2.

$$AP + PA - LWL - \frac{M^*}{\varepsilon_1}P^2 - PB\Sigma_1^{-1}B^T P > 0, \ QD + DQ - KTK - \frac{N^*}{\varepsilon_2}Q^2 - QC\Sigma_2^{-1}C^T Q > 0;$$

Equation (1.10).

$$\dot{V}(x_t, y_t)|_{(1.5)} \leq e^{2kt}\left\{ x^T(t)\left[2kP - PA - AP + LWL\right]x(t) + 2x^T(t)PBg(y(t-\tau)) \right.$$

$$+ y^T(t)\left[2kQ - QD - DQ + KTK\right]y(t) + 2y^T(t)QCf(x(t-\sigma))$$

$$+ 2x^T(t)P\Gamma^T\Pi g(y(t-\tau)) - e^{-2k\sigma}f^T(x(t-\sigma))Wf(x(t-\sigma))$$

$$\left. + 2y^T(t)Q\Theta^T\Omega f(x(t-\sigma)) - e^{-2k\tau}g^T(y(t-\tau))Tg(y(t-\tau)) \right\}$$

Equations (1.11) – (1.14).

$$2x^T(t)PBg(y(t-\tau)) \leq x^T(t)PB\Sigma_1^{-1}B^T Px(t) + g^T(y(t-\tau))\Sigma_1 g(y(t-\tau))$$

$$2y^T(t)QCf(x(t-\sigma)) \leq y^T(t)QC\Sigma_2^{-1}C^T Qy(t) + f^T(x(t-\sigma))\Sigma_2 f(x(t-\sigma))$$

$$2x^T(t)P\Gamma^T\Pi g(y(t-\tau)) \leq \tfrac{1}{\varepsilon_1}x^T(t)P\Gamma^T\Gamma Px(t) + \varepsilon_1 g^T(y(t-\tau))\Pi^T\Pi g(y(t-\tau))$$

$$2y^T(t)Q\Theta^T\Omega f(x(t-\sigma)) \leq \tfrac{1}{\varepsilon_2}y^T(t)Q\Theta^T\Theta Qy(t) + \varepsilon_2 f^T(x(t-\sigma))\Omega^T\Omega f(x(t-\sigma))$$

Substituting (1.11)–(1.16) into (1.10), and from conditions (1.8) and (1.9), we have Equation (1.17), which means:

$$V(x_t, y_t) \leq V(x_0, y_0), \quad t \geq 0$$

Since (Box 3), then we easily obtain (Box 4) for all t $\geq$ 0, where $\gamma \geq 1$ is a constant. By Definition 1.1.1, this completes the proof. □

Theorem 1.2.2 Under assumptions (H_1) and (H'_2), the equilibrium point (u^*, v^*) of system (1.1) is unique and globally exponentially stable if there

Equation (1.17).

$$
\begin{aligned}
\dot{V}(x_t, y_t)\big|_{(1.5)} &\leq e^{2kt} \Big\{ x(t)^T \Big[2kP - PA - AP + LWL + PB\Sigma_1^{-1}B^T P + \tfrac{M^*}{\varepsilon_1}P^2 \Big] x(t) \\
&\quad + y(t)^T \Big[2kQ - QD - DQ + KTK + QC\Sigma_2^{-1}C^T Q + \tfrac{N^*}{\varepsilon_2}Q^2 \Big] y(t) \\
&\quad + f^T(x(t-\sigma)) \Big[\Sigma_2 + \varepsilon_2 \Omega^T \Omega - e^{-2k\sigma}W \Big] f(x(t-\sigma)) \\
&\quad + g^T(y(t-\tau)) \Big[\Sigma_1 + \varepsilon_1 \Pi^T \Pi - e^{-2k\tau}T \Big] g(y(t-\tau)) \Big\} \leq 0
\end{aligned}
$$

Box 3.

$$
V(x_t, y_t) \geq e^{2kt}\Big[\lambda_{\min}(P)\|x(t)\|^2 + \lambda_{\min}(Q)\|y(t)\|^2 \Big], \quad t \geq 0
$$

$$
\begin{aligned}
V(x_0, y_0) &\leq \lambda_{\max}(P)\|x(0)\|^2 + \lambda_{\max}(Q)\|y(0)\|^2 \\
&\quad + \int_{-\tau}^0 e^{2ks}g^T(y(s))Tg(y(s))ds + \int_{-\sigma}^0 e^{2ks}f^T(x(s))Wf(x(s))ds \\
&\leq \Big(\lambda_{\max}(P) + \sigma\|W\|\|L\|^2\Big)\sup_{s\in[-\sigma,0]}\|x(s)\|^2 + \Big(\lambda_{\max}(Q) + \tau\|T\|\|K\|^2\Big)\sup_{s\in[-\tau,0]}\|y(s)\|^2
\end{aligned}
$$

Box 4.

$$
\|x(t)\| + \|y(t)\| \leq \sqrt{2}\Big(\|x(t)\|^2 + \|y(t)\|^2\Big)^{\frac{1}{2}} \leq \gamma \left(\sup_{s\in[-\tau^*,0]}\|x(s)\| + \sup_{s\in[-\tau^*,0]}\|y(s)\| \right)e^{-kt}
$$

Equation (1.18).

$$
\begin{pmatrix}
AP + PA - 2R_1 - \beta\big(A + LRARL + LR^2L\big) & P & \sqrt{\beta}\,LR & PB \\
P & \tfrac{\varepsilon_1}{M^*}I_{n\times n} & 0 & 0 \\
\sqrt{\beta}\,RL & 0 & \tfrac{\varepsilon_3}{M^*}I_{n\times n} & 0 \\
B^T P & 0 & 0 & \Sigma_1
\end{pmatrix} > 0
$$

$$
\begin{pmatrix}
QD + DQ - 2R_2 - \alpha\big(D + KWDWK + KW^2K\big) & Q & \sqrt{\alpha}\,KW & QC \\
Q & \tfrac{\varepsilon_2}{N^*}I_{m\times m} & 0 & 0 \\
\sqrt{\alpha}\,WK & 0 & \tfrac{\varepsilon_4}{N^*}I_{m\times m} & 0 \\
C^T Q & 0 & 0 & \Sigma_2
\end{pmatrix} > 0
$$

exist positive definite matrices P, Q, Σ_1, Σ_2, positive diagonal matrices $R_1, R_2, R = diag(r_1, r_2, ..., r_n)$, $W = diag(w_1, w_2, ..., w_n)$ and positive constants α, β, ξ_i ($i = 1,2,3,4$) such that Equations (1.18) and:

$$\varepsilon_1 \Pi^T \Pi + \Sigma_1 + \beta \left(\varepsilon_3 \Pi^T \Pi + B^T B\right) - 2R_2 K^{-2} < 0,$$

$$\varepsilon_2 \Omega^T \Omega + \Sigma_2 + \alpha \left(\varepsilon_4 \Omega^T \Omega + C^T C\right) - 2R_1 L^{-2} < 0 \tag{1.19}$$

are generated.

Proof: From Lemma 1.2.1, condition (1.18) is equivalent to Box 5, then there exists a scalar $k > 0$ such as Equations (1.20) and (1.21).

Define the Lyapunov functional as Box 6. Under assumption (H'_2), we have Equations (1.22) and (1.23), and:

$$f^T(x(t-\sigma))R_1 L^{-2} f(x(t-\sigma)) \leq x^T(t-\sigma)R_1 x(t-\sigma) \tag{1.24}$$

Box 5.

$$AP + PA - 2R_1 - \beta\left(A + LRARL + LR^2 L\right) - \tfrac{M^*}{\varepsilon_1} P^2 - \tfrac{M^*}{\varepsilon_3}\beta LR^2 L - PB\Sigma_1^{-1}B^T P > 0,$$

$$QD + DQ - 2R_2 - \alpha\left(D + KWDWK + KW^2 K\right) - \tfrac{N^*}{\varepsilon_2} Q^2 - \tfrac{N^*}{\varepsilon_4}\alpha KW^2 K - QC\Sigma_2^{-1}C^T Q > 0$$

Equation (1.20)

$$AP + PA - 2kP - 2R_1 - 2kLR - \beta\left(A + LRARL + LR^2 L\right) - \tfrac{M^*}{\varepsilon_1} P^2 - \tfrac{M^*}{\varepsilon_3}\beta LR^2 L - PB\Sigma_1^{-1}B^T P > 0,$$

$$QD + DQ - 2kQ - 2R_2 - 2kKW - \alpha\left(D + KWDWK + KW^2 K\right) - \tfrac{N^*}{\varepsilon_2} Q^2 - \tfrac{N^*}{\varepsilon_4}\alpha KW^2 K - QC\Sigma_2^{-1}C^T Q > 0$$

Equation (1.21)

$$\varepsilon_1 \Pi^T \Pi + \Sigma_1 + \beta(\varepsilon_3 \Pi^T \Pi + B^T B) - 2e^{-2k\tau} R_2 K^{-2} \leq 0,$$

$$\varepsilon_2 \Omega^T \Omega + \Sigma_2 + \alpha(\varepsilon_4 \Omega^T \Omega + C^T C) - 2e^{-2k\sigma} R_1 L^{-2} \leq 0$$

Box 6.

$$V(x_t, y_t) = e^{2kt} x^T(t)Px(t) + e^{2kt} y^T(t)Qy(t) + 2\beta e^{2kt}\sum_{i=1}^{n} r_i \int_0^{x_i(t)} f_i(s)ds$$

$$+ 2\alpha e^{2kt}\sum_{j=1}^{m} w_j \int_0^{y_i(t)} g_j(s)ds + 2\int_{t-\sigma}^{t} e^{2ks} x^T(s)R_1 x(s)ds + 2\int_{t-\tau}^{t} e^{2ks} y^T(s)R_2 y(s)ds$$

Equation (1.22)

$$0 \leq \sum_{i=1}^{n} r_i \int_0^{x_i(t)} f_i(s)ds \leq \sum_{i=1}^{n} r_i L_i \int_0^{x_i(t)} sds \leq \frac{1}{2}\sum_{i=1}^{n} r_i L_i x_i^2(t) = \frac{1}{2} x^T(t)RLx(t)$$

Equation (1.23)

$$0 \leq \sum_{j=1}^{m} w_i \int_0^{y_i(t)} g_j(s)ds \leq \sum_{j=1}^{m} w_i K_j \int_0^{y_i(t)} sds \leq \frac{1}{2}\sum_{j=1}^{m} w_j K_j y_j^2(t) = \frac{1}{2} y^T(t)WKy(t)$$

$$g^T(y(t-\tau))R_2K^{-2}g(y(t-\tau)) \leq y^T(t-\tau)R_2y(t-\tau)$$

$$(1.25)$$

Calculate the derivative of $V(x_t,y_t)$ along the solutions of (1.5) and substitute inequalities (1.22)–(1.25) into it, we obtain Equation (1.26). On the other hand, from Lemma 1.2.1, we have Equations (1.27) through (1.32).

Substitute inequalities (1.11)–(1.16) and (1.27)–(1.32) into (1.26), and from (1.19)–(1.20), we obtain Equation (1.33). This means, $V(x_t,y_t) < V(x_0,y_0)$ for all $t \geq 0$. The remaining part of the proof is similar to that of Theorem 1.2.1 and is omitted. $\square$

Equation (1.26)

$$
\begin{aligned}
\dot{V}(x_t,y_t)\big|_{(1.5)} &\leq e^{2kt}\Big\{ x^T(t)\big[2kP - PA - AP + 2k\beta RL + 2R_1\big]x(t) + 2x^T(t)PBg(y(t-\tau)) \\
&\quad + y^T(t)\big[2kQ - QD - DQ + 2k\alpha WK + 2R_2\big]y(t) + 2y^T(t)QCf(x(t-\sigma)) \\
&\quad + 2x^T(t)P\Gamma^T\Pi g(y(t-\tau)) - 2\beta f^T(x(t))RAx(t) + 2\beta f^T(x(t))RBg(y(t-\tau)) \\
&\quad + 2y^T(t)Q\Theta^T\Omega f(x(t-\sigma)) - 2\alpha g^T(y(t))WDy(t) + 2\alpha g^T(y(t))WCf(x(t-\sigma)) \\
&\quad + 2\beta f^T(x(t))R\Gamma^T\Pi g(y(t-\tau)) - 2e^{-2k\sigma}f^T(x(t-\sigma))R_1L^{-2}f(x(t-\sigma)) \\
&\quad + 2\alpha g^T(y(t))W\Theta^T\Omega f(x(t-\sigma)) - 2e^{-2k\tau}g^T(y(t-\tau))R_2K^{-2}g(y(t-\tau))\Big\}
\end{aligned}
$$

Equation (1.27)

$$
\begin{aligned}
2\beta f^T(x(t))R\Gamma^T\Pi g(y(t-\tau)) &\leq \frac{\beta}{\varepsilon_3}f^T(x(t))R\Gamma^T\Gamma Rf(x(t)) + \varepsilon_3\beta g^T(y(t-\tau))\Pi^T\Pi g(y(t-\tau)) \\
&\leq \frac{M^*}{\varepsilon_3}\beta x^T(t)LR^2Lx(t) + \varepsilon_3\beta g^T(y(t-\tau))\Pi^T\Pi g(y(t-\tau))
\end{aligned}
$$

Equation (1.28)

$$
\begin{aligned}
2\alpha g^T(y(t))W\Theta^T\Omega f(x(t-\sigma)) &\leq \frac{\alpha}{\varepsilon_4}g^T(y(t))W\Theta^T\Theta Wg(y(t)) + \varepsilon_4\alpha f^T(x(t-\sigma))\Omega^T\Omega f(x(t-\sigma)) \\
&\leq \frac{N^*}{\varepsilon_4}\alpha y^T(t)KW^2Ky(t) + \varepsilon_4\alpha f^T(x(t-\sigma))\Omega^T\Omega f(x(t-\sigma))
\end{aligned}
$$

Equation (1.29)

$$-2\beta f^T(x(t))RAx(t) \leq \beta x^T(t)Ax(t) + \beta f^T(x(t))RARf(x(t)) \leq \beta x^T(t)\big(A + LRARL\big)x(t)$$

Equation (1.30)

$$-2\alpha g^T(y(t))WDy(t) \leq \alpha y^T(t)\big(D + KWDWK\big)y(t)$$

Equation (1.31)

$$2\beta f^T(x(t))RBg(y(t-\tau)) \leq \beta x^T(t)LR^2Lx(t) + \beta g^T(y(t-\tau))B^TBg(y(t-\tau))$$

Equation (1.32)

$$2\alpha g^T(y(t))WCf(x(t-\sigma)) \le \alpha y^T(t)KW^2Ky(t) + \alpha f^T(x(t-\sigma))C^TCf(x(t-\sigma))$$

Equation (1.33)

$$\dot{V}(x_t, y_t)\Big|_{(1.5)} \le e^{2kt}\Big\{ x^T(t)\Big[2kP - PA - AP + 2R_1 + 2kLR + \beta\left(A + LRARL + LR^2L\right)$$

$$+ \frac{M^*}{\varepsilon_1}P^2 + \frac{M^*}{\varepsilon_3}\beta LR^2L + PB\Sigma_1^{-1}B^TP \Big]x(t)$$

$$+ y^T(t)\Big[2kQ - QD - DQ + 2R_2 + 2kKW + \alpha\left(D + KWDWK + KW^2K\right)$$

$$+ \frac{N^*}{\varepsilon_2}Q^2 + \frac{N^*}{\varepsilon_4}\alpha KW^2K + QC\Sigma_2^{-1}C^TQ \Big]y(t)$$

$$+ f^T(x(t-\sigma))\Big[\varepsilon_2\Omega^T\Omega + \Sigma_2 + \alpha(\varepsilon_4\Omega^T\Omega + C^TC) - 2e^{-2k\sigma}R_1L^{-2} \Big]f(x(t-\sigma))$$

$$+ g^T(y(t-\tau))\Big[\varepsilon_1\Pi^T\Pi + \Sigma_1 + \beta(\varepsilon_3\Pi^T\Pi + B^TB) - 2e^{-2kt}R_2K^{-2} \Big]g(y(t-\tau)) \Big\}$$

Remark 1.2.1. Theorems 1.2.1 and 1.2.2 are developed under different assumptions and the use of various Lyapunov functions. They provided two different sufficient conditions ensuring the equilibrium point of system (1.5) to be unique and globally exponentially stable. Generally speaking, both have advantages in different problems and applications.

Example 1.2.1. Consider the higher order BAM neural networks (1.1) with $m = 2$, $n = 3$; $A = diag(48,54,42)$, $D = diag(40,44)$; $L = diag(0.7,0.8,0.9)$, $K = diag(0.6,0.7)$; $\sigma = \tau = 0.5$; $N = [N_1,N_2,N_3]^T = [1,1,1]^T$, $M = [M_1,M_2]^T = [1,1]^T$;

$$B = \begin{bmatrix} 0.5 & 0.6 \\ -0.1 & 0.2 \\ 0.7 & -0.3 \end{bmatrix}, \quad C = \begin{bmatrix} 0.2 & -0.3 & 0.4 \\ -0.1 & 0.2 & 0.5 \end{bmatrix};$$

$$E_1 = \begin{bmatrix} 0.9501 & 0.6068 \\ 0.2311 & 0.4860 \end{bmatrix}, E_2 = \begin{bmatrix} 0.8913 & 0.4565 \\ 0.7621 & 0.0185 \end{bmatrix},$$

$$E_3 = \begin{bmatrix} 0.8214 & 0.6154 \\ 0.4447 & 0.7919 \end{bmatrix};$$

$$S_1 = \begin{bmatrix} 0.9218 & 0.4057 & 0.4103 \\ 0.7382 & 0.9355 & 0.8936 \\ 0.1763 & 0.9169 & 0.0579 \end{bmatrix},$$

$$S_2 = \begin{bmatrix} 0.3529 & 0.1389 & 0.6038 \\ 0.8132 & 0.2028 & 0.2722 \\ 0.0099 & 0.1987 & 0.1988 \end{bmatrix}$$

then:

$$\Pi = \begin{bmatrix} 1.9003 & 0.8380 \\ 0.8380 & 0.9720 \\ 1.7826 & 1.2186 \\ 1.2186 & 0.0370 \\ 1.6428 & 1.0601 \\ 1.0601 & 1.5839 \end{bmatrix}, \Omega = \begin{bmatrix} 1.8436 & 1.1439 & 0.5865 \\ 1.1439 & 1.8709 & 1.8106 \\ 0.5865 & 1.8106 & 0.1158 \\ 0.7057 & 0.9521 & 0.6137 \\ 0.9521 & 0.4055 & 0.4709 \\ 0.6137 & 0.4709 & 0.3976 \end{bmatrix}$$

Using standard numerical software, it is found that there exist $\varepsilon_1 = 5.5086$, $\varepsilon_2 = 2.7019$; $W = diag(124.2670,121.1546,129.2524)$, $T = diag(153.1128,150.8543;$

$$P = \begin{bmatrix} 1.5747 & -0.0000 & -0.0001 \\ -0.0000 & 1.5347 & 0.0003 \\ -0.0001 & 0.0003 & 2.3328 \end{bmatrix},$$

$$Q = \begin{bmatrix} 1.8582 & -0.0001 \\ -0.0001 & 1.8786 \end{bmatrix};$$

$$\Sigma_1 = \begin{bmatrix} 41.1091 & -21.9732 \\ -21.9732 & 56.6327 \end{bmatrix},$$

$$\Sigma_2 = \begin{bmatrix} 52.9019 & -8.9928 & -5.8702 \\ -8.9928 & 47.9032 & -7.0662 \\ -5.8702 & -7.0662 & 58.6923 \end{bmatrix}$$

such that conditions (1.6) and (1.7) in Theorem 1.2.1 hold, therefore, the equilibrium point of this system is unique and globally exponentially stable.

Example 1.2.2. Consider the higher order BAM neural networks (1.1) with $m = 2 = n$; $A = diag(23,15)$, $D = diag(18,21)$; $L = diag(2.0, 1.5)$, $K = diag(2.1,2.7)$; $N = [N_1,N_2] = \left[\sqrt{2},\sqrt{2}\right]^T$, $M = [M_1,M_2]^T = \left[\sqrt{2},\sqrt{2}\right]^T$; $\sigma = 1$, $\tau = 0.5$;

$$B = \begin{bmatrix} 0.5 & 1.6 \\ 0.2 & -2.3 \end{bmatrix}, C = \begin{bmatrix} -0.3 & 0.4 \\ -0.1 & 1.5 \end{bmatrix},$$

$$E_1 = \begin{bmatrix} 0.6992 & 0.4784 \\ 0.7275 & 0.5548 \end{bmatrix};$$

$$E_2 = \begin{bmatrix} 0.1210 & 0.7159 \\ 0.4508 & 0.8928 \end{bmatrix}, S_1 = \begin{bmatrix} 0.2731 & 0.8656 \\ 0.2548 & 0.2324 \end{bmatrix},$$

$$S_2 = \begin{bmatrix} 0.8049 & 0.2319 \\ 0.9048 & 0.2393 \end{bmatrix};$$

then:

$$\Pi = \begin{bmatrix} 1.3984 & 1.2059 \\ 1.2059 & 1.1097 \\ 0.2421 & 1.1666 \\ 1.1666 & 1.7857 \end{bmatrix}, \Omega = \begin{bmatrix} 0.5462 & 1.1204 \\ 1.2804 & 0.4647 \\ 1.6097 & 1.1403 \\ 1.1403 & 0.4786 \end{bmatrix}$$

by taking $\alpha = 0.0223$, $\beta = 0.0303$; we can find the following feasible solutions $\varepsilon_1 = 2.5665$, $\varepsilon_2 = 4.4301$, $\varepsilon_3 = 8.7175$; $W = diag(2.4359, 0.6083)$, $R = diag(0.8997, 0.8606)$, $R_1 = diag(97.8737, 45.4553)$, $R_2 = diag(101.3219, 161.6616)$; $\varepsilon_4 = 18.2510$;

$$P = \begin{bmatrix} 7.3061 & -0.5999 \\ -0.5999 & 6.0078 \end{bmatrix}, Q = \begin{bmatrix} 9.5724 & 0.1274 \\ 0.1274 & 12.6656 \end{bmatrix};$$

$$\Sigma_2 = \begin{bmatrix} 11.4886 & -8.9369 \\ -8.9369 & 17.1113 \end{bmatrix}$$

according to Theorem 1.2.2, the equilibrium point of this system is unique and globally exponentially stable.

Periodic Oscillation of Higher Order Bam Neural Networks with Periodic Coefficients and Delays

In this subsection, we consider higher order BAM neural networks shown in Equation (1.34), with initial conditions (1.3); where $i = 1,2,...,n$; $j = 1,2,...,m$. In addition, $b_{ij}(t), c_{ji}(t), e_{ijl}(t), s_{jil}(t), I_i(t)$ and $J_i(t)$ are all ω-periodic functions.

Equation (1.34)

$$\begin{cases} u_i'(t) = -a_i u_i(t) + \sum_{j=1}^{m} b_{ij}(t)\tilde{g}_j(v_j(t-\tau)) + \sum_{j=1}^{m}\sum_{l=1}^{m} e_{ijl}(t)\tilde{g}_j(v_j(t-\tau))\tilde{g}_l(v_l(t-\tau)) + I_i(t), \\ v_j'(t) = -d_j v_j(t) + \sum_{j=1}^{n} c_{ji}(t)\tilde{f}_i(u_i(t-\sigma)) + \sum_{i=1}^{n}\sum_{l=1}^{n} s_{jil}(t)\tilde{f}_i(u_i(t-\sigma))\tilde{f}_l(u_l(t-\sigma)) + J_j(t) \end{cases}$$

The following notations and lemmas are used in this subsection. Let $A = (a_{ij})_{n \times n} \in R^{n \times n}$ be a matrix, $A > 0$ $(A \geq 0)$ denotes each element a_{ij} is positive (nonnegative, respectively). For $x = [x_1, x_2, ..., x_n]^T \in R^n$, $x > 0$ $(x \geq 0)$ means each element x_i is positive (nonnegative, respectively). We use E_n to represent the n×n identity matrix. For every continuous ω- periodic function φ, define $\varphi^+ = \max_{0 \leq t \leq \omega} |\varphi(t)|$; $T^{n \times n} = \{A = (a_{ij})_{n \times n} \in R^{n \times n}: a_{ij} \leq 0 (i \neq j)\}$.

Lemma 1.2.2: (Berman and Plemmons, 1979). Let $A \in T^{n \times n}$, then A is a nonsingular M-matrix if one of the following conditions holds:

1. All of the principal minors of A are positive.

2. A has all positive diagonal elements and there exists a positive diagonal matrix D such that AD is strictly diagonally dominant; that is:

$$a_{ii} d_i > \sum_{j \neq i} |a_{ij}| d_j, \quad i = 1, 2, \cdots, n \qquad (1.35)$$

3. A has positive inverse; that is, A^{-1} exists and $A^{-1} \geq 0$.

Let X and Z be two Banach spaces, $L: DomL \subset X \to Z$ be a linear mapping and $N: X \to Z$ be a continuous mapping. L is called a **Fredholm mapping of index zero** if $KerL = co$ dim ImL $< +\infty$ and ImL is closed in Z. If L is a Fredholm mapping of index zero and there exist continuous projectors:

$$P: X \to X \text{ and } Q: Z \to Z$$

such that ImP = $KerL$, $KerQ$ = ImL = Im$(I - Q)$, it follows that the mapping $L|_{DomL \cap KerP}: (I - P)X \to$ ImL is invertible, and we use K_p to denote this inverse mapping. If Ω is an open bounded subset of X, the mapping N is called L-**compact** on $\bar{\Omega}$ if $QN(\bar{\Omega})$ is bounded and $K_P(I - Q)N: \bar{\Omega} \to X$ is compact. Since ImQ is isomorphic to $KerL$, there must exist an isomorphism J: Im$Q \to KerL$.

Lemma 1.2.3: (Mawhin's Continuation Theorem) (Gaines and Mawhin, 1977). Let X and Z be two Banach spaces and L be a Fredholm mapping of index zero. Assume that $\Omega \subset X$ is an open bounded set and $N: X \to Z$ is a continuous operator which is L-compact on $\bar{\Omega}$. Then $Lx = Nx$ has at least one solution in DomL $\cap \bar{\Omega}$, if the following two conditions are satisfied:

1. For each $\lambda \in (0,1)$, $x \in \partial\Omega \cap DomL$, $Lx \neq \lambda Nx$

2. For each $x \in \partial\Omega \cap KerL$, $QNx \neq 0$ and $\deg(JQNx, \Omega \cap KerL, 0) \neq 0$.

Lemma 1.2.4: (Gopalsamy, 1992). Let $f(\cdot): [0, +\infty) \to R^+$ be a continuous function, and $f(\cdot)$ is integrable and uniformly continuous on $[0, +\infty)$, then $\lim_{t \to +\infty} f(t) = 0$.

EXISTENCE OF PERIODIC SOLUTIONS

Theorem 1.2.3 Under the assumptions (H_1) and (H_2), system (1.34) has at least one ω-periodic solution if:

$$\Gamma = \begin{bmatrix} E_n & -W \\ -V & E_m \end{bmatrix} \qquad (1.36)$$

is a nonsingular M-matrix, where:

$$W = (w_{ij})_{n \times m}, V = (v_{ji})_{m \times n},$$

$$w_{ij} = \frac{1}{a_i}(b_{ij}^+ K_j + \sum_{l=1}^{m} e_{ijl}^+ M_l K_j),$$

$$v_{ji} = \frac{1}{d_j}(c_{ji}^+ L_i + \sum_{l=1}^{n} s_{jil}^+ N_l L_i).$$

Proof: We first construct the set Ω in Lemma 1.2.3 by the method of a priori bounds. Denote:

$$w(t) \triangleq [u^T(t), v^T(t)]^T$$

where $u^T(t) = [u_1(t), u_2(t), \cdots, u_n(t)]^T$, $v^T(t) = [v_1(t), v_2(t), \cdots, v_m(t)]^T$. Let:

$$X = \{[u^T(t), v^T(t)]^T \in C(R, R^{n+m}):$$
$$u(t+\omega) = u(t), v(t+\omega) = v(t)\} = Z$$

equipped with the norm:

$$\left\| (u^T(t), v^T(t))^T \right\| = \sum_{i=1}^{n} \max_{t \in [0,\omega]} |u_i(t)| + \sum_{j=1}^{m} \max_{t \in [0,\omega]} |v_j(t)|$$

then X is a Banach space. $L: Doml \subset X \to Z$, $P: X \cap DomL \to KerL$, $N: X \to Z$ and Q: $X \to X/\mathrm{Im}L$ are given as follows, and in Box 7:

$$L \begin{bmatrix} u_1 \\ \cdots \\ u_n \\ v_1 \\ \cdots \\ v_m \end{bmatrix} = \begin{bmatrix} u_1'(t) \\ \cdots \\ u_n'(t) \\ v_1'(t) \\ \cdots \\ v_m'(t) \end{bmatrix},$$

$$P \begin{bmatrix} u_1(t) \\ \cdots \\ u_n(t) \\ v_1(t) \\ \cdots \\ v_m(t) \end{bmatrix} = Q \begin{bmatrix} u_1(t) \\ \cdots \\ u_n(t) \\ v_1(t) \\ \cdots \\ v_m(t) \end{bmatrix} = \begin{bmatrix} \frac{1}{\omega}\int_0^\omega u_1(t)dt \\ \cdots \\ \frac{1}{\omega}\int_0^\omega u_n(t)dt \\ \frac{1}{\omega}\int_0^\omega v_1(t)dt \\ \cdots \\ \frac{1}{\omega}\int_0^\omega v_m(t)dt \end{bmatrix}$$

It is easy to see that L is a linear operator with $KerL = \{w(t)|w(t) = w(0) \in R^{n+m}\}$; $\mathrm{Im}L = \{w(t) \in Z, \int_0^\omega w(t)dt = 0\}$ is closed in Z, P and Q are continuous projectors satisfying $\mathrm{Im}P = KerL$, $\mathrm{Im}L = KerQ = (I - Q)$ and $\dim KerL = n = co \dim \mathrm{Im}L$, then it follows that L is a Fredholm mapping of index zero. Furthermore, the inverse (with respect to $L|_{DomL \cap KerP}$) $K_P: \mathrm{Im}L \to KerP \cap DomL$ exists, which has the forms shown in Box 8.

By using the Arzela-Ascoli theorem, it is easy to prove that for every bounded subset $\Omega \in X$, $K_P(I-Q)N$ is relatively compact on $\bar{\Omega}$ in X, that is, N is L-compact on $\bar{\Omega}$.

Consider the operator equation $Lw = \lambda Nw$, $\lambda \in (0,1)$, that is (see Equation (1.37)),

Box 7.

$$N[u_1, \cdots, u_n, v_1, \cdots v_m]^T$$

$$= \begin{bmatrix} -a_1 u_1(t) + \sum_{j=1}^{m} b_{1j}(t)\tilde{g}_j(v_j(t-\tau)) + \sum_{j=1}^{m}\sum_{l=1}^{m} e_{1jl}(t)\tilde{g}_j(v_j(t-\tau))\tilde{g}_l(v_l(t-\tau)) + I_1(t) \\ \cdots \\ -a_n u_n(t) + \sum_{j=1}^{m} b_{nj}\tilde{g}_j(v_j(t-\tau)) + \sum_{j=1}^{m}\sum_{l=1}^{m} e_{njl}(t)\tilde{g}_j(v_j(t-\tau))\tilde{g}_l(v_l(t-\tau)) + I_n(t) \\ -d_1 v_1(t) + \sum_{i=1}^{n} c_{1i}(t)\tilde{f}_i(u_i(t-\sigma)) + \sum_{i=1}^{n}\sum_{l=1}^{n} s_{1il}(t)\tilde{f}_i(u_i(t-\sigma))\tilde{f}_l(u_l(t-\sigma)) + J_1(t) \\ \cdots \\ -d_m v_m(t) + \sum_{i=1}^{n} c_{mi}(t)\tilde{f}_i(u_i(t-\sigma)) + \sum_{i=1}^{n}\sum_{l=1}^{n} s_{mil}(t)\tilde{f}_i(u_i(t-\sigma))\tilde{f}_l(u_l(t-\sigma)) + J_m(t) \end{bmatrix}$$

$$\triangleq [\nabla u_1(t), \cdots, \nabla u_n(t), \nabla v_1(t), \cdots, \nabla v_m(t)]^T.$$

Box 8.

$$K_P \begin{bmatrix} u_1 \\ \cdots \\ u_n \\ v_1 \\ \cdots \\ v_m \end{bmatrix} = \begin{bmatrix} \int_0^t u_1(s)ds - \frac{1}{\omega}\int_0^\omega \int_0^t u_1(s)dsdt \\ \cdots \\ \int_0^t u_n(s)ds - \frac{1}{\omega}\int_0^\omega \int_0^t u_n(s)dsdt \\ \int_0^t v_1(s)ds - \frac{1}{\omega}\int_0^\omega \int_0^t v_1(s)dsdt \\ \cdots \\ \int_0^t v_m(s)ds - \frac{1}{\omega}\int_0^\omega \int_0^t v_m(s)dsds \end{bmatrix} \quad and \quad QN \begin{bmatrix} u_1 \\ \cdots \\ u_n \\ v_1 \\ \cdots \\ v_m \end{bmatrix} = \begin{bmatrix} \frac{1}{\omega}\int_0^\omega \nabla u_1(t)dt \\ \cdots \\ \frac{1}{\omega}\int_0^\omega \nabla u_n(t)dt \\ \frac{1}{\omega}\int_0^\omega \nabla v_1(t)dt \\ \cdots \\ \frac{1}{\omega}\int_0^\omega \nabla v_m(t)dt \end{bmatrix},$$

$$K_P(I-Q)N[u_1,\cdots,u_n,v_1,\cdots v_m]^T$$

$$= \begin{bmatrix} \int_0^t [\nabla u_1(s) - \frac{1}{\omega}\int_0^\omega \nabla u_1(\theta)d\theta]ds - \frac{1}{\omega}\int_0^\omega \int_0^t [\nabla u_1(s) - \frac{1}{\omega}\int_0^\omega \nabla u_1(\theta)d\theta]dsdt \\ \cdots \\ \int_0^t [\nabla u_n(s) - \frac{1}{\omega}\int_0^\omega \nabla u_n(\theta)d\theta]ds - \frac{1}{\omega}\int_0^\omega \int_0^t [\nabla u_n(s) - \frac{1}{\omega}\int_0^\omega \nabla u_n(\theta)d\theta]dsdt \\ \int_0^t [\nabla v_1(s) - \frac{1}{\omega}\int_0^\omega \nabla v_1(\theta)d\theta]ds - \frac{1}{\omega}\int_0^\omega \int_0^t [\nabla v_1(s) - \frac{1}{\omega}\int_0^\omega \nabla v_1(\theta)d\theta]dsdt \\ \cdots \\ \int_0^t [\nabla v_m(s) - \frac{1}{\omega}\int_0^\omega \nabla v_m(\theta)d\theta]ds - \frac{1}{\omega}\int_0^\omega \int_0^t [\nabla v_m(s) - \frac{1}{\omega}\int_0^\omega \nabla v_m(\theta)d\theta]dsdt \end{bmatrix}$$

Equation (1.37).

$$\begin{cases} u_i'(t) = -\lambda a_i u_i(t) + \lambda \sum_{j=1}^m b_{ij}(t)\tilde{g}_j(v_j(t-\tau)) + \lambda \sum_{j=1}^m \sum_{l=1}^m e_{ijl}(t)\tilde{g}_j(v_j(t-\tau))\tilde{g}_l(v_l(t-\tau)) + \lambda I_i(t), \\ v_j'(t) = -\lambda d_j v_j(t) + \lambda \sum_{i=1}^n c_{ji}(t)\tilde{f}_i(u_i(t-\sigma)) + \lambda \sum_{i=1}^n \sum_{l=1}^n s_{jil}(t)\tilde{f}_i(u_i(t-\sigma))\tilde{f}_l(u_l(t-\sigma)) + \lambda J_j(t) \end{cases}$$

where $i = 1,2,...,n$; $j = 1,2,...,m$. Suppose that $[u_1(t),\cdots,u_n(t),v_1(t),\cdots,v_m(t)]^T \in X$ is a periodic solution of system (1.37) for a certain $\lambda \in (0,1)$. Multiplying both sides of the ith equation of system (1.37) by $u_i(t)$ ($i = 1,2,...,n$) and integrating from 0 to ω. From (H_1) and (H_2), Equation (1.38) follows.

For the sake of convenience, define $\|\psi\|_2 = \left(\int_0^\omega |\psi(t)|^2 dt\right)^{1/2}$ where $\psi \in C(R,R)$; and noting that:

$$\left(\int_0^\omega |v_j(t-\tau)|^2 dt\right)^{1/2} = \left(\int_0^\omega |v_j(t)|^2 dt\right)^{1/2}$$

from (1.38), we have Equation (1.39), where $r_i \triangleq (1/a_i)I_i^+\sqrt{\omega}$. Multiplying both sides of the $(n+j)$th equation of system (1.37) by $v_j(t)$ ($j = 1,2,...,m$) and integrating on interval $[0,\omega]$, similarly, one has Equation (1.40), where $r_{n+j} = (1/d_j)J_j^+\sqrt{\omega}$. (1.39) combining with (1.40) derives that:

Equation (1.38).

$$a_i \int_0^\infty u_i^2(t)dt \leq \sum_{j=1}^m K_j b_{ij}^+ \int_0^\infty |u_i(t)||v_j(t-\tau)| \, dt + I_i^+ \int_0^\infty |u_i(t)| \, dt$$

$$+ \sum_{j=1}^m \sum_{l=1}^m e_{ijl}^+ M_l K_j \int_0^\infty |u_i(t)||v_j(t-\tau)| \, dt$$

$$\leq \sum_{j=1}^m K_j b_{ij}^+ \left(\int_0^\infty |u_i(t)|^2 \, dt \right)^{1/2} \left(\int_0^\infty |v_j(t-\tau)|^2 \, dt \right)^{1/2}$$

$$+ \sum_{j=1}^m \sum_{l=1}^m e_{ijl}^+ M_l K_j \left(\int_0^\infty |u_i(t)|^2 \, dt \right)^{1/2} \left(\int_0^\infty |v_j(t-\tau)|^2 \, dt \right)^{1/2}$$

$$+ I_i^+ \sqrt{\omega} \left(\int_0^\infty |u_i(t)|^2 \, dt \right)^{1/2}$$

Equation (1.39).

$$\|u_i\|_2 \leq \sum_{j=1}^m \frac{1}{a_i} (b_{ij}^+ K_j + \sum_{l=1}^m e_{ijl}^+ M_l K_j) \|v_j\|_2 + \frac{1}{a_i} I_i^+ \sqrt{\omega} \triangleq \sum_{j=1}^m w_{ij} \|v_j\|_2 + r_i$$

Equation (1.40).

$$\|v_j\|_2 \leq \sum_{i=1}^n \frac{1}{d_j} (c_{ji}^+ L_i + \sum_{l=1}^m s_{jil}^+ N_l L_i) \|u_i\|_2 + \frac{1}{d_j} J_j^+ \sqrt{\omega} \triangleq \sum_{i=1}^n v_{ji} \|u_i\|_2 + r_{n+j}$$

Equation (1.42).

$$|u_i(t_i)| \leq T_i / \sqrt{\omega} \triangleq T_i^*, \ (i=1,2,\cdots,n) \quad |v_j(t_j^*)| \leq T_{n+j} / \sqrt{\omega} \triangleq T_{n+j}^*. \ (j=1,2,\cdots m)$$

$$\Gamma h \leq r \qquad\qquad (1.41)$$

w h e r e $h = [\|u_1\|_2, \cdots, \|u_n\|_2, \|v_1\|_2, \cdots, \|v_m\|_2]^T$, $r = [r_1, r_2, \cdots, r_{m+n}]^T$. An application of Lemma 1.2.2 yields:

$$h \leq \Gamma^{-1} r \triangleq [T_1, T_2, \cdots, T_{m+n}]^T,$$

which implies that:

$$\left(\int_0^\infty |u_i(t)|^2 \, dt \right)^{1/2} \leq T_i, \left(\int_0^\infty |v_j(t)|^2 \, dt \right)^{1/2} \leq T_{n+j}$$

$$(i=1,2,...,n; j=1,2,...,m)$$

It is not difficult to check that there exist t_i, t_j^* $[0,\omega]$ such that Equation (1.42) occurs.

Utilizing with the Leibniz-Newton formula $u_i(t) = u_i(t_i) + \int_{t_i}^t u_i'(s)ds$, from (1.42) one has:

$$|u_i(t)| \leq T_i^* + \int_0^\infty |u_i'(s)| \, ds$$

From (1.37), we have Box 9, which implies:

$$|u_i(t)| \leq T_i^* + R_i$$

By a similar argument, one has:

$$|v_j(t)| \leq T_{n+j}^* + R_{n+j}$$

Box 9.

$$\int_0^\infty u_i'(s)ds \le a_i \int_0^\infty |u_i(s)| \, ds + \sum_{j=1}^m b_{ij}^+ K_j \int_0^\infty |v_j(s-\tau)| \, ds$$

$$+ \sum_{j=1}^m \sum_{l=1}^m e_{ijl}^+ M_l K_j \int_0^\infty |v_j(s-\tau)| \, ds + I_i^+ \omega$$

$$\le a_i \sqrt{\omega} \|u_i\|_2 + \sum_{j=1}^m b_{ij}^+ K_j \sqrt{\omega} \|v_j\|_2 + \sum_{j=1}^m \sum_{l=1}^m e_{ijl}^+ M_l K_j \sqrt{\omega} \|v_j\|_2 + I_i^+ \omega$$

$$\le a_i \sqrt{\omega} T_i + \sum_{j=1}^m b_{ij}^+ K_j \sqrt{\omega} T_{n+j} + \sum_{j=1}^m \sum_{l=1}^m e_{ijl}^+ M_l K_j \sqrt{\omega} T_{n+j} + I_i^+ \omega$$

$$= a_i \sqrt{\omega} T_i + a_i \sqrt{\omega} \sum_{j=1}^m w_{ij} T_{n+j} + I_i^+ \omega \triangleq R_i$$

Box 10.

$$-a_i u_i^2 + \sum_{j=1}^m \frac{1}{\omega} u_i \tilde{g}_j(v_j) \int_0^\infty b_{ij}(s)ds + \sum_{j=1}^m \sum_{l=1}^m \frac{1}{\omega} u_i \tilde{g}_j(v_j)\tilde{g}_l(v_l) \int_0^\infty e_{ijl}(s)ds + \frac{1}{\omega} u_i \int_0^\infty I_i(s)ds \ge 0$$

Box 11.

$$a_i u_i^2 \le \sum_{j=1}^m \frac{1}{\omega} u_i \tilde{g}_j(v_j) \int_0^\infty b_{ij}(s)ds + \sum_{j=1}^m \sum_{l=1}^m \frac{1}{\omega} u_i \tilde{g}_j(v_j)\tilde{g}_l(v_l) \int_0^\infty e_{ijl}(s)ds + \frac{1}{\omega} u_i \int_0^\infty I_i(s)ds$$

$$\le |u_i| \sum_{j=1}^m (b_{ij}^+ K_j + \sum_{l=1}^m M_l K_j e_{ijl}^+) |v_j| + |u_i| I_i^+$$

Denote $R_i^* = T_i^* + R_i + \frac{1}{m+n}$ and $R_{n+j}^* = T_{n+j}^* + R_{n+j} + \frac{1}{m+n}$, take:

$$\Omega = \left\{ w = [u_1, \cdots, u_n, v_1, \cdots, v_m]^T \right.$$

$$\left. \in X \, \middle| \, |u_i(t)| < R_i^*, |v_j(t)| < R_{n+j}^* \text{ for all } t \right\}$$

If $w = [u_1, ..., u_n, v_1, ..., v_m]^T \, \partial\Omega \cap KerL = \partial\Omega \cap R^{n+m}$, then w is a constant vector in R^{n+m} with $|u_i| = R_i^*$, $|v_j| = R_{n+j}^*$, for $i = 1,2,...,n; j = 1,2,...,m$. Therefore:

$$u_i(QNw)_i = -a_i u_i^2 + \sum_{j=1}^m \frac{1}{\omega} u_i \tilde{g}_i(v_j) \int_0^\infty b_{ij}(s)ds$$

$$+ \sum_{j=1}^m \sum_{l=1}^m \frac{1}{\omega} u_i \tilde{g}_j(v_j)\tilde{g}_l(v_l) \int_0^\infty e_{ijl}(s)ds + \frac{1}{\omega} u_i \int_0^\infty I_i(s)ds$$

(1.43)

$$v_j(QNw)_{n+j} = -d_j v_j^2 + \sum_{i=1}^n \frac{1}{\omega} v_j \tilde{f}_i(u_i) \int_0^\infty c_{ji}(s)ds$$

$$+ \sum_{i=1}^n \sum_{l=1}^n \frac{1}{\omega} v_j \tilde{f}_i(u_i)\tilde{f}_l(u_l) \int_0^\infty s_{jil}(s)ds + \frac{1}{\omega} v_j \int_0^\infty J_j(s)ds$$

(1.44)

We claim that there exists some $i \in \{1,2,...,n\}$ or $j \in \{1,2,...,m\}$ such that:

$$u_i(QNw)_i < 0, \text{ or } v_j(QNw)_{n+j} < 0 \qquad (1.45)$$

Suppose that $u_i(QNw)_i \ge 0$ and $v_j(QNw)_{n+j} \ge 0$, then Box 10 occurs; this leads to Box 11, which implies Equation (1.46). By a similar argument, we have Equation (1.47).

Equation (1.46).

for all $i = 1,2,...,n$:

$$R_i^* \leq \sum_{j=1}^{m} \frac{1}{a_i}(b_{ij}^+ K_j + \sum_{l=1}^{m} M_l K_j e_{ijl}^+)R_{n+j}^* + \frac{1}{a_i}I_i^+ = \sum_{j=1}^{m} w_{ij}R_{n+j}^* + r_i/\sqrt{\omega}$$

Equation (1.47).

$$R_{n+j}^* \leq \sum_{i=1}^{n} \frac{1}{d_j}(c_{ji}^+ L_i + \sum_{l=1}^{n} N_l L_i s_{jil}^+)R_{n+j}^* + \frac{1}{d_j}J_j^+ = \sum_{i=1}^{n} v_{ji}R_i^* + r_{n+j}/\sqrt{\omega} \quad (j = 1,2,\cdots,m)$$

Equation (1.50).

$$\left\| QN(u_1,u_2,...,u_n,v_1,v_2,...,v_m)^T \right\| = \sum_{i=1}^{n} |(QNw)_i| + \sum_{j=1}^{m} |(QNw)_{n+j}| > 0$$

Box 12.

$$\left\| H(w,\theta) \right\| = \sum_{i=1}^{n} \left| -\theta u_i + (1-\theta)(QNw)_i \right| + \sum_{j=1}^{m} \left| -\theta v_j + (1-\theta)(QNw)_{n+j} \right| > 0$$

On the other hand:

$$R^* > T^* = T/\sqrt{\omega} = \Gamma^{-1} r/\sqrt{\omega} \tag{1.48}$$

where:

$$R^* = \left[R_1^*, R_2^*, \cdots, R_{n+m}^* \right]^T,$$
$$T^* = \left[T_1^*, T_2^*, \cdots, T_{n+m}^* \right]^T,$$
$$T = \left[T_1, T_2, \cdots, T_{n+m} \right]^T$$

which means that there exists some i or j such that:

$$R_i^* > \sum_{j=1}^{m} w_{ij}R_{n+j}^* + r_i/\sqrt{\omega}$$

or

$$R_{n+j}^* > \sum_{i=1}^{n} v_{ji}R_i^* + r_{n+j}/\sqrt{\omega}$$

which is a contradiction. And so there must exist some $i \in \{1,2,...,n\}$ or $j \in \{1,2,...,m\}$ such that:

$$u_i(QNw)_i < 0, \quad \text{or} \quad v_j(QNw)_{n+j} < 0 \tag{1.49}$$

This leads to Equation (1.50). Consequently:

$$QNw \neq 0 \quad \text{for} \quad w \in \partial\Omega \cap \text{Ker}L$$

Define:

$$H(w,\theta) = -\theta w + (1-\theta)QNw, \theta \in [0,1]$$

where:

$$w = [u_1,u_2,...,u_n,v_1,v_2,...,v_m]^T \in R^{n+m}$$

If $w \in \text{Ker}L \cap \partial\Omega$, Box 12 follows from (1.49); that is, $H(w,\theta) \neq 0$. According to the invariant of homology, we have:

$$\deg\{JQNw,\Omega \cap \text{Ker}L,0\} = \deg\{-w,\Omega \cap \text{Ker}L,0\} \neq 0$$

where $J: \text{Im}Q \to \text{Ker}L$ is an isomorphism. Therefore, by the continuation theorem of Gaines and Mawhin, system (1.34) has at least one ω-periodic solution. This completes the proof. □

Global Attractivity of Periodic Solution

In this subsection, the global attractivity of (1.34) is discussed. Under assumptions of Theorem 1.2.3, (1.34) has at least one ω-periodic solution $\omega^*(t) = [u_1^*(t), u_2^*(t), \ldots, u_n^*(t), \ v_1^*(t), v_2^*(t), \ldots, v_m^*(t)]^T$. Let $x_i(t) = u_i(t) - u_i^*(t)$, $y_j(t) = v_j(t) - v_j^*(t)$; $x_i(t) = u_i(t) - u_i^*(t)$, $f_i(x_i(t)) = \tilde{f}_i(x_i(t) + u_i^*(t)) - \tilde{f}_i(u_i^*(t))$ and $g_j(y_j(t)) = \tilde{g}_j(y_j(t) + v_j^*(t)) - \tilde{g}_j(v_j^*(t))$; then system (1.34) is transformed into Equation (1.51), where $\xi_i(t)$ and $\eta_i(t)$ are defined similar as those of (1.4).

Theorem 1.2.4: Assume that all conditions of Theorem 1.2.3 hold. System (1.34) has a unique, globally attractive ω-periodic solution if Θ is a nonsingular M-matrix; where:

$$\Theta = \begin{bmatrix} -H & -R \\ -P & -K \end{bmatrix}$$

(1.52)

in which $R = (r_{ij})_{n \times m}$ and:

$$r_{ij} = \frac{1}{2}[b_{ij}^+ + \sum_{l=1}^{m}(e_{ijl}^+ + e_{ilj}^+)[\xi_l]^+]K_j,$$

$$[\xi_l]^+ = \sup_{t \in [0, +\infty)} |\xi_l(t)|;$$

$P = (p_{ji})_{m \times n}$ and

$$p_{ji} = \frac{1}{2}[c_{ji}^+ + \sum_{l=1}^{n}(s_{jil}^+ + s_{jli}^+)[\eta_l]^+]L_i;$$

$H = diag\{h_1, h_2, \ldots, h_n\}$ and

$$h_i = -a_i + \frac{1}{2}\sum_{j=1}^{m}[b_{ij}^+ + \sum_{l=1}^{m}(e_{ijl}^+ + e_{ilj}^+)[\xi_l]^+]K_j;$$

$K = diag\{k_1, k_2, \ldots, k_m\}$ and

$$k_j = -d_j + \frac{1}{2}\sum_{i=1}^{n}[c_{ji}^+ + \sum_{l=1}^{n}(s_{jil}^+ + s_{jli}^+)[\eta_l]^+]L_i,$$

$$[\eta_l]^+ = \sup_{t \in [0, +\infty)} |\eta_l(t)|$$

Proof. Box 13 follows from (1.51), where D^+ denotes the upper right Dini derivative. Define the Lyapunov functionals as Equations (1.53) and (1.54). Calculating the derivatives of $V_k(t)$ ($k = 1, 2, \ldots, n+m$), one obtains Equations (1.55)

Equation (1.51).

$$\begin{cases} \dfrac{dx_i(t)}{dt} = -a_i x_i(t) + \sum_{j=1}^{m}[b_{ij}(t) + \sum_{l=1}^{m}(e_{ijl}(t) + e_{ilj}(t))\xi_l(t)]g_j(y_j(t-\tau)), \\[4mm] \dfrac{dy_j(t)}{dt} = -d_j y_j(t) + \sum_{i=1}^{n}[c_{ji}(t) + \sum_{l=1}^{n}(s_{jil}(t) + s_{jli}(t))\eta_l(t)]f_i(x_i(t-\sigma)) \end{cases}$$

Box 13.

$$|x_i(t)|D^+|x_i(t)| \leq -a_i|x_i(t)|^2 + \sum_{j=1}^{m}\left[b_{ij}^+ + \sum_{l=1}^{m}(e_{ijl}^+ + e_{ilj}^+)[\xi_l]^+\right]K_j|y_j(t-\tau)||x_i(t)|$$

$$\leq -a_i|x_i(t)|^2 + \sum_{j=1}^{m}\left[b_{ij}^+ + \sum_{l=1}^{m}(e_{ijl}^+ + e_{ilj}^+)[\xi_l]^+\right]K_j\frac{|y_j(t-\tau)|^2 + |x_i(t)|^2}{2},$$

$$|y_j(t)|D^+|y_j(t)| \leq -d_j|y_j(t)|^2 + \sum_{i=1}^{n}\left[c_{ji}^+ + \sum_{l=1}^{n}(s_{jil}^+ + s_{jli}^+)[\eta_l]^+\right]L_i\frac{|x_i(t-\sigma)|^2 + |y_j(t)|^2}{2}$$

Equation (1.53).

$$V_i(t) = \frac{|x_i(t)|^2}{2} + \frac{1}{2}\sum_{j=1}^{m}\left[b_{ij}^+ + \sum_{l=1}^{m}(e_{ijl}^+ + e_{ilj}^+)[\xi_l]^+\right]K_j\int_{t-\tau}^{t}|y_j(s)|^2\,ds,\ i=1,2,\cdots n$$

Equation (1.54).

$$V_{n+j}(t) = \frac{|y_j(t)|^2}{2} + \frac{1}{2}\sum_{i=1}^{n}\left[c_{ji}^+ + \sum_{l=1}^{n}(s_{jil}^+ + s_{jli}^+)[\eta_l]^+\right]L_i\int_{t-\sigma}^{t}|x_i(s)|^2\,ds,\quad j=1,2,\cdots m$$

Equation (1.55).

$$V'_i(t) \le -a_i|x_i(t)|^2 + \sum_{j=1}^{m}\left[b_{ij}^+ + \sum_{l=1}^{m}(e_{ijl}^+ + e_{ilj}^+)[\xi_l]^+\right]K_j\frac{|y_j(t-\tau)|^2 + |x_i(t)|^2}{2}$$

$$+\frac{1}{2}\sum_{j=1}^{m}\left[b_{ij}^+ + \sum_{l=1}^{m}(e_{ijl}^+ + e_{ilj}^+)[\xi_l]^+\right]K_j\left[|y_j(t)|^2 - |y_j(t-\tau)|^2\right]$$

$$\le\left\{-a_i + \frac{1}{2}\sum_{j=1}^{m}\left[b_{ij}^+ + \sum_{l=1}^{m}(e_{ijl}^+ + e_{ilj}^+)[\xi_l]^+\right]K_j\right\}|x_i(t)|^2$$

$$+\frac{1}{2}\sum_{j=1}^{m}\left[b_{ij}^+ + \sum_{l=1}^{m}(e_{ijl}^+ + e_{ilj}^+)[\xi_l]^+\right]K_j|y_j(t)|^2$$

$$= h_i|x_i(t)|^2 + \sum_{j=1}^{m}r_{ij}|y_j(t)|^2$$

Equation (1.56).

$$V'_{n+j} \le\left\{-d_j + \frac{1}{2}\sum_{i=1}^{n}\left[c_{ji}^+ + \sum_{l=1}^{n}(s_{jil}^+ + s_{jli}^+)[\eta_l]^+\right]L_i\right\}|y_j(t)|^2$$

$$+\frac{1}{2}\sum_{i=1}^{n}\left[c_{ji}^+ + \sum_{l=1}^{n}(s_{jil}^+ + s_{jli}^+)[\eta_l]^+\right]L_i|x_i(t)|^2$$

$$= k_j|y_j(t)|^2 + \sum_{i=1}^{n}p_{ji}|x_i(t)|^2$$

and (1.56). Let $V(t) = (V_1(t), V_2(t),\ldots,V_{n+m}(t))^T$, it follows from (1.55) and (1.56) that:

$$V'(t) \le -\Theta\gamma(t)$$

where $V'(t) = [V'_1(t), V'_2(t),\ldots,V'_{n+m}(t)]^T$; $\gamma(t) = [|x_1(t)|^2, |x_2(t)|^2,\ldots,|x_n(t)|^2, |y_1(t)|^2, |y_2(t)|^2,\ldots,|y_m(t)|^2]^T$.

Since Θ is a nonsingular M-matrix and by Lemma 1.2.2, we have $\Theta^{-1}V'(t) \le -\gamma(t)$. By defining the vector:

$$\tilde{V}(t) = [\tilde{V}_1(t), \tilde{V}_2(t),\ldots,\tilde{V}_{n+m}(t)]^T = \Theta^{-1}V(t) \ge 0 \tag{1.57}$$

we obtain:

$$\tilde{V}_i'(t) \leq -\left|x_i(t)\right|^2, \qquad i = 1, 2, \ldots, n \qquad (1.58)$$

$$\tilde{V}_{n+j}'(t) \leq -\left|y_j(t)\right|^2, \qquad j = 1, 2, \ldots, m \qquad (1.59)$$

Integrating both sides of (1.58) and (1.59) from 0 to t results in:

$$\tilde{V}_i(t) + \int_0^t \left|x_i(s)\right|^2 ds \leq \tilde{V}_i(0) < +\infty,$$

$$\tilde{V}_{n+j}(t) + \int_0^t \left|y_j(s)\right|^2 ds \leq \tilde{V}_{n+j}(0) < +\infty$$

and hence:

$$\int_0^t \left|x_i(s)\right|^2 ds \leq \tilde{V}_i(0) < +\infty,$$

$$\int_0^t \left|y_j(s)\right|^2 ds \leq \tilde{V}_{n+j}(0) < +\infty$$

which implies that $|x_i(s)|^2$ and $|y_j(s)|^2$ are integrable on $[0, +\infty)$ for all $i = 1, 2, \ldots, n; j = 1, 2, \ldots, m$. It follows from (1.53) and (1.54) that $|x_i(s)|^2 \leq 2V_i(t)$, $|y_j(s)|^2 \leq 2V_{n+j}(t)$; namely $\gamma(t) \leq 2V(t)$. Combining with (1.57), we obtain $\gamma(t) \leq 2\Theta\tilde{V}(t)$, which means that $\Theta^{-1}\gamma(t) \leq 2\tilde{V}(t) \leq 2\tilde{V}(0) < +\infty$. And so $|x_i(t)|^2 < +\infty$, $|y_j(t)|^2 < +\infty$; which implies that $|u_i(t) - u_i^*(t)|^2 < +\infty$, $|v_j(t) - v_j^*(t)|^2 < +\infty$; that is, $|u_i(t)|$ and $|v_j(t)|$ are also bounded for $|u_i^*(t)|$ and $|v_j^*(t)|$ are bounded. This, together with (1.36), leads to the boundedness

of $u_i'(t)$ and $v_j'(t)$, then $|\gamma_r(t)|^2$ $(r = 1, 2, \ldots, n+m)$ is uniformly continuous on $[0, +\infty)$. By Lemma 1.2.4, we have:

$$\lim_{t \to +\infty} \left|u_i(t) - u_i^*(t)\right|^2 = 0,$$

$$\lim_{t \to +\infty} \left|v_j(t) - v_j^*(t)\right|^2 = 0$$

Thus, the proof is complete. $\quad\square$

GLOBAL ASYMPTOTIC STABILITY OF PERIODIC SOLUTION

Theorem 1.2.5: Assume that (H_1) and (H_2) hold. System (1.34) has a unique, globally asymptotically stable ω-periodic solution if there exist constants $\lambda_i > 0$, $\lambda_{n+j} > 0$ such that appears in Box 14, where K_j, L_i are the constants defined in the assumption (H_1).

Proof. Consider the Lyapunov functional in Box 15. Calculating the upper right derivate $D^+V(t)$ of V along the solution of (1.51), and estimating it via the assumptions, we have Box 16, where $\varepsilon = \min(\alpha, \beta) > 0$; and this means that periodic solution of system (1.34) is globally asymptotically stable (Hale, 1977). This completes the proof. $\quad\square$

Example 1.2.3. Consider the higher order BAM neural networks displayed in Equation

Box 14.

$$-\lambda_i a_i + \sum_{j=1}^m \lambda_{n+j}\left(c_{ji}^+ + \sum_{l=1}^m (s_{jil}^+ + s_{jli}^+)[\eta_l]^+\right)L_i \triangleq -\alpha < 0; i = 1, 2, \ldots, n$$

$$-\lambda_{n+j} d_j + \sum_{i=1}^n \lambda_i\left(b_{ij}^+ + \sum_{l=1}^n (e_{ijl}^+ + e_{ilj}^+)[\xi_l]^+\right)K_j \triangleq -\beta < 0; j = 1, 2, \ldots, m$$

Box 15.

$$V(t) = \sum_{i=1}^n \lambda_i\left[\left|x_i(t)\right| + \sum_{j=1}^m\left(b_{ij}^+ + \sum_{l=1}^m(e_{ijl}^+ + e_{ilj}^+)[\xi_l]^+\right)\int_{t-\tau}^t\left|g_j(y_j(s))\right|ds\right]$$

$$+ \sum_{j=1}^m \lambda_{n+j}\left[\left|y_j(t)\right| + \sum_{i=1}^n\left(c_{ji}^+ + \sum_{l=1}^n(s_{jil}^+ + s_{jli}^+)[\eta_l]^+\right)\int_{t-\sigma}^t\left|f_i(x_i(s))\right|ds\right]$$

(1.60), where $[a_1, a_2, a_3]^T = [6,5,4]^T$, $[d_1, d_2]^T = [7,5]^T$, $[L_1, L_2, L_3]^T = [0.7, 0.8, 0.9]^T$, $[K_1, K_2]^T = [0.6, 0.7]^T$, $[N_1, N_2, N_3]^T = [1,1,1]^T$, $[M_1, M_2]^T = [1,1]^T$;

$$\left(c_{ji}\right)_{2\times 3} = \begin{bmatrix} 0.2 & 0.3 & 0.4 \\ 0.1 & 0.2 & 0.5 \end{bmatrix},$$

$$\left(e_{1jl}\right)_{2\times 2} = \begin{bmatrix} 0.9501 & 0.6068 \\ 0.2311 & 0.4860 \end{bmatrix},$$

$$\left(e_{2jl}\right)_{2\times 2} = \begin{bmatrix} 0.8913 & 0.4565 \\ 0.7621 & 0.0185 \end{bmatrix},$$

Equation (1.60).

$$\begin{cases} \dfrac{du_i(t)}{dt} = -a_i u_i(t) + \sum_{j=1}^{2} b_{ij} \tilde{g}_j(v_j(t-\tau)) + \sum_{j=1}^{2}\sum_{l=1}^{2} e_{ijl} \tilde{g}_j(v_j(t-\tau))\tilde{g}_l(v_l(t-\tau)) + \sin(\pi), \\ \dfrac{dv_j(t)}{dt} = -d_j v_j(t) + \sum_{i=1}^{3} c_{ji} \tilde{f}_i(u_i(t-\sigma)) + \sum_{i=1}^{3}\sum_{l=1}^{3} s_{jil} \tilde{f}_i(u_i(t-\sigma))\tilde{f}_l(u_l(t-\sigma)) + \cos(\pi) \end{cases}$$

Box 16.

$$\begin{aligned} D^+V(t) \le{} & \sum_{i=1}^{n} \lambda_i \Bigg[-a_i |x_i(t)| + \sum_{j=1}^{m} \Bigg(b_{ij}^+ + \sum_{l=1}^{m} (e_{ijl}^+ + e_{ilj}^+)[\xi_l]^+ \Bigg) |g_j(y_j(t-\tau))| \\ & + \sum_{j=1}^{m} \Bigg(b_{ij}^+ + \sum_{l=1}^{m} (e_{ijl}^+ + e_{ilj}^+)[\xi_l]^+ \Bigg) \big(|g_j(y_j(t))| - |g_j(y_j(t-\tau))| \big) \Bigg] \\ & + \sum_{j=1}^{m} \lambda_{n+j} \Bigg[-d_j |y_j(t)| + \sum_{i=1}^{n} \Bigg(c_{ji}^+ + \sum_{l=1}^{n} (s_{jil}^+ + s_{jli}^+)[\eta_l]^+ \Bigg) |f_i(x_i(t-\sigma))| \\ & + \sum_{i=1}^{n} \Bigg(c_{ji}^+ + \sum_{l=1}^{n} (s_{jil}^+ + s_{jli}^+)[\eta_l]^+ \Bigg) \big(|f_i(x_i(t))| - |f_i(x_i(t-\sigma))| \big) \Bigg] \\ \le{} & -\varepsilon \Bigg(\sum_{i=1}^{n} |u_i(t) - u_i^*(t)| + \sum_{j=1}^{m} |v_j(t) - v_j^*(t)| \Bigg) \end{aligned}$$

Figure 1. Transient response of state variable $u_1(t)$

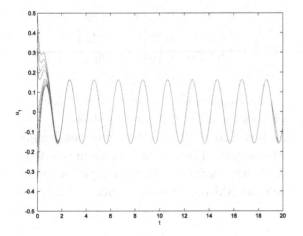

Figure 2. Transient response of state variable $u_2(t)$

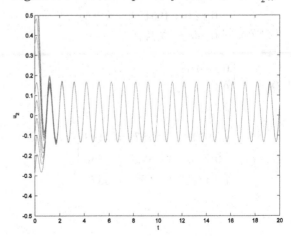

Box 17.

$$\Gamma = \begin{bmatrix} 1 & 0 & 0 & -0.2057 & -0.1537 \\ 0 & 1 & 0 & -0.1737 & -0.1373 \\ 0 & 0 & 1 & -0.3205 & -0.2689 \\ -0.1938 & -0.3277 & -0.1994 & 1 & 0 \\ -0.1674 & -0.2381 & -0.1633 & 0 & 1 \end{bmatrix},$$

$$\Theta = \begin{bmatrix} 4.1851 & 0 & 0 & -0.9714 & -0.8435 \\ 0 & 3.5602 & 0 & -0.9304 & -0.5095 \\ 0 & 0 & 1.9488 & -1.0209 & -1.0304 \\ -1.3209 & -2.0502 & -1.3108 & 2.3181 & 0 \\ -0.8301 & -0.8114 & -0.8920 & 0 & 2.4665 \end{bmatrix}$$

Box 18.

$$\Gamma^{-1} = \begin{bmatrix} 1.0890 & 0.1411 & 0.0897 & 0.2773 & 0.2108 \\ 0.0769 & 1.1216 & 0.0774 & 0.2355 & 0.1866 \\ 0.1453 & 0.2295 & 1.1463 & 0.4372 & 0.3621 \\ 0.2652 & 0.4406 & 0.2714 & 1.2181 & 0.1742 \\ 0.2243 & 0.3282 & 0.2207 & 0.1739 & 1.1389 \end{bmatrix},$$

$$\Theta^{-1} = \begin{bmatrix} 1.2851 & 1.6753 & 2.2904 & 2.2196 & 1.7423 \\ 1.0376 & 1.9456 & 2.2710 & 2.2158 & 1.7054 \\ 2.4845 & 3.9760 & 5.9535 & 5.2588 & 4.1579 \\ 3.0548 & 4.9236 & 6.6802 & 6.6295 & 4.8522 \\ 1.6723 & 2.6417 & 3.6710 & 3.3777 & 3.0565 \end{bmatrix}$$

$$\left(e_{3jl} \right)_{2\times 2} = \begin{bmatrix} 0.8214 & 0.6154 \\ 0.4447 & 0.7919 \end{bmatrix};$$

$$\left(b_{ij} \right)_{3\times 2} = \begin{bmatrix} 0.5 & 0.6 \\ 0.1 & 0.2 \\ 0.7 & 0.3 \end{bmatrix},$$

$$\left(s_{1ij} \right)_{3\times 3} = \begin{bmatrix} 0.9218 & 0.4057 & 0.4103 \\ 0.7382 & 0.9355 & 0.8936 \\ 0.1763 & 0.9169 & 0.0579 \end{bmatrix},$$

$$\left(s_{2ij} \right)_{3\times 3} = \begin{bmatrix} 0.3529 & 0.1389 & 0.6038 \\ 0.8132 & 0.2028 & 0.2722 \\ 0.0099 & 0.1987 & 0.1988 \end{bmatrix}$$

By computation, we have what follows in Figures 1 and 2, and Boxes 17 and 18.

It is clear that Γ and Θ are both nonsingular M-matrices. Thus, it follows from Theorem 1.2.4 that system (1.60) has a unique 2-periodic solution which is globally attractive. Let $f(u) =$

Figure 3. Transient response of state variable $u_3(t)$

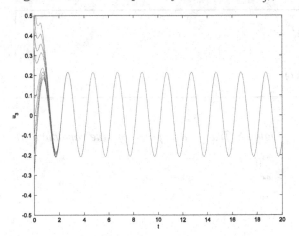

Figure 4. Transient response of state variable $v_1(t)$

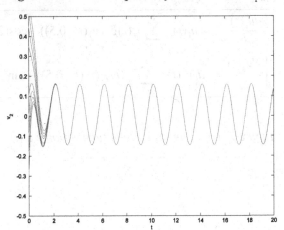

Figure 5. Transient response of state variable $v_2(t)$

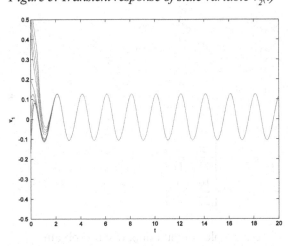

Figure 6. Phase plots of state variables

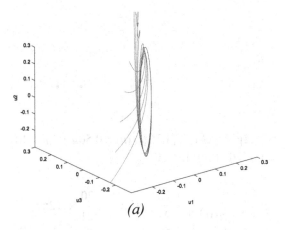

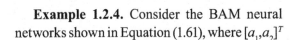

$0.5(|u+1|u-1|), \tilde{f}_1(u_1) = 0.7f(u), \tilde{f}_2(u_2) = 0.8f(u), \tilde{f}_3(u_3) = 0.9f(u), \tilde{g}_1(v_1) = 0.6f(u), \tilde{g}_2(v_2) = 0.7f(u), \tau = \sigma = 0.5$. Figure 1 – Figure 5 depict the time responses of state variables $u_1(t)$, $u_2(t)$, $u_3(t)$, $v_1(t)$ and $v_2(t)$ with nine different initial values respectively. Figure 6 depicts the phase plots of state variables $u_1(t)$, $u_2(t)$, $u_3(t)$, $v_1(t)$, $v_2(t)$. It confirms that the proposed conditions in Theorem 1.2.4 lead to the unique and globally attractive 2-periodic solution for system (1.60).

Example 1.2.4. Consider the BAM neural networks shown in Equation (1.61), where $[a_1, a_2]^T$

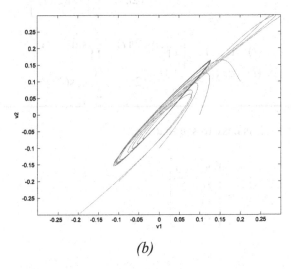

(b)

Equation (1.61).

$$\begin{cases} \dfrac{du_i(t)}{dt} = -a_i u_i(t) + \displaystyle\sum_{j=1}^{2} b_{ij}(t)\tilde{g}_j(v_j(t-0.5)) + \cos(2\pi t), \\[3mm] \dfrac{dv_j(t)}{dt} = -d_j v_j(t) + \displaystyle\sum_{i=1}^{3} c_{ji}(t)\tilde{f}_i(u_i(t-0.5)) + \sin(2\pi t) \end{cases}$$

Figure 7. Transient response of state variable $u_1(t)$

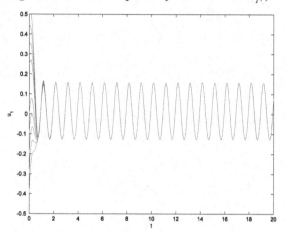

Figure 8. Transient response of state variable $u_2(t)$

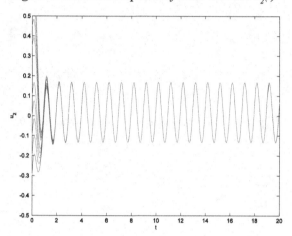

$= [3,2]^T$, $[d_1, d_2]^T = [4,3]^T$; $\tilde{f}_i(u) = 0.5(|u+1||u-1|)$, $\tilde{g}_j(v) = 0.5(|v+1||v-1|)$;

$$\begin{bmatrix} b_{11}(t) & b_{12}(t) \\ b_{21}(t) & b_{22}(t) \end{bmatrix} = \begin{bmatrix} \dfrac{20}{21}\sin(2\pi t) & \dfrac{20}{21}\cos(2\pi t) \\[3mm] \dfrac{20}{21}\cos(2\pi t) & \dfrac{20}{21}\sin(2\pi t) \end{bmatrix},$$

$$\begin{bmatrix} c_{11}(t) & c_{12}(t) \\ c_{21}(t) & c_{22}(t) \end{bmatrix} = \begin{bmatrix} \dfrac{5}{11}\cos(2\pi t) & \dfrac{5}{11}\sin(2\pi t) \\[3mm] \dfrac{10}{23}\sin(2\pi t) & \dfrac{10}{23}\cos(2\pi t) \end{bmatrix}$$

It is easy to see that:

$$\begin{bmatrix} b_{11}^+ & b_{12}^+ \\ b_{21}^+ & b_{22}^+ \end{bmatrix} = \begin{bmatrix} \dfrac{20}{21} & \dfrac{20}{21} \\[3mm] \dfrac{20}{21} & \dfrac{20}{21} \end{bmatrix},$$

$$\begin{bmatrix} c_{11}^+ & c_{12}^+ \\ c_{21}^+ & c_{22}^+ \end{bmatrix} = \begin{bmatrix} \dfrac{5}{11} & \dfrac{5}{11} \\[3mm] \dfrac{10}{23} & \dfrac{10}{23} \end{bmatrix}$$

By simple computation, one can obtain:

$$\Gamma = \begin{bmatrix} 1 & 0 & -0.3175 & -0.3175 \\ 0 & 1 & -0.4762 & -0.4762 \\ -0.1136 & -0.1136 & 1 & 0 \\ -0.1449 & -0.1449 & 0 & 1 \end{bmatrix},$$

$$\Theta = \begin{bmatrix} 2.0476 & 0 & -0.4762 & -0.4762 \\ 0 & 1.0476 & -0.4762 & -0.4762 \\ -0.2273 & -0.2273 & 3.5455 & 0 \\ -0.2174 & -0.2174 & 0 & 2.5652 \end{bmatrix}$$

and:

Figure 9. Transient response of state variable $v_1(t)$

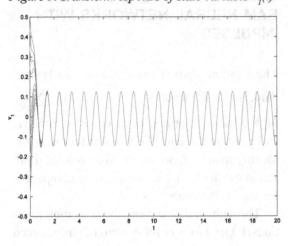

Figure 10. Transient response of state variable $v_2(t)$

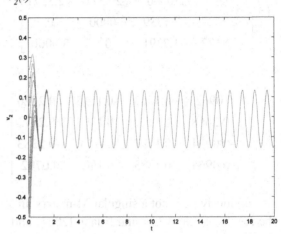

Figure 11. Phase plots of state variables

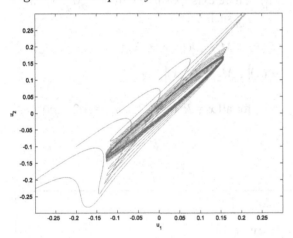

$$\Gamma^{-1} = \begin{bmatrix} 1.1033 & 0.1033 & 0.3994 & 0.3994 \\ 0.1549 & 1.1549 & 0.5991 & 0.5991 \\ 0.1430 & 0.1430 & 1.1135 & 0.1135 \\ 0.1823 & 0.1823 & 0.1447 & 1.1447 \end{bmatrix},$$

$$\Theta^{-1} = \begin{bmatrix} 0.5072 & 0.0368 & 0.0731 & 0.1010 \\ 0.0368 & 1.0265 & 0.1428 & 0.1974 \\ 0.0349 & 0.0682 & 0.2959 & 0.0191 \\ 0.0461 & 0.0901 & 0.0183 & 0.4151 \end{bmatrix}$$

Therefore, Γ and Θ are nonsingular M-matrices, it follows from Theorem 1.2.4 that system

(1.61) has a unique 1-periodic solution which is globally attractive. Figure 7 – Figure 10 depict the time responses of state variables $u_1(t)$, $u_2(t)$, $v_1(t)$ and $v_2(t)$ with nine different initial values respectively. Figure 11 depicts the phase plots of state variables $u_1(t)$, $u_2(t)$, $v_1(t)$ and $v_2(t)$. It confirms that the proposed conditions in Theorem 1.2.4 lead to the unique and globally attractive 1-periodic solution for system (1.61). According to Theorem 1 in Liu, Chen and Huang, (2004) and Chen, Huang, Liu and Cao, (2006), we have:

$$A = \begin{bmatrix} 3.0000 & 0 & -3.8095 & -3.8095 \\ 0 & 2.0000 & -2.8571 & -2.8571 \\ -2.2727 & -2.1739 & 4.0000 & 0 \\ -1.8182 & -1.7391 & 0 & 3.0000 \end{bmatrix},$$

$$A^{-1} = \begin{bmatrix} 0.0962 & -0.3403 & -0.1515 & -0.2020 \\ -0.2668 & 0.1172 & -0.1704 & -0.2272 \\ -0.0904 & -0.1297 & 0.0713 & -0.2383 \\ -0.0964 & -0.1383 & -0.1906 & 0.0792 \end{bmatrix}$$

Obviously, A is not a singular M-matrix and the results in Liu, Chen and Huang (2004) and Chen, Huang, Liu and Cao (2006) are not available, which means that the results are more effective than the ones in Liu, Chen and Huang (2004) and Chen, Huang, Liu and Cao (2006) for some neural networks.

STABILITY OF HIGHER ORDER BAM NEURAL NETWORKS WITH IMPULSES

The notations used in this section are fairly standard. For $x \in R^n$, denote $\|x\| = \sqrt{x^T x}$ and $|x| = \sum_{i=1}^{n} |x_i|$. $M > 0$ means that matrix M is real symmetric and positive definite. We use I to represent the identity matrix. Also, matrix dimensions, if not stated explicitly, are assumed to be compatible for algebraic manipulations.

Throughout this section, the activation functions $f_j(\cdot), g_i(\cdot), h_j(\cdot), s_i(\cdot)$ of system (1.2) are assumed to possess the following properties:

(A_1) There exist positive numbers M_{1j}, N_{1i}, M_{2j}, N_{2i} such that:

$$|f_j(x)| \le M_{1j} \ , \ |(g_i \ x)| \le N_{1i};$$
$$|h_j(x)| \le M_{2j} \ , \ |(s_i \ x)| \le N_{2i}$$

for all $x \in R^n$ $(i = 1,2,...,n; j = 1,2,...,m)$.

Box 19.

$$x(t) = \left[x_1(t), x_2(t),...,x_n(t)\right]^T, \ \Delta x(t) = \left[\Delta x_1(t), \Delta x_2(t),...,\Delta x_n(t)\right]^T;$$

$$y(t) = \left[y_1(t), y_2(t),...,y_m(t)\right]^T, \ \Delta y(t) = \left[\Delta y_1(t), \Delta y_2(t),...,\Delta y_m(t)\right]^T;$$

$$f(y(t-\tau(t))) = \left[f_1(y_1(t-\tau(t))), f_2(y_2(t-\tau(t))),...,f_m(y_m(t-\tau(t)))\right]^T,$$

$$g(x(t-\sigma(t))) = \left[g_1(x_1(t-\sigma(t))), g_2(x_2(t-\sigma(t))),...,g_n(x_n(t-\sigma(t)))\right]^T;$$

$$h(y(t^- -\tau(t))) = \left[h_1(y_1(t^- -\tau(t))), h_2(y_2(t^- -\tau(t))),...,h_m(y_m(t^- -\tau(t)))\right]^T,$$

$$s(x(t^- -\sigma(t))) = \left[s_1(x_1(t^- -\sigma(t))), s_2(x_2(t^- -\sigma(t))),...,s_n(x_n(t^- -\sigma(t)))\right]^T;$$

$$A = diag(a_1,a_2,...,a_n), \ D = diag(d_1,d_2,...,d_m); \ B = (b_{ij})_{n \times m}, \ C = (c_{ji})_{m \times n};$$

$$E = diag(e_1,e_2,...,e_n), \ R = diag(r_1,r_2,...,r_m); \ W = (w_{ij})_{n \times m}, \ U = (u_{ji})_{m \times n};$$

$$\Gamma_1 = diag(f(y(t-\tau(t))), f(y(t-\tau(t))),...,f(y(t-\tau(t))))_{n \times n},$$

$$\Theta_1 = diag(g(x(t-\sigma(t))), g(x(t-\sigma(t))),...,g(x(t-\sigma(t))))_{m \times m};$$

$$\Gamma_2 = diag(h(y(t^- -\tau(t))), h(y(t^- -\tau(t))),...,h(y(t^- -\tau(t))))_{n \times n},$$

$$\Theta_2 = diag(s(x(t^- -\sigma(t))), s(x(t^- -\sigma(t))),...,s(x(t^- -\sigma(t))))_{m \times m};$$

(A_2) $f_j(0) = g_i(0) = h_j(0) = s_i(0) = 0$, $i = 1,2,...,n$; $j = 1,2,...,m$

(A_3) There exist positive numbers $K_{1j}, L_{1i}, K_{2j}, L_{2i}$ such that:

$$|f_j(x) - f_j(y)| \leq K_{1j}|x - y|,$$

$$|g_i(x) - g_i(y)| \leq L_{1i}|x - y|;$$

$$|h_j(x) - h_j(y)| \leq K_{2j}|x - y|,$$

$$|s_i(x) - s_i(y)| \leq L_{2i}|x - y|$$

for all $x,y \in R^n$ ($i = 1,2,...,n$; $j = 1,2,...,m$).

The initial conditions associated with (1.2) are of the form:

$$x_i(t) = \varphi_i(t),\ y_j(t) = \psi_j(t);\ t_0 - \tau^* \leq t \leq t_0 \tag{1.62}$$

in which $\varphi_i(t), \psi_j(t)(i = 1,2,...,n; j = 1,2,...,m)$ are continuous functions.

Denote Box 19, and $\Pi_1 = \left[B_1^T, B_2^T,...,B_n^T\right]^T$, where $B_i = (b_{ijl})_{m \times m}, \Sigma_1 = \left[C_1^T, C_2^T,...,C_m^T\right]^T$, where $C_j = (c_{jil})_{n \times n}$; $\Pi_2 = \left[W_1^T, W_2^T,...,W_n^T\right]^T$ where $W_i = (w_{ijl})_{m \times m}$, $\Sigma_2 = \left[U_1^T, U_2^T,...,U_m^T\right]^T$, where $U_j = (w_{jil})_{n \times n}$. Hence system (1.2) can be rewritten in the following vector-matrix form shown in Equation (1.63).

Also, for later development, denote $K_1 = diag(K_{11}, K_{12},...,K_{1m})$, $M_1^* = \sum_{j=1}^{m} M_{1j}^2$, $L_1 = diag(L_{11}, L_{12},...,L_{1n})$; $K_2 = diag(K_{21}, K_{22},...,K_{2m})$, $N_1^* = \sum_{i=1}^{n} N_{1i}^2$, $M_2^* = \sum_{j=1}^{m} M_{2j}^2$, $L_2 = diag(L_{21}, L_{22},...,L_{2n})$, $N_2^* = \sum_{i=1}^{n} N_{2i}^2$.

Lemma 1.3.1: Differential Inequality with Delay and Impulse (Yue, Xu and Liu, 1999). Consider the following differential inequalities:

$$\begin{cases} \dfrac{df(t)}{dt} \leq -\alpha f(t) + \beta \|f_t\|, & t \neq t_k \\ f(t_k) \leq a_k f(t_k^-) + b_k \|f_{t_k}\|; & \end{cases} \tag{1.64}$$

where $f(t) \geq 0$; $f_t(s) = f(t+s)$, $s \in [-\tau^*,0]$;

$\|f_t\| = \sup_{t-\tau^* \leq s \leq t} f(s)$, $\|f_{t^-}\| = \sup_{t-\tau^* \leq s < t} f(s)$, and $f_{t_0}(\cdot)$ is a continuous function. Suppose that $\alpha > \beta \geq 0$ and there exists a scalar $\delta > 1$ such that $t_k - t_{k-1} > \delta\tau^*$, then $f(t) \leq \rho_1\rho_2...\rho_{k+1} \exp\{\kappa\lambda\tau^*\}\|f_{t_0}\| \exp\{-\lambda(t-t_0)\}$, where $t \in [t_k, t_{k+1}]$, $\rho_i = \max\{1, a_i + b_i \exp\{\lambda\tau^*\}\}$, ($i = 1,2,...,k + 1$) and λ is the unique positive root of

Equation (1.63).

$$\begin{cases} \dfrac{dx(t)}{dt} = -Ax(t) + Bf(y(t-\tau(t))) + \Gamma_1^T\Pi_1 f(y(t-\tau(t))), & t \neq t_k \\ \dfrac{dy(t)}{dt} = -Dy(t) + Cg(x(t-\sigma(t))) + \Theta_1^T\Sigma_1 g(x(t-\sigma(t))); & t \neq t_k \\ \Delta x(t) = Ex(t^-) + Wh(y(t^- - \tau(t))) + \Gamma_2^T\Pi_2 h(y(t^- - \tau(t))), & t = t_k \\ \Delta y(t) = Ry(t^-) + Us(x(t^- - \sigma(t))) + \Theta_2^T\Sigma_2 s(x(t^- - \sigma(t))). & t = t_k \end{cases}$$

Box 20.

$$f(t) \leq \vartheta \|f_{t_0}\| \exp\left\{-\left(\lambda - \frac{\ln(\vartheta \exp\{\lambda\tau^*\})}{\delta\tau^*}\right)(t - t_0)\right\}, \qquad \forall t \geq t_0$$

Equation (A.2).

$$
\begin{aligned}
f(t_1) &\leq a_1 f(t_1^-) + b_1 \left\| f_{t_1^-} \right\| \\
&\leq a_1 \left\| f_{t_0} \right\| \exp\{-\lambda(t_1 - t_0)\} + b_1 \exp\{\lambda\tau^*\} \left\| f_{t_0} \right\| \exp\{-\lambda(t_1 - t_0)\} \\
&= (a_1 + b_1 \exp\{\lambda\tau^*\}) \left\| f_{t_0} \right\| \exp\{-\lambda(t_1 - t_0)\} \\
&\leq \rho_1 \left\| f_{t_0} \right\| \exp\{-\lambda(t_1 - t_0)\}
\end{aligned}
$$

Box 21.

$$
\begin{cases}
f(t) \leq g_1(t) & t \in [t_1 - \tau^*, t_1] \\
\left\| g_{1t_1} \right\| = \sup_{s \in [t_1 - \tau^*, t_1]} g_1(s) = \rho_1 \exp\{\lambda\tau^*\} \left\| f_{t_0} \right\| \exp\{-\lambda(t_1 - t_0)\}
\end{cases}
$$

Box 22.

$$
g_1(t) \leq \left\| g_{1t_1} \right\| \exp\{-\lambda(t - t_1)\} \leq \rho_1 \exp\{\lambda\tau^*\} \left\| f_{t_0} \right\| \exp\{-\lambda(t - t_0)\}, \quad t \in [t_1, t_2)
$$

equation $\lambda = \alpha - \beta \exp\{\lambda\tau^*\}$. In particular, if

$$
\vartheta = \sup_{k=1,2,\ldots} \{1, a_k + b_k \exp\{\lambda\tau^*\}\}
$$

then Box 20 occurs.

Proof. Since $\alpha > \beta \geq 0$ the transcendental equation $\lambda = \alpha - \beta \exp\{\lambda\tau^*\}$ has a unique positive root. In the following, we take three steps to prove our result.

Step 1. When $t \in [t_0, t_1)$, since:

$$
\frac{df(t)}{dt} \leq -af(t) + \beta \left\| f_t \right\|
$$

from Driver (1977), we know:

$$
f(t) \leq \left\| f_{t_0} \right\| \exp\{-\lambda(t - t_0)\} \tag{A.1}
$$

When $t = t_1$, we have Equation (A.2).

Step 2. Construct a continuous function $g_1(t)$ on interval $[t_1 - \tau^*, t_1]$ such as shown in Box 21.

In fact, such a function does exist, for example, we could take it as $g_1(t) = \rho_1 \left\| f_{t_0} \right\| \exp\{-\lambda(t_1 - t_0)\}$. Now consider the following dynamical system:

$$
\begin{cases}
\dfrac{dg_1(t)}{dt} = -\alpha g_1(t) + \beta \left\| g_{1t} \right\|, & t \in [t_1, t_2) \\
g_1(s) = \rho_1 \left\| f_{t_0} \right\| \exp\{-\lambda(s - t_0)\}. & s \in [t_1 - \tau^*, t_1]
\end{cases}
$$

From Driver (1977), we have Box 22.

Next, we will show that $f(t) < rg_1(t)$ where constant $r > 1$ and $t \in [t_1 - \tau^*, t_2)$.

When $t \in [t_1 - \tau^*, t_1]$ since $r > 1$, we easily have $f(t) < rg_1(t)$.

When $t \in [t_1, t_2)$, suppose the conclusion is not correct, then there must exist a $t' \in (t_1, t_2)$ such that

$f(t') < rg_1(t')$ and $f(t) < rg_1(t)$ $t \in [t_1, t')$. And we obtain $\dfrac{df(t')}{dt} > r \dfrac{dg_1(t')}{dt}$ On the other hand:

$$
\frac{df(t')}{dt} \leq -\alpha f(t') + \beta \left\| f_{t'} \right\| \leq -\alpha rg_1(t') + \beta r \left\| g_{1t'} \right\| = r \frac{dg_1(t')}{dt}
$$

a contradiction is shown.

Let $r \to 1^+$, and we have:

Box 23.

$$\begin{cases} f(t) \le g_k(t), & t \in [t_k - \tau^*, t_k] \\ \|g_{k_{t_k}}\| = \sup_{s \in [t_k - \tau^*, t_k]} g_k(s) = \rho_1 \rho_2 ... \rho_k \exp\{k\,\lambda\tau^*\} \|f_{t_0}\| \exp\{-\lambda(t_k - t_0)\} \end{cases}$$

Box 24.

$$\begin{cases} \dfrac{dg_k(t)}{dt} = -\alpha\,g_k(t) + \beta\|g_{kt}\|, & t \in [t_k, t_{k+1}) \\ g_k(s) = \rho_1 \rho_2 ... \rho_k \exp\{(k-1)\,\lambda\tau^*\} \|f_{t_0}\| \exp\{-\lambda(s - t_0)\} & s \in [t_k - \tau^*, t_k] \end{cases}$$

$$f(t) \le g_1(t) \le \rho_1 \exp\{\lambda\tau^*\} \|f_{t_0}\| \exp\{-\lambda(t - t_0)\},$$
$$t \in [t_1, t_2)$$

$$f(t_2) \le a_2 f(t_2^-) + b_2 \|f_{t_2^-}\| \tag{A.3}$$

$$\le (a_2 + b_2 \exp\{\lambda\tau^*\}) \rho_1 \exp\{\lambda\tau^*\} \|f_{t_0}\| \exp\{-\lambda(t - t_0)\}$$
$$\le \rho_1 \rho_2 \exp\{\lambda\tau^*\} \|f_{t_0}\| \exp\{-\lambda(t - t_0)\} \tag{A.4}$$

Step 3. Suppose when $t \in [t_{k-1}, t_k)$, we have:

$$f(t) \le \rho_1 \rho_2 ... \rho_{k-1} \exp\{(k-1)\,\lambda\tau^*\} \|f_{t_0}\| \exp\{-\lambda(t - t_0)\} \tag{A.5}$$

and

$$f(t_k) \le \rho_1 \rho_2 ... \rho_k \exp\{(k-1)\,\lambda\tau^*\} \|f_{t_0}\| \exp\{-\lambda(t - t_0)\} \tag{A.6}$$

Construct a continuous function $g_k(t)$ on the interval $t \in [t_k - \tau^*, t_k]$ such as shown in Box 23.

In fact, such a function does exist, for example, we could take it as $g_k(t) = \rho_1 \rho_2 ... \rho_k \exp\{(k-1)\lambda\tau^*\}$ $\|f_{t_0}\| \exp\{-\lambda(t - t_0)\}$. Now consider the dynamical system shown in Box 24.

Using the similar method as that of Step 2 and we can obtain:

$$f(t) \le \rho_1 \rho_2 ... \rho_k \exp\{k\,\lambda\tau^*\} \|f_{t_0}\| \exp\{-\lambda(t - t_0)\};$$
$$t \in [t_k, t_{k+1}) \tag{A.7}$$

$$f(t_{k+1}) \le \rho_1 \rho_2 ... \rho_{k+1} \exp\{k\,\lambda\tau^*\} \|f_{t_0}\| \exp\{-\lambda(t_{k+1} - t_0)\} \tag{A.8}$$

Accordingly, from the above three steps, we conclude:

$$f(t) \le \rho_1 \rho_2 ... \rho_{k+1} \exp\{k\,\lambda\tau^*\} \|f_{t_0}\| \exp\{-\lambda(t - t_0)\},$$
$$t \in [t_k, t_{k+1}]$$

and the proof is completed. □

Remark 1.3.1. It should be noted that in Lemma 1.3.1, when $\delta > \ln(\vartheta \exp\{\lambda\tau^*\})/\lambda\tau^*$, then system (1.64) is exponentially stable.

Remark 1.3.2. When there is no impulse in formula (1.64), then the differential inequality with delay and impulse reduces into the well known Halanay inequality (Halanay, 1966), see Zhou and Cao (2002).

In the following, it will be shown that, under some conditions, the equilibrium point of system (1.2) is unique and globally exponentially stable.

Theorem 1.3.1: Under assumptions $(A_1 - A_3)$, the equilibrium point of system (1.2) is unique and globally exponentially stable if the following conditions are satisfied:

1. There exist matrices P > 0, Q > 0, $\Psi_1 > 0$, $\Psi_2 > 0$ and scalars $\varepsilon_i > 0$ ($i = 1,2$) such that:

$$\Omega_1 = PA + AP - PB\Psi_1^{-1}B^T P - \frac{M_1^*}{\varepsilon_1}P^2 > 0,$$

$$\Omega_2 = QD + DQ - QC\Psi_2^{-1}C^T Q - \frac{N_1^*}{\varepsilon_2}Q^2 > 0$$

$$\begin{bmatrix} AP + PA & PB & P \\ B^T P & \Psi_1 & 0 \\ P & 0 & \dfrac{\varepsilon_1}{M_1^*}I \end{bmatrix} > 0,$$

$$(1.65)$$

or equivalently:

$$\begin{bmatrix} QD + DQ & QC & Q \\ C^T Q & \Psi_2 & 0 \\ Q & 0 & \dfrac{\varepsilon_2}{N_1^*}I \end{bmatrix} > 0$$

2. $\alpha > \beta \geq 0$ $\qquad\qquad$ (1.66)

Box 25.

$$\beta = 2\max\left\{ \frac{\lambda_{\max}(\Psi_1 + \varepsilon_1\Pi_1^T\Pi_1)\max\limits_{1\leq j\leq m}K_{1j}^2}{\lambda_{\min}(Q)}, \frac{\lambda_{\max}(\Psi_2 + \varepsilon_1\Sigma_1^T\Sigma_1)\max\limits_{1\leq i\leq n}L_{1i}^2}{\lambda_{\min}(P)} \right\}$$

Box 26.

$$a = 2\max\left\{ \frac{\lambda_{\max}(P)\|I + E\|^2}{\lambda_{\min}(P)}, \frac{\lambda_{\min}(Q)\|I + R\|^2}{\lambda_{\min}(Q)} \right\},$$

$$b = 4\max\left\{ \frac{\lambda_{\max}(P)(\|W\| + \sqrt{M_2^*}\|\Pi_2\|)^2\max\limits_{1\leq j\leq m}K_{2j}^2}{\lambda_{\min}(Q)}, \frac{\lambda_{\max}(Q)(\|U\| + \sqrt{N_2^*}\|\Sigma_2\|)^2\max\limits_{1\leq i\leq n}L_{2i}^2}{\lambda_{\min}(P)} \right\}$$

Equation (1.68).

$$\lambda_{\min}(P)\|x(t)\|^2 + \lambda_{\min}(Q)\|y(t)\|^2 \leq V(t) \leq \lambda_{\max}(P)\|x(t)\|^2 + \lambda_{\max}(Q)\|y(t)\|^2$$

Equation (1.69).

$$\dot{V}(t)\big|_{(1.63)} = 2x^T(t)P[-Ax(t) + Bf(y(t-\tau(t))) + \Gamma_1^T\Pi_1 f(y(t-\tau(t)))]$$
$$+ 2y^T(t)Q[-Dy(t) + Cg(x(t-\sigma(t))) + \Theta_1^T\Sigma_1 g(x(t-\sigma(t)))]$$

Equation (1.70).

$$2x^T(t)PBf(y(t-\tau(t))) \leq x^T(t)PB\Psi_1^{-1}B^T Px(t) + f^T(y(t-\tau(t)))\Psi_1 f(y(t-\tau(t)))$$

Equation (1.71).

$$2y^T(t)QCg(x(t-\sigma(t))) \leq y^T QC\Psi_2^{-1}C^T Qy(t) + g^T(x(t-\sigma(t)))\Psi_2 g(x(t-\sigma(t)))$$

where $\alpha = \min\left\{\dfrac{\lambda_{\min}(\Omega_1)}{\lambda_{\max}(P)}, \dfrac{\lambda_{\min}(\Omega_2)}{\lambda_{\max}(Q)}\right\}$ and Box 25 are true.

3. There exists a scalar $\delta > \ln(\rho \exp\{\lambda \tau^*\}) / \lambda \tau^*$ such that:

$$\inf_{k=1,2\dots} \{t_k - t_{k-1}\} > \tau^* \delta \qquad (1.67)$$

where λ is the unique positive solution of $\lambda = \alpha - \beta \exp\{\lambda \tau^*\}$ and $\rho = \max\{1, a - b \exp\{\lambda \tau^*\}\}$, in which Box 26 occurs.

Proof: Define the Lyapunov function as:

$$V(t) = x^T(t)Px(t) + y^T(t)Qy(t)$$

Obviously (see Equation (1.68)).

Firstly, we consider the case of $t \neq t_k$. Calculate the derivative of V (t) along the solutions of (1.63) and we obtain Equation (1.69).

From Lemma 1.2.1, we have Equations (1.70) – (1.73).

Since $\Gamma_1^T \Gamma_1 = \| f(y(t - \tau(t))) \|^2 I$ and:

$$\| f(y(t - \tau(t))) \|^2 \le \sum_{j=1}^m M_{1j}^2 = M_1^*$$

it follows that:

$$x^T(t)P\Gamma_1^T \Gamma_1 Px(t) \le M_1^* x^T(t)P^2 x(t) \qquad (1.74)$$

Equation (1.72).

$$\boxed{\begin{aligned}
& 2x^T(t)P\Gamma_1^T \Pi_1 f(y(t - \tau(t))) \\
& \le \frac{1}{\varepsilon_1} x^T(t)P\Gamma_1^T \Gamma_1 Px(t) + \varepsilon_1 f^T(y(t - \tau(t)))\Pi_1^T \Pi_1 f(y(t - \tau(t)))
\end{aligned}}$$

Equation (1.73).

$$\boxed{\begin{aligned}
& 2y^T(t)Q\Theta_1^T \Sigma_1 g(x(t - \sigma(t))) \\
& \le \frac{1}{\varepsilon_2} y^T(t)Q\Theta_1^T \Theta_1 Qy(t) + \varepsilon_2 g^T(x(t - \sigma(t)))\Sigma_1^T \Sigma_1 g(x(t - \sigma(t)))
\end{aligned}}$$

Equation (1.76).

$$\boxed{\begin{aligned}
\dot{V}(t)\big|_{(1.63)} & \le -x^T(t)\Omega_1 x(t) + \lambda_{\max}(\Psi_2 + \varepsilon_2 \Sigma_1^T \Sigma_1)\max_{1 \le i \le n} L_{1i}^2 \| x(t - \sigma(t)) \|^2 \\
& \quad - y^T(t)\Omega_2 y(t) + \lambda_{\max}(\Psi_1 + \varepsilon_1 \Pi_1^T \Pi_1)\max_{1 \le j \le n} K_{1j}^2 \| y(t - \tau(t)) \|^2 \\
& \le -\alpha V(t) + \beta \overline{V}(t),
\end{aligned}}$$

Equation (1.77).

$$\boxed{\begin{aligned}
V(t_k) & = (x(t_k^-) + \Delta x(t_k))^T P(x(t_k^-) + \Delta x(t_k)) + (y(t_k^-) + \Delta y(t_k))^T Q(y(t_k^-) + \Delta y(t_k)) \\
& \le \lambda_{\max}(P)\| (I + E)x(t_k^-) + (W + \Gamma_2^T \Pi_2)h(y(t_k^- - \tau(t_k))) \|^2 \\
& \quad + \lambda_{\max}(Q)\| (I + R)y(t_k^-) + (U + \Theta_2^T \Sigma_2)s(x(t_k^- - \sigma(t_k))) \|^2 \\
& \le aV(t_k^-) + b\overline{V}(t_k^-)
\end{aligned}}$$

The fact $\Theta_1^T \Theta_1 = \|g(x(t-\sigma(t)))\|^2$ and:

$$\|g(x(t-\sigma(t)))\|^2 \le \sum_{i=1}^{n} N_{1i}^2 = N_1^*$$

leads to:

$$y^T(t)Q\Theta_1^T \Theta_1 Qy(t) \le N_1^* y^T(t)Q^2 y(t) \qquad (1.75)$$

Substituting (1.70)–(1.75) into (1.69), and from (1.65), (1.66), (1.68), we obtain Equation (1.76), where $\overline{V}(t) = \sup_{t-\tau^* \le s \le t} V(s)$.

Secondly, we consider the case of $t = t_k$, by (1.63), we have Equation (1.77), where $\overline{V}(t_k^-) = \sup_{t_k - \tau^* \le s \le t_k} V(s)$.

By (1.66), (1.67), (1.76), (1.77), and Lemma 1.3.1, we obtain:

$$V(t) \le \rho \overline{V}(t_0) \exp\left\{ -\left(\lambda - \frac{\ln(\rho \exp\{\lambda^* \tilde{\tau}\})}{\delta \tau^*} \right)(t-t_0) \right\},$$

$$t \ge t_0$$

and from (1.68) we have Box 27, and this completes the proof. □

Theorem 1.3.2: Under assumptions $(A_1 - A_3)$ the equilibrium point of system (1.2) is unique and globally exponentially stable if the following conditions are satisfied:

1. $\alpha > \beta \ge 0$ (1.78)
   where $\alpha = \min\{\min_{1 \le i \le n} a_i, \min_{1 \le j \le m} d_j\}$, and Box 28 are true.

Box 27.

$$\|x(t)\|^2 + \|y(t)\|^2 \le \frac{\rho \max\{\lambda_{\max}(P), \lambda_{\max}(Q)\}}{\min\{\lambda_{\min}(P)\lambda_{\min}(Q)\}} (\|x_{t_0}\|^2 + \|y_{t_0}\|^2) \exp\left\{ -\left(\lambda - \frac{\ln(\rho \exp\{\lambda \tau^*\})}{\delta \tau^*} \right)(t-t_0) \right\}$$

Box 28.

$$\beta = 2\max\left\{ \max_{1 \le j \le m}\{\sum_{i=1}^{n}(|b_{ij}| + \sum_{l=1}^{m}|b_{ijl}|M_{1l})K_{1j}\}, \max_{1 \le i \le n}\{\sum_{j=1}^{m}(|c_{ji}| + \sum_{l=1}^{n}|c_{jil}|N_{1l})L_{1i}\} \right\}$$

Box 29.

$$a = \max\{\max_{1 \le i \le n}|1+e_i|, \max_{1 \le j \le m}|1+r_j|\},$$

$$b = 2\max\left\{ \max_{1 \le j \le m}\{\sum_{i=1}^{n}(|w_{ij}| + \sum_{l=1}^{m}|w_{ijl}|M_{2l})K_{2j}\}, \max_{1 \le i \le n}\{\sum_{j=1}^{m}(|u_{ji}| + \sum_{l=1}^{n}|u_{jil}|N_{2l})L_{2i}\} \right\}$$

Equation (1.80).

$$D^+V(t)|_{(1.63)} \le -\sum_{i=1}^{n} a_i |x_i(t)| + \sum_{j=1}^{m}\sum_{i=1}^{n}(|c_{ji}| + \sum_{l=1}^{n}|c_{jil}|N_{1l})|x_i(t-\sigma(t))|L_{1i}$$

$$-\sum_{j=1}^{m} d_j |y_j(t)| + \sum_{i=1}^{n}\sum_{j=1}^{m}(|b_{ij}| + \sum_{l=1}^{m}|b_{ijl}|M_{1l})|y_j(t-\tau(t))|K_{1j}$$

$$\le -\alpha V(t) + \beta \overline{V}(t)$$

2. There exists a scalar $\delta > \ln(\rho \exp\{\lambda\tau^*\}) / \lambda\tau^*$ such that:

$$\inf_{k=1,2\ldots} \{t_k - t_{k-1}\} > \tau^*\delta \qquad (1.79)$$

where λ is the unique positive solution of $\lambda = \alpha - \beta \exp\{\lambda\tau^*\}$ and $\rho = \max\{1, a + b \exp\{\lambda\tau^*\}\}$ in which Box 29 occurs.

Proof: Define the Lyapunov function as:

$$V(t) = \sum_{i=1}^{n} |x_i(t)| + \sum_{j=1}^{m} |y_j(t)|$$

Firstly, we consider the case of $t \neq t_k$. Calculate the upper right Dini derivative of $V(t)$ along the solutions of (1.63), and from (1.78), we obtain Equation (1.80).

Secondly, we consider the case of $t = t_k$, by (1.63) and condition (2) we have Equation (1.81).

By (1.80), (1.81), and Lemma 1.3.1, we obtain:

$$V(t) \leq \rho\overline{V}(t_0)\exp\{-(\lambda - \frac{\ln(\rho \exp\{\lambda\tau^*\})}{\delta\tau^*})(t - t_0)\}, \quad t \geq t_0$$

From (1.79), we have Box 30, and this completes the proof. □

When there is no impulse in system (1.63), then it reduces into the model shown in Equation (1.82).

From Theorems 1.3.1 and 1.3.2 above, it is easy to show that the following corollaries hold.

Equation (1.81).

$$V(t_k) = \sum_{i=1}^{n} \left| (1+e_i)x_i(t_k^-) + \sum_{j=1}^{m} \left(w_{ij} + \sum_{l=1}^{m} w_{ijl} h_l(y_l(t_k^- - \tau(t_k)))) h_j(y_j(t_k^- - \tau(t_k))) \right) \right|$$

$$+ \sum_{j=1}^{m} \left| (1+r_j)y_j(t_k^-) + \sum_{i=1}^{n} \left(u_{ji} + \sum_{l=1}^{n} u_{jil} s_l(x_l(t_k^- - \tau(t_k)))) s_i(x_i(t_k^- - \tau(t_k))) \right) \right|$$

$$\leq aV(t_k^-) + b\overline{V}(t_k^-)$$

Box 30.

$$|x(t)| + |y(t)| \leq \frac{\rho \max\{\lambda_{max}(P), \lambda_{max}(Q)\}}{\min\{\lambda_{min}(P), \lambda_{min}(Q)\}} (|x_{t_0}| + |y_{t_0}|)\exp\{-(\lambda - \frac{\ln(\rho \exp\{\lambda\tau^*\})}{\delta\tau^*})(t - t_0)\}$$

Equation (1.82).

$$\begin{cases} \dfrac{dx(t)}{dt} = -Ax(t) + Bf(y(t - \tau(t))) + \Gamma_1^T \Pi_1 f(y(t - \tau(t))), \\ \dfrac{dy(t)}{dt} = -Dy(t) + Cg(x(t - \tau(t))) + \Theta_1^T \Sigma_1 g(x(t - \tau(t))) \end{cases}$$

Box 31.

$$\beta = 2\max\left\{ \frac{\lambda_{max}(\Psi_1 + \varepsilon_1\Pi_1^T\Pi_1)\max_{1 \leq j \leq m} K_{1j}^2}{\lambda_{min}(Q)}, \frac{\lambda_{max}(\Psi_2 + \varepsilon_2\Sigma_1^T\Sigma_1)\max_{1 \leq i \leq n} L_{1i}^2}{\lambda_{min}(P)} \right\}$$

Box 32.

$$\beta = 2\max\left\{\max_{1\leq j\leq m}\left\{\sum_{i=1}^{n}(|b_{ij}| + \sum_{l=1}^{m}|b_{ijl}|M_{1l})K_{1j}\right\}, \max_{1\leq i\leq n}\left\{\sum_{j=1}^{m}(|c_{ji}| + \sum_{l=1}^{n}|c_{jil}|N_{1l})L_{1i}\right\}\right\}$$

Box 33.

$$\beta = 2\max\left\{\lambda_{max}(Y_1)\max_{1\leq j\leq m}K_{1j}^2\Big/\lambda_{min}(Q), \lambda_{max}(Y_2)\max_{1\leq i\leq n}L_{1i}^2\Big/\lambda_{min}(P)\right\};$$

$$\alpha = \min\{\lambda_{min}(\Omega_1)/\lambda_{max}(P), \lambda_{min}(\Omega_2)/\lambda_{max}(Q)\}$$

Corollary 1.3.1. Under assumptions $(A_1 - A_3)$ the equilibrium point of system (1.82) is unique and globally exponentially stable if the following conditions are satisfied:

1. There exist matrices $P > 0$, $Q > 0$, $\Psi_1 > 0$, $\Psi_2 > 0$ and scalars $\varepsilon_i > 0$ ($i = 1,2$) such that:

$$\Omega_1 = PA + AP - PB\Psi_1^{-1}B^T P - \frac{M_1^*}{\varepsilon_1}P^2 > 0,$$

$$\Omega_2 = QD + DQ - QC\Psi_2^{-1}C^T Q - \frac{N_1^*}{\varepsilon_2}Q^2 > 0$$

2. $\alpha > \beta \geq 0$
   where $\alpha = \min\left\{\dfrac{\lambda_{min}(\Omega_1)}{\lambda_{max}(P)}, \dfrac{\lambda_{min}(\Omega_2)}{\lambda_{max}(Q)}\right\}$ and Box 31 occur.

Corollary 1.3.2 Under assumptions $(A_1 - A_3)$, the equilibrium point of system (1.82) is unique and globally exponentially stable if $\alpha > \beta \geq 0$, where $\alpha = \min\left\{\min_{1\leq i\leq n} a_i, \min_{1\leq j\leq m} d_j\right\}$, and Box 32.

When Π_1 and Σ_1 all disappear in system (1.82), that is, $\Pi_1 = \Sigma_1 = 0$, then it reduces into the extensively studied lower order BAM neural networks:

$$\begin{cases} \dfrac{dx(t)}{dt} = -Ax(t) + Bf(y(t - \tau(t))), \\ \dfrac{dy(t)}{dt} = -Dy(t) + Cg(x(t - \sigma(t))) \end{cases} \quad (1.83)$$

Corollary 1.3.3. Under assumptions $(A_1 - A_3)$, the equilibrium point of system (1.83) is unique and globally exponentially stable if the following conditions are satisfied:

1. There exist matrices $P > 0$, $Q > 0$, $Y_1 > 0$, $Y_2 > 0$ and scalars $\varepsilon_i > 0$ ($i = 1,2$) such that:

$$\Omega_1 = PA + AP - PBY_1^{-1}B^T P - \frac{M_1^*}{\varepsilon_1}P^2 > 0,$$

$$\Omega_2 = QD + DQ - QCY_2^{-1}C^T Q - \frac{N_1^*}{\varepsilon_2}Q^2 > 0$$

$$(1.84)$$

2. $\alpha > \beta \geq 0$, where Box 33 occurs.

Corollary 1.3.4 Under assumptions $(A_1 - A_3)$, the equilibrium point of system (1.83) is unique and globally exponentially stable if $\alpha > \beta \geq 0$, where:

$$\alpha = \min\left\{\min_{1\leq i\leq n} a_i, \min_{1\leq j\leq m} d_j\right\},$$

$$\beta = 2\max\left\{\max_{1\leq j\leq m}(K_{1j}\sum_{i=1}^{n}|b_{ij}|), \max_{1\leq i\leq n}(L_{1i}\sum_{j=1}^{m}|c_{ji}|)\right\}$$

Example 1.3.1. Consider the impulsive higher order BAM neural networks (1.2) with $m = 2$, $n = 3$; $A=diag(16,18,14)$, $D=diag(20,22)$; $E=diag(0.7,-1.1,0.9)$, $R=diag(-1.3,1.4)$; $L_1=diag(0.1,0.08,0.1)$, $K_1=diag(0.06,0.07)$; $L_2=diag(1.2,1.4,1.6)$, $K_2=diag(0.7,0.9)$; $N_1^* = N_2^* = 3$, $M_1^* = M_2^* = 2$; $\tau^* = 3$;

$$B=\begin{bmatrix} 0.5 & 0.6 \\ -0.1 & 0.2 \\ 0.7 & -0.3 \end{bmatrix}, \quad C=\begin{bmatrix} 0.2 & -0.3 & 0.4 \\ -0.1 & 0.2 & 0.5 \end{bmatrix}; \quad W=\begin{bmatrix} 0.35 & 0.66 \\ -0.21 & 0.12 \\ 0.37 & -0.53 \end{bmatrix},$$

$$U=\begin{bmatrix} 0.22 & -0.33 & 0.54 \\ -0.17 & 0.28 & 0.45 \end{bmatrix}; \quad B_1=\begin{bmatrix} 0.1210 & 0.7159 \\ 0.4508 & 0.8928 \end{bmatrix},$$

$$B_2=\begin{bmatrix} 0.2731 & 0.8656 \\ 0.2548 & 0.2324 \end{bmatrix}, B_3=\begin{bmatrix} 0.8049 & 0.2319 \\ 0.9084 & 0.2393 \end{bmatrix},$$

$$C_1=\begin{bmatrix} 0.0498 & 0.1909 & 0.1708 \\ 0.0784 & 0.8439 & 0.9943 \\ 0.6408 & 0.1739 & 0.4398 \end{bmatrix}, \quad C_2=\begin{bmatrix} 0.3400 & 0.3932 & 0.0381 \\ 0.3142 & 0.5915 & 0.4586 \\ 0.3651 & 0.1197 & 0.8699 \end{bmatrix},$$

$$W_1=\begin{bmatrix} 0.9342 & 0.1603 \\ 0.2644 & 0.8729 \end{bmatrix}, \quad W_2=\begin{bmatrix} 0.2379 & 0.9669 \\ 0.6458 & 0.6649 \end{bmatrix},$$

$$W_3=\begin{bmatrix} 0.8704 & 0.1370 \\ 0.0099 & 0.8188 \end{bmatrix},$$

$$U_1=\begin{bmatrix} 0.4302 & 0.6873 & 0.1556 \\ 0.8903 & 0.3461 & 0.1911 \\ 0.7349 & 0.1660 & 0.4225 \end{bmatrix}, \quad U_2=\begin{bmatrix} 0.8560 & 0.4608 & 0.4122 \\ 0.4902 & 0.4574 & 0.9016 \\ 0.8159 & 0.4507 & 0.0056 \end{bmatrix}$$

then

$$\Pi_1=\begin{bmatrix} 0.1210 & 0.7159 \\ 0.4508 & 0.8928 \\ 0.2731 & 0.8656 \\ 0.2548 & 0.2324 \\ 0.8049 & 0.2319 \\ 0.9084 & 0.2393 \end{bmatrix}, \quad \Sigma_1=\begin{bmatrix} 0.0498 & 0.1909 & 0.1708 \\ 0.0784 & 0.8439 & 0.9943 \\ 0.6408 & 0.1739 & 0.4398 \\ 0.3400 & 0.3932 & 0.0381 \\ 0.3142 & 0.5915 & 0.4586 \\ 0.3651 & 0.1197 & 0.8699 \end{bmatrix}$$

$$\Pi_2=\begin{bmatrix} 0.9342 & 0.1603 \\ 0.2644 & 0.8729 \\ 0.2379 & 0.9669 \\ 0.6458 & 0.6649 \\ 0.8704 & 0.1370 \\ 0.0099 & 0.8188 \end{bmatrix}, \quad \Sigma_2=\begin{bmatrix} 0.4302 & 0.6873 & 0.1556 \\ 0.8903 & 0.3461 & 0.1911 \\ 0.7349 & 0.1660 & 0.4225 \\ 0.8560 & 0.4608 & 0.4122 \\ 0.4902 & 0.4574 & 0.9016 \\ 0.8159 & 0.4507 & 0.0056 \end{bmatrix}$$

By letting $\delta > 4.6200$ and using standard numerical software, it is found that $\varepsilon_1 = 2.0776$, $\varepsilon_2 = 1.2466$; $P=diag(0.0333,0.0296,0.0382)$, $Q=diag(0.0266,0.0241)$; $Y_2=diag(1.0388, 1.0388,1.0388)$, $Y_1=diag(1.0388,1.0388)$ satisfy conditions (1)-(3) in Theorem 1.3.1 with $\alpha = 27.8508$, $\beta = 3.6633$; $a = 21.7150$, $b = 189.0985$. Therefore, the equilibrium point of this system is unique and globally exponentially stable.

Example 1.3.2. Consider the impulsive higher order BAM neural networks (1.2) with $n=m=2$ and $A=diag(5,6)$, $D=diag(7,8)$; $E=diag(6,-8)$, $R=diag(-7,4)$; $L_1=diag(0.3,0.6)$, $K_1=diag(0.5,0.5)$, $L_2=diag(0.9,1.2)$, $K_2=diag(1,0.7)$, $N_{ij} = M_{ij} = (i,j = 1,2)$, $\tau^* = 3$;

$$B=\begin{bmatrix} 0.9003 & 1.2137 \\ 0.4623 & -0.0280 \end{bmatrix}, \quad C=\begin{bmatrix} -0.6541 & 0.5429 \\ 1.9595 & -0.4953 \end{bmatrix},$$

$$B_1=\begin{bmatrix} -0.4556 & 0.0305 \\ 0.3976 & 0.4936 \end{bmatrix}; \quad B_2=\begin{bmatrix} -0.2433 & 1.7073 \\ 1.7200 & 0.1871 \end{bmatrix},$$

$$C_1=\begin{bmatrix} 0.5667 & 0.9222 \\ 1.3617 & 0.1357 \end{bmatrix}, \quad C_2=\begin{bmatrix} 0.3667 & 1.6785 \\ 0.4251 & 0.2576 \end{bmatrix};$$

$$W=\begin{bmatrix} -0.7222 & 0.3974 \\ 0.4055 & 0.2076 \end{bmatrix}, \quad U=\begin{bmatrix} 0.0596 & 0.4181 \\ 1.2811 & -0.2404 \end{bmatrix},$$

Equation (1.85).

$$\begin{cases} \dfrac{dx(t)}{dt} = -ax(t)+bf(y(t-\tau(t)))+b_1 f^2(y(t-\tau(t))), & t \neq t_k \\[2ex] \dfrac{dy(t)}{dt} = -dx(t)+cg(x(t-\sigma(t)))+c_1 g^2(y(t-\sigma(t))); & t \neq t_k \\[2ex] \Delta x(t) = ex(t^-)+wh(y(t^--\tau(t)))+w_1 h^2(y(t^--\tau(t))), & t = t_k \\[1ex] \Delta y(t) = ry(t^-)+us(x(t^--\sigma(t)))+u_1 s^2(x(t^--\sigma(t))); & t = t_k \end{cases}$$

$$W_1 = \begin{bmatrix} -0.3945 & 0.3017 \\ 1.0833 & 0.3958 \end{bmatrix}; \; W_2 = \begin{bmatrix} 0.5896 & 1.0452 \\ 1.9137 & 0.7603 \end{bmatrix},$$

$$U_1 = \begin{bmatrix} 0.4891 & 0.8798 \\ 0.5359 & 0.8668 \end{bmatrix}, \quad U_2 = \begin{bmatrix} 0.1738 & 0.7351 \\ 0.1152 & 0.2629 \end{bmatrix}$$

It is found that if we take $\delta > 14.7009$, then conditions (1) and (2) in Theorem 1.3.2 hold with $\alpha = 5$, $\beta = 4.04$, $\lambda = 0.0666$; $\rho = 15.4472$; $a = 7$, $b = 6.9174$. Therefore, the equilibrium point of system (1.2) satisfying the given condition is unique and globally exponentially stable.

Example 1.3.3. Consider the two-dimensional impulse higher order BAM neural networks shown in Equation (1.85), where $a = 0.2999$, $b = 8.8501$, $b_1 = 0.1680$, $d = 0.21$, $c = 8.2311$, $c_1 = 1.1860$, $e = 2$, $w = 0.8913$, $w_1 = 0.4565$, $r = 3$, $u = 0.7621$, $u_1 = 0.0185$, $K_1 = L_1 = K_2 = L_2 = 0.01$, $M_1 = N_1 = 1$, $\tau^* = 3$, $M_2 = N_2 = 1$. By letting $\delta > 723.0342$, and using standard numerical software, it is found that $\varepsilon_1 = \varepsilon_2 = 60.4811$; $P = 0.0984$, $Q = 0.0799$; $Y_1 = 26.4811$, $Y_2 = 64.4811$ satisfy conditions (1)-(3) in Theorem 1.3.1 with $\alpha = 0.3071$, $\beta = 0.3040$; $a = 32$, $b = 0.0009$. Therefore, the equilibrium

point of system (1.85) is unique and globally exponentially stable.

When there is no impulse in system (1.85), it reduces into the following higher order BAM neural networks:

$$\begin{cases} \dfrac{dx(t)}{dt} = -ax(t) + bf(y(t - \tau(t))) + b_1 f^2(y(t - \tau(t))), \\ \dfrac{dy(t)}{dt} = -dy(t) + cg(x(t - \sigma(t))) + c_1 g^2(x(t - \sigma(t))) \end{cases}$$

(1.86)

For (1.86), if we take the same parameters as in (1.85), from Corollary 1.3.1, it can be deduced that (1.86) is globally exponentially stable; while it is found that the conditions in Cao, Liang and Lam (2004) are not feasible for this system. Hence, it is seen that our results improve and extend the earlier works.

For model (1.86), when $b_1 = c_1 = 0$, it reduces into the following extensively studied lower order BAM neural networks:

$$\begin{cases} \dfrac{dx(t)}{dt} = -ax(t) + bf(y(t - \tau(t))), \\ \dfrac{dy(t)}{dt} = -dy(t) + cg(x(t - \sigma(t))) \end{cases}$$

(1.87)

Figure 12. State response of HOBAMNNs (1.86)

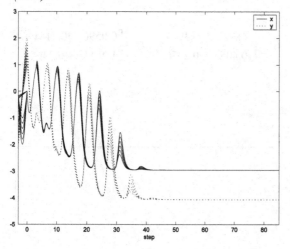

Figure 13. State response of lower order BAMNNs (1.87)

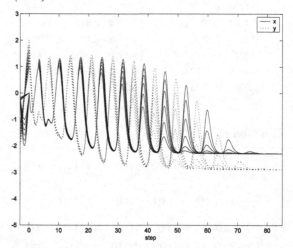

By letting a=1.9220, b=9.8501, b_1 = –4, d=1.1631, c=8.2311, c_1 = –5, $\tau(t) = \sigma(t) = 3$ and $f(x)$ = $1/(1 + \exp(-x)) - 1/2$ in system (1.86) and (1.87), from the following Figures, one may have a better understanding of the effect of higher order terms on the properties of the system such as convergence rate. For more details, one can see Simpson (1990), Kosmatopoulos, Polycarpou, Christodoulou and Ioannou (1995), Kosmatopoulos and Christodoulou (1995) and the references therein.

FUTURE RESEARCH DIRECTIONS

In this chapter, we have studied the dynamical behaviors of some kinds of HONNs (second order). Due to the time delays and the higher order structure, this kind of system has complex dynamics which have not been analyzed thoroughly so far. In the future, we think there are a lot of things for us to do:

1. The relation between the complexity of the dynamics and the order of the system should be considered. It should be investigated how and to what extent does the order of the system affect its dynamical behaviors.
2. Real life systems are usually affected by external perturbations which in many cases are of great importance and can be treated as randoms. As pointed out by Haykin: "in real nervous systems, synaptic transmission is a noisy process brought on by random fluctuations form the release of neurotransmitters and other probabilistic causes, therefore, stochastic effects should be taken into account." Therefore, it is of great necessity to study the dynamics of stochastic HONNs.
3. For the complex structure of HONNs, bifurcation and chaos do exist in such systems, and we believe that they are much more complex than the first order case. Up till now, there have not been any results on these topics.

4. The synchronization problem of dynamical systems has received a great deal of research interest in the past decade. Special attention has been focused on the synchronization of chaotic dynamical systems, particularly those large-scale and complex networks of chaotic oscillators. To the best of our knowledge, synchronization on HONN systems has not been discussed.
5. Periodic solutions are studied in this chapter for HONNs. When applying neural networks in optimization problems or for the storage of images, multi-equilibrium points and multi-periodic solutions are needed. The notion of multistability of a neural network is used to describe coexistence of multiple stable patterns such as equilibria or periodic orbits. Results on these topics have yet to emerge, therefore, we will consider these problems in the future.

CONCLUSION

In this chapter, firstly, by employing the Lyapunov technique, the LMI approach, and a differential inequality with delays and impulses, sufficient conditions are obtained to ensure that higher order BAM networks with or without impulses are globally exponentially stable. The new results are easily tested in practice. Furthermore, the methods employed in this chapter are useful to study some other neural systems. Secondly, several sufficient criteria are derived ensuring the existence, global attractivity and global asymptotic stability of the periodic solution for higher order BAM neural networks with periodic coefficients and delays by using coincidence degree theory and the properties of the nonsingular M-matrix. In the end, we show that HONNs satisfying some conditions are exponentially stable and have periodic solutions by using the Lyapunov method and LMI techniques. These results play an important role in design and applications of high quality neural networks.

ACKNOWLEDGMENT

This work was jointly supported by the National Natural Science Foundation of China under Grant No. 60574043, the Natural Science Foundation of Jiangsu Province of China under Grant No. BK2006093, International Joint Project funded by NSFC and the Royal Society of the United Kingdom, and the Foundation for Excellent Doctoral Dissertation of Southeast University YBJJ0705.

REFERENCES

Abu-Mostafa, Y., & Jacques, J. (1985). Information capacity of the Hopfield model. *IEEE Transactions on Information Theory, 31*(4), 461-464.

Baldi, P. (1988)}. Neural networks, orientations of the hypercube, and algebraic threshold functions. *IEEE Transactions on Information Theory, 34*(3), 523-530.

Berman, A., & Plemmons, R. J. (1979). *Nonnegative matrices in the mathematical science*. New York: Academic Press.

Boyd, S., Ghaoui, L. E., Feron, E., & Balakrishnan, V. (1994). *Linear matrix inequalities in system and control theory*. Philadephia: SIAM.

Cao, J. (1999). On stability of delayed cellular neural networks. *Physics Letters A, 261*, 303-308.

Cao, J. (2001). Global exponential stability of Hopfield neural networks. *International Journal of Systems Science, 32*(2), 233-236.

Cao, J. (2003). Global asymptotic stability of delayed bi-directional associative memory neural networks. *Applied Mathematics and Computation, 142*, 333-339.

Cao, J., & Dong, M. (2003). Exponential stability of delayed bidirectional associative memory networks. *Applied Mathematics and Computation, 135*, 105-112.

Cao, J., Liang, J., & Lam J. (2004). Exponential stability of high-order bidirectional associative memory neural networks with time delays. *Physica D, 199*, 425-436.

Cao, J., & Tao, Q. (2001). Estimation on domain of attraction and convergence rate of Hopfield continuous feedback neural networks. *Journal of Computer and System Sciences, 62*, 528-534.

Cao, J., & Wang, L. (2002). Exponential stability and periodic oscillatory solution in BAM networks with delays. *IEEE Transactions on Neural Networks, 13*(2), 457-463.

Cao, J., & Wang, J. (2004). Absolute exponential stability of recurrent neural networks with Lipschitz-continuous activation functions and time delays. *Neural Networks, 17*, 379-390.

Cao, J., Wang J., & Liao, X. (2003). Novel stability criteria of delayed cellular neural networks. *International Journal Neural Systems, 13*(5), 367-375.

Chen, A., Cao, J., & Huang, L. (2004). Exponential stability of BAM neural networks with transmission delays. *Neurocomputing, 57*, 435-454.

Chen, A., Huang, L., Liu, Z., & Cao, J. (2006). Periodic bidirectional associative memory neural networks with distributed delays. *Journal of Mathematical Analysis and Applications, 317*(1), 80-102.

Chua, L. O., & Yang, L. (1988). Cellular neural networks: Theory. *IEEE Transactions on Circuits and Systems, 35*(10), 1257-1272.

Cohen, M. A., & Grossberg, S. (1983). Absolute stability and global pattern formation and parallel memory storage by competitive neural networks. *IEEE Transactions on Systems, Man and Cybernetics, 13*(5), 815-826.

Dembo, A., Farotimi, O., & Kailath, T. (1991). High-order absolutely stable neural networks. *IEEE Transactions on Circuits and Systems, 38*(1), 57-65.

van den Driessche, P., & Zou, X. (1998). Global attractivity in delayed Hopfield neural network models. *SIAM Journal on Applied Mathematics, 58*(6), 1878-1890.

Driver, R. D. (1977). *Ordinary and delay differential equations.* New York: Springer-Verlag.

Gaines, R. E., & Mawhin, J. L. (1977). *Coincidence degree and nonlinear differential equations.* Berlin: Springer-Verlag.

Gopalsamy, K. (1992). *Stability and oscillation in delay equation of population dynamics.* Dordrecht: Kluwer Academic Publishers.

Halanay, A. (1966). *Differential equation: Stability oscillations time-lags.* New York: Academic Press.

Hale, J. K. (1977). *Theory of functional differential equations.* New York: Springer-Verlag.

Ho, D. W. C., Lam, J., Xu, J., & Tam, H. K. (1999). Neural computation for robust approximate pole assignment. *Neurocomputing, 25,* 191-211.

Hopfield, J. J. (1984). Neurons with graded response have collective computational properties like those of two-state neurons. *Proceedings of National Academy of Sciences of the United States of America, Biophysics, 81*(10), 3088-3092.

Kamp, Y., & Hasler, M. (1990). *Recursive neural networks for associative memory.* New York: Wiley.

Kosko, B. (1988). Bidirectional associative memories. *IEEE Transactions on Systems, Man, and Cybernetics, 18*(1), 49-60.

Kosmatopoulos, E. B., & Christodoulou, M. A., (1995). Structural properties of gradient recurrent high-order neural networks. *IEEE Transactions on Circuits Systems-II, 42*(9), 592-603.

Kosmatopoulos, E. B., Polycarpou, M. M., Christodoulou, M. A., & Ioannou, P. A. (1995). High-order neural network structures for identification on

dynamical systems. *IEEE Transactions on Neural Networks, 6,* 422-431.

Liao, X. F., & Yu, J. B. (1998). Qualitative analysis of bi-directional associative memory with time delays. *International Journal of Circuit Theory and Applications, 26*(3), 219-229.

Liu, Z., Chen, A. & Huang, L. (2004). Existence and global exponential stability of periodic solution to self-connection BAM neural networks with delays. *Physics Letters A, 328,* 127-43.

Marcus, C. M., & Westervelt, R. M. (1989). Stability of analog neural networks with delay. *Physical Review A, 39,* 347-359.

McEliece, R., Posner, E., Rodemich, E., & Venkatesh, S. (1987). The capacity of the Hopfield associative memory. *IEEE Transactions on Information Theory, 33*(4), 461-482.

Mohamad, S. (2001). Global exponential stability in continuous-time and discrete-time delay bidirectional neural networks. *Physica D, 159,* 233-251.

Peretto, P., & Niez, J. J. (1986). Long term memory storage capacity of multiconnected neural networks. *Biological Cybernetics, 54*(1), 53-63.

Personnaz, L., Guyon, I., & Dreyfus, G. (1987). High-order neural networks: Information storage without errors. *Europhysics Letters, 4*(8), 863-867.

Psaltis, D., Park, C. H., & Hong, J. (1988). Higher-order associative memories and their optical implementations. *Neural Networks, 1*(2), 149-163.

Ren, F. L., & Cao, J. (2006). LMI-based criteria for stability of high-order neural networks with time-varying delay. *Nonlinear Analysis, Series B, 7*(5), 967-979.

Ren, F. L., & Cao, J. (2007a). Periodic oscillation of higher-order BAM neural networks with periodic coefficients and delays. *Nonlinearity, 20*(3), 605-629.

Ren, F. L., & Cao, J. (2007b). Periodic solutions for a class of higher-order Cohen-Grossberg type neural networks with delays. *Computer and Mathematics with Application,54*(6), *826-839.*

Simpson, P. K. (1990). Higher-ordered and intra-connected bidirectional associative memories. *IEEE Transactions on Systems, Man, and Cybernetics, 20*(3), 637-653.

Vidyasagar, M. (1993). *Nonliear Systems Analysis (second edition).* Englewood Cliffs, New Jersey.

Xu, B., Liu, X., & Liao, X. (2003). Global asymptotic stability of high-order Hopfield type neural networks with time delays. *Computers and Mathematics with Applications, 45*(10), 1729-1737.

Yue, D., Xu, S. F., & Liu, Y. Q. (1999). Differential inequality with delay and impulse and its applications to design of robust control. *Control Theory and Applications, 16,* 519-524, (in Chinese).

Zhou, D., & Cao, J. (2002). Globally exponential stability conditions for cellular neural networks with time-varying delays. *Applied Mathematics and Computation, 131,* 487-496.

ADDITIONAL READING

Barbashin, E. A. (1970). *Introduction to the theory of stability.* Walters-Noordhoff.

Boyd, S., Ghaoui, L. E., Feron, E., & Balakrishnan, V. (1994). *Linear matrix inequalities in system and control theory.* SIAM, Philadephia.

Cao, J., Ho, D. W. C., & Huang, X. (2007). LMI-based criteria for global robust stability of bidirectional associative memory networks with time delay. *Nonlinear Analysis, Series A, 66*(7), 1558-1572.

Cao, J., & Song, Q. (2006). Stability in Cohen-Grossberg type BAM neural networks with time-varying delays. *Nonlinearity, 19*(7), 1601-1617.

Cao, J., & Xiao, M. (2007). Stability and Hopf bifurcation in a simplified BAM neural network with two time delays. *IEEE Transactions on Neural Networks, 18*(2), 416-430.

Cao J., Yuan, K., & Li, H. X. (2006). Global asymptotical stability of generalized recurrent neural networks with multiple discrete delays and distributed delays. *IEEE Transactions on Neural Networks, 17*(6), 1646-1651.

Cheng, C. Y., Lin, K. H., & Shih, C. W. (2006). Multistability in recurrent neural networks. *SIAM Journal on Applied Mathematics, 66*(4), 1301-1320.

Gahinet, P., Nemirovski, A., Laub, J., & Chilali, M. (1995). *LMI control toolbox.* [M]. Natick: The Math Works Inc.

Hale, J. K., & Lunel, S. M. V. (1991). *Introduction to functional differential equations.* New York: Springer-Verlag.

Ho, D. W. C., Liang, J., & Lam, J. (2006). Global exponential stability of impulsive high-order BAM neural networks with time-varying delays. *Neural Networks, 19*(10), 1581-1590.

Huang, X., & Cao, J. (2006). Generalized synchronization for delayed chaotic neural networks: a novel coupling scheme. *Nonlinearity, 19*(12), 2797-2811.

Lakshmikantham, V., Bainov, D. D., & Simeonov, P. S. (1989). *Theory of impulsive differential equations.* Singapore: World Scientific.

Sun, Y., & Cao, J. (2007). Adaptive lag synchronization of unknown chaotic delayed neural networks with noise perturbation. *Physics Letters A, 364,* 277-285.

Yuan, K., Cao, J., & Li, H. X. (2006). Robust stability of switched Cohen-Grossberg neural networks with mixed time-varying delays. *IEEE Transactions on Systems, Man, and Cybernetics-B, 36* (6), 1356-1363.

Zeng, Z., & Wang, J. (2006). Multiperiodicity of discrete-time delayed neural networks evoked by periodic external inputs. *IEEE Transactions on Neural Networks, 17*(5), 1141-1151.

Zeng, Z., & Wang, J. (2006). Multiperiodicity and exponential attractivity evoked by periodic external inputs in delayed cellular neural networks. *Neural Computation, 18*(4), 848-870.

Zhang, Y., Tan, K. K., & Lee, T. H. (2003). Multi-stability analysis for recurrent neural networks with unsaturating piecewise linear transfer functions. *Neural Computation, 15*(3), 639-662.

Chapter XIX
A New Topology for Artificial Higher Order Neural Networks:
Polynomial Kernel Networks

Zhao Lu
Tuskegee University, USA

Leang-san Shieh
University of Houston, USA

Guanrong Chen
City University of Hong Kong, China

ABSTRACT

Aiming to develop a systematic approach for optimizing the structure of artificial higher order neural networks (HONN) for system modeling and function approximation, a new HONN topology, namely polynomial kernel network, is proposed in this chapter. Structurally, the polynomial kernel network can be viewed as a three-layer feedforward neural network with a special polynomial activation function for the nodes in the hidden layer. The new network is equivalent to a HONN; however, due to the underlying connections with polynomial kernel support vector machines, the weights and the structure of the network can be determined simultaneously using structural risk minimization. The advantage of the topology of the polynomial kernel network and the use of a support vector kernel expansion pave the way to represent nonlinear functions or systems, and underpins some advanced analysis of the network performance. In this chapter, from the perspective of network complexity, both quadratic programming and linear programming based training of the polynomial kernel network are investigated.

INTRODUCTION

As an important neural processing topology, artificial higher order neural networks (HONNs) have demonstrated great potential for approximating unknown functions and modeling unknown systems (Kosmatopoulos et al., 1995; Kosmatopoulos and Christodoulou, 1997). In particular, HONNs have been adopted as basic modules in the construction of dynamic system identifiers and also controllers for highly uncertain systems (Rovithakis, 1999; Lu et al., 2006). Nevertheless, as an important factor that affects the performance of neural networks, the structure of a network is usually hard to determine appropriately in any specific application. It is possible to reduce modeling errors by increasing the complexity of the network; however, increasing the complexity may overfit the data leading to a degradation of its generalization ability. As a consequence, in practice the choice of network structure is often a compromise between modeling errors and the network complexity. Some efforts have been made in the attempt to determine the optimal topological structure of HONN by using for example genetic algorithms (Rovithakis et al., 2004).

Recently, there has been a trend in the machine learning community to construct a nonlinear version of a linear algorithm using the so-called 'kernel method' (Schölkopf and Smola, 2002; Vert et al., 2004). As a new generation of learning algorithms, the kernel method utilizes techniques from optimization, statistics, and functional analysis to achieve maximal generality, flexibility, and performance. The kernel machine allows high-dimensional inner-product computations to be performed with very little overhead and brings all the benefits of the mature linear estimation theory. Of particular significance is the Support Vector Machine (SVM) that forms an important subject in the learning theory. SVM is derived from statistical learning theory (Evgeniou et al., 2000; Cristianini and Shawe-Taylor, 2000), which is a two-layer network with inputs transformed by the kernels corresponding to a subset of the input data, while its output is a linear function of the weights and kernels. The weights and the structure of the SVM are obtained simultaneously by a constrained minimization at a given precision level of the modeling errors. For all these reasons, the kernel methods have become more and more popular as an alternative to neural-network approaches. However, due to the fact that SVM is basically a non-parametric technique, its effective use in dynamical systems and control theory remains to be seen.

Actually, SVM includes a number of heuristic algorithms as special cases. The relationships between SVM and radial basis function (RBF) networks, neuro-fuzzy networks and multilayer perceptron have been accentuated and utilized for developing new learning algorithms (Chan et al., 2001; Chan et al., 2002; Suykens and Vandewalle, 1999). Of particular interest is a recent observation that Wiener and Volterra theories, which extend the standard convolution description of linear systems by a series of polynomial integral operators with increasing degrees of nonlinearity, can be put into a kernel regression framework (Franz and Schölkopf, 2006).

Inspired by the unifying view of Weiner and Volterra theories and polynomial kernel regression, provided by (Franz and Schölkopf, 2006), and by the fact that the Wiener expansion decomposes a signal according to the order of interaction of its input elements, in this chapter a new topology for HONN, called the polynomial kernel network, is proposed and investigated, which bridges the gap between the parametric HONN model and the non-parametric support vector regression model.

Structurally, the polynomial kernel network can be viewed as a three-layer feedforward neural network with a special polynomial activation function for the nodes in the hidden layer. Due to the equivalence between the proposed polynomial kernel network and the support vector machine with an inhomogeneous polynomial kernel, the training for a polynomial kernel network can be carried out under the framework of structural risk minimization, which results in an excellent generalization capability. In contrast to other kernels, polynomial kernel solutions can be directly transformed into their corresponding Wiener or Volterra representation. Many entries in Volterra kernels, for instance, have a direct interpretation in signal processing applications, but this nice interpretability is lost when other kernels are used.

Throughout this chapter, lower case symbols such as x, y, α,... refer to scalar-valued objects, lower case boldfaced symbols such as $\boldsymbol{x}$, $\boldsymbol{y}$, $\boldsymbol{\beta}$,... refer to vector-valued objects, and finally capital symbols will be used for matrices.

POLYNOMIAL KERNEL NETWORKS

It is well known that using a kernel function in an SVM aims at effectively computing the dot-product in a space. A kernel, capable of representing a dot-product in a space, has to satisfy Mercer's condition, namely, for all square-integrable functions $g(\boldsymbol{x})$ the real-valued kernel function $k(\boldsymbol{x},\boldsymbol{y})$ has to satisfy $\iint k(\boldsymbol{x},\boldsymbol{y})g(\boldsymbol{x})g(\boldsymbol{y})d\boldsymbol{x}d\boldsymbol{y} \geq 0$. It is also well known that Mercer's condition only tells whether or not a prospective kernel is actually a dot product in a given space, but it does not tell how to construct the feature mapping and the images of the input examples in the mapping feature space, not even what the high-dimensional feature space is. Although the construction of the feature mapping cannot be done in general, one can still construct the mapping and form the feature space for the case of a simple kernel. For instance, with a homogeneous polynomial kernel, one can explicitly construct the mapping and show that the corresponding space is just a Euclidean space of dimension C^d_{d+n-1} (the combinatorial of choosing d from d + n − 1), where d is the degree of the homogeneous polynomial and

n is the dimension of the input space. Therefore, by applying a kernel function in place of the dot product, one is able to obtain an SVM rather than unnecessarily constructing the feature mapping explicitly related to the kernel function, which is obviously advantageous.

Polynomial Kernel and Product Feature Space

According to Mercer's condition, one has several possibilities for choosing this kernel function, including linear, polynomial, spline, RBF, etc., among which homogeneous and inhomogeneous polynomials are popular choices:

$$k_{poly1}(\boldsymbol{x},\boldsymbol{x}_i) = \langle \boldsymbol{x},\boldsymbol{x}_i \rangle^d \qquad (1)$$

$$k_{poly2}(\boldsymbol{x},\boldsymbol{x}_i) = (\langle \boldsymbol{x},\boldsymbol{x}_i \rangle + 1)^d \qquad (2)$$

where $d \geq 0$ is the degree of the polynomial and the inner product is defined by $\langle \boldsymbol{x},\boldsymbol{x}_i \rangle = \boldsymbol{x}^T \boldsymbol{x}_i$. The inhomogeneous kernel is usually preferable as it can avoid technical problem with the Hessian becoming zero.

The feature space induced by the kernel was defined as the space spanned by $\{(\varphi_p(\boldsymbol{x}))_{p=1}^m, \boldsymbol{x} \in R^n\}$ that is, the feature space where the data $\boldsymbol{x}$ are "mapped" was determined by the choice of the φ_p functions. Specifically, the polynomial kernel k_{poly1} of degree 2 corresponds to a feature space spanned by all products of 2 variables, that is, $\{x_1^2, x_1x_2, x_2^2\}$. It is easy to see that the kernel k_{poly2} of degree 2 corresponds to a feature space spanned by all products of at most 2 variables; that is, $\{1, x_1, x_2, x_1^2, x_1x_2, x_2^2\}$. More generally, the kernel k_{poly1} corresponds to a feature space whose dimensions are spanned by all possible dth-order monomials in input coordinates, and all the different dimensions are scaled with the square root of the number of ordered products of the respective d entries.

The feature map induced by the homogeneous polynomial kernel can be characterized by the following theorem:

Theorem 1: (Schölkopf and Smola, 2002). The feature map induced by the homogeneous polynomial kernel $k_{poly1}(x,x') = \langle x,x'\rangle^d$ can be defined coordinate-wise by:

$$\varphi_p(x) = \sqrt{\frac{d!}{\prod_{i=1}^{n} p_i!}} \prod_{i=1}^{n} x_i^{p_i} \tag{3}$$

for every $p = (p_1,p_2,...,p_n) \in \mathbb{N}^n$ and $\sum_{i=1}^{n} p_i = d$.

On the other hand, the inhomogeneous kernel k_{poly2} can be expanded by using the multinomial formula, as:

$$\left(\langle x,x_i\rangle + 1\right)^d = \sum_{j=0}^{d} C_d^j \langle x,x_i\rangle^j \tag{4}$$

which is a linear combination of the homogeneous polynomial kernel with positive coefficients, resulting in a feature space spanned by all monomials up to degree d, and the dimension of the induced feature space is:

$$\sum_{j=0}^{d} C_{d+j+1}^j$$

Often, these monomials are referred to as *product features*, and the corresponding feature space as *product features space*. Evidently, the dimension of the feature space is equal to the number of basis elements φ_p, which does not necessarily have to be finite. For example, when the kernel k is a Gaussian, the dimension of the feature space is infinite, while when the kernel k is a polynomial of degree d, the dimension of the feature space is finite.

A New Topology for HONN: Polynomial Kernel Network

HONN is a fully interconnected network, containing high-order connections of sigmoid functions in its neurons. Defining by x, y its input and output,

respectively, with $x \in R^n$ and $y \in R$, the input-output representation of the HONN is ruled by:

$$y = w^T s(x) \tag{5}$$

where w is an L–dimensional vector of the adjustable synaptic weights and $s(x)$ is an L–dimensional vector with elements $s_i(x)$, $i = 1,2,...,L$, of the form:

$$s_i(x) = \prod_{j \in I_i} \left[s(x_j) \right]^{d_j(i)} \tag{6}$$

where I_i, $i = 1,2,...,L$, are collections of L unordered subsets of $\{1,2,...,n\}$ and $d_j(i)$ are nonnegative integers. In equation (6), $s(x_j)$ is a monotone increasing smooth function, which is usually represented by sigmoidals of the form:

$$s(x_j) = \frac{\mu}{1 + e^{-l(x_j - c)}} + \lambda, j = 1,2,...,n \tag{7}$$

In equation (7), the parameters μ, l represent the bound and the maximum slope of the sigmoidal curvature and λ, c, the vertical and horizontal shifts, respectively.

For the HONN model described above, it is known (Rovithakis and Christodoulou, 2000) that there exist integers L, $d_j(i)$ and optimal weight values w^*, such that for any smooth unknown function $f(x)$ and for any given $\varepsilon > 0$, one has $|f(x) - w^{*T} s(x)| \le \varepsilon$, $\forall x \in \mathbb{Z}$, where $\mathbb{Z} \subset R^n$ is a known compact region. In other words, for sufficiently high-order terms, there exist weight values w^* such that the HONN structure $w^{*T} s(x)$ can approximate $f(x)$ to any degree of accuracy over a compact domain.

In an attempt to develop a kernel-based network architecture equivalent to HONN, a kernel capable to induce the feature map equivalent to equation (6) needs to be first determined. Inspired by the similarity between the monomial features in equation (3) and the high-order connections of sigmoid functions described by equation (6), a variation of the inhomogeneous polynomial kernel is chosen below, in order to induce a feature map consisting of the monomials of sigmoidals:

$$k(\boldsymbol{x}, \boldsymbol{x}_i) = k_{ploy2}(s(\boldsymbol{x}), s(\boldsymbol{x}_i)) = (\langle s(\boldsymbol{x}), s(\boldsymbol{x}_i) \rangle + 1)^d \tag{8}$$

The following theorem guarantees the positive definiteness of the kernel shown in (8).

Theorem 2: (Schölkopf and Smola, 2002). If $\sigma: X \to X$ is a bijection mapping (a transformation which is one-to-one and onto), and if $k(x, x_i)$ is a kernel, then $k(\sigma(x), \sigma(x_i))$ is also a kernel.

Obviously, the sigmoid function given by equation (7) is a bijection mapping; therefore, the $k(x, x_i)$ in equation (8) is a kernel. It then follows from Theorem 1 that the feature map induced by kernel (8) corresponds to the scaled high-order connections of sigmoid functions. Hence, a new three-layer network topology equivalent to HONN, called the polynomial kernel network, can be defined as follows:

- Input-layer: $\boldsymbol{net}^1 = s(\boldsymbol{x})$, where $\boldsymbol{x}$ is the input vector
- Hidden-layer: $net_j^2 = (1 + s(\boldsymbol{x}_j)^T \boldsymbol{net}^1)^d$, where $s(\boldsymbol{x}_j)$ is the weights vector connecting the jth node in the hidden layer to the input-layer, and $\boldsymbol{x}_j$ is the selected training point; $[s(\boldsymbol{x}_1), \cdots, s(\boldsymbol{x}_h)]^T$ is the interconnection matrix, where h is the number of hidden nodes.
- Output-layer: $y = \boldsymbol{\beta}^T \boldsymbol{net}^2 = \sum_{i=1}^{h} \beta_i net_i^2$

   where $\boldsymbol{net}^2 = [net_1^2, \cdots, net_h^2]^T$ and $\boldsymbol{\beta} = [\beta_1, \ldots, \beta_h]$ is the weight vector of the output layer

In summary, the mathematical representation of a polynomial kernel network is:

$$y = \sum_{i=1}^{h} \beta_i (1 + s(\boldsymbol{x}_j)^T s(\boldsymbol{x}))^d = \sum_{i=1}^{h} \beta_i k_{poly2}(s(\boldsymbol{x}), s(\boldsymbol{x}_j)) \tag{9}$$

The main advantage of this polynomial kernel network over HONN lies in the availability of systematic learning methods for determining its optimal topological structure and weights using structural risk minimization. Learning algorithms based on quadratic programming and linear programming will be discussed respectively in the following two sections.

DETERMINING THE OPTIMAL TOPOLOGICAL STRUCTURE OF POLYNOMIAL KERNEL NETWORKS VIA QUADRATIC PROGRAMMING

Formulation of Quadratic Programming Support Vector Regression

In this section, basic ideas of the conventional quadratic programming support vector method for function approximation, that is, quadratic programming support vector regression (QP-SVR), are first reviewed.

SVR fits a continuous-valued function to data in a way that shares many of the advantages of support vector machine classification. Consider regression in the following set of functions:

$$f(\boldsymbol{x}) = \boldsymbol{w}^T \varphi(\boldsymbol{x}) + b \tag{10}$$

with given training data $\{(\boldsymbol{x}_1, y_1), \ldots, (\boldsymbol{x}_\ell, y_\ell)\}$, where ℓ denotes the total number of exemplars, $\boldsymbol{x}_i \in R^n$ are the input, $y_i \in R$ are the target output data, the nonlinear mapping $\varphi: R^n \to R^m$ $(m > n)$ maps the input data into a high- or infinite-dimensional feature space, and $\boldsymbol{w} \in R^m$, $b \in R$. In ε–SV regression (Smola and Schölkopf, 2004), the goal is to find a function $f(\boldsymbol{x})$ that has at most ε deviation from the actually obtained targets y_i for all the training data, and at the same time is as flat as possible. In the support vector method, one aims at minimizing the empirical risk subject to elements of the structure:

minimize $\quad \dfrac{1}{2}\|w\|^2$

subject to $\quad \begin{cases} y_i - \langle w, \varphi(x_i) \rangle - b \le \varepsilon \\ \langle w, \varphi(x_i) \rangle + b - y_i \le \varepsilon \end{cases}$

$$(11)$$

Similarly to the "soft margin" loss function, which is used in support vector classifiers, the slack variables ζ_i and ζ_i^* correspond to the sizes of the excess deviations for positive and negative deviations, respectively, and they can be introduced to cope with otherwise infeasible constraints of the optimization problem (11). Hence, one has the following formulation:

minimize $\quad \dfrac{1}{2}\|w\|^2 + C\sum_{i=1}^{\ell}(\zeta_i + \zeta_i^*)$

subject to $\begin{cases} y_i - \langle w, \varphi(x_i) \rangle - b \le \varepsilon + \zeta_i \\ \langle w \;\; \varphi(x_i) \rangle + b - y_i \le \varepsilon + \zeta_i^* \\ \qquad \zeta_i, \zeta_i^* \ge 0 \end{cases}$

$$(12)$$

This is a classical quadratic optimization problem with inequality constraints, and the optimization criterion penalizes the data points whose y–values differ from $f(x)$ by more than ε. The constant $C > 0$ determines the trade-off between the flatness of f and the amount up to which deviations larger than ε are tolerated, and the ε-insensitive zone is usually called as ε-tube.

Introducing the Lagrange multipliers $\boldsymbol{\alpha}$, $\boldsymbol{\alpha}^*$, $\boldsymbol{\eta}$ and $\boldsymbol{\eta}^*$, one can write the corresponding Lagrangian, as:

$$L = \frac{1}{2}\|w\|^2 + C\sum_{i=1}^{\ell}(\zeta_i + \zeta_i^*) - \sum_{i=1}^{\ell}(\eta_i \zeta_i + \eta_i^* \zeta_i^*)$$

$$- \sum_{i=1}^{\ell}\alpha_i(\varepsilon + \zeta_i - y_i + \langle w, \varphi(x_i) \rangle + b)$$

$$- \sum_{i=1}^{\ell}\alpha_i^*(\varepsilon + \zeta_i^* + y_i - \langle w, \varphi(x_i) \rangle - b)$$

$$(13)$$

$s.\ t.\ \ \alpha_i, \alpha_i^*, \eta_i, \eta_i^* \ge 0$

It follows from the saddle-point condition that the partial derivatives of L with respect to the primal variables $(w, b, \zeta_i, \zeta_i^*)$ have to vanish for optimality:

$$\partial_b L = \sum_{i=1}^{\ell}(\alpha_i^* - \alpha_i) = 0$$

$$(14)$$

$$\partial_w L = w - \sum_{i=1}^{\ell}(\alpha_i - \alpha_i^*)\varphi(x_i) = 0$$

$$(15)$$

$$\partial_\zeta L = C - \alpha_i - \eta_i = 0$$

$$(16)$$

$$\partial_{\zeta^*} L = C - \alpha_i^* - \eta_i^* = 0$$

$$(17)$$

Substituting (14–17) into (13) yields the following dual optimization problem shown in equation (18). It can be inferred from equation (15) that:

$$w = \sum_{i=1}^{\ell}(\alpha_i - \alpha_i^*)\varphi(x_i)$$

$$(19)$$

where α_i, α_i^* are obtained by solving the quadratic programming problem (18). The data points corresponding to non-zero values of $(\alpha_i - \alpha_i^*)$ are called *support vectors*. Typically, many of these

Equation (18).

---

maxmize $\quad -\dfrac{1}{2}\sum_{i,j=1}^{\ell}(\alpha_i - \alpha_i^*)(\alpha_j - \alpha_j^*)\langle\varphi(x_i), \varphi(x_j)\rangle - \varepsilon\sum_{i=1}^{\ell}(\alpha_i - \alpha_i^*) + \sum_{i=1}^{\ell}y_i(\alpha_i - \alpha_i^*)$

subject to $\quad \sum_{i=1}^{\ell}(\alpha_i - \alpha_i^*) = 0 \quad$ and $\quad \alpha_i, \alpha_i^* \in [0, C]$

---

values are equal to zero. Finally, by substituting (19) into (10), the function $f(x)$ can be expressed in the dual space as:

$$f(\boldsymbol{x}) = \sum_{i=1}^{l} (\alpha_i - \alpha_i^*) k(\boldsymbol{x}, \boldsymbol{x}_i) + b = \sum_{i \in SV} (\alpha_i - \alpha_i^*) k(\boldsymbol{x}, \boldsymbol{x}_i) + b$$

(20)

where SV is the set of support vectors and the kernel function k corresponds to:

$$k(\boldsymbol{x}, \boldsymbol{x}_i) = \langle \varphi(\boldsymbol{x}), \varphi(\boldsymbol{x}_i) \rangle \qquad (21)$$

Support vector learning algorithms yield the prediction functions that are expanded on a subset of training vectors, or support vectors, which gave their names.

Note that the complete algorithm consisting of the optimization problem (18) and regression function (20) can be presented in terms of inner products between data. If the kernel (8) is used for support vector learning, equation (20) can be written as:

$$f(\boldsymbol{x}) = \sum_{i \in SV} \beta_i \left(\langle s(\boldsymbol{x}), s(\boldsymbol{x}_i) \rangle + 1 \right)^d + b \qquad (22)$$

$$\beta_i = \alpha_i - \alpha_i^*$$

which corresponds to a mathematical representation of the polynomial kernel network given by equation (9).

Obviously, the selection of the support vectors plays a crucial role in determining the complexity of equation (22), hence the topological structure of the polynomial kernel network: the number of nodes in the hidden-layer h is specified by the cardinal number of the support vector set $|SV|$, and the interconnection matrix $[s(\boldsymbol{x}_1),...,s(\boldsymbol{x}_h)]^T$ is also assigned by the sigmoid transformation of the selected support vectors. Further, the weight vector of the output layer is given by the coefficients of the kernel expansion, that is, $\boldsymbol{\beta} = [\beta_1,...,\beta_h]^T$.

Networks Complexity and the Sparsity of QP-SVR

Apparently, the form of the prediction function (22) determines the complexity of the corresponding polynomial kernel network. Notice also that in the conventional quadratic programming support vector learning scheme, the prediction function often contains redundant terms. The complexity or simplicity of an SVM prediction function depends on a sparse subset of the training data being selected as support vectors by an optimization technique. In many practical applications, the inefficiency of the conventional SVM scheme for selecting support vectors can be more crucial, as witnessed by those regression applications where the entire training set can be selected if error insensitivity is not included (Drezet and Harrison, 2001).

A recent study has compared standard support vector learning and the uniformly regularized orthogonal least squares (UROLS) algorithms by using time series predictions, leading to the finding that both methods have similar excellent generalization performance but the resulting model from SVM is not sparse enough (Lee and Billings, 2002). It is explained that the number of support vectors found by the quadratic programming support vector learning algorithm is only an upper bound on the number of necessary and sufficient support vectors, and the reason for this effect is the linear dependence among the support vectors in the feature space. For linear approximation, it has been pointed out (Ancona, 1999) that the solution found by SVM for regression is a tradeoff between the sparsity of the representation and the closeness to the data. SVM extends this linear interpretation to nonlinear approximation by mapping into a higher-dimensional feature space. Some efforts have been made attempting to control the sparsity in support vector machines (Drezet and Harrison, 2001).

Among a number of successful applications of SVM in practice, it has been shown (Rojo-

Alvarez et al., 2006; Drezet and Harrison, 1998) that the use of a support vector kernel expansion also provides a potential avenue to represent non-linear functions or systems and underpin some advanced analysis. Although it is believed that the formulation of SVM embodies the structural risk minimization principle, thus combining excellent generalization properties with a sparse model representation, data modeling practitioners have begun to realize that the capability of the standard quadratic programming SVR (QP-SVR) method in producing sparse models has perhaps been overstated. For example, it has been shown that the standard SVM technique is not always able to construct parsimonious models in nonlinear systems identification (Drezet and Harrison, 1998).

In the scenario of constructing a polynomial kernel network, the sparsity in model representation is crucial due to its important role in determining the complexity of the network. Due to the distinct mechanism for selecting support vectors from the QP-SVR, linear programming support vector regression (LP-SVR) is advantageous over QP-SVR in model sparsity, an ability to use more general kernel functions and achieve fast learning based on linear programming (Kecman, 2001; Hadzic and Kecman, 2000). The idea of LP-SVM is to use the kernel expansion as an ansatz for the solution, but to use a different regularizer, namely the ℓ_1 norm of the coefficient vector. In other words, for LP-SVR, the nonlinear regression problem is treated as a linear one in kernel space, rather than in feature space as in the case of QP-SVR.

DETERMINING THE OPTIMAL TOPOLOGICAL STRUCTURE OF POLYNOMIAL KERNEL NETWORKS VIA LINEAR PROGRAMMING

Conceptually, there are some similarities between LP-SVR and QP-SVR. Both algorithms adopt the

ε-insensitive loss function and use kernel functions in their feature spaces.

Consider formulation (12) for soft-margin QP-SVR, with the loss function defined by

$$L(y_i - f(\boldsymbol{x}_i)) = \begin{cases} 0, & if \ |y_i - f(\boldsymbol{x}_i)| \le \varepsilon \\ |y_i - f(\boldsymbol{x}_i)| - \varepsilon, & otherwise \end{cases}$$

$$(23)$$

The optimization problem (12) is equivalent to the following regularization problem:

$$minimize \ R_{reg}[f] = \sum_{i=1}^{\ell} L(y_i - f(\boldsymbol{x}_i)) + \lambda \|w\|^2$$

$$(24)$$

where $f(\boldsymbol{x})$ is in the form of (10) and $\lambda \|w\|^2$ is the regularization term. According to the celebrated *Representer Theorem* (Schölkopf and Smola, 2002), an explicit form of the solution to the regularization problem (24) can be obtained and expressed by the following SV kernel expansion:

$$f(\boldsymbol{x}) = \sum_{i=1}^{\ell} \beta_i k(\boldsymbol{x}_i, \boldsymbol{x})$$

$$(25)$$

where $k(x_i, x)$ is the kernel function. The significance of the Representer Theorem is that although one might try to solve an optimization problem in an infinite-dimensional space, containing linear combinations of kernels centered at some arbitrary points, it points out that the solution lies in the span of ℓ particular kernels — those centered at the training points. By defining:

$$\boldsymbol{\beta} = [\beta_1 \ \beta_2 \cdots \beta_\ell]^T.$$

the LP-SVR replaces (24) by:

$$minimize \ R_{reg}[f] = \sum_{i=1}^{\ell} L(y_i - f(\boldsymbol{x}_i)) + \lambda \|\boldsymbol{\beta}\|_1$$

$$(26)$$

where $f(\boldsymbol{x})$ is in the form of (25) and $\|\boldsymbol{\beta}\|_1$ denotes the ℓ_1 norm in the coefficient space. This regularization problem is equivalent to the following constrained optimization problem:

$$minimize \quad \frac{1}{2}\|\boldsymbol{\beta}\|_1 + C\sum_{i=1}^{\ell}(\xi_i + \xi_i^*)$$

$$subject\ to \quad \begin{cases} y_i - \sum_{j=1}^{\ell}\beta_j k(\boldsymbol{x}_j,\boldsymbol{x}_i) \le \varepsilon +\xi_i \\ \sum_{j=1}^{\ell}\beta_j k(\boldsymbol{x}_j,\boldsymbol{x}_i) - y_i \le \varepsilon +\xi_i^* \\ \xi_i,\ \xi_i^* \ge 0 \end{cases}$$

$$(27)$$

From the geometric perspective, it follows that $\xi_i\xi_i^* = 0$ in the SV regression. Therefore, it suffices to introduce a slack ξ_i in the constrained optimization problem (27), thus arriving at the following formulation of SV regression with fewer slack variables:

$$minimize \quad \frac{1}{2}\|\boldsymbol{\beta}\|_1 + 2C\sum_{i=1}^{\ell}\xi_i$$

$$subject\ to \quad \begin{cases} y_i - \sum_{j=1}^{\ell}\beta_j k(\boldsymbol{x}_j,\boldsymbol{x}_i) \le \varepsilon +\xi_i \\ \sum_{j=1}^{\ell}\beta_j k(\boldsymbol{x}_j,\boldsymbol{x}_i) - y_i \le \varepsilon +\xi_i \\ \xi_i \ge 0 \end{cases}$$

$$(28)$$

To convert the above optimization problem into a linear programming problem, one may decompose β_i and $|\beta_i|$ as follows:

$$\beta_i = \alpha_i^+ - \alpha_i^-,\ |\beta_i| = \alpha_i^+ + \alpha_i^- \qquad (29)$$

where $\alpha_i^+, \alpha_i^- \ge 0$.

It is worth noting that the decompositions in (29) are unique, i.e., for a given β_i there is only one pair (α_i^+, α_i^-) that fulfils both equations. Note also that both variables cannot be larger than zero at the same time, that is, $\alpha_i^+ \cdot \alpha_i^- = 0$. In this way, the ℓ_1 norm of β can be written as:

$$\|\boldsymbol{\beta}\|_1 = \left(\underbrace{1,\ 1,\ \cdots,1}_{\ell},\ \underbrace{1,\ 1,\ \cdots,1}_{\ell}\right)\begin{pmatrix}\boldsymbol{\alpha}^+ \\ \boldsymbol{\alpha}^-\end{pmatrix} \qquad (30)$$

where $\boldsymbol{\alpha}^+ = (\alpha_1^+, \alpha_2^+, \cdots, \alpha_\ell^+)^T$ and $\boldsymbol{\alpha}^- = (\alpha_1^-, \alpha_2^-, ..., \alpha_\ell^-)^T$. Furthermore, the constraints in the formulation (28) can also be written in the following vector form:

$$\begin{pmatrix} K & -K & -I \\ -K & K & -I \end{pmatrix} \cdot \begin{pmatrix}\boldsymbol{\alpha}^+ \\ \boldsymbol{\alpha}^- \\ \boldsymbol{\xi}\end{pmatrix} \le \begin{pmatrix} y+\varepsilon \\ \varepsilon - y \end{pmatrix} \qquad (31)$$

where $K_{ij} = k(x_i, x_j)$, $\boldsymbol{\xi} = (\xi_1,\xi_2,...,\xi_\ell)^T$, and I is the $\ell \times \ell$ identity matrix. Thus, the constrained optimization problem (28) can be implemented by the following linear programming problem:

$$minimize \quad c^T \begin{pmatrix}\boldsymbol{\alpha}^+ \\ \boldsymbol{\alpha}^- \\ \boldsymbol{\xi}\end{pmatrix}$$

$$subject\ to \quad \begin{pmatrix} K & -K & -I \\ -K & K & -I \end{pmatrix} \cdot \begin{pmatrix}\boldsymbol{\alpha}^+ \\ \boldsymbol{\alpha}^- \\ \boldsymbol{\xi}\end{pmatrix} \le \begin{pmatrix} y+\varepsilon \\ \varepsilon - y \end{pmatrix}$$

$$(32)$$

where:

$$c = \left(\underbrace{1,\ 1,\ \cdots,\ 1}_{\ell},\ \underbrace{1,\ 1,\ \cdots,\ 1}_{\ell},\ \underbrace{2C,\ 2C,\ \cdots,\ 2C}_{\ell}\right)^T$$

In the QP-SVR case, a squared penalty on the coefficients α_i has the disadvantage that even though some kernel functions $k(x_i,x)$ may not contribute much to the overall solution, they still appear in the function expansion. This is due to the fact that the gradient of α_i^2 tends to 0 as $\alpha_i \to 0$. On the other hand, a regularizer whose derivative does not vanish in the neighborhood of 0 will not exhibit such a problem. This is why the sparsity of the solution could be greatly improved in LP-SVR.

Geometrically, for QP-SVR, the set of points not inside the tube coincides with the set of SVs. However within the LP context, this is no longer true—although the solution is still sparse, any point could be an SV even if it is inside the tube (Smola et al., 1999). Actually, a sparse solution can still be obtained in LP-SVR, even though the size of the insensitive tube was set to zero due to the soft constraints used (Drezet and Harrison, 2001). But usually a more sparse solution can be obtained by using a non-zero ε.

CONCLUSION

In this chapter, by introducing a new kernel function as a variation of the inhomogeneous polynomial kernel, a connection between HONN and kernel machines is established. From the equivalence between high-order connections of sigmoid functions in HONN and the product feature space induced by the kernel function, a new topology for HONN—polynomial kernel network—is proposed and analyzed, which enables in a systematic way to determine the network structure and the connecting weights based on the idea of structural risk minimization.

To reduce the complexity of the networks and to represent the nonlinear functions or systems in a compact form, QP-SVR based and LP-SVR based training algorithms have been discussed respectively. Of particular importance is their roles and mechanisms in selecting support vectors and in generating sparse approximation models, which have also been analyzed and compared.

FUTURE RESEARCH OUTLOOK

Although this chapter discusses high-order neural networks and the polynomial kernel network mainly in the context of nonlinear function or system approximation, the product feature associated with them has proven quite effective in visual pattern recognition, among others. Visual patterns are usually represented as vectors with entries being pixel intensities. Taking products of the entries of these vectors therefore corresponds to taking products of pixel intensities, which is akin to taking logical "and" operations on the pixels. Clearly, future research along this direction may include investigation of the potential of the polynomial kernel network in the realm of visual pattern recognition. For applications of HONN in pattern recognition, some references were given in the section of additional reading.

On the other hand, the fact that the proposed polynomial kernel network is parameterized by the interconnection matrix and output layer weights enables the development of some effective on-line training algorithms, where the training may comprise two phases: firstly the topological structure and initial weights of the polynomial kernel networks can be assigned by SV learning algorithm; then on-line training methods can be developed for updating the network weights.

REFERENCES

Ancona, N. (1999). *Properties of support vector machines for regression*. Tech. Report, Cambridge, MA: Massachusetts Institute of Technology, Center for Biological and Computational Learning.

Chan, W. C., Chan, C. W., Cheung, K. C., & Harris, C. J. (2001). On the modelling of nonlinear dynamic systems using support vector neural networks. *Engineering Applications of Artificial Intelligence, 14*, 105-113.

Chan, W. C., Chan, C. W., Jayawardena, A.W., & Harris, C. J. (2002). Structure selection of neurofuzzy networks based on support vector regression. *International Journal of Systems Science, 33*, 715-722.

Cristianini, N., & Shawe-Taylor, J. (2000). *An introduction to support vector machines and other kernel-based learning methods.* Cambridge, UK: Cambridge University Press.

Drezet, P. M. L., & Harrison, R. F. (2001). A new method for sparsity control in support vector classification and regression. *Pattern Recognition, 34,* 111-125.

Drezet, P.M.L., & Harrison, R. F. (1998). Support vector machines for system identification. *UKACC International Conference on Control.*

Evgeniou, T., Pontil, M., & Poggio, T. (2000). Statistical learning theory: A primer. *International Journal Computer Vision, 38,* 9-13.

Franz, M. O., & Schölkopf, B. (2006). A unifying view of Wiener and Volterra theory and polynomial kernel regression. *Neural Computation, 18,* 3097-3118.

Hadzic, I., & Kecman, V. (2000). Support vector machines trained by linear programming: Theory and application in image compression and data classification. In *IEEE 5th Seminar on Neural Network Applications in Electrical Engineering.*

Kecman, V. (2001). *Learning and soft computing: Support vector machines, neural networks, and fuzzy logic models.* Cambridge, MA: MIT Press.

Kosmatopoulos, E. B., & Christodoulou, M. A. (1997). High-order neural networks for the learning of robot contact surface shape. *IEEE Trans. Robotics and Automation, 13,* 451-455.

Kosmatopoulos, E. B., Polycarpou, M. M., Christodoulou, M. A., & Ioannou, P. A. (1995). High-order neural network structures for identification of dynamical systems. *IEEE Trans. Neural Networks, 6,* 422-431.

Lee, K. L., & Billings, S. A. (2002). Time series prediction using support vector machines, the orthogonal and the regularized orthogonal le-ast-squares algorithms. *International Journal of Systems Science, 33,* 811-821.

Lu, Z., Shieh, L. S., Chen, G., & Coleman, N. P. (2006). Adaptive feedback linearization control of chaotic systems via recurrent high-order neural networks. *Information Sciences, 176,* 2337-2354.

Rojo-Alvarez, J. L., Martinez-Ramon, M., Prado-Cumplido, M., Artes-Rodriguez, A., & Figueiras-Vidal, A.R. (2006). Support vector machines for nonlinear kernel ARMA system identification. *IEEE Trans. on Neural Networks, 17,* 1617-1622.

Rovithakis, G. A. (1999). Robustifying nonlinear systems using high-order neural network controllers. *IEEE Trans. Automatic Control, 44,* 102-108.

Rovithakis, G. A., & Christodoulou, M. A. (2000). *Adaptive control with recurrent high-order neural networks.* Berlin, Germany: Springer-Verlag.

Rovithakis, G. A., Chalkiadakis, I., & Zervakis, M. E. (2004). High-order neural network structure selection for function approximation applications using genetic algorithms. *IEEE Trans. Systems, Man and Cybernetics, 34,* 150-158.

Schölkopf, B., & Smola, A. J. (2002). *Learning with kernels: Support vector machines, regularization, optimization, and beyond.* Cambridge, MA: MIT Press.

Smola, A. J., & Schölkopf, B. (2004). A tutorial on support vector regression. *Statistics and Computing, 14,* 199-222.

Smola, A. J., Schölkopf, B., & Rätsch, G. (1999). Linear programs for automatic accuracy control in regression. In *9th International Conference on Artificial Neural Networks* (pp. 575–580), London.

Suykens, J. A. K., & Vandewalle, J. (1999). Training multilayer perceptron classifiers based on a modified support vector method. *IEEE Trans. Neural Networks*, *10*, 907-911.

Vert, J. P., Tsuda, K., & Schölkopf, B. (2004). A primer on kernel methods. In J. P. Vert, K. Tsuda, B. Schölkopf (Ed.), *Kernel methods in computational biology* (pp. 35-70). Cambridge, MA: MIT Press.

ADDITIONAL READING

Pandya, A.S., & Uwechue, O.A. (1997). *Human face recognition using third-order synthetic neural networks*. Kluwer Academic Publishing.

Zhang, S. J., Jing, Z. L., & Li, J. X. (2004). Fast learning high-order neural networks for pattern recognition. *Electronics Letters*, *40*(19), 1207-1208.

Chapter XX
High Speed Optical Higher Order Neural Networks for Discovering Data Trends and Patterns in Very Large Databases

David R. Selviah
University College London, UK

ABSTRACT

This chapter describes the progress in using optical technology to construct high-speed artificial higher order neural network systems. The chapter reviews how optical technology can speed up searches within large databases in order to identify relationships and dependencies between individual data records, such as financial or business time-series, as well as trends and relationships within them. Two distinct approaches in which optics may be used are reviewed. In the first approach, the chapter reviews current research replacing copper connections in a conventional data storage system, such as a several terabyte RAID array of magnetic hard discs, by optical waveguides to achieve very high data rates with low crosstalk interference. In the second approach, the chapter reviews how high speed optical correlators with feedback can be used to realize artificial higher order neural networks using Fourier Transform free space optics and holographic database storage.

INTRODUCTION

The problem of searching very large financial or business databases consisting of many variables and the way they have previously changed over time in order to discover relationships between them is difficult and time consuming. One example of this type of problem would be to analyze, the movements of specific equity share values based on how they depend on other variables and, hence, to predict their future behavior. Trends and patterns need to be found within the time-series of the variable. In addition, the relationships and dependencies between the changes in the time-series of the chosen variable and other time-series need to be found bearing in mind that there may be time lags between them. For example, the value of a specific equity share may depend on the time history of other shares, the oil price, the exchange rates, the bank base interest rates, economic variables such as the UK retail prices index (RPI), UK consumer prices index (CPI), the mortgage rates. It may also depend on the weather behavior, the occurrence of natural and manmade disasters and tax and import duty changes. When the time history of all of these variables and many more for all countries is stored it results in a very large database which is slow to search and analyze.

Several terabyte RAID arrays of magnetic hard discs mounted in racks are in demand for storage and backup of crucial financial, business and medical data and to archive all internet web pages and internet traffic. Very impressive simulations of 8 million neurons with 6,300 synapses in the 1 TB main memory on an IBM Blue Gene L supercomputer having 4,096 processors each having 256 MB have recently been reported (Frye, 2007). However, the demand is for similar fast performance at somewhat lower cost and in a more compact system for office use. The speed at which very large databases can be searched is also becoming limited by the speed at which the copper interconnections on the printed circuit boards inside the racks can operate. As speeds approach 10 Gb/s (10,000,000,000 bits per second) the copper tracks act as aerials and broadcast microwaves to each other causing so much cross-talk interference that the systems cannot operate. The radiated signal also causes power loss so the signal cannot travel very far (Grözing, 2006). In addition, the square shaped pulses transmitted degrade due to dispersion and limited bandwidth of the copper tracks so that the emerging pulse is

spread in time interfering with adjacent bits causing intersymbol interference (ISI). The solution here is to use optical technology as optical beams can travel next to one another without significant crosstalk interference and suffer much less loss and signal degradation. This solution is discussed in the first part of the chapter in which the copper tracks are replaced by optical waveguides, rather like optical fibers, but more amenable to mass manufacturing as part of the printed circuit board fabrication process.

Artificial Higher Order Neural Networks are particularly good at discovering trends, patterns, and relationships between values of a variable at one time and values of the same variable at another time. This is because they multiply elements of the input data, time-series, vector together to identify correlations and dependencies between the different elements. This may be carried out directly before entering the data into a neural network or may be performed by appropriate hidden layer neurons in the network. In either case, the main problem of Artificial Higher Order Neural Networks is that the number of possible element combinations increases much faster than the number of elements in the input vector. The calculation speed and storage capacity of computers limits the number of combinations and, hence, the number of elements in the input vectors that can be considered and so many of the possible inter-relationships cannot be found nor used. In another chapter by the same author in this book, it is shown how the number of combinations can be dramatically reduced by summing selections of them by forming a new input vector of the inner and outer product correlations and this even gives better performance than using the higher order multiples of the variables themselves. The act of calculating the inner and outer product correlations also discovers the relationships and dependencies between the time-series data set for one variable and that for another including the effect of time lags. Such inner and outer product correlations of time-series datasets take several calculation steps on a computer, but in a free space optical system can be performed at the speed of light. This solution is discussed in the second part of the chapter where optical higher order neural network systems consisting of lasers, lenses, liquid crystal spatial light modulators, and cameras are described. These higher order neural networks also have recursive feedback. In addition, it is described how holographic memory storage can be used in such systems to make available a very large and dense storage capacity. All of the stored datasets in the holographic database can be searched *in parallel* and so incurs no additional time penalty as occurs in traditional magnetic hard disc storage arrays.

The text concentrates on the research of the author and his research group as they have led research in both these areas and the research of other groups is indicated where appropriate by references.

OPTICAL WAVEGUIDE CHIP-TO-CHIP INTERCONNECTION TECHNOLOGY

Electronic systems are often designed as a vertical rack of several units. The rack provides the power supply to the units and external optical fiber interconnections to the internet and local area network. Each unit has a "backplane" placed centrally or at the back of a system unit. The backplane or "motherboard" is the main large area printed circuit board (PCB) with up to 20 layers of copper tracks. A large number of other smaller printed circuit boards are plugged into the backplane at right angles to its surface. These smaller boards are variously called mezzanine boards, line cards (in telecommunication multiway switching units), drive cards (in storage arrays), blade servers (in computer arrays) or daughter cards. Since we are concentrating on storage arrays, we will refer to them as drive cards. In this case, each drive card has several "hard" or

magnetic spinning disc drives on which data is stored. To preserve the data in the event of hard disc drive or drive card failures the same data is spread across several disc drives on several cards using a format known as RAID. It is common for the drive cards to be plugged in horizontally or vertically from the front of the unit into the backplane and for additional cards such as dual power supplies and dual controllers to be plugged in from the back. In this case, the backplane is really in the middle of the unit but still tends to be called the backplane. The controllers provide communications to the local area network through optical fibers and format incoming data into the RAID format. All units are doubled to provide backup in case of failure and so provide high reliability. If a drive card or controller card fails it is easy to unplug it from the backplane and to replace it. However, the backplane is in the center of the unit so is too costly to replace and it is quicker to replace the whole unit rather than to extract the backplane. Therefore, it is common to avoid putting active components such as integrated circuits or lasers onto the backplane as these are the most likely causes of failure. The active components are all put onto the drive cards which can easily be pulled out and replaced in case of failure. The backplane, therefore, only performs interconnections between all of the drive cards and the controllers by means of its multiple layers of copper tracks or traces. The backplane also physically supports the drive cards which plug into connectors arrayed on the backplane and so the backplane is usually up to 1 cm thick and it is perforated by large holes to allow forced cooling air flow from fans to pass around the drive cards. The data from several drives on one drive card is aggregated and sent along the copper tracks on the backplane so the highest data rates and the highest interconnectivity is required on the backplane. So this is where the copper track or trace limitations are noticed first but as drives continue to become smaller and more are integrated onto the drive cards the copper track limitations will soon be noticed on the drive cards themselves.

As a result of the difficulty and cost of overcoming the problems of copper tracks or traces on printed circuit boards to allow propagation over reasonable distances, and mainly as a result of the severe crosstalk between the copper tracks that can prevent such a system working, other technological solutions are being investigated. Optics is the ideal technology to use as beams of photons pass through each other without interacting unlike electric currents in which the electrons are charged and interact through their electric fields. Therefore, optics is the ideal technology for interconnects, whereas electronics is the ideal technology for switches and non-linear elements, which require strong interactions. Perhaps the most obvious and low risk way to use optics is simply to replace the copper tracks or traces by optical waveguides (Uhlig, 2006; Schröder, 2006). In this section, we give a highly simplified explanation of this technology for non-scientists. Texts for more accurate and detailed explanations may be found in the references at the end of the chapter.

In optical waveguide technology light is used to carry the digital data by switching it on an off to create optical bits and these are transmitted through optical waveguides. An optical waveguide is very similar to an optical fiber in construction but is confined to travel within a single layer within or on the printed circuit board. An optical fiber consists of two materials, one forming a cylindrical core and the other around it forming a cylindrical cladding. The two materials are chosen so that the speed of light is slightly slower in the core than in the cladding. This has the effect of binding the light so that it cannot escape from the core being forced to reflect back and forth at the boundary between the core and the cladding. The waveguide is rather like an optical fiber, which has been glued down onto the surface of the PCB, and so light can travel through it carrying signals similar to copper tracks carrying electron current.

One drawback of optical communications is that the optical beam cannot carry an electronic power supply and present integrated circuits require an electrical power supply. Therefore, the optimum technology is a hybrid technology in which most of the data carrying copper tracks are replaced by optical waveguides but some copper tracks are preserved to carry electrical power to the integrated circuits and to provide low data rate control signals. The control signals, for example, may be used to monitor the temperature and to control cooling fans as high bit rate integrated circuits become very hot in use.

However, waveguides differ from fibers in that they can be fabricated cheaply using the same processes already used to fabricate integrated circuits and PCBs and so are compatible with their manufacturing and could be integrated into the PCB manufacturers production lines. Printed circuit boards are made of FR4 which is a composite material made from woven glass fiber in an epoxy matrix and often the weave and weft of the fibers cause undulations in the surface of the board which would cause loss if the waveguides were to be made directly on it (Chang, 2007). So first, a planarizing layer of lower cladding polymer is deposited on the board surface. This is also needed to ensure that the cladding material surrounds the core polymer. The core polymer layer is then deposited and patterned before being covered in another layer of cladding polymer that encloses it. The waveguides fabricated by these processes have almost square cross sectional cores as opposed to the circular cores of optical fibers and share the same cladding material which surrounds and buries all of them whereas each optical fiber has its own cladding. Waveguides are sometimes divided into to distinct types in the same way as fibers have two distinct types: single mode with tiny cores of 5 to 9 micron diameters and multimode with 50 or 62.5 micron diameters (Hamam, 2007). The modes of the waveguides and fibers are distinct distributions of light across the waveguide each having its own velocity along the length of the waveguide or fiber. The number of modes that can exist within the core of the optical fiber or waveguide reduces as the core width reduces until in a single mode fiber or waveguide only one mode remains. The energy in a pulse of light, which enters a multimode fiber or waveguide, is distributed between all of the modes. In the ray model of light low order modes correspond to rays of light traveling almost directly along the axis of the waveguide whereas higher order modes correspond to those having rays at increasing angles from the waveguide axis which have to reflect more often at the core/cladding interface and so, simplistically, travel a further distance. Since the modes travel at different velocities, the input pulse is split into a number of pulses, which arrive at slightly different times and usually overlap one another so that the output is a much longer spread out pulse, which is known as modal dispersion. In multimode waveguides and fibers, this means that a single pulse of light spreads in time the further it travels in the waveguide and so begins to overlap and interfere with pulses before and after. This has a more serious effect for shorter pulses of light so there is a limit on the maximum bit rate that multimode waveguides and fibers can transmit, which depends on their lengths. Therefore, for high bit rate telecommunications single mode fibers and waveguides are preferred. However, costly connectors with high tolerances are required to precisely align the tiny 5 to 9 micron cores reproducibly or manual or robotic alignment to maximize the light coupled is needed which is also costly and time consuming. So in optical backplanes multimode waveguides are preferred to ease the alignment tolerances required and as the communication distances are rather short modal dispersion has not been found to be a problem up to reasonable bit rates.

Single mode waveguide technology is well developed for high bit rate applications and waveguides formed in silica have been formed to allow light from several different wavelength lasers to be combined at the transmitter and separated at the receiver. This technology is often called "silicon microbench" technology or "Optoelectronic Integrated Circuits (OIC or OEIC)" or "Planar Lightwave Circuits (PLC)" (Xerox, 2007) or "integrated optics (IO)" or "Silicon Photonics" (Rattner, 2007) and provides a test bed onto which lasers, modulators, photodiodes, and optical switch active elements can be accurately aligned and interconnected. More recently waveguides formed in silicon have been formed on integrated circuits themselves by such leading companies as Intel (Young, 2004; Liu, 2007), IBM (Xia, 2006) and Xerox (Xerox, 2007) to provide optical input and output pin-out to overcome the limitations of copper input and output integrated circuit package pins which are similar to those for copper tracks. However, due to the connector cost and cost of fabricating waveguides in silica and silicon it cannot be directly transferred to use in optical backplanes. In optical printed circuit board backplanes, waveguides made from polymer are preferred due to its lower inherent cost and lower fabrication costs and ability to fabricated waveguides over large areas of 0.5 – 1 meter dimensions.

Polymer Multimode Optical Waveguide Interconnects

Although many companies in several countries (Milward, 2006; Schröder, 2007; Ahn, 2006) have decided that multimode waveguides combined with copper tracks on hybrid printed circuit boards are the most promising way forwards to overcome the copper track bottleneck on backplanes there are differences in the approaches being investigated.

The polymer type must be chosen to withstand high lamination temperatures in the PCB manufacturing process and to withstand reflow soldering temperatures and must withstand cycles of high humidity and wide fluctuations in temperature without delaminating. It must have low loss at the wavelength of light being used and be able to be fabricated by conventional PCB processes without major changes to the productions lines. Two polymers are currently receiving a lot of interest: Acrylate and Polysiloxane. The Truemode™ acrylate polymer formulation provided by Exxelis Ltd. offers low loss at 850 nm, which corresponds to the most readily available low cost vertical cavity surface emitting lasers (VCSELs). Polysiloxane formulations provided by Dow Corning and Rohm and Haas have low loss over a wider range of wavelengths.

The optical connector is an essential component but until recently a sufficiently low cost one had not been demonstrated and so this represented a hurdle to any further progress in the introduction of optical waveguide technology. This was recently put right as a result of the connector research carried out in the collaborative UK EPSRC "Storlite" project by Xyratex Technology Ltd. and University College London (UCL) which designed and demonstrated an operational low cost prototype connector (Papakonstantinou, 2007; Pitwon, 2004; Pitwon, 2004; Pitwon 2006). The active connector contained 4 VCSEL lasers and 4 photodiodes giving 4 output channels and 4 input channels. It used a patented low cost self-aligning technique to realize a pluggable connector, which can be simply unplugged and reconnected with high alignment accuracy (± 6 microns) easily sufficient for multimode waveguides. 10 Gb/s Ethernet traffic was sent through one connector, through a 10 cm waveguide and through a second connector without any errors and it was demonstrated at several commercial trade shows (Pitwon, 2004; Pitwon, 2004; Pitwon, 2006). This connector has now been licensed and commercialized for manufacture and will soon be widely available.

Although the design rules for single mode waveguides are well known those for multimode waveguides are currently being established by experimentation using various polymers and fabrication techniques and by theoretical modeling in the University College London (UCL)

and Xyratex led UK EPSRC IeMRC Flagship OPCB project consortium of 3 universities and 9 companies forming a supply chain. Design rules are also being investigated by Dow Corning in collaboration with Cambridge University, UK. Design rules are needed to establish, for example, the minimum radius of a waveguide bend (Papakonstantinou, 2006; Papakonstantinou, 2007) and the loss when two waveguides cross and when one waveguide splits into two. Other waveguide elements also need to be investigated such as tapered waveguides (Rashed, 2004) bent tapered waveguides (Papakonstantinou, 2004), Thermo-optic switches (Rashed, 2004), Power splitters (Rashed, 2004) and the effects of misalignment at connectors and couplers (Yu, 2004). There are also major programs of research into polymer multimode optical waveguides in USA, Germany and Japan.

The simplest interconnections by waveguides and lowest risk approach are point-to-point interconnections. In higher order neural networks, each connection could be performed using one waveguide. However, it would be more efficient to use one waveguide to carry data, which would have traveled along several interconnections. This can be done by time multiplexing or even wavelength multiplexing the data so although it travels through a single waveguide it can be separated at the other end and so effectively represents several connections.

In a higher order neural network the same signal from one neuron must be sent to several, say N, receiving neurons along differently weighted paths. It is most effective for the weighting to be applied in the electronic domain rather than along the optical waveguide path. Although the loss through the waveguide depends on its length and the number of bends and crossings, it would constrain the layout if the weight were to be built into the propagation path and it would also not be programmable. Therefore, the weights can be applied at the transmitting integrated circuit and then sent through N outgoing waveguides or multiplexed into one outgoing waveguide. Alternatively, the weights can be applied at the receiving end so the same signal is sent through the N outgoing waveguides and a weight applied to each one after reception. Since sending the same signal through N waveguides is not very efficient, it could be sent through one waveguide and used multiple times at the receiver.

More complicated interconnection patterns are also possible but introduce an increased element of risk. The output from a single neuron in an integrated circuit could be sent through one waveguide, which then splits into many channels for the N output neurons. This can be done using multiway splitters (Rashed, 2004; Rashed, 2005) or by cascading 1:2 splitters until the desired split ratio of 1:N is achieved. Of course splitting the optical signal in this way results in the power being split so each receiving channel receives 1/N of the original power and care must be taken to ensure that this is well above the receiver noise floor otherwise a number of errors will ensue.

The weights can also be applied in the optical domain using programmable optical splitters or switches. Such devices have been described (Rashed, 2004; Rashed, 2005) which use heating (Rashed, 2004) to cause the switching or to change the splitting ratio. Thermal switching is not as fast as transistor switching but is sufficiently fast for a higher order neural network, as the weights do not need to change after training.

FREE SPACE OPTICAL CORRELATOR HIGHER ORDER NEURAL NETWORKS

Rather than simply replacing copper wires and tracks by optical waveguides the optical technology can be more fully exploited by not restricting the light to travel through waveguides. For example, in a telescope or microscope or pair of spectacles or in an eye the light is free to travel in any direction in a three dimensional space.

Restricting light to travel through waveguides may be convenient for existing printed circuit board manufacturing processes but allowing light its full potential opens up the possibility of novel neural network architectures instead of forcing them to match the architectures of computers. When light is restricted to travel in waveguides the maximum bit rate is limited particularly for multimode guides. Its speed is reduced and the light suffers attenuation and loss but when light travels through free space its bit rate is almost unlimited, it has no loss (at least in a vacuum), and its speed is the maximum speed possible. Waveguides are limited as they can only lie in a plane or in several planes and cross talk between the waveguides must be minimized. However, in free space optics the full parallelism of light can be used in which multiple parallel beams of light travel, being spatially separated, and additional functionality become available. Two types of light are available: incoherent light which has a wide spectral bandwidth and behaves like daylight with which we are familiar in everyday life and coherent light which has a very narrow spectral bandwidth and which comes from lasers and possesses surprising properties which cannot be inferred from our knowledge of everyday daylight.

In the following, we begin by describing the calculation primitives that can easily be carried out using free space optics and then go on to combine them in ever increasing complexity to arrive finally at an optical higher order neural network. A number of key free space optical devices are also introduced through the discussion, Lens, Liquid crystal Display (LCD), Spatial Light Modulator (SLM), digital cameras, multiplexed holograms:

- **Addition:** When two unrelated light beams fall onto the same photodetector the detector measures the sum of the powers of the two beams. A photodetector outputs an electrical current which is proportional to the power of the light falling onto it as long as the photodetector is operated in its linear region and is not in saturation and as long as the incident light wavelength is within its wavelength range of detection. If the two incident beams have different wavelengths then because the efficiency of generation of photocurrent depends on the wavelength, the sum will be weighted by the relative efficiencies. Unfortunately, many photodetectors do not have uniform efficiency across their receiving surface so care must be taken to illuminate the same area with the two beams.

- **Subtraction:** If two incident beams falling on the same photodetector are coherent and come from the same laser then they may interfere producing fringes and speckle on the photodetector. If the photodetector is sufficiently large, it will average out the fringes and speckle. However, if the two beams travel in the same direction towards the photodetector then interference can occur across the whole wavefront of the beams resulting in something between constructive or destructive interference at the two extremes depending on their relative phases. In a simple system, the phase of the two beams depends on the distance that they have traveled and on the speed of light along their respective paths. So, subtraction can be realized by arranging for the two beams to be in antiphase so that they cancel on another. However, such a system is very sensitive to vibration as changes in position of the optical components by a fraction of a wavelength (~633 nm for red light) will change their relative phases and so would not give a simple subtraction. Moreover, convection currents in the air through which the laser beams travel or sound waves or dust perturb the path of the optical beams affecting the subtraction so that this is not really a viable technique unless the light beams travel short paths inside an isolated material.

- **Multiplication and Division:** If a light beam passes through an absorbing material the power of the light beam will reduce with distance traveled.. Therefore, if a material lets through ¼ of the light then the output light will be the product of the power of the input light and ¼. This can be considered to be multiplication by 0.25 or division by 4. In the case of absorbing materials, the power is always reduced. If the absorption varies across the field of view such as in a photographic transparency or an image copied onto an overhead transparency foil then a spatially uniform input backlight will multiply by the image on the transparency and output that image. If the input backlight is not uniform, for example, if it has already passed though one transparency and then passes through a second transparency placed close after it the output image will be the product of the images on the two transparencies. Modulators are available in which the absorption of the material may be changed by changing an applied voltage. For example, a nematic liquid crystal display consists of pixels whose attenuation can be varied to give gray levels in the display. If a first image formed by passing a spatial uniform backlight illumination through a first liquid crystal display is passed through a second liquid crystal display (LCD) displaying a second image placed close after the first display the output image will be the product of the two input images since the corresponding pixels are multiplied. There is often a difficulty in placing the two LCDs close enough together to avoid the light passing through any one pixel spreading by diffraction before reaching the second LCD. If coherent light is used then an additional problem arises that the light passing through the display may take very slightly longer to pass through some regions than others resulting in phase changes across the wavefront. Manufactures have tightened their manufacturing tolerances for LCDs for this application so that the time taken for light to pass through any part of the display is the same and such displays are usually called spatial light modulators (SLMs) to distinguish them from the more usual displays.

- **Imaging and Scale Change:** If a beam of light from a distant source passes through a lens, it focuses to a point at a distance known as the "focal length" which is a measure of the strength of the lens. If the light is incoherent and diffuse, say daylight passing through a window, then a converging lens will focus the light to form an image in the "focal plane", at a distance of the focal length from the lens. The image will be of a window inverted. If the light is direct from the sun, then an inverted image of the sun is formed. A first image can be copied to a plane some distance away using a lens in a process known as "imaging". If the first image, usually called the "object", is placed twice the focal length away from the lens then the image formed on a plane twice the focal length on the other side of the lens is the same size. If the original image consisted of "pixels" or picture elements in a two-dimensional square array the pixels in the image will be the same without serious crosstalk between pixels if correctly designed to take account of the divergence of light. So, a lens can be used to image one LCD to another to avoid the problem of the divergence of light when they cannot be placed closely enough together. If the input object is moved closer or further from the lens than twice the focal length then the output image is enlarged or reduced in size.
- **Two Dimensional Fourier Transform:** If the light source is a laser then a valuable additional functionality becomes available. A lens performs a two dimensional Fourier

Transform of an input object placed at its focal length away, onto an image plane a distance of the focal length away on the other side of the lens. This is a very powerful operation unavailable to guided wave optics or incoherent optics. The Fourier Transform performed in this way is a true complex Fourier transform of the amplitude *and* phase of the light emerging from each pixel of the input SLM. In such a case care must be taken to ensure that the laser illuminates the input SLM so that the output from it has a plane wavefront with all points having the same phase otherwise the Fourier Transform will be affected by the actual phase front. Fourier Transforms can also be performed by lenses in other arrangements but these are not fully correct complex Fourier Transforms. For example, if a lens is placed touching an SLM then in the focal plane a Fourier Transform will be achieved but it will not have a correct phase factor.

Two Dimensional Correlation and Convolution for Inner and Outer Products

The mathematical definitions of correlation and convolution for two-dimensional images (Selviah, 1989) are very similar apart from a minus sign. Although the full definition has complex conjugates in it, if the pattern is entirely real then the complex conjugate is just the pattern itself so the conjugates will be neglected in the rest of this discussion. In each case, there are two functions or in two dimensions, images, which are moved across each other in the vertical and horizontal directions and at each position, are multiplied and the values summed across the plane. The only difference is that in the case of correlation of one image with itself then both images are the same way around so that they can exactly overlap and match point by point. In the convolution of the two images, one image is inverted or reflected through its center of symmetry as if it had been flipped about a vertical and horizontal axis so that the two images never exactly match. In the case of correlation, when the two images are in alignment and if they are the same, then the highest value of the correlation is achieved and so it is a measure of the alignment and similarity of the two images and so can be used for pattern recognition. When the images are in alignment, each pixel value is multiplied by itself to give squared values and these could be summed by a lens to give the inner product. When the images are relatively displaced in horizontal or vertical alignment, the products give the cross products, which could be summed by a lens to give the outer product correlation.

As an example of how this may be used to discover trends, patterns, relationships and dependencies in financial and business data let us start by considering a more simple case of an input one dimensional vector representing a time-series of a variable such as the stock market share price. The database, in this example, also contains multiple time-series of different variable such as other share value time-series. The inner products of the whole time-series reveal similarities in trends between variables while the outer products reveal time-lagged trends between variables. The input need not be a real variable but could be a trend or pattern so that the correlations reveal the variables, which have this trend or pattern in them. As an extension of this the one dimensional vector time-series can be changed into a two dimensional covariance matrix containing second order cross products and this can be used as the input image. The database in this example also contains multiple covariance matrix images of different variable time-series such as other share value time-series. The covariance matrix reveals inter relationships within the time-series of the variable while the correlation of different covariance matrices compares these with those of other stored time-

series to look for occurrences of the same pattern in the case of the inner product and time lagged occurrences in the case of the outer product. A time lag dependency would be shown by a lateral translation along the diagonal of the covariance matrix giving the strongest output signal value. The following discussion is written assuming the inputs are one-dimensional vectors, for simplicity, but it should be remembered that the order of the higher order neural network described could be increased by using two dimensional covariance matrix images instead.

It is possible to use the Fourier Transform property of a lens in coherent light to perform convolution and correlation by using the convolution theorem which states that the inverse Fourier Transform of the product of two Fourier transformed functions is the convolution of the two functions. A number of designs of optical system can be used to realize the convolution, or by inverting images through their centers of symmetry, the correlation. Let us concentrate on the one shown in Figure 1.

In this system two images, labeled s and p are to be correlated. The two-dimensional Fourier Transform of each image is correspondingly labeled S and P. The first image, s, is put onto the first SLM towards the left. The second image, p, is Fourier Transformed in two dimensions in a computer and its Fourier Transform, P, is put onto the second SLM near the center of the figure. The first SLM on the left is illuminated using a laser with a beam sufficiently wide to illuminate the whole SLM with a parallel (collimated) uniform beam of intensity, A, so that it has a plane wavefront. The light emerging from the first SLM, with the first image imposed on it, is Fourier Transformed by the first lens which is a distance of its focal length from each of the SLMs. The Fourier Transform of the first image is formed on the second SLM and passes through it. The output of the second SLM is then the product of the Fourier Transforms of the two images. This product then passes through a second Fourier Transforming lens used to ef-

Figure 1. Optical inner product correlation of two images

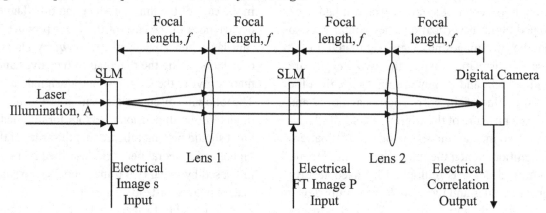

Figure 2. Block diagram showing order of mathematical operations being performed

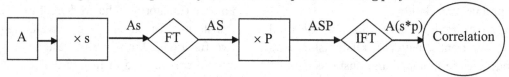

fectively perform an inverse Fourier Transform so that on the output plane at the right hand of the figure is formed the convolution of the two images. If the first image on the first SLM and the Fourier transform of the second image on the second SLM are correctly inverted then the output falling on the digital camera becomes the correlation rather than the convolution.

If the input laser beam has parallel rays (is collimated), and if an ideal SLM is used, the output will also be a parallel laser beam but modulated across its cross section by the SLM. So the first pattern, s, is projected along the system axis so that its Fourier Transform, S, falls onto the central SLM exactly in alignment with the Fourier transform pattern, P, already there. If the central SLM was not there the pattern would be inverse Fourier transformed by the second lens and the original pattern would appear at the output of the system on the camera. Likewise, if only the central SLM were present and uniformly illuminated then the Fourier Transform of the pattern, P, on

it would spatially modulate the beam and would be inverse Fourier Transformed by the second lens and so pattern, p, would appear on the output digital camera. The positions of the pattern, p, and the pattern, s, would be in exact alignment. This type of ideal alignment means that the only multiplication of the two patterns that occurs is when the two patterns are in alignment, which is the position for the inner product so only the inner product is obtained. This is fine if this system is to represent one layer of a neural network (Selviah, 1989), however, for a higher order neural network the outer product terms must also be formed.

If the input laser beam is angled with respect to the system axis, as shown in Figure 3, this has the effect of imposing a phase slope across the image emerging from the first SLM. When this is Fourier Transformed by the first lens it results in a translation or lateral shift of the image of the Fourier Transform of the first pattern, S, across the face of the middle SLM. Following this through the system, this results in the calculation of an

Figure 3. Optical inner and outer product correlation of two images

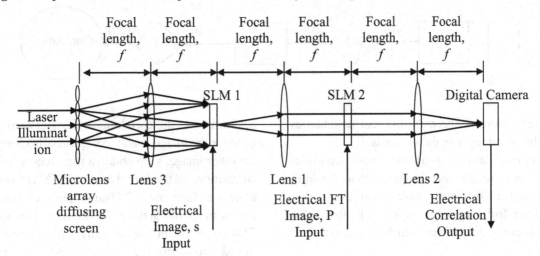

outer product term in the correlation on the digital camera. Therefore, in order to calculate all the outer and inner products the input illumination needs to be a series of parallel beams at a range of angles around the system axis. This can be achieved in many ways, one of which is shown in Figure 3, in which the initial laser beam illuminates a microlens array diffusing screen (Poon, 1992; Poon, 1993), which is then Fourier Transformed, by a lens to obtain the required illumination for the first SLM. The lateral positions of each microlens result after Fourier Transformation in a correspondingly angled beam on the SLM.

On the output plane face of the digital camera is formed the correlation, the central value represents the inner product correlation which would be the largest value if the two input images were the same and the points in the area around that central point give the outer product values. Therefore, this system calculates the inner and outer products required for a higher order neural network. If a pinhole is placed at the position of the inner product correlation bright spot so that only this passes through and the outer product terms are blocked, then the system only performs the inner product correlation as required for a first order neural network (Selviah, 1989).

In fact, there are several ways to arrange this system. Another variant of this system is obtained if the two images are interchanged. Mathematically the same output function is obtained, as the correlation operation is commutative but having possible inversions about the vertical and/or horizontal axes depending on the initial inversions of the original images about these axes. A further variant of the original system described is obtained by replacing each of the original images by their Fourier Transform as shown in Figure 4.

In this case, the system is set up so that the input images, s and p, are in alignment pixel by pixel at the central SLM. The output correlation in this case is a correlation of the Fourier Transforms of the original images rather than being the correlation of the original images themselves. By Parsival's Theorem, the inner products in both cases have the same value although the arrangement of the outer products on the output correlation plane may differ. This can be used as one layer of a new type of higher order neural network in which the cross product or outer product terms are formed not between the original images but between the Fourier Transforms of the original images. Such a layer seeks cross correlations or

Figure 4. Block diagram for a variant of the original system

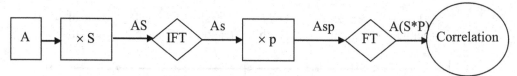

cross relationships between different periodicities in the two images or data records.

This is just one way to perform optical correlation, as there are other designs such as the Joint Transform Correlators described in the further reading. To distinguish this system it is often called the 4*f* correlator system (which is its length).

Multiplexed Correlators for one Layer of Interconnections for a Higher Order Neural Network

Selviah (1989) showed that rather than considering individual weights and interconnections each layer of a neural network is equivalent to a series of parallel correlations. In this model, the input data or image is correlated with a large number of images formed indirectly from and representing the weights of the interconnections. The output correlation images are then summed in alignment pixel by pixel and the value for each pixel is sent to a neuron for the next layer. This result, which is not immediately obvious from the outset, is very helpful for optical implementation. In order to implement one layer of a neural network or a higher order neural network it is necessary to implement a parallel bank or array of correlators and, as has been shown in the last section, free space optics can easily perform a two dimensional correlation.

One of the images can be taken to represent the input "pattern", p, and the other image to represent one of the "stored" images representing the weights, s_i, where i=1,…,M. M is the number of images required to fully represent all of the weights of the neural interconnection layer. One way to

perform all of the correlations necessary would be to fix the image, p and to sequentially change the other image, s_i, to obtain a time sequence of correlations on the digital camera. SLMs can operate at a video rate of 30 frames per second and some can operate at up to 100 frames per second. This may be sufficient for many applications but in order to obtain the highest speed, all of the correlations should be performed simultaneously. The system described could be duplicated many times and placed side by side with each system having the same input pattern, p, but different stored patterns, s_i, so each system calculates one of the required correlations. However, this would multiply up the cost of the components.

Alternatively the Fourier Transforms of the stored images, S_i, could be placed side by side in an array to form a large compound image made up of tiles, each one being one of the stored images. The input image pattern, p, could be placed on the central SLM as in Figure 3. The inverse Fourier Transforms of the stored images give the original stored patterns exactly aligned with the pixels of the central SLM. These stored patterns, s_i, would be simultaneously multiplied by the input pattern, p, as they pass through the SLM. The key point is that although the stored patterns are all projected onto the input image they are *distinguishable* from each other because the rays for each stored pattern arrive at the central SLM from a different *angle* in two dimensions corresponding to the position of that pattern's Fourier Transform on the original SLM. The result of this is that after a further Fourier Transform the correlations would be distinguishable being formed simultaneously in a square two-dimensional array on the digital camera. This system uses space multiplexing of the stored images, s_i, on the first SLM and results in space multiplexing of the output correlations.

This system design requires some trade-offs. In a first order neural network, only the inner products are needed and these could be placed very close together in the output correlation plane to form an image in their own right assuming the system is designed to minimize diffraction from the first SLM. However, in a higher order neural network the outer product cross product points surrounding each inner product correlation peak are also required so this limits the proximity of the patterns in the input plane which means that the stored images in the input plane cannot overlap which they would not do if placed side by side in an array. Large liquid crystal displays with many pixels are now available for use as televisions and are made on production lines to tight tolerances so this could be used for the first SLM. A phase correction film may need to be applied to correct for any phase variation across to the display to ensure that any optical phase front incident would be maintained in orientation after passing through the SLM. However, the maximum size of the display, the minimum size of the pixels and the maximum size of reasonably priced lenses are limited. Therefore, the number of stored images, which is related to the size of the database that can be searched, is limited although it can be searched very quickly.

High-Density Holographic Storage

In order to search a vast database at high speed using the optical systems described it is necessary to have a high-density optical database. Digital discs (CDs and DVDs) offer high-density storage of bits particularly when the discs contain multiple layers, with data on both sides of the disc. The number of layers is limited as the surface indentations partially obscure the deeper layers. Although the data capacity of such digital discs can be increased, the readout time is limited, as individual tracks must be read out at the rotation speed of the disc. Multiple tracks can be read out simultaneously and high disc rotation speeds can be used, but ultimately the total data that can be read is limited. Generally the data is read out to RAM memory and once all of the necessary data has been read out then it can be used to train or to input into a high order neural network.

Holographically stored data can be stored just as densely, if not more so, but can be stored in areas so that the whole database can be read out simultaneously. Therefore, researchers are investigating the idea of holographic databases. The data is not stored as indentations on the surface or on layers within the disc. The full volume of the disc material is used and in effect, individual atoms share the data. One piece of data is recorded on an area of a disc and when recorded as a far field hologram, it can be recovered from any portion of the area onto which it was recorded. So if the disc is broken, even a small piece can be used to recover the data or if part of the disc is damaged the data is not lost as it is also stored elsewhere. This is similar to the use of RAID magnetic hard disc technology in conventional data storage systems although the data is not spread between discs but spread within a single disc. In fact, work on holographic databases began before digital discs were invented but the higher cost of the holographic recording material compared to polymer embossed discs meant that the digital technology was first introduced to the market. However, recently new lower cost polymer recording materials have been developed and this now opens the way for holographic databases.

Very simply, a hologram is rather like a photograph, in that it can record an image, but in addition, it can record the directions of the beams passing through the original image. When it is replayed correctly, it recreates the original image *and* the directions of the original beams. In order to record a hologram coherent light from a laser is usually required. The laser beam is split and part used to illuminate the object or passed through an SLM to provide the data or signal beam. The scattered light from the object or passing through the SLM is allowed to illuminate the recording material. The other "reference" beam, from the initially split laser beam, is also set to illuminate the recording material. The paths of both of the beams are usually set to be similar lengths to the recording material. The two laser beams interfere constructively and destructively within the recording material to create bright and dark, very closely spaced, fringes that are recorded within the volume of the material forming the hologram. The recording material sometimes needs to be developed depending on the choice of material. The recording material may be the same as those used to record photographs but of a higher quality or may be certain photorefractive crystals or polymers. After developing, and perhaps fixing, if either of the original beams used to record the hologram, again illuminates the hologram, the other beam used to record it is regenerated just as if it had passed through the hologram material. So, if the reference beam is again set to illuminate the hologram the other signal recording beam will be generated as if it had come from the original object or SLM. Anyone viewing that beam would think it *had* come from the original object and so see a three dimensional object. In the case being considered here, however, the object seen will be the two dimensional SLM.

Multiple images can be recorded holographically inside the same volume of material and distinguished if the original images had different initial beam directions (angle multiplexing) and very large numbers of images can be stored by this means inside a small volume. Images can also be stored side by side in different areas of the holographic recording material (space multiplexing). Moreover, unlike the images being placed side by side on the SLM, image areas can be allowed to overlap, provided the angle of the rays in the original images are different. This form of multiplexing is known as Spatio-Angular Multiplexing (SAM) and its introduction by Tao,

(1993); Tao,(1995) has led to far higher densities of holographic storage and to the first practical commercial holographic storage system products (Psaltis, 1988) In Phase Technologies (Anderson, 2004; Anderson, 2007; Anderson, 2007). In the ensuing high-density holographic storage products, the recording material is usually in the form of disc that is rotated and the input image from an SLM is used to interfere with a reference beam in a small area on the disc. As the disc turns overlapping recording regions are used to record different data as the reference beam angle to the data beam is changed. However, the importance of Spatio-Angular Multiplexing (SAM) goes beyond its ability to densely store images as all of the stored images can be simultaneously read out and projected at different angles onto an SLM as part of a correlator.

Opto-Electronic High Order Feedback Neural Network (HOFNET)

One of the first optical higher order neural networks and the first demonstrated having an order higher than second order was the High Order Feedback Neural Network (HOFNET) (Selviah, 1990; Mao, 1991; Selviah 1991; Mao 1992; Mao, 1992) described in detail below. The limited dynamic range and noise present in free space optics limited earlier optical higher order neural networks (Athale, 1986; Owechko, 1987; Psaltis, 1988; Jang, 1988; Jang, 1989; Lin 1989; Horan, 1990) to second order. The HOFNET circumvented these problems by introducing electronic feedback to raise the order of the non-linearity on successive iterations.

In order to make a higher order neural network having a large number of interconnections and weights for high speed analysis of a very large database the large SLM used in the system described above for realizing multiplexed correlators is replaced by a space multiplexed array of holograms. Each hologram in the array is a recording of the Fourier Transform of a different stored image, S_i. The recordings are made as shown in Figure 5.

After the Fourier Transform of each stored image, S_i, is recorded, the hologram recording material is moved laterally and the recording of the next stored image is made. In the case of space multiplexing the angles between the reference beam and the signal beam are unchanged between recordings. This hologram is placed

back into the multiplexed correlator system as shown in Figure 6.

The system in Figure 6 is similar to the inner product correlator in Figure 1 except that this time the SLM is not used to display an image but instead is used to control the intensity of illumination to the holographic image store. So the SLM does not need so many pixels, or such small pixels as before, as it only needs the same number

Figure 5. The recording method for space multiplexed holograms

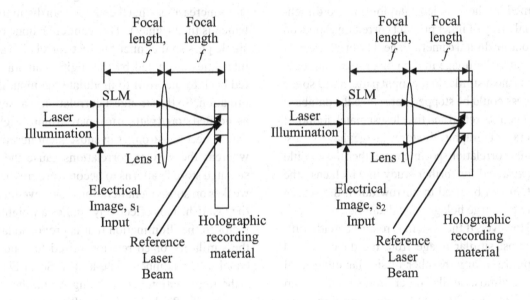

Figure 6. The opto-electronic high order feedback optical neural network (HOFNET)

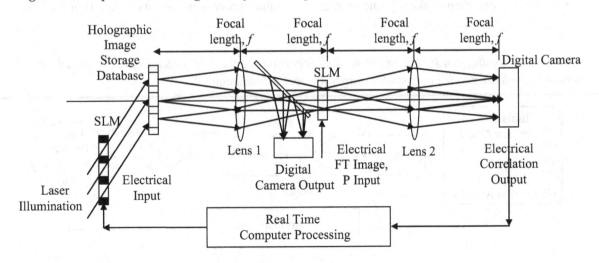

as the number of stored holographic images. The illumination must be at the same angle as the reference beam used to record the holograms. When replayed in this way, each hologram replays the Fourier Transform of the image, which is then inverse Fourier Transformed by the lens, so that all of the original images, s_i, are superimposed in alignment on the central SLM and pass through it, at separate distinguishable angles, multiplying by the input image, p, on it. Figure 7 shows the order of mathematical operations.

Finally, these products are Fourier Transformed by the final lens and form a two dimensional array of inner product correlation spots on the output digital camera plane. The brightest spot indicates the image in the holographic database that is most similar to the input pattern and so the process could be stopped here since the database has been searched and the closest match found. If several holographically stored images have almost similar correlation spot intensities then those could be extracted for further study in which case the system can be used to narrow down the search of a very large holographic database.

However, if the system is required to identify the most similar image from the database and there are a large number of similar images all giving almost similar inner product correlation spot intensities then the system must identify which of the spots is the most intense. If the digital camera can clearly identify one spot as

being the most intense there is no problem, but in practice the system has a minimum difference or resolution between spot intensities that it can distinguish due to random electrical noise in the digital camera and random optical speckle noise in the system and input electrical noise to the SLMs. This is where the higher order aspects of the neural network come into play. If all of the correlation spot intensities are squared or raised to a higher order power then the highest spot intensities increase most so that the difference between them and the next brightest correlation spots increases so that the system can distinguish which is the brightest. This cannot be done on a single pass so the inner product correlation spot intensities are noted by the digital camera and fed back to the SLM to modulate the input illumination. So the strongest correlations cause the associated stored pattern to replayed more brightly and so become stronger in subsequent iterations whereas the weaker correlations cause the associated stored patterns to become progressively weaker on subsequent iterations until eventually they vanish. This effectively applies a weighting factor to the illumination that is proportional to the similarity or correlation raised to a power equal to the number of iterations. So in Figure 7 the illumination begins being A and then becomes $A(S_i*P)$, $A(S_i*P)^2$, $A(S_i*P)^3$, and so on in subsequent iterations. The feedback causes this higher order non-linearity in the HOFNET but

Figure 7. Block diagram for the mathematical operations of the high order feedback optical neural network which are carried out simultaneously for each stored image, S_i

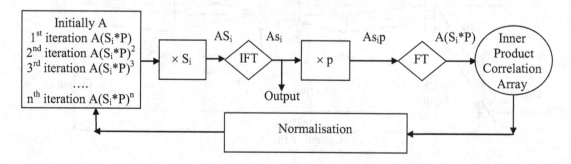

it could equally well be implemented as a power law non-linear function in a neuron in a feed forward network. Finally, after several iterations only one stored pattern is being replayed from the holographic image database.

Optical and electrical systems have a fixed dynamic range so the input cannot be allowed to exceed some value otherwise saturation occurs and cannot be allowed to be too small otherwise it will be below the noise floor of the system. Therefore, the feedback loop needs to incorporate some form of normalization. For example, the strongest correlation peaks whose difference could not be resolved by the system could set the left hand SLM to fully open so that the most laser light illuminated their stored patterns in which case the illumination for the other patterns would gradually drop to zero on repeated iterations. Once the dissimilar patterns in the database gradually are reduced in intensity and vanish, the noise arising from their extra light disappears and so the noise gradually reduces. Then the difference between the strongest correlations becomes discernable as the noise has reduced and the weaker of those correlations then also reduces to zero leaving only one pattern iterating.

The output is taken from the image being replayed onto the central SLM and can be easily taken out using a beam splitter as shown in Figure 6 onto a second digital camera. The image on this output digital camera gradually changes during the iterations as it becomes most similar to the pattern in the database that most resembles the input image.

In the system described, if the electronic feedback were through a real time embedded computer it could identify the weaker correlations in the first pass and set them to zero after one pass, and the same after subsequent passes so converging more quickly. However, the intention here is that the computer will be replaced in the future by two dimensional arrays of smart pixels acting as neuron thresholding elements and they may have more limited computing power only

being able to raise to a power and normalize. If lateral inhibition is also activated in the electronic smart pixel neuron array then faster convergence can occur.

The process of phase conjugation, which reflects back a light ray from whence it came reversing the phase front exactly, can be used to good effect in forming more efficient holograms (Chang, 1994) and in providing a direct optical feedback mechanism in a phase conjugate resonator (Owechko, 1987; Chang, 1995) without the need for an electronic feedback path.

FUTURE RESEARCH DIRECTIONS

Polymer Multimode Optical Waveguide Interconnects

In long distance connections between mezzanine cards on the backplane, several interconnections between neurons can be aggregated together or "time multiplexed" so each waveguide represents many such connections. This will enable very complex interconnection patterns with multiple interconnections to become possible which is particularly suitable for implementation of higher order neural networks.

Optical waveguide technology will soon be available to system designers so the challenge for hardware designers is to design appropriate interconnection patterns for an optical backplane to connect simulated neurons or arrays of simulated neurons on integrated circuits on mezzanine cards. In this way, the system architecture will more closely resemble that of the higher order neural network resulting in improvements in training times and operational speed. Multiple layers of optical waveguides with interconnecting optical "vias" are also becoming available which will allow more complex interconnection patterns to be realized.

The challenge for software designers is to appropriately partition the neural network between the integrated circuits to make full use of the high-speed optical connections. Ideally, there will be no difference in the speed of the short distance connections between simulated neurons within a single integrated circuit and those neuron arrays on mezzanine cards further along the backplane. So, near and far connections need not be considered differently.

High speed optical interconnections open the possibility of implementation of higher order neural networks having far higher orders than simply partial or full second order which have not been seriously considered for practical applications due to the large number of interconnections and the resulting training times and operational times.

Free Space Optical Correlator Higher Order Neural Networks

In the High Order Feedback Optical Neural Network (HOFNET) demonstrated, only the inner products were calculated. Figure 3 showed how both inner and outer products could be calculated and this could be incorporated into the HOFNET to substantially extend its operation to have not only high order inner products but also higher order outer products towards being a fully higher order neural network. This requires recording additional holograms using Spatio-Angular Multiplexing (SAM).

The development of smart pixel arrays and artificial retinas opens the possibility of constructing feedforward multilayer networks using the multiplexed inner and outer product correlators of Figure 3 for each layer.

ACKNOWLEDGMENT

The author thanks his research fellows and research students for carrying out, under his direction, much of the experimental and computational work reviewed in this chapter. Particular thanks are due to Dr. Zhi Qiang 'Frank' Mao, Prof. Shiquan Tao, Dr. Guoyu Yu, Ioannis Papakonstantinou and Kai Wang. The author also thanks Dave Milward, Steve Thompson, Richard Pitwon, Ken Hopkins and Tim Courtney of Xyratex Technology Ltd UK for collaborative research on the optical waveguide connector.

REFERENCES

High Speed Waveguide Optical Interconnect References

Ahn, S. H., Cho, I. K., Han, S. P., Yoon, K. B., & Lee, M. S. (2006, August). Demonstration of high-speed transmission through waveguide-embedded optical backplane. *Optical Engineering, 45*(8), 085401

Chang, Y. J., Gaylord, T. K., & Chang, G. K. (2007). Attenuation in waveguides on FR-4 boards due to periodic substrate undulations. *Applied Optics, 46*(12), 2234-2243

Frye, J., Ananthanarayanan, R., & Modha, D. S. (2007, February). *Towards real-time, mouse-scale cortical simulations.* IBM Research Report, RJ10404, (A0702-001) Computer Science, Accessed on 2nd May 2007, http://www.modha.org/papers/rj10404.pdf

Grözing, M., Philipp, B., Neher, & Berroth, M. M. (2006, September). *Sampling receive equalizer with bit-rate flexible operation up to 10 Gbit/s.* Paper presented at the European Solid-State Circuits Conference, ESSCIRC 2006, Montreux, Switzerland, 16-19.

Hamam, H. (2007). Optical fiber communications, Volume I: Key concepts, data transmission, digital and optical networks, Part 3: Digital and optical networks. In H. Bidgoli, (Ed.), *The handbook of computer networks.* John Wiley & Sons, Inc.

Liu, A. (2007) *Announcing the world's first 40G silicon laser modulator!* Accessed on 21st Aug

2007 from http://blogs.intel.com/research/2007/07/40g_modulator.html

Milward, D., & Selviah, D. R. (2006). Data connections see the light: Optical links promise faster data transfer. *UK Department of Trade and Industry Photonic Focus Newsletter* (5), 8-9, http://www.photonics.org.uk/newsletter/featureArticles3.php

Papakonstantinou, I., Selviah, D. R., & Fernandez, F. A. (2004). Multimode laterally tapered bent waveguide modelling. *LEOS 2004, 17th Annual Meeting of the IEEE Lasers and Electro-Optic Society*, Puerto Rico, USA: IEEE, 2, 983-984

Papakonstantinou, I., Wang, K., Selviah, D. R., & Fernández, F. A. (2006, May). Experimental study of bend and propagation loss in curved polymer channel waveguides for high bit rate optical interconnections. *IEEE Workshop on High Speed Digital Systems*, Santa Fe, New Mexico, USA: IEEE

Papakonstantinou, I., Selviah, D. R., Pitwon, R. A., & Milward, D. (2007). Low cost, precision, self-alignment technique for coupling laser and photodiode arrays to waveguide arrays. *IEEE Transactions on Advanced Packaging*.

Papakonstantinou, I., Wang, K., Selviah, D.R., & Fernandez, A. F. (2007). Transition, radiation and propagation loss in polymer multimode waveguide bends. *Optics Express*, 15(2), 669-679.

Pitwon, R., Hopkins, K., Milward, D., Papakonstantinou, I., Selviah, D.R. (2005). *Optical connector*. Photonex UK.

Pitwon, R., Hopkins, K., Milward, D., Selviah, D. R.Papakonstantinou, I. (2005). Storlite optical backplane demonstrator optical connector. *Exhibition Centre, 31st European Conference on Optical Communication, ECOC*.

Pitwon, R., Hopkins, K., Milward, D., Selviah, D. R, Papakonstantinou, I., Wang, K., & Fernández, A. F. (2006). High speed pluggable optical backplane connector. *Fraunhofer IZM and VDI/VDE-IT International Symposium on Photonic Packaging: Electrical Optical Circuit Board and Optical Backplane, Electronica*, Messe Munchen: Fraunhofer IZM and VDI/VDE-IT

Rashed, A. M., & Selviah, D. R. (2004). Modelling of polymer taper waveguide for optical backplane. *Semiconductor and Integrated Opto-Electronics Conference (SIOE'04)*, Cardiff, UK: SIOE'04, paper 40.

Rashed, A. M., Papakonstantinou, I., & Selviah, D. R. (2004, November). Modelling of polymer thermo-optic switch with tapered input for optical backplane. *LEOS 2004, 17th Annual Meeting of the IEEE Lasers and Electro-Optic Society*, IEEE LEOS, Puerto Rico: IEEE, 2, 457- 458

Rashed, A. M., & Selviah, D. R. (2004). Modelling of Polymer 1×3 MMI power splitter for optical backplane. *IEEE LEOS Conference on Optoelectronic and Microelectronic materials and devices, Commad'04*, Brisbane, Australia: IEEE, 281- 284

Rashed, A. M., & Selviah, D. R. (2004). Modelling of the effects of thermal gradients on optical propagation in polymer multimode tapered waveguides in optical backplanes. *Photonics North 2004, Software and Modelling in Optics*, Ottawa, Canada: SPIE, International Society for Optical Engineering, USA, 5579 (1 and 2), 359-366

Rattner, J. (2007) *Hybrid silicon laser: Intel platform research*. Accessed on 31st Aug. 2007 http://techresearch.intel.com/articles/TeraScale/1448.htm

Schröder, H., Bauer, J., Ebling, F., Franke, M., Beier, A., Demmer, P., Süllau, W., Kostelnik, J., Mödinger, R., Pfeiffer, K., Ostrzinski, U., & Griese, E. (2006, January). Waveguide and packaging technology for optical backplanes and hybrid electrical-optical circuit boards. *Integrated Optics: Devices, Materials, and Technologies X, Photonics West*, San Jose, USA

Schröder, H. (2007). *Planar integrated optical interconnects for hybride electrical-optical circuit boards und optical backplanes.* Retrieved April 24, 2007 from http://www.pb.izm.fhg.de/mdi-bit/060_Publikationen/Vortraege/030_2006/ad-don/oit/Schroeder%20ICO%20top%20Meeting%20St%20Petersburg%202006%2002%20color.pdf

Uhlig, S., Frohlich, L., Chen, M., Arndt-Staufen-biel, N., Lang, G., Schroder, H., Houbertz, R., Popall, M., & Robertsson, M. (2006). Polymer optical interconnects: A scalable large-area panel processing approach. *IEEE Transactions on Advanced Packaging, 29*(1), 158-170

Xerox (2007). *Optical MEMS.* Accessed 31st Aug 2007 http://www.xeroxtechnology.com/moems

Xia, F. Sekaric, L. & Vlasov, Y. (2006). Ultracom-pact optical buffers on a silicon chip. *Nature Photonics 1,* 65 – 71. doi:10.1038/nphoton.2006.42

Young, I. (2004). Intel introduces chip-to-chip optical I/O interconnect. *Prototype Technology@ Intel Magazine,* 1-7, Accessed on 31st Aug 2007 http://www.intel.com/technology/magazine/re-search/it04041.pdf

Yu, G., Selviah, D. R., & Papakonstantinou, I. (2004, November). Modelling of optical cou-pling to multimode polymer waveguides: Axial and lateral misalignment tolerance. *LEOS 2004, 17th Annual Meeting of the IEEE Lasers and Electro-Optic Society,* Puerto Rico, USA:IEEE, 2, 981- 982

Free Space Optical Correlator Higher Order Neural Network References

Anderson, K. & Curtis, K. (2004). Polytopic mul-tiplexing. *Optics Letters, 29*(12), 1402-1404

Anderson, K., Fotheringham, E., Hill, A., Sissom, B. & Curtis, K. (2007). *High speed holographic data storage at 500 Gbit/in². Accessed on 31st Aug. 2007 http://www.inphase-technologies.com/downloads/pdf/technology/HighSpeed-HDS500Gbin2.pdf

Anderson, K., Fotheringham, E., Weaver, S., Sis-som, B., & Curtis, K. (2007). *How to write good books.* Accessed on 31st Aug. 2007 http://www.inphase-technologies.com/downloads/pdf/tech-nology/How_to_write_good_books.pdf

Athale, R. A., Szu, H. H., & Friedlander, C. B. (1986). Optical implementation of associative memory with controlled nonlinearity in the cor-relation domain. *Optics Letters, 11,* 482-484

Chang, C. C., & Selviah, D. R. (1994). High ef-ficiency photorefractive storage for multimode phase conjugate resonators. *Institute of Physics Optical Computing Conference, Edinburgh*: In-stitute of Physics, UK, PD12.27-PD12.28

Chang, C. C., & Selviah, D. R. (1995). High ef-ficiency photorefractive storage for multimode phase conjugate resonators. *Optical Comput-ing, Institute of Physics Conference Series, 139,* 439-442.

Horan, P., Uecker, D. & Arimoto, A. (1990). Optical implementation of a second-order neural network discriminator model. *Japanese Journal of Applied Physics, 29,* 361-365;

Jang, J., Shin, S., & Lee, S. (1988) Optical implementation of quadratic associative memory with outer-product storage. *Optics Letters, 13,* 693-695

Jang, J., Shin, S., & Lee, S. (1989). Programmable quadratic associative memory using holographic lenslet arrays. *Optics Letters, 14,* 838-840.

Lin, S. & Liu, L. (1989). Opto-electronic imple-mentation of a neural network with a third-order interconnection for quadratic associative memory, *Optics Communications, 73,* 268-272

Mao, Z. Q., Selviah, D. R., & Midwinter, J. E. (1992, June). Optoelectronic High Order Feedback Neural Net with parallel optical feedback. Paper presented at *Institute of Physics Conference on Opto-Electronic Neural Networks*. Sharp Laboratories of Europe, Oxford Science Park.

Mao, Z. Q., Selviah, D. R., & Midwinter, J. E. (1992). Optical high order feedback neural network using an optical fibre amplifier. *International Conference on Artificial Neural Networks, ICANN'92*, I. Aleksander, J. Taylor (Ed.): Elsevier Science Publishers, 2, 1479-1482

Mao, Z. Q., Selviah, D. R., Tao, S., & Midwinter, J. E. (1991). Holographic high order associative memory system. *Third IEE International Conference on Holographic Systems, Components and Applications*, Heriot Watt University, Edinburgh, Scotland, 342, 132-136

Owechko, Y., Dunning, G. D., Marom, E., & Soffer, B. H. (1987). Holographic associative memory with non-linearities in the correlation domain. *Applied Optics*, *26*, 1900-1910

Poon, P. C. H., Selviah, D. R., Midwinter, J. E., Daly, D., & Robinson, M. G. (1993). Design of a microlens based total interconnection for optical neural networks. *Optical Society of America Optical Computing Conference*, Palm Springs, USA: OSA, 7, 46-49

Poon, P. C. H., Selviah, D. R., Robinson, M. G., & Midwinter, J. E. (1992, June). *Free space interconnection elements for opto-electronic neural networks*. Paper presented at Institute of Physics Conference on Opto-electronic Neural Networks, Sharp Laboratories of Europe, Oxford Science Park

Psaltis, D., Park, C. H., & Hong, J. (1988). Higher order associative memories and their optical implementations. *Neural Networks*, *1*, 149-163

Selviah, D. R., Mao, Z.Q., & Midwinter, J.E. (1990). Opto-electronic high order feedback neural network. *Electronics Letters,* 26(23), 1954-1955.

Selviah, D. R., Mao, Z. Q., & Midwinter, J. E. (1991). An Opto-electronic high order feedback net (HOFNET) with variable non-linearity. *Second IEE International Conference on Artificial Neural Networks*, Bournemouth: IEE, 349, 59-63

Selviah, D. R., Midwinter, J. E., Rivers, A. W., & Lung, K. W. (1989). Correlating matched filter model for analysis and optimisation of neural networks. *IEE Proceedings, Part F Radar and Signal Processing, 136*(3), 143-148.

Tao, S., Selviah, D. R., & Midwinter, J.E. (1993). Spatioangular multiplexed storage of 750 holograms in an Fe:LiNbO$_3$ crystal. *Optics Letters, 18*(11), 912-914.

Tao, S., Song, Z. H., Selviah, D. R., Midwinter, J. E. (1995). Spatioangular-multiplexing scheme for dense holographic storage. *Applied Optics 34*(29), 6729-6737.

ADDITIONAL READING

Bishop, C. M. (1995). Neural networks for pattern recognition. In *Higher-order networks*, 133-134.

Denz, C., & Tschudi, T. (Ed.)(1998). *Optical neural networks*. Braunschweig : Vieweg.

Gardner, M. C., Kilpatrick, R. E., Day, S. E., Renton, R. E., & Selviah, D. R. (1999). Experimental verification of a computer model for optimising a liquid crystal display for spatial phase modulation. *Journal of Optics A: Pure and Applied Optics 1*(2), 299-303.

Gardner, M. C., Kilpatrick, R. E., Day, S. E., Renton, R. E., & Selviah, D. R. (1998). Experimental verification of a computer model for optimising a liquid crystal TV for spatial phase modulation.

In P. Chavel, D. A. B. Miller, H. Thienpont (Eds.), *Optics in computing '98,* SPIE, 3490, 475-478

Giles, C. L., Griffin, R. D., & Maxwell, T. (1988) Encoding geometric invariances in higher-order neural networks. *Neural information processing systems, Proceedings of the First IEEE Conference*, Denver, CO; 301-309.

Giles, C. L., & Maxwell, T. (1987) Learning, invariance, and generalization in high-order neural networks. *Applied Optics, 26*(23), 4972-4978.

Kilpatrick, R. E., Gilby, J. H., Day, S. E., & Selviah, D. R. (1998). Liquid crystal televisions for use as spatial light modulators in a complex optical correlator. In D. P. Casasent, T. H. Chao (Eds.), *Optical Pattern Recognition IX*, Orlando, USA: SPIE, 3386, 70-77

Lee, Y. C. et al. (1986). Machine learning using a higher order correlation network. *Physica, 22D.* North-Holland, 276-306

Mendel, J.M. (1991) Tutorial on higher-order statistics (spectra) in signal processing and system theory: theoretical results and some applications. *Proceedings of the IEEE, 79*(3), 278-305

Midwinter, J. E., & Selviah, D. R. (1989). Digital neural networks, matched filters and optical implementations. In I. Aleksander (Ed.), *Neural Computing Architectures* (pp. 258-278). Kogan Page.

Perantonis, S. J., & Lisboa, P. J. G. (1992). Translation, rotation, and scale invariant pattern recognition by high-order neural networks and moment classifiers. *IEEE Transactions on Neural Networks, 3*(2), 241-251.

Reid, M. B., Spirkovska, L., & Ochoa, E., (1989) Rapid training of higher-order neural networks for invariant pattern recognition. *IJCNN., International Joint Conference on Neural Networks*, Vol.1, Washington, DC, USA, 689-692

Selviah, D. R., & Midwinter, J. E. (1989). Extension of the Hamming neural network to a multilayer architecture for optical implementation. *First IEE international Conference on Artificial Neural Networks*: IEE, 313, 280-283

Selviah, D. R., & Midwinter, J. E. (1989). Memory Capacity of a novel optical neural net architecture. *ONERA-CERT Optics in Computing International Symposium*, Toulouse: ONERA-CERT, 195-201

Selviah, D. R., & Midwinter, J. E. (1989). Matched filter model for design of neural networks. In J. G. Taylor, C. L. T. Mannion (Eds.) *Institute of Physics Conference New Developments in Neural Computing*, IOP, 141-148

Selviah, D. R., & Chang, C. C. (1995). Self-pumped phase conjugate resonators and mirrors for use in optical associative memories. *Optics and Lasers in Engineering 23*(2-3), 145-166.

Selviah, D. R. (1994). Invited author: Optical computing. In Bloor, D., Brook, R. J., Flemings, M. C., Mahajan, S. (Eds.) *Encyclopaedia of Advanced Materials Volume 3*. Pergamon Press, 1820-1825.

Selviah, D. R. (1996). Invited author: Optical implementations of neural networks. *Second International Conference on Optical Information Processing*, St Petersburg, Russia

Selviah, D. R. (1995). Invited author: Optical implementations of neural networks. *8th International Conference on Laser Optics '95*, St Petersburg, Russia, 2, 172-173

Selviah, D. R., & Midwinter, J. E. (1987). Pattern recognition using opto-electronic neural networks. *IEE colloquium digest*, IEE, 1867/105, 6/1-6/4

Selviah, D. R., & Stamos, E. (2002). Invited paper: Similarity suppression algorithm for designing pattern discrimination filters. *Asian Journal of Physics, 11*(3), 367-389.

Selviah, D. R., Tao, S., & Midwinter, J. E. (1993). Holographic storage of 750 holograms in a photorefractive crystal memory. *Optical Society of America Optical Computing Conference*, Palm Springs, USA: OSA, 7, PD2-1-PD2-5

Selviah, D. R., Twaij, A. H. A. A., & Stamos, E. (1996). Invited author: Development of a feature enhancement encoding algorithm for holographic memories. *International Symposium on Holographic Memories*, Athens.

Shin, Y., & Ghosh, J. (1991) The pi-sigma network: An efficient higher-order neural network for pattern classification and function approximation. *IJCNN-91-Seattle International Joint Conference on Neural Networks*, Vol.1, Seattle, WA, USA, 13-18.

Spirkovska, L., & Reid, M. B. (1993) Coarse-coded higher-order neural networks for PSRI object recognition, *IEEE Transactions on Neural Networks*, 4(2), 276-283.

Spirkovska, L., & Reid, M. B., (1990) Connectivity strategies for higher-order neural networks applied to pattern recognition. *IJCNN International Joint Conference on Neural Networks*, San Diego, CA, USA, 1, 21-26.

Spirkovska, L., & Reid, M. B. (1992) Robust position, scale, and rotation invariant object recognition using higher-order neural networks, *Pattern Recognition*, 25(9), 975-985

Stamos, E., & Selviah, D. R. (1998). Feature enhancement and similarity suppression algorithm for noisy pattern recognition. In D. P. Casasent,

T. H. Chao (Eds.), *Optical Pattern Recognition IX*. Orlando, USA: SPIE, 3386, 182-189

Tao, S., Selviah, D. R., & Midwinter, J. E. (1993). High capacity, compact holographic storage in a photorefractive crystal. *OSA Photorefractive materials, Effects, and Devices conference*, Kiev, Ukraine: OSA, 578-581

Tao, S., Selviah, D. R., & Midwinter, J. E. (1993). Optimum replay angle for maximum diffraction efficiency of holographic gratings in $Fe:LiNbO_3$ crystals. *OSA Photorefractive materials, Effects, and Devices conference*, Kiev, Ukraine: OSA, 474-477.

Tao, S., Song, Z. H., & Selviah, D. R. (1994). Bragg Shift of holographic gratings in photorefractive $Fe:LiNbO_3$ crystals. *Optics Communications, 108*(1-3), 144-152.

Twaij, A. H., Selviah, D. R., & Midwinter, J. E. (1992, June). *Feature refinement learning algorithm for opto-electronic neural networks*. Paper presented at Institute of Physics Conference on Opto-Electronic Neural Networks, Sharp Laboratories of Europe, Oxford Science Park.

Twaij, A. H., Selviah, D. R., & Midwinter, J. E. (1992). An introduction to the optical implementation of the Hopfield network via the matched filter formalism. *University of London Centre for Neural Networks Newsletter* (3).

Yu, F. T. S., & Jutamulia, S. (1992). *Optical signal processing, computing, and neural network*. New York: Wiley.

Chapter XXI
On Complex Artificial Higher Order Neural Networks:
Dealing with Stochasticity, Jumps and Delays

Zidong Wang
Brunel University, UK

Yurong Liu
Yangzhou University, China

Xiaohui Liu
Brunel University, UK

ABSTRACT

This chapter deals with the analysis problem of the global exponential stability for a general class of stochastic artificial higher order neural networks with multiple mixed time delays and Markovian jumping parameters. The mixed time delays under consideration comprise both the discrete time-varying delays and the distributed time-delays. The main purpose of this chapter is to establish easily verifiable conditions under which the delayed high-order stochastic jumping neural network is exponentially stable in the mean square in the presence of both the mixed time delays and Markovian switching. By employing a new Lyapunov-Krasovskii functional and conducting stochastic analysis, a linear matrix inequality (LMI) approach is developed to derive the criteria ensuring the exponential stability. Furthermore, the criteria are dependent on both the discrete time-delay and distributed time-delay, hence less conservative. The proposed criteria can be readily checked by using some standard numerical packages such as the Matlab LMI Toolbox. A simple example is provided to demonstrate the effectiveness and applicability of the proposed testing criteria.

INTRODUCTION

Artificial neural networks are known to have successful applications in pattern recognition, pattern matching and mathematical function approximation. Comparing to the traditional first-order neural networks, artificial higher order neural networks (HONNs) allow high-order interactions between neurons, and therefore have stronger approximation property, faster convergence rate, greater storage capacity, and higher fault tolerance, see Artyomov & Yadid-Pecht (2005), Dembo et al. (1991), Karayiannis & Venetsanopoulos (1995), Lu et al (2006), and Psaltis et al. (1988). As pointed out in Giles & Maxwell (1987), HONNs have been shown to have impressive learning capability because the order or structure of a HONN can be tailored to the order or structure of the problem and also the knowledge can be encoded in HONNs. Due to the fact that time delays exist naturally in neural processing and signal transmission (Arik, 2005; Cao & Chen, 2004; Cao et al., 2005; Zhao, 2004a; Zhao, 2004b), the stability analysis problems for HONNs with discrete and/or distributed delays have drawn particular research attention, see e.g. Cao et al. (2004), Ren and Cao (2006), Wang et al. (2007) and Xu et al. (2005) for some recent results.

In real nervous systems, the synaptic transmission is a noisy process brought on by random fluctuations from the release of neurotransmitters and other probabilistic causes (Kappen, 2001). Indeed, such a phenomenon always appears in the electrical circuit design when implementing the neural networks. Also, the nervous systems are often subjected to external perturbations which are of a random nature. Stochastic neural networks have been extensively applied in many areas, such as pattern classification (Kappen, 2001) and time series prediction (Lai and Wong, 2001). In Kappen (2001), the application of stochastic neural networks based on Boltzmann machine learning has been demonstrated on a digit recognition problem, where the data consists of 11000 examples of handwriting digits (0-9) complied by the U.S. Postal Service Office of Advanced Technology, and the examples are pre-processed to produce 8 binary images. The main idea in Kappen (2001) is to model each of the digits using a separate Boltzmann Machine with a flat stochastic distribution, which gives rise to a special kind of stochastic neural networks with stochastically binary neurons. It has been shown in Kappen (2001) that the classification error rate for the test data set of handwriting digits using the stochastic neural networks is much lower than that using the traditional neural networks (e.g. nearest neighbour, back-propagation, wake-sleep, sigmoid belief). Furthermore, in Lai and Wong (2001), the stochastic neural network has been used to approximate complex nonlinear time series with much lower computational complexity than those for conventional neural networks, and the stochastic neural networks have been shown in Lai and Wong (2001) to have the universal approximation property of neural networks, and successfully improve post-sample forecasts over conventional neural networks and other nonlinear and nonparametric models. In addition, it has recently been revealed in Blythe et al. (2001) that a neural network could be stabilized or destabilized by certain stochastic inputs. Therefore, it is of practical significance to study the stability for delayed stochastic neural networks, and some preliminary results have been published, for example, in Huang et al. (2005), Wan and Sun (2005), Wang et al. (2006a), Wang et al. (2006b), Wang et al. (2006c) and Zhang et al. (2007). Note that, in Wang et al. (2006a) and Wang et al. (2006b), both the discrete and distributed time delays have been taken into account in the stochastic neural network models.

On the other hand, neural networks often exhibit a special characteristic of *network mode switching*. In other words, a neural network sometimes has finite modes that switch from one to another at different times (Casey, 1996; Huang et al, 2005; Tino et al, 2004), and such a switching (or jumping) can be governed by a *Markovian chain* (Tino et al, 2004). An ideal assumption with the conventional recurrent neural networks (RNNs) is that the continuous variables propagate from one processing unit to the next. Such an assumption, unfortunately, does not hold for the case when an RNN switches within several modes, and therefore RNNs sometimes suffer from the problems in catching long-term dependencies in the input stream. Such a phenomenon is referred to as the problem of information latching (Bengio et al., 1993). Recently, it has been revealed in Tino et al. (2004) that, the switching (or jumping) between different RNN modes can be governed by a Markovian chain. Specifically, the class of RNNs with Markovian jump parameters has two components in the state vector. The first one which varies continuously is referred to be the continuous state of the RNN, and the second one which varies discretely is referred to be the mode of the RNN. Markovian RNNs have great application potentials. For example, in Tino et al. (2004), the Markovian neural networks have been effectively applied on a sequence of quantized activations of a laser in a chaotic regime and an artificial language exhibiting deep recursive structures, where the laser sequence has been modelled quite successfully with finite memory predictors, although the predictive contexts of variable memory depth are necessary. Note that the control and filtering problems for dynamical systems with Markovian jumping parameters have already been widely studied, see e.g. Ji and Chizeck (1990). In Wang et al. (2006c), the exponential stability has been studied for delayed recurrent neural networks with Markovian jumping parameters. However, to the best of the authors' knowledge, the stability analysis problem for *stochastic* HONNs with *Markovian switching* and *multiple mixed time delays* has not been fully investigated, and such a situation motivates our current research.

In this chapter, we aim to investigate the global exponential stability analysis problem for a class of stochastic high-order jumping neural networks with *simultaneous* discrete and distributed time-delays. By utilizing a Lyapunov-Krasovskii functional and conducting the stochastic analysis, we recast the addressed stability analysis problem into a numerically solvability problem. Different from the commonly used matrix norm theories (such as the *M*-matrix method), a unified *linear matrix inequality* (LMI) approach is developed to establish sufficient conditions for the neural networks to be globally exponentially stable in the mean square. Note that LMIs can be easily solved by using the Matlab LMI toolbox, and no tuning of parameters is required (Boyd et al, 1994). A numerical example is provided to show the usefulness of the proposed global stability condition.

Notations

Throughout this chapter, $\mathbb{R}^n$ and $\mathbb{R}^{n\times m}$ denote, respectively, the n dimensional Euclidean space and the set of all $n\times m$ real matrices. The superscript "T" denotes the transpose and the notation $X \geq Y$ (respectively, $X > Y$) where X and Y are symmetric matrices, means that $X - Y$ is positive semi-definite (respectively, positive definite). I is the identity matrix with compatible dimension. For $h > 0$, $C([-h,0]; \mathbb{R}^n)$ denotes the family of continuous functions φ from $[-h,0]$ to $\mathbb{R}^n$ with the norm $\|\varphi\| = \sup_{-h\leq\theta\leq0}|\varphi(\theta)|$, where $|\cdot|$ is the Euclidean norm in $\mathbb{R}^n$. If A is a matrix, denote by $\|A\|$ its operator norm, that is, $\|A\| = \sup\{|Ax| : |x|=1\} = \sqrt{\lambda_{\max}(A^TA)}$, where $\lambda_{max}(\cdot)$ (respectively, $\lambda_{min}(\cdot)$ means the largest (respectively, smallest) eigenvalue of A. $l_2[0,\infty]$ is the space of square integrable vector. Moreover, let $(\Omega, F, \{F_t\}_{t\geq0}, P)$ be a complete probability space with a filtration $\{F_t\}_{t\geq0}$ satisfying the usual conditions (i.e., the filtration contains all P-null sets and is right continuous). Denote by $L^p_{F_0}([-h,0];\mathbb{R}^n)$ the family of all F_0-measurable $C([-h,0]; \mathbb{R}^n)$-valued random variables $\xi = \{\xi(\theta): -h \leq \theta \leq 0$ such that $\sup_{-h\leq\theta\leq0}\mathbb{E}|\xi(\theta)|^p < \infty$ where $\mathbb{E}\{\cdot\}$ stands for the mathematical expectation operator with respect to the given probability measure P. Sometimes, the arguments of a function will be omitted in the analysis when no confusion can arise.

PROBLEM FORMULATION

Let $r(t)$ $(t \geq 0)$ be a right-continuous Markov chain on the probability space $(\Omega, F, \{F\}_{t \geq 0}, P)$ taking values in a finite state space with $S = 1,2,...,N$ generator $\Gamma = (\gamma_{ij})_{N \times N}$ given by Box 1.

Here $\Delta > 0$ and γ_{ij} is the transition rate from i to j if $i \neq j$, while:

$$\gamma_{ii} = -\sum_{j \neq i} \gamma_{ij}.$$

$$(1)$$

In this chapter, based on the model in Wang et al. (2007), we consider the stochastic delayed

HONN with Markovian switching shown in Equation (2), or equivalently Equation (3), where $x(t) = [x_1(t), x_2(t), \cdots, x_n(t)]^T \in \mathbb{R}^n$ is the state vector associated with the n neurons, $I_j(j = 1,2,...,L)$ is a set of $\{1,2,...,n\}$, L and $d_m(j)$ are positive integers, and $g_m(\cdot)$ is the activation function with $g(0) = 0$. In the neural network (3), the matrix $A(i) = \text{diag}(a_1(i), a_2(i)),..., a_n(i))$ has positive entries $a_k(i) > 0$. The $n \times n$ matrices $B(i) = [b_{kj}(i)]_{n \times n}$, $C(i,s) = [c_{kj}(i,s)]_{n \times n}$, and $D(i,s) = [d_{kj}(i,s)]_{n \times n}$ are, respectively, the connection weight matrix, the discretely delayed connection weight matrix, and the distributively delayed connection weight matrix. $F(x(t)) = [f_1(x(t)), f_2(x(t))..., f_L(x(t))]^T$ with $f_j(x(t)) = \prod_{m \in I_j} [g_m(x_m(t))]^{d_m(j)}$ is the product of L activation functions that reflects the high-order characteristics. The scalar constant τ_{1s} ($s = 1,...N_1$) denotes the discrete time delay, whereas scalar $\tau_{2s} \geq 0$ ($s = 1,...N_2$) describes the distributed time delay.

Box 1.

$$P\{r(t+\Delta) = j \mid r(t) = i\} = \begin{cases} \gamma_{ij}\Delta + o(\Delta), & \text{if } i \neq j; \\ 1 + \gamma_{ii}\Delta + o(\Delta), & \text{if } i = j. \end{cases}$$

Equation (2).

$$dx_k(t) = \left\{ -a_k(r(t))x_k(t) + \sum_{j=1}^{L} b_{kj}(r(t)) \prod_{m \in I_j} [g_m(x_m(t))]^{d_m(j)} \right.$$

$$+ \sum_{j=1}^{L} \sum_{s=1}^{N_1} c_{kj}(r(t), s) \prod_{m \in I_j} [g_m(x_m(t - \tau_{1s}))]^{d_m(j)}$$

$$\left. + \sum_{j=1}^{L} \sum_{s=1}^{N_2} d_{kj}(r(t), s) \int_{t-\tau_{2s}}^{t} \prod_{m \in I_j} [g_m(x_m(s))]^{d_m(j)} ds \right\} dt$$

$$+ \sigma_k(x_k(t), x_k(t - \tau_{11}),..., x_k(t - \tau_{1N_1}), r(t), t)dw_k(t)$$

Equation (3).

$$dx(t) = \left[-A(r(t))x(t) + B(r(t))F(x(t)) + \sum_{v=1}^{N_1} C(r(t), v)F(x(t-\tau_{iv})) + \sum_{v=1}^{N_2} D(r(t), v) \int_{t-\tau_{2v}}^{t} F(x(s))ds \right] dt$$

$$+ \sigma(x(t), x_t, t, r(t))dw(t),$$

For convenience, let:

$$\tau_1 = \max_{1 \le s \le N_1} \{\tau_{1s}\}, \quad \tau_2 = \max_{1 \le s \le N_2} \{\tau_{2s}\}, \quad \tau = \max\{\tau_1, \tau_2\}$$

(4)

In the neural network (3), $w(t)$ is a scalar Wiener process (Brownian Motion) on $(\Omega, F, \{F_t\}_{t \ge 0}, P)$ which is independent of the Markov chain $r(\cdot)$ and satisfies:

$$\mathbb{E}[w(t)] = 0, \quad \mathbb{E}[w^2(t)] = t.$$ (5)

The function $\sigma: \mathbb{R}^n \times \ldots \times \mathbb{R}^n \times \mathbb{R}_+ \times S \to \mathbb{R}^n$ is Borel measurable and is assumed to satisfy Equation (6), where $\rho_0 > 0$ and $\rho_s > 0$ $(s = 1, \ldots, N_1)$ are scalar constants.

In this chapter, as in Ren and Cao (2006) and Wang et al. (2008), we make the following assumptions.

Assumption 1: There exist constants $\mu_k > 0$ such that:

$$|g_m(x)| \le \mu_m|x|, \quad \forall x \in \mathbb{R}, \quad m = 1, 2, \ldots, n$$

(7)

Assumption 2: The following holds for all:

$$|g_m(x)| \le 1, \quad \forall x \in \mathbb{R}, \quad n = 1, 2, \ldots, m.$$ (8)

Remark 1: Under Assumption 1 and Assumption 2, it is easy to check that functions F and σ satisfy the linear growth condition (cf. Khasminskii, 1980; Skorohod, 1989). Therefore, for any initial data $\xi \in L^2_{\mathcal{F}_0}([-\tau, 0]; \mathbb{R}^n)$, the system (3) has a unique solution denoted by $x(t;\xi)$, or $x(t)$ (cf. Khasminskii, 1980; Skorohod, 1989),

and it is obvious that the system (3) has a trivial solution, that is, $x(t) \equiv 0$ corresponding to the initial data $\xi = 0$.

Definition 1: The neural network (3) is said to be stable in the mean square if, for any $\varepsilon > 0$, there is a $\delta(\varepsilon) > 0$ such that:

$$\mathbb{E}|x(t;\xi)|^2 < \varepsilon, \ t > 0 \ \text{when} \ \sup_{-\tau \le s \le 0} \mathbb{E}|\xi(s)|^2 < \delta.$$

(9)

If, in addition to (9), the relation $\lim_{t \to 0} \mathbb{E}|x(t;\xi)|^2 = 0$ holds, then the neural network (3) is said to be asymptotically stable in the mean square.

Definition 2: The neural network (3) is said to be exponentially stable in the mean square if there exist positive constants $\alpha > 0$ and $\mu > 0$ such that every solution $x(t;\xi)$ of (3) satisfies:

$$\mathbb{E}|x(t;\xi)|^2 \le \mu e^{-\alpha t} \sup_{-\tau \le s \le 0} \mathbb{E}|\xi(s)|^2, \quad \forall t > 0.$$

The main purpose of this chapter is to deal with the problem of exponential stability analysis for the neural network (3). By constructing new Lyapunov-Krasovskii functional, we shall establish LMI-based sufficient conditions under which the global exponential stability in the mean square is guaranteed for the stochastic HONN (3) with mixed time delays and Markovian switching.

MAIN RESULTS AND PROOFS

The following lemmas will be used in establishing our main results.

Equation (6).

$$\sigma^T(x(t), x_t, t, r(t))\sigma(x(t), x_t, t, r(t)) \le \rho_0 x^T(t)x(t) + \sum_{s=1}^{N_1} \rho_s x^T(t - \tau_{1s})x(t - \tau_{1s}),$$

Lemma 1: Let x, y be any n-dimensional real vectors and P be a $n \times n$ positive semi-definite matrix. Then, for any scalar $\varepsilon > 0$ the following matrix inequality holds:

$$2x^T P y \le \varepsilon^T x^T P x + \varepsilon^{-1} y^T P y.$$

Lemma 2: (Gu, 2000). For any positive definite matrix $M > 0$, scalar $\gamma > 0$, vector function ω: $[0,\gamma] \to \mathbb{R}^n$ such that the integrations concerned are well defined, the following inequality holds:

$$\left(\int_0^\gamma \omega(s)ds \right)^T M \left(\int_0^\gamma \omega(s)ds \right) \le \gamma \left(\int_0^\gamma \omega^T(s)M\omega(s)ds \right)$$

(10)

Lemma 3: (Schur Complement). Given constant matrices $\Omega_1, \Omega_2, \Omega_3$ where $\Omega_1 = \Omega_1^T$ and $\Omega_2 > 0$, then:

$$\Omega_1 + \Omega_3^T \Omega_2^{-1} \Omega_3 < 0$$

if and only if:

$$\begin{bmatrix} \Omega_1 & \Omega_3^T \\ \Omega_3 & -\Omega_2 \end{bmatrix} < 0.$$

Lemma 4: (Ren and Cao, 2006). Let $\Sigma_\mu = \text{diag}(\mu_1, \mu_2, ..., \mu_n)$ be a positive diagonal matrix. Then, for the function $F = [f_1(x), f_2(x), ..., f_L(x)]^T$ ($x \in \mathbb{R}^n$), the following inequality holds:

$$F^T(x)F(x) \le Lx^T \Sigma_\mu \Sigma_\mu x.$$

(11)

The main results of this chapter are given in the following theorem.

Theorem 1: Let $\epsilon_0(0 < \epsilon_0 < 1)$ be a fixed constant and let Assumption 1 and Assumption 2 hold. Then, the stochastic HONN (3) with mixed time delays and Markovian switching is globally exponentially stable in the mean square if there exist constants $\lambda_0 > 0, \lambda_{1s} > 0$ ($s = 1,...,N_1$) and $\lambda_{2s} > 0$ ($s = 1,...,N_2$), positive definite matrices Q_s ($s = 1,...,N_1$), R_s ($s = 1,...,N_2$), and $P_i (i \in S)$ such that the following LMIs hold:

$$P_i < \lambda_0 I, \quad Q_s < \lambda_{1s} I, \quad R_s < \lambda_{2s} I,$$

(12)

$$\Phi(i) < 0, \ (i \in \mathcal{S})$$

(13)

where Box 2 occurs with Equation (14).

Box 2.

$$\Phi(i) = \begin{bmatrix} \Pi(i) & P_i C(i,1) & \cdots & P_i C(i,N_1) & P_i D(i,1) & \cdots & P_i D(i,N_2) & P_i B(i) \\ C^T(i,1)P_i & -Q_1 & \cdots & 0 & 0 & \cdots & 0 & 0 \\ \vdots & \vdots & & \vdots & \vdots & & \vdots & \vdots \\ C^T(i,N_1)P_i & 0 & \cdots & -Q_{N_1} & 0 & \cdots & 0 & 0 \\ D^T(i,1)P_i & 0 & \cdots & 0 & -\frac{1}{\tau_{21}}R_1 & \cdots & 0 & 0 \\ \vdots & \vdots & & \vdots & \vdots & & \vdots & \vdots \\ D^T(i,N_2)P_i & 0 & \cdots & 0 & 0 & \cdots & -\frac{1}{\tau_{2N_2}}R_{N_2} & 0 \\ B^T(i)P_i & 0 \cdots & 0 & 0 & \cdots & 0 & 0 & -I \end{bmatrix}$$

Equation (14).

$$\Pi(i) = -P_i A(i) - A(i)P_i + \sum_{j=1}^{N} \gamma_{ij} P_j + (\varepsilon_0 \tau + \lambda_0 \sum_{v=0}^{N_1} \rho_v)I + (1 + \sum_{v=1}^{N_1} \lambda_{1v} + \sum_{v=1}^{N_2} \tau_{2v}\lambda_{2v})L\Sigma_\mu\Sigma_\mu.$$

Equation (15).

$$V(x(t),t,r(t)=i) = x^T(t)P_ix(t) + \lambda_0 \sum_{v=1}^{N_1} \rho_v \int_{t-\tau_{1v}}^t x^T(s)x(s)ds + \varepsilon_0 \int_{t-\tau}^t \int_s^t x^T(\theta)x(\theta)d\theta ds$$

$$+ \sum_{v=1}^{N_1} \int_{t-\tau_{1v}}^t F^T(x(s))Q_vF(x(s))ds + \sum_{v=1}^{N_2} \int_{t-\tau_{2v}}^t \int_s^t F^T(x(\theta))R_vF(x(\theta))d\theta ds.$$

Equation (16).

$$\mathcal{L}V(x(t),t,i)$$

$$:= \lim_{\Delta \to 0^+} \sup \left[\{V(x(t+\Delta),t+\Delta,r(t+\Delta)) \mid x(t),r(t)=i\} - V(x(t),t,r(t)=i) \right]$$

$$= 2x^T(t)P_i \left[-A(i)x(t) + B(i)F(x(t)) + \sum_{v=1}^{N_1} C(i,v)F(x(t-\tau_{iv})) + \sum_{v=1}^{N_2} D(i,v) \int_{t-\tau_{2v}}^t F(x(s))ds \right]$$

$$+ \sum_{j=1}^N \gamma_{ij}V(x(t),t,j) + \sigma^T(x(t),x_t,t,i)P_i\sigma(x(t),x_t,t,i) + \lambda_0 \sum_{v=1}^{N_1} \rho_v x^T(t)x(t)$$

$$-\lambda_0 \sum_{v=1}^{N_1} \rho_v x^T(t-\tau_{1v})x(t-\tau_{1v}) + \varepsilon_0 \tau x^T(t)x(t) - \varepsilon_0 \int_{t-\tau}^t x^T(s)x(s)ds + \sum_{v=1}^{N_1} F^T(x(t))Q_vF(x(t))$$

$$- \sum_{v=1}^{N_1} F^T(x(t-\tau_{1v}))Q_vF(x(t-\tau_{1v})) + \sum_{v=1}^{N_2} \tau_{2v}F^T(x(t))R_vF(x(t)) - \sum_{v=1}^{N_2} \int_{t-\tau_{2v}}^t F^T(x(s))R_vF(x(s))ds$$

$$- \sum_{v=1}^{N_1} F^T(x(t-\tau_{1v}))Q_vF(x(t-\tau_{1v})) + \sum_{v=1}^{N_2} \tau_{2v}F^T(x(t))R_vF(x(t)) - \sum_{v=1}^{N_2} \int_{t-\tau_{2v}}^t F^T(x(s))R_vF(x(s))ds$$

Proof: Denote by $C^{2,1}(\mathbb{R}^n \times \mathbb{R}_+ \times S; \mathbb{R}^n)$ the family of all nonnegative functions $V(x,t,i)$ on $\mathbb{R}^n \times \mathbb{R}_+ \times S$ which are twice differentiable with respect to the first variable x and once differentiable with respect to the second variable t.

In order to establish the stability conditions, we introduce the following Lyapunov-Krasovskii functional candidate $V(x(t),t,r(t)=i) := V(x(t),t,i) \in C^{2,1}(\mathbb{R}^n \times \mathbb{R}_+ \times S; \mathbb{R}^n)$ by Equation (15).

The weak infinitesimal operator LV (Khasminskii, 1980; Skorohod, 1989) along (3) from $\mathbb{R}^n \times \mathbb{R}_+ \times S$ to $\mathbb{R}$ is given by Equation (16).

By (1), it is clear that:

$$\sum_{j=1}^N \gamma_{ij}V(x(t),t,j) = \sum_{j=1}^N \gamma_{ij}x^T(t)P_jx(t). \tag{17}$$

It follows readily from (6) that:

$$\sigma^T(x(t),x_t,t,i)P_i\sigma(x(t),x_t,t,i)$$
$$\leq \lambda_{\max}(P_i)\sigma^T(x(t),x_t,t,i)P_i\sigma(x(t),x_t,t,i)$$
$$\leq \lambda_0 \left[\rho_0 x^T(t)x(t) + \sum_{v=1}^{N_1} \rho_v x^T(t-\tau_{1v})x(t-\tau_{1v}) \right]. \tag{18}$$

Furthermore, it follows from Lemma 1 that:

$$2x^T(t)P_iB(i)F(x(t)) \leq$$
$$x^T(t)P_iB(i)B^T(i)P_ix(t) + F^T(x(t))F(x(t)) \tag{19}$$

Substituting (17)- (19) into (16) yields Equation (20).

By Lemma 4, we have:

$$F^T(x(t))F(x(t)) \leq Lx^T(t)\Sigma_\mu\Sigma_\mu x(t) \tag{21}$$

and:

Equation (20).

$$\mathcal{L}V(x(t),t,i)$$
$$= 2x^T(t)P_i\left[-A(i)x(t)+B(i)F(x(t))+\sum_{v=1}^{N_1}C(i,v)F(x(t-\tau_{iv}))+\sum_{v=1}^{N_2}D(i,v)\int_{t-\tau_{2v}}^{t}F(x(s))ds\right]$$
$$+x^T(t)P_iB(i)B^T(i)P_ix(t)+\sum_{j=1}^{N}\gamma_{ij}x^T(t)P_jx(t)+\lambda_0\sum_{v=0}^{N_1}\rho_v x^T(t)x(t)$$
$$+\varepsilon_0\tau x^T(t)x(t)-\varepsilon_0\int_{t-\tau}^{t}x^T(s)x(s)ds+\sum_{v=1}^{N_1}F^T(x(t))Q_vF(x(t))-\sum_{v=1}^{N_1}F^T(x(t-\tau_{1v}))Q_vF(x(t-\tau_{1v}))$$
$$+\sum_{v=1}^{N_2}\tau_{2v}F^T(x(t))R_vF(x(t))-\sum_{v=1}^{N_2}\int_{t-\tau_{2v}}^{t}F^T(x(s))R_vF(x(s))ds$$

Equation (24).

$$\int_{t-\tau_{2v}}^{t}F^T(x(s))R_vF(x(s))ds\geq\frac{1}{\tau_{2v}}\left[\int_{t-\tau_{2v}}^{t}F(x(s))ds\right]^T R_v\left[\int_{t-\tau_{2v}}^{t}F(x(s))ds\right].$$

Equation (25).

$$\mathcal{L}V(x(t),t,i)$$
$$= 2x^T(t)P_i\left[-A(i)x(t)+B(i)F(x(t))+\sum_{v=1}^{N_1}C(i,v)F(x(t-\tau_{iv}))+\sum_{v=1}^{N_2}D(i,v)\int_{t-\tau_{2v}}^{t}F(x(s))ds\right]$$
$$+x^T(t)P_iB(i)B^T(i)P_ix(t)+(1+\sum_{v=1}^{N_1}\lambda_{1v}+\sum_{v=1}^{N_2}\tau_{2v}\lambda_{2v})Lx^T(t)\Sigma_\mu\Sigma_\mu x(t)+\sum_{j=1}^{N}\gamma_{ij}x^T(t)P_jx(t)$$
$$+\lambda_0\sum_{v=0}^{N_1}\rho_v x^T(t)x(t)+\varepsilon_0\tau x^T(t)x(t)-\varepsilon_0\int_{t-\tau}^{t}x^T(s)x(s)ds-\sum_{v=1}^{N_1}F^T(x(t-\tau_{1v}))Q_vF(x(t-\tau_{1v}))$$
$$-\sum_{v=1}^{N_2}\frac{1}{\tau_{2v}}\left[\int_{t-\tau_{2v}}^{t}F(x(s))ds\right]^T R_v\left[\int_{t-\tau_{2v}}^{t}F(x(s))ds\right]$$
$$= \xi^T(t)\Psi(i)\xi(t)-\varepsilon_0\int_{t-\tau}^{t}x^T(s)x(s)ds,$$

$$F^T(x(t))Q_vF(x(t))\leq\lambda_{\max}(Q_v)F^T(x(t))F(x(t))$$

$$\leq\lambda_{1v}Lx^T(t)\Sigma_\mu\Sigma_\mu x(t). \tag{22}$$

Similarly, we can obtain:

$$F^T(x(t))R_vF(x(t))\leq\lambda_{2v}Lx^T(t)\Sigma_\mu\Sigma_\mu x(t). \tag{23}$$

Also, Equation (24) follows easily from Lemma 2.

Combining (20) with (21)-(24), we can establish Equation (25), where Box 3 occurs, with $\Pi(i)$ being defined in (14).

From the inequality (13) and Lemma 3, Equation (26) follows readily. Together with (25), this implies that:

Box 3.

$$\xi(t) = \left[\begin{array}{cccccc} x^T(t) & F^T(x(t-\tau_{11})) & \cdots & F^T(x(t-\tau_{1N_1})) & \int_{t-\tau_{21}}^t F^T(x(s))ds & \cdots & \int_{t-\tau_{2N_2}}^t F^T(x(s))ds \end{array}\right]^T$$

$$\Psi(i) = \begin{bmatrix} \Pi(i) + P_i B(i) B^T(i) P_i & P_i C(i,1) & \cdots & P_i C(i,N_1) & P_i D(i,1) & \cdots & P_i D(i,N_2) \\ C^T(i,1)P_i & -Q_1 & \cdots & 0 & 0 & \cdots & 0 \\ \vdots & \vdots & & \vdots & \vdots & & \vdots \\ C^T(i,N_1)P_i & 0 & \cdots & -Q_{N_1} & 0 & \cdots & 0 \\ D^T(i,1)P_i & 0 & \cdots & 0 & -\frac{1}{\tau_{21}}R_1 & \cdots & 0 \\ \vdots & \vdots & & \vdots & \vdots & & \vdots \\ D^T(i,N_2)P_i & 0 & \cdots & 0 & 0 & \cdots & -\frac{1}{\tau_{2N_2}}R_{N_2} \end{bmatrix}$$

Equation (26).

$$\Psi(i) = \begin{bmatrix} \Pi(i) & P_i C(i,1) & \cdots & P_i C(i,N_1) & P_i D(i,1) & \cdots & P_i D(i,N_2) \\ C^T(i,1)P_i & -Q_1 & \cdots & 0 & 0 & \cdots & 0 \\ \vdots & \vdots & & \vdots & \vdots & & \vdots \\ C^T(i,N_1)P_i & 0 & \cdots & -Q_{N_1} & 0 & \cdots & 0 \\ D^T(i,1)P_i & 0 & \cdots & 0 & -\frac{1}{\tau_{21}}R_1 & \cdots & 0 \\ \vdots & \vdots & & \vdots & \vdots & & \vdots \\ D^T(i,N_2)P_i & 0 & \cdots & 0 & 0 & \cdots & -\frac{1}{\tau_{2N_2}}R_{N_2} \end{bmatrix}$$

$$+ \left[\begin{array}{cccccc} B^T(i)P_i & 0 & \cdots & 0 & 0 & \cdots & 0 \end{array}\right]^T \left[\begin{array}{cccccc} B^T(i)P_i & 0 & \cdots & 0 & 0 & \cdots & 0 \end{array}\right],$$

$$\mathcal{L}V(x(t),t,i) \le \xi^T(t)\Psi(i)\xi(t) - \varepsilon_0 \int_{t-\tau}^t x^T(s)x(s)ds$$

$$\le \lambda_{\max}(\Psi(i))|\xi(t)|^2 - \varepsilon_0 \int_{t-\tau}^t x^T(s)x(s)ds$$

$$\le \lambda_{\max}(\Psi(i))|x(t)|^2 - \varepsilon_0 \int_{t-\tau}^t x^T(s)x(s), \tag{27}$$

with $\lambda_{\max}(\Psi(i)) < 0$.

In order to deal with the exponential stability of (3), we define the weak infinitesimal operator along (3) as follows:

$$\mathcal{L}[e^{\alpha t}V(x(t),t,i)] = e^{\alpha t}[\alpha V(x(t),t,i) + \mathcal{L}V(x(t),t,i)]. \tag{28}$$

where α is a positive constant to be determined.

Regarding the terms in the function $V(x(t),t,i)$, it is easy to see that:

$$x^T(t)P_i x(t) \le \lambda_{\max}(P_i)|x(t)|^2. \tag{29}$$

$$\lambda_0 \sum_{v=1}^{N_1} \rho_v \int_{t-\tau_{1v}}^t x^T(s)x(s)ds \le \lambda_0 \sum_{v=1}^{N_1} \rho_v \int_{t-\tau}^t x^T(s)x(s)ds \tag{30}$$

$$\varepsilon_0 \int_{t-\tau}^t \int_s^t x^T(\theta)x(\theta)d\theta ds \le \varepsilon_0 \tau \int_{t-\tau}^t x^T(s)x(s)ds. \tag{31}$$

Also, from Lemma 4, we have Equation (32). Similarly, we can obtain Equation (33).

Substituting (29)-(33) into (15) results in:

$$V(x(t),t,i) \le \lambda_{\max}(P_i)|x(t)|^2 + \kappa_0 \int_{t-\tau}^t x^T(s)x(s)ds. \tag{34}$$

where Box 4 is true.

Equation (35) can now follow from (27), (28) and (34). Choose a constant $\alpha = \alpha_0$ which is sufficiently small such that the following inequalities hold:

$$\begin{cases} \lambda_{\max}(\Phi(i)) + \alpha_0 \lambda_{\max}(P_i) &< 0. \\ -\varepsilon_0 + \alpha_0 \kappa_0 &< 0. \end{cases} \quad (36)$$

By the generalized Itô formula (Khasminskii, 1980; Skorohod, 1989), we have Equation (37).

Let:

$$\beta_1 = \max_{1 \le i \le N} \lambda_{\max}(P_i), \quad \beta_2 = \min_{1 \le i \le N} \lambda_{\min}(P_i).$$

From (34), it follows that:

$$\mathbb{E}V(x(0), r(0)) \le \beta_1 |x(0)|^2 + \kappa_0 \mathbb{E} \int_{-\tau}^{0} x^T(s)x(s)ds$$

$$\le (\beta_1 + \kappa_0 \tau) \sup_{-\tau \le s \le 0} \mathbb{E}|x(s)|^2. \quad (38)$$

On the other hand, it is obvious that:

$$\mathbb{E}V(t) \ge \beta_2 \mathbb{E}|x(t)|^2. \quad (39)$$

Equation (32).

$$\int_{t-\tau_{1v}}^{t} F^T(x(s))Q_v F(x(s))ds \le \lambda_{\max}(Q_v) \int_{t-\tau}^{t} F^T(x(s))F(x(s))ds$$

$$\le L\lambda_{1v} \int_{t-\tau}^{t} x(s)\Sigma_\mu \Sigma_\mu x(s)ds$$

$$\le L\lambda_{1v} \lambda_{\max}(\Sigma_\mu \Sigma_\mu) \int_{t-\tau}^{t} x(s)x(s)ds.$$

Equation (33).

$$\int_{t-\tau_{2v}}^{t} \int_{s}^{t} F^T(x(\theta))RF(x(\theta))d\theta ds \le \tau_{2v}\lambda_{\max}(R) \int_{t-\tau_{2v}}^{t} F^T(x(s))F(x(s))ds$$

$$\le \tau_{2v}L\lambda_{2v}\lambda_{\max}(\Sigma_\mu \Sigma_\mu) \int_{t-\tau_2}^{t} x^T(s)x(s)ds.$$

Box 4.

$$\kappa_0 = \varepsilon_0 \tau + L \sum_{v=1}^{N_1} \lambda_{1v}\lambda_{\max}(\Sigma_\mu \Sigma_\mu) + \tau_2 L \sum_{v=1}^{N_2} \lambda_{2v}\lambda_{\max}(\Sigma_\mu \Sigma_\mu) + \lambda_0 \sum_{v=1}^{N_1} \rho_v.$$

Equation (35).

$$\mathcal{L}[e^{\alpha t}V(x(t), t, i)] \le e^{\alpha t}\left[(\lambda_{\max}(\Phi(i)) + \alpha\lambda_{\max}(P_i)) |x(t)|^2 + (-\varepsilon_0 + \alpha\kappa_0) \int_{t-\tau}^{t} x^T(s)x(s)ds \right].$$

Equation (37).

$$e^{\alpha_0 t}\mathbb{E}V(x(t), t, r(t)) \le \mathbb{E}V(x(0), 0, r(0)) + \int_{0}^{t} LV(x(s), r(s))ds$$

$$\le \mathbb{E}V(x(0), 0, r(0)).$$

and then from (37), (38) and (39) it follows that:

$$\mathbb{E}|x(t;\xi)|^2 \le (\beta_1 + \kappa_0\tau)\beta_2 e^{-\alpha_0 t} \sup_{-\tau \le s \le 0} \mathbb{E}|\xi(s)|^2,$$

(40)

which completes the proof of Theorem 1.

Remark 2: In Theorem 1, sufficient conditions are provided for the neural network (3) to be globally exponentially stable in mean square. It should be pointed out that, such conditions are expressed in the form of LMIs, which could be easily checked by utilizing the recently developed interior-point methods available in Matlab toolbox, and no tuning of parameters will be needed (Gahinet et al., 1995).

In what follows, we specialize our results to two cases. Both corollaries given below are easy consequences of Theorem 1, hence the proofs are omitted.

Case 1: We first consider the delayed stochastic HONN (3) with $N_1 = N_2 = 1$. That is, consider the delayed stochastic HONN shown in Equation (41).

The following corollary can be obtained directly.

Corollary 1: Let $\epsilon_0(0 < \epsilon_0 < 1)$ be a fixed constant and let Assumption 1 and Assumption 2 hold. Then, the delayed stochastic HONN (41) is globally exponentially stable in the mean square if there exist three constants $\lambda_0 > 0, \lambda_1 > 0$ and $\lambda_2 > 0$, two positive definite matrices Q and R, and a set of positive matrices $P_i(i \in S)$ such that the LMIs shown in Box 5 hold.

Case 2: In this case, we consider the delayed stochastic HONN (3) without distributed time delay given by Equation (42), and can then get the following corollary easily.

Corollary 2: Let $\epsilon_0(0 < \epsilon_0 < 1)$ be a fixed constant and let Assumption 1 and Assumption 2 hold. Then, the delayed stochastic HONN (42) is globally exponentially stable in the mean square if there exist constants $\lambda_0 > 0$ and $\lambda_{1s} > 0$ ($s = 1,...,N_1$), positive definite matrices Q_s ($s = 1,...,N_1$) and R_s ($s = 1,...,N_2$), and $P_i(i \in S)$ such that the LMIs shown in Box 6 hold.

Equation (41).

$$dx(t) = \left[-A(r(t))x(t) + B(r(t))F(x(t)) + C(r(t))F(x(t-\tau_1)) + D(r(t)) \int_{t-\tau_2}^{t} F(x(s))ds \right] dt$$
$$+ \sigma(x(t), x_t, t, r(t))dw(t)$$

Box 5.

$$P_i < \lambda_0 I, \quad Q < \lambda_1 I, \quad R < \lambda_2 I,$$

$$\hat{\Phi}(i) := \begin{bmatrix} \hat{\Pi}(i) & P_iC(i) & P_iD(i) & P_iB(i) \\ C^T(i)P_i & -Q & 0 & 0 \\ D^T(i)P_i & 0 & -\frac{1}{\tau_2}R & 0 \\ B^T(i)P_i & 0 & 0 & -I \end{bmatrix} < 0, \ (i \in S)$$

where:

$$\hat{\Pi}(i) = -P_iA(i) - A(i)P_i + \sum_{j=1}^{N}\gamma_{ij}P_j + (\varepsilon_0\tau + \lambda_0\rho_0 + \lambda_0\rho_1)I + (1+\lambda_1+\tau_2\lambda_2)L\Sigma_\mu\Sigma_\mu.$$

Following the same line of Theorem 1, we can also deal with the analysis problem of asymptotic stability for the neural network (3), and obtain the following result.

Corollary 3: Suppose Assumption 1 and Assumption 2 hold. Then, the delayed stochastic HONN (3) with the mixed multiple time delays and Markovian switching is globally asymptotically stable in the mean square if there exist constants $\lambda_0 > 0, \lambda_{1s} > 0$ ($s = 1,...,N_1$) and $\lambda_{2s} > 0$ ($s = 1,...,N_2$), positive definite matrices Q_s ($s = 1,...,N_1$) and R_s ($s = 1,...,N_2$), and $P_i (i \in S)$ such that the LMIs shown in Box 7 hold.

Equation (42).

$$
dx(t) = \left[-A(r(t))x(t) + B(r(t))F(x(t)) + \sum_{v=1}^{N_1} C(r(t),v)F(x(t-\tau_{iv})) \right] dt
$$
$$
+\sigma(x(t), x_t, t, r(t))dw(t).
$$

Box 6.

$$
P_i < \lambda_0 I, \quad Q_s < \lambda_{1s} I.
$$

$$
\Phi(i) = \begin{bmatrix}
\bar{\Pi}(i) & P_i C(i,1) & \cdots & P_i C(i,N_1) & P_i B(i) \\
C^T(i,1)P_i & -Q_1 & \cdots & 0 & 0 \\
\vdots & \vdots & & \vdots & \vdots \\
C^T(i,N_1)P_i & 0 & \cdots & -Q_{N_1} & 0 \\
B^T(i)P_i & 0\cdots & 0 & 0 & -I
\end{bmatrix},
$$

where:

$$
\bar{\Pi}(i) = -P_i A(i) - A(i)P_i + \sum_{j=1}^{N} \gamma_{ij} P_j + (\varepsilon_0 \tau + \lambda_0 \sum_{v=0}^{N_1} \rho_v)I + (1 + \sum_{v=1}^{N_1} \lambda_{1v})L\Sigma_\mu \Sigma_\mu.
$$

Box 7.

$$
P_i < \lambda_0 I, \quad Q_s < \lambda_{1s} I, \quad R_s < \lambda_{2s} I,
$$

$$
\tilde{\Phi}(i) = \begin{bmatrix}
\tilde{\Pi}(i) & P_i C(i,1) & \cdots & P_i C(i,N_1) & P_i D(i,1) & \cdots & P_i D(i,N_2) & P_i B(i) \\
C^T(i,1)P_i & -Q_1 & \cdots & 0 & 0 & \cdots & 0 & 0 \\
\vdots & \vdots & & \vdots & \vdots & & \vdots & \vdots \\
C^T(i,N_1)P_i & 0 & \cdots & -Q_{N_1} & 0 & \cdots & 0 & 0 \\
D^T(i,1)P_i & 0 & \cdots & 0 & -\frac{1}{\tau_{21}}R_1 & \cdots & 0 & 0 \\
\vdots & \vdots & & \vdots & \vdots & & \vdots & \vdots \\
D^T(i,N_2)P_i & 0 & \cdots & 0 & 0 & \cdots & -\frac{1}{\tau_{2N_2}}R_{N_2} & 0 \\
B^T(i)P_i & 0\cdots & 0 & 0 & & 0 & 0 & -I
\end{bmatrix} < 0
$$

where:

$$
\tilde{\Pi}(i) = -P_i A(i) - A(i)P_i + \sum_{j=1}^{N} \gamma_{ij} P_j + (\lambda_0 \sum_{v=0}^{N_1} \rho_v)I + (1 + \sum_{v=1}^{N_1} \lambda_{1v} + \sum_{v=1}^{N_2} \tau_{2v} \lambda_{2v})L\Sigma_\mu \Sigma_\mu.
$$

Remark 3: In our results, the stability analysis problems are dealt with for several classes of stochastic HONNs with mixed multiple time delays and Markovian jumping parameters. An LMI-based sufficient condition is derived for the stability of the neural networks addressed. The exponential as well as asymptotical stability can be readily checked by the solvability of a set of LMIs, which can be done by resorting to the Matlab LMI toolbox. In next section, an illustrative example will be provided to show the potential of the proposed criteria.

A NUMERICAL EXAMPLE

In this section, a simple example is presented here to demonstrate the effectiveness of our main results.

Consider a two-neuron stochastic HONN (3) with $N_1 = N_2 = 2$ and the parameters shown in Box 8.

With the given parameters, by using Matlab LMI Toolbox, we solve the LMIs (12) and (13), and obtain the feasible solution as shown in Box 9.

It follows from Theorem 1 that the delayed stochastic HONN (3) with the given parameters is globally exponentially stable in the mean square.

CONCLUSION

In this chapter, the global exponential stability analysis problem has been studied for a general class of stochastic HONNs with mixed time delays and Markovian switching. The mixed time delays under consideration comprise both the discrete time-varying delays and the distributed time-delays. We have established easily verifiable conditions under which the delayed high-order stochastic neural network is exponentially stable in the mean square in the presence of both the mixed time delays and Markovian switching. By

Box 8.

$$A(1) = \begin{bmatrix} 3 & 0 \\ 0 & 3.5 \end{bmatrix}, \ A(2) = \begin{bmatrix} 2.5 & 0 \\ 0 & 3 \end{bmatrix}, \ B(1) = \begin{bmatrix} 0.4 & 1 \\ -0.6 & -0.8 \end{bmatrix}, \ B(2) = \begin{bmatrix} 0.6 & -0.5 \\ -0.4 & -0.3 \end{bmatrix},$$

$$C(1,1) = \begin{bmatrix} -0.7 & -0.5 \\ 0.4 & 0.6 \end{bmatrix}, \ C(1,2) = \begin{bmatrix} -0.2 & 0.3 \\ 0.1 & 0.2 \end{bmatrix}, \ C(2,1) = \begin{bmatrix} 0.7 & 0.5 \\ -0.3 & 0.3 \end{bmatrix},$$

$$C(2,2) = \begin{bmatrix} 0.3 & 0 \\ -0.1 & -0.2 \end{bmatrix}, \ D(1,1) = \begin{bmatrix} 0.5 & -0.4 \\ -0.2 & 0.6 \end{bmatrix}, \ D(1,2) = \begin{bmatrix} 0.2 & -0.3 \\ 0 & 0.3 \end{bmatrix},$$

$$D(2,1) = \begin{bmatrix} -0.2 & 0.4 \\ -0.5 & 0.8 \end{bmatrix}, \ D(2,2) = \begin{bmatrix} 0.3 & -0.1 \\ -0.3 & 0.2 \end{bmatrix}, \ \Sigma_\mu = (0.3, 0.2), \ L = 3, \ \varepsilon_0 = 0.01,$$

$$\rho_0 = \rho_1 = \rho_2 = 0.2, \ \tau_1(t) = 0.1(1+\sin t), \ \tau_{21} = 0.2, \ \tau_{22} = 0.1, \ \tau = 0.2, \ \gamma_{11} = -3,$$
$$\gamma_{12} = 3, \ \gamma_{21} = 4, \ \gamma_{22} = -4.$$

Box 9.

$$P_1 = \begin{bmatrix} 0.6565 & -0.0269 \\ -0.0269 & 0.4306 \end{bmatrix}, \ P_2 = \begin{bmatrix} 0.6397 & 0.0062 \\ 0.0062 & 0.4275 \end{bmatrix}, \ Q_1 = \begin{bmatrix} 1.1087 & 0.0445 \\ 0.0445 & 1.0827 \end{bmatrix},$$

$$Q_2 = \begin{bmatrix} 1.0298 & -0.0022 \\ -0.0022 & 1.0291 \end{bmatrix}, \ R_1 = \begin{bmatrix} 0.2959 & -0.0109 \\ -0.0109 & 0.3034 \end{bmatrix}, \ R_2 = \begin{bmatrix} 0.1399 & -0.0061 \\ -0.0061 & 0.1441 \end{bmatrix},$$

$$\lambda_0 = 1.4872, \ \lambda_{11} = 1.8964, \ \lambda_{12} = 1.8378, \ \lambda_{21} = 1.3321, \ \lambda_{22} = 1.2448.$$

employing new Lyapunov-Krasovskii functionals and conducting stochastic analysis, a linear matrix inequality (LMI) approach has been developed to derive the criteria for the exponential stability, where the criteria are dependent on both the discrete time delay and distributed time delay. A simple example has been provided to demonstrate the effectiveness and applicability of the proposed testing criteria.

FUTURE RESEARCH DIRECTIONS

Higher-order neural networks (HONNs), which include both the Cohen-Grossberg neural network and the Hopfield neural network as special cases, allow high-order interactions between neurons, and therefore have stronger approximation property, faster convergence rate, greater storage capacity, and higher fault tolerance than the traditional first-order neural networks. In the past years, HONNs have been successfully applied in many areas, such as biological science, pattern recognition and optimization. However, in a real world, the system ever becomes more and more complex. In addition to the stochasticity, Markovian jumps and mixed time-delays considered in this chapter, there are still many other kinds of complexity that must be addressed.

Advances in computing have contributed much to the successful handling of certain problems in biology, physics, economics etc that until recently were thought too difficult to be analysed. These complex systems problems tend to share a number of interesting properties. For example, they have many components that interact in some *interesting* way and these components or agents may be similar or differ in important characteristics. The systems are *dynamic* in nature, interact with their environments and *adapt* their internal structures as a consequence of such interaction. A key feature of such a system is that the *non-linear* interactions among its components can lead to interesting *emergent* behaviour.

The study of complexity has benefited from knowledge and advance in virtually all traditional disciplines of science, engineering, economics, and medicine. Much of the current computational work for analysis and control of such systems is based on methods from artificial intelligence, mathematics, statistics, operational research, and engineering, including non-linear dynamics, time series analysis, dynamic systems, cellular automata, artificial life, evolutionary computation, game theory, neural networks, multi-agents, and heuristic search methods. These methods have provided solutions, or early promises, to many real-world complex systems problems, including protein folding in bioinformatics, collaborative design of complex products, and the analysis of economic systems. However, there are fundamental limitations to the existing methodologies. For example, mathematical models for these systems tend to be constructed with assumptions that are rarely justified by real-world characteristics. The methods for understanding non-linear dynamic systems or time series are still under-developed to cope with rich dynamics of the complex system. The incorporation of domain knowledge or problem solving heuristics in the analysis of such systems is still yet to be done in a rigorous manner. Last but not least, there have been few associations between the individual complex systems methods and their impact on the development of novel computational paradigms. Neural network is one of the few exceptions that led to the development of connection machines, so is the push towards molecular computing and quantum computing that would lead to non-traditional computational paradigms. But many real world problems may demand an integration of methods from different fields and it would be an interesting challenge to see if a new computational paradigm may be born out of a coherent computational framework, capable of addressing key complex systems issues effectively.

In order to better understand the dynamical behaviours of different kinds of complexity, we should make use of the great capacity of HONNs, where complexity consists of nonlinearities, uncertainties, stochasticity, couplings, time-varying delays and external disturbances. The work reported in this chapter aims to study the global exponential stability analysis problem for a general class of stochastic HONNs with mixed time delays and Markovian switching. While the main focus of this chapter is to establish a theoretical framework that takes into account several typical complexities, we understand that ideal real-time applications are very important to validate the criteria and complete experiments can support the conclusion in solving real problems. Real-time application would be our main research topics in the future. More specifically, we list some of the future research topics as follows:

- Investigate the dynamics of more powerful HONNs that involves uncertainties, stochasticity, couplings, time-varying delays and external disturbances
- Design adaptive observers with which an array of HONNs is synchronized.
- Investigate how the HONN topology, specifically a small-world network structure, affects both the qualitative and quantitative synchronization behaviours.
- Derive the criteria under which certain HONNs become chaotic synchronized with different measures.
- Determine whether the model for synchronization behaviour observe characteristics of self-organization criticality and decide how the size and frequency of synchronization events fit a power law distribution.
- Apply the results obtained in optimization problem and designing a secure communication scheme and conduct experiments for benchmark models.

ACKNOWLEDGMENT

This work was supported in part by the Engineering and Physical Sciences Research Council (EPSRC) of the U.K. under Grant GR/S27658/01, an International Joint Project sponsored by the Royal Society of the U.K. and the NSFC of China, the Alexander von Humboldt Foundation of Germany, the Natural Science Foundation of Jiangsu Province of China under Grant BK2007075, the Natural Science Foundation of Jiangsu Education Committee of China under Grant 06KJD110206, the National Natural Science Foundation of China under Grants 10471119 and 10671172, and the Scientific Innovation Fund of Yangzhou University of China under Grant 2006CXJ002.

REFERENCES

Arik, S. (2005). Global robust stability analysis of neural networks with discrete time delays. *Chaos, Solitons and Fractals*, *26*(5), 1407-1414.

Artyomov, E., & Yadid-Pecht, O. (2005). Modified high-order neural network for invariant pattern recognition. *Pattern Recognition Letters*, *26*(6), 843-851.

Bengio, Y., Frasconi, P., & Simard, P. (1993). The problem of learning long-term dependencies in recurrent networks. In *Proc. 1993 IEEE Int. Conf. Neural Networks*, vol. 3, pp.1183–1188.

Blythe, S., Mao, X. & Liao, X. (2001). Stability of stochastic delay neural networks. *Journal of the Franklin Institute*, *338*, 481-495.

Boyd, S., EI Ghaoui, L., Feron, E. & Balakrishnan, V. (1994). *Linear matrix inequalities in system and control theory*. Philadelphia, PA: SIAM.

Cao, J., & Chen, T. (2004). Globally exponentially robust stability and periodicity of delayed neural networks. *Chaos, Solitons and Fractals*, *22*(4), 957-963.

Cao, J., Huang, D.-S. & Qu, Y. (2005). Global robust stability of delayed recurrent neural networks. *Chaos, Solitons and Fractals*, *23*, 221-229.

Cao, J., Liang, J., & Lam, J. (2004). Exponential stability of high-order bidirectional associative memory neural networks with time delays. *Physica D: Nonlinear Phenomena*, *199*(3-4), 425-436.

Casey, M.P. (1996). The dynamics of discrete-time computation with application to recurrent neural networks and finite state machine extraction. *Neural Comput.*, *8*(6), 1135-1178.

Dembo, A., Farotimi, O., & Kailath, T. (1991). High-order absolutely stable neural networks. *IEEE Trans. Circuits Syst.*, *38*(1), 57-65.

Gahinet, P., Nemirovsky, A., Laub A.J., & Chilali, M. (1995). *LMI control toolbox: For use with Matlab*. The Math Works, Inc.

Giles, C.L., & Maxwell T. (1987). Learning, invariance, and generalization in high-order neural networks. *Appl. Optics*, *26*(23), 4972-4978.

Gu, K. (2000). An integral inequality in the stability problem of time-delay systems. In *Proceedings of 39th IEEE Conference on Decision and Control*, December 2000, Sydney, Australia, pp. 2805-2810.

Hale, J.K. (1977). *Theory of functional differential equations*. New York: Springer-Verlag.

Huang, H., Ho, D. W. C, & Lam, J. (2005). Stochastic stability analysis of fuzzy Hopfield neural networks with time-varying delays. *IEEE Trans. Circuits and Systems: Part II*, *52*(5), 251-255.

Huang, H., Qu, Y., & Li, H.X. (2005). Robust stability analysis of switched Hopfield neural networks with time-varying delay under uncertainty. *Physics Letters A*, *345*(4-6), 345-354.

Ji, Y., & Chizeck, H.J. (1990). Controllability, stabilizability, and continuous-time Markovian jump linear quadratic control. *IEEE Trans. Automat. Control*, *35*, 777-788.

Kappen, H. J. (2001). An introduction to stochastic neural networks. In Stan Gielen and Frank Moss (Eds.), *Handbook of biological physics*, pp.517-552. Elsevier.

Karayiannis, N. B., & Venetsanopoulos, A. N. (1995). On the training and performance of high-order neural networks. *Mathematical Biosciences*, *129*(2), 143-168.

Khasminskii, R. Z. (1980). *Stochastic stability of differential equations*. Alphen aan den Rijn, Sijthoffand Noor, Khasminskiidhoff.

Lai, T.L., & Wong, P.S. (2001). Stochastic neural networks with applications to nonlinear time series. *Journal of the American Statistical Association*, *96*(455), 968-981.

Lu, Z., Shieh, L.-S., Chen G., & Coleman, N. P. (2006). Adaptive feedback linearization control of chaotic systems via recurrent high-order neural networks. *Information Sciences*, *176*(16), 2337-2354.

Psaltis D., Park, C. H., & Hong, J. (1988). Higher order associative memories and their optical implementations. *Neural Networks*, *1*, 143-163.

Ren, F., & Cao, J. (2006). LMI-based criteria for stability of high-order neural networks with time-varying delay. *Nonlinear Analysis Series B: Real World Applications*, *7*(5), 967-979.

Skorohod, A. V. (1989). *Asymptotic methods in the theory of stochastic differential equations*. Providence, RI: Amer. Math. Soc.

Tino, P., Cernansky, M. & Benuskova, L. (2004). Markovian architectural bias of recurrent neural networks. *IEEE Trans. Neural Networks*, *15*(1), 6-15.

Wan, L., & Sun, J. (2005). Mean square exponential stability of stochastic delayed Hopfield neural networks. *Physics Letters A*, *343*(4), 306-318.

Wang, Z., Fang, J. & Liu, X. (2008). Global stability of stochastic high-order neural networks with discrete and distributed delays. *Chaos, Soliton & Fractals, 36*(2), pp. 388-396.

Wang, Z., Liu, Y., Li, M., & Liu, X. (2006a). Stability analysis for stochastic Cohen-Grossberg neural networks with mixed time delays. *IEEE Trans. Neural Networks, 17*(3), 814-820.

Wang, Z., Liu, Y., Fraser, K., & Liu, X. (2006b). Stochastic stability of uncertain Hopfield neural networks with discrete and distributed delays. *Physics Letters A, 354*(4), 288-297.

Wang, Z., Liu, Y., Yu, L., & Liu, X. (2006c). Exponential stability of delayed recurrent neural networks with Markovian jumping parameters, *Physics Letters A, 356*(4-5), 346-352.

Xu, B., Liu, X., & Liao, X. (2005). Global asymptotic stability of high-order Hopfield type neural networks with time delays. *Computers & Mathematics with Applications, 45*(10-11), 1729-1737.

Zhang, J., Shi, P., & Qiu, J. (2007). Novel robust stability criteria for uncertain stochastic Hopfield neural networks with time-varying delays. *Nonlinear Analysis: Real World Applications, 8*(4), 1349-1357

Zhao, H. (2004a). Global asymptotic stability of Hopfield neural network involving distributed delays. *Neural Networks, 17*, 47-53.

Zhao, H. (2004b). Existence and global attractivity of almost periodic solution for cellular neural network with distributed delays. *Applied Mathematics and Computation, 154*, 683-695.

ADDITIONAL READING

Arik, S. (2003). Global asymptotic stability of a larger class of neural networks with constant time delay. *Phys. Lett. A, 311*, 504–511.

Arik, S. (2002). An analysis of global asymptotic stability of delayed cellular neural networks. *IEEE Trans. Neural Networks, 13*(5), 1239–1242.

Arik, S., & Tavsanoglu, V. (2000). On the global asymptotic stability of delayed cellular neural networks. *IEEE Trans. Circuits Syst. I, 47*(4), 571–574.

Cao, J. (2001). Global exponential stability of Hopfield neural networks. *Int. J. Systems Sci., 32*, 233–236.

Gopalsamy, K., & He, X. Z. (1994). Stability in asymmetric Hopfield nets with transmission delays. *Phys. D, 76*(4), 344–358.

Ho, D.W.C., Lam, J., Xu, J., & Tam, H.K. (1999). Neural computation for robust approximate pole assignment, *Neurocomputing*, vol. 25, pp. 191–211.

Hopfield, J.J. (1982). Neural networks and physical systems with emergent collective computational abilities. *Proc. Natl. Acad. Sci., 79*, 2554–2558.

Hopfield, J. J. (1984) Neurons with graded response have collective computational properties like those of two-state neurons. *Proc. Natl. Acad. Sci., 81*, 3088–3092.

Khalil, H. K. (1988). *Nonlinear systems*. New York: Mcmillan.

Liu, X. Z., & Teo, K. L. (2005). Exponential stability of impulsive high-order Hopfield-type neural networks with time-varying delays. *IEEE Trans. Neural Networks, 16*(6), 1329–1339.

Sanchez, E.N., & Perez, J.P. (1999). Input-to-state stability (ISS) analysis for dynamic NN. *IEEE Trans. Circuits Syst. I , 46*, 1395–1398.

Simpson, P.K. (1990). Higher-ordered and intra-connected bidirectional associative memories, *IEEE Trans. Syst. Man Cybernet., 20*, 637–653.

Xu, B .J., Liu, X .Z., & Liao, X.X. (2003). Global asymptotic stability of high-order Hopfield type neural networks with time delays. *Comput. Math. Appl., 45*, 1729–1737.

Xu, Z. B. (1995). Global convergence and asymptotic stability of asymmetric Hopfield neural networks. *J. Math. Anal. Appl., 191*, 405–427.

Zhang, Q., Wei, X. P., & Xu, J. (2003). Global asymptotic stability of Hopfield neural networks with transmission delays. *Phys. Lett. A, 318*, 399–405.

Zhang, J.Y., & Jin, X.S. (2000). Global stability analysis in delayed Hopfield neural network models. *Neural Networks, 13*, 745–753.

Chapter XXII
Trigonometric Polynomial Higher Order Neural Network Group Models and Weighted Kernel Models for Financial Data Simulation and Prediction

Lei Zhang
University of Technology, Sydney, Australia

Simeon J. Simoff
University of Western Sydney, Australia

Jing Chun Zhang
IBM, Australia

ABSTRACT

This chapter introduces trigonometric polynomial higher order neural network models. In the area of financial data simulation and prediction, there is no single neural network model that could handle the wide variety of data and perform well in the real world. A way of solving this difficulty is to develop a number of new models, with different algorithms. A wider variety of models would give financial operators more chances to find a suitable model when they process their data. That was the major motivation for this chapter. The theoretical principles of these improved models are presented and demonstrated and experiments are conducted by using real-life financial data.

INTRODUCTION

Financial operators have nowadays access to an extremely large amount of data, quantitative and qualitative, real-time or historical, and use this information to support their investment decision-making process.

Quantitative data, such as historical price database or real-time price information is largely processed by computer programs. However, there are only few programs based on artificial intelligence techniques for financial analysis intended for the end user. Financial operators have only a limited choice of models for the data.

Until now, in the area of financial data simulation and prediction, there is no single neural network model that could handle the wide variety of data and perform well in the real world.

A way of solving this difficulty is to develop a number of new models, with different algorithms. A wider variety of models would give financial operators more chances to find a suitable model when they process their data. That was the major motivation for this chapter.

The degree of accuracy is the most important characteristic of a simulation and prediction model. A way to increase the degree of accuracy of a model is provided in this chapter. Group theory with trigonometric polynomial higher order neural network models and weighted kernel models are used in this chapter to improve accuracy.

In the artificial intelligence area, the traditional way of operating is the Questions and Answers (Q&A) method. The neural network model looks like a 'black box' for the financial operators. Within the Q&A method, financial operators do not need to know much about the underlying model without outside intervention, given the relevant training data. This kind of process is called 'model-free inference'. For situations where it is too difficult or time consuming to derive an accurate mathematical representation for the physical model, such a system would be ideal in practice.

The difficulty is due to the dual nature of the estimation of error in a problem. An incorrect model that has insufficient or inappropriate representational ability will have a high bias. On the other hand, a model able to be truly bias free must have a high variance to ensure its encoding flexibility, and hence will require a prohibitively large training set to provide a good approximation.

The dilemma is that, the more representational power a neural network model is given, the more difficult it is for it to learn concepts correctly. Each neural network model has an inherent underlying process that is used to construct its internal model and, as a consequence, any solution that is found will be naturally biased by the representational power of the learning system. Such bias includes the architecture type, connection topology and perhaps the input and output representations. Consequently the estimation of these parameters relies on the prior knowledge or biases of the researcher about the problem, annihilating the original goal of bias free learning.

To achieve low variance while simultaneously estimating a large variety of parameters requires an impractical number of training examples.

One possible solution to this problem is to develop a new model that is visible to the operator. The proposed program in this chapter will allow the operator to watch every aspect of the model during the training process.

BACKGROUND

The basic ideas behind Artificial Neural Networks (ANNs) are not new. McCulloch & Pitts developed their simplified single neuron model over 50 years ago. Widrow developed his 'ADALINE' and Posenblatt the 'PERCEPTRON' during the 1960's. Multi-layer feed-forward networks (Multi-Layer Perceptrons or MLPs) and the back-propagation algorithm were developed during the late 1970's, and Hopfield devised his recurrent (feed back) network during the early 1980's. The development of MLPs and 'Hopfiled nets' heralded a resurgence of worldwide interest in ANNs, which has continued unabated ever since.

ANNs are new types of computers based on (inspired by) models of biological neural networks (brains). It should be emphasized that nobody fully understands how biological neural networks work. Despite this, ANN has captured the imagination of both research scientists and practitioners alike - the prospect of producing computers based on the workings of the human brain is truly inspiring.

Despite a flurry of activity during the previous decades, ANNs remains a young field of research. It offers a new approach to computing which develops mathematical structures with the ability to learn. The methods are loosely inspired by academic investigations into modelling the nervous system's learning processes. It has been repeatedly demonstrated that ANNs can be used to solve many real-world problems, and indeed are excellent for pattern recognition/classification tasks in particular.

What is a Neural Network?

- A new form of computing, inspired by biological models.
- A mathematical model composed of a large number of processing elements organized into layers.
- "... a computing system made-up of a number of simple, highly interconnected processing elements, which processes information by its dynamic state response to external inputs" (Maureen Caudill [1991]'s paraphrase of Robert Hecht -Nielsen).

There are many different types of models that can be labeled 'artificial neural networks'. Before going into each specific network type, we will introduce some notations and graphical representations in networks commonly used in the literature. It is the best to start with the most

basic processing unit in the network: the neuron. As a processing unit, it will receive inputs. Then, some transformation will be made to the inputs to obtain an output.

The transformation can be carried out in two stages. In the first stage, either a linear combination of all the inputs or a norm of the difference between the inputs and the center of the hidden unit will be applied to obtain a scalar, called the net.

The coefficients of the linear transformation or the center of the hidden units are called the weights. The processing structure of the neuron can be divided into two different types and two different modeling functions. The global approximation and the local approximation can also be introduced here. The details will be discussed in later sections.

In the second stage, a non-linear transformation will be carried out on the net to obtain the output. The function used for the non-linear transformation is called the transfer function. To sum up, the whole process is stated in equation 2.1:

$$y = f(\sum_{i=1}^{n} x_i w_i + w_0)$$

or (2.1)

$$y = f\{[\sum_{i=1}^{n} (x_i - w_i)^2] / w_0\}$$

where y is the output of the unit, x_i is its ith input, w_i is the weight associated with the ith input, n is the number of inputs and f is the transfer function. The graphical representation of the process is given in Figure 2.1.

Most network structures can be organised in layers. A layer consists of a number of neurons. There are no connections between the neurons in the same layer but the neurons belonging to different layers are connected. A typical network structure with two layers is given by equation 2.2.

Figure 2.1. A single node with weighted inputs

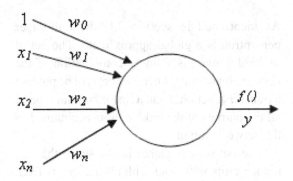

Figure 2.2. The structure of the artificial neural network

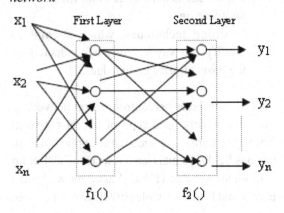

The first layer is called the input layer, and contains one node (or neuron) for each of the training data entry. The last layer is called the output layer and contains one neuron for each of the network outputs. Between the input and output layers are an arbitrary number of hidden layers each containing an arbitrary number of neurons. Each neuron is connected to every other neuron in adjacent layers by a set of weights.

The weights define the 'strength' of the flow of information from one layer to the next through the network. Each weight can take on any positive or negative value. 'Training' a neural network is simply the process of determining an appropriate set of weights so that the network accurately approximates the input/output relationship of the training data.

Equation 2.2 corresponds to the graphical representation shown in Figure 2.2.

First layer: $f_k^1 = f_1(\sum_{i=1}^{n} w_{i,k}^1 + x_{0,k}^1)$

$$(2.2)$$

Second layer: $y_j = f_2(\sum_{k=1}^{n} w_{k,j}^2 y_k^1 + w_{0,k}^2)$

where:

yj   The jth network output
yj1   The jth output of the first layer
xI   The Ith network input
wlI,k The weight between Ith input and the kth hidden unit

w2k,j the weight between the kth hidden unit and the jth output
f1   the transfer function in the first layer
f2   the transfer function in the second layer
p   the number of network outputs
r1   the number of network inputs and r2 is the number of hidden units

Techniques for Prior Knowledge Usage

For any learner with a representational ability, learning can be viewed as a search through the range of implementable functions, to find the function that most closely approximates the desired problem. Methods for utilizing the information contained in prior knowledge can thus be viewed as attempting to restrict or bias the space of implementable functions for a particular learner.

Previous attempts at practical methods for the incorporation or transferal of prior knowledge in neural networks can be divided roughly into three groups: weight techniques, structural techniques and learning techniques:

- Weight techniques, where the prior knowledge to be used is encoded in the weights of trained neural networks.

- Structural techniques in which the prior knowledge is hard-coded into the network architecture.
- Learning techniques, which attempt to modify the way learning is conducted on the basis of prior knowledge.

The multilayer perceptron neural network is the most widely used type of neural network. There are numerous successful applications in various fields. To mention a few: Hong C. Leung and Victor W. Zue (1989), Yeshwant K. Muthusamy and Ronald A.Cole (1992) have done some applications in speech recognition. Timothy S. Wilkinson, Dorothy A. Mighell and Joseph W. Goodman (1989) have done a good job by applying it to image processing. Charles Schlay, Yves Chanvin, Van Henkle and Richard Golden (1995) have used it in control applications.

In finance, Apostolos Nicholas Refenes, Achileas Zapranis and Gavin Francis (1994) applied it to assets allocations. In this application, the multi-layer perceptron network is compared with a classical method for stock ranking, that is, multiple linear regression. It was found that the network outperforms regression in terms of out-sample mean-square-error. Also, the performance was tested and found to be stable for various network architectures and training parameters. The sensitivity of the output to various inputs is also examined in detail in this work.

Structural Techniques

As mentioned in section 2.1, the multilayer perceptron is a global approximate. The net of its hidden units is a linear combination of the network input units. Then, the net will be put into a transfer function. Last, a linear combination of all the outputs of the hidden units is obtained as the network output.

The network is global in the sense that the hidden units will react with all the inputs from any part of the input space, rather than with some of them. In detail, each hidden unit divides the whole input space into two regions and assigns two different values to the inputs from the two different regions. The overall process of the network is summarised in equation 2.3 and is represented by Figure 2.3.

$$y_j = f_m(......f_2(\sum_{k=1}^{n} w_{k,j}^2 y_k^1 + w_{0,k}^2 f_1(\sum_{i=1}^{n} w_{i,k}^1 + x_{0,k}^1)))$$

(2.3)

where:
yj   the jth network output
xi   the ith network input
wmi,k   the weight between the ith input and the kth unit in the mth layer
fm   the transfer function in the mth layer
q   the number of layers
p   the number of network outputs

Figure 2.3. The multilayer the artificial neural network structure

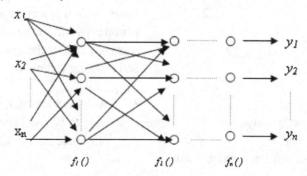

rm   the number of inputs in the mth layer
woi,k   the weights associated with a
    constant input are called bias

In practice, nearly all applications of the multilayer perceptron network have only one hidden layer. Moreover, according to a theorem in Tianping Chen and Hong Chen (1995), a multilayer perceptron network can approximate nearly any function with only one hidden layer. This result means that a solution always exists from a single hidden layer network but it says nothing about how difficult it is to obtain that solution.

It is possible that the solution for a particular problem can be obtained in an easier way if we use more hidden layers. To sum up, we need to pay special attention to the single layer network but need not reject other possible structures.

Besides the number of hidden layers, the number of hidden units in each layer needs to be determined. It depends on the complexity of the system being modeled. For a more complex system, a larger number of hidden units are needed. In practice, the optimal number of hidden units is found by trial and error. Let us see some examples in the real word.

A speculative paper by Schmidhuber deals with issues concerning the embedding of 'meta'-levels in neural network architecture (Schmidhurber J., 1993). It is based on the idea that a network could examine binary values of 0 and 1, and then changes its own internal state by the use of appropriate feedback. No experimental results were given for this technique, however it is an interesting idea.

Brown (Brown R.H., T.L. Ruchti, and Gray 1992), in the paper Gray Layer Technology: Incorporating A Prior Knowledge into Feed forward Artificial Neural Networks demonstrates the use of a technique that constrains the weights within a hidden 'grey' layer according to the prior knowledge that is known about the desired function approximation. Good results are demonstrated for a single example where the non-linear dynamics of a control system is to be approximated. A method for constraining the weights on general problems is not suggested within the paper.

Weight sharing, where several network connections are forced to share the same weight value, has been successfully applied to the problem of building symmetry invariance into networks. Improvements in both the generalisation ability and learning times for problems requiring such invariance have been found (Shawe-Taylor J. 1993).

It can be shown that the network structure and weights for approximating both linear and non-linear differential equations can be calculated by using a generalisation of the Taylor series (Cozzio R. 1995). This technique allows the direct integration of any a priori knowledge about the differential equation to be factored into the network design. It is however limited to application domains that use differential equations, such as the prediction of time series.

Probably the most generally applicable of the structural techniques is problem decomposition. Here, a problem is broken down into smaller tasks and trained on separate smaller networks before being recombined into one large network. The methods described in the 'weight techniques' can still be applied to these modular networks to yield even greater performance increases.

Weight Techniques

According to Tianping Chen and Hong Chen (1995), a multilayer perceptron network with any Tauber-Wiener functions, is a universal approximator. A necessary and sufficient condition for being a Tauber-Wiener function is that it is not a ploynomial.

As described in later sections, the training of a multilayer perceptron network can by easily implement by gradient methods. A derivative of the transfer function is needed for training. Thus, a differentiable transfer function is widely used in order to facilitate training. One commonly used transfer function for multilayer perceptrons is the sigmoid function, given by equation 2.4:

$$f(x) = f(x)(1 - f(x)) \qquad (2.4)$$

Another commonly used transfer function is the hyperbolic tangent function given by equation 2.5:

$$f(x) = 1 - f(x)2 \qquad (2.5)$$

Probably the simplest type of transfer known is the literal transfer, where the source weights are copied directly for use as the initial weights for training a new problem. Sharkey (Sharkey N.E. 1991) has examined this situation for some simple classification problems.

He found that both positive transfers, leading to decreased training times, and negative transfers, which increase training times, could occur over random initialisation, under certain circumstances. Negative transfers tended to occur when the type of output classification was changed between tasks, and positive transfer was more likely in the case where only the input classification was changed.

All the networks considered in this chapter have either consistent inputs or consistent outputs (e.g. for character recognition, a character will be classified with the same output, independently of the training set font). The consistent use of inputs and/or outputs is a necessary feature of training within the same problem environment.

Discriminality Based Transfer (DBT) (Pratt L.Y. 1993) uses the relevance of input layer hyperplanes (as determined by the weight values into the neurons) on the new task to determine whether the weights for each input neuron layer should be allowed to change.

All other weights in higher layers are randomly initialised. The hyperplane relevance is determined by using an entropy measure or mutual information metric, which relies on determining class boundaries in the training data.

Enhanced training speed, relative to a small subset of randomly initialised networks, were shown across a range of real world classification tasks. DBT is constrained to systems in which a target class can be assigned for each of the inputs, and so cannot be used for problems such as surface approximation or regression.

Some other weight-based methods of utilising prior knowledge revolve around the use of traditional AI methods to generate appropriate weights (Thrun S. & Mitchell T. 1993). These systems rely on the knowledge of a human expert to initialise weight vectors. In the same way the similarity between fuzzy systems and radial basis functions also allows the direct incorporation of fuzzy rules into neural type systems (Gupta 1994). The direct incorporation of these 'expert' rules into a neural network is presented in (Mitra 1995), so these techniques are not discussed further.

Learning Techniques

Learning is the process by which a neural network modifies its weights in response to external inputs. In traditional programming, where highly structured programs such as FORTRAN are used, the programmer will be given the inputs, some type of processing requirements (what to do with the inputs), and the desired output. The programmer's job is to apply the necessary, minute, step-by-step instructions to develop the required relationship between the input and output.

Knowledge-based programming techniques (expert systems) use higher-level concepts to specify relationships between inputs and outputs. These higher-level concepts are referred to as heuristics, or more commonly, rules.

In contrast, neural networks do not require any instructions, rules, or processing requirements about how to process the input data. In fact, neural networks determine the relationship between input and output by looking at examples of many input-output pairs. This unique ability to determine how to process data is usually referred to as self-organisation. The process of self-organising is called adaptation, or learning.

Pairs of inputs and outputs are applied to the neural network. These pairs of data are used to teach or train the network, and as such are referred to as the training set. Knowing what output is expected from each of the inputs, the network learns by automatically adjusting or adapting the strengths of the connections between process elements. The method used for the adjusting process is called the learning rule.

How fast does learning occur? That depends on several things. There are trade-offs in the rates of learning. Obviously, a lower rate means that a lot more time is spent in accomplishing the off-line learning to produce a trained system. With a faster rate however, the network may not be able to make the fine discriminations possible with a system that learns slower. Researchers are working on giving us the best of both worlds.

Consider accuracy and speed with the following illustration. Once a system had learned a 500-matrix image consisting of 500 three-digit decimals ranging from .000 to 1.000 in less than three minutes, we purposely altered one digit of a three-digit decimal. Upon recall, the neural network detected this change every time. This is analogous to learning the image of a dollar bill in pixel form. Now, if we alter one pixel in George Washington's eye, the neural network will detect it instantly.

Finally, the learning rule and the modification of the weights play a smaller but sometimes lengthy role in the training effort. Again, it depends on the particular problem for which the network was developed. We do find that, as before, imaging or pattern classification networks are several orders of magnitude simpler to train: little or no adjustment to the weights is required, and learning rules do not have to be changed.

Most learning equations have some provision for a learning rate, or learning constant. Usually this term is positive and between 0 and 1. If the learning rate is greater than 1, it is easy for the learning algorithm to "overshoot" in correcting the weights, and the network may oscillate.

Small values of learning rate will not correct the error as quickly, but if small steps are taken in correcting errors, there is a better chance of arriving at the minimum error and thus the optimum weight settings. The learning rate is, then, a measure of the speed of convergence of the network.

A 'Meta' Neural Network (MNN) that learns to adjust the learning parameters by observing the changes in weights during training is presented in Meta-Neural Networks that learn by learning (Naik D.K. 1992). This technique is intended to allow the overall training speed on similar problems to be increased, by getting the MNN to choose an optimum step size and direction vector for a gradient descent learning algorithm. On simple four-bit parity and two-class problems this technique was shown to have significant speed improvement, however no follow-up work has been published to date.

Abu-Mostaf in the papers of Hints and the VC Dimension and Hints (Abu-Mostafa Y.S. 1993 & 1995) show how hints can be integrated into the learning process by generating additional training examples from the prior knowledge. This can be an effective technique in environments where limited training data is available (Al-Mashouq K.A. 1991).

To train a network for a specific problem from within this environment, the new network is placed 'on-top' of the environment network such that its inputs are connected to the environment networks outputs. These outputs are intended to be invariant under the similarity transforms applicable to a particular environment. The research is backed by some rigorous theoretical justification but is demonstrated only on toy problems.

Kernel Techniques

The panorama of Kernel techniques is quiet large. Kernels can be used in almost every aspect in

Artificial Intelligent, including classification and regression trees, predictive rules (for association or prediction), distance-based models, probabilistic models (e.g. Bayesian networks) (David Heckerman, Dan Geiger and David M. Chickering 1995), neural networks and kernel-based learning machines, e.g. Support Vector Machines (SVMs) (Christopher J.C. Burges 1998). In this chapter, we briefly describe how kernels are considered as functions in the neural networks context.

Kernel methods can be described as a large family of models sharing the use of a kernel function. The idea underpinning the use of a kernel function is to focus on the representation and processing of pairwise comparisons rather than on the representation and processing of a single object. In other words, when considering several objects, instead of representing each object via a real-valued vector, a real-valued function K (obj1,obj2) is defined in order to "compare" the two objects obj1 and obj2.

As an example of kernel function, let us consider the Gaussian radial basis kernel function defined as:

$$K_{RBF}(u,u') = \exp\left(-\frac{d(u,u')^2}{2v^2}\right)$$

where v is a parameter and d(·,·) is the Euclidean distance.

The strategy to focus on pairwise comparisons shared by all kernel methods leads to some advantages that are worth mentioning here. First of all, it is typically easier to compare two objects instead of defining some abstract space of features where to represent a single object. This is especially true if the objects are complex and possibly of different size. A second advantage is the fact that the hypothesis space is defined on the basis of the kernel matrix, which is always nXn, that is, independent from the complexity and size of the objects involved. Finally, when considering positive defined kernels, it is possible to exploit the so called kernel trick: any (learn-ing) method defined for vectorial data which just exploits dot products of the input vectors, can be applied implicitly in the feature space associated with a kernel, by replacing each dot product by a kernel evaluation. This allows to "transform" linear methods into non-linear methods.

TRIGONOMETRIC POPLYNOMIAL HIGHER ORDER NEURAL NETWORK GROUP MODELS

Suppose we define two sets of vectors $x_t \in R^n$ and $y_t \in R^m$ for $t = 0(1)p - 1$ where R is the set of real numbers. The pairs (x_t, y_t) can be regarded as the required input-output mapping of some neural networks. There are $n > 0$ individual inputs and $m > 0$ individual outputs denoted by $x_{t,i}$ for $i = 1(1)n$ and $y_{t,j}$ for $j = 1(1)m$. Of course there maybe a large number of possible inputs and outputs, but $p > 0$ is a representative selection which defines a training set. Our objective is to determine a mapping function g such that:

$$y_{t,j} = g_i(x_t)$$
$$\text{for } t = 0(1)p-1, j = 1(1)m \qquad (3.1)$$

and produces $y_{v,j} \approx g_j(x_v)$ for some pattern not in the training set. Infect we will accept the less stringent requirement that g simply minimizes the least-square error (or energy function) of the mapping for the training set. In addition we also demand that g has an algebraic or computational form that can be mapped on to a massively parallel connection structure in which nodes (or neurons) require modular and easily computed functions. This distributed form of the computation leads to highly desirable fault tolerant features and low latency between presentation of the input and the production of the output. Competing mappings (or networks) are compared with respect to the number of neurons required and their ability to generalize to previously unseen patterns.

Figure 3.1 shows a typical three layers network with three inputs and three outputs. Each neuron computes the inner product of weights w_j and the actual input value i_j on each of the input connections, this net value is then applied to an activation or squashing function f() chosen to map the neuron output into a specific range (for example [-1, 1] or [0, 1]). Normally we assume that the input layer passes its input directly to the output. Finally the value θ is a bias which shifts (or offsets) the neuron output within the range of activation.

Learning algorithms have evolved from a basic two-layer linear model. For example, suppose that the xt patterns in our training set are mutually orthogonal and normalized so that:

$$x_i^T x_j = \begin{cases} 1 \text{ if } i = j \\ 0 \text{ otherwise} \end{cases} \quad (3.2)$$

we can write:

$$y_t = y_t x_t^T x_t = (y_t x_t^T) x_t = W_t x_t \quad (3.3)$$

where W_t is the so-called weight matrix. Furthermore by applying (3.3) to all the patterns in the training set we can write:

$$y_t = W x_t = W_t x_t + \dots + W_t x_t + \dots w_{p-1} x_t = W_t x_t \quad (3.4)$$

where:

$$W = \sum_{i=0}^{p-1} W_i$$

Equation (3.4) is the well-known Hebb learning rule and can be implemented by a network similar to Figure 1 with just two-layers and an activation function of the form $f(net_j) = net_j$ where net_j is the net input to neuron j in the output layer. Clearly the elements w_{ij} of W correspond to the weights on the network connections. Thus W contains all the information about the mapping between xt and yt for $t = 0(1)p-1$. In the network this knowledge is distributed across all the connections.

The Hebb rule works only when the xt vectors are mutually orthogonal. For vectors that are linearly independent the more powerful delta rule is employed. Here we use the equations:

$$W(n) = W(n - 1) + \eta\delta(n) \, x^T(n)$$
$$\delta(n) = y(n) - W(n - 1)x(n) \quad (3.5)$$

where η is scalar and represents the learning rate, and W(n), y(n), x(n) are the weight matrix, output, and input patterns on the nth presentation step of the method (patterns being selected cyclically or at random). The convergence of (3.5) is proved in a number of papers, we simply note that the final

Figure 3.1. Three Layer Neural Network

Output

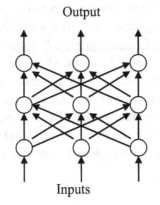

Inputs

$O = f(\Sigma_j \, w_j i_j + \theta)$

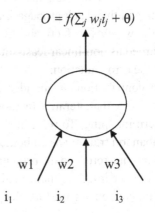

w1   w2   w3

i_1 i_2 i_3

weight matrix is the least-squares solution for the require mapping in (3.1).

Minksy (Minksy M.L. 1988) in the famous work demonstrated that two-layer networks were severely limited in their learning capabilities. For example the XOR problem cannot be learned because the input patterns are neither orthogonal nor linearly independent. More powerful multi-layer networks are required. The generalized delta-rule extends (3.5) into the realm of multi-layer networks. The method can be summarized by the following equations

$$\Delta_t w_{j,i} = \eta (y_{t,j} - o_{t,j}) \, x_t i = \eta \delta_{t,j} x_{t,i} \qquad (3.6)$$

where $o_{t,j}$ is the jth network output for pattern t. Clearly $\delta_{t,j}$ represents the error made by the network for this component and $\Delta_t w_{j,i}$ is the change to the weight connecting neurons i and j in the network.

For a two-layer network (3.6) and (3.5) are equivalent but for multi-layer networks we have no way of modifying weights on hidden layer connections. This problem is solved by the formula:

$$\delta_{t,j} = \begin{cases} (y_{t,j} - o_{t,j}) f'_j (net_{t,j}) & \text{for output nodes} \\ f'_j (net_{t,j}) \sum_k \delta_{t,k} w_{k,j} & \text{for hidden nodes} \end{cases}$$

$$(3.7)$$

where f() and f'() are the activation function and its derivative. Training proceeds by repeatedly passing patterns forward through the network to find the output and then back propagating the error to adjust the weights. Effectively the process can be regarded as non-linear least-squares optimization of the error-function.

So the main contribution of our idea is to describe a direct rather than iterative method for coding the pattern mapping. To reach this goal we essentially abandon training as embodied by (3.5)-(3.7) in favour of a return to the principle of orthogonality expressed in (3.2), which remains as elegant method for condensing the knowledge of

classification into only a few parameters. Central to our scheme (as in other schemes) is the idea of linearly separable input patterns.

Very little artificial neural network research has concentrated on the precursors of neural network group models. Examples of such work are the integrated neural network (Matsuoka T., Hamada H. & Nakatsu R. 1989), or Pentland and Turk's holistic model (Denver Colorado, 1992). Lumer (Lumer E.D. 1992) proposed a new mechanism, selective attention among perceptual groups, as part of his early vision on computational models. In his model, perceptual grouping is initially performed in 'connectionist networks' by dynamically binding the neural activities triggered in response to related image features.

Lie Groups were used in Tsao's (Tsao Tien-Ren 1989) group sets approach to the computer simulation of 3D rigid motion. More specifically, motion is expressed as an exponential mapping of the linear combination of six infinitesimal generators of the one-parameter Lie subgroup.

Hu (Hu Shengfa & Pingfan Yan 1992) proposed a level-by-level learning scheme for artificial neural groups. This learning method closely resembles the process of knowledge growth observed in both human individuals and society. Further, it leads to improved generalisation and learning efficiency.

The neural network hierarchical model (Willcox C.R. 1991) consists of binary-state neurons grouped into clusters, and can be analysed using a Renormalisation Group (RG) approach.

Unlike the research previously described, Yang (Yang Xiahua 1992) pays attention to the activities of neuron groups. His work, together with Naimark's (Naimark M. A. & A.I. Stern 1982) earlier theory of group representations, is used as the basis for neural network group sets, which is developed in the following sections.

The reasons for using Neural Network Group Sets as the proposed algorithm are three-fold:

1. Neural network-based models developed so far are not yet sufficiently powerful to characterise complex systems. Moreover, a gap exists in the research literature between complex systems and general systems. A step towards bridging this gap can be made using neural network group sets.

2. As mentioned earlier, neural networks can effectively simulate a function if it varies in a continuous and smooth fashion with respect to the input variables. However, in the real word such variations can be discontinuous and non-smooth. Accordingly, if we use only simple neural networks to simulate these functions, then accuracy is a problem.

3. Neural networks are massively parallel architectures. Thus, by using parallel, ANN-based reasoning networks, we can compute all the rules, models, knowledge and facts stored in the different weights simultaneously. However, real-world reasoning is invariably complex, nonlinear and discontinuous. Thus, simple neural network models may not always yield correct reasoning, whereas neural network groups, possibly may.

A theory of artificial neural network group models has been developed by Ming Zhang, John Fulcher and Roderick A. Sofield. Neural network groups are able to approximate a continuous function, and to what degree of accuracy. These principles are then illustrated by way of the THONG models developed for financial data simulation. The accuracy of the models used in the THONG program is about 2 to 4 times better then QwikNet program.

In order to handle real life cases of input training data, the Trigonometric polynomial Higher Order Neural network Group model (THONG) has been developed as follows.

THONG is one kind of neural network group, in which each element is a trigonometric polynomial higher order neural network, such as model-0,

model-1, and model-2 proposed in this chapter. THONG can be defined as:

$$THONG \subset N \tag{3.8}$$

where THONG = {model-0, model-1, model-2,......}.

Let us use last section's format to express 3.1 as follows:

$$THONN \in THONG \tag{3.9}$$

where THONN = $f : Rn \rightarrow Rm$.

In the formula (3.9), THONG is a trigonometric polynomial higher order neural network group model. And THONN is an element of the THONG set, which is a trigonometric polynomial higher order neural network model.

The domain of the THONN inputs is the n-dimensional real number Rn. Likewise, the THONN outputs belong to the m-dimensional real number Rm. The neural network function f is a mapping from the inputs of THONN to its outputs. The Backpropagation algorithm has been used in the trigonometric higher order polynomial neural network models. There is no problem with the convergence. Based on the inference (Zhang Ming & Fulcher John 1996), such neural network group can approximate any kind of piece-wise continues function, and to any degree of accuracy. Hence, THONG, as shown in Figure 3.2 is able to simulate discontinuous data.

In the THONG, Model-0, Model-1, and Model-2 are the main three different models. Model-0 is the general trigonometric polynomial neural network model. Model-1 and model-2 are the improved trigonometric polynomial higher order neural network models.

General Trigonometric Polynomial Neural Network Model (Model-0)

First, we set up the general model (THONN model-0). The other models that I have devel-

Figure 3.2. Trigonometric Polynomial Higher Order Neural Network Group Models

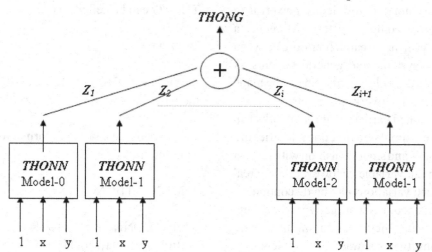

oped are based on this general model. Model-0 is a very basic model in the group models. We suppose that Model-0 can be useful for handling linear input data.

THONN Model-0 is a general multilayer type of neural network model. It uses the trigonometric functions neurons, ie., the linear, multiply and power neurons based on the trigonometric polynomial form. The equation is given in (3.2), as shown in equation (3.10), where aij, are the weights of the network. All the weights on the layer can be derived directly from the coefficients of the discrete analog form of the trigonometric polynomial. In the following, we show model-0's structure in graphical form.

Improved Trigonometric Polynomial Neural Network Models (Model-1)

In order to simulate and prediction higher frequency, high order non-linear and discontinuous data, I can improve upon the general trigonometric polynomial neural network models by using the Sampling Theorem.

The sampling theorem tells us that it is possible to establish a generalisation applicable to any kind of signal. This is because any analog signal - with a low-pass spectrum of maximum

frequency fmax - can be totally represented by the complete sequence of its instantaneous values x(tk) sampled at regular time intervals t provided that te is less than or equal to 1/(2fmax). In other words, the reversibility condition is satisfied if:

$$fe = 1/te \geq 2fmax \tag{3.11}$$

where te is the sampling time interval and fe the sampling frequency. If $nx(tk) \geq fe$ is selected, the sampling frequency will be higher than twice the maximum frequency of the data. Hence the improved trigonometric polynomial neural network model will be able to simulate higher frequency data.

Based on the sampling theorem, several improved models have been designed within the trigonometric polynomial neural network domain. First formulate the THONG Model-1. The equations are as follows:

$$z = \sum_{k1,k2=0}^{n} a_{k1k2} \cos^{k1}(a_{k1k2}^{x} x) \sin^{k2}(a_{k1k2}^{y} y)$$
$$= \sum_{k1,k2=0}^{n} (a_{k1k2}^{o})\{ a_{k1k2}^{hx}[\cos(a_{k1k2}^{x}x)]^{k1} \} \{a_{k1k2}^{hy}[\sin(a_{k1k2}^{y}y)]^{k2} \}$$

$$\tag{3.12}$$

Figure 3.3. The structure of the THONN Model-0

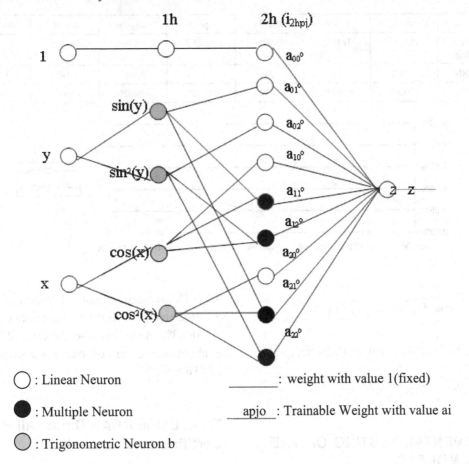

⃝ : Linear Neuron

● : Multiple Neuron

◗ : Trigonometric Neuron b

_____ : weight with value 1(fixed)

apjo : Trainable Weight with value ai

where:

$$a_{k1k2} = (a_{k1k2}{}^{o})(a_{k1k2}{}^{hx})(a_{k1k2}{}^{hy})$$

Second Hidden Layer Weights: $(a_{k1k2}{}^{x})$ and $(a_{k1k2}{}^{y})$

First Hidden Layer Weights: $(a_{k1k2}{}^{hx})$ and $(a_{k1k2}{}^{hy})$

Output Layer Weights: $(a_{k1k2}{}^{o})$

Trigonometric Polynomial Higher Order Neural Network (Model – 2)

To simulate higher order nonlinear data, the improved trigonometric polynomial neural network model (equation 3.12) still does not perform very well. Accordingly, we built another trigonometric

polynomial higher order neural network (Model - 2).

The THONN Model-2 uses trigonometric function neurons, linear-, multiply- and power-neurons based on the trigonometric polynomial form. THONN Model-2 also uses Sigmoid Neurons as output neurons and Logarithm Neurons to convert outputs to their original form:

$$Z = \ln\left(\frac{Z'}{1-Z'}\right)$$

$$where: \quad Z' = \frac{1}{1+e^{-e}}.$$

497

Figure 4.1.1. All banks lending to persons ($ million)

	Jan-96	Feb-96	Mar-96	Apr-96	May-96	Jun-96	Average
Total Lending	183417	184558	185031	186597	187898	189601	
THONN	1.34%	5.27%	8.76%	1.80%	2.94%	1.14%	3.54%
THONG	0.0000%	0.0000%	0.0000%	0.0015%	0.0002%	0.0000%	0.0003%

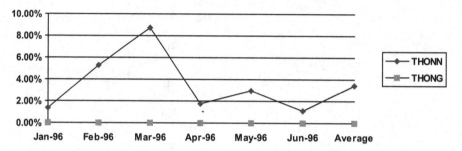

$$Z = \sum_{k_1 k_2 = 0}^{n} a_{k_1 k_2} \cos^{k_1}(a_{k_1 k_2}^x x) \sin^{k_2}(a_{k_1 k_2}^y y)$$

$$= \sum_{k_1 k_2 = 0}^{n} (a_{k_1 k_2}^0)\{a_{k_1 k_2}^{hx}[\cos(a_{k_1 k_2}^x x)]^{k_1}\}\{a_{k_1 k_2}^{hy}[\sin(a_{k_1 k_2}^y y)]^{k_2}\}$$

$$where: \quad a_{k_1 k_2} = (a_{k_1 k_2}^0)(a_{k_1 k_2}^{hx})(a_{k_1 k_2}^{hy})$$

EXPERIMENTAL TESTING OF THE THONG MODELS

The experimental tests compare THONN (single models without group models, which include Model-0, Model-1 and Model-2) with THONG.

The THONG models have been trained and tested on different groups of real-life data. All these data have been extracted from the Reserve Bank of Australia Bulletin (RBAB), August 1996.

Tests Using RBAB Data: "All Banks Lending to Persons"

The models of the THONG program have been tested by using the data of All Banks Lending to Persons, 1996 (Reserve Bank of Australia Bulletin, August 1996, p. s7, reproduced in Figure

4.1.1. The average error of THONN is 3.54%. The average error of THONG, which uses group sets is 0.0003%. So in this case, the error of THONG is about four orders of magnitude smaller than of THONN.

Tests Using RBAB Data: "All Banks Certificates of Deposit"

In this test, the data of All Banks Certifications of Deposit (1995) are also extracted from the Reserve Bank of Australia Bulletin, August 1996, p. s15.

In Figure 4.1.2 one can see that the average error of THONN is 22.45%. The average error of THONG is 2.75%. So in this case, again the accuracy of the THONG model is much superior to the THONN models.

Tests Using RBAB Data: "Australia Dollar Vs USA Dollar"

Here, THONG models have been tested using the data of Australia Dollar Vs USA Dollar (1995/96) (Reserve Bank of Australia Bulletin, August 1996, p. s50).

Figure 4.1.2. All banks certificates of deposit ($ million)

	Jan-95	Feb-95	Mar-95	Apr-95	May-95	Jun-95	Average
Deposits Certificates	4032	4268	4669	4513	4217	4079	
THONN	42.44%	1.93%	14.21%	0.49%	5.55%	70.10%	22.45%
THONG	6.50%	1.00%	3.80%	0.00%	1.20%	4.00%	2.75%

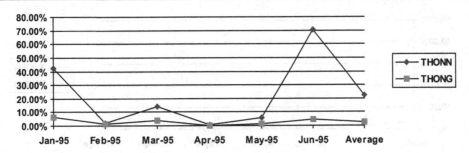

Figure 4.3. Australia dollar vs USA dollar

	Jan-96	Feb-96	Mar-96	Apr-96	May-96	Jun-96	Average
A$/USA$ Rates	0.7447	0.7635	0.7793	0.7854	0.7983	0.7890	
THONN	5.4%	26.5%	0.8%	3.4%	13.7%	0.3%	8.35%
THONG	15.39%	2.48%	3.22%	5.42%	2.90%	0.33%	4.96%

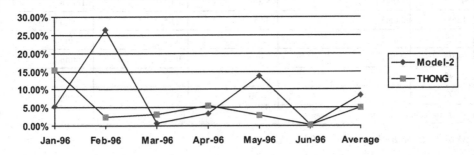

Please see Figure 4.3. The average error of THONN is 8.35%. The average error of the THONG is 4.96%. So in this case, the accuracy of the THONG program is about twice as good as the THONN.

Gold Price

The THONG program has been tested by using the data of Gold Price (1995) (Reserve Bank of Australia Bulletin, August 1996, p. s52).

Please see Figure 4.4. The average error of THONN is 8.18%. The average error of THONG is 0.90%. So, in this case, the accuracy of the THONG is about ten times better than the THONN.

Japan Economic Statistics

The THONN and THONG models have been used to predict 09/1995 and 12/1995 Japan Economic Statistics (Real gross domestic product 1990 =

Figure 4.4. Gold price (USA$ per fine ounce)

	Jan-95	Feb-95	Mar-95	Apr-95	May-95	Jun-95	Average
USA$ per fine ounce	374.9	376.4	392	389.75	384.3	387.05	
THONN	42.59%	2.7%	0.81%	0.71%	0.95%	1.31%	8.18%
THONG	3.60%	1.20%	0.00%	0.20%	0.00%	0.40%	0.90%

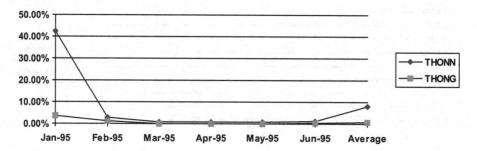

Table 1. 12/1993-12/1995 Japan economic statistics

Month/Year	RGDP	THONN |Error|%	THONG |Error|%	Case
12/93	104.9	16.6	0.04	Training
03/94	105.3	4.2	0.01	Training
06/94	105.8	1.7	0.01	Training
09/94	106.5	5.8	0.01	Training
12/94	105.3	27.5	27.5	Training
03/95	105.5	4.3	3.06	Training
06/95	106.1	4.9	0.27	Training
09/95	106.7	8.68	7.59	Testing
12/95	108.0	16.70	3.56	Testing
Average Testing |Error|		12.69%	5.58%	

Reserve Bank of Australia Bulletin (August 1996, page s64)

100). The data from 12/93 to 06/95 are training data. Prediction results showed that the THONN model average error is 12.69 and THONG model (higher order neural network group model) only had 5.58% average error.

The average error of THONN is 10.2%. The average error of THONG is 5.5%. So in this case, the accuracy of THONG is about twice times better than THONN.

FUTURE TRENDS

Models should fit data files automatically. There are many different kinds of models in 'THONG'. Which one is the best suited for a particular input training data file?

The best choice is dependent on the problem, and usually trail-and-error is needed to determine the best method. In this conventional method, we

Figure 4.5. 12/1993-12/1995 Japan economic statistics

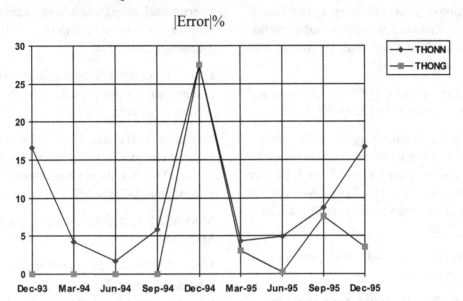

have to try in turn each model, with a number of different set parameters. Then one has to compare the results to select the best model and the best set of parameters for that model. Of course, the procedure is very tedious and slow.

Maybe, we can find some other ways, to search and fit automatically the best model with the best set of the parameters to an input data file. The simplest and best way would be to add a function in the THONG program, to choose the best model for an input data file automatically, based on minimising the simulation errors.

Giving the financial operators the choice of either the conventional method (manual fitting) or the new method (automatic fitting), as desired, would make the THONG program more attractive.

CONCLUSION

In this chapter we have introduced for the first time Trigonometric Polynomial Higher Order Neural Network Group Models - THONG, for financial data simulation and prediction. Within the group theory of THONG, two improved models have been developed. These models are constructed with three layer trigonometric polynomial higher order neural networks. The weights of the THONG models are derived directly from the coefficients of the trigonometric polynomial form.

The results of the experiments using real-life data show that the simulation and prediction accuracy of is satisfactory. A comparative analysis of data processing by THONG with that of available commercial programs has proven that the new program works faster and is more accurate.

REFERENCES

Abu-Mostafa, Y.S. (1993). Hints and the VC Dimension. *Neural Computation*, 5(2), 278-288.

Abu-Mostafa, Y.S. (1995). Hints. *Neural Computation*, 7(4), 639-671.

Al-Mashouq, K.A. (1991). Including hints in training neural nets. *Neural Computation*, 3(3), 418-427.

Brown, R.H., Ruchti, T.L., & Ruchti, G. (1992). Layer technology: Incorporating a prior knowledge into feedforward artificial neural networks. *International Joint Conference on Neural Networks*, Vol. I, pp. 806-811.

Burges, Christopher J.C. (1998). *Data mining and knowledge discovery*, Vol 2, pp. 121-167.

Carpenter, G., & Grossberg, S. (1986). Absolutely Stable learning of recognition codes by a self-organizing neural network. In J. Denker (Ed.), *AIP Conf. Proc.151: Neural Network for Computing*, American Institute of Physics, New York, pp. 77-85.

Caudill, M. (1991). Naturally intelligent systems. *AI Expert*, 6, 56 - 61.

Chen, T., & Chen, H. (1995). Approximation capability to functions of several variables,nonlinear functionals, and operators by radial basis function neuralnetworks. *Neural Networks*, 6, 904-910.

Chiang, C.C., & Fu, H.C. (1992). A fast learning multilayer neural network model and its Array processor implementation. *Journal of Information Science & Engineering*, 8(2), 283 - 305.

Colorado, D. (1992). Neural information processing systems - natural & synthetic. *Proceedings NIPS'92.*

Cozzio, R. (1995). *Neural network design using a priori knowledge*. Ph.D. Thesis, Swiss Federal Institute of Technology.

Gupta, M. (1994). On the principles of fuzzy neural networks (Invited Review). *Fuzzy Sets And Systems*, 61(1), 1-18.

Heckerman, D., Geiger, D., & Chickering, D. M. (1995). Learning Bayesian networks: The combination of knowledge and statistical data. *Machine Learning*, 20, 197-243.

Hu, S., & Yan P. (1992). Level-by-level learning for artificial neural groups, Acta Electron. *Sinica*, 20(10), 39-43.

Leung, H. C., & Zue, V. W. (1989). Applications of error back-propagation to phonetic classification. *Advances in Neural Information Processing Systems*, 1, 206 – 214.

Lumer, E.D. (1992). Selective attention to perceptual groups: the phase tracking mechanism. *Int. J. Neural Systems*, 3(1) 1-17.

Matsuoka, T., Hamada, H., & Nakatsu, R. (1989). Syllable recognition using integrated neural networks. *Proc. Int. Joint Conf. Neural Networks*, Washington, DC, pp. 251-258.

Minksy, M. L. (1988). *SA papert*. Cambridge: MIT-Press.

Mitra, A. (1995). Fuzzy multilayer perceptron, inferencing and rule generation. *IEEE Transactions on Neural Networks*, 6(1), 51-63.

Muthusamy, Y. K., & Cole, R. A. (1992). The Ogi multi-language telephone speech corpus. *Proceedings of the International Conference on Spoken Language Processing* , vol 2, pp. 895 -898, Banff, Alberta, Canada.

Naik, D. K. (1992). Meta-neural networks that learn by learning. *International Joint Conference on Neural Networks*, Vol. I pp. 437-444.

Naimark, M. A., & Stern, A. I. (1982). *Theory of group representations*. Springer, Berlin.

Pratt, L.Y. (1993). Transferring previously learned backpropagation results to new learning tasks. Ph.D. Thesis, Rutgers University.

Refenes, A. N., Zapranis, A., & Francis, G. (1994). Stock performance modeling using neural networks: A comparative study with regression models. *Neural Networks*, 7(2), 375 – 388.

Schlay, C., Chanvin, Y., Henkle, V., & Golden, R. (1995). *Back propagation: Theory, architectures, and applications*. Hillsdale, NJ: Lawrence Erlbaum Associates.

Schmidhurber, J. (1993.) A neural network that embeds its own meta-levels. *International Conference on Neural Networks*, pp. 407-412.

Sharkey, N. E. (1991). Connectionist representation techniques. *The Artificial Intelligence Review*, *5*(3), 143-148.

Shawe-Taylor, J. (1993). Symmetries and discriminability in feed forward neural architectures. *IEEE Transactions on Neural Networks*, *4*(5) 816-826.

Thrun, S., & Mitchell, T. (1993). *Integrating inductive and explanation based learning: Advances in neural information processing systems 5*. Morgan Kaufmann

Timothy, S., Wilkinson, D., Mighell, A., & Goodman, J. W. (1989). Backpropagation and its application to handwritten signature verification. *Advances in neural information processing systems 1*, pp. 340 – 347.

Tsao, T. (1989). A group theory approach to neural network computing of 3d rigid motion. *Proc. Int. Joint Conf. Neural Networks*, Vol. 2, pp.275-280.

Willcox, C.R. (1991). Understanding hierarchical neural network behavior: A re-normalization group approach. *J. Phys. A*, *24*, 2635-2644.

Yang, X. (1992). A convenient Method to Prune Multilayer Neural Networks via Transform Domain Backpropagation Algorithm, International Joint conference on Neural Networks Volume 3 pp.817-822.

Zhang, M. & Fulcher, J. (1996). Neural network group models for financial data simulation. *World Congress on Neural Networks*, San Diego, California, USA.

About the Contributors

Ming Zhang was born in Shanghai, China. He received the MS degree in information processing and PhD degree in the research area of computer vision from East China Normal University, Shanghai, China, in 1982 and 1989, respectively. He held postdoctoral fellowships in artificial neural networks with the Chinese Academy of the Sciences in 1989 and the USA National Research Council in 1991. He was a face recognition airport security system project manager and PhD co-supervisor at the University of Wollongong, Australia in 1992. Since 1994, he was a lecturer at the Monash University, Australia, with a research area of artificial neural network financial information system. From 1995 to 1999, he was a senior lecturer and PhD supervisor at the University of Western Sydney, Australia, with the research interest of artificial neural networks. He also held senior research associate fellowship in artificial neural networks with the USA National Research Council in 1999. He is currently a full professor and graduate student supervisor in computer science at the Christopher Newport University, VA, USA. With more than 100 papers published, his current research includes artificial neural network models for face recognition, weather forecasting, financial data simulation, and management.

* * *

Alma Y. Alanis was born in Durango, Durango, Mexico, in 1980. She received the BSc degree from Instituto Tecnologico de Durango (ITD), Durango Campus, Durango, Durango, in 2002, and the MSc and PhD degrees in electrical engineering from the Advanced Studies and Research Center of the National Polytechnic Institute (CINVESTAV), Guadalajara Campus, Mexico, in 2004 and 2007 respectively. Her research interest centers on time series forecasting using neural networks, neural control, back-stepping control, block control, chaos reproduction and their applications to electrical machines and power systems.

Dhiya Al-Jumeily was awarded his PhD in intelligent tutoring systems from John Moores University in 2000. He originally obtained a first class degree from the University of Baghdad in Mathematics (1987), a diploma in science from the University of Liverpool (1991) and an MPhil from Liverpool John Moores University (1994). Dhiya's research interests include: Computer algebra systems, technology and mathematics education; The effect of computer algebra on the learning and teaching of mathematics. Dhiya is a member of the British Computer Society (BCS) and the Institute of Electrical and Electronic Engineers (IEEE)

Jinde Cao received the BS degree from Anhui Normal University, Wuhu, China, the MS degree from Yunnan University, Kunming, China, and the PhD degree from Sichuan University, Chengdu,

China, all in mathematics/applied mathematics, in 1986, 1989, and 1998, respectively. From March 1989 to May 2000, he was with Yunnan University. In May 2000, he joined the Department of Mathematics, Southeast University, Nanjing, China. From July 2001 to June 2002, he was a post-doctoral research fellow in the Department of Automation and Computer-Aided Engineering, Chinese University of Hong Kong, Hong Kong. From July 2006 to September 2006, he was a visiting research fellow of Royal Society in the School of Information Systems, Computing and Mathematics, Brunel University, UK.

Guanrong Chen received the MSc degree in Computer Science from Zhongshan University, China and the PhD degree in applied mathematics from Texas A&M University, USA. After working at the University of Houston for ten some years, currently he is a chair professor and the founding director of the Centre for Chaos Control and Synchronization at the City University of Hong Kong. He has been a fellow of the IEEE since 1996 for his fundamental contributions to the theory and applications of chaos control and bifurcation analysis.

Yuehui Chen received his BSc degree in the Department of mathematics (major in control theory) from the Shandong University in 1985, and Master and PhD degree in the School of Electrical Engineering and Computer Science from the Kumamoto University of Japan in 1999 and 2001. During 2001–2003, he had worked as the senior researcher at the Memory-Tech Corporation, Tokyo. Since 2003 he has been a member at the Faculty of School of Information Science and Engineering, Jinan University, where he currently heads the Computational Intelligence Laboratory. His research interests include evolutionary computation, neural networks, fuzzy logic systems, hybrid computational intelligence, computational intelligence grid and their applications in time-series prediction, system identification, intelligent control, intrusion detection systems, web intelligence and bioinformatics. He is the author and co-author of more than 80 technique papers.

Christian L. Dunis is professor of Banking & Finance and head of the Doctoral Programme at the Business School of Liverpool John Moores University, where he also heads the Centre for International Banking, Economics and Finance (CIBEF). He is also a consultant to asset management firms, specialising in the application of nonlinear methods to financial management problems and an official reviewer attached to the European Commission for the evaluation of applications to finance of emerging software technologies. He is an editor of the European Journal of Finance and has published widely in the field of financial markets analysis and forecasting. He has organised the annual Forecasting Financial Markets Conference since 1994.

Wael El-Deredy received a BSc in electrical engineering from Ain Shams University, Egypt, in 1988, a MSc in communications and signal processing from Imperial College London, in 1993, and a PhD from the Institute of Neurology, University College London in 1998. From 1988 to 1991, he was with IBM as a computer engineer, and from 1997 to 2002, he was with Unilever as a research scientist. Since 2005 he hold a lectureship in cognitive neuroscience at the University of Manchester where his research interests include brain dynamics; inverse problem of the electroencephalography; probabilistic models and neural complexity.

Ben Evans completed his PhD in forecasting commodity spread markets in 2006. His current research interests are non-linear forecasting methods applied to risk neutral portfolios, with special emphasis on commodity markets and market relationships.His work has been published in numerous journals including *Applied Financial Economics, Neural Network World* and *European Journal of Finance*. His work has also been presented at the Forecasting Financial Markets Conference 2003-2006 and the 2005 Connectionist Conference. Ben currently works as a commodity risk analyst at Dresdner Kleinwort Investment Bank in Frankfurt and as a specialist consultant to Morris Lubricants LTD in England.

Shuzhi Sam Ge, IEEE Fellow, PEng, is a professor with the National University of Singapore. He received his BSc degree from Beijing University of Aeronautics and Astronautics (BUAA), and the PhD degree and the diploma of Imperial College (DIC) from Imperial College of Science, Technology and Medicine. He has served/been serving as an associate editor for a number of flagship journals including *IEEE Transactions on Automatic Control, IEEE Transactions on Control Systems Technology, IEEE Transactions on Neural Networks*, and *Automatica*. He also serves as an editor of the Taylor & Francis Automation and Control Engineering Series. His current research interests include social robotics, multimedia fusion, adaptive control, and intelligent systems.

Rozaida Ghazali received the BSc (Hons) degree in computer science from Universiti Sains Malaysia (1997), and the MSc degree in Computer Science from Universiti Teknologi Malaysia (2003). She is a member of teaching staff at information technology and multimedia faculty, Universiti Tun Hussein Onn, Johor, Malaysia, and currently pursuing a PhD degree in Higher Order Neural Networks for financial time series prediction at School of Computing and Mathematical Sciences, Liverpool John Moores University, UK. Her research areas include neural networks for financial time series prediction and physical time series forecasting.

Takakuni Goto received the BE, ME and PhD degrees in electrical engineering from Tohoku University, Sendai, Japan, in 2001, 2003 and 2006, respectively.

Madan M. Gupta is a professor (Emeritus) in the College of Engineering and the director of the Intelligent Systems Research Laboratory at the University of Saskatchewan, Canada. He received his BE (Hons.) and ME degrees from the Birla Engineering College, India in 1961 and 1962, respectively. He received his PhD degree from the University of Warwick, United Kingdom in 1967. In the fall of 1998, Dr. Gupta was awarded an earned Doctor of science (DSc) degree by the University of Saskatchewan. His current research interests are in the areas of neural systems, integration of fuzzy-neural systems, intelligent and cognitive robotic systems, new paradigms in information and signal processing, and chaos in neural systems. He has authored or co-authored over 800 published research papers and 3 books, and edited or co-edited 19 other books. He has been a postdoctoral research fellow at the Department of Functional Brain Imaging, He is currently a professor and doctoral advisor at the Southeast University. Prior to this, he was a professor at Yunnan University from 1996 to 2000. He is the author or coauthor of more than 130 journal papers and five edited books and a reviewer of *Mathematical Reviews* and *Zentralblatt-Math*. His research interests include nonlinear systems, neural networks, complex systems and complex networks, control theory, and applied mathematics. His current research interests include computational intelligence, ergonomics and neuroscience.

Noriyasu Homma received a BA, MA, and PhD in electrical and communication engineering from Tohoku University, Japan, in 1990, 1992, and 1995, respectively. From 1995 to 1998, he was a lecturer at the Tohoku University, Japan. He is currently an associate professor of the faculty of medicine at the Tohoku University. From 2000 to 2001, he was a visiting professor at the Intelligent Systems Research Laboratory, University of Saskatchewan, Canada. His current research interests include neural networks, complex and chaotic systems, soft-computing, cognitive sciences, and brain sciences. He has published over 70 papers, and co-authored 1 book and 3 chapters in 3 research books in these fields.

Zeng-Guang Hou received the BE and ME degrees in electrical engineering from Yanshan University (formerly Northeast Heavy Machinery Institute), Qinhuangdao, China, in 1991 and 1993, respectively, and the PhD degree in electrical engineering from Beijing Institute of Technology, Beijing, China, in 1997. From May 1997 to June 1999, he was a postdoctoral research fellow at the Laboratory of Systems and Control, Institute of Development Aiging and Cancer, Tohoku University, Sendai, Japan, since October 2006. From January 2007 to March 2007, he was a visiting postdoctoral fellow at Center for Molecular and Behavioral Neuroscience, Rugters University, Newark, New Jersey, USA. He was a research assistant at the Hong Kong Polytechnic University, Hong Kong SAR, China, from May 2000 to January 2001. From July 1999 to May 2004, he was an associate professor at the Institute of Automation, Chinese Academy of Sciences, and has been a full professor since June 2004. From September 2003 to October 2004, he was a visiting professor at the Intelligent Systems Research Laboratory, College of Engineering, University of Saskatchewan, Saskatoon, SK, Canada. He has published over 80 papers in journals and conference proceedings. His current research interests include computational intelligence, robotics, and intelligent control systems. Dr. Hou is an associate editor of the *IEEE Computational Intelligence* Magazine, and an editorial board member of the *International Journal of Intelligent Systems Technologies and Applications* (IJISTA), *Journal of Intelligent and Fuzzy Systems*, and *International Journal of Cognitive Informatics and Natural Intelligence*. He was a guest editor for special issues of the *International Journal of Vehicle Autonomous Systems on Computational Intelligence and Its Applications to Mobile Robots and Autonomous Systems* and for *Soft Computing* (Springer) *on Fuzzy-Neural Computation and Robotics*.

Abir Jaafar Hussain is a full time senior lecturer at the School of Computer and Mathematical Sciences at John Moores University. Her main research interests are neural networks, signal prediction, telecommunication fraud detection and image processing. She completed her BSc degree at the Department of Electronic and Electrical Engineering at Salford University. She then joined the control systems centre at UMIST to complete her MSc degree in control and information technology. The MSc dissertation was in collaboration with the Department of Paper Science where fractal simulations of martial damage accumulation in cellulosic fibres were investigated. Then she pursued a PhD research project at the Control Systems Centre at the University of Manchester (UMIST). Her PhD was awarded in 2000 for a thesis entitled *Polynomial Neural Networks and Applications to Image Compression and Signal Prediction*. In November 2001 Dr. Abir Hussain joined the Distributed Multimedia Systems (DMS) at Liverpool John Moores University as a full-time senior lecturer.

Adam Knowles received BSc (Hons) and MSc degrees in computer science, from the University of Birmingham, UK, in 2002 and 2003 respectively. In 2005 he received a MPhil degree from Liverpool John Moores University, UK, for research on higher-order and pipelined neural networks. He is currently a research student at the Department of Electronics, University of York, UK, where his research is being sponsored by NCR. His research interests include: data fusion and biologically inspired algorithms.

Jason Laws is a reader in finance at Liverpool JMU and the programme leader for the specialist Master's in international banking and finance. Jason has taught finance at all levels in the UK, Hong Kong and Singapore. Jason is also the co-author of *Applied quantitative methods for trading and investment* (John Wiley, 2003), and has recent publications in the *European Journal of Operations Research*, *European Journal of Finance*, *Applied Financial Economics*, *Neural Network World* and *The Journal of Forecasting*.

Jinling Liang was born in Henan, China, in 1974. She received the BS degree in 1997, the MS degree in 1999, both in mathematics from Northwest University, Xi'an China, and the PhD degree in applied mathematics in 2006 from Southeast University, Nanjing, China. She was appointed as lecturer in 2002 and associate professor in 2007 at Southeast University. From January to March and March to April in 2004, she was a research assistant in the Department of Mechanical Engineering, University of Hong Kong, and the Department of Mathematics, City University of Hong Kong, Hong Kong, respectively. Now, she is working toward the post-doctoral research fellow in the Department of Information Systems and Computing, Brunel University, UK. Her current research interests include neural networks, nonlinear analysis and complex networks.

Paulo Lisboa is professor in industrial mathematics at Liverpool John Moores University. His main research interests are applications of artificial neural network methods to medical decision support and computational marketing. He leads collaborative research nationally and internationally, including the cancer track for the FP6 Network of Excellence Biopattern. He has over 150 refereed publications and 4 edited books. He is associate editor for *Neural Networks*, *Neural Computing Applications*, *Applied Soft Computing* and *Source Code for Biology and Medicine*. He also serves on the executive committees of the Healthcare Technologies Professional Network of the IET and in the Royal Academy of Engineering's UK focus for biomedical engineering. He is an expert evaluator for the European Community and senior consultant with global organisations in the manufacturing, medical devices and clinical research sectors.

Panos Liatsis graduated with a dipl. eng in electrical engineering from the Democritos University of Thrace, Greece and a PhD in computer vision and neural networks from the Control Systems Centre at UMIST. In April 1994, he was appointed a lecturer in the Control Systems Centre at UMIST, where he worked with various industrial partners including British Aerospace, Lucas Industries, and TRW Automotive. In November 2003, he moved to the School of Engineering & Mathematical Sciences at City University, where he is currently a senior lecturer and director of the Information and Biomedical Engineering Centre (IBEC). He is a regular expert evaluator working for the European Commission, a member of the EPSRC Peer Review College, the IEEE, the IET, the InstMC and a European engineer (Eur Ing). He is a member of various International Conference Programme Committees including the International Conference on Video Processing & Multimedia Communications, EURASIP Conference on Video & Image Processing and the International Conference on Systems, Signals and Image Processing. His main research interests are neural networks, genetic algorithms, computer vision and pattern recognition. He has published over 90 scientific papers in international journals and conferences and edited two international conference proceedings.

Xiaohui Liu is a professor of computing at Brunel University where he directs the Centre for Intelligent Data Analysis, conducting interdisciplinary research concerned with the effective analysis of data, particularly in biomedical areas. He is a charted engineer, life member of the Association for the Advancement of Artificial Intelligence, fellow of the Royal Statistical Society, and fellow of the British Computer Society. Professor Liu has over 180 refereed publications in data mining, bioinformatics, intelligent systems and time series.

Yurong Liu is an associate professor at the Department of Mathematics, Yangzhou University, China. His current interests include neural networks, nonlinear dynamics, time-delay systems, and chaotic dynamics.

Zhao Lu received his MS degree in the major of control theory and engineering from Nankai University, Tianjin, China, in 2000, and his PhD degree in electrical engineering from University of Houston, USA, in 2004. From 2004 to 2006, he has been working as a post-doctoral research fellow in the Department of Electrical and Computer Engineering at Wayne State University, Detroit, USA, and the Department of Naval Architecture and Marine Engineering at University of Michigan, Ann Arbor, USA, respectively. Since 2007, he has joined the faculty of the Department of Electrical Engineering at Tuskegee University, Tuskegee, USA. His research interests mainly include nonlinear control theory, machine learning, and pattern recognition.

Efstathios Milonidis received his first degree in electrical engineering from the National Technical University of Athens, his MSc in control engineering and his MPhil in aerodynamics and flight mechanics from Cranfield Institute of Technology, and his PhD in control theory and design from City University. Prior to his present appointment as a lecturer in control and information systems at the School of Engineering & Mathematical Sciences he was an associate research professor at the Institute of Automation, Danish Technical University, Copenhagen, and an associate professor at the Department of Electronics at the Technical University of Thessaloniki, Greece. His research experience is in the areas of Control systems design, algebraic control synthesis methods, and sampled and discrete time systems. He has contributed in the development of a methodology for synthesis of discrete time control schemes based on the problem of "finite settling time stabilisation" (FSTS) and the development of control based methodology for Control Structure Selection. His main research interests are in discrete time control, modelling and simulation of dynamical systems, systems theory and graph methods for multivariable control systems.

Godfrey C. Onwubolu is professor of engineering, School of Engineering & Physics, faculty of science & technology, at the University of the South Pacific, Suva, Fiji. He holds a BEng from the University of Benin, MSc and PhD from the University of Aston in Birmingham, UK. His current areas of teaching and research are mechatronics, modern manufacturing, modern optimization, modern inductive modeling techniques, and modern data mining techniques (5M). He is the author of three books: *Emerging optimization techniques in production planning & control*: Imperial College Press: London; *New optimization techniques in engineering*: Springer-Verlag, Heidelberg, Germany; and *Mechatronics: Principles & applications*: Elsevier: Oxford. He has published over 100 articles in international journals and conference proceedings. As a chartered engineer (CEng) and a chartered member British Computer

Society (CMBCS), he is also a senior member of the Institute of Industrial Engineers (SMIIE), a senior member of the Institute of Industrial Engineers (SMIIE), and a senior member of the American Society of Manufacturing Engineers (SASME).

Fengli Ren was born in Henan Province, China. She received her BS degree in mathematics from Zhengzhou University, Zhengzhou, China, in 2001, and her MS degree in mathematics from Southeast University, Nanjing, China, in 2006. She is working toward her PhD degree at Southeast University, Nanjing, China. Her research interests include stability theory, nonlinear systems, neural networks, chaos synchronization and genetic regulatory networks.

Jesus Rico was born in Purepero Michoacán, México. He received the BSc, MSc and a PhD from the University of Michoacan, the University of Nuevo Leon and the University of Glasgow, respectively; all in the area of power system. He has been teaching at the University of Michoacan since 1990 and form part of the powers system group of the postgraduate studies in the faculty of engineering. He is also with the utility company of Mexico, CFE where he undertakes electric distribution projects. He also has done postdoctoral stays at the University of Glasgow and Arizona State University.

Edgar N. Sanchez obtained the BSEE from Universidad Industrial de Santander (UIS), Bucaramanga, Colombia in 1971, the MSEE from CINVESTAV-IPN (Advanced Studies and Research Center of the National Polytechnic Institute), Mexico City, Mexico, in 1974 and the Docteur Ingenieur degree in automatic control from Institut Nationale Polytechnique de Grenoble, France in 1980. He was granted an USA National Research Council Award as a research associate at NASA Langley Research Center, Hampton, Virginia, USA (January 1985 to March 1987). His research interest center in Neural Networks and Fuzzy Logic as applied to Automatic Control systems. He has been advisors of 6 PhD theses and 33 MSc theses. Since January 1997, he is professor of CINVESTAV_IPN, Guadalajara Campus, Mexico.

John Seiffertt, currently a PhD candidate in the Applied Computational Intelligence Laboratory at the University of Missouri-Rolla. John holds graduate degrees in applied mathematics and economics and has worked as a resarch analyst at the Federal Reserve Bank of St Louis and spent a summer in research at Los Alamos National Laboratory. Additionally, he has worked in institutional asset allocation at Bank of America Capital Management, as a pension actuary for Buck Consultants, and taught as a member of the mathematics and computer science faculty at the University of Missouri-St Louis.

David R. Selviah studied at Trinity College Cambridge University, UK and Christ Church, Oxford University, UK and developed surface acoustic wave radar correlators and pulse compression filters at Plessey Research (Caswell) Ltd, UK. Thereafter, at the Department of Electronic and Electrical Engineering, UCL he has researched into optical devices, interconnections, algorithms and systems for 20 years and has over 100 publications and patents. His research includes image, signal and data processing, pattern recognition algorithms, 10 Gb/s multimode polymer waveguide optical printed circuit boards with self aligning multi-channel connectors, optical higher order neural networks, holographic multiplexed storage, variable focal length microlenses.

Janti Shawash achieved his Bachelor's honors degree in electronic engineering at the Princess Sumaya University for Technology in Amman, Jordan. He was ranked top (in the top 1%), in his final project "Image Processing Using Nonlinear Two-Dimensional Spatial Filters." Thereafter, he studied for an MSc in technologies for broadband communications at Department of Electronic and Electrical Engineering, UCL and carried out a project on "Real Time Image Processing Techniques using Graphical Processing Units." He was awarded the MSc degree and began his PhD studies in October 2006 winning an overseas research scholarship and a UCL graduate school scholarship.

Da Shi, IEEE student member, received his BSc degree in computer science and engineering from the Northeast University of China. He is currently working toward the PhD degree in the State Key Laboratory of Machine Perception of the Peking University of China. His research interests include intelligent modeling and machine learning, especially learning Bayesian networks and applying it to financial problems.

Leang-San Shieh received his MS and PhD degrees from the University of Houston, USA. He is a professor and the director of the Computer and Systems Engineering. He was the recipient of the 1973 and 1997 College Teaching Excellence Awards, the 1988 College Senior Faculty Research Excellence Award, and the 2003-2004 Fluor Daniel Faculty Excellence Award, the highest award given in the college, from the UH Cullen College of Engineering. In addition, he was the recipient of the 1976 University Teaching Excellence Award and the 2001-2002 El Paso Faculty Achievement Award from the University of Houston. His fields of interest are digital control, optimal control, self-tuning control and hybrid control of uncertain systems. He authored and co-authored more than two hundred and fifty articles in various referred scientific journals.

Simeon J. Simoff is professor of information technology and head of the School of Computing and Mathematics at the University of Western Sydney. He is also head of the e-Markets Research Group at the University of Technology, Sydney. He is also a founding co-director of the Institute of Analytic Professionals of Australia. He is known for the unique blend of interdisciplinary scholarship and innovation, which integrates the areas of data mining, design computing, virtual worlds and digital media, with application in the area of electronic trading environments. His work in these fields has resulted in 11 co-authored/edited books and more than 170 research papers, and a number of cross-disciplinary educational programs in information technology and computing. He is co-editor of the CRPIT series "Conferences of Research and Practice in Information Technology." He has initiated and co-chaired several international conference series in the area of data mining, including The Australasian data mining series AusDM, and the ACM SIGKDD Multimedia Data Mining and Visual Data Mining series.

Ashu M. G. Solo is an electrical and computer engineer, mathematician, writer, and entrepreneur. His primary research interests are in intelligent systems, public policy, and the application of intelligent systems in control systems, computer architecture, power systems, optimization, pattern recognition, decision making, and public policy. Solo has about 100 publications in these and other fields. He co-developed some of the best published methods for maintaining power flow in and multi-objective optimization of radial power distribution system operations. Solo has served on 52 international program committees for 50 research conferences and 2 research multi-conferences. He is the principal of Maverick Technologies America Inc. Solo previously served honorably as an infantry officer and platoon commander understudy in the Cdn. Army Reserve.

Shaohua Tan received his PhD degree from the Katholieke Universiteit Leuven of Belgium in 1987. He is currently professor, Centre for Information Science, Peking University, China. He was IEEE senior member and served as deputy director of the State Key Laboratory of Machine Perception and Centre for Information Science, Peking University. He has been working in the areas of systems and control, digital signal processing, speech processing and artificial neural networks, where he has published over 100 papers in the journals and conferences in these areas. His current research interests include intelligent modeling of complex systems and machine learning using Bayesian networks.

Zidong Wang is a professor of dynamical systems and computing at Brunel University of the UK. His research interests include dynamical systems, signal processing, bioinformatics, control theory and applications. He has published more than 100 papers in refereed international journals, and was awarded research fellowships from Germany, Japan and Hong Kong. He is currently serving as an associate editor or editorial board member for 10 international journals including 4 IEEE Transactions.

Peng Wu was born in 1980. He received BSc and Master's degree in School of Information Science and Engineering University of Jinan in 2002 and 2007. Since 2002 he has worked as a teacher in School of Computer Engineering University of Jinan. His research interests include evolutionary computation, neural networks, fuzzy logic systems, hybrid computational intelligence their applications in time-series prediction, system identification, and intelligent control.

Qiang Wu was born in 1982. He received BSc degree in School of Information Science and Engineering University of Jinan in 2005, and he has approximately two years of experience in computational intelligence and time series forecasting. Present he is pursuing a master degree in laboratory of computational intelligence at School of Information Science and Engineering, University of Jinan. His research interest includes Computational Intelligence, time series prediction, neural networks and evolutionary computation.

Donald C. Wunsch II is from 1999 – present the Mary K. Finley Missouri distinguished professor of electrical & computer engineering at the Missouri University of Science & Technology. His prior positions were associate professor at Texas Tech, senior principal scientist at Boeing, consultant for Rockwell International, and technician for International Laser Systems. He has an Executive MBA from Washington University in St. Louis, PhD in electrical engineering from the University of Washington (Seattle), MS in applied mathematics from the same institution, BS in applied mathematics from the University of New Mexico, and he also completed a humanities honors program at Seattle University. He has over 250 publications in his research field of computational intelligence, and has attracted over $5.5 million in research funding. He has produced thirteen PhDs: seven in electrical engineering, five in computer engineering, and one in computer science. His research interests include neural networks, and their applications in: the game of Go, reinforcement learning, approximate dynamic programming, financial engineering, representation of knowledge and uncertainty, collective robotics, computer security, critical infrastructure protection, biomedical applications, and smart sensor networks. Selected key contributions (in collaboration with other researchers) include the first hardware implementation of an adaptive resonance neural network, a theoretical unification and applications of reinforcement learning architectures, fuzzy number neural networks training and regression for surety assessment, performance improvements in heuristic approaches to the traveling salesman problem, and clustering applications. He chairs the UMR Information Technology and Computing Committee and the Computer Security Task Force, as well as the CIO Search Committee, and served as a board member of the International Neural Networks Society, the University of Missouri Bioinformatics Consortium, the Idaho EPSCOR Project Advisory Board, and the IEEE Neural Networks Council. He also served as technical program co-chair for IJCNN 02, general chair for IJCNN 03, and president of the International Neural Networks Society

Shuxiang Xu won from the Australian government a scholarship (Overseas Postgraduate Research Award) to research a PhD at the University of Western Sydney, Sydney, Australia in 1996, and was awarded a PhD in computing by this university in 2000. He received a MSc in applied mathematics and a BSc in mathematics in 1989 and 1996, respectively, from the University of Electronic Science and Technology of China, Chengdu, China. His current interests include the theory and applications of artificial neural networks, genetic algorithms, data mining, and pattern recognition. He is currently a lecturer at the School of Computing, University of Tasmania, Tasmania, Australia.

Jean X. Zhang is currently a PhD candidate at The George Washington University. She received a BBA in accounting from the College of William and Mary in 2004 and a MS in accounting from the University of Virginia in 2005. She received the Outstanding Research Paper Award in the government and nonprofit section, American Accounting Association 2007 Annual Meeting. Her research interests are corporate governance, governmental accounting and new generation computing techniques.

Jing Chun Zhang is IT security specialist at IBM Australia. He is also recognized by the Oracle Certificated Professional Program as an Oracle8i/9i certified database administrator and Unix administrator. He has graduated from the Beijing University of Technology. He received his Master's degree in Science with honors at the University of Western Sydney. He has been working for the IBM Australia for more than ten years and currently is taking the responsible for security section. His research areas include neural networks, database applications and security issues.

Lei Zhang is a PhD candidate in the information technology faculty at the University of Information Technology, Sydney. He has graduated from the Beijing Capital Normal University majored in Information Engineering in 2001. He received his Master's degree in computer studies at the University of New England in 2004. He worked as a designer at the Beijing Telecommunication Designing and Planning Institution. He is currently working in the e-Markets Research Group at the University of Technology, Sydney. His research areas include data/text mining, machine learning and artificial intelligence areas.

Index